CLARENCE BYRD

Clarence Byrd Inc.

IDA CHEN

Clarence Byrd Inc.

With contributions by

GARY DONELL

Byrd & Chen's
Canadian
Tax
Principles

2017–2018 EDITION

Volume I

 Pearson

ISBN 978-0-13-449820-1

Vice-President, Editorial: Anne Williams
Marketing Manager: Spencer Snell
Manager, Project Management: Avinash Chandra
Manager of Content Development: Suzanne Schaan
Developmental Editor: Suzanne Simpson Millar
Media Developer: Bogdan Kosenko
Production Editor: Leanne Rancourt
Permissions Project Manager: Joanne Tang
Cover Designer: Anthony Leung

Vice-President, Cross Media and Publishing Services: Gary Bennett

10 9 8 7 6 5 4 3 2 1

ISBN 978-0-13-449820-1

PREFACE

Objectives Of Canadian Tax Principles Package

The Text

Subject Coverage

The objective of this text is to provide coverage of all the tax subjects that are taught in Canadian college and university tax courses. In so doing, it also provides comprehensive coverage of all the tax issues that are required in the educational programs of CPA Canada.

This material is designed to be used in a two semester university or college course and is far too extensive to be completely covered in a single one semester course. The traditional split in the material would be to cover Chapters 1 through 11 in a first course dealing with the determination of Net Income For Tax Purposes for all taxpayers, as well as the calculation of Taxable Income and Tax Payable for individuals. This could be followed by a second course where the focus is primarily on the taxation of corporations. The relevant material on corporations is found in Chapters 12 through 17. The remaining Chapters 18 through 21 deal with partnerships, trusts, international taxation, and GST/HST.

Level Of Coverage

In terms of style, we have attempted to strike a balance between the kind of complete documentation that can render the material incomprehensible to anyone other than a tax professional, and the total elimination of references that would make it impossible for readers to expand their understanding of particular points. In those situations where we feel the issue is sufficiently complex that further investigation could be helpful, we have provided a list of references to the relevant Sections of the *Income Tax Act* or other related materials. In contrast, no direction has been provided when the material is either very straightforward, or where the relevant parts of the *Act* would be obvious.

This book can be used with or without additional source material. Some instructors require students to acquire a copy of the *Income Tax Act* and permit its use as a reference during examinations. For instructors wishing to take this approach, frequent references to the *Act* have been included. In addition, access to an electronic version of the *Income Tax Act* is available on the Companion Website.

For instructors not wishing to require the use of the *Income Tax Act*, we have designed the problem material so that students should be able to solve all of the included problems relying solely on the text as a reference.

The Need For Two Volumes

In the over 30 years that we have been writing this text, we have seen the content grow from about 400 pages to more than 1,500 pages. We initially dealt with this increase in size by providing a separate Study Guide. However, the text alone has grown to over 1,000 pages and, while accommodating this in a single volume is feasible, the result would be far less useful to students than dividing the material into two reasonably sized volumes.

If there was any consensus among our users as to which subjects should be dealt with in each volume, they could be made available separately. However, virtually all of our users omit material from Volume I and include material from Volume II. Further, there is no consistent pattern as to which material is omitted and which material is included. Given this, it would not be possible to produce separate volumes that meet the needs of all of our users.

Pearson eText

In response to concerns over the growing size (and weight) of the paper edition of this text, access to the **Pearson eText** is included with the print version. This eText gives users access to the text wherever and whenever there is access to the Internet. It contains the content of both volumes of the text, as well as the content of the Study Guide. The eText pages look just like the printed text and, in addition, offers powerful functionality. See the **Student Supplements** section of this preface for more information.

Note that the electronic text embedded in the FITAC Research Library continues to be available. Designed for references purposes, it provides electronic links from the text material to the various sources contained in FITAC (e.g., the *Income Tax Act*). Note however, it only includes the text and does not provide the Exercises and other problem material that are provided with the printed text. See the **Student Supplements** section of this preface for more information.

The Study Guide

The major objective of the Study Guide is to provide students with convenient access to the solutions for the Exercises and Self Study Problems. Having these solutions in a separate volume makes it much easier for students to simultaneously view the problem while solving it and then consult its complete and detailed solution.

The Study Guide also provides a number of additional features to enhance the learning experience. These can be described as follows:

- Detailed instructions on "How To Work Through" each Chapter in the text. This includes guidance on when to attempt Exercises and Self Study Problems as the student reads through the text.

- A detailed list of "Learning Objectives" for each Chapter. This allows the student to ensure that he/she has understood all of the relevant subjects covered in the Chapter.

- Sample completed tax returns for both individuals and corporations. These are useful practice for students using the ProFile tax software that is available with this text.

- At the end of each Chapter in the text, there is a list of key terms that were used in that Chapter. All of these terms are alphabetically listed in a Glossary that is at the back of the Study Guide. This provides an easy way to find the meaning of a term that was introduced in one Chapter, but is being referred to again in a subsequent Chapter.

Problem Material Available

For Students - Problems and Detailed Solutions

Canadian Tax Principles contains a large number of problems that have complete and detailed solutions available to students. The various types of problems are as follows:

Exercises   These are short problems that are focused on a single issue. Each Exercise is presented in the text of *Canadian Tax Principles* text, directly following the material that is relevant to its solution. This provides you with immediate feedback as to whether you have understood the material that you have just read. Solutions to these Exercises can be found in the Study Guide.

Self Study Problems   These problems are more complex than the Exercises and sometimes deal with more than one subject. While the actual problems are available only on the Companion Website, within the text we have provided an indication of when it would be appropriate to work each problem. Solutions to the Self Study Problems are included in the Study Guide.

Tax Software Self Study Problems   These problems are designed to be solved using the ProFile software that is available with *Canadian Tax Principles*. These problems, along with their solutions, are found in the Study Guide. The completed tax returns are available on the Companion Website.

Supplementary Self Study Problems   For each of the 21 chapters, additional Self Study Problems, along with solutions, are available on the Companion Website.

Practice Examinations   A 90 minute practice examination, along with a solution and suggested marking guide, is available on the Companion Website for each of the 21 chapters. These examinations contain various types of problems, including multiple choice, true/false and essay questions, as well as longer problems.

For Instructors - Assignment Problems And Test Items

Canadian Tax Principles contains several types of problems designed for instructors:

Assignment Problems   These problems vary in difficulty and include the most difficult non-comprehensive problems in the text. They are found at the end of each chapter of *Canadian Tax Principles*. They are sometimes adapted from professional examinations and may involve a number of different issues. Solutions to these problems are available only to instructors. These solutions are not available to students.

Assignment Problems (Comprehensive)   These comprehensive problems are the most challenging type of problem material in the text. They are cumulative in that they incorporate issues from previous chapters. There are two comprehensive assignment problems per chapter in Chapters 6 through 11 and they are found at the end of the Assignment Problems for the chapter. Solutions to these problems are available only to instructors.

Assignment Tax Software Problems   Assignment Tax Software Problems dealing with personal tax returns are found at the end of Chapters 4 and 11. An additional Assignment Tax Software Problem, involving a corporate tax return, is located at the end of Chapter 14. Solutions to Assignment Tax Software Problems are available only to instructors.

Examination Problems   For instructors adopting *Canadian Tax Principles*, a large and comprehensive selection of problems and solutions for use on examinations is available. These include multiple choice questions (over 700), true/false questions (over 200), essay questions (over 400), exercises (over 400), as well as more than 350 comprehensive types of problem ranging in difficulty from easy to very difficult.

Student Supplements

Student Companion Website

The Companion Website for *Canadian Tax Principles* holds a great deal of additional material that will provide significant assistance to students and others using this text. Instructions on how to access the Companion Website can be found on the access card provided with this package. The URL for this Companion Website is:

www.pearsoncanada.ca/byrdchen/ctp2018

With respect to the content of this Companion Website, the various items that are included can be described as follows:

- **Self Study Problems** Within the text we have provided an indication of when it would be appropriate to work each Self Study Problem. The problems themselves are available on the Companion Website. Their solutions are included in the Study Guide.

- **Pearson eText**   The Pearson eText gives you access to the text whenever and wherever you have access to the Internet. eText pages look exactly like the printed text, offering powerful functionality. You can create notes, highlight text in different colours, create bookmarks, zoom, and search. The Pearson eText can also be accessed on mobile devices. Unlike the electronic text version in the FITAC research library, the Pearson eText includes the same problem material that is found in the printed text.

- **CPA Canada's Federal Income Tax Collection (FITAC)** This comprehensive electronic tax research library contains the *Income Tax Act, Income Tax Folios,* and other official materials. In addition, it includes an electronic copy of the *Canadian Tax Principles* text. Unlike the Pearson eText, it does not include the problem material that is found in the print text. However, it does have the advantage of being electronically linked to the *Income Tax Act*, as well as other CRA publications that are included in the FITAC.

- **ProFile Tax Return Preparation Software** Intuit's professional tax preparation software, ProFile, is available free of charge to users of *Canadian Tax Principles*. This software includes tax preparation capabilities for individuals, corporations, and trusts. Note that this software is provided in a form that is for educational use only. It cannot be used to file actual tax returns.

- **Corrections and Updates** Any corrections to the text, Study Guide, or other student material are provided here throughout the year.

- **Supplementary Self Study Problems** For each chapter, additional Self Study Problems, along with detailed solutions, are available for further practice in problem solving.

- **Practice Examinations** A 90-minute practice examination, along with a solution and suggested marking guide, is available for each chapter. These examinations contain a variety of problems, including multiple choice, essay questions and longer problems.

- **Power Point Presentations** There is a PowerPoint presentation for each chapter. These provide the basis for a quick review of the material covered in the chapter.

- **Glossary Flashcards** These flashcards help test understanding of key terms in each chapter.

- **2017 Tax Rates, Credits and Common CCA Classes** This is available as a PDF file, for reference. This tax information is also available at the front of Volumes 1 and 2, and CCA classes are available in the Chapter 5 Appendix.

- **Tax Returns** The Study Guide contains tax return examples and Self Study tax software problems, along with notes to their solutions. The completed tax returns are available on the Companion Website, to download and use with your ProFile software, or to view in PDF files.

Instructor Supplements

In addition to all of the materials that are available to students, instructors will be provided with the following additional resources through the Pearson online catalogue:

- **Solutions Manual** A full solutions manual is available to instructors. This manual includes solutions to all of the Assignment Problems, including those that use the ProFile software. It also includes a problem concordance which correlates all problems from the last edition to this one. This is provided to assist instructors who have used the last edition with revising their courses.

- **Test Item File** For instructors adopting *Canadian Tax Principles*, a large and comprehensive selection of problems and solutions for use on examinations is available (see previous description).

The Federal Budget

The Process

One of the great difficulties in preparing material on Canadian taxation is the fact that changes in the relevant legislation are made each year. This is complicated by the fact that the date for each year's budget is not entirely predictable. Between 2002 and 2017, the arrival date has ranged from December 10th of the preceding year (the 2002 budget) to May 2nd of the budget year (the 2006 budget). For 2017, the budget was presented on March 22, 2017.

Proposed Changes In The March 22, 2017 Budget

Repealed As Of 2017   We would remind you that the repeal of these measures as of January 1, 2017 was presented in the 2016 budget:

- the cumulative eligible capital rules (transitional rules are covered in Chapter 5)
- the children's arts and fitness tax credits
- the education and textbook tax credits

The major changes proposed in the March 22, 2017 budget are as follows:

Personal Tax Measures

Public Transit Tax Credit The provision for this credit was repealed as of July 1, 2017.

Home Relocation Loans Deduction   The provision for the home relocation loans deduction is repealed as of January 1, 2018.

Canada Caregiver Credit   The 2017 budget greatly simplified the system of tax measures for caregivers by replacing the existing caregiver credit, infirm dependant credit and family caregiver tax credit with a new Canada Caregiver Credit. The new credit provides tax assistance to caregivers for dependants who have an infirmity and are dependent on the caregiver for support by reason of that infirmity.

Disability Tax Credit   The budget added nurse practitioners to the list of medical practitioners that could certify eligibility for the disability tax credit. A nurse practitioner is permitted to certify for all types of impairments that are within the scope of their practice.

Medical Expense Tax Credit   To recognize that some individuals may need to incur costs related to the use of reproductive technologies, the budget clarifies the application of the medical expense tax credit so that individuals who require medical intervention in order to conceive a child are eligible to claim the same expenses that would generally be eligible for individuals on account of medical infertility.

Tuition Tax Credit   The 2017 budget extends the eligibility criteria for the tuition tax credit to tuition fees paid to a university, college or other post-secondary institution in Canada for occupational skills courses that are not at the post secondary level.

Business Tax Measures

Investment Tax Credit For Child Care Spaces   The provision for this investment tax credit for expenditures on child care spaces is repealed as of the Budget Day (March 22, 2017). To provide transitional relief, the credit will be available in respect of eligible expenditures incurred before 2020 pursuant to a written agreement entered into before Budget Day.

Billed Basis Accounting   The 2017 budget eliminates the use of the billed basis accounting. This measure is effective for the first fiscal year of a business that begins after Budget Day (March 22, 2017).

Gains And Losses On Derivatives   The 2017 budget included two measures that affect the recognition of gains and losses on derivatives. The first provides for the elective use of the market-to-market method. The second is an anti-avoidance provision related to the straddle transactions. Coverage of these provisions goes beyond the scope of this text.

Acknowledgments

We would like to thank the many students who have used this book, the instructors who have adopted it at colleges and universities throughout Canada, as well as the assistants and tutors who have been involved in these courses.

In terms of the content of the book, we would like to give special thanks to:

Gary Donell   After many years with the CRA, Gary is now affiliated with the Ottawa office of Welch LLP. Gary has been a significant contributor to this text for nearly 20 years, bringing to it an outstanding knowledge of income tax issues. He has made many valuable suggestions that have contributed greatly to the accuracy and clarity of the material. In addition, he was responsible for writing much of the Chapter 18 material on partnerships and the Chapter 20 material on international taxation. Mr. Donell has undertaken this work independently of his work with either the CRA or Welch LLP. The views that are contained in this publication do not, in any way, reflect the policies of these organizations.

Also of great help in improving the text over the years were the comments and corrections provided by the following instructors:

- **Joseph Armanious** - McGill University (Montreal)
- **Laura Cumming** - Dalhousie University (Halifax)
- **Larry Goldsman** - McGill University (Montreal)
- **Susan Hurley** - NAIT (Edmonton)
- **Miles Laing** - Okanagan College (Kelowna)
- **Jay Perry** - Niagara College (Niagara-On-The-Lake)
- **Ruth Ann Strickland** - Western University (London)
- **Victor Waese** - BCIT (Burnaby)
- **Ronald Wong** - Capilano University (Vancouver)

It's Our Fault

As always, we have made every effort to accurately reflect appropriate tax rules. Every word in the text, problems, and solutions has been read by at least two and, in most cases three, individuals. However, it is virtually certain that errors remain. These errors are solely the responsibility of the authors and we apologize for any confusion that they may cause you.

We welcome any corrections or suggestions for additions or improvements. These can be sent to us at:

byrdinc@sympatico.ca

Clarence Byrd, Clarence Byrd Inc.

Ida Chen, Clarence Byrd Inc.

July, 2017

2017 Rates, Credits And Other Data

> For your convenience, this information, as well as the Chapter 5
> Appendix of common CCA rates, is available **online** as a .PDF file.

Information Applicable To Individuals

Federal Tax Rates For Individuals

Taxable Income In Excess Of	Federal Tax	Marginal Rate On Excess
$ -0-	$ -0-	15.0%
45,916	6,887	20.5%
91,831	16,300	26.0%
142,353	29,436	29.0%
202,800	46,966	33.0%

Federal Tax Credits For Individuals - Personal Credits (ITA 118)

Reference

118(1)(a) **Married Persons** 15% of $11,635 ($1,745).

118(1)(a) **Spousal** 15% of $11,635 ($1,745), less 15% of the spouse's Net Income For Tax Purposes. Base amount increased by $2,150 (to $13,785) if the spouse is mentally or physically infirm. Not available when the spouse's income is more than $11,635 (or $13,785).

118(1)(b) **Eligible Dependant** 15% of $11,635 ($1,745), less 15% of the eligible dependant's Net Income For Tax Purposes. Base amount increased by $2,150 (to $13,785) if the eligible dependant is mentally or physically infirm. Not available when the eligible dependant's income is more than $11,635 (or $13,785).

118(1)(b.1) **Canada Caregiver For Child Under 18** 15% of $2,150 ($323).

118(1)(c) **Single Persons** 15% of $11,635 ($1,745).

118(1)(d) **Canada Caregiver** 15% of $6,883 ($1,032), reduced by 15% of the dependant's income in excess of $16,163.

118(1)(e) **Canada Caregiver - Additional Amount** If either the income adjusted infirm spousal credit base or the income adjusted infirm eligible dependant credit base is less than the spouse or eligible dependant's income adjusted credit base ($6,883 - less the spouse or dependant's income in excess of $16,163), an additional Canada caregiver credit is available based on 15% of the deficiency.

118(2) **Age** 15% of $7,225 ($1,084). The base for this credit is reduced by the lesser of $7,225 and 15% of the individual's net income in excess of $36,430. Not available when income is more than $84,597. If the individual cannot use this credit, it can be transferred to a spouse or common-law partner.

118(3) **Pension** 15% of up to $2,000 of eligible pension income for a maximum credit of $300 [(15%)($2,000)]. If the individual cannot use this credit, it can be transferred to a spouse or common-law partner.

118(10) **Canada Employment Credit** 15% of up to $1,178. This produces a maximum credit of $177.

Other Common Federal Personal Credits (Various ITA)

118.01 **Adoption Expenses Credit** 15% of eligible expenses (reduced by any reimbursements) up to a maximum of $15,670 per adoption. This results in a maximum credit of $2,351.

118.02 **Public Transit Passes Credit** 15% of the cost of monthly or longer transit passes acquired prior to July 1, 2017. Unavailable for passes acquired subsequent to that date.

118.031 **Children's Arts Credit** Repealed for 2017 and subsequent years.

118.041 **Home Accessibility Credit** 15% of lesser of $10,000 and the amount of qualifying expenditures for the year.

118.05 **First Time Home Buyer's Credit** 15% of $5,000 ($750) of the cost of an eligible home.

118.06 **Volunteer Firefighters Credit** 15% of $3,000 ($450) for qualifying volunteers.

118.07 **Volunteer Search And Rescue Workers Credit** 15% of $3,000 ($450) for qualifying volunteers.

118.1 **Charitable Donations - Regular** The general limit on amounts for this credit is 75% of Net Income. There is an addition to this general limit equal to 25% of any taxable capital gains and 25% of any recapture of CCA resulting from a gift of capital property. In addition, the income inclusion on capital gains arising from a gift of some publicly traded shares is reduced from one-half to nil. For individuals, the credit is equal to:

$$[(15\%)(A)] + [(33\%)(B)] + [(29\%)(C)] \text{ where:}$$

A = The first $200 of eligible gifts.
B = The lesser of:
  • Total gifts, less $200; and
  • Taxable Income, less $202,800.
C = The excess, if any, by which the individual's total gifts exceed the sum of $200 plus the amount determined in B.

118.1(3.1) **Charitable Donations - First-Time Donor's Super Credit** For qualified "first-time" donors, a maximum of 25% of $1,000 ($250) credit which is added to the regular donations tax credit. This credit can only be claimed one time during the years 2013 through 2017.

118.2 **Medical Expenses** The medical expense tax credit is determined by the following formula:

$$[15\%] [(B - C) + D], \text{ where:}$$

B is the total of an individual's medical expenses for himself, his spouse or common-law partner, and any of his children who have not reached 18 years of age at the end of the year.
C is the lesser of 3% of the individual's Net Income For Tax Purposes and $2,268 (2017 figure).
D is the total of all amounts each of which is, in respect of a dependant of the individual (other than a child of the individual who has not attained the age of 18 years before the end of the taxation year), an amount determined by the formula:

$$E - F, \text{ where:}$$

E is the total of the dependant's medical expenses
F is the lesser of 3% of the dependant's Net Income For Tax Purposes and $2,268 (2017 figure).

118.3 **Disability - All Ages** 15% of $8,113 ($1,217). If not used by the disabled individual, it can be transferred to a person claiming that individual as a dependant.

118.3   **Disability Supplement - Under 18 And Qualifies For The Disability Tax Credit** 15% of $4,733 ($710), reduced by the total of amounts paid for attendant care or supervision in excess of $2,772 that are deducted as child care costs, deducted as a disability support amount, or claimed as a medical expense in calculating the medical expense tax credit.

Education Related Credits

118.5   • **Tuition Fees Which Includes Examination And Ancillary Fees**
  • 15% of qualifying tuition fees
  • 15% of examination fees for both post-secondary examinations and examinations required in a professional program
  • 15% of ancillary fees that are imposed by a post-secondary educational institution on all of their full or part-time students. Up to $250 in such ancillary fees can be claimed even if not required of all students.

118.6(2)   • **Education**   Repealed for 2017 and subsequent years.

118.6(2.1)   • **Textbook**   Repealed for 2017 and subsequent years.

118.62   • **Interest On Student Loans**
  15% of interest paid on qualifying student loans.

118.9   • **Transfer Of Tuition Credit**
  If the individual cannot use the credit, is not claimed as a dependant by his spouse, and does not transfer the unused credit to a spouse or common-law partner, then a parent or grandparent of the individual can claim up to $750 [(15%)($5,000)] of any unused tuition credit. The amount that can be transferred is reduced by the amount of the credit claimed by the student for the year.

118.7   **Employment Insurance** 15% of amounts paid by employees up to the maximum Employment Insurance premium of $836 (1.63% of $51,300). This produces a maximum tax credit of $125 [(15%)($836)].

118.7   **Canada Pension Plan** 15% of amounts paid by employees up to the maximum Canada Pension Plan contribution of $2,564 [4.95% of ($55,300 less $3,500)]. This produces a maximum tax credit of $385 [(15%)($2,564)]. For self-employed individuals, the payment is $5,128 ($2,564 times 2).

122.51   **Refundable Medical Expense Supplement** The individual claiming this amount must be over 17 and have earned income of at least $3,514. The amount is equal to the lesser of $1,203 and 25/15 of the medical expense tax credit (25% of allowable medical expenses). The refundable amount is then reduced by 5% of family Net Income in excess of $26,644. Not available when family income is more than $50,704.

122.8   **Refundable Child Fitness Credit**   Repealed for 2017 and subsequent years.

122.9   **Refundable Teacher And Early Childhood Educator School Supply Tax Credit**   A maximum of 15% of up to $1,000 ($150) of eligible expenditures that are made by eligible educators.

127(3)   **Political Donations** Three-quarters of the first $400, one-half of the next $350, one-third of the next $525, to a maximum credit of $650 on donations of $1,275.

127.4   **Labour Sponsored Venture Capital Corporations (LSVCC) Credit** The federal credit is equal to 15 percent of acquisitions of provincially registered LSVCCs.

ITA 82 and ITA 121

Dividend Tax Credit

- **Eligible Dividends** These dividends are grossed up by 38%. The federal dividend tax credit is equal to 6/11 of the gross up. The credit can also be calculated as 15.02% of the grossed up dividends, or 20.7272% of the actual dividends received.

- **Non-Eligible Dividends** These dividends are grossed up by 17%. The federal dividend tax credit is equal to 21/29 of the gross up. The credit can also be calculated as 10.52% of the grossed up dividends, or 12.31% of the actual dividends received.

Other Data For Individuals

ITA 82

Dividend Gross Up

Eligible Dividends For these dividends, the gross up is 38% of dividends received.

Non-Eligible Dividends For these dividends, the gross up is 17% of dividends received.

Chapter 4

OAS Clawback Limits The tax (clawback) on Old Age Security (OAS) benefits is based on the lesser of 100% of OAS benefits received, and 15% of the amount by which "threshold income" (Net Income For Tax Purposes, calculated without the OAS clawback) exceeds $74,788.

Chapter 4

EI Clawback Limits The tax (clawback) on Employment Insurance (EI) benefits under the *Employment Insurance Act* is based on the lesser of 30% of the EI benefits received, and 30% of the amount by which "threshold income" exceeds $64,125 (1.25 times the maximum insurable earnings of $51,300). For this purpose, "threshold income" is Net Income For Tax Purposes, calculated without the OAS or EI clawbacks.

Chapter 9

Child Care Expenses The least of three amounts:

1. The amount actually paid for child care services. If the child is at a camp or boarding school, this amount is limited to a weekly amount $275 (any age if eligible for disability tax credit), $200 (under 7 year of age), or $125 (age 7 through 16 or over 16 with a mental or physical impairment).

2. The sum of the **Annual Child Care Expense Amounts** for the taxpayer's eligible children. The per child amounts are $11,000 (any age if eligible for disability tax credit), $8,000 (under 7 year of age), or $5,000 (age 7 through 16 or over 16 with a mental or physical impairment).

3. 2/3 of the taxpayer's **Earned Income** (for child care expenses purposes).

Chapter 10

RRSP Deduction Room For 2017, the addition to RRSP deduction room is equal to:

- the lesser of $26,010 and 18% of 2016 Earned Income,
- reduced by the 2016 Pension Adjustment and any 2017 Past Service Pension Adjustment,
- and increased by any 2017 Pension Adjustment Reversal.

Chapter 11

Lifetime Capital Gains Deduction For 2017, the deduction limit for dispositions of shares of qualified small business corporations is $835,716. There is an additional amount for farm or fishing properties of $164,284, providing a total of $1,000,000 for such properties.

Provincial Tax Rates And Provincial Credits For Individuals Provincial taxes are based on Taxable Income, with most provinces adopting multiple rates. The number of brackets range from three to five. Provincial tax credits are generally based on the minimum provincial rate applied to a credit base that is similar to that used for federal credits. In addition to regular rates, several provinces use surtaxes.

Information Applicable To Individuals And Corporations

ITR 4301 **Prescribed Rate** The following figures show the base rate that would be used in calculations such as imputed interest on loans. It also shows the rates applicable on amounts owing to and from the CRA. For recent quarters, the interest rates were as follows:

Year	Quarter	Base Rate	Owing From*	Owing To
2015	All	1%	3%	5%
2016	All	1%	3%	5%
2017	I and II	**1%**	**3%**	**5%**

*The rate on refunds to corporations is limited to the base rate, without the additional 2%.

Automobile Deduction Limits

- CCA is limited to the first $30,000 of the automobiles cost, plus applicable GST/HST/PST (not including amounts that will be refunded through input tax credits).
- Interest on financing of automobiles is limited to $10 per day.
- Deductible leasing costs are limited to $800 per month (other constraints apply).
- Operating Cost Benefit = $0.25 per kilometre.
- Deductible Rates = $0.54 for first 5,000 kilometres, $0.48 for additional kilometres.

CCA Rates See Appendix to Chapter 5.

Quick Method Rates (GST Only)

	Percentage On GST Included Sales	
	First $30,000	On Excess
Retailers And Wholesalers	0.8%	1.8%
Service Providers And Manufacturers	2.6%	3.6%

Note Different rates apply in the provinces that have adopted an HST system.

Information Applicable To Corporations

Federal Corporate Tax Rates are as follows (federal tax abatement removed):

General Business (Before General Rate Reduction)	28%
General Business (After General Rate Reduction Of 13%)	15%
Income Eligible For M&P Deduction	15%
Income Eligible For Small Business Deduction	10.5%
Part IV Refundable Tax	38-1/3%
Part I Refundable Tax On Investment Income Of CCPC (ART)	10-2/3%

Reference 125(1) **Small Business Deduction** is equal to 17.5% of the least of:

A. Net Canadian active business income.

B. Taxable Income, less:

1. 100/28 times the ITA 126(1) credit for taxes paid on foreign non-business income, calculated without consideration of the additional refundable tax under ITA 123.3 or the general rate reduction under ITA 123.4; and

2. 4 times the ITA 126(2) credit for taxes paid on foreign business income, calculated without consideration of the general rate reduction under ITA 123.4.

C. The annual business limit of $500,000, less any portion allocated to associated corporations, less the reduction for large corporations.

125.1   **Manufacturing And Processing Deduction** is equal to 13% of the lesser of:

A. Manufacturing and processing profits, less amounts eligible for the small business deduction; and

B. Taxable Income, less the sum of:
1. the amount eligible for the small business deduction;
2. 4 times the foreign tax credit for business income calculated without consideration of the ITA 123.4 general rate reduction; and
3. "aggregate investment income" (of CCPCs) as defined in ITA 129(4).

123.4(2)   **General Rate Reduction** is equal to 13% of Full Rate Taxable Income. This is Taxable Income, reduced by; income eligible for the small business deduction, income eligible for the M&P deduction and the corporation's "aggregate investment income" for the year.

126(1)   **Foreign Tax Credits For Corporations** The Foreign Non-Business Income Tax Credit is the lesser of:

- The tax paid to the foreign government (for corporations, there is no 15% limit on the foreign non-business taxes paid); and

- An amount determined by the following formula:

$$\left[\frac{\text{Foreign Non} - \text{Business Income}}{\text{Adjusted Division B Income}} \right] [\text{Tax Otherwise Payable}]$$

126(2)   The Foreign Business Income Tax Credit is equal to the least of:

- The tax paid to the foreign government;

- An amount determined by the following formula:

$$\left[\frac{\text{Foreign Business Income}}{\text{Adjusted Division B Income}} \right] [\text{Tax Otherwise Payable}] ; \quad \text{and}$$

- Tax Otherwise Payable for the year, less any foreign tax credit taken on non-business income under ITA 126(1).

129(4)   **Aggregate Investment Income** is the sum of:

- net taxable capital gains for the year, reduced by any net capital loss carry overs deducted during the year; and

- income from property including interest, rents, and royalties, but excluding dividends that are deductible in computing Taxable Income. Since foreign dividends are generally not deductible, they would be included in aggregate investment income.

123.3   **Additional Refundable Tax On Investment Income (ART)** is equal to 10-2/3% of the lesser of:

- the corporation's "aggregate investment income" for the year [as defined in ITA 129(4)]; and

- the amount, if any, by which the corporation's Taxable Income for the year exceeds the amount that is eligible for the small business deduction.

186(1)   **Part IV Tax** is assessed at a rate of 38-1/3% of portfolio dividends, plus dividends received from a connected company that gave rise to a dividend refund for the connected company as a result of the payment.

129(3)(a) **Refundable Portion Of Part I Tax Payable** is defined as the least of three items:

    1. the amount determined by the formula

$$A - B, \text{ where}$$

    A is 30-2/3% of the corporation's aggregate investment income for the year, and

    B is the amount, if any, by which the foreign non-business income tax credit exceeds 8% of its foreign investment income for the year.

    2. 30-2/3% of the amount, if any, by which the corporation's taxable income for the year exceeds the total of:

- the amount eligible for the small business deduction;
- 100 ÷ 38-2/3 of the tax credit for foreign non-business income; and
- 4 times the tax credit for foreign business income.

    3. the corporation's tax for the year payable under Part I.

129(3) **Refundable Dividend Tax On Hand (RDTOH)** is defined as follows:

- The corporation's RDTOH at the end of the preceding year; less
- The corporation's dividend refund for its preceding taxation year; plus
- The Refundable Portion Of Part I tax for the year; plus
- The total of the taxes under Part IV for the year.

89(1) **General Rate Income Pool** A CCPC's General Rate Income Pool (GRIP) is defined as follows:

- The GRIP balance at the end of the preceding year; plus
- 72% of the CCPC's Taxable Income after it has been reduced by amounts eligible for the small business deduction and aggregate investment income; plus
- eligible dividends received during the year; plus
- adjustments related to amalgamations and wind-ups; less
- eligible dividends paid during the preceding year.

Tax Related Web Sites

GOVERNMENT

Canada Revenue Agency www.cra.gc.ca
Department of Finance Canada www.fin.gc.ca

CPA FIRMS

BDO https://www.bdo.ca/en-ca/services/tax/domestic-tax-services/overview/

Ernst & Young www.ey.com/CA/en/Services/Tax

KPMG www.kpmg.com/ca/en/services/tax

PricewaterhouseCoopers www.pwc.com/ca/en/tax/publications.jhtml

OTHER

CPA Canada www.CPAcanada.ca

Canadian Tax Foundation www.ctf.ca

ProFile Tax Suite www.intuit.ca/professional-tax-software/index.jsp

CONTENTS

The textbook is published in two Volumes:	Volume I = Chapters 1 to 10 Volume II = Chapters 11 to 21

CHAPTER 3

Income Or Loss From An Office Or Employment

Chapter 3, continued

CHAPTER 4

Taxable Income And Tax Payable For Individuals

(continued)

Chapter 4, continued

CHAPTER 5
Capital Cost Allowance

CHAPTER 6
Income Or Loss From A Business

CHAPTER 7
Income From Property

CHAPTER 8
Capital Gains And Capital Losses

CHAPTER 9
Other Income, Other Deductions, And Other Issues

CHAPTER 10

Retirement Savings And Other Special Income Arrangements

Study Guide

Your two volume textbook is accompanied by a separate Study Guide that is available in print and online.

The chapters of this Study Guide correspond to the chapters of **Byrd & Chen's Canadian Tax Principles.**

Each of these Study Guide chapters contains the following:

- Detailed guidance on how to work through the text and problems in the chapter.
- Detailed solutions to the Exercises and Self Study Problems in the textbook for the chapter.
- A list of learning objectives for the material in the chapter.

In addition, the Study Guide contains:

- Two sample personal tax returns and two Self Study Tax Software Problems in Chapters 4 and 11.
- A sample corporate tax return in Chapter 13.
- An extensive Glossary.

CHAPTER 1

Introduction To Federal Taxation In Canada

The Canadian Tax System

Alternative Tax Bases

1-1.   There are a variety of ways in which taxes can be classified. One possible basis of classification would be the economic feature or event that is to be taxed. Such features or events are referred to as the base for taxation and a large number of different bases are used in different tax systems throughout the world. Some of the more common tax bases are as follows:

Income Tax   A tax on the income of certain defined entities.

Property Tax   A tax on the ownership of some particular set of goods.

Consumption Tax   A tax levied on the consumption or use of a good or service. Also referred to as sales tax or commodity tax.

Value Added Tax   A tax levied on the increase in value of a good or service that has been created by the taxpayer's stage of the production or distribution cycle.

Tariffs or Customs Duties   A tax imposed on the importation or exportation of certain goods or services.

Transfer Tax   A tax on the transfer of property from one owner to another.

User Tax   A tax levied on the user of some facility such as a road or airport.

Capital Tax   A tax on the invested capital of a corporation.

Head Tax   A tax on the very existence of some classified group of individuals.

1-2.   At one time or another, some level of Canadian government has used, or is still using, all of these bases for taxation. For example, the Canadian federal government currently has, in addition to income taxes on corporations, individuals, and trusts, such taxes as the Goods and Services Tax (GST), an alcoholic beverages tax, special transaction taxes, a gasoline tax, as well as others. However, the dominant form of Canadian taxation at the federal level is the income taxes levied on both corporations and individuals. This fact is reflected in Figure 1-1 (following page) which provides a percentage distribution of the $304.7 billion in budgetary revenues that the federal government expects to collect during fiscal 2017-2018.

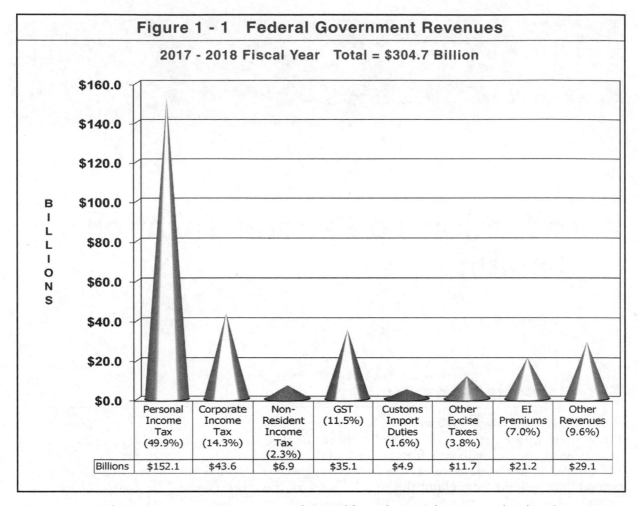

Figure 1 - 1   Federal Government Revenues

2017 - 2018 Fiscal Year   Total = $304.7 Billion

	Personal Income Tax (49.9%)	Corporate Income Tax (14.3%)	Non-Resident Income Tax (2.3%)	GST (11.5%)	Customs Import Duties (1.6%)	Other Excise Taxes (3.8%)	EI Premiums (7.0%)	Other Revenues (9.6%)
Billions	$152.1	$43.6	$6.9	$35.1	$4.9	$11.7	$21.2	$29.1

1-3.   The statistics in Figure 1-1 were obtained from the March, 2017 Federal Budget papers.

1-4.   Figure 1-1 makes it clear that personal income taxes constitute, by far, the most important source of federal government revenues. The share of federal government revenues provided by personal income taxes is expected to be 49.9 percent of the total in 2017-2018. This is virtually the same as for 2016-2017, when this source of revenues was 50 percent of the total.

1-5.   Corporate income taxes are forecast at 14.3 percent of 2017-2018 federal government revenues. This is higher than the 13.2 percent that this source of revenues produced in 2016-2017. The GST (Goods and Services Tax) is an important source of federal government revenues. The share of federal government revenues provided by GST is expected to be 11.5 percent of the total in 2017-2018. This source of revenues was 11.6 percent of the total in 2016-2017.

1-6.   Other revenues consist of revenues from Crown corporations, other programs and net foreign exchange.

Taxable Entities In Canada
Federal Income Tax
1-7.   Three types of entities are subject to federal income taxation. These are:

- Individuals (human beings)
- Corporations
- Trusts

1-8. You should note that the *Income Tax Act* uses the term "person" to refer to all three types of taxable entities. This can be a bit confusing in that the dictionary defines person as "a human being, whether man, woman, or child". Despite this conventional usage of the term person, the *Income Tax Act* applies it to both corporations and trusts. When the *Act* wishes to refer to a human taxpayer, it uses the term "individual".

1-9. For income tax purposes, unincorporated businesses such as partnerships and proprietorships are not viewed as taxable entities. Rather, income earned by an unincorporated business organization is taxed in the hands of the proprietor (who would be an individual) or the partner. Note that members of a partnership may be individuals, trusts, or corporations.

1-10. As discussed in Chapter 2, "Procedures And Administration", all three types of taxable entities are required to file income tax returns. The return for an individual is referred to as a T1, for a corporation, a T2, and for a trust, a T3. Proprietorships and partnerships do not file income tax returns as they are not taxable entities.

GST

1-11. The requirement to register to collect and remit GST generally extends to any person engaged in commercial activity in Canada. You should note that the definition of a person for GST purposes is different from that used in the *Income Tax Act*. For income tax purposes, a "person" is restricted to an individual, a corporation, or a trust. Unincorporated businesses do not file separate income tax returns.

1-12. Under GST legislation, the concept of a person is much broader, including individuals, partnerships, corporations, estates of deceased individuals, trusts, charities, societies, unions, clubs, associations, commissions, and other organizations. Chapter 21, "GST/HST" includes detailed coverage of the Goods And Services Tax and the Harmonized Sales Tax.

Exercise One - 1

Subject: Taxable Entities For Income Tax Purposes

Which of the following entities could be required to file an income tax return?

- Max Jordan (an individual)
- Jordan's Hardware Store (an unincorporated business)
- Jordan & Jordan (a partnership)
- The Jordan family trust (a trust)
- Jordan Enterprises Ltd. (a corporation)
- The Jordan Foundation (an unincorporated charity)

Exercise One - 2

Subject: Taxable Entities For GST Purposes

Which of the following entities could be required to file a GST return?

- Max Jordan (an individual)
- Jordan's Hardware Store (an unincorporated business)
- Jordan & Jordan (a partnership)
- The Jordan family trust (a trust)
- Jordan Enterprises Ltd. (a corporation)
- The Jordan Foundation (an unincorporated charity)

SOLUTIONS available in print and online Study Guide.

Federal Taxation And The Provinces
Personal Income Taxes

1-13.   Under the Constitution Act, the federal, provincial, and territorial governments have the power to impose taxes. The provinces and territories are limited to direct taxation as delegated in the Act, a constraint that leaves all residual taxation powers to the federal government. The provinces are further limited to the taxation of income earned in the particular province and the income of persons resident in that province. Within these limitations, all of the provinces and territories impose both personal and corporate income taxes.

1-14.   Under the federal/provincial tax collection agreement, provincial taxes are calculated by applying a provincial tax rate to a Taxable Income figure. With the exception of Quebec, all of the provinces use the same Taxable Income figure that is used at the federal level.

1-15.   Despite the use of the federal Taxable Income figure, the provinces have retained considerable flexibility in their individual tax systems. This flexibility is achieved in two ways:

- Each province can apply different rates and surtaxes to as many tax brackets as it wishes.

- More importantly, each province is able to set different provincial credits to apply against provincial Tax Payable. While most provinces have provincial credits that are similar to credits that are established at the federal level, the value of these credits varies considerably at the provincial level. For example, the 2017 base for the basic personal tax credit varies from $8,000 in Prince Edward Island to $18,690 in Alberta. In addition, many provinces have additional types of credits. As an example of this, Ontario has a property tax credit for its residents.

1-16.   The provincial differences complicate the preparation of tax returns. The level of complication varies from province to province, depending on the degree to which provincial tax brackets and provincial tax credits resemble those applicable at the federal level.

1-17.   Because of these complications, the problem material in this text will, in general, not require the calculation of provincial taxes for individuals. However, because the combined federal/provincial rate is important in many tax-based decisions (e.g., selecting between alternative investments), we will continue to refer to overall combined rates, despite the fact that such figures are very specific to the province in which the income is taxed, as well as the characteristics associated with the individual filing the return.

Exercise One - 3

Subject: Federal And Provincial Taxes Payable

John Forsyth has Taxable Income of $27,000. For the current year, his federal tax rate is 15 percent, while the corresponding provincial rate is 7.5 percent. Determine Mr. Forsyth's combined federal and provincial tax payable, before consideration of any available credits against Tax Payable.

SOLUTION available in print and online Study Guide.

Corporate Income Taxes

1-18.   The system used to calculate provincial corporate income tax payable is similar to the system that is applicable to individuals. Provincial corporate income tax is levied on Taxable Income. All of the provinces, with the exception of Alberta and Quebec, use the federal *Income Tax Act* to compute Taxable Income. Even in Alberta and Quebec, the respective provincial Tax Acts have many of the same features as the federal *Act*.

1-19.   With respect to the collection of corporate income taxes, only Alberta and Quebec collect their own corporate income taxes. In all other provinces and territories, corporate income taxes are collected by the federal government on behalf of the provinces.

GST, HST And PST

1-20. Although detailed coverage of GST and HST can be found in Chapter 21, GST/HST, we will provide a short overview here as part of our introduction to federal taxation. When the federal government proposed a joint federal/provincial goods and services tax (GST) in 1987, the lack of interest by provincial governments meant that the GST was introduced only at the federal level. Provincial sales taxes remained in place without significant alteration. As a result, two different sales taxes were collected, accounted for, and remitted.

1-21. This situation was very costly and time consuming for businesses operating in more than one province, as they had to file multiple sales tax returns under different sets of rules. This was clearly an inefficient way to generate tax revenues and, not surprisingly, considerable pressure developed for the harmonization of the separate federal and provincial sales taxes.

1-22. Despite the obvious efficiencies that would result from harmonization, it has not been accepted across Canada. Quebec administers its own Quebec sales tax (QST) which is a somewhat harmonized system. While its coverage is similar to the GST, it is not identical.

1-23. In several provinces there is a harmonized sales tax (HST) which is, in effect, a combined federal/provincial sales tax. These systems differ from the Quebec model in that the HST is a single tax administered by the federal government. The HST provinces are New Brunswick, Nova Scotia, Newfoundland, Prince Edward Island and Ontario.

1-24. Since each HST province chooses the rate for the provincial portion of the HST and the provinces have selected different rates, the HST is not a single rate throughout the HST provinces. As a result, even among the HST provinces, the application of the HST on a sale can result in a sales tax figure that varies depending on the province of sale.

1-25. The various provincial sales tax regimes have left Canada with a fragmented sales tax system. As of March 1, 2017, the different sales tax rates in the provinces are:

- HST Rates (Includes 5 Percent GST)
    - **13%** (5% + 8%) for Ontario
    - **15%** (5% + 10%) for New Brunswick, Newfoundland, Nova Scotia, and Prince Edward Island
- GST Plus Provincial Sales Tax
    - **10%** (5% + 5%) for Saskatchewan
    - **12%** (5% + 7%) for British Columbia
    - **13%** (5% + 8%) for Manitoba
    - **14.975%** (5% + 9.975%) for Quebec
- GST Only
    - **5%** for Alberta

Tax Policy Concepts

Taxation And Economic Policy

1-26. The traditional goal of tax legislation has been to generate revenues for the relevant taxing authority. However, it is clear that today's approach to tax legislation is multi-faceted. We use tax legislation as a tool to facilitate a number of economic policy objectives:

Resource Allocation Tax revenues are used to provide public goods and services. Pure public goods such as the cost of our national defense system are thought to benefit all taxpayers. As it is not possible to allocate costs to individuals on the basis of benefits received, such costs must be supported with general tax revenues. Similar allocations occur with such widely used public goods as education, health care, and pollution control. In some cases, the tax system also has an influence on the allocation of private goods. For example, excise taxes are used to discourage the consumption of alcohol and tobacco products.

Distribution Effects   Our tax system is used to redistribute income and wealth among taxpayers. Such provisions as the federal GST tax credit and provincial sales tax exemptions on food and low priced clothing have the effect of taking taxes paid by higher income taxpayers and distributing them to lower income wage earners or taxpayers with higher basic living costs in proportion to their income.

Stabilization Effects   Taxes may also be used to achieve macroeconomic objectives. At various times, tax policy has been used to encourage economic expansion, increase employment, and to assist in holding inflation in check. An example of this is the emphasis on stimulating the economy that is found in recent budgets.

Fiscal Federalism   This term refers to the various procedures that are used to allocate resources among different levels of government. For 2016-2017, it is estimated that transfers to other levels of government will amount to $68.6 billion, as compared to transfers to persons of $91.4 billion, and direct program spending of $131.3 billion. In the next step in the chain, a portion of provincial tax revenue is transferred to municipal governments.

Taxation And Income Levels

General Approaches

1-27.   Policy makers are concerned about the relationship between income levels and rates of taxation. Taxes can be proportional, in that a constant rate is applied at all levels of income. In theory, this is our general approach to taxing the income of corporations. For public companies, the system is based on a flat rate that is applicable to all income earned by the company. However, a wide variety of provisions act to modify the application of this rate, resulting in a situation where many Canadian companies are not subject to this notional flat rate.

1-28.   As an alternative, taxation can be regressive, resulting in lower effective rates of taxation as higher income levels are reached. Sales taxes generally fall into this regressive category as lower income individuals spend a larger portion of their total income and, as a consequence, pay a greater portion of their total income as sales taxes levied on their expenditures.

EXAMPLE   Consider the Werner sisters:

Gertrude Werner has income of $200,000 and spends $40,000 of this amount. She lives in a province with a 13 percent harmonized sales tax (HST) on expenditures, resulting in the payment of $5,200 in HST. This represents a 2.6 percent effective tax rate on her $200,000 income.

Ingrid Werner has income of $40,000 and spends all of this amount. She lives in the same province as her sister, resulting in the payment of $5,200 in HST. This represents a 13 percent effective tax rate on her $40,000 income.

Exercise One - 4

Subject: Regressive Taxes

Margie Jones has Taxable Income for the current year of $895,000, of which $172,000 is spent on goods and services that are subject to Harmonized Sales Tax (HST) at a rate of 13 percent. Her sister, Jane Jones, is a part-time student living in the same province and has Taxable Income of $18,000. During the current year, as a result of using some of her savings, she spends $27,500 on goods and services that are all subject to HST. Determine the effective sales tax rate as a percentage of the income of the two sisters.

SOLUTION available in print and online Study Guide.

We suggest you work Self Study Problem One-1 at this point.

1-29.   In contrast to the regressive nature of sales taxes, the present system of personal income taxation is designed to be progressive, since higher rates are applied to higher levels of income.   For 2017, the federal rates range from a low of 15 percent on the first $45,916 of Taxable Income to a high of 33 percent on Taxable Income in excess of $202,800.

Progressive Vs. Regressive

1-30.   As noted in the preceding paragraph, the federal income tax system taxes individuals using a progressive system.   The major arguments in favour of this approach can be described as follows:

Equity   Higher income individuals have a greater ability to pay taxes.   As their income is above their basic consumption needs, the relative cost to the individual of having a portion of this income taxed away is less than the relative cost to lower income individuals, where additional taxation removes funds required for such essentials as food and housing.

Stability   Progressive tax rates help maintain after-tax income stability by shifting people to lower tax brackets in times of economic downturn and to higher brackets when there is economic expansion.   The resulting decreases or increases in income taxes serve to cushion the economic swings.

1-31.   There are, however, a number of problems that can be associated with progressive rates.   These can be briefly described as follows:

Complexity   With progressive rates in place, efforts will be made to divide income among as many individuals (usually family members) as possible.   These efforts to make maximum use of the lower tax brackets necessitate the use of complex anti-avoidance rules by taxation authorities.

Income Fluctuations   In the absence of relieving provisions, progressive rates discriminate against individuals with highly variable income streams.   That is, under a progressive system, an individual with $1,000,000 in income in one year and no income for the next three years will pay substantially more in taxes than an individual with the same $1,000,000 total earned over four years at a rate of $250,000 per year.

Family Unit Problems   Progressive tax rates discriminate against single income family units.   A family unit in which one spouse makes $200,000 and the other has no Taxable Income would pay significantly more in taxes than would be the case if each spouse earned $100,000.

Economic Growth   It is clear that the high tax brackets that can be associated with a progressive system can discourage both employment and investment efforts.   This could serve to limit economic growth.

Tax Concessions   The high brackets associated with progressive systems lead to pressure for various types of tax concessions to be made available.   Because high income individuals have a greater ability to take advantage of favourable provisions in the income tax legislation, they may actually wind up paying taxes at lower effective rates.   In response to the possibility that, in extreme cases, some high income individuals pay no income taxes at all, there is an alternative minimum income tax that is imposed on certain taxpayers (see Chapter 11).

Tax Avoidance And Evasion   Progressive rates discourage income reporting and encourage the creation of various means to evade taxation.   Evasion strategies range from simple bartering, to cash only transactions, to offshore tax havens and finally to criminal activities.

Reduced Tax Revenues   There is evidence that, if tax rates are too high, the result may be reduced aggregate tax revenues.   Some authorities believe that this begins to occur at tax rates between 40 and 50 percent.

We would note that, with the 2016 increase in the maximum federal rate to 33 percent, the maximum combined federal/provincial rate in most provinces now exceeds 50 percent, going as high as 54 percent. While it is difficult to predict the degree to which this will encourage tax evasion, it is almost certain that tax rates at this level will result in significant amounts of income being moved out of Canada. Individuals with income in excess of the maximum threshold, often have great flexibility in where they reside and how they invest.

Of particular importance is the possibility of moving to the U.S. where the combined federal/state rate on income in excess of $200,000 can be as low as 33 percent. When Canadian tax rates over 50 percent are combined with Florida's mild winters (Florida has no state income tax), it is likely that many individuals who are able to do so will at least consider a change in venue.

Flat Tax Systems

1-32.   While progressive tax systems continue to be pervasive, there has been a worldwide trend towards flattening rate schedules. One of the reasons for this trend is the fact that effective tax rates are not as progressive as the rate schedules indicate. As mentioned in the preceding paragraph, high bracket taxpayers tend to have better access to various types of tax concessions which can significantly reduce the effective rates for these individuals.

1-33.   Given this situation, it has been suggested that we could achieve results similar to those which, in fact, prevail under the current system by applying a single or flat rate of tax to a broadened taxation base. In this context, the term base broadening refers to the elimination of tax concessions, resulting in tax rates that are applied to a larger income figure.

1-34.   There is currently no flat provincial tax system in place in Canada. Alberta's 10 percent rate on the income of individuals was in place until 2015. However, faced with the financial difficulties generated by falling oil prices, the Alberta government introduced a progressive system in 2016.

We suggest you work Self Study Problem One-2 at this point.

Tax Incidence

1-35.   Tax incidence refers to the issue of who really pays a particular tax. While statutory incidence refers to the initial legal liability for tax payment, the actual economic burden may be passed on to a different group. For example, certain taxes on production might be the legal liability of the producer. However, they may be partly or entirely shifted to consumers through price increases on the goods produced.

1-36.   Policy makers must be concerned with this to ensure that the system is working as intended. It is generally assumed that the incidence of personal income tax falls on individuals. In addition, in their role as consumers, individuals also assume the responsibility for a large portion of the various sales taxes that are levied in Canada. The incidence of corporate taxes is more open to speculation. Shareholders may bear the burden of corporate taxes in the short run. However, most authorities believe that, in the long run, this burden is shared by employees and consumers.

Tax Expenditures

1-37.   In contrast to government funding programs that provide payments to various entities in the economy, tax expenditures reflect revenues that have been given up by the government through the use of tax preferences, concessions, and other tax breaks. These expenditures may favour selected individuals or groups (senior citizens), certain kinds of income (capital gains), or certain characteristics of some taxpayers (the disabled).

1-38.   In an effort to quantify the importance of these expenditures, the Department of Finance produces the publication, "Tax Expenditures And Evaluations" each year. The 2017 edition contains figures for the years 2011 through 2018 (projected). Examples of the 2011 estimates and 2017 projections of the cost of some of these expenditures include:

Tax Expenditure	2011	2017
Charitable donations tax credit	$2.4 billion	$2.9 billion
Tax credit for spouse	$1.6 billion	$1.6 billion
Partial inclusion of capital gains	$3.8 billion	$6.0 billion
The deduction of RRSP contributions	$10.0 billion	$16.3 billion
Tax free gains on principal residences	$4.7 billion	$6.8 billion

1-39.   It is clear that such tax expenditures are of considerable significance in the management of federal finances. It is equally clear that the provision of this type of government benefit has become entrenched in our tax system. This situation can be explained by a number of factors:

- It is less costly to administer tax expenditures than it is to administer government funding programs.

- More decisions are left to the private sector so that funds may be allocated more efficiently.

- Tax expenditures reduce the visibility of certain government actions. This is particularly beneficial if some social stigma is attached to the programs. For example, a child tax benefit system is more acceptable than increasing social assistance (welfare) payments.

- Tax expenditures reduce the progressivity of the tax system. As many of the tax expenditures, such as tax shelters, are more available to higher income taxpayers, they serve to reduce effective tax rates in the higher rate brackets.

1-40.   Tax expenditures are not only very substantial, they are also difficult to control. This was expressed several years ago by a former auditor general, as follows:

A cost conscious Parliament is in the position of a team of engineers trying to design a more fuel efficient automobile. They think they have succeeded, but the engine seems to go on consuming as much gas as it did before. They cannot understand the problem until they notice that, hidden from view, a myriad of small holes have been punched through the bottom of the gas tank. This is too often the way of tax expenditures. Revenue leaks away, and MPs do not know about it until it is too late.

Qualitative Characteristics Of Tax Systems
General Concepts
1-41.   Accounting standard setting bodies have established such concepts as relevance and reliability as being desirable qualitative characteristics of accounting information. While not established with the same degree of formality, it is clear that there are similar concepts that can be used to evaluate tax systems. Some of these desirable qualitative characteristics can be described as follows:

Equity Or Fairness   Horizontal equity entails assessing similar levels of taxation for people in similar economic circumstances. If two individuals each have Taxable Income of $50,000, horizontal equity would require that they each pay the same amount of taxes.

In contrast, vertical equity means dissimilar tax treatment of people in different circumstances. If an individual has Taxable Income of $100,000, he should pay more taxes than an individual with Taxable Income of $50,000.

Neutrality   The concept of neutrality calls for a tax system that interferes as little as possible with decision making. An overriding economic assumption is that decisions are always made to maximize the use of resources. This may not be achieved when tax factors affect how taxpayers save, invest, or consume.   Taxes, by influencing economic decisions, may cause a less than optimal allocation of resources.

Adequacy   A good tax system should meet the funding requirements of the taxing authority. It is also desirable that these revenues be produced in a fashion that is dependable and relatively predictable from year to year.

Elasticity   Tax revenues should be capable of being adjusted to meet changes in economic conditions, without necessitating tax rate changes.

Flexibility   This refers to the ease with which the tax system can be adjusted to meet changing economic or social conditions.

Simplicity And Ease Of Compliance   A good tax system is easy to comply with and does not present significant administrative problems for the people enforcing the system.

Certainty   Individual taxpayers should know how much tax they have to pay, the basis for payments, and the due date. Such certainty also helps taxing authorities estimate tax revenues and facilitates forecasting of budgetary expenditures.

Balance Between Sectors   A good tax system should not be overly reliant on either corporate or individual taxation. Attention should also be given to balance within these sectors, insuring that no type of business or type of individual is asked to assume a disproportionate share of the tax burden.

International Competitiveness   If a country's tax system has rates that are out of line with those in comparable countries, the result will be an outflow of both business and skilled individuals to those countries that have more favourable tax rates.

Conflicts Among Characteristics

1-42.   In designing a tax system, many compromises are required. Examples include the fact that flexibility is often in conflict with certainty, equity requires trade-offs in simplicity and neutrality, and some taxes with very positive objectives are very non-neutral in nature. An example of this last conflict is that the rates available to small businesses are very favourable because the government believes that this attracts investment to this sector, thereby encouraging employment and the development of active business efforts. However, this may not result in the optimal allocation of resources to the business sector as a whole.

Evaluation Of The Canadian System

1-43.   Canadian policy makers often refer to the preceding qualitative characteristics in discussions involving taxation policies. This would make it appropriate to consider how the current system of federal taxation stacks up against these criteria. While any comprehensive evaluation of this question goes well beyond the objectives of this text, we offer the following brief comments:

• With respect to equity, Canada continues to have situations in which high income individuals pay little or no tax and relatively low income individuals are subjected to fairly high effective rates. While the alternative minimum tax was instituted to correct this problem, inequity is unlikely to be eliminated in a tax system that attempts to accomplish as many diverse objectives as does the current Canadian system.

• As noted previously, the Canadian system has a very heavy reliance on the taxation of personal income and receives a very low portion of its revenues from the corporate income tax. Also on the low side is the contribution of the GST.

• The Canadian system has had problems with stability and dependability of revenues.

• The Canadian tax system is very complex, making compliance difficult for many taxpayers. In addition, administration of the legislation is made more difficult by the large number of provisions and the lack of clarity in their content.

The inability to achieve a harmonized GST/HST system has made this situation much worse. As we have noted, different provinces have adopted different systems, thereby complicating inter-provincial transactions. Further, in a given province, there are significant variations in the types of goods and services that are subject to taxation within a given system.

- With respect to international competitiveness, the situation is different for corporations and individuals.

    - Over the last few years, tax rates on Canadian corporations have been reduced. These reductions leave Canada with corporate rates that compare very favorably with most foreign jurisdictions.

    - In contrast, increasing the maximum federal tax rate on individuals to 33 percent in 2016 has made Canada less competitive with other venues, particularly the United States.

We suggest you work Self Study Problem One-3 at this point.

Income Tax Reference Materials

Introduction

1-44. To this point in our discussion of the Canadian tax system and related tax policy concepts, we have considered a variety of taxation bases as they apply at both the federal and provincial level. However, with the exception of Chapter 21 which deals with the goods and services tax, the focus of this book is on the federal taxes that are assessed on the income of individuals, corporations, and trusts.

1-45. Reference materials related to the federal income tax are very extensive. In addition to the *Income Tax Act* there are many other sources of information. These include other legislative materials, other publications of the Canada Revenue Agency (CRA), documents related to court decisions, as well as interpretive materials from a wide variety of sources.

1-46. If presented in paper format, a complete library of these materials would run to thousands of pages and would have to be included in a large number of separate volumes. Given this, almost all tax practitioners work with an electronic database that provides for easy access through key word searches.

1-47. These electronic databases are published by several Canadian organizations, including CCH, Carswell, and CPA Canada. Through our affiliation with CPA Canada, we are able to provide you with access to their Federal Income Tax Collection (FITAC). This electronic database can be accessed from the Companion Website for this text. It includes:

- The *Income Tax Act* and *Income Tax Regulations*.
- Most CRA publications including Income Tax Folios, Interpretation Bulletins, Information Circulars, Guides, and forms.
- An electronic copy of this text that is searchable and has electronic links to other reference materials in the database.

1-48. A description of all of these materials will be found in the sections which follow.

The Income Tax Act

Importance

1-49. This is the most important source of information for dealing with matters related to the federal income tax. Interpretation and guidance can be found in many other sources. However, at the end of the day, this document provides the basis for any final decision related to the amount of income tax that will have to be paid by an individual, corporation, or trust.

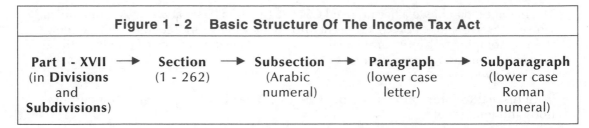

Figure 1 - 2   Basic Structure Of The Income Tax Act

| Part I - XVII (in **Divisions** and **Subdivisions**) | → | Section (1 - 262) | → | Subsection (Arabic numeral) | → | Paragraph (lower case letter) | → | Subparagraph (lower case Roman numeral) |

1-50.   It is a very long document, running over 2,500 pages in paper format. It is also written in a very legalistic style which, in our opinion, cannot be readily understood by most individuals. Given this, the design of our text is such that it does not require the use of the *Income Tax Act* in order to understand its content or complete the related problem material.

1-51.   While the design of this text does not require the use of the *Income Tax Act* as a reference, it is still important to have some understanding of the structure of this document. One reason for this is that the organization of this book generally follows the structure of the *Income Tax Act*. In addition, you will find many references to the *Act* embedded as part of the text. There are two reasons for this:

- The most important reason for these references is to allow interested individuals to explore a particular issue to a depth that goes beyond the scope of this text. The presence of *Income Tax Act* references greatly facilitates this process.
- The use of references can also be convenient. In dealing with a particular subject, it is often more efficient to refer to a subject with a reference to the *Act* than to repeatedly use the full description of the subject.

1-52.   Given these considerations, we will provide a description of the basic structure and content of this important legislation.

Structure Of The Federal Income Tax Act

1-53.   Figure 1-2 diagrams the basic structure of the *Act*. As can be seen in this diagram, the major divisions of the *Income Tax Act* are referred to as Parts. Some, but not all of these Parts, contain two or more Divisions (e.g., Part I of the *Act* contains Divisions A through J). Some Divisions, but again not all of them, contain Subdivisions. For example, Division B of Part I contains Subdivisions a through k. Note that, while the Parts are numbered I through XVII, there are more than 17 Parts. This reflects the fact that when a new Part is added, it has been more convenient to attach a decimal designation to the new Part, as opposed to renumbering all of the Parts that follow the new Section. For example, Part I is followed by Part I.01, Part I.1, Part I.2, and Part I.3.

1-54.   All of the Parts contain at least one Section. However, there is considerable variance in the size of the Parts. Part I.2, "Tax On Old Age Security Benefits", contains only one Section. In contrast, Part I, the largest and most important Part of the *Act*, contains Sections 2 to 180.

1-55.   The Sections are labeled 1 through 262. However, as was the case with Parts of the *Act*, decimals are used to label new Sections. For example, Section 12 is followed by Section 12.1, Section 12.2, Section 12.3 (repealed), Section 12.4, Section 12.5, and Section 12.6.

1-56.   Sections may be further subdivided into Subsections [designated with Arabic numerals as in Subsection 84(1)]. This is followed by Paragraphs [designated with lower case letters as in Paragraph 84(1)(b)], and by Subparagraphs [designated with lower case Roman numerals as in Subparagraph 84(1)(b)(i)]. In some cases, the outlining process goes even further with Clauses (designated with upper case letters) and Subclauses (designated with upper case Roman numerals). Putting all of this together means that the reference:

ITA 115(1)(a)(i)(A)(I)

would be read as *Income Tax Act* Section 115, Subsection (1), Paragraph (a), Subparagraph (i), Clause A, Subclause I. Normally the relevant Part of the *Act* (Part I in this case) is not indicated in such references.

Parts Of The Act

1-57.   The Parts of the *Income Tax Act* are numbered I through XVII. As noted, because of the use of decimal designations there are more than 17 Parts.

1-58.   About 70 percent of the Sections of the *Income Tax Act* are found in Part I, which is titled "Income Tax". This Part contains Sections 2 through 180 of the *Act* and, because of its importance, we will provide a more detailed description of this Part in the following material.

1-59.   Parts I.01 through XIX cover a variety of special taxes as well as rules related to matters of administration, enforcement, and interpretation. For example, Part V is titled "Tax And Penalties In Respect Of Qualified Donees" and Part XII.3 is titled "Tax On Investment Income Of Life Insurers". As the great bulk of our attention in this text will be focused on Part I of the *Act*, there is little point in providing a list of these Parts for you to read. However, if you have further interest in their content, we would refer you to the complete copy of the *Income Tax Act* that is included in the FITAC database, which can be installed from the Companion Website for this text.

Part I Of The Act

1-60.   Part I, the largest and most important Part of the *Income Tax Act*, is divided into eleven Divisions. Some of these Divisions are further divided into Subdivisions. The Divisions and their more significant Subdivisions are described in the following paragraphs:

Division A: "Liability For Tax" (ITA Section 2)   This short Division is concerned with the question of who is liable for payment of income tax in Canada. This Division will be covered in this Chapter 1.

Division B: "Computation Of Income" (ITA Sections 3 through 108)   This is the longest Division in Part I and concerns itself with the determination of Net Income For Tax Purposes. Its first five Subdivisions describe the major sources of income and deductions and are as follows:

- **Subdivision a** - "Income Or Loss From An Office Or Employment"   This Subdivision deals with the ordinary wages and salaries that are earned by individuals while as an employee. The material in this Subdivision provides the basis for Chapter 3.

- **Subdivision b** - "Income Or Loss From A Business Or Property"   This Subdivision deals with business income earned by corporations, trusts, and by individuals through proprietorship or partnership arrangements. Also covered in this Subdivision is property income which includes rents, interest, dividends, and royalties. The material in this Subdivision provides the basis for Chapters 5, 6, and 7.

- **Subdivision c** - "Taxable Capital Gains And Allowable Capital Losses"   This Subdivision deals with gains and losses resulting from the disposal of capital property. The material in this Subdivision is dealt with in Chapter 8.

- **Subdivision d** - "Other Sources Of Income"   Covered here are miscellaneous income sources, such as spousal support received and various types of pension income, that do not fit into any of the major categories dealt with in Subdivisions a, b, and c. This material is covered in Chapter 9.

- **Subdivision e** - "Deductions In Computing Income"   Covered here are miscellaneous deductions such as moving expenses, child care costs, and spousal support paid. These are deductions that do not fit into any of the categories in Subdivisions a, b, and c. This material is also covered in Chapter 9.

Subdivisions a, b, and c each provide for both inclusions and deductions and, as a consequence, require the calculation of a net income figure. The deductions that are specified in Subdivisions a, b and c can only be deducted from inclusions in that same Subdivision. That is, deductions related to business income (Subdivision b) cannot be deducted from the inclusions for employment income (Subdivision a). This becomes a very important point when the inclusions in a particular Subdivision are not sufficient to support all of the available deductions in that Subdivision.

The remaining six Subdivisions of Division B do not provide new sources of income but, rather, provide additional rules related to the determination of Net Income. These remaining Subdivisions are as follows:

- **Subdivision f** - "Rules Relating To Computation Of Income"   This Subdivision contains a variety of rules related to the deductibility of expenses, income attribution, and the death of a taxpayer. These rules are covered in Chapters 6 and 9.

- **Subdivision g** - "Amounts Not Included In Computing Income"   This is a very specialized Subdivision, dealing with certain types of exempt income. It is not given significant coverage in this text.

- **Subdivision h** - "Corporations Resident In Canada And Their Shareholders" This Subdivision presents a number of rules related to the taxation of Canadian resident corporations. This material is covered in Chapters 12, 13, and 14.

- **Subdivision i** - "Shareholders Of Corporations Not Resident In Canada"   This is a specialized Subdivision. Limited coverage is available in Chapter 20.

- **Subdivision j** - "Partnerships And Their Members"   This Subdivision, dealing with rules related to partnerships, is given detailed coverage in Chapter 18.

- **Subdivision k** - "Trusts And Their Beneficiaries"   This Subdivision, dealing with the taxation of trusts, is given detailed consideration in Chapter 19.

Division C: "Computation Of Taxable Income" (ITA Sections 109 through 114.2) This Division covers the conversion of Division B income (commonly referred to as Net Income For Tax Purposes, or simply Net Income) into Taxable Income for residents. For individuals, it is given initial coverage in Chapter 4, followed by more detailed coverage in Chapter 11. For corporations, the coverage is in Chapter 12.

Division D: "Taxable Income Earned In Canada By Non-Residents" (ITA Sections 115 through 116)   Coverage of this material can be found in Chapter 20.

Division E: "Computation Of Tax" (Sections 117 through 127.41)   This Division is concerned with determining the taxes that are payable on the Taxable Income determined in Divisions C and D. It has five Subdivisions as follows:

- Subdivision a   - Rules applicable to individuals
- Subdivision a.1 - Canada Child Benefit
- Subdivision a.2 - Working Income Tax Benefit
- Subdivision b   - Rules applicable to corporations
- Subdivision c   - Rules applicable to all taxpayers

The computation of tax for individuals is largely covered in Chapter 4, with some additional coverage in Chapter 11. The corresponding material for corporations is found in Chapters 12 and 13.

Division E.1:   "Minimum Tax" (Sections 127.5 through 127.55)   This Division is concerned with the obligation of individuals to pay a minimum amount of tax, as well as the computation of this alternative minimum tax. This material is covered in Chapter 11.

Division F: "Special Rules Applicable In Certain Circumstances" (Sections 128 through 143.4)   Much of this Division is devoted to very specialized situations (bankruptcies) or organizations (cooperative corporations). While these situations are not given coverage in this text, the Division overs two subjects that are of more general importance. These are immigration to, and emigration from, Canada which are covered in Chapter 20, and refundable dividends for private corporations which is covered in Chapter 13.

Division G: "Deferred And Other Special Income Arrangements" (Sections 144 through 148.1) This important Division covers the rules related to Registered Retirement Savings Plans, Registered Pension Plans, Deferred Profit Sharing Plans, as well as other deferred income arrangements. Detailed attention is given to this material in Chapter 10.

Division H: "Exemptions" (Sections 149, through 149.2) Covered here are exemptions for individuals and organizations such as certain employees of foreign countries, pension trusts, and charitable organizations. These topics are not given coverage in this text.

Divisions I And J: "Returns, Assessments, Payment And Appeals" and "Appeals To The Tax Court Of Canada And The Federal Court" (Sections 150 through 180) These Divisions deal with the resolution of disputes between taxpayers and the Canada Revenue Agency (CRA). Limited coverage of this material is found in Chapter 2.

Other Income Tax Legislation

1-61. While the *Income Tax Act* constitutes the major source of legislation relevant to the study of federal income tax, there are three other sources of legislative materials that are relevant. These are draft legislation, the Income Tax Regulations and a group of International Tax Treaties between Canada and other countries. A general description of these legislative materials follows.

Draft Legislation

1-62. It is traditional for the federal government to issue a Budget in the first half of each year. Budgets are presented as a Notice Of Ways And Means Motion. As such, its content is of a general nature and does not contain the actual legislative provisions that are required to implement the proposals that are being put forward. The preparation of this legislation takes a considerable period of time and, when it is completed, it is presented as draft legislation. Additional time will pass before this draft legislation is passed by Parliament.

1-63. These time lags sometimes create a somewhat awkward situation in which returns for a particular taxation year must sometimes be filed prior to the actual passage of the legislation relevant to that year. Tax planning can be further complicated by an election call by the governing party. If the election is scheduled after a budget statement, but prior to the passage of the relevant legislation, there will be uncertainty as to whether the budget proposals will, in fact, be implemented.

Income Tax Regulations

1-64. Section 221 of the *Income Tax Act* allows the Governor In Council to make Regulations concerning the administration and enforcement of the *Income Tax Act*. Some of the items listed in this Section include:

- prescribing the evidence required to establish facts relevant to assessments under this *Act*;

- requiring any class of persons to make information returns respecting any class of information required in connection with assessments under this *Act*;

- prescribing anything that, by this *Act*, is to be prescribed or is to be determined or regulated by regulation; and

- defining the classes of persons who may be regarded as dependent for the purposes of this *Act*.

1-65. While these Regulations cannot extend the limits of the law, they can serve to fill in details and, to some extent, modify the statutes. For example, most of the rules for determining the amount of Capital Cost Allowance that can be deducted are established in the Regulations. Such Regulations provide an essential element of flexibility in the administration of the *Act* in that they can be issued without going through a more formal legislative process.

1-66.   You should also note that references to material in the Regulations are often referred to in the *Income Tax Act* as "prescribed". For example, the rate the CRA charges on late tax payments, a "prescribed" rate of interest, is determined by a procedure that is described in Regulations 4301 and 4302.

International Tax Treaties

1-67.   Canada currently has tax treaties (also known as tax conventions) with nearly 100 countries. The most important of these are the Tax Conventions with the United States and the United Kingdom. While there is considerable variation in the agreements, most of them are based on the model convention developed by the Organization For Economic Co-operation And Development (OECD).

1-68.   The purpose of these treaties is twofold. First, they attempt to avoid double taxation of taxpayers who may have reason to pay taxes in more than one jurisdiction and, second, they try to prevent international evasion of taxes. In situations where there is a conflict between the Canadian *Income Tax Act* and an international tax treaty, the terms of the international tax treaty prevail.

1-69.   Chapter 20 will provide additional discussion of Canada's tax treaties. Particular attention will be given to the treaty between the U.S. and Canada.

Income Tax Application Rules, 1971

1-70.   When capital gains taxation was introduced in Canada in 1972 (more than 40 years ago), a large number of transitional rules were required, primarily to ensure that the effects of the new legislation were not retroactive. These transitional rules are called the Income Tax Application Rules, 1971, and they can be of some significance in certain situations involving pre-1972 assets.

Other Sources Of Income Tax Information

Electronic Library Resources

1-71.   As noted in Paragraph 1-46, most tax practitioners rely on an electronic library for their tax reference materials. Also as noted, the Companion Website for this text provides access to one of these libraries — CPA Canada's Federal Income Tax Collection (FITAC).

CRA Website

1-72.   The CRA has an extensive website at **www.cra-arc.gc.ca**. Almost all of the forms, Guides, Income Tax Folios, Interpretation Bulletins and other documents provided by the CRA that are described in Paragraph 1-73 are available on the website. The forms and publications can be viewed and printed online or downloaded to a computer in one or more formats. There is also an online request service available to have printed forms or publications mailed out. The website is constantly being expanded to provide more forms and publications and more information on electronic services such as EFILE and NETFILE.

CRA Publications

1-73.   The CRA provides several publications to the public which, while they do not have the force of law, can be extremely helpful and influential in making decisions related to income taxes. These can be described as follows:

> **Income Tax Folios**   In 2013, the CRA introduced a new type of technical publication, called Income Tax Folios, a.k.a. IT Folios or simply Folios. Their goal is to update the information currently found in Interpretation Bulletins and to introduce improved web functionality. The new publications are organized into seven Series with each Series divided into Folios that contain Chapters on specific topics. For example, under Series 1, Individuals, Folio 1 is Health and Medical, and Chapter 1 covers the Medical Expense Tax Credit. This Chapter is designated S1-F1-C1, which stands for Series 1, Folio 1, Chapter 1.

This is, of course, a huge project that will require a number of years to complete. As an indication of this, as of April 1, 2017, only 37 Chapters have been released.

Interpretation Bulletins   Over 500 Interpretation Bulletins were issued by the CRA prior to 2013, though many of these have been cancelled. The objective of these Bulletins was to give the CRA's interpretation of particular sections of the law that it administers and to announce significant changes in departmental interpretation along with the effective dates of any such changes. An example of an important Interpretation Bulletin still in effect at the time of writing (April, 2017) is IT-63R5 which deals with an employee's personal use of an automobile supplied by an employer.

The CRA stopped issuing new Interpretation Bulletins in 2003, but continued to issue many revisions until 2013. The content of the existing Bulletins is being gradually replaced by the series titled Income Tax Folios (see preceding material).

Information Circulars   While over 300 of these circulars have been issued, there are currently about 60 in effect. The objective of these publications is to provide information regarding procedural matters that relate to both the *Income Tax Act* and the provisions of the Canada Pension Plan, and to announce changes in organization, personnel, operating programs, and other administrative developments.

Guides And Pamphlets   The CRA publishes a large number of non-technical Pamphlets and Guides that provide information on particular topics of interest to taxpayers. Examples of Pamphlets are "Canadian Residents Going Down South" (P151) and "Tax Information For People With Disabilities" (P149). Examples of Guides are "Business And Professional Income" (T4002), "Preparing Returns For Deceased Persons" (T4011), and "RRSPs And Other Registered Plans For Retirement" (T4040).

CRA News Releases, Tax Tips, And Fact Sheets   The CRA publishes News Releases on a variety of subjects, such as prescribed interest rates, corporate EFILE, deferral of taxation on employee stock options, and maximum pensionable earnings. They also provide information on when monthly payments will be released under the Canada Child Tax Benefit system and when quarterly payments will be released under the GST tax credit program. Some of the News Releases take the form of questions and answers, while others deal with the subject in some depth.

Advance Income Tax Rulings And Technical Interpretations   In recognition of the considerable complexity involved in the interpretation of many portions of the *Income Tax Act*, the Income Tax Rulings Directorate of the CRA will, for a fee, provide an Advance Income Tax Ruling on how it will tax a proposed transaction, subject to certain limitations and qualifications. Advance Income Tax Rulings are available to the public, but only in severed format with much of the relevant information that may permit identification of the parties deleted. The result is that such publications are of questionable value.

The Income Tax Rulings Directorate of the CRA also provides both written and telephone Technical Interpretations to the public (other than for proposed transactions where an Advance Income Tax Ruling is required) free of charge. Such interpretations however are not considered binding on the CRA.

Income Tax Technical News   Prior to 2012, the CRA issued newsletters titled *Income Tax Technical News* which provided up-to-date information on current tax issues. None have been issued since 2011 and existing newsletters are being cancelled as new Income Tax Folios are gradually incorporating their content.

Court Decisions

1-74.   Despite the huge volume of information available for dealing with income tax matters, disputes between taxpayers and the CRA regularly find their way into the Canadian court system. Of the hundreds of tax cases that are reported each year, the great majority do not involve tax evasion or other criminal offences. Rather, they involve an honest difference of opinion between the taxpayer and the CRA. Common areas of litigation include:

- the deductibility of both business and employment related expenses;
- whether an individual is working as an employee or an independent contractor;
- establishing a property's fair market value;
- the question of whether a transaction took place at arm's length;
- the deductibility of support payments;
- distinguishing between profits that are capital in nature and those that are ordinary business income; and
- the deductibility of farm losses against other sources of income.

1-75.   With the large number of court cases and the fact that they cover the great majority of issues that might arise in the application of income tax legislation, attention must be given to the precedents that have been established in the court decisions. While court decisions cannot be used to change the actual tax law, court decisions may call into question the reasonableness of interpretations of the ITA made by either the CRA or tax practitioners. Given the volume and complexity of court cases on income tax, we will cite only very important cases in our coverage of the various subjects in this text. However, a careful review of all relevant case material would be essential in researching any complex tax issue.

> **We suggest you work Self Study Problem One-4 at this point.**

Liability For Part I Income Tax

Background

1-76.   The *Income Tax Act* contains a number of Parts that deal with assessing taxes on various taxpayers. For example, Part VI assesses a tax on the capital of financial institutions, while Part XIII provides for a tax that is assessed largely on the property income of non-residents.

1-77.   While recognizing that these other types of taxes exist, the focus of this Chapter is on Part I tax. In terms of terminology, the portion of any tax legislation that specifies who is liable to pay tax is called a charging provision. With respect to Part I tax, the relevant charging provision is found in ITA 2. There are two components to this charging provision. The first, ITA 2(1) specifies the applicability of Part I tax to residents. The second, ITA 2(3), specifies the situations where non-residents will be taxed under Part I.

1-78.   In this Chapter we will give detailed consideration to the application of Part I tax to residents, including a complete discussion of the meaning of "resident". Some attention will also be given to the Part I tax liability of non-residents. Detailed consideration of this topic is available to Chapter 20, "International Issues In Taxation".

1-79.   We would note that taxes assessed under other Parts of the *Income Tax Act* will be given some attention in other Chapters. In particular, Chapter 20 will deal with taxation of foreign source income of Canadian residents, as well as the application of Part XIII to non-residents.

Charging Provision For Canadian Residents

1-80.   The Part I charging provision for Canadian residents is as follows:

ITA 2(1)   An income tax shall be paid, as required by this *Act*, on the taxable income for each taxation year of every person resident in Canada at any time in the year.

1-81.   There are several terms used in this charging provision that require further explanation:

Person   The charging provision makes it clear that responsibility for paying the federal income tax lies with "persons". As explained in Paragraph 1-8, in contrast to its usual dictionary meaning (i.e., human being), the *Income Tax Act* uses this term to refer to individuals, corporations, and trusts. When a provision of the *Act* is directed at human taxpayers, the term "individual" is generally used.

This reference establishes the fact that there are three entities which must file income tax returns — individuals, corporations, and trusts.

Resident ITA 2(1) also establishes that Canadian residents are liable for Canadian income tax, without regard to their citizenship. This is in contrast to the situation in the United States where U.S. citizens are liable for U.S. income taxes, without regard to where they reside.

While the *Income Tax Act* does not provide a definition of resident, in many cases the application of this concept is self-evident. For an individual who has lived and worked in Red Deer, Alberta for his entire life, never leaving Canada even for short vacations, it is not difficult to establish Canadian residency.

However, for corporations and trusts, as well as for individuals in certain types of circumstances, determining residency can become a fairly complex process. It is also, because of the large differences in tax rates in alternative jurisdictions, a matter of some importance. Detailed consideration of the issues related to residency can be found in the next major Section of this Chapter.

Taxation Year The term taxation year is defined in ITA 249(1). The general rule, which applies to all individuals and to most trusts, is that the taxation year is a calendar year. There are, however, two exceptions to this general rule:

Corporations For a corporation, the taxation year is defined as a "fiscal period". ITA 249.1 goes on to define fiscal period as a period for which accounts are made up that does not exceed 53 weeks. These definitions establish the fact that corporations are not required to use the calendar year as their taxation year.

Graduated Rate Estates Without going into detail, a "graduated rate estate" is a trust that arises at the time of an individual's death. Such trusts can continue for up to 36 months after the date of death and, during that 36 month period, such trusts can use a non-calendar taxation year. For more information on this type of trust, see Chapter 19, Trusts And Estate Planning.

Taxable Income Taxable income is defined in Section 2 of the *Act* as follows:

ITA 2(2) The taxable income of a taxpayer for a taxation year is the taxpayer's income for the year plus the additions and minus the deductions permitted by Division C.

The process of converting Net Income For Tax Purposes into Taxable Income will be given some attention at a later point in this Chapter. However, detailed coverage will be found in Chapters 4 and 11.

Charging Provision For Non-Residents
General Charging Provision
1-82. The second charging provision in the *Income Tax Act* deals with the taxation of non-residents. It is as follows:

ITA 2(3) Where a person who is not taxable under subsection (1) for a taxation year

(a) was **employed** in Canada,
(b) carried on a **business** in Canada, or
(c) disposed of a **taxable Canadian property**,

at any time in the year or a previous year, an income tax shall be paid, as required by this *Act*, on the person's taxable income earned in Canada for the year determined in accordance with Division D.

1-83. As noted, we will give very limited attention to the taxation of non-residents in this Chapter. The comments in this Chapter are very general and do not take into consideration the many complexities that exist in this area. In particular, the significant influence that tax treaties with other countries can have on the taxation of non-residents is given only superficial consideration in this Chapter 1. Detailed consideration of the issues associated with the taxation of non-residents, under Part I as well as other Parts of the *Income Tax Act*, will be found in Chapter 20.

Employment Income Earned By Non-Residents

1-84.   As the term is used in ITA 2(3)(a), Canadian employment income refers to income earned by a non-resident while working as an employee in Canada, generally without regard to the location of the employer. An example of this would be a U.S. citizen who is a resident of Detroit, Michigan, but is employed at an automobile plant in Windsor, Ontario. Such an individual would, in general, be subject to Canadian taxes on his employment income. However, as the individual is a non-resident, his other sources of income would not be taxed in Canada.

Business Income Earned By Non-Residents

1-85.   The second situation in which non-residents are subject to Canadian taxes is specified in ITA 2(3)(b). This paragraph indicates that persons who carried on business in Canada during a taxation year are subject to Canadian taxes on that income. Many of the difficulties associated with implementing this provision are related to determining what constitutes "carrying on business in Canada". This clearly includes producing or manufacturing products in Canada. In addition, ITA 253 indicates that it includes situations where a business is offering things for sale in Canada through an employee.

1-86.   This broad interpretation is, however, mitigated in those circumstances where the non-resident is a resident of a country with which Canada has a tax treaty. For example, if a U.S. corporation had sales staff selling products in Canada, ITA 253 would suggest that it should be taxed as a non-resident carrying on business in Canada. However, the Canada-U.S. tax treaty overrides ITA 253 in that this agreement exempts a U.S. enterprise from Canadian taxation unless it is carrying on business through permanent establishments in Canada.

1-87.   It is also important to distinguish between those situations in which a non-resident is offering something for sale in Canada through an employee and those situations in which a non-resident is selling to an independent contractor who resells the item in Canada. In the former case, the non-resident person is carrying on business in Canada, while in the latter case the non-resident is not.

Dispositions Of Taxable Canadian Property By Non-Residents

1-88.   ITA 2(3)(c) specifies the third situation in which non-residents are subject to Canadian taxation. This provision indicates that non-residents are subject to Canadian taxation on gains resulting from the disposition of "taxable Canadian property".

1-89.   The concept of taxable Canadian property is discussed more completely in Chapter 20. However, you should note at this point that the major items included in taxable Canadian property are:

- Real property, a.k.a., real estate situated in Canada.

- Certain capital property and inventories of a business carried on in Canada.

- A share of an unlisted corporation, an interest in a partnership, or an interest in a trust if, at any time within the preceding 60 months, more than 50 percent of the fair market value of the share or interest was derived from certain properties including Canadian real property, Canadian resource properties and timber resource properties.

- A share of a listed corporation only if, at any time within the preceding 60 months, at least 25 percent of the issued shares of any class were owned by the non-resident taxpayer and/or non-arm's length persons, and more than 50 percent of the shares' fair market value was derived from certain properties including Canadian real property, Canadian resource properties and timber resource properties.

1-90. This provision means that, if a resident of the state of Washington sells a vacation property that he owns in Whistler, British Columbia, any gain on that sale will be subject to Canadian taxation.

1-91. To help solve the problems arising from difficulties associated with collecting taxes from non-residents, ITA 116(5) indicates that, if there is a gain from the sale of taxable Canadian property by a non-resident, the person purchasing the property is responsible for the required taxes (see Chapter 20 for a discussion of the relevant 25 percent tax withholding). Exceptions to this occur if:

- the purchaser had no reason to believe that the seller of the property was a non-resident;

- the minister has issued a clearance certificate indicating that the non-resident has made arrangements for paying the taxes.

Property Income Earned By Non-Residents

1-92. The charging provisions in ITA 2 do not cover Canadian source property income of non-residents (e.g., rents, interest, or royalties). However, this type of income is covered in Part XIII of the *Act*. The general provision in Part XIII requires a flat 25 percent tax be withheld on Canadian property income paid to non-residents. This 25 percent tax rate is usually reduced for payments to non-residents in countries where Canada has a tax treaty.

1-93. This tax is withheld at the source of income, is based on the gross amount of such income, and no provision is made for any expenses related to acquiring the income. Since this inability to deduct expenses could result in serious inequities, there are provisions that allow a non-resident to elect to file a Canadian tax return for certain types of property income under Part I of the *Act*. These Part XIII tax provisions are discussed more thoroughly in Chapter 20 which deals with international issues in taxation.

Exercise One - 5

Subject: Non-Resident Liability For Tax

Ms. Laurie Lacombe, a U.S. citizen, has Canadian employment income of $22,000. She lives in Blaine, Washington and is a resident of the United States for the entire year. Ms. Lacombe does not believe that she is subject to taxation in Canada. Is she correct? Explain your conclusion.

SOLUTION available in print and online Study Guide.

Residence

Importance

1-94. As discussed, the charging provision for Part I of the *Income Tax Act* indicates that this tax is applicable to any person that is a resident of Canada. If a person is considered a resident of Canada in a given year, that person will be subject to Part I for that year on all sources of income, regardless of where that income is earned. Alternatively, if the person is a non-resident, Part I tax will only apply to Canadian employment income, Canadian business income, and gains on the disposition of Taxable Canadian Property.

1-95. Residency status is determined by applying certain rules and guidelines that originate from jurisprudence, common law, the *Income Tax Act*, and tax treaties. These rules vary depending on whether the person is an individual, corporation, or trust. In the material that follows, we will give detailed consideration to the rules applicable to each of these categories of taxpayers.

Residence Of Individuals

General Concept

1-96.   For the average Canadian individual whose job, family, dwelling place, and other personal property are all located in Canada, the concept of residence is not at all ambiguous. Such individuals would clearly be Canadian residents and, as a result, they would be liable for Canadian taxation on their worldwide income. Short departures from the country for holidays or business activities would not have any effect on this conclusion.

1-97.   However, for a growing number of individuals, the question of residence is more complex. It is also an important question. As tax rates and tax rules in different countries vary tremendously, the location of a person's residence can have a significant impact on the amount of taxes that will have to be paid.

1-98.   While the term resident is not specifically defined in the *Income Tax Act*, Income Tax Folio, S5-F1-C1, *Determining An Individual's Residence*, provides extensive guidance in this area. The most generally applicable statement in this IT Folio is as follows:

> **Paragraph 1.10**   The most important factor to be considered in determining whether an individual leaving Canada remains resident in Canada for tax purposes is whether the individual maintains residential ties with Canada while abroad. While the residence status of an individual can only be determined on a case by case basis after taking into consideration all of the relevant facts, generally, unless an individual severs all significant residential ties with Canada upon leaving Canada, the individual will continue to be a factual resident of Canada and subject to Canadian tax on his or her worldwide income.

1-99.   Paragraph 1.11 of S5-F1-C1 goes on to point out that the ties that will almost always be considered significant are:

> **Dwelling**   If an individual maintains a dwelling place in Canada, it will generally result in the individual being considered a resident. One possible exception to this rule would be when an individual who leaves Canada rents out a former dwelling place to an arm's length party. In this type of situation, owning a Canadian residence may not be considered a residential tie.

> **Spouse Or Common-Law Partner**   If an individual has a spouse or common-law partner who remains in Canada, it will generally result in the individual being considered a Canadian resident. An exception here would be when the individual was living separate or apart from the spouse or common-law partner prior to their departure from Canada.

> **Dependants**   If an individual has dependants, such as minor children, who remain in Canada, it will generally result in the individual being considered a Canadian resident.

1-100.   S5-F1-C1 also implies that, even in the absence of one of the preceding ties, an individual may still be considered to be a resident of Canada on the basis of secondary residential ties. Paragraph 1.14 contains the following examples of residential ties:

- personal property in Canada (such as furniture, clothing, automobiles, and recreational vehicles);
- social ties with Canada (such as memberships in Canadian recreational or religious organizations);
- economic ties with Canada (such as employment with a Canadian employer and active involvement in a Canadian business, and Canadian bank accounts, retirement savings plans, credit cards, and securities accounts);
- landed immigrant status or appropriate work permits in Canada;
- hospitalization and medical insurance coverage from a province or territory of Canada;
- a driver's license from a province or territory of Canada;
- a vehicle registered in a province or territory of Canada;
- a seasonal dwelling place in Canada or a leased dwelling place;

• a Canadian passport; and

• memberships in Canadian unions or professional organizations.

1-101.   S5-F1-C1 notes that these secondary ties must be looked at collectively and that it would be unusual for a single secondary tie to be sufficient for an individual to be classified as a Canadian resident.

Exercise One - 6

Subject: Residential Ties

At the end of the current year, Simon Farr departed from Canada in order to take a permanent position in Ireland. He was accompanied by his wife and children, as well as all of his personal property. Due to depressed real estate prices in his region, he was unable to sell his residence at a satisfactory price. However, he was able to rent it for a period of two years. He also retained his membership in CPA (Chartered Public Accountants) Ontario. After his departure, would he still be considered a Canadian resident for tax purposes? Explain your conclusion.

SOLUTION available in print and online Study Guide.

Temporary Absences

1-102.   Many of the problems associated with establishing residency involve situations where an individual leaves Canada for a temporary period of time. The issue here is, under what circumstances should an individual be viewed as having retained their Canadian residency status during the period of their absence from Canada?

1-103.   It is an important issue in that, if they are viewed as having retained their Canadian residency status, they will be subject to Canadian taxation on their worldwide income during the period of absence from Canada. While credits against Canadian income tax payable would usually be available for any income taxes paid in the foreign jurisdiction, the foreign taxes paid may be insufficient to cover the full Canadian tax liability.

1-104.   S5-F1-C1 makes it clear that the length of the period of time during which the individual is absent from Canada is not a determining factor with respect to residency. If an individual severs all primary and secondary residential ties, it appears that he will cease to be a Canadian resident without regard to the period of his absence.

1-105.   If some residential ties are retained during a temporary absence, other factors will be considered. As described in S5-F1-C1, these are as follows:

Intent   The issue here is whether the individual intended to permanently sever residential ties with Canada. If, for example, the individual has a contract for employment, if and when he returns to Canada, this could be viewed as evidence that he did not intend to permanently depart. Another factor would be whether the individual complied with the rules related to permanent departures (i.e., as noted in Chapter 8, there is a deemed disposition of an individual's property at the time of departure from Canada, resulting in the need to pay taxes on any gains).

Frequency Of Visits   If the individual continues to visit Canada on a regular and continuing basis, particularly if other secondary residential ties are present, this would suggest that he did not intend to permanently depart from Canada.

Residential Ties Outside Of Canada   A further consideration is whether or not the individual establishes residential ties in another country. If someone leaves Canada and travels for an extensive period of time without settling in any one location, it will be considered as evidence that he has not permanently departed from Canada.

1-106.   It is clear that there is considerable room for differences of opinion as to whether an individual has ceased to be a Canadian resident during a temporary absence from Canada. It is equally clear that the issue should be given careful attention by taxpayers who find themselves in this situation. The potential tax consequences of failing to deal properly with residency issues can be significant.

Exercise One - 7

Subject: Temporary Absences

Jane is a Canadian citizen who is employed by a multi-national corporation. While she has worked for many years in the Canadian office of this organization, she agreed to transfer to the corporation's office in Florida. Before leaving, she disposed of her residence and other personal property that she did not wish to move. She canceled her Alberta driver's licence and health care card, and closed all of her Canadian banking and brokerage accounts.

Because her boyfriend remained in Edmonton, she flew back to Canada at least once a month. After 26 months, she decided that between the excessive heat and humidity in Florida and the travel required to maintain the relationship with her boyfriend, she would return to Canada. At this point, her boyfriend is not her common-law partner. Would Jane be considered a Canadian resident during the 26 months that she was absent from Canada? Explain your conclusion.

SOLUTION available in print and online Study Guide.

Part Year Residence

1-107.   In a year in which a person clearly commences or terminates residency in Canada, they will be taxed in Canada on their worldwide income for the part of the year in which they are resident in Canada. While the courts have indicated that establishing residence is a complex matter that involves many considerations, the date of entry will often be based on the immigration rules. However, for departures from Canada, Paragraph 1.22 of S5-F1-C1 indicates that the date on which an individual becomes a non-resident is the latest of:

- the date the individual leaves Canada,
- the date the spouse or common-law partner and/or other dependants of the individual leave Canada, and
- the date the individual becomes a resident of the country to which they are immigrating.

1-108.   Situations involving part year residency require a fairly complex prorating of income, deductions, and personal tax credits. For example, an individual who is a resident of Canada for only part of the year will not be entitled to a full personal tax credit (see Chapter 4). The process for prorating such deductions and credits is specified in ITA 114 and ITA 118.91.

Exercise One - 8

Subject: Part Year Residence

Mark is a Canadian citizen and, since graduating from university, has been employed in Vancouver. He has accepted a new position in the United States and, as of February 1 of the current year flies to Los Angeles to assume his responsibilities. (He has been granted a green card to enable him to work in the U.S.) His wife remains behind with their children until June 15, the end of their school year. On that date, they fly to Los Angeles to join Mark. Their residence is sold on August 1 of the current year, at which time a moving company picks up their furniture and other personal possessions.

The moving company delivers these possessions to their new house in Los Angeles on August 15. Explain how Mark will be taxed in Canada during the current year.

Exercise One - 9

Subject: Part Year Residence

Mr. Jonathan Kirsh was born in Kansas and, until the current year, had lived in various parts of the United States. On September 1 of the current year he moves to Lethbridge, Alberta to begin work at a new job. He brings his family and all of his personal property with him. However, he continues to have both a chequing and a savings account in a U. S. financial institution. Explain how Mr. Kirsh will be taxed in Canada during the current taxation year.

SOLUTIONS available in print and online Study Guide.

Sojourners And Other Deemed Residents

1-109.   Individuals who are considered Canadian residents on the basis of the residential ties that we have discussed are generally referred to as factual residents. ITA 250(1) extends the meaning of resident to include certain other individuals who are considered deemed residents. As we shall see, an individual can be a deemed resident even if they do not set foot in Canada in the relevant taxation years.

1-110.   There are two important tax consequences associated with deemed residents:

• Deemed residents are taxed on their worldwide income for the entire taxation year. This is in contrast to part year residents who are only subject to Canadian taxation during that portion of the taxation year that they are present in Canada.

• Deemed residents are not deemed to reside in a specific province and, as a consequence, they are not subject to provincial taxes. In order to maintain fairness with other Canadian taxpayers, ITA 120(1) requires deemed residents to pay an additional federal tax equal to 48 percent of the basic federal tax that is otherwise payable. This will result in an overall tax liability that is either lower or higher than that of a factual resident, depending on the province that is being compared.

1-111.   Included on the list of deemed residents of Canada are the following:

1.   Sojourners in Canada for 183 days or more.

2.   Members, at any time during the year, of the Canadian armed forces when stationed outside of Canada.

3.   Ambassadors, ministers, high commissioners, officers or servants of Canada, as well as agents general, officers, or servants of a province, provided they were Canadian residents immediately prior to their appointment.

4.   An individual performing services, at any time in the year, in a country other than Canada under a prescribed international development assistance program of the Government of Canada, provided they were resident in Canada at any time in the 3 month period preceding the day on which those services commenced.

5.   A child of a deemed resident, provided they are also a dependant whose net income for the year was less than the base for the basic personal tax credit ($11,635 for 2017).

6.   An individual who was at any time in the year, under an agreement or a convention with one or more other countries, entitled to an exemption from tax on substantially all of their income in any of those countries, because at that time the person was related to, or a member of the family of, an individual who was resident in Canada.

1-112.   Of these items, numbers 1 and 6 require further explanation. With respect to item 1, a sojourner is an individual who is temporarily present in Canada for a period of 183 days or more during any one calendar year. Because of ITA 250(1), this person is deemed to be a Canadian resident for the entire year.

1-113.   For this sojourner rule to apply, the individual must be a resident of another country during the 183 days in question. This means that an individual who gives up his residence in another country and moves to Canada early in a taxation year will be considered a part year resident, not a sojourner. Correspondingly, a Canadian resident who leaves Canada to take up residence in another country on September 1 will not be a sojourner, despite the fact that he is in Canada for more than 183 days in the year. As noted, this is an important distinction because the sojourner is liable for Canadian tax on his worldwide income for the entire year, not just the portion of the year when he was in Canada.

1-114.   S5-F1-C1 indicates that sojourning means establishing a temporary residence and would include days spent in Canada on vacation trips. However, the Bulletin makes it clear that individuals who, for employment purposes, commute to Canada on a daily basis, are not considered to be sojourning.

1-115.   Item 6 refers to situations where someone is exempt from tax in a foreign country because they are related to an individual who is a Canadian resident. For example, the spouse of a Canadian diplomat working in the U.S. would be exempt from U.S. income taxes under the governing international tax treaty because she is the spouse of the diplomat. As the diplomat would be a deemed resident of Canada under item 3, the spouse would be a deemed resident of Canada under item 6.

Exercise One - 10

Subject: Individual Residency

Ms. Suzanne Blakey was born 24 years ago in Paris, France. She is the daughter of a Canadian High Commissioner serving in that country. Her father still holds this position. However, Ms. Blakey is now working in London. The only income that she earns in the year is from her London marketing job and is subject to taxes in England. She has never visited Canada. Determine the residency status of Suzanne Blakey.

SOLUTION available in print and online Study Guide.

Individuals With Dual Residency

1-116.   There are situations in which the application of the normal residency rules would result in an individual being considered a resident of more than one country. For example, a member of the Canadian armed forces is deemed to be a resident of Canada, but might also be considered a resident by the country in which he is stationed.

1-117.   In the absence of some mechanism for dealing with the problem, such an individual could be subject to double taxation, with each country of residence assessing taxes on the basis of their domestic legislation. In such situations, the presence of an international tax treaty becomes crucial. These bilateral treaties contain provisions, generally referred to as tie-breaker rules, which are designed to provide relief from the potential double taxation that is inherent in dual residence situations.

1-118.   While there is a general presumption that the provisions of international treaties override domestic tax legislation, these tie-breaker rules are of such importance that they are formally acknowledged in Canada's *Income Tax Act*. Specifically, ITA 250(5) indicates that a person is deemed not to be a resident of Canada if the terms of a particular tax treaty make him a resident of another country and not a resident of Canada.

1-119. As an example of a typical set of tie-breaker rules, the Canada/U.S. tax treaty resolves the dual residency problem for individuals by examining a list of factors. These factors are applied in the following order:

Permanent Home If the individual has a permanent home available in only one country, the individual will be considered a resident of that country. A permanent home means a dwelling, rented or purchased, that is continuously available at all times. For this purpose, a home that would only be used for a short duration would not be considered a permanent home.

Centre of Vital Interests If the individual has permanent homes in both countries, or in neither, then this test looks to the country in which the individual's personal and economic relations are greatest. Such relations are virtually identical to the ties that are examined when determining factual residence for individuals.

Habitual Abode If the first two tests do not yield a determination, then the country where the individual spends more time will be considered the country of residence.

Citizenship If the tie-breaker rules still fail to resolve the issue, then the individual will be considered a resident of the country where the individual is a citizen.

Competent Authority If none of the preceding tests resolve the question of residency then, as a last resort, the so-called "competent authority procedures" are used. Without describing them in detail, these procedures are aimed at opening a dialogue between the two countries for the purpose of resolving the conflict.

Exercise One - 11

Subject: Dual Residency - Individuals

Using the tie breaker rules, determine the resident status of Dizzy and Donna for 2017 in the following two Cases:

Case 1 Dizzy Jones is an unmarried saxophone player from Los Angeles who has always lived in the U.S. He decides to spend some time in Canada and arrives in Vancouver on May 5, 2017, looking for work in various nightclubs. A friend watches his home in Los Angeles while he is gone. He lives in boarding rooms and hotels throughout his time in Canada and returns to Los Angeles on February 14, 2018.

Case 2 Donna, a U.S. citizen, lives in the state of New York. In the fall of 2016, while attending a business convention in Toronto, she met Donald. They decided to get married the following year and live permanently in the U.S. as soon as Donald could arrange his business affairs in Canada. In December, 2016, Donna took an eight month leave of absence from her job and gave notice to her landlord. On January 1, 2017, they moved in together, sharing an apartment in Toronto which was leased on a monthly basis while Donald finalized his business affairs. In August, 2017, they terminated the lease and returned to New York where they were married and purchased a house.

SOLUTION available in print and online Study Guide.

Residence Vs. Citizenship

1-120. While Canada assesses taxes on the basis of residence, some other countries base the liability for tax on citizenship. Of particular importance in this regard is the United States. There are a significant number of Canadian resident individuals who are also citizens of the U.S. In the absence of mitigating legislation, such individuals would be taxed twice on most types of income.

1-121.   Fortunately, the Canada/U.S. tax treaty provides for this situation. In very simplified terms, such individuals are allowed to credit Canadian taxes paid against their U.S. tax liability. As, in many cases, Canadian taxes on individuals are higher than U.S. taxes on a given amount of income, the U.S. tax liability may be eliminated.

1-122.   Despite the fact that the balance owing to the U.S. is usually nil, U.S. citizens who are Canadian residents must file a U.S. tax return each year. If this important requirement is overlooked, it can lead to significant difficulties with U.S. tax authorities.

> **We suggest you work Self Study Problems One-5, 6, and 7 at this point.**

Residence Of Corporations

1-123.   Being an artificial legal entity, a corporation does not reside anywhere in the same physical sense that the term applies to an individual. To some extent, the jurisdiction of incorporation can assist in finding an answer to the residency question. More specifically, ITA 250(4)(a) indicates that corporations which are incorporated in Canada after April 26, 1965 are deemed to be resident in Canada.

1-124.   For corporations incorporated in Canada prior to April 27, 1965, ITA 250(4)(c) indicates that these corporations would also be treated as residents if at any time, in any taxation year ending after April 26, 1965:

- they were resident in Canada (under the mind and management concept discussed in the following Paragraphs), or
- carried on business in Canada.

1-125.   What jurisdiction a company was incorporated in is not, however, the end of the story. If this were the case, it would be possible to escape Canadian taxation by the simple act of incorporating outside of the country. Beyond the rules described in the preceding Paragraph, a well established common law principle applies.

1-126.   This is the idea that a corporation is resident in the jurisdiction in which the mind and management of the company are located. If the conclusion is that the mind and management of a corporation is in Canada, then a corporation that is not incorporated in Canada will be considered a resident for Canadian tax purposes. Note that, as this rule has been interpreted by the courts, mind and management resides where the highest functional decisions of a corporation are made, not where day-to-day decisions are made. It would appear that the most important factor in making this decision would be residence of the board of directors.

1-127.   This "mind and management" criteria would also apply to a corporation that was incorporated in Canada prior to April 27, 1965. Such a corporation would become a resident if, at any time after April 26, 1965, its mind and management was located within Canada. Unlike the foreign jurisdiction corporation, which would be considered to be a Canadian resident only as long as the mind and management remained in Canada, a pre-April 27, 1965 Canadian corporation that became a resident because of the mind and management criteria would remain a Canadian resident, even if the mind and management were moved to a different jurisdiction.

Corporations - Dual Residency

1-128.   As was the case with individuals, a corporation may be considered to be resident in more than one country. For example, a corporation that was incorporated in Canada after April 26, 1965 might have its mind and management located in the U.S. This would make this company a deemed resident of Canada and a factual resident of the U.S.

1-129.   In situations such as this, tax treaties again become very important. In the absence of such treaties, companies could be subject to taxation in both the countries where they are considered to be resident. As an example of such treaty provisions, the Canada/U.S. tax treaty indicates that, in situations where a company is considered to be a resident of both countries, the corporation will be deemed to be a resident only in the country in which it is incorporated.

Exercise One - 12

Subject: Corporate Residency

Roswell Ltd. was incorporated in the state of New York in 2013. It carries on business in both the United States and Canada. However, all of the directors of the Company live in Kemptville, Ontario and, as a consequence, all of the directors meetings are held in Kemptville. Determine the residency status of Roswell Ltd.

Exercise One - 13

Subject: Corporate Residency

Sateen Inc. was incorporated in Manitoba in 2012. However, since 2015, all of the Company's business has been carried on outside of Canada. Determine the residency status of Sateen Inc.

Exercise One - 14

Subject: Dual Residency - Corporations

Using the tie breaker rules, determine the resident status of the corporations in the following two Cases:

Case 1 Taxco is a company incorporated in Nova Scotia in 2015 to hold investments in other Canadian companies. Taxco never carried on business in Canada. All the shareholders and members of the board of directors are residents of the U.S. All board of directors meetings are held in the U.S.

Case 2 Junkco is a company incorporated in Delaware in 2016. The majority of the members of the board of directors, however, reside in Montreal, where all board of directors meetings take place. Junkco does not carry on any business in Canada.

SOLUTIONS available in print and online Study Guide.

We suggest you work Self Study Problems One-8 and 9 at this point.

Residence Of Trusts

1-130. The residence of a trust can only be determined by examining the circumstances involved in each case. In general, however, Income Tax Folio S6-F1-C1, *Residence Of A Trust Or Estate*, indicates that, similar to the case for corporations, a trust resides where the central management and control of the trust actually takes place.

1-131. Usually the management and control of the trust rests with, and is exercised by, the trustee, executor, liquidator, administrator, heir or other legal representative of the trust. However, the residence of the trustee does not always determine the residence of a trust. For example, if trustees reside in different jurisdictions, the trust will reside where the more substantial central management and control actually takes place.

1-132. In addition, if a substantial portion of the central management and control of the trust rests with someone other than the trustee, such as the settlor or the beneficiaries of the trust, the actions of these other persons must also be considered. It is where the central management and control is factually exercised that will determine the residence of the trust.

Alternative Concepts Of Income

The Economist's View

1-133.   In the past, economists have viewed income as being limited to rents, profits, and wages. In general, capital gains, gratuitous receipts, and other such increases in net worth were not included. In this context, most economists perceived income to be a net concept. That is, income is equal to revenues, less any related expenses.

1-134.   In more recent times, the economist's concept of income has moved in the direction of including measures of net worth or capital maintenance. The oft cited quotation "Income is the amount that can be spent during the period and still be as well off at the end of the period as at the beginning." is perhaps as good a description of the current concept as any available.

1-135.   This broader concept of income is based on the idea that income should include all increases in net economic power that occur during the relevant measurement period.

The Accountant's View

1-136.   What we currently view as Net Income from an accounting point of view is the result of applying a fairly flexible group of rules that are referred to as generally accepted accounting principles (GAAP). In general, Net Income is determined by establishing the amount of revenue on the basis of point of sale revenue recognition. Then, by using a variety of cash flows, accruals, and allocations, the cost of assets used up in producing these revenues is matched against these revenues, with this total deducted to produce the accounting Net Income for the period.

1-137.   If this same process is viewed from the perspective of the Balance Sheet, Net Income is measured as the increase in net assets for the period under consideration, plus any distributions that were made to the owners of the business during that period.

1-138.   The current accounting model continues to value many assets at historical cost and records changes in value only when supported by an arm's length transaction. This means that many of the increases in wealth that would be included in the economist's concept of income would not be included in accounting Net Income.

1-139.   However, the gap between the two approaches is gradually being narrowed as accounting standard setters show an increased willingness to incorporate fair value measurement into their pronouncements, both with respect to Balance Sheet values and with respect to inclusions in Net Income.

The Income Tax Act View

1-140.   As was the case with the determination of accounting income, the *Income Tax Act* uses a complex set of rules to arrive at a figure that we will refer to as Net Income For Tax Purposes. While tax references often refer to this figure simply as Net Income, we will use the lengthier designation in order to distinguish this figure from accounting Net Income.

1-141.   Net Income For Tax Purposes is made up of several different types of income and, in addition, these different types of income must be combined using what tax practitioners refer to as an ordering rule. While the detailed computation of Net Income For Tax Purposes will occupy us through most of the first half of this text, we will provide a general discussion of its various components, as well as the ordering rule for combining these components, in the next section of this Chapter.

Net Income For Tax Purposes

Structure

1-142.   The procedures for determining Net Income For Tax Purposes are specified in Division B of the *Income Tax Act*. In fact, this figure is sometimes referred to in tax literature as Division B Income. Once Net Income For Tax Purposes has been established, the items specified in Division C of the *Income Tax Act* are subtracted to determine Taxable Income. This Taxable Income figure provides the basis for calculating the federal income tax that is payable by individuals, corporations, and trusts that are resident in Canada.

1-143.   Net Income For Tax Purposes is made up of four basic types of income, each of which requires a separate calculation of a net amount. Each net calculation is based on a group of inclusions and deductions that are specific to that type of income. For example, net employment income is made up of inclusions for items such as wages or salaries received, along with deductions for items such as union dues and the costs of required travel. Note that if an individual had business income deductions in excess of business income inclusions, this excess could not be applied directly in the calculation of net employment income.

1-144.   In addition to the net calculations required for the four types of income, Net Income For Tax Purposes includes a group of other inclusions that do not fit in the four basic income categories, as well as a group of other deductions that are not related to the major categories of income.

Components

1-145.   The four types of income that are included as components of Net Income For Tax Purposes can be described as follows:

Net Employment Income (Loss)   Net employment income is made up of inclusions related to the activities of individuals who are serving as employees, less deductions related to that activity. These inclusions and deductions are specified in Division B, subdivision a, of the *Income Tax Act*. While it is possible to have a negative amount (employment loss), this would be fairly unusual. Note that, unlike the situation with other types of income, only individuals can earn employment income.

Net Business Income (Loss)   Net business income is made up of inclusions related to carrying on a business, less deductions related to that activity. These inclusions and deductions are specified in Division B, subdivision b, of the *Income Tax Act*. The business income rules are generally the same for individuals, corporations, and trusts.

Net Property Income (Loss)   Net property income is made up of inclusions related to the holding of property, less deductions related to holding such property. Examples of property income would include interest received on debt securities, dividends received on equity securities, and lease payments received on rental property. Note that, as the term is used in tax work, property income does not include capital gains or capital losses.

As was the case with net business income, inclusions and deductions related to property income are covered in Division B, subdivision b, of the *Income Tax Act*. While there are some differences in the rules for determining property income and those for determining business income, the calculations are sufficiently similar that they are included in a single subdivision. Like business income, property income can be earned by individuals, corporations, and trusts.

Capital Gains and Capital Losses   Capital gains and losses arise when an asset that has been used to produce business or property income is sold. The inclusions and deductions related to this type of income are specified in Division B, subdivision c, of the *Income Tax Act*. As was true with business and property income, capital gains and losses can arise on dispositions by individuals, corporations, and trusts.

As you may already be aware, in Canada only one-half of capital gains are taxed and only one-half of capital losses are deductible. This has created the need for the use of special terminology. More specifically:

- The term "**taxable** capital gain" is used when referring to the taxable **one-half** of a capital gain. When the term capital gain (without the taxable) is used, it is a reference to 100 percent of the gain.

- The term "**allowable** capital loss" is used when referring to the deductible **one-half** of a capital loss. When the term capital loss (without the allowable) is used, it is a reference to 100 percent of the loss.

Unlike employment, business, and property losses, a net allowable capital loss (allowable capital losses in excess of taxable capital gains) cannot be deducted against any other type of income. This will be explained in more detail in the next section.

1-146.   The remaining two components of Net Income For Tax Purposes can be described as follows:

Other Sources Of Income   There are some additional sources of income that do not fit into any of the basic categories of income. These inclusions, which are largely applicable to individual taxpayers, are specified in Division B, subdivision d, of the *Income Tax Act*. Examples of these subdivision d inclusions would be pension income received, spousal support received, and social assistance payments received.

Other Deductions From Income   Similar to the situation with inclusions, there are some deductions that do not relate to any of the basic income categories. These deductions, which are again largely related to individuals, are specified in Division B, subdivision e of the *Income Tax Act*. Examples of these subdivision e deductions include spousal support paid, child care costs, moving expenses, and RRSP contributions.

1-147.   As a final point here, we would note that, if an amount received does not fall into one of these categories, it is not part of Net Income For Tax Purposes and, in general, it would not be subject to federal income tax. Examples of this would include lottery winnings, amounts inherited, and gambling profits. An "exception" to gambling profits being non-taxable could arise if the CRA concluded that an individual's gambling activities were so extensive that the individual was carrying on a gambling business.

Combining The Components - ITA Section 3

Ordering Rules

1-148.   In the previous section we noted that four types of income are included in Net Income For Tax Purposes, along with two other components which deal with miscellaneous inclusions and miscellaneous deductions. While it would be possible to simply add up these figures, this is not the approach that is required by the *Income Tax Act*. Section 3 of the *Income Tax Act* requires that these various components be combined in a very specific manner.

1-149.   This type of Section is referred to in tax work as an ordering rule and, while we will encounter several other such rules in the course of this text, we are concerned here with Section 3 which is the ordering rule for combining the various components of Net Income For Tax Purposes. This rule is applied to individuals, corporations and trusts.

1-150.   While some of the ideas involved in applying this formula will not be fully explained until later in the text, it is useful at this stage to provide the basic structure of this formula in order to enhance your understanding of how the material on the various components of Net Income For Tax Purposes is organized.

1-151.   The Section 3 rules are made up of four basic paragraphs, ITA 3(a), 3(b), 3(c), and 3(d). A discussion of each of these paragraphs follows. In addition, the ITA 3 rules are presented graphically in Figure 1-3 (following page).

ITA 3(a) Sources Of Income

1-152.   The ordering process begins in ITA 3(a) with the addition of all **Positive** sources of income other than taxable capital gains. This includes positive amounts of employment income, business income, property income, and other miscellaneous inclusions from Subdivision d of Division B.

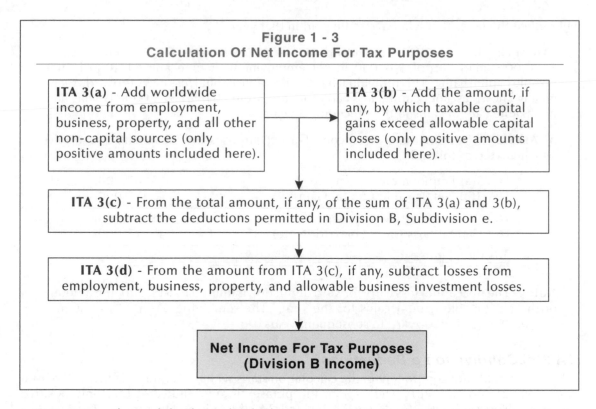

Figure 1 - 3
Calculation Of Net Income For Tax Purposes

ITA 3(a) - Add worldwide income from employment, business, property, and all other non-capital sources (only positive amounts included here).

ITA 3(b) - Add the amount, if any, by which taxable capital gains exceed allowable capital losses (only positive amounts included here).

ITA 3(c) - From the total amount, if any, of the sum of ITA 3(a) and 3(b), subtract the deductions permitted in Division B, Subdivision e.

ITA 3(d) - From the amount from ITA 3(c), if any, subtract losses from employment, business, property, and allowable business investment losses.

Net Income For Tax Purposes (Division B Income)

1-153.   Note that, while the individual components of this total are net amounts (e.g., employment income is made up of inclusions, net of deductions), the total is not a net calculation.   For example, a business loss would not be deducted against a positive employment income under ITA 3(a). Rather, such losses would be deducted at a later point in the calculation of Net Income For Tax Purposes.

ITA 3(b) Net Taxable Capital Gains

1-154.   To the total determined in ITA 3(a), ITA 3(b) requires that you "determine the amount, if any, by which" taxable capital gains exceed allowable capital losses. The phrase "if any" is commonly used in tax legislation to indicate that negative amounts are ignored.

1-155.   It is of particular importance here, since the fact that ITA 3(b) cannot be negative establishes the very important rule that the current year's allowable capital losses can only be deducted to the extent of taxable capital gains that have been recognized in the calculation of Net Income For Tax Purposes for the current year.

> **EXAMPLE**   During the current year, an individual has dispositions that result in taxable capital gains of $12,000 and allowable capital losses of $15,000.

> **ANALYSIS**   As there is no excess of taxable capital gains over allowable capital losses, the amount that will be added under ITA 3(b) will be nil.

1-156.   The $3,000 excess of allowable capital losses over taxable capital gains does not disappear. As is explained in detail in Chapters 4 and 11, current year allowable capital losses that are in excess of current year taxable capital gains can be deducted in the calculation of Taxable Income in past or future years. Note, however, that this carry over allowable capital loss deduction is limited to the amount of net taxable capital gains that are included in the Net Income For Tax Purposes of the carry over year.

1-157.   Unused allowable capital losses can be carried back to any of the preceding three taxation years. This will result in an amended Tax Payable for that year and a claim for a refund. If there are not sufficient taxable capital gains in the three preceding years to absorb the unused losses, they can then be carried forward to any subsequent taxation year. In a subsequent year, they will be deducted in the calculation of that year's Taxable Income, which will reduce the taxes that will have to be paid in that year.

EXAMPLE During 2017, an individual has a Net Income For Tax Purposes of $100,000, made up of $85,000 in net employment income and $15,000 in net taxable capital gains. This individual has an allowable capital loss carry forward, technically known as a net capital loss carry forward, from 2016 of $25,000. He has had no taxable capital gains in the preceding 3 years.

ANALYSIS The individual's Net Income For Tax Purposes and Taxable Income would be calculated as follows:

ITA 3(a) Employment Income	$ 85,000
ITA 3(b) Net Taxable Capital Gains	15,000
Net Income For Tax Purposes	$100,000
Net Capital Loss Carry Forward (Note)	(15,000)
Taxable Income	$ 85,000

Note The net capital loss carry forward deduction is limited to $15,000, the amount of the net taxable capital gains for the year. The remaining $10,000 ($25,000 - $15,000) is carried forward to subsequent years.

ITA 3(c) Subdivision e Deductions

1-158.   The ITA 3(c) component of the calculation starts with the amount, if any, of the total from ITA 3(a) and ITA 3(b). Here again, the phrase "if any" indicates that only positive amounts will be used. If the total from ITA 3(a) and ITA 3(b) is nil, Net Income For Tax Purposes is nil and the calculation is complete.

1-159.   Alternatively, if the total is positive, it is reduced by any Division B, Subdivision e deductions that are available. These deductions will be covered in detail in Chapters 9 and 10. Common examples of such deductions include spousal support paid, moving expenses, child care costs, and RRSP contributions.

1-160.   Note the importance of order here. ITA 3(c) requires that subdivision e amounts be deducted prior to business and property losses. This is important because subdivision e deductions are, in many cases, only deductible in the year to which they relate (e.g., if you cannot deduct spousal support in the current year, you cannot deduct it in a past or future year). In contrast, if you cannot use a business or property loss in the current year, it can be carried over to a past year or a future year.

ITA 3(d) Losses

1-161.   ITA 3(d) begins with any positive amount carried over from ITA 3(c). From this amount, any current year losses, other than allowable capital losses, will be deducted. This would include the deduction of any current year business losses, property losses, employment losses, and allowable business investment losses (allowable business investment losses are a special type of allowable capital loss that can be deducted against any type of income). Current period farm losses are also deductible here, subject to certain restrictions that are described in Chapter 6 (see the section on Income For Farmers).

Loss Carry Overs

1-162.   As we have noted, allowable capital losses that arise in the current year can only be deducted to the extent of taxable capital gains. Also as noted, other types of losses that arise in the current year can only be deducted to the extent that there is a positive total of other types of income and deductions after ITA 3(c). We have also mentioned the fact that these losses do not disappear — they can be carried back to claim a refund of taxes paid or forward to reduce future taxes payable.

1-163. Regardless of the type of loss, the carry back period is limited to the preceding 3 years. For example, a 2017 business loss can be deducted against amounts of Taxable Income that were recorded in 2015, 2015, or 2016.

1-164. In contrast, the limit on the carry forward period varies with the type of loss. In somewhat simplified form the rules are as follows:

Carry Forward Of Allowable Capital Losses Unused allowable capital losses can be carried forward and deducted in the determination of Taxable Income in any future taxation year, but only to the extent of the net taxable capital gains, if any, in the carry forward year.

Carry Forward Of Other Types Of Losses Employment, business, and property losses that cannot be used in the year in which they arise, can be carried forward and deducted in the determination of Taxable Income in any of the next 20 years. With the exception of certain types of farm losses (a type of business loss), the carry forward amounts can be applied against any type of income.

1-165. The detailed rules for this carry forward process are fairly complex, involving a number of rules that are not described in this brief summary. These rules are given detailed consideration in Chapter 11.

Net Income For Tax Purposes - Example

1-166. The following example provides an illustration of how the ITA 3 rules are applied.

EXAMPLE Jonathan Morley has the following income and loss components for the year:

Net Employment Income	$17,000
Business Loss (From Restaurant)	(21,000)
Net Property Income	9,000
Taxable Capital Gains	14,000
Allowable Capital Losses	(19,000)
Subdivision e Deductions (Spousal Support Paid)	(9,000)

ANALYSIS Mr. Morley's Net Income For Tax Purposes would be calculated as follows:

Income Under ITA 3(a):		
Net Employment Income	$17,000	
Net Property Income	9,000	$26,000
Income Under ITA 3(b):		
Taxable Capital Gains	$14,000	
Allowable Capital Losses	(19,000)	Nil
Balance From ITA 3(a) And (b)		$26,000
Subdivision e Deductions		(9,000)
Balance Under ITA 3(c)		$17,000
Deduction Under ITA 3(d):		
Business Loss		(21,000)
Net Income For Tax Purposes (Division B Income)		**Nil**

1-167. Mr. Morley's Business Loss exceeds the amount calculated under ITA 3(c), resulting in a Net Income For Tax Purposes of nil. However, there would be a carry over of the unused business loss equal to $4,000 ($21,000 - $17,000), and of the unused allowable capital loss in the amount of $5,000 ($14,000 - $19,000).

Exercise One - 15

Subject: Net Income For Tax Purposes

For the current year, Mr. Norris Blanton has net employment income of $42,000, a business loss of $15,000, taxable capital gains of $24,000, and Subdivision e deductions of $13,000. What is the amount of Mr. Blanton's Net Income For Tax Purposes for the current year?

Exercise One - 16

Subject: Net Income For Tax Purposes

For the current year, Ms. Cheryl Stodard has interest income of $33,240, taxable capital gains of $24,750, allowable capital losses of $19,500, and a net rental loss of $48,970. What is the amount of Ms. Stodard's Net Income For Tax Purposes for the current year? Indicate the amount and type of any loss carry overs that would be available at the end of the current year.

Exercise One - 17

Subject: Net Income For Tax Purposes

For the current year, Mrs. Marie Bergeron has net employment income of $42,680, taxable capital gains of $27,400, allowable capital losses of $33,280, Subdivision e deductions of $8,460, and a business loss of $26,326. What is the amount of Mrs. Bergeron's Net Income For Tax Purposes for the current year? Indicate the amount and type of any loss carry overs that would be available at the end of the current year.

SOLUTIONS available in print and online Study Guide.

We suggest you work Self Study Problems One-10, 11 and 12 at this point.

Net Income To Taxable Income

1-168. Once we have determined the amount of Net Income For Tax Purposes, it must then be converted into Taxable Income by deducting the items specified in Division C of the *Income Tax Act*. This is, in fact, a fairly complex process that will be covered in detail in Chapters 4 and 11.

1-169. While we are deferring detailed coverage of this subject, it is useful as part of this overview for you to be aware of the major items that will be involved in the conversion of Net Income For Tax Purposes to Taxable Income. They are as follows:

- A deduction for losses carried over from other years.
- A deduction for social assistance and worker's compensation payments that have been included in Net Income For Tax Purposes.
- A deduction related to amounts of employment income resulting from the exercise or sale of stock options.
- A deduction related to the employment income benefit that can result from an employer-provided home relocation loan.
- A deduction related to capital gains on qualified property (the lifetime capital gains deduction).
- A deduction related to the costs of living in certain areas of the Canadian north.

Principles Of Tax Planning

Introduction

1-170.   Throughout this text, there will be a great deal of emphasis on tax planning and, while many of the specific techniques that are involved can only be fully explained after the more detailed provisions of tax legislation have been covered, there are some basic tax planning principles that can be described at this point.

1-171.   Our objective here is simply to provide a general understanding of the results that can be achieved through tax planning so that you will be able to recognize the goal of more specific tax planning techniques when they are examined. In addition, this general understanding should enable you to identify other opportunities for tax planning as you become more familiar with this material.

1-172.   The basic goals of tax planning can be summarized as follows:

- Tax avoidance or reduction.
- Tax deferral.
- Income splitting.

1-173.   While these classifications can be used to describe the goals of all tax planning arrangements, such arrangements seldom involve a clear cut attempt to achieve only one of these goals. For example, the principal reason for making contributions to a Registered Retirement Savings Plan is to defer taxes until later taxation years. However, such a deferral can result in the taxpayer avoiding some amount of taxes if he is taxed at a lower rate in those later years.

Tax Avoidance Or Reduction

1-174.   The most desirable result of tax planning is to permanently avoid the payment of some amount of tax. This very desirability is probably the most important explanation for the scarcity of such arrangements and, while the number of possibilities in this area is limited, they do exist.

1-175.   An outstanding example of tax avoidance is the capital gains deduction that is available on the disposition of qualified farming or fishing property, and qualified small business corporation shares. For 2017, the deduction limit for dispositions of shares of qualified small business corporations is $835,716. There is an additional amount for farm or fishing properties of $164,284, providing a total of $1,000,000 for all such qualified properties. These capital gains can be received by an individual taxpayer on a completely tax free basis For individuals in a position to enjoy the benefits of this provision, it is one of the best tax avoidance mechanisms available (see Chapter 11 for a detailed discussion of this provision).

1-176.   Other forms of complete tax avoidance can be found in the employee benefits area, in that some types of benefits can be given to employees without being considered taxable. These would include an employer's contributions to disability and private health care insurance, and the provision of discounts to employees on products or services normally sold by the employer (see Chapter 3).

1-177.   Additional opportunities in this area require more complex arrangements. Such arrangements involve the use of trusts and private corporations and cannot be described in a meaningful manner at this stage of the material.

Tax Deferral

1-178.   The basic concept behind tax planning arrangements involving the deferral of tax payments is the very simple idea that it is better to pay taxes later rather than sooner. This is related to the time value of money and also involves the possibility that some permanent avoidance of taxes may result from the taxpayer being taxed at a lower marginal income tax rate at the time the deferred amounts are brought into taxable income.

1-179.   Such deferral arrangements may involve either the delayed recognition of certain types of income or, alternatively, accelerated recognition of deductions. As an example of delayed recognition of income, an employer can provide a benefit to an employee in the form of contributions to a registered pension plan. Such benefits will not be taxed in the year in which they are earned. Rather, they will be taxed at a later point in time when the employee begins to receive benefits from the registered pension plan.

1-180.   As an example of expense acceleration, the ownership of a rental property may allow the owner to deduct its capital cost at a rate that is usually in excess of any decline in the physical condition or economic worth of the building. While this excess deduction will normally be added back to the taxpayer's income when the building is sold, the payment of taxes on some part of the rental income from the property has been deferred.

1-181.   Deferral arrangements are available in a number of different situations and currently represent one of the more prevalent forms of tax planning.

Income Splitting
General Idea
1-182.   Progressive rates are built into Canadian federal income tax legislation. This means that, in general, the taxes payable on a given amount of taxable income will be greater if that amount accrues to one taxpayer, than would be the case if that same total amount of taxable income is split between two or more people. While not technically a form of income splitting, the same effect can be achieved by having a given sum of taxable income taxed in the hands of an individual in a low tax bracket rather than an individual in a high tax bracket.

1-183.   This does not mean that it would be advantageous to give part of your income away to perfect strangers. What it does mean is that, within a family or other related group, it is desirable to have the group's aggregate taxable income allocated as evenly as possible among the members of the group.

Example
1-184.   The tax savings that can be achieved through income splitting are among the most dramatic examples of the effectiveness of tax planning. For example, if Mr. Jordan had taxable income of $811,200 (this is four times $202,800, the bottom threshold of the highest federal tax bracket in 2017 of 33 percent), his basic federal tax payable in 2017 would be $247,738 (this simplified calculation does not take into consideration the various tax credits that would be available to Mr. Jordan).

1-185.   Alternatively, if Mr. Jordan was married and the $811,200 could be split on the basis of $405,600 to him and $405,600 to his wife, the federal taxes payable would total $227,780 [(2)($113,890)], a savings of $19,958 ($247,738 - $227,780).

1-186.   If we carry this one step further and assume that Mr. Jordan is married and has two children, and that the $811,200 in taxable income can be allocated on the basis of $202,800 to each individual, the total federal taxes payable will be reduced to $187,864 [(4)($46,966)]. This represents a savings at the federal level of $59,874 ($247,738 - $187,864) when compared to the amount of taxes that would have been paid if Mr. Jordan alone had been taxed on the entire $811,200.

1-187.   When we add provincial effects, the potential savings could be close to $100,000, a substantial reduction on income of $811,200. Making this savings even more impressive is the fact that it is not a one shot phenomena but, rather, a savings that could occur in each year that the income splitting plan is in effect.

Note To Students   You will learn how to calculate the tax payable amounts shown in the preceding paragraphs in Chapter 4 of the text.

Problems With Income Splitting

1-188. While income splitting can be one of the most powerful planning tools available to taxpayers, there are several problems associated with implementing such arrangements:

- Splitting income with children often involves losing control over assets, a process that is emotionally difficult for some individuals.
- Splitting income involves decisions as to which family members are worthy of receiving benefits and how much those benefits should be.
- The tax on split income, a.k.a., the "kiddie tax", a high rate tax assessed on certain types of income received by related minors can make income splitting very difficult in some situations. This tax is described in detail in Chapter 11.

Exercise One - 18

Subject: Tax Planning

Mr. Stephen Chung, a successful flamenco dancer, has decided to make contributions to an RRSP in the name of his spouse, the mother of his twelve children, rather than making contributions to his own plan. What type of tax planning is involved in this decision? Explain your conclusion.

Exercise One - 19

Subject: Tax Planning

Mr. Green's employer pays all of the premiums on a private dental plan that covers Mr. Green and his family. What type of tax planning is illustrated by this employee benefit? Explain your conclusion.

SOLUTIONS available in print and online Study Guide.

Additional Supplementary Self Study Problems Are Available Online.

Abbreviations To Be Used

1-189. In our writing, we try to avoid using abbreviations because we believe that there is a tendency in accounting and tax writing to use so many of them that the material can become unreadable. However, in the tax area, some sources are so commonly cited that it is clearly inefficient to continue using their full description. As a result, in the remainder of this text, we will use the following abbreviations on a regular basis:

Abbreviation	Meaning
CRA	Canada Revenue Agency
ITA	Federal *Income Tax Act*
ITF S#-F#-C#	A Chapter in an Income Tax Folio that is part of a Series
IT	Interpretation Bulletin
IC	Information Circular
GST	Goods and Services Tax
HST	Harmonized Sales Tax
GAAP	Generally Accepted Accounting Principles
CCA	Capital Cost Allowance (see Chapter 5)
UCC	Undepreciated Capital Cost (see Chapter 5)

Key Terms Used In This Chapter

1-190.   The following is a list of the key terms used in this Chapter. These terms, and their meanings, are compiled in the Glossary Of Key Terms located at the back of the separate paper Study Guide.

Advance Tax Ruling	Net Income For Tax Purposes
Allowable Capital Loss	Non-Resident
Business Income	Ordering Rule
Capital Asset	Part Year Resident
Capital Gain/Loss	Person
Capital Tax	Progressive Tax System
Consumption Tax	Property Income
Customs Duties	Property Tax
Deemed Resident	Qualitative Characteristics
Division B Income	Regressive Tax System
Dual Resident	Residential Ties
Employment Income	Resident
Fiscal Period	Sojourner
Flat Tax System	Tariffs
Goods And Services Tax	Tax Base
GST	Tax Deferral
Harmonized Sales Tax (HST)	Tax Expenditure
Head Tax	Tax Incidence
Income	Tax Planning
Income Splitting	Taxable Canadian Property
Income Tax	Taxable Capital Gain
Income Tax Application Rules	Taxable Entity
Income Tax Folios	Taxable Income
Income Tax Regulations	Taxation Year
Income Tax Technical News	Tie Breaker Rules
Individual	Transfer Tax
Information Circulars	Value Added Tax
Interpretation Bulletins	

References

1-191. For more detailed study of the material in this Chapter, we would refer you to the following:

ITA 2(1)	Tax Payable By Persons Resident In Canada
ITA 2(3)	Tax Payable By Non-Resident Persons
ITA 3	Income For Taxation Year
ITA 114	Individual Resident In Canada For Only Part Of Year
ITA 115	Non-Resident's Taxable Income In Canada
ITA 116	Disposition By Non-Resident Person Of Certain Property
ITA 118.91	Part-Year Residents
ITA 118.94	Tax Payable By Non-Resident (Tax Credits)
ITA 248(1)	Definitions (Taxable Canadian Property)
ITA 249	Definition Of "Taxation Year"
ITA 250(1)	Person Deemed Resident
S5-F1-C1	Determining An Individual's Residency Status
S6-F1-C1	Residence of a Trust or Estate
IT-168R3	Athletes And Players Employed By Football, Hockey And Similar Clubs
IT-420R3	Non-Residents - Income Earned In Canada

Problems For Self Study (Online)

To provide practice in problem solving, there are Self Study and Supplementary Self Study problems available on the Companion Website.

Within the text we have provided an indication of when it would be appropriate to work each Self Study problem. The detailed solutions for Self Study problems can be found in the print and online Study Guide.

We provide the Supplementary Self Study problems for those who would like additional practice in problem solving. The detailed solutions for the Supplementary Self Study problems are available online, not in the Study Guide.

The .PDF file "Self Study Problems for Volume 1" on the Companion Website contains the following for Chapter 1:

- 12 Self Study problems,
- 5 Supplementary Self Study problems, and
- detailed solutions for the Supplementary Self Study problems.

Assignment Problems

(The solutions to these problems are only available in
the solutions manual that has been provided to your instructor.)

Assignment Problem One - 1
(Application Of General Tax Principles)

Many of the provisions of the *Income Tax Act* are written in very general terms. For example, ITA 18 lists a number of general characteristics that must apply before a particular expense can be deducted in the computation of business income.

Required: Indicate the situations in which such generally worded provisions of the *Income Tax Act* will be overridden.

Assignment Problem One - 2
(Conflicting Objectives)

The tax systems of various countries are designed to meet a variety of objectives. In addition to raising revenues, we call on our tax systems to provide fairness, to have the characteristic of simplicity, to meet social or economic goals, to balance regional disparities, and to be competitive on an international basis. While it would be a fairly simple matter to design a system that would meet any single one of these objectives, we frequently encounter conflicts when we attempt to create a system that meets several of these objectives.

Required: Discuss the possible conflicts that can arise when a tax system is designed to meet more than a single objective.

Assignment Problem One - 3
(Qualitative Characteristics Of Tax Systems)

Discuss whether the following situations meet the objectives and match the characteristics of a good tax system. Identify any conflicts that exist and the probable economic incidence of the tax or tax expenditure.

A. Diamonds are South Africa's major export. Assume that a tax is levied on diamond production of Par Excellence Inc., which has a monopoly in the country. Movements of diamonds are closely monitored and accounted for.

B. Chimeree Inc. owns the largest diamond mine in Sierra Leone. A tax is levied on diamond production. Movements of diamonds are not closely controlled, and helicopters pick up shipments under the cover of darkness.

C. Gains on dispositions of principal residences are exempt from income tax in Canada.

D. A rule stipulates that only 50 percent of the cost of business meals can be deducted in calculating Canadian business income for personal and corporate Taxable Income.

E. A newly created country levies a head tax which requires every resident adult to pay an annual tax.

Assignment Problem One - 4
(Introduction Of Head Tax)

Concerned with her inability to control the deficit, the Minister of Finance has indicated that she is considering the introduction of a head tax. This would be a tax of $200 per year, assessed on every living Canadian resident who, on December 31 of each year, has a head. In order to enforce the tax, all Canadian residents would be required to have a Head Administration Tax identification number (HAT, for short) tattooed in an inconspicuous location on their scalp. A newly formed special division of the RCMP, the Head Enforcement Administration Division (HEAD, for short), would run spot checks throughout the country in order to ensure that everyone has registered and received their HAT.

The Minister is very enthusiastic about the plan, anticipating that it will produce additional revenues of $5 billion per year. It is also expected to spur economic growth through increased sales of Canadian made toques.

As the Minister's senior policy advisor, you have been asked to prepare a memorandum evaluating this proposed new head tax.

Required: Prepare the memorandum.

Assignment Problem One - 5
(Residency After Departure From Canada)

Mr. Valone is a U.S. citizen. However, since obtaining permanent residence status in 2003, he has been employed on a full time basis in London, Ontario. His employer is a Canadian subsidiary of a multi-national corporation that operates in a number of different countries. The head office of the company is in the United States.

Mr. Valone has been very successful in his position with the Canadian subsidiary. Based on this, he has been offered a promotion which involves a significant increase in salary. However, this promotion is conditional on his moving to the company's head office in Philadelphia no later than March 1, 2017. Given the sizable increase in remuneration, Mr. Valone finds this offer too good to pass up.

As he is a U.S. citizen, he has no difficulty getting the appropriate documentation to establish his residency in the U.S. He relinquishes his Canadian driver's licence, as well as his provincial health care card. As required by his employer, he is at his desk in the new work location in the U.S. on March 1.

Mr. Valone and his spouse have two children who are attending a private school in London. The current semester at this school lasts until June 15, 2017. In order to provide continuity in their education, Mrs. Valone decides that she and children will remain in Canada until the current semester is finished. They depart on June 20, 2017.

The real estate market in London has been somewhat slow of late. As a consequence, the Valone's house is not sold until October 5, 2017.

Required For purposes of assessing Canadian income taxes, determine when Mr. Valone ceased to be a Canadian resident and the portion of his annual income which would be assessed for Canadian taxes. Explain your conclusions.

Assignment Problem One - 6
(Residency After Departure From Canada)

Mr. David Hamilton was a long-time resident of Canada. On January 13, 2016, he departed from Canada to work in Qatar. The work was done under a contract of employment with an American company that was operating in Qatar.

1. Mr. Hamilton did not obtain resident status in Qatar or in any other country. He did not have a postal address in Qatar.

2. Mr. Hamilton obtained a work permit in Qatar that was valid until August 13, 2017.

3. After the work permit expired, Mr. Hamilton had to leave Qatar. He subsequently returned several times to meet with friends and business associates there.

4. Mr. Hamilton's Canadian driver's licence expired in August, 2015 and was not renewed.

5. After taking intensive driving courses, Mr. Hamilton acquired a driver's licence in Qatar in December, 2016 that was valid for 5 years.

6. Mr. Hamilton gave up his Canadian health card in 2017.

7. Mr. Hamilton had two sons who remained in Canada. One of the sons, Harold, had significant health issues.

8. Mr. Hamilton kept a credit card, bank account, an RRSP and investments in Canada when he began work in Qatar.

9. Mr. Hamilton continued to hold a Canadian passport.

10. He visited Canada four times in 2016 and three times during 2017. Each visit was for 2 weeks. His visits were largely to see his sons and mother. The relationship with his wife was strained before he left for Qatar and deteriorated significantly afterwards. This led to their divorce in 2017. After his son Harold advised him to follow his dream of leaving Canada, he began the process of permanently leaving Canada. To this end, on July 1, 2017, he gave his share of the family home to his wife and closed all of his Canadian financial accounts. He paid regular support payments after the divorce occurred.

11. During his visits to Canada, he stayed in hotels and used rented vehicles.

12. In 2016, Mr. Hamilton's accountant filed a tax return for him as a resident of Canada.

13. Mr. Hamilton is well respected in his profession and considered to be a very responsible employee.

Despite filing a tax return in 2016 as a resident of Canada, Mr. Hamilton believes that he gave up his Canadian residency on January 13, 2016 and wishes to revise his 2016 tax return to reflect this.

Required: Determine whether Mr. Hamilton is a resident of Canada. If you conclude he is not, provide the date that he ceased to be a Canadian resident. Provide reasons for your conclusion.

Assignment Problem One - 7
(Residency Of Individuals - 5 Cases)

For each of the following persons, indicate how they would be taxed in Canada for the year ending December 31, 2017. Your answer should explain whether the person is a Canadian resident, what parts of their income would be subject to Canadian taxation, and the basis for your conclusions.

Case A   John is a citizen of the U.K. who has landed immigrant status in Canada. He has been employed in Canada for over 15 years. In 2016, he won $1.5 million in a lottery. He has decided to use these funds to spend two years touring Europe and Asia. His wife and children will remain at the family home in New Brunswick. He was not present in Canada during any part of 2017.

Case B   In 2016, Jane's Canadian employer asked her to spend three years working in their Hong Kong office. Her employment contract requires her to return to Canada in 2019. Jane severs all of her residential ties with Canada and moves to Hong Kong in November, 2016. She is not present in Canada during any part of 2017.

Case C   Laura is married to a member of the Canadian armed forces who is serving in Ghana. She is a citizen of Ghana and has never visited Canada. During 2017, because her husband is a member of the Canadian armed forces, she is not subject to taxation in Ghana.

Case D   Martha Mendoza is a U.S. citizen who lives in Buffalo, New York. During 2017 she is employed 5 days per week in Fort Erie, Ontario. Her 2017 salary is $52,000. In addition, she has $2,000 (Canadian) of interest on a savings account with a Buffalo bank.

Case E   Barry Long is a Canadian citizen who has lived and worked in Canada all of his life. When he is offered a significant increase in salary if he accepts a position in Spain, he accepts this position and on March 1, 2017, he moves to Spain. While he immediately establishes residency in Spain, he is not joined by his wife and children until July 1, 2017. As they are unable to sell their Canadian home at an acceptable price, the property is rented under a long-term residential lease.

Assignment Problem One - 8
(Residency Of Corporations - 4 Cases)

Each of the following cases provides information about an individual corporation. For each case, indicate whether the corporation would be considered a Canadian resident for the current year. Explain your conclusions.

Case A   The Allor Company was incorporated in North Dakota in 1999. Currently, however, the head office of the corporation is in Regina, Saskatchewan. As all of the directors of the corporation are residents of this Canadian city, all of the meetings of the board of directors are held in Regina.

Case B   Kodar Ltd. was incorporated in Canada in 2005. However, as its directors have come to hate Canadian winters, they have all moved permanently to the southern United States. Because of this, they hold all of their Board of Directors meetings in Phoenix, Arizona.

Case C   The Karlos Company was incorporated in Minnesota in 1998. The two directors lived in Winnipeg, Manitoba and for several years, all of the Board of Directors and shareholders meetings were held in Winnipeg, Manitoba. In early 2005, the directors were replaced by residents of St. Paul, Minnesota. After this, all of the Board of Directors and shareholders meetings were held in St. Paul.

Case D   Bradlee Inc. was incorporated in Canada in 1961. While it operated in Canada for a number of years, all of its operations, management and directors relocated to the United States in 2008.

Assignment Problem One - 9

(Residency/Dual Residency - Individuals)

Determine the residency status of the individuals in the following Cases. Use the tie-breaker rules found in the Canada/U.S. tax treaty where appropriate.

Case A Ty Breaker is a citizen of the United States. He is a professional athlete, a successful entrepreneur and very single. During 2017, he plays for a Canadian soccer team and, as a consequence, he spends 194 days in Canada. Because of his extensive travel, he stores his few personal items in his mother's basement and lives in short term rentals of hotel suites in both Canada and the U.S. As he owns corporations in both countries, he has office space in both Canada and the U.S. In previous years, Ty has played for a U.S. soccer team and has spent less than 100 days per year in Canada.

Case B Jordan Marsh is a U.S. citizen who does construction work as an independent contractor. He has a home in Kalispell, Montana which he has owned for many years. As work has been slow in that city in recent years, he decides to temporarily move to Lethbridge after hearing work is plentiful there. He moves on March 31, 2017. He does not sell his Kalispell residence as his brother needs a temporary home while he renovates. Jordan lives in a Lethbridge hotel until February 12, 2018. By this time he has realized that the work situation is worse in Lethbridge than it was in Kalispell. Given this, he returns to Kalispell.

Assignment Problem One - 10

(Net Income And Taxable Income)

Explain the terms Net Income For Tax Purposes and Taxable Income.

Assignment Problem One - 11

(Alternative Views Of Income)

Distinguish between the accountant's, the economist's, and the *Income Tax Act* views of income.

Assignment Problem One - 12

(Net Income For Tax Purposes - Two Cases)

Karla Gomez is a Canadian resident who lives in Toronto. In the following two Cases, different assumptions are made with respect to the amounts and types of income she will include in her tax return for the current year. Information is also provided on the deductions that will be available to her for the year.

Case One Karla had net employment income of $62,350. Unfortunately, her unincorporated flower shop suffered a net business loss of $115,600. In contrast, she had a very good year in the stock market, realizing the following gains and losses:

Capital Gains	$97,650
Capital Losses	5,430

Also during the current year, Karla made deductible contributions of $4,560 to her RRSP.

Case Two   Karla had net employment income during the year of $45,600, as well as net business income of $27,310 and a net rental loss of $4,600. As part of a divorce agreement from a previous year, Karla paid spousal support of $600 per month to her former common-law partner, Lucretia Smart for the entire year. She realized the following results in the stock market during the year:

Capital Gains	$31,620
Capital Losses	41,650

While Karla does not gamble on a regular basis, she enjoys the ambiance of the local casino. Given this, two or three times a year, she spends an evening dining and gambling with friends there. In March of this year, she got very lucky, winning $46,000 by hitting a slot machine jackpot.

Required: For each Case, calculate Karla's Net Income For Tax Purposes (Division B income) for the current year. Indicate the amount and type of any loss carry overs that would be available at the end of the year.

Assignment Problem One - 13

(Net Income For Tax Purposes - Four Cases)

The following four Cases make different assumptions with respect to the amounts of income and deductions available to Mr. Emerson Comfort for the current taxation year:

Case 1

During the year, Emerson has net employment income of $123,480, interest income of $4,622, and taxable capital gains of $24,246. He has allowable capital losses of $4,835. He has deductible child care costs of $9,372.

Case 2

During the year, Emerson has net business income of $72,438 and a net rental loss of $9,846. His taxable capital gains for the year total $4,233, while his allowable capital losses for the year are $7,489. Because of his very high Earned Income in the previous year, he is able to make $22,000 deductible RRSP contribution.

Case 3

During the year, Emerson has net employment income of $47,234 and a net business loss of $68,672. Capital gains for the year total $12,472 while capital losses are realized in the amount of $9,332. He has deductible child care costs of $3,922.

Case 4

During the year, Emerson has interest income of $6,250, net business income of $43,962, and capital gains of $12,376. He also has a net rental loss of $72,460 and capital losses of $23,874. As he moved to a new work location during the year, he has deductible moving expenses of $7,387.

Required   For each Case, calculate Emerson's Net Income For Tax Purposes (Division B income). Indicate the amount and type of any loss carry overs that would be available at the end of the current year, or state that no carry overs are available.

CHAPTER 2

Procedures And Administration

Introduction

2-1.   This Chapter begins with a brief overview of the administration of the Canada Revenue Agency (CRA). This is followed by a description of filing and tax payment procedures applicable to individuals, corporations, and trusts.

2-2.   This material on filing and tax payment procedures will be followed by a description of the assessment and reassessment process, including the various avenues that can be followed in appealing unfavourable assessments. Attention will also be given to issues related to tax avoidance and tax evasion, collection and enforcement procedures, and taxpayer relief provisions.

Administration Of The Department

2-3.   The CRA has the responsibility for carrying out the tax policies that are enacted by Parliament. In carrying out these policies, the chief executive officer of the CRA is the Commissioner of Revenue. The duties of the Minister of National Revenue, as well as those of the Commissioner of Revenue, are described in the *Act* as follows:

> **ITA 220(1)**   The Minister shall administer and enforce this Act and the Commissioner of Revenue may exercise all the powers and perform the duties of the Minister under this Act.

2-4.   The Minister of National Revenue is responsible for the CRA and is accountable to Parliament for all of its activities, including the administration and enforcement of program legislation such as the *Income Tax Act* and the *Excise Tax Act*. The Minister has the authority to ensure that the CRA operates within the overall government framework and treats its clients with fairness, integrity, and consistency.

2-5.   The CRA has a Board of Management consisting of 15 members appointed by the Governor in Council, 11 of whom have been nominated by the provinces and territories. The Board has the responsibility of overseeing the management of the CRA, including the development of the Corporate Business Plan, and the management of policies related to resources, services, property, personnel, and contracts. The Commissioner of the CRA, who is a member of the CRA Board, is responsible for the CRA's day-to-day operations.

2-6.   Unlike the boards of Crown corporations, the CRA Board is not involved in all the activities of the CRA. In particular, the CRA Board has no authority in the administration and enforcement of legislation, which includes the *Income Tax Act* and the *Excise Tax Act*, for which the CRA remains fully accountable to the Minister of National Revenue. In addition, the CRA Board is denied access to confidential client information.

2-7.   Following the ministerial mandate found in ITA 220(1), ITA 221(1) provides that the Governor in Council has the power to make Income Tax Regulations for various specific purposes or for the purpose of carrying out other provisions of the *Income Tax Act*. Unlike the provisions of the *Income Tax Act*, these Regulations may be passed by Order-In-Council without ratification by Parliament. They generally become effective when they are published in the Canada Gazette.

Returns And Payments - Individuals

Requirement To File - ITA 150

2-8.   ITA 150(1) is a general rule that requires all persons (individuals, corporations, and trusts) to file a tax return. Although ITA 150(1.1)(b) exempts individuals from filing tax returns except where certain conditions are met, there are still other provisions in the *Income Tax Act* that require returns to be filed. The CRA website lists many reasons why an individual would be required to file an individual tax return, a.k.a., T1, the most common reasons being if, in the year, the individual:

- has Tax Payable;
- is requested by the CRA to file a tax return;
- has disposed of a capital property, or realized a taxable capital gain;
- and his spouse or common-law partner have elected to split pension income; or
- has to contribute to the Canada Pension Plan or pay Employment Insurance premiums.

2-9.   In addition to these requirements for residents, non-resident individuals must generally file a T1 tax return if, during the year, they have a taxable capital gain or dispose of a Taxable Canadian Property (See Chapter 20, International Issues In Taxation for more details.)

2-10.   Even when there is no requirement to file, if an individual is entitled to a refund, it will only be available if a return is filed. Further, it is beneficial for others to file, especially low income taxpayers, in order to be eligible for income-based benefits such as the Canada Child Benefit, the GST credit and the Guaranteed Income Supplement. If they fail to file, they will not receive these amounts, even if they qualify.

2-11.   Individuals can either file a paper form or, alternatively, use an electronic filing method. The advantage of electronic filing for the taxpayer, particularly if he is entitled to a refund, is that the return will be processed more quickly. For the CRA, electronic filing eliminates the possibility of errors in the process of transferring information from paper forms to their electronic records. While supporting documents (e.g., a charitable donation receipt) cannot be included with an electronic filing, the CRA has the right to request that such receipts be provided.

2-12.   The CRA website has detailed coverage of the two alternatives for electronic filing. Both EFILE and NETFILE are automated transmission services that permit the filing of tax returns online. The main difference between them can be described as follows:

NETFILE allows a taxpayer to file their own personal income tax return directly to the CRA online through the use of a CRA certified tax software program. It is intended for use by those who prepare their own tax returns. This system can be used by almost all Canadian resident individuals.

EFILE allows tax preparation service providers who are registered with the CRA to file tax returns for clients online. It is designed for those who prepare and file tax returns for clients. The NETFILE system cannot be used to file returns for clients.

2-13.   CRA's filing statistics for the 2016 personal tax-filing season covering the period from February 15, 2016 to August 1, 2016 are shown in the following table. There is a significant decline in the percentage of taxpayers using paper filing over the 3 years.

	Electronically Filed	Paper Filed	Total T1 Returns
2016	23,507,132 (85%)	4,177,253 (15%)	27,684,385
2015	23,383,313 (81%)	5,397,643 (19%)	28,780,956
2014	21,936,593 (78%)	6,162,087 (22%)	28,296,680

Due Date For Individual Returns

General Rule

2-14.   As noted in Chapter 1, individuals must use the calendar year as their taxation year. This means that for every individual, the taxation year ends on December 31. Given this, ITA 150(1)(d)(i) indicates that, in general, individuals must file their tax return for a particular year on or before April 30 of the following year. Although the filing due date is extended to the next business day if the due date falls on a weekend, we will use April 30 (or June 15 if applicable as explained in the following material) as the due date in our examples and problems.

Individuals Who Are Partners Or Proprietors

2-15.   Recognizing that individuals who are involved in an unincorporated business may need more time to determine their income for a taxation year, the *Income Tax Act* provides a deferral of the filing deadline. If an individual, or his cohabiting spouse or common-law partner, carried on a business during the year, ITA 150(1)(d)(ii) extends the due date for filing to June 15 of the calendar year following the relevant taxation year.

2-16.   An interesting feature of this provision is that, while the return does not have to be filed until June 15, payment of all taxes owing is required by the usual date of April 30. Any amounts that are not paid by April 30 will be assessed interest until the outstanding balance is paid. The relevant interest rate is described later in this Chapter.

Exercise Two - 1

Subject: Individual Tax Payment Date

Brandon Katarski's 2017 Net Income includes business income. When is his 2017 tax return due? By what date must his 2017 tax liability be paid in order to avoid the assessment of interest on amounts due?

SOLUTION available in print and online Study Guide.

Deceased Taxpayers

2-17.   As will be discussed in Chapter 9, there are many tax related complications that arise when an individual dies. In order to provide the deceased individual's representatives with sufficient time to deal with these complications, the *Act* indicates the following:

ITA 150(1)(b)   in the case of an individual who dies after October of the year and before the day that would be the individual's filing due date for the year if the individual had not died, by the individual's legal representatives on or before the day that is the later of the day on or before which the return would otherwise be required to be filed and the day that is 6 months after the day of death

2-18.   For an individual whose filing due date is April 30, this provision means that if death occurs between November 1 of the previous year and April 30 of the current year, the return for the previous year does not have to be filed until six months after the date of death.

> **EXAMPLE**   A single individual who is not involved in an unincorporated business dies on March 1, 2018 without having filed a 2017 return.
>
> **ANALYSIS**   The due date for the 2017 return is September 1, 2018, six months after the individual's death.   The due date for the 2018 final return is April 30, 2019.

2-19.   The provision works somewhat differently for an individual who has a June 15 filing due date due to business income. If such an individual dies between November 1 and December 15 of a taxation year, the later of six months after the date of death and the normal filing due date, will be the normal filing date of June 15. This means that for decedents who would normally have a June 15 filing due date, the six month extension is available if they die between December 16 of a taxation year and June 15 of the following year.

> **EXAMPLE**   An individual whose wife owns an unincorporated business dies on May 2, 2018 without having filed a 2017 tax return.
>
> **ANALYSIS**   The due date for the 2017 return is November 2, 2018, six months after the individual's death. The due date for the 2018 final return is June 15, 2019.

Exercise Two - 2

Subject: Deceased Taxpayer Filing Date

Sally Cheung dies on February 15, 2018. Sally's only income for 2017 and 2018 was from investments. Her husband's Net Income for these years included income from an unincorporated business. Her representatives must file her 2017 and 2018 tax returns by what dates?   Explain your answer.

SOLUTION available in print and online Study Guide.

Withholdings For Income Tax - ITA 153
Salaries And Wages
2-20.   A large portion of the income taxes paid by individuals employed in Canada is collected through source deductions. Under ITA 153, any individual who earns employment income will have the estimated taxes on this income withheld from gross pay through payroll deductions made by their employer. The tax withheld is related to the amount of the individual's income, with the required withholdings intended to cover the tax payable on this income. However, it would be unusual for such withholding to be exactly equal to the taxes payable for the year. As a consequence, most individuals will either owe taxes and be required to file a tax return or, alternatively, be entitled to a refund that can only be obtained by filing a tax return.

2-21.   The amount withheld by an employer is based on a form that is filled out by each employee, Form TD1, "Personal Tax Credits Return". This form lists personal and other credits that are available to an individual and asks the employee to indicate which of these he will be claiming.

2-22.   Also on Form TD1, an individual can request to have the amount withheld increased beyond the required amount. An individual might choose to do this if his employment income withholding is based on rates in a low tax rate province, but his residence is in a high tax rate province (e.g., an individual who works in Alberta, but lives in Saskatchewan). Another situation where this might be desirable would be if an individual received large taxable spousal support payments as these are not subject to withholding. In either of these cases, requesting additional withholding would allow the individual to pay extra taxes each pay period and avoid a large tax liability on filing, or the requirement to pay instalments.

2-23.   A different type of problem can arise when an employed individual has significant deductions from income, losses, or non-refundable tax credits not listed on the TD1, that can be used to offset the taxes on employment income.

> **EXAMPLE** Monica Kinney has 2017 employment income of $91,831. She lives in Alberta where a 10 percent provincial rate is applicable to her income. Her employer would normally withhold based on the assumption that she will owe income taxes totalling $25,483 ($16,300 federal, plus $9,183 provincial, ignoring all tax credits). However, if Ms. Kinney has annual deductible spousal support payments of $20,000, her income will be reduced to $71,831 and her actual 2017 federal and provincial taxes payable will only be $19,383 ($12,200 + $7,183). As will be explained later, the government will not pay interest on the extra $6,100 in taxes withheld.

2-24.   Monica can request a reduction in the amount of tax withheld by her employer by using Form T1213, "Request To Reduce Tax Deductions At Source". As long as the deductions (e.g., payroll deductions for an RRSP), losses (e.g., rental loss) or tax credits (e.g. for charitable donations) can be documented in a reasonable fashion, the CRA will normally authorize the employer to reduce the tax withheld from the employee's remuneration.

Withholdings By Other Payers

2-25.   In addition to requiring employers to withhold specified amounts from the salaries and wages of employees, ITA 153 contains a fairly long list of other types of payments from which the payer must withhold prescribed amounts. These include:

- retiring allowances
- death benefits
- payments from Registered Retirement Savings Plans
- payments from Registered Education Savings Plans
- distributions under retirement compensation arrangements

2-26.   In addition to payments listed in ITA 153, withholding is required on certain payments to non-residents. While the general rate of tax on the Canadian source income of non-residents is established in ITA 212 as 25 percent, the amount that will actually be withheld is usually modified by international tax treaties. For a more complete discussion of this type of withholding, see Chapter 20, International Issues In Taxation.

Instalment Payments For Individuals - ITA 156
Basis For Requiring Instalments

2-27.   As discussed in the previous section, amounts to be applied to future tax liabilities must be withheld by the payer from certain types of income. Such income includes employment income, as well as other less common sources.

2-28.   For many individuals, particularly those earning employment income, the withholding of taxes constitutes the major form of tax payment in any taxation year. However, in situations where an individual has large amounts of income that are not subject to withholding (e.g., self-employment income or investment income), quarterly instalment payments may have to be made towards the current year's tax liability.

2-29.   In the *Income Tax Act*, the requirement for paying instalments is stated in terms of when instalments are not required. Specifically, no instalments are required if:

> **ITA 156.1(2)(b)**   The individual's net tax owing for the particular year, or for each of the 2 preceding taxation years, does not exceed the individual's instalment threshold for that year.

2-30.   In provinces other than Quebec, "net tax owing" is the amount, if any, by which the total federal and provincial tax owing for a particular year, exceeds all tax withheld for that year. An "individual's instalment threshold" is defined in ITA 156.1(1) as $3,000. In Quebec, net tax owing only includes federal taxes and the instalment threshold is $1,800.

2-31.   While the legislation is based on when instalments are not required, it is usually more useful to give guidance in terms of when instalments are required. The requirement could be restated as follows:

> You are required to make instalment payments for 2017 if your **net tax owing** is more than $3,000:
>
> - in 2017; **and**
> - in **either** 2016 **or** 2015.
>
> Note that **net tax owing** is not equal to **Tax Payable** if any income tax has been withheld.

Due Dates For Individuals

2-32.   For individuals required to pay instalments, the quarterly payments are due on March 15, June 15, September 15, and December 15.

Determining Amounts Of Instalments

2-33.   In simple terms, the required instalments will be based on the net tax owing for the current year, the preceding year, or a combination of the first and second preceding years. The *Canada Pension Plan Act* and the *Employment Insurance Act* provide for instalments on the same basis as that of the *Income Tax Act*. Since the CRA administers the Canada Pension Plan (CPP) and Employment Insurance (EI), where an individual has CPP contributions and/or EI premiums payable on self-employed income (see Chapter 3), the instalments are based on the total of net tax owing plus any CPP contributions and EI premiums payable.

2-34.   In determining the amount to be paid as instalments, individuals have a choice of three alternatives for calculating the required quarterly instalments. These alternatives are as follows:

> **Alternative 1 - Current Year**   One-quarter of the estimated net tax owing (which is not necessarily equal to Tax Payable) for the current taxation year [ITA 156(1)(a)(i)].
>
> **Alternative 2 - Preceding Year**   One-quarter of the net tax owing for the immediately preceding taxation year [ITA 156(1)(a)(ii)].
>
> **Alternative 3 - Second And First Preceding Year**   The first two instalments (March 15 and June 15) based on one-quarter of the net tax owing for the second preceding taxation year. The remaining two instalments (September 15 and December 15) equal the excess of the net tax owing for the preceding year over one-half of the net tax owing for the second preceding year [ITA 156(1)(b)], divided by two. Note that one-half of the net tax owing for the second preceding year is the amount that should have been paid in the first two instalments under this approach.
>
> In effect, in almost all situations, Alternative 3 requires the same total instalments as Alternative 2. However, if the net tax owing in the second preceding year is less than the net tax owing in the preceding year, there is some amount of tax deferral.

2-35.   The individual taxpayer can select the most advantageous of these alternatives. The basic rules for this selection are as follows:

- If the net tax owing is lowest in the current year, Alternative 1 is best.
- If the net tax owing is lowest in the preceding year, Alternative 2 is best.
- If the net tax owing is lowest in the second preceding year:
    - and the net tax owing in the first preceding year is higher than the current year, Alternative 1 is best.
    - and the net tax owing in the first preceding year is lower than the current year, Alternative 3 is best. While the total amount of the instalments will be the same as in Alternative 2, their present value will be less because of the reduced amount for the first two payments.

CRA's Instalment Reminder

2-36. It is likely that many individual taxpayers are not capable of calculating their required instalments. To assist all individuals, the CRA sends out Instalment Reminders that calculate quarterly instalments. Taxpayers are assured that, if they pay the amounts specified in these reminders by the required dates, no interest will be assessed for late instalments.

2-37. The amounts specified in these Instalment Reminders are based on Alternative 3. The reason that the CRA has adopted this approach is based on information availability:

Alternative 1 The CRA would not know the current year's Tax Payable until April 30 or June 15 of the following year. This would be too late for advising a taxpayer as to any of the current year's instalments under this approach.

Alternative 2 The CRA would not know the previous year's Tax Payable until April 30 or June 15 of the current year. This would too late for advising a taxpayer as to the first required instalment for the current year and, in the case of June 15 filers, too late to provide information on the second required instalment for the current year.

2-38. Given this situation, Alternative 3 is the only approach that could be used by the CRA to provide taxpayers with instalment information that would unequivocally avoid any assessment of interest.

2-39. While using the amounts specified in the Instalment Reminder is a risk free solution to remitting instalments, it may not be the best answer for an individual taxpayer.

EXAMPLE Ali Kern, a self-employed general contractor, had Taxable Income in both 2015 and 2016 that was in excess of $200,000. Unfortunately, in early 2017 he was in a serious accident and could not work all year. His business experienced significant losses which ultimately resulted in a Taxable Income of nil.

ANALYSIS The CRA's Instalment Reminders would base its calculations on the high levels of income for 2015 and 2016. Paying these amounts would be a very poor choice as it would, in essence, constitute an interest free loan to the government. As Ali knew early in the year that he would have little or no income, his best choice would be to make no instalments based on his estimated current year net tax owing of nil.

2-40. However, if an individual does not pay the amounts calculated in the CRA's Instalment Reminders, the taxpayer is basing some or all of his payments on estimates. If his estimates are too low, he will be assessed interest on any insufficient instalments.

Example Of Instalments For Individuals

2-41. A simple example will serve to illustrate the alternative approaches to calculating instalments.

EXAMPLE Mr. Hruba is not subject to any withholding and has the following amounts of net tax owing:

2015	$20,000
2016	32,000
2017 (Estimated)	24,000

ANALYSIS The use of alternative 1 based on the 2017 estimate of $24,000 would result in quarterly instalments of $6,000 ($24,000 ÷ 4), totaling $24,000 for the year.

Alternative 2, based on the 2016 figure of $32,000 is the worst alternative. The quarterly instalments would be $8,000 ($32,000 ÷ 4), totaling $32,000 for the year.

Under alternative 3 (used in the CRA's Instalment Reminders), instalments 1 and 2 would each be $5,000 ($20,000 ÷ 4). However, instalments 3 and 4 would each be $11,000 [($32,000 - $10,000) ÷ 2], resulting in a total of $32,000.

This analysis would suggest that alternative 1 provides the best solution. While the first two payments under alternative 3 are somewhat lower ($5,000 vs. $6,000), the total amount under alternative 1 is significantly lower ($24,000 vs. $32,000).

2-42.   The CRA will calculate interest based on each instalment that should have been paid using the payment option that requires the least amount of interest to a specific date. The CRA will then calculate interest based on the instalments that were paid. If the former amount exceeds the latter, the individual will be assessed interest on the difference, provided the amount involved exceeds $25. Note that contra interest as explained in Paragraph 2-45 could also be relevant in calculating the applicable interest.

Exercise Two - 3

Subject: Individual Instalments

Marlene Carter, a resident of Ontario, had net tax owing for 2015 of $3,500, net tax owing for 2016 of $4,000, and expects to have net tax owing for 2017 of $1,500. Is she required to make instalment payments for 2017? If so, what would be the minimum quarterly payment and when would they be due?

Exercise Two - 4

Subject: Individual Instalments

John Lee, a resident of Newfoundland, had net tax owing for 2015 of $3,500, net tax owing for 2016 of $1,500, and expects to have net tax owing for 2017 of $4,500. Is he required to make instalment payments for 2017? If so, what would be the minimum quarterly payment and when would they be due?

Exercise Two - 5

Subject: Individual Instalments

At the beginning of 2017, the following information relates to Jesse Forbes:

Year	Tax Payable	Amounts Withheld
2015	$53,000	$52,000
2016	59,000	52,000
2017 (Estimated)	64,000	60,000

Is Jesse required to make instalment payments during 2017? If he is required to make instalment payments, indicate the amounts that would be required under each of the three alternative methods of calculating instalments. Indicate which alternative would be preferable.

SOLUTIONS available in print and online Study Guide.

We suggest you work Self Study Problem Two-1 at this point.

Interest

When Interest Is Charged

2-43.   Interest is assessed on any amounts that are not paid when they are due. For individuals, this would include:

• Any balance owing on April 30th of the current year for the taxes of the preceding year. We would remind you that the amount owing is due on April 30th, without regard to whether the taxpayer's filing due date is April 30 or June 15.

- Any portion of a required instalment payment that is not remitted on the required instalment due date.

- On some penalties. For example, interest is charged on penalties for late filing (see following discussion of this penalty).

2-44. Compound daily interest is charged on these amounts. In the case of amounts owing on April 30th, the start date for interest is May 1, with the accrual continuing until the amounts are paid. For deficient instalment amounts, the interest clock starts ticking on the date the instalment is due. This accrual would continue until an offset occurs (see next paragraph) or the due date for the balance owing. At this latter date, further interest would be based on the amount owing at that date.

2-45. A further important point here is that interest accrued on late or deficient instalments can be offset by making instalment payments prior to their due date, or by paying an amount in excess of the amount required (creating contra interest). Note, however, if early or excess payments are made when there is no accrual of interest owed on late or deficient instalments, the government will not pay interest to the taxpayer on the excess.

Prescribed Rates Of Interest

2-46. There are a number of provisions in the *Income Tax Act* which require the use of an assumed rate of interest. What we refer to as the prescribed base rate is an annual rate that is calculated each quarter, based on the effective yield on three month Government of Canada treasury bills during the first month of the preceding quarter. The CRA announces this prescribed base rate for each quarter a few weeks before the start of the quarter.

2-47. Many years ago there was a single prescribed rate. However, the government felt that this rate was sufficiently low that too many taxpayers chose not to make required tax payments. To try to solve this problem, on amounts owing to the government, 4 percentage points were added to the prescribed base rate as described in the preceding paragraph. At the same time, a third rate was established for amounts owed to taxpayers. As a result, there are now multiple prescribed interest rates and ITR 4301 contains the calculations for these rates. The rates that concern us here are:

Base Rate This rate, described in Paragraph 2-46, is applicable for all purposes except amounts owing to and from the CRA (e.g., the determination of the taxable benefit for an employee who receives an interest free loan from an employer). For the first quarter of 2017, this rate was 1 percent.

Base Rate Plus 2 Percent This rate is applicable when calculating interest on refunds to individuals and trusts, but not corporations. For the first quarter of 2017, this rate was 3 percent.

In recent years, interest rates on short term investments have been much lower than the prescribed rate plus 2 percent. To prevent corporations from overpaying instalments to take advantage of the higher interest rates paid by the CRA, the rate on amounts owed to corporations is only the base rate and does not include the extra 2 percent.

Base Rate Plus 4 Percent This rate is applicable when calculating interest on late or deficient instalments, unpaid source deductions, and other amounts owing to the CRA by all taxpayers. For the first quarter of 2017, this rate was 5 percent. Note that amounts paid to the CRA under this provision are not deductible for any taxpayer.

2-48. The prescribed base rate was set at 1 percent on April 1, 2009. With the single exception of the fourth quarter of 2013 when the base rate rose to 2 percent for a single quarter, the rate has remained at 1 percent through the first quarter of 2017.

2-49. Many individuals are faced with the choice of either making their instalment payments or, alternatively, paying off other types of liabilities that they have accumulated. In many cases, the interest rate on other debts is higher than 5 percent.

EXAMPLE   Jasmine Ho has determined that her March instalment for 2017 will be $7,500. She owes $7,500 on her Visa credit card for personal expenditures. Jasmine does not have the funds to pay both the credit card debt and her tax instalment.

ANALYSIS   The annual interest rate that will be charged on her Visa balance is likely to be around 20 percent. This compares to a current rate on late tax instalments of 5 percent. Without regard to financial planning issues, Jasmine would clearly reduce her interest costs by paying off the credit card debt, as opposed to making her instalment payment.

Penalties

Late Filing Penalty

2-50.   If the deadline for filing an income tax return is not met, the CRA assesses a penalty. For a first offence, this penalty amounts to 5 percent of the tax that was unpaid at the filing due date, plus 1 percent for each complete month (part months do not count) the unpaid tax is outstanding up to a maximum of 12 months. This penalty would be in addition to interest on the amounts due. If there are no taxes owed on the due date, or if the taxpayer is entitled to a refund, the late filing penalty would be nil.

2-51.   If the taxpayer has been charged a late filing penalty in any of the three preceding taxation years, the CRA can double the penalty on the second offence to 10 percent of the tax owing, plus 2 percent per month up to a maximum of 20 months. This will happen if the second late filed return is filed after the CRA has already sent a demand to file that return.

2-52.   In terms of tax planning, the penalty for late filing is sufficiently severe that individuals should make every effort to file their income tax returns no later than the deadline (April 30 or June 15), even if all of the taxes owing cannot be paid at that time. This is of particular importance if they have filed late in one of the three preceding years.

2-53.   This point is sometimes forgotten when the previous offence resulted in a negligible penalty. The penalty for a second offence will double, even if the amount involved in the first penalty was very small.

Late Or Deficient Instalments Penalty

2-54.   There is no penalty for late payment of income taxes or on moderate amounts of late or deficient instalments. However, there is a penalty when large amounts of late or deficient instalments are involved. This penalty is specified in ITA 163.1 and is equal to 50 percent of the amount by which the interest owing on the late or deficient instalments exceeds the greater of $1,000 and 25 percent of the interest that would be owing if no instalments were made. As this penalty does not kick in unless the amount of interest exceeds $1,000, it would only apply to fairly large amounts of late or deficient instalments.

Exercise Two - 6

Subject: Penalties And Interest For Individuals

Despite the fact that her net tax owing has been between $3,000 and $4,000 in the two previous years, and is expected to be a similar amount during 2017, Mary Carlos has made no instalment payments for 2017. While her normal filing date would be April 30, 2018, she does not file her 2017 return or pay the balance owing until July 20, 2018. What penalties and interest will be assessed for the 2017 taxation year?

SOLUTION available in print and online Study Guide.

Due Date For Balance Owing - Living Individuals

2-55. If the combination of amounts withheld and instalments paid falls short of the total taxes payable for the taxation year, there will be a balance owing. For living individuals, ITA 248(1) defines the "balance due date" as April 30, without regard to whether the taxpayer qualifies for the June 15 filing due date because of business income.

Deceased Taxpayers - Balance Due Dates And Final Returns

Balance Due Dates - Deceased Taxpayer

2-56. The due date for the amount owing for the year of death is generally April 30th of the year following death. However, if the taxpayer is eligible for the six month extension of the filing due date for the current or previous year's return, the balance due date for that return is also extended to the revised filing due date.

> **EXAMPLE** Before filing her 2017 tax return, Joanne Rivers dies on March 31, 2018. For 2017 and 2018, her income was from her business. No instalments were required. There is a balance owing for both years. What are the due dates for these amounts?

> **ANALYSIS** Her 2017 return will be due on September 30, 2018, six months after her death. Any balance owing for 2017 will be due at that time. Although her final return for 2018 will be due on June 15, 2019, any balance owing for 2018 will be due on April 30, 2019.

Final Returns - Special Rules Applicable At Death

2-57. Dealing with the death of a taxpayer is a very complex area of tax practice. In fact, for an individual with a substantial estate and/or a number of beneficiaries, it usually requires the services of a tax practitioner who specializes in the area. Complete coverage of this subject goes well beyond the scope of this general text.

2-58. However, we will provide some coverage of a few of the more important issues that arise when an individual dies. For example, in Chapter 9 we discuss the deemed disposition of capital assets at death and in Chapter 11 we cover the special rules that apply to net capital losses in the year of death.

2-59. Additional filing issues related to the deceased taxpayers, such as returns to be filed and available credits, are covered in an Appendix to Chapter 11.

Returns And Payments - Corporations

Due Date For Corporate Returns - ITA 150

2-60. Unlike the case with individuals, the taxation year of a corporation can end on any day of the calendar year. This makes it impossible to have a uniform filing date and, as a consequence, the filing deadline for corporations is specified as six months after the fiscal year end of the company.

2-61. Under ITA 150(1)(a), corporations (other than corporations that are registered charities) that are resident in Canada at any time in the year, carry on business in Canada, have a taxable capital gain, dispose of Taxable Canadian Property, or would be subject to Canadian tax if not for an international tax treaty, are required to file a corporate tax return, a.k.a. T2, within this specified period. Information from the financial statements must accompany this form, along with other required schedules.

Filing Alternatives For Corporations

Paper Vs. Electronic Filing

2-62. ITA 150.1(2.1) indicates that prescribed corporations must file their returns electronically. They do not have the option to paper file. For this purpose, prescribed corporations are those that have gross revenues in excess of $1 million. Corporations with gross revenues of $1 million or less can choose to paper file or to file their return electronically.

Use Of Functional Currency

2-63.   If a Canadian enterprise has foreign operations, it is likely that some of their records will be maintained in a foreign currency. If these records are translated into Canadian dollars in order to file the required return, there may be a problem. The use of some translation procedures can introduce what many analysts believe are distortions in the reported results.

2-64.   To correct this situation, ITA 261 allows the determination of Canadian tax liabilities on the basis of financial statements prepared in the corporation's functional currency. For this purpose, functional currency is defined as follows:

> "**functional currency**" of a taxpayer for a taxation year means the currency of a country other than Canada if that currency is, throughout the taxation year,
>
> (a) a qualifying currency; and
> (b) the primary currency in which the taxpayer maintains its records and books of account for financial reporting purposes.

2-65.   ITA 261 provides the following definition of qualifying currency:

> "**qualifying currency**" at any time means each of
> (a) the currency of the United States of America;
> (b) the currency of the European Monetary Union;
> (c) the currency of the United Kingdom;
> (d) the currency of Australia; and
> (e) a prescribed currency.

2-66.   You should also note that the term "functional currency" has a different meaning in the *Income Tax Act* than it does in Canadian and International Financial Reporting Standards. Financial reporting standards use this term to refer to the currency of the primary economic environment in which the corporation operates, without regard to the currency in which the corporation keeps its records.

Instalment Payments For Corporations

Instalment Threshold

2-67.   Corporations are generally required to make monthly instalment payments throughout their taxation year. However, this requirement is eliminated if either the estimated Tax Payable for the current year or the Tax Payable for the preceding taxation year does not exceed $3,000 (combined federal and provincial). In addition, special rules apply to some "Canadian Controlled Private Corporations", or CCPCs. While CCPCs will be defined more precisely in Chapter 12, at this point we would note that a CCPC is a private corporation that is controlled by residents of Canada and does not have any of its shares traded in public markets. The special instalment rules applicable to these CCPCs will be discussed beginning at Paragraph 2-70.

Calculating The Amount - General Rules (Excluding Small CCPCs)

2-68.   When instalments are required, they must be paid on or before the last day of each month, with the amount being calculated on the basis of one of three alternatives. As laid out in ITA 157(1)(a), these alternatives are as follows:

1. **Current Year** - 12 instalments, each based on 1/12 of the estimated tax payable for the current year.

2. **Preceding Year** - 12 instalments, each based on 1/12 of the tax that was payable in the immediately preceding year.

3. **Second And First Preceding Year** - 2 instalments, each based on 1/12 of the tax that was payable in the second preceding year, followed by 10 instalments based on 1/10 of the amount by which the taxes paid in the immediately preceding year exceeds the sum of the first two instalments.

2-69.   Choosing between these alternatives is usually a relatively simple matter. The choice should be the instalment base that provides the minimum total cash outflow or, in those cases where alternative bases result in the same total cash outflow, the alternative that provides the greatest amount of deferral. For businesses that are experiencing year to year increases in their taxes payable, the third alternative will generally meet this objective. Note, however, the total cash outflow under the third alternative will usually be the same as the total cash outflow under the second alternative.

> **EXAMPLE** The Marshall Company, a public company, estimates that its 2017 taxes payable will be $153,000. In 2016, the Company paid taxes of $126,000. The corresponding figure for 2015 was $96,000.
>
> **ANALYSIS** The choices for instalment payments for Marshall Company would be:
>
> 1.   12 instalments of $12,750 each ($153,000 ÷ 12) totaling $153,000.
> 2.   12 instalments of $10,500 each ($126,000 ÷ 12) totaling $126,000.
> 3.   2 instalments of $8,000 each ($96,000 ÷ 12) and 10 instalments of $11,000 each [($126,000 - $16,000) ÷ 10] totaling $126,000.
>
> While the cash outflows under alternative 3 total the same amount as those under alternative 2, alternative 3 would be selected because the first two payments are smaller and provide a deferral to the last 10 payments.

Calculating The Amount - Small CCPCs

2-70.   "Small" CCPCs are allowed to pay instalments on a quarterly basis. ITA 157(1.2) defines a small CCPC as one for which:

• the Taxable Income of the corporation and its associated corporations does not exceed $500,000 during the current or the previous taxation year;

• the Taxable Capital Employed In Canada of the corporation and its associated corporations does not exceed $10 million for the current or previous year;

• an amount has been deducted under ITA 125 (the small business deduction) for the current or previous year; and

• a perfect compliance record has been maintained with respect to payments and filings (for GST, source deductions and income taxes) during the last 12 months.

2-71.   For CCPCs that meet this definition, ITA 157(1.1) provides three alternatives for calculating instalments:

1.   **Current Year** - 4 instalments, each based on 1/4 of the estimated tax payable for the current taxation year.

2.   **Preceding Year** - 4 instalments, each based on 1/4 of the tax that was payable in the immediately preceding taxation year.

3.   **Second And First Preceding Year** - 1 instalment based on 1/4 of the tax that was payable in the second preceding taxation year, followed by 3 instalments based on 1/3 of the amount by which the taxes paid in the immediately preceding taxation year exceeds the first instalment.

2-72.   The payments are required on or before the last day of each of the fiscal quarters.

Exercise Two - 7

Subject: Corporate Instalments

Madco Ltd. is not a small CCPC. It has a December 31 year end. For 2015, its tax payable was $32,000, while for 2016, the amount was $59,000. For 2017, its estimated tax payable is $74,000. What would be the minimum instalments for 2017 and when would they be due? How would your answer differ if Madco Ltd. was a small CCPC?

Exercise Two - 8

Subject: Corporate Instalments

Fadco Inc. is not a small CCPC. It has a November 30 year end. For the taxation year ending November 30, 2014, its tax payable was $102,000, while for the 2016 taxation year, the amount was $54,000. For the 2017 taxation year, its estimated tax payable is $17,000. What would be the minimum instalments for 2017 and when would they be due? How would your answer differ if Fadco Inc. was a small CCPC?

SOLUTIONS available in print and online Study Guide.

Due Date For Balance Owing - Corporations

2-73.   Regardless of the instalment base selected, any remaining taxes are due within two months of the corporation's fiscal year end. An exception is made in the case of Canadian controlled private corporations (CCPCs) that have claimed the small business deduction in the current or preceding taxation year. For these corporations, the due date is three months after their fiscal year end, provided their Taxable Income did not exceed $500,000 for the previous year. Note that to qualify for this deferred due date, the corporation only has to be a CCPC. It does not have to be a "small" CCPC as described in Paragraph 2-70.

2-74.   Note that the final due date for payment is earlier than the due date for filing returns. For example, a company with a March 31 year end that is not eligible for the small business deduction would not have to file its tax return until September 30. However, all of its taxes would be due on May 31. This means that this final payment will often have to be based on an estimate of the total amount of taxes payable.

Exercise Two - 9

Subject: Corporate Due Date

The taxation year end for Radco Inc. is January 31, 2017. Indicate the date on which the corporate tax return must be filed, as well as the date on which any final payment of taxes is due.

SOLUTION available in print and online Study Guide.

Interest And
Penalties For Corporations

2-75.   The basic rules for interest on corporate balances owing or receivable are generally the same as those applicable to individuals. These were covered beginning in Paragraph 2-43. However, as described in Paragraph 2-47, interest paid to corporations on overpayments is calculated at the regular rate, not at the higher rate applicable to individuals and trusts.

2-76. Note that it is especially important that corporations avoid interest on late tax or instalment payments. Since corporations can usually deduct any interest expense that they incur, the payment of non-deductible interest on late tax payments represents a high cost source of financing. For example, if a corporation is paying taxes at a rate of 25 percent, interest at a non-deductible rate of 5 percent is the equivalent of a deductible interest rate of 6.7 percent [5% ÷ (1 - .25)]. Many corporations, particularly those that are publicly traded, are able to access financing at rates that are lower than this.

2-77. The previously covered penalties applicable to individuals for late filing of returns and for large amounts of late instalments (see Paragraph 2-50 and 2-54) are equally applicable to corporations. In addition to the penalties applicable to individuals, ITA 235 contains a further penalty applicable to large corporations. It calls for a penalty equal to .0005 percent per month of a corporation's Taxable Capital Employed In Canada. This will be assessed for a maximum period of 40 months.

2-78. This is a fairly harsh penalty in that, unlike the usual penalties that are based on any additional tax payable at the time the return should have been filed, this penalty is based on the capital of the enterprise, without regard to earnings or tax payable for the year. For example, CNR has Shareholders' Equity (roughly the equivalent of Taxable Capital Employed In Canada) of $4.857 billion. If the .0005 percent penalty was applied to this balance for 40 months, the total penalty would be $971,400.

> **We suggest you work Self Study Problems Two-2, 3, and 4 at this point.**

Returns And Payments - Trusts

Types Of Trusts

2-79. As defined in the Glossary to this text, a testamentary trust is a trust that arises on, and as a consequence of, the death of an individual. All other trusts are referred to as inter vivos trusts. As will be discussed in Chapter 19, "Trusts And Estate Planning", major changes in the rules for testamentary trusts became effective for 2016, including the introduction of a special category of testamentary trust referred to as a "graduated rate estate". What follows here is based on the rules applicable for 2017 and subsequent years.

Filing Requirements

2-80. In general, a trust must file a trust income tax return, a.k.a., T3 if it:

- has Tax Payable for the year;
- is requested by the CRA to file a tax return;
- has disposed of a capital property during the year; or
- has a taxable capital gain during the year.

2-81. There are other reasons for filing listed in the T3 Trust Guide. However, none are of sufficient importance to deal with here.

Due Dates For Returns

2-82. In general, all inter vivos and testamentary trusts, other than graduated rate estates, must use the calendar year as their taxation year. A testamentary trust designated as a graduated rate estate can use a non-calendar fiscal period for the duration of its limited life. All trusts must file their tax returns within 90 days of the end of their taxation year.

Payment Of Taxes

2-83. Legislation generally requires that all trusts, except graduated rate estates, make instalment payments. In the past, the CRA has not enforced instalment requirements against any type of trust. It appears that this approach will continue.

2-84. With respect to determining the amount of the instalments, the rules in ITA 156(1) cover both individuals and trusts. This means that, as was discussed in Paragraph 2-34 for individuals, trusts have three alternatives for calculating instalment amounts and the due dates are March 15, June 15, September 15 and December 15.

2-85. Any balance owing when the return is filed must be remitted with the return. Stated alternatively, the balance is due 90 days after the end of the trust's taxation year, generally March 31.

Interest And Penalties

2-86. For both testamentary and inter vivos trusts, interest on late final balance payments is calculated using the same rules as those applicable to individuals. In addition, late filing penalties for trusts are the same as those for individuals. However, it is the administrative practice of the CRA not to assess interest or penalties on late instalments.

We suggest you work Self Study Problem Two-5 at this point.

Income Tax Information Returns

2-87. ITA 221(1)(d) gives the CRA the right to require certain taxpayers to file information returns in addition to the returns in which they report their taxable income. These information returns are described in Part II of the Income Tax Regulations and must be filed using a prescribed form. Common examples of these returns and the related prescribed form would be as follows:

- **T3** This form is used by trustees (which includes trustees of some mutual funds) and executors to report the allocation of the trust's income.
- **T4** This form is used by employers to report remuneration and taxable benefits paid to employees and the various amounts withheld for source deductions.
- **T5** This form is used by organizations to report interest, dividend, and royalty payments.
- **T4RSP** This form is used by trustees to report payments out of Registered Retirement Savings Plans.

Books And Records

2-88. As indicated in IC78-10R5, "Books And Records Retention/Destruction":

> Books and records have to be kept for the period or periods provided by subsections 230(4) to (7) and section 5800 of the *Income Tax Regulations* ...

2-89. While for many of these documents, the specified retention period is 6 years, there are many variations in the length of the retention period, with both longer and shorter periods being specified in the sources cited in Paragraph 2-88.

Assessments And The CRA My Account Service

CRA Website - My Account Service

2-90. The CRA invests considerable resources on continual improvements to its website and electronic services. The goal is to reduce costs and provide faster, more efficient services to taxpayers. For example, the Auto-Fill My Return service allows individuals and authorized representatives to automatically fill in parts of a current year income tax return. The CRA website contains the My Account service which is a secure online portal that allows registered individuals to see many of their tax accounts online and manage their tax information. There is a similar My Business Account service available for businesses. The CRA website contains a list of its ever expanding electronic services. For the My Account service, the available information includes access to Notices of Assessment, RRSP and TFSA contribution limits, instalments paid and payable and many other past and present balances.

Notice Of Assessment

2-91.   After a tax return has been filed, the CRA runs a number of tests on the return, such as verifying the eligibility for various deductions (e.g., RRSP deductions) and tax credits (e.g., age credit). After processing a return, the CRA completes a Notice of Assessment which contains the amount, if any, of taxes to be paid or refunded, an explanation of any changes it has made to the return, and any interest and penalties that were assessed. For individuals, it also contains additional information such as the taxpayer's RRSP deduction limit. For individuals, the Notice of Assessment is available online in the My Account service, often within a few weeks of filing. A somewhat longer period is normally required for corporate income tax assessments and more complicated individual returns. The CRA will mail out the Notice of Assessment unless the taxpayer has opted instead to have e-mail notification as soon as it is available to be viewed online.

Notice Of Reassessment

2-92.   The Notice of Assessment does not free the taxpayer from additional scrutiny of the return. The CRA is under pressure to issue Notice of Assessments quickly so the initial assessment is not in-depth. A more detailed review of many returns is done after the Notice of Assessment has been completed. The CRA has a matching program that compares information the CRA has received from third parties, such as employers and financial institutions with the relevant returns. The CRA will issue a Notice of Reassessment with a revised amount payable or refunded and an explanation if a change is made to a taxpayer's return for any reason such as amounts not matching or duplicate claims on a spouse's return. The Notice of Reassessment can also be viewed online in the My Account service.

2-93.   The normal reassessment period is the period that ends 3 years after the date on the Notice of Assessment for individuals, most trusts, and Canadian controlled private corporations. This normal reassessment period is extended to 4 years for other corporations because of the greater complexity that may be involved in the review process. There are a number of exceptions to this normal 3 year reassessment period that include the following:

- Reassessment can occur at any time:
  - if the taxpayer or person filing the return has made any misrepresentation that is attributable to neglect, carelessness or willful default, or has committed any fraud in filing the return or in supplying information,
  - if the taxpayer has filed a waiver of the 3 year time limit.

- Reassessment can occur outside the normal reassessment period:
  - if an individual or testamentary trust has requested a reduction in taxes, interest, or penalties. The ability to use this provision is limited to 10 years after the particular year in question,
  - when reassessment within the normal period affects a balance outside of this period,
  - in situations where the taxpayer is claiming certain specified deductions. An example of this would be a listed personal property loss being carried back to claim a refund of taxes paid.

Refunds

2-94.   When tax has been withheld from income and/or instalments have been paid, the CRA's Notice of Assessment may show that there has been an overpayment of income tax. In this situation, the taxpayer is entitled to a refund of any excess payments and, in the great majority of cases, such refunds are sent without any further action being taken. If, for some reason, the refund is not made, the taxpayer can apply for it in writing within the normal reassessment period. However, if there are other tax liabilities outstanding, such as amounts owing from prior years, the CRA has the right to apply the refund against these liabilities.

2-95.   A further point here is that refunds will not generally be made if the return is filed more than 3 years after the end of the relevant taxation year (e.g., a refund on a 2012 tax return that is filed in 2017 will normally not be paid).

2-96.   Interest is paid on overpayments of income tax at the prescribed rate (see Paragraph 2-47). For individuals, interest at the prescribed base rate, plus 2 percentage points, begins to accrue on the later of two dates:

- 30 days after the balance due date (generally, April 30); or
- 30 days after the return is filed.

2-97.   For an individual with business or professional income, the normal filing date would be June 15. If such an individual was entitled to a refund and waited until this date to file, interest would not begin to accrue until July 15.

2-98.   For corporations, interest on refunds at the prescribed base rate, without the additional 2 percentage points, begins to accrue at the later of two dates. These are:

- 120 days after the corporate year end; or
- 30 days after the corporation's tax return is filed (unless it is not filed prior to the due date, in which case the due date is applicable).

2-99.   Taxpayers can request that any refund due to them be transferred to their tax instalment account. The advantage of this is that the transfer would normally occur more quickly than the issuance of a refund. This option is available on the corporate tax return, but is only available through a separate written request in the case of personal tax returns. This is one reason it is not commonly used by individuals.

Adjustments To Income Tax Returns

2-100.   There is no general provision in the *Income Tax Act* for filing an amended return. However, this does not mean that amounts included in the returns of previous years cannot be altered. It simply means that the adjustment process normally takes place after the return has been processed and a Notice of Assessment has been received.

2-101.   There are many reasons why adjustments to a previously filed return could be necessary. Besides the obvious omissions or errors (i.e., omitting a charitable donation receipt or making an error in recording the information on a T4), there are many other possible reasons. Information received after the return was filed, for example, learning through a tax course that a parent should have been claimed as a dependant, would make an adjustment of a prior return advantageous.

2-102.   IC 75-7R3, "Reassessment of a Return of Income", permits such adjustments if the following conditions are met:

- the CRA is satisfied that the previous assessment was incorrect;

- the reassessment can be made within the normal reassessment period or the taxpayer has filed a waiver;

- the requested decrease in taxable income does not solely depend on an increase in a permissive deduction such as capital cost allowance;

- the change is not based solely on a successful appeal to the courts by another taxpayer; and

- the taxpayer's return has been filed within 3 years of the end of the year to which it relates.

2-103.   For individuals, changes can be requested through the CRA website by using the My Account service, or by mailing Form T1-ADJ, "T1 Adjustment Request" or a letter detailing the adjustment requested. The calculations required to issue a reassessment are taken care of by the CRA. This informal procedure can be used any time within the normal reassessment period, provided the return has been filed within 3 years of the end of the year to which it relates.

Disputes And Appeals

Representation By Others

2-104. At the initial stages of any dispute, a taxpayer may wish to represent himself. However, if complex issues are involved, or if the dispute progresses to a later stage where procedures require more formal representation, a taxpayer is likely to authorize some other party to act as their representative.

2-105. The CRA's "Represent A Client" service is designed to provide online access to both individual and business tax information by authorized representatives registered with the CRA. The registration process is relatively simple as this service is not designed solely for tax professionals, but can also be used by friends and family members of the taxpayer.

2-106. There are many services available through "Represent A Client". The list is available on the CRA website and includes most of the services available through My Account.

2-107. In order for the CRA to discuss any matter, including the issue in dispute, with anyone other than the taxpayer, the taxpayer must either:

- have on file with the CRA Form T1013, "Authorizing Or Canceling A Representative" (for individuals) or RC59 "Business Consent" (for businesses), or

- have authorized a representative through My Account or My Business Account to access their account using the "Represent A Client" service.

Informal Request For Adjustments

2-108. If a taxpayer disagrees with an assessment or reassessment, the usual first step is to contact the CRA immediately. In some cases the proposed change is the result of a simple error on the part of the taxpayer or a lack of information and can be corrected or resolved through telephone contact or by letter.

Notice Of Objection

General Rules

2-109. If the informal contact does not resolve the issue in question, a taxpayer has the right to file a notice of objection. The three methods available for filing one are:

- by accessing My Account or My Business Account from the CRA website and selecting the option "Register my formal dispute" (also available through Represent A Client),
- using Form T400A, "Objection – Income Tax Act", or,
- writing a letter to the Chief of Appeals at the relevant Appeals Intake Centre explaining the reasons for your objection.

2-110. For corporations and inter vivos trusts, a notice of objection must be filed within 90 days of the date on the Notice of Assessment or Reassessment. For individuals and testamentary trusts, the rules are more generous. For these taxpayers, the notice of objection must be filed before the later of:

- 90 days from the date on the Notice of Assessment or Reassessment; or
- one year from the filing due date for the return under assessment or reassessment.

EXAMPLE An individual required to file on April 30, 2017, files on March 26, 2017. The Notice of Assessment is dated May 14, 2017 and contains a change by the CRA. The Notice of Reassessment is dated August 1, 2018 and contains another change.

ANALYSIS A notice of objection related to the Notice of Assessment must be filed before the later of August 12, 2017 (90 days after the date on the Notice) and April 30, 2018 (one year after the filing due date). The deadline would be April 30, 2018, without regard for the fact that the return was actually filed on March 26, 2017. Since the Notice of Reassessment was received after April 30, 2018, the notice of objection for it must be filed by October 30, 2018 (90 days after the date on the Notice).

2-111.   When an individual dies after October of the year and before May of the following year, you will recall that the filing date for the return is extended to six months after the date of death, thereby extending the date for filing a notice of objection by the same number of months.

2-112.   A taxpayer can request an extension of the filing deadline for the notice of objection. Since many of the disputed issues result from a Notice of Reassessment mailed more than a year after the filing due date of the return, the relevant deadline is then 90 days from the date on the Notice of Reassessment. If the matter is complicated and requires professional help, 90 days may not be sufficient time to respond to the reassessment. The application for an extension must be made within one year of the deadline to file the notice of objection.

2-113.   After the notice of objection is received, the CRA is required to reply to the taxpayer:

- vacating the assessment,
- confirming it (i.e., refusing to change it),
- varying the amount, or
- reassessing.

2-114.   Unresolved objections are subject to review by the Chief of Appeals. These appeals sections are instructed to operate independently of the assessing divisions and should provide an unbiased second opinion. If the matter remains unresolved after this review, the taxpayer must either accept the CRA's assessment or, alternatively, continue to pursue the matter to a higher level of appeal.

2-115.   The CRA has a pamphlet covering the dispute process, Resolving Your Dispute: Objections and Appeal Rights under the Income Tax Act (P148). It contains coverage of the procedures needed to file a Notice of Assessment, including a sample, as well as information on how to proceed with an appeal.

Rules For Large Corporations

2-116.   The CRA appears to believe that it has been the practice of certain corporate taxpayers to delay the dispute process by filing vague objections in the first instance, and subsequently bringing in fresh issues as the appeal process moves forward.

2-117.   To prevent this perceived abuse, a corporation must specify each issue to be decided, the dollar amount of relief sought for each issue, and the facts and reasons relied on by the corporation in respect of each issue when filing a notice of objection.

2-118.   If the corporation objects to a reassessment or additional reassessment made by the CRA, or appeals to the Tax Court of Canada, the objection or appeal can be only with respect to issues and dollar amounts properly dealt with in the original notice of objection. There is an exception to this general rule for new issues that are raised by the CRA on assessment or reassessment. These limitations are only applicable to "large corporations", defined as a corporation with Taxable Capital Employed In Canada that is in excess of $10 million at the end of the year to which the objection relates.

Exercise Two - 10

Subject: Notice Of Objection

Jerry Fall filed his 2017 tax return as required on April 30, 2018. His Notice of Assessment dated May 20, 2018 indicated that his return was accepted as filed. On May 22, 2019, he receives a Notice of Reassessment dated May 15, 2019 indicating that he owes additional taxes, as well as interest on the unpaid amounts. What is the latest date for filing a notice of objection for this reassessment? Explain your answer.

SOLUTION available in print and online Study Guide.

Tax Court Of Canada

Deadline For Appeal

2-119.   A taxpayer who does not find satisfaction through the notice of objection procedure may then proceed to the next level of the appeal procedure, the Tax Court of Canada. Appeals to the Tax Court of Canada must be made within 90 days of the date on the CRA's response to the notice of objection (which would confirm the assessment or reassessment), or 90 days after the notice of objection has been filed if the CRA has not replied. It is not possible to bypass the Tax Court of Canada and appeal directly to the Federal Court level, except in very limited circumstances.

Informal Procedure

2-120.   On appeal to the Tax Court of Canada, the general procedure will automatically apply unless the taxpayer elects to have his case heard under the informal procedure. The informal procedure can be elected for appeals in which the total amount of federal tax and penalty involved for a given year is less than $25,000, or where the loss in question is less than $50,000.

2-121.   Advantages of the informal procedure include:

- The rules of evidence remain fairly informal, allowing the taxpayer to represent himself, or be represented by an agent other than a lawyer.
- Under the informal procedure, even if the taxpayer is unsuccessful, he cannot be asked to pay court costs.
- The informal procedure is designed as a fast-track procedure that is usually completed within 6 or 7 months whereas the general procedure may take many years.

2-122.   The major disadvantage of the informal procedure is that the taxpayer generally gives up all rights to further appeals if the Court decision is unfavourable.

General Procedure

2-123.   If the general procedure applies, formal rules of evidence must be used, resulting in a situation where the taxpayer has to be represented by either himself, or legal counsel. In practical terms, this means that for cases involving substantial amounts, lawyers will usually be involved.

2-124.   Under the general procedure, if the taxpayer is unsuccessful, the Court may require the taxpayer to pay costs to the CRA. Under either procedure, if the taxpayer is more than 50 percent successful (e.g., if he is claiming $10,000 and is awarded more than $5,000), the judge can order the CRA to pay all or part of the taxpayer's costs. However, there is a Tariff structure that can severely limit the costs that can be awarded by the court.

Appeals By The Minister

2-125.   There are situations in which the CRA may pursue a matter because of its general implications for broad groups of taxpayers. The individual taxpayer is given protection from the costs associated with this type of appeal by the requirement that the CRA be responsible for the taxpayer's reasonable legal fees when the amount of taxes payable in question does not exceed $25,000 or the loss in dispute does not exceed $50,000. This is without regard to whether the appeal is successful.

Resolution

2-126.   Prior to the hearing by the Tax Court of Canada, discussions between the taxpayer and the CRA are likely to continue. It would appear that, in the majority of cases, the dispute will be resolved prior to the actual hearing. However, if a hearing proceeds, the Court may dispose of an appeal by:

- dismissing it; or
- allowing it and
  - vacating the assessment,
  - varying the assessment, or
  - referring the assessment back to the CRA for reconsideration and reassessment.

Federal Court And Supreme Court Of Canada

2-127.   Either the CRA or the taxpayer can appeal a general procedure decision of the Tax Court of Canada to the Federal Court of Appeal. The appeal must be made within 30 days of the date on which the Tax Court of Canada makes its decision.

2-128.   It is possible to pursue a matter beyond the Federal Court to the Supreme Court of Canada. This can be done if the Federal Court of Appeal refers the issue to the higher Court, or if the Supreme Court authorizes the appeal. These actions will not usually happen unless there are new issues or legal precedents to be dealt with and, as a result, such appeals are not common. However, when tax cases do reach the Supreme Court, they often attract a great deal of public attention.

We suggest you work Self Study Problem Two-6 at this point.

Tax Evasion, Avoidance And Planning

Tax Evasion

2-129.   The concept of tax evasion is not difficult to understand. It is described on the CRA website as follows:

> Tax evasion typically involves deliberately ignoring a specific part of the law. For example, those participating in tax evasion may under-report taxable receipts or claim expenses that are non-deductible or overstated. They might also attempt to evade taxes by wilfully refusing to comply with legislated reporting requirements.
>
> Tax evasion, unlike tax avoidance, has criminal consequences. Tax evaders face prosecution in criminal court.

2-130.   There is little ambiguity in this description as it involves deliberate attempts to deceive the taxation authorities. The most common of the offenses that fall under this description of tax evasion is probably the failure to report revenues. This may involve individuals receiving income in the form of cash (common in the home renovation business). Many of the more important cases involve income from assets held offshore.

2-131.   You should note the severity of the possible punishments associated with tax evasion. The facts in a recent example illustrate this point:

> **Ottawa, Ontario, October 19, 2016...** The Canada Revenue Agency (CRA) announced today that, on October 17, 2016, Tania Kovaluk was sentenced in the Superior Court of Justice in Ottawa to 1,825 days (5 years) in jail for deliberately choosing not to pay a court-imposed fine for criminal tax evasion. On November 20, 2012, Kovaluk pleaded guilty to multiple counts related to income tax and GST evasion. She was sentenced to two years and five months in jail, and was fined $887,328, which was payable in full by June 30, 2014. Since she was released from jail she has made no attempt to pay her court-imposed fine. Kovaluk, a dentist, knowingly failed to report $2,578,987 in income she earned from 2003 to 2007, thereby evading $721,617 in federal taxes.

Tax Avoidance And Tax Planning
A Fuzzy Concept

2-132.   Despite the fact that disputes may arise with respect to its implementation, the concept of tax evasion is clear — tax evasion involves deliberately breaking the law. Working from this concept, it could be argued that any tax arrangement that is within the law should be considered tax planning.

2-133.   However, there is a longstanding view within the government that there are tax arrangements that, while they do not break the law, violate the "spirit" of the law. Such transactions are commonly referred to as avoidance transactions. In an attempt to support this view, the CRA website describes the difference between tax planning and tax avoidance as follows:

> Tax avoidance and tax planning both involve tax reduction arrangements that may meet the specific wording of the relevant legislation. **Effective tax planning** occurs when the results of these arrangements are consistent with the intent of the law. When tax planning reduces taxes in a way that is inconsistent with the overall spirit of the law, the arrangements are referred to as **Tax Avoidance**. The Canada Revenue Agency's interpretation of the term "tax avoidance" includes all unacceptable and abusive tax planning. Aggressive tax planning refers to arrangements that "push the limits" of acceptable tax planning.

> Tax avoidance occurs when a person undertakes transactions that contravene specific anti-avoidance provisions. Tax avoidance also includes situations where a person reduces or eliminates tax through a transaction or a series of transactions that comply with the letter of the law but violate the spirit and intent of the law. It was to address these latter situations that the general anti-avoidance rule was enacted in 1988.

> Tax avoidance results when actions are taken to minimize tax, while within the letter of the law, those actions contravene the object and spirit of the law.

2-134.   For many years, the CRA tried to enforce this tax avoidance concept through the use of a "business purpose test". That is, if a transaction had no business purpose other than the avoidance or reduction of taxes, it was not acceptable for tax purposes. However, the courts consistently rejected this concept, leaving the CRA with little ability to enforce what it viewed as tax avoidance. An attempt to solve this problem was put forward in 1988 as a General Anti-Avoidance Rule (GAAR).

General Anti-Avoidance Rule (GAAR)
Basic Provisions

2-135.   The basic GAAR provision is as follows:

> **Paragraph 245(2)** Where a transaction is an avoidance transaction, the tax consequences to a person shall be determined as is reasonable in the circumstances in order to deny a tax benefit that, but for this section, would result, directly or indirectly, from that transaction or from a series of transactions that includes that transaction.

2-136. The Section goes on to describe an avoidance transaction as follows:

> **ITA 245(3)**   An avoidance transaction means any transaction

> (a) that, but for this section, would result, directly or indirectly, in a tax benefit, unless the transaction may reasonably be considered to have been undertaken or arranged primarily for bona fide purposes other than to obtain the tax benefit; or

> (b) that is part of a series of transactions, which series, but for this section, would result, directly or indirectly, in a tax benefit, unless the transaction may reasonably be considered to have been undertaken or arranged primarily for bona fide purposes other than to obtain the tax benefit.

2-137.   Taken together, these provisions mean that the GAAR will apply to any transaction other than those where there is a bona fide non-tax purpose, or where there is no misuse or abuse of the *Act*. If a transaction is judged to be an avoidance transaction, the consequences may involve:

* The disallowance of a deduction in whole or in part.
* Deductions or losses being allocated to a different person.
* The nature of some payments being re-characterized.
* Some tax effects (e.g., a loss) that might otherwise be recognized being ignored.

2-138.   The interpretation of these rules is generally left to lawyers, rather than to accountants. Given this, we will not provide any detailed coverage of this subject in this text. However, GAAR is of sufficient importance that anyone involved in tax work should be aware of the existence of this provision.

Collection And Enforcement

Taxpayer Property

2-139.   The CRA has enforcement powers under the provisions of ITA 231.1, "Inspections" and ITA 231.2, "Requirement To Provide Documents Or Information".

2-140.   Tax officials or other persons authorized by the CRA have the right to enter a taxpayer's place of business, locations where anything is done in connection with the business, or any place where records related to the business are kept. Tax officials may also examine any document of another taxpayer that relates, or may relate to, the information that is, or should be, in the books and records of the taxpayer who is being audited. However, in those cases where the place of business is also a dwelling, the officials must either obtain the permission of the occupant or have a court issued warrant. In this process, the officials may audit the books and records, examine all property, and require that the taxpayer answer questions and provide assistance.

2-141.   Seizure of books and records requires a court issued warrant. If this occurs, a taxpayer may apply to have the records returned. Also requiring judicial authorization is demands for information about unnamed persons from third parties. This could include information from the files of the taxpayer's lawyer or accountant. There are additional confidentiality rules in this area that protect solicitor/client communications. However, accountant/client privilege is not protected unless they are part of the solicitor/client privilege. This usually occurs when a lawyer directs the activities of the accountant.

Collections

2-142.   As noted earlier in the Chapter, the due date for the payment of personal income taxes for a taxation year is April 30 of the following year. The due date for corporate income taxes is two months after the corporate year end (three months for qualifying Canadian controlled private corporations). Additional taxes may become payable as a result of an assessment or reassessment. If this is the case, these taxes are due at the time the notice of assessment is mailed.

2-143.   Initial collection procedures will not normally extend beyond communicating with the taxpayer about his liability and the related interest that will be charged. In the case of taxes resulting from an assessment or reassessment, the CRA cannot exercise its collection powers until:

* 90 days after the assessment or reassessment date when no objection is filed;
* 90 days from the date of the notice from the CRA appeals division confirming or varying the assessment or reassessment where an objection has been filed and no further appeal has been made; or
* 90 days after a court decision has been made and there are no further appeals.

2-144.   If informal procedures fail to result in payment of the tax owing by the defaulter, the CRA can request that a taxpayer owing money to the defaulter make payments to the CRA in settlement of the defaulter's liability. A common example of this would be garnishment of a defaulter's wages to pay income taxes owed. The CRA can go even further and obtain a judgment against a defaulter that can be enforced by seizure and sale of the taxpayer's property.

Other Penalties
Examples
2-145.   We have previously discussed the penalties associated with the late payment of instalments and the late filing of tax returns. There are a number of other penalties that are specified in tax legislation. Examples of such penalties would be as follows:

Repeated Failure To Report Income   This penalty applies when there is a failure to report at least $500 in income in the current year, and in any of the three preceding years. The penalty is the lesser of:

- 10 percent of the unreported amount (not the taxes owing); and
- an amount equal to 50 percent of the difference between the understatement of related to the omission and the amount of any tax paid in respect of the unreported amount (e.g., withholdings by an employer).

False Statements Or Omissions   This penalty applies in cases of gross negligence where there is an intention to disregard the *Income Tax Act*. The penalty is the greater of $100 and 50 percent of the understated tax.

Evasion   Penalties here range from 50 percent to 200 percent of the relevant tax and, in addition, imprisonment for a period not exceeding two years.

Tax Advisors And Tax Return Preparers
2-146.   Tax preparers who prepare more than 10 returns for a fee are required to register with the CRA and file them electronically. Mandatory electronic filing applies to both the filing of T1 individual returns and T2 corporate returns. Individual taxpayers and volunteers who do not charge a fee to prepare tax returns for others are not required to register for an EFILE number. Tax preparers who do not efile may be charged a penalty of $25 for each paper-filed T1 and $100 for each paper-filed T2.

2-147.   Civil penalties for tax advisors and tax return preparers who encourage or assist clients with tax evasive practices are found in ITA 163.2, titled "Misrepresentation of a Tax Matter by a Third Party". The penalty of most concern to accountants is the one for participating in a misrepresentation in the preparation of a return. The penalty is the greater of $1,000 and the penalty assessed on the tax return preparer's client for making the false statement or omission. The penalty on the client is equal to 50 percent of the amount of tax avoided as a result of the misrepresentation. The total amount of the penalty is capped at $100,000, plus the gross compensation to which the tax return preparer is entitled to receive.

2-148.   IC 01-1, "Third-Party Civil Penalties", is an extensive Information Circular that contains 18 examples of the application of third-party penalties. While the examples cited in the IC illustrate clear cut abuses, there are many situations in which it is to the taxpayer's advantage to pursue a more aggressive stance in claiming deductions. It is believed that these penalties discourage tax return preparers from suggesting or condoning this type of approach, out of fear that they may be liable for the third party penalties if the returns are audited. In addition, it appears that an increasing number of tax return preparers are refusing to service certain types of high risk clients.

Promoters Of Abusive Tax Shelters And Tax Planning Arrangements
2-149.   The CRA has a number of penalties applicable to tax advisors and promoters of what they consider to be abusive tax shelters and tax planning arrangements. For example, for many years the CRA has been actively pursuing taxpayers participating in "gifting tax shelter schemes" and promoters of these schemes.

2-150. The penalties in this complex area can arise from a number of misdeeds such as participating in a misrepresentation, making or furnishing false or misleading statements and being involved with the development of an "abusive" tax shelter. In addition to promoters, the penalties can apply to a tax advisor who, in the course of providing tax advice, is responsible for and contributes to the design of any of the tax avoidance elements of the arrangement.

We suggest you work Self Study Problem Two-7 at this point.

Additional Supplementary Self Study Problems Are Available Online.

Taxpayer Relief Provisions (Fairness Package)

Basic Rules

2-151. There is a widespread perception that the application of some of the CRA's rules on interest and penalties, as well as certain other rules, can result in individuals and other taxpayers being treated in an unfair manner. Reflecting this concern, a "fairness package" is described in IC 07-1, "Taxpayer Relief Provisions". In general terms, the content of IC 07-1 is as follows:

Part I describes the relevant legislation and limits claims to 10 years from the end of the calendar year in which the tax issue occurred.

Part II - Guidelines For The Cancellation Or Waiver Of Penalties And Interest indicates that penalties or interest may be waived in the following situations:

- **Extraordinary Circumstances** - Examples include natural disasters or serious illness.

- **Actions Of The CRA** - Examples here include processing delays and errors in materials made available to the public

- **Inability To Pay Or Financial Hardship** - Examples here include the need to provide extended payment arrangements or the inability of an individual to provide basic necessities for his family.

Part III - Guidelines for Accepting Late, Amended, or Revoked Elections While the *Act* contains numerous elections, there is rarely any provision for revoking, amending, or making them after the specified time period has passed. The Appendix to IC 07-01 provides a fairly long list of prescribed elections for which the CRA has discretionary authority to extend the statutory time limit for their filing, amending, or revoking.

Part IV - Guidelines For Refunds Or Reduction In Amounts Payable Beyond The Normal Three Year Period The *Act* sets a three year limitation period from the end of the tax year of an individual to file an income tax return to claim a tax refund and a three year limitation period from the date of the Notice of Assessment to ask for an adjustment to an assessment issued for a previous tax year. The information in Part IV of this IC deals with the CRA's discretion to relieve an individual and a testamentary trust from the limitation period and, in certain circumstances, to accept late requests to give the individual or testamentary trust a refund or reduction in tax.

Part V - Rules and Procedures When Relief is Granted or Denied This is a more technical section, setting out the procedures related to granting relief, as well as the procedures associated with administrative and judicial reviews of fairness decisions.

Application

2-152.   Very little has been written about the application of the taxpayer relief provisions. Perhaps the most useful information is a guide that was prepared by the CRA for internal use. This *Taxpayer Relief Guide,* which is available as the result of a request made under the Federal *Access To Information Act*, provides a very extensive discussion of the application of the taxpayer relief provisions. At this time, however, this *Guide* does not appear to be available on the CRA web site.

2-153.   We would note that it has become commonplace for decisions made under the authority of the taxpayer relief legislation to be challenged in court through an application for judicial review. This may result in the decision being returned to the CRA for reconsideration. For example, in both Meier v. CRA [2011 DTC 5127] and NRT Technology Corp v. Canada [2013 DTC 5056], the fairness decision of the CRA was overturned and returned to the CRA for consideration.

2-154.   We would also note that the CRA has taken a number of steps that are designed to ensure that taxpayers are, in fact, treated fairly. These include the publication of a fairness pledge as well as a taxpayer bill of rights. More information about this subject is available on the CRA website.

Key Terms Used In This Chapter

2-155.   The following is a list of the key terms used in this Chapter. These terms, and their meanings, are compiled in the Glossary located at the back of the Study Guide.

Assessment	Notice Of Objection
Consent Form	Penalties
EFILE	Prescribed Rate
Fairness Package	Reassessment
GAAR	Small CCPC
Information Return	Source Deductions
Instalment Threshold	Tax Avoidance
Instalments	Tax Court Of Canada
My Account (CRA Website)	Tax Evasion
Net Tax Owing	Tax Planning
NETFILE	Taxpayer
Notice Of Assessment	Taxpayer Relief Provisions

References

2-156.   For more detailed study of the material in this Chapter, we would refer you to the following:

ITA 150   Filing Returns Of Income - General Rule
ITA 151   Estimate Of Tax
ITA 152   Assessment
ITA 153(1)   Withholding
ITA 156   Other Individuals (Instalments)
ITA 156.1   Definitions (Instalments)
ITA 157   Payment By Corporation (Instalments)
ITA 161   Interest (General)

ITA 162-163.1 Penalties
ITA 163.2   Misrepresentation Of A Tax Matter By A Third Party
ITA 164(1)   Refunds
ITA 165   Objections To Assessment
ITA 169-180   Appeals To The Tax Court Of Canada And The Federal Court Of Appeal
ITA 220   Minister's Duty
ITA 221   Regulations
ITA 222   Definitions (Collections)
ITA 223   Definitions (Seizure Of Property)
ITA 224   Garnishment
ITA 227   Withholding Taxes
ITA 230   Records And Books
ITA 231.1   Inspections
ITA 231.2   Requirement To Provide Documents Or Information
ITA 261   Definitions (Functional Currency)
ITA 245-246   Tax Avoidance

ITR Part II   Information Returns
ITR 4301   Prescribed Rate of Interest
ITR 5300   Instalments (Individuals)
ITR 5301   Instalments (Corporations)
ITR 5800   Retention Of Books And Records

IC 01-1   Third-Party Civil Penalties
IC 07-1   Taxpayer Relief Provisions
IC 71-14R3   The Tax Audit
IC 75-6R2   Required Withholding From Amounts Paid To Non-Resident
                 Persons Providing Services In Canada
IC 75-7R3   Reassessment Of A Return Of Income
IC 78-10R5   Books And Records Retention/Destruction
IC 84-1   Revision Of CCA Claims And Other Permissive Deductions
IC 88-2   General Anti-Avoidance Rule: Section 245 Of The Income Tax Act
IC 98-1R6   Collection Policies

S5-F4-C1   Income Tax Reporting Currency

P148   Resolving Your Dispute: Objection And Appeal Rights Under The Income Tax
                 Act

Problems For Self Study (Online)

To provide practice in problem solving, there are Self Study and Supplementary Self Study problems available on the Companion Website.

Within the text we have provided an indication of when it would be appropriate to work each Self Study problem. The detailed solutions for Self Study problems can be found in the print and online Study Guide.

We provide the Supplementary Self Study problems for those who would like additional practice in problem solving. The detailed solutions for the Supplementary Self Study problems are available online, not in the Study Guide.

The .PDF file "Self Study Problems for Volume 1" on the Companion Website contains the following for Chapter 2:

- 7 Self Study problems,
- 5 Supplementary Self Study problems, and
- detailed solutions for the Supplementary Self Study problems.

Assignment Problems

(The solutions for these problems are only available in
the solutions manual that has been provided to your instructor.)

Assignment Problem Two - 1
(Individual Tax Instalments)

For 2015, Mr. Mason Boardman has combined federal and provincial Tax Payable of $62,350. For this year, his employer withheld $61,600.

For 2016, his combined federal and provincial Tax Payable is $29,760. For this year, his employer withheld $13,740.

For 2017, he anticipates having combined federal and provincial Tax Payable of $52,370. He expects that his employer will withhold $47,390.

In January, 2017, you are asked to provide tax advice to Mr. Boardman. He has asked you whether it will be necessary for him to pay instalments in 2017 and, if so, what the minimum amounts that should be paid are, along with the dates on which these amounts are due.

Required: Provide the information requested by Mr. Boardman. Show all your calculations.

Assignment Problem Two - 2
(Instalments, Interest And Penalties For Corporations)

For both tax and accounting purposes Ledux Inc. has a January 31 year end. Ledux is a publicly traded Canadian company.

For the year ending January 31, 2015, Ledux Inc. had federal Tax Payable of $193,420. During the following year ending January 31, 2016, the federal Tax Payable was $215,567. While final figures are not available at this time, it is estimated that federal Tax Payable for the year ending January 31, 2017 will be $203,345.

Required:

A. Calculate the instalment payments that are required for the year ending January 31, 2017 under each of the alternative methods available. Indicate which of the alternatives would be preferable.

B. If the Company did not make any instalment payments towards its 2017 taxes payable, and did not file its corporate tax return or pay its taxes payable on time, indicate how the interest and penalty amounts assessed against it would be determined (a detailed calculation is not required).

Assignment Problem Two - 3
(Individual Tax Instalments)

For the three taxation years ending December 31, 2015, 2016, and 2017, assume that Bronson James had the following actual and estimated amounts of federal and provincial Tax Payable withheld by his employer:

2015	$8,946
2016	9,672
2017 (Estimated)	10,476

In order to illustrate the calculation of required instalments, consider the following three independent cases. In each case, Bronson's combined federal/provincial Tax Payable is provided.

Year	Case 1	Case 2	Case 3
2015	$ 7,843	$ 8,116	$13,146
2016	12,862	13,846	12,842
2017 (Estimated)	14,327	13,542	13,676

Required: For each of the three Cases:

* indicate whether instalments are required for the 2017 taxation year;
* in those Cases where instalments are required, calculate the amount of the instalments that would be required under each of the three acceptable methods;
* in those cases where instalments are required, indicate which of the three acceptable methods would be the best alternative; and
* in those Cases where instalments are required, indicate the dates on which the payments will be due.

Assignment Problem Two - 4
(Corporate Tax Instalments)

For the three years ending December 31, 2015 through December 31, 2017, a corporation's combined federal and provincial Tax Payable is as follows:

2015 = $153,640
2016 = $186,540
2017 = $172,340 (Estimated)

Case One   The taxpayer is a small CCPC.

Case Two   The taxpayer is a small CCPC. Assume that its combined federal and provincial taxes payable for the year ending December 31, 2016 were $163,420, instead of the $186,540 given in the problem.

Case Three The taxpayer is a publicly traded corporation.

Case Four   The taxpayer is a publicly traded corporation. Assume that its combined federal and provincial taxes payable for the year ending December 31, 2016 were $163,420, instead of the $186,540 given in the problem.

Required: For each of the preceding independent Cases, provide the following information:

1. Indicate whether instalments are required during 2017. Provide a brief explanation of your conclusion.

2. Calculate the amount of instalments that would be required under each of the acceptable methods available.

3. Indicate which of the available methods would best serve to minimize instalment payments during 2017. If instalments must be paid, indicate the dates on which they are due.

Assignment Problem Two - 5
(Filing Dates)

In addition to interest charges on any late payment of taxes, penalties may be assessed for failure to file a return within the prescribed deadlines. These deadlines vary depending on the taxpayer.

Required: Indicate when income tax returns must be filed for each of the following types of taxpayers:

    A. Living individuals.
    B. Deceased individuals.
    C. Trusts.
    D. Corporations.

Assignment Problem Two - 6
(Appeals)

Mr. James Simon has asked for your services with respect to dealing with a Notice of Reassessment requesting additional tax for the 2013 taxation year which he says he has just received. Your first interview takes place a week later, on April 25, 2017, and Mr. Simon informs you that he has had considerable difficulty with the CRA in past years and, on two occasions in the past five years, he has been required to pay penalties as well as interest.

With respect to the current reassessment, he assures you that he has complied with the law and that there is a misunderstanding on the part of the assessor. After listening to him describe the situation, you decide it is likely that his analysis of the situation is correct.

Required: Indicate what additional information should be obtained during the interview with Mr. Simon and what steps should be taken if you decide to accept him as a client.

Assignment Problem Two - 7
(Tax Preparer's Penalties)

For each of the following independent cases, indicate whether you believe any penalty would be assessed under ITA 163.2 on any of the parties involved. Explain your conclusion.

Case 1

In preparing a tax return for one of his established clients, an accountant relies on the financial statements that another accountant has prepared for the client's business income. Nothing in these statements seemed unreasonable.

On audit, the CRA finds that the business income financial statements prepared by the other accountant contained material misrepresentations.

Case 2

An accountant is asked to prepare tax return for a new client. The accountant had no previous acquaintance with the individual.

Assignment Problems

The client provides statements, prepared using the appropriate tax figures, showing a net business income of $45,000. He has no other income. He indicates that, during the current year, he made a $32,000 contribution to a registered Canadian charity, but has lost the receipt and has requested a duplicate. As it is now April 29, in order to avoid a late filing penalty, the accountant e-files the tax return, claiming a tax credit for the contribution without seeing the receipt.

Case 3

An accountant has been engaged by a new client to use his records to prepare an income statement and to use the information in this statement to prepare a tax return. As part of this engagement, the accountant reviews both the expense and revenue information that has been provided to him by the new client. He finds revenues of $285,000 and expenses of $201,000. The information used to arrive at these figures seems reasonable and, given this, the accountant files the required tax return.

When the client is audited, the CRA finds a large proportion of the expenses claimed cannot be substantiated by adequate documentation and may not have been incurred. Furthermore, it appears that the client has a substantial amount of unreported revenues.

Case 4

An accountant who lives in an expensive neighbourhood notices that the house next door has just been sold. It was listed for $1 million. The accountant introduces himself to the new neighbour and they become friends.

At tax time the friend hires the accountant to prepare his return. The accountant is given a T4 with $25,000 in income reported. Thinking that the gross income is on the low side, the accountant asks if this is all the income he has and the friend replies that it is so. The accountant is still not satisfied with the answer as the income seems to be out of proportion with the living standard of the friend, so he then asks him if he has received money from any source other than his employment and the friend replies that he received a substantial inheritance from his mother last year.

The accountant does not ask any further questions and prepares and files the return. When the friend is audited it is discovered that he has over $200,000 in unreported income.

Case 5

Units in a new limited partnership tax shelter are being sold by a company. The company has established this limited partnership by acquiring a software application in the open market for $100,000. However, the prospectus prepared by the company states that the fair market value of the application is $5,000,000, a value that was supported by an independent appraiser. The tax shelter is registered with the CRA and is available as an investment opportunity in the current year.

On audit, the CRA determines that the $100,000 that was paid for the software application is, in fact, its fair market value on the date of the transfer. In discussing the matter with the independent appraiser, the CRA finds that the appraisal was not prepared using normal valuation procedures. In addition, the appraiser based his work entirely on assumptions and facts that were provided by the company. The appraiser was paid $50,000 for his work.

Case 6 (Requires Basic GST/HST Knowledge)

An accountant is asked to file a HST return for a client who has not kept records of the HST paid or payable on her business purchases for the year. However, the client does have financial statements for her business which, after a brief review, the accountant finds to be reasonable.

In his review, the accountant found that these statements contain large amounts for wages and interest expense, as well as a significant amount of purchases that are zero-rated. (HST is not paid on any of these types of expenses). In preparing the HST return, the accountant applies a factor of 13/113 to all of the expenses shown in the income statement. This results in an overstatement of input tax credits reported on the HST return.

CHAPTER 3

Income Or Loss From An Office Or Employment

Employment Income Defined

General Rules

3-1.   Income or loss from an office or employment (employment income, hereafter) is covered in Part I, Division B, Subdivision a of the *Income Tax Act*. This relatively short Subdivision is made up of Sections 5 through 8, the general contents of which can be described as follows:

> **Section 5** contains a definition of employment income.

> **Section 6** provides detailed information on what amounts must be included in the determination of employment income.

> **Section 7** is a more specialized Section that provides the tax rules associated with stock options granted to employees.

> **Section 8** provides detailed information on what amounts can be deducted in the determination of employment income.

3-2.   The basic description of employment income is as follows:

> **ITA 5(1)** Subject to this Part, a taxpayer's income for a taxation year from an office or employment is the salary, wages and other remuneration, including gratuities, received by the taxpayer in the year.

3-3.   While ITA 5(2) contemplates the possibility of a loss from an office or employment, the limited amount of deductions that can be made against employment income inclusions would make such an event very unusual.

3-4.   "Employment" is generally defined in ITA 248(1) as the position of an individual in the service of some other person. Similarly, "office" is defined as the position of an individual entitling him to a fixed or ascertainable stipend or remuneration. As will be discussed later, determining whether an individual is, or is not, an employee can be a contentious issue.

3-5.   As to what is included in employment income, the terms "salary" and "wages" generally refer to monetary amounts provided in return for employment services. However, the term "remuneration" is somewhat broader and includes any type of reward or benefit associated with employment services. With the specific inclusion of gratuities, it is clear that employment income includes not only payments from an employer but, in addition, includes any other payments or benefits that result from a taxpayer's position as an employee, without regard to the source of the payment or benefit.

3-6. While it would not be common, it is possible that an individual could receive a payment from an employer that is not related to the quantity or quality of services performed as an employee. For example, if the employee made a personal loan to the employer, any interest paid by the employer to the employee on the loan would not be considered employment income.

Cash Basis And The Use Of Bonus Arrangements
Amounts Received
3-7. As presented in Paragraph 3-2, the definition of an employee's income states that it is made up of amounts "received by the taxpayer in the year". The use of the term "received" serves to establish that employment income must be reported on a cash basis, not on an accrual basis.

Tax Planning Opportunity
3-8. This fact, when combined with the fact that business income for tax purposes is calculated on an accrual basis (see Chapter 6), provides a tax planning opportunity. A business can declare a bonus to one of its employees and, because it is on an accrual basis, deduct it for tax purposes by simply recognizing a firm obligation to pay the amount. In contrast, the employee who has earned the bonus will not have to include it in employment income until it is actually received.

> **EXAMPLE** A business with a December 31 year end declares a bonus to an employee in December, 2017, but stipulates that it will not be paid until January, 2018.

> **ANALYSIS** While the business would get the deduction in 2017, the employee would not include the amount in income until the 2018 taxation year. If the bonus had been paid in December, 2017, the employee would have had to include it in income in 2017. In effect, this arrangement defers the taxation applicable to the employee by one taxation year even though the payment has been deferred by only a few days.

Limits On Deferral
3-9. There are, however, limits to this deferral. ITA 78(4) indicates that, where such a bonus is paid more than 180 days after the employer's year end (note that this is not always December 31), but less than three years, the employer will not be able to deduct the amount until it is paid.

> **EXAMPLE** An employer with a June 30 year end declares a bonus for an employee on June 30, 2017 that is payable on January 1, 2018.

> **ANALYSIS** As January 1, 2018 is more than 180 days after the employer's year end on June 30, 2017, the employer will not be able to deduct the bonus in the fiscal year ending June 30, 2017. It will have to be deducted in the fiscal year ending June 30, 2018.

3-10. A different situation can arise when a "bonus" will not be paid until more than three years after the end of the calendar year in which the employee's services were rendered. In this case, the "bonus" may become a "salary deferral arrangement", resulting in the employee being taxed on the relevant amounts in the calendar year in which the services were rendered. The employer deducts the bonus in the fiscal year it is declared. This type of arrangement is discussed in more detail in Chapter 10, Retirement Savings And Other Special Income Arrangements.

3-11.   The tax consequences associated with the three types of bonus arrangements are summarized in the following Figure 3-1:

Figure 3 - 1 Bonus Arrangements	
Type Of Bonus Arrangement	**Tax Consequences**
Standard Bonus (Paid within 180 days of business year end.)	Employer deducts when declared. Employee includes when received.
Other Bonus (Paid more than 180 days after the employer's year end, but prior to 3 years after the end of the year in which the bonus was earned.)	Employer deducts when paid. Employee includes when received.
Salary Deferral Arrangement (Paid more than 3 years after the end of the year in which services were rendered.)	Employer deducts when declared. Employee includes when services rendered. (See Chapter 10)

Exercise Three - 1

Subject: Bonus

Neelson Inc. has a September 30 year end. On August 1, 2017, it declares a bonus of $100,000 payable to Mr. Sam Neelson, an executive of the Company. The bonus is payable on May 1, 2018. Describe the tax consequences of this bonus to both Neelson Inc. and Mr. Neelson.

SOLUTION available in print and online Study Guide.

We suggest you work Self Study Problem Three-1 at this point.

Net Concept

3-12.   Employment income is a net income concept. That is, it is made up of both inclusions (e.g., salaries and wages) and deductions (e.g., registered pension plan contributions and union dues). In conjunction with this, we would point out that the deductions that are described in ITA 8 can only be deducted against employment income inclusions. Given the limited deductions available in the determination of employment income, it would be very rare for these deductions to exceed the inclusions.

3-13.   If an employment loss were to occur, the excess ITA 8 deductions could not be applied against any other source of income. However, if other sources of income are available, the same result can be accomplished by deducting the net employment loss under ITA 3(d) as per the calculation of Net Income For Tax Purposes that is described in Chapter 1.

EXAMPLE   An individual has employment income of $3,000 and employment expenses of $4,500, resulting in a net employment loss of $1,500. His only other source of income is $20,000 in interest income. He has no Subdivision e deductions.

ANALYSIS   The individual's Net Income For Tax Purposes would be calculated as follows:

Income Under ITA 3(a)	$20,000
Losses Under ITA 3(d)	(1,500)
Net Income For Tax Purposes	$18,500

Employee Versus Self-Employed

Introduction

3-14.   An individual doing work for an organization will be undertaking this activity in one of two possible roles. He may be working as an employee. If this is the case, he is earning employment income and is subject to the rules discussed in this Chapter.

3-15.   In contrast, he may be working as a self-employed individual, often referred to as an independent contractor. From the point of view of the organization using the individual's services, such arrangements are often referred to as contracting out. The payments made to such self-employed individuals are classified as business income and are subject to the rules that are covered in Chapter 6, Business Income.

3-16.   This distinction is of considerable importance, both to the individual worker and to the organization using his services. Given this importance, the following material describes the tax features of these alternatives, both from the point of view of the worker and from the point of view of the organization using his services.

3-17.   In terms of tax planning, structuring a working relationship to achieve the desired classification of the individual doing the work may result in tax avoidance for both parties. For the worker, being classified as a self-employed individual will generally result in larger deductions against income, thereby reducing Tax Payable. From the point of view of the organization using the individual's services, the independent contractor classification can reduce the costs of using those services.

Employee Perspective

Deductions Available

3-18.   As will be discussed later in this Chapter, an individual's ability to deduct expenses from employment income is quite limited when compared to self-employed individuals. If an individual is self-employed, any income that he earns is classified as business income, making it eligible for the wider range of deductions that is available under the business income provisions of the *Income Tax Act*. For example, a self-employed professional can generally deduct the costs of driving to work. If this individual were classified as an employee, this deduction would typically not be available.

CPP Contributions

3-19.   If an individual is an employee, his employer will be required to withhold a portion of his pay for Canada Pension Plan (CPP) contributions and Employment Insurance (EI) premiums. With respect to CPP contributions, for 2017 both the employee and the employer are required to contribute 4.95 percent of up to $55,300 of gross wages reduced by a basic exemption of $3,500. This results in maximum contributions by both the employee and employer of $2,564, or a total of $5,128.

3-20.   In contrast, if an individual is self-employed, there will be no withholding of CPP from the amounts received as business income. However, this does not mean that this individual can escape these costs. A self-employed individual must make contributions on the same basis as an employee. Further, self-employed individuals are required to pay both an employee share and an employer share, resulting in a potential maximum payment of $5,128. We would note that, despite the larger contributions required of self-employed individuals, the pension benefits will be the same as for the employed individual.

3-21.   As noted in Chapter 2, CPP amounts for the self-employed are collected by the CRA. They are calculated on the T1 tax return where they become part of the amount owing. Further, the CRA includes them in the instalment base when instalments are required which means that they may be a factor in determining the size of quarterly instalments. This could be viewed as a modest advantage of being self-employed as there is some deferral of the required CPP payments, as compared to their payment through payroll deductions.

3-22.   However, any benefit resulting from deferral of the CPP payments is clearly offset by the fact that the self-employed individual has to pay double the CPP contributions (both the employee and the employer share) with no higher future pension benefit than employees. There is clearly an overall disadvantage to the self-employed individual.

EI Premiums

3-23.   With respect to EI premiums, the amount that will be withheld from employee earnings amounts to 1.63 percent of the first $51,300 in gross wages, with a maximum annual value of $836. The employer is assessed 1.4 times this amount, a maximum of $1,170. This represents an effective rate for the employer of 2.28 percent.

3-24.   Employees are generally required to participate in the EI program. One exception is for employees owning more than 40 percent of the voting shares of the employer. In that case, since no EI can be collected, no EI premiums are paid. The EI rules are complex which can make the determination of insurable employment difficult, especially in the case of an owner-manager employing family members. A non-arm's length employee (such as an adult child or a spouse) would only be eligible for participation in the EI program if it is reasonable to conclude that the owner would have hired an arm's length person under a similar contract of employment.

3-25.   Self-employed individuals can opt into the EI program on a voluntary basis for special (restricted) EI benefits, such as maternity benefits. They must opt in at least 12 months prior to making a claim, but once they opt in, they are committed for the taxation year. Further, if a claim is made under this program, the individual is committed for life, or until they stop being self-employed. The good news is that self-employed individuals do not have to pay the employer's share of EI premiums. This means the maximum cost for 2017 would be $836.

3-26.   As is the case with CPP payments for self-employed individuals, EI premiums for self-employed individuals are collected by the CRA. This means that payments are paid through instalments or on the balance due date for the return, thereby providing a small amount of deferral. More importantly, with participation voluntary, a self-employed individual can choose whether or not to participate in this program. Since the self-employed individual does not pay the employer's share of the EI (unlike the situation with the CPP), the EI rules appear to be advantageous to self-employed individuals who are eligible.

Fringe Benefits

3-27.   A significant disadvantage of being classified as an independent contractor rather than an employee is the fact that independent contractors do not receive fringe benefits. An employee may receive a wide variety of benefits such as dental and drug plans, membership in a registered pension plan, vacation pay, or life insurance coverage. Such benefits have a significant value, in some cases adding as much as 20 percent to an employee's remuneration. Further, even if the self-employed individual were willing to pay for such benefits, some benefits may not be available to a single individual at a reasonable cost (e.g., extended medical coverage). In any case, a self-employed individual will have to receive significantly higher basic remuneration to be in the same economic position as an individual working as an employee who has generous benefits.

Opportunity For Tax Evasion

3-28.   While we certainly do not condone this, as a practical matter, in some situations, being self-employed can offer significantly larger opportunities for tax evasion. There are stringent reporting requirements that make it difficult for an employee to avoid detection if he fails to report employment income.

3-29.   In contrast, self-employment income is sometimes received partially or wholly in cash, depending on the clients. Usually when cash is received, the work is being done for an individual who cannot deduct the cost of the work and does not require a receipt to be issued. A common example of this would be an individual who hires a self-employed contractor to do renovations on his principal residence and pays cash to avoid paying the HST.

3-30.   If the self-employed individual is willing to evade income and sales taxes by not reporting these revenues, then the lack of income tax withholding on self-employment earnings becomes a permanent reduction in taxes. Although it is clearly illegal, for some individuals, not reporting earnings received in cash is one of the main motivations behind being self-employed.

Conclusion

3-31.   As the preceding indicates, the desirability of self-employed status is not clear cut. For an individual with limited deductible expenses, self-employment may not be advantageous from an economic point of view. Alternatively, if an individual's work is such that large amounts of business expenses are generated, it is probably desirable to be taxed as a self-employed contractor.

3-32.   Non-tax advantages could include the ability to set work schedules and the freedom to choose the amount and type of work accepted. The added cost of accounting for the business and the implications of the GST/HST would also have to be considered. As noted in Chapter 21, in most cases, a self-employed individual would have to register for the GST/HST if he is not a small supplier.

Employer Perspective

3-33.   There are several advantages to a business from using the services of self-employed individuals as opposed to employees. One of the major advantages associated with the hiring of these independent contractors (a.k.a. contracting out) is that the employer avoids payments for Canada Pension Plan (CPP), Employment Insurance (EI), Workers' Compensation, and Provincial Health Care (where applicable).

3-34.   The amounts involved here are consequential. CPP and EI payments alone can add more than 7 percent to the wage costs. Provincial payroll taxes can push the total of these costs above 10 percent of wage costs. Further cost savings result from the fact that the employer will avoid the administrative costs associated with having to withhold and remit income taxes and the employee's share of CPP and EI payments.

3-35.   Also in favour of using independent contractors is the fact that the business will avoid the costs of any fringe benefits that it normally extends to its employees. A less measurable benefit is that employers are freed from ongoing commitments to individuals because there is generally no long-term contract with self-employed workers.

3-36.   An additional and less direct advantage of using independent contractors is that the business is not legally responsible for their work. If an employee does work that results in some type of legal liability for damages, it is the employer that will be responsible for any costs that arise. In contrast, if such work is carried out by an independent contractor, the organization may escape any legal responsibility.

3-37.   Given all of these advantages, it is not surprising to find more businesses contracting out in order to control labour costs and limit liability.

Making The Distinction

Intent

3-38.   The general approach to distinguishing between an employee and an independent contractor is the question of whether an employer/employee relationship exists. As there is no clear definition of employer/employee relationships, disputes between taxpayers and the CRA are very common. To avoid such disputes, and to assist taxpayers in determining whether or not an individual is an employee, the CRA provides a Guide titled "Employee Or Self-Employed?" (RC4110).

3-39.   As described in this Guide, the first step in making this distinction is to determine the intent of both parties. Both the worker and the payer must be clear as to whether there is a contract of service (employee/employer) or alternatively, a contract for services (business relationship). This intent may or may not be in the form of a written agreement.

Other Factors - Employee Vs. Self-Employed

3-40.   In many cases, the intent is clear. However, the worker and payer must ensure that their intent is reflected in the actual terms and conditions of their relationship. In making this determination, the Guide indicates that the following factors will be considered by the CRA:

Control   In an employer/employee relationship, the employer usually controls, directly or indirectly, the way the work is done and the work methods used. The employer assigns specific tasks that define the real framework within which the work is to be done.

Ownership Of Tools And Equipment   In an employer/employee relationship, the employer usually supplies the equipment and tools required by the employee. In addition, the employer covers the following costs related to their use: repairs, insurance, transport, rental, and operations (e.g., fuel).

In some trades, however, it is customary for employees to supply their own tools. This is generally the case for garage mechanics, painters, and carpenters. Similarly, employed computer scientists, architects, and surveyors sometimes supply their own software and instruments.

Ability To Subcontract Or Hire Assistants   If the individual must personally perform the services, he is likely to be considered an employee. Alternatively, if the individual can hire assistants, with the payer having no control over the identity of the assistants, the individual is likely to be considered self-employed.

Financial Risk   In general, employees will not have any financial risks associated with their work. In contrast, self-employed individuals can have risk and can incur losses. Responsibility for fixed monthly costs is a good indicator that an individual is self-employed.

Responsibility For Investment And Management   If the individual has no capital investment in the business of the payer and no presence in management, he is likely to be considered an employee. Alternatively, if the individual has made an investment and is active in managing his business, he should be considered self-employed.

Opportunity For Profit   In an employer/employee relationship, the employer alone normally assumes the risk of loss. The employer also usually covers operating costs, which may include office expenses, employee wages and benefits, insurance premiums, and delivery and shipping costs. The employee does not assume any financial risk, and is entitled to his full salary or wages regardless of the financial health of the business.

Correspondingly, an employee will have little or no opportunity for profit. While there may be productivity bonuses for exceptional work, such amounts are not generally viewed as profit.

3-41.   The CRA Guide includes a long list of indicators for each of the preceding factors that could affect whether an individual was considered an employee or self-employed. This Guide can be quite helpful if more detailed information in this area is required.

3-42.   We would point out that it is extremely important for a business to be sure that any individual who is being treated as a self-employed contractor qualifies for that status. Actions that can be taken to ensure self-employed status for the individual include:

- Having the individual register for the GST.
- Having the individual work for other businesses.
- Having the individual advertise his services.
- To the extent possible, having the individual cover his own overhead, including phone service, letterhead, equipment, and supplies.
- Having the individual prepare periodic invoices, preferably on an irregular basis.
- Having a lawyer prepare an independent contractor agreement.
- If feasible, having the individual incorporate.

Request A CPP/EI Ruling

3-43.   A failure to correctly determine whether a worker should be considered an employee or, alternatively, self-employed, could prove to be very costly to a business using the services of that individual. It is possible that, if the CRA judges the individual to be an employee, the business could be held liable for CPP and EI amounts that should have been withheld from the individual's earnings, as well as the employer's share of these amounts.

3-44.   As evidenced by the large number of court cases involving this issue, it is clear that wrong classifications are not uncommon. A fairly reliable way of avoiding this problem is to request a CPP/EI ruling from the CRA. Such a ruling can be requested either by the business or the worker by sending a letter, or completing Form CPT1, *Request for a Ruling as to the Status of a Worker Under the Canada Pension Plan and/or the Employment Insurance Act.*

We suggest you work Self Study Problem Three-2 at this point.

Inclusions - Employee Benefits

Basic Concepts

3-45.   As noted in the Employer's Guide, "Taxable Benefits And Allowances" (T4130), a benefit arises if an employer pays for, or gives something, that is personal in nature:

- directly to an employee; or
- to a person who does not deal at arm's length with the employee (e.g., a spouse, child or sibling).

3-46.   This would include any goods or services that the employer arranges for a third party to give to an employee, as well as any allowance or reimbursement for an employee's personal expenses.

3-47.   It would not include reimbursement for employment related expenses, nor would it include reasonable allowances to cover employment related expenses. For a more complete discussion of allowances, see the later section in this chapter that deals with this subject beginning at Paragraph 3-125.

3-48.   As such, benefits may be taxable or non-taxable. To the extent a benefit is taxable, it must be included in employment income. As the name implies, non-taxable benefits will not be included in employment income.

3-49.   Segregation of benefits into taxable and non-taxable amounts is a fairly complex process, involving both legislative provisions and administrative practices. As a result, employee benefit planning is an important component of any large tax practice.

3-50.   The amount to be included in employment income is, in general, its fair market value. If GST, PST, or HST is applicable, these amounts would be included in the amount that is added to employment income. This is discussed in beginning at Paragraph 3-77.

Inclusions - Salaries And Wages

3-51.   We have noted that ITA 5 specifies that employment income includes salaries, wages, and other remuneration. When only salaries or wages are involved, there is little need to elaborate on employment income inclusions. Such amounts clearly must be included in the determination of employment income and, as the amounts are monetary in nature, there are no issues associated with their valuation.

Inclusions - Non-Salary Benefits

Introduction

3-52.   If salaries and wages were the only benefits provided by employers, this would be the shortest and least complex chapter in this text. However, this is not the case. Employers use a wide variety of other benefits, commonly referred to as fringe benefits.

3-53.   There are three basic reasons for using these alternative forms of compensation:

Tax Considerations   Different benefits have different tax consequences for employees. Through careful planning, an employee's tax bill can be reduced, often at no cost to the employer. An example of this would be the provision of private health care which can be received by employees on a tax free basis.

Employee Motivation   Employers believe that some forms of compensation moti-vate employees to apply greater effort to their employment duties, e.g., the granting of stock options. These securities only have value if the market value of an employer's stock goes up. Given this, it is thought that employees will work harder towards increasing the value of the company's stock if they are granted such options.

Employee Retention   Studies show that properly planned non-salary benefits play a major role in employee retention. For example, an employee who uses employer provided day care would be more inclined to reject a job offer from a competitor who doesn't offer day care even though the monetary compensation would be higher.

3-54.   While these are worthy objectives, they significantly complicate the determination of the appropriate values to be included in employment income. In addition to determining which benefits are taxable, there are often issues associated with the determination of the value that should be attached to these non-salary benefits.

3-55.   Some guidance in this area is provided by the content of ITA 6, *Inclusions*. However, this legislative guidance does not resolve many of the issues that are associated with fringe benefits and, as a consequence, additional non-legislative guidance is required. We will give fairly detailed attention to both the legislative guidance found in ITA 6, as well as to the other sources that are relevant to the determination of employment income.

Legislative Guidance
ITA 6(1)

3-56.   ITA 6(1) is the largest subsection in ITA 6. As such it contains a number of paragraphs which list specific items that must be included in employment income. The more important are as follows.

ITA 6(1) Inclusions

- ITA 6(1)(b)   Amounts received as an allowance for personal or living expenses.
- ITA 6(1)(c)   Director's or other fees.
- ITA 6(1)(d)   Allocations under profit sharing plans.
- ITA 6(1)(e)   Standby charge for automobiles.
- ITA 6(1)(f)   Wage loss replacement plans, provided they are received on a periodic basis and are intended to replace employment income.
- ITA 6(1)(g)   Employee benefit plan benefits.
- ITA 6(1)(h)   Allocations under employee trusts.
- ITA 6(1)(i)   Salary deferral arrangement payments (to the extent they have not previ-ously been included in income).
- ITA 6(1)(j)   Reimbursements and awards.
- ITA 6(1)(k)   Automobile operating expense benefit.

3-57.   Accompanying these specific inclusions, ITA 6(1)(a) notes a number of items that can be received without being included in employment income. The more important of these are as follows:

ITA 6(1)(a) Exclusions

- Employer's contributions to:
  - registered pension plans;
  - group sickness or accident insurance plans, provided that any benefits received under the plan will be taxed under ITA 6(1)(f);
  - private health services plans;
  - supplementary unemployment benefit plans;
  - deferred profit sharing plans;
  - employee life and health trusts.

- Counseling services related to the mental or physical health of the employee or a related party, or related to re-employment or retirement of the employee.

- Benefits under a retirement compensation arrangement, employee benefit plans (e.g. death benefit plans), and employee trusts. However actual payments or allocations from such plans or arrangements are taxable elsewhere.

- Benefits resulting from reduced tuition provided to the children of teachers at private schools, provided the teacher is dealing at arm's length with the school and the reduction is not a substitute for salary or other remuneration from the school.

  Note   If you were to read ITA 6(1)(a), you would find that the listed exclusions include both group term life insurance, as well as benefits related to automobiles. This gives the illusion these items are not taxable benefits. However, this is not the case. In a somewhat awkward approach to this issue, these benefits are excluded under ITA 6(1)(a), but included under other provisions. Automobile benefits are included under ITA 6(1)(e) and (k) as listed in the following paragraph, and group term life insurance premiums are included under ITA 6(4).

Other ITA 6 Inclusions

3-58.   As noted, ITA 6(1) includes fairly long lists of inclusions and exclusions. In contrast, the other subsections of ITA 6 deal with inclusions in employment income. The more important of these are as follows:

- ITA 6(2) and (2.1) **"Reasonable Standby Charges"**.

- ITA 6(3) and (3.1) **"Payments By Employer To Employee"**, which requires the inclusion of amounts paid either immediately before employment begins, or subsequent to the period of employment.

- ITA 6(4) **"Group Term Life Insurance"**.

- ITA 6(6) **"Employment At Special Work Site Or Remote Location"**.

- ITA 6(7) **"Cost Of Property Or Service"**, which requires the addition of applicable GST/HST/PST to the amount of some taxable benefits.

- ITA 6(9) **"Amount In Respect Of Interest On Employee Debt"**.

- ITA 6(11) **"Salary Deferral Arrangements"**.

- ITA 6(15) and (15.1) **"Forgiveness Of Employee Debt And Forgiven Amount"**, which require that employee debt forgiven by an employer must be included in employment income.

- ITA 6(16) through (18) **"Disability Related Employee Benefits"**

- ITA 6(19) through (22) **"Housing Loss And Eligible Housing Loss"** limit the amount that can be reimbursed on a tax free basis to an employee who has suffered a housing loss as the result of a required move.

3-59.   Most of these items will be covered in more detail later in this Chapter or in other Chapters of the text.

Non-Legislative Guidance
Sources
3-60.   While it appears extensive, the guidance in ITA 6 has not been adequate to guide employers in making the distinction between taxable and non-taxable benefits. Because of this, the CRA provides a significant amount of additional guidance.

3-61.   For many years, this guidance was found in IT-470, "Employee's Fringe Benefits". This IT Bulletin has been replaced by IT Folio S2-F3-C2, "Benefits And Allowances Received From Employment".

3-62.   We have found this IT Folio to be a rather weak document that provides less clarity than the IT Bulletin that it replaced. Given this, we have looked to the CRA Employers' Guide, "Taxable Benefits And Allowances" (T4130). In our view, the Guide is far more useful than IT Folio S2-F3-C2 in clarifying taxable vs. non-taxable benefits. The material which follows is largely based on the content of the Employers' Guide.

Specific Items
3-63.   What follows is a description of the various benefits that are discussed in the Employers' Guide. The benefits are listed in alphabetical order. In some cases, the specific item will be discussed in more detail in a later section of this Chapter. We would also note that the descriptions here are very general. If you are dealing with a real world situation, you should consult the detailed information provided in the Employers' Guide.

Automobile Benefits   When an employee is allowed to make personal use of an automobile that is provided by his employer, a taxable benefit must be recorded. The determination of these benefits is complex and will be covered in a separate section of this Chapter beginning at Paragraph 3-79.

Board And Lodging   If an employer provides an employee with free board or lodging, its fair market value must, in general, be treated as a taxable benefit. If the board or lodging is subsidized rather than free, the fair market value will be reduced by any amounts paid by the employee.

The major exceptions to this general rule are as follows:

- Board or lodging provided at a **special work site**. A special work site is defined as an area where temporary duties are performed by an employee who keeps a self-contained domestic establishment at another location as his or her principal place of residence. Because of the distance between the two areas, the employee is not expected to return daily from the work site to his or her principal place of residence.

- Board or lodging provided at a **remote work site**. A remote work site is defined as remote when it is 80 kilometers or more from the nearest established community with a population of at least 1,000 people.

Board or lodging provided at these sites is not considered to be a taxable benefit.

Cell Phone And Internet Benefits   If an employee makes some personal use of an employer provided cell phone or employer provided internet services, a pro rata share of the cost is considered a taxable benefit.

Employer Provided Child Care   If an employer provides, at his place of business, child care that is not available to the general public, it is not considered to be a taxable benefit.

Discounts On Merchandise   In general, if an employer provides discounts on merchandise, it is not considered a taxable benefit. However, the discounts must be available to all employees and the discounted price cannot be below cost.

Education Related Benefits   There are several types of benefits that relate to education.

- If an employer provides an allowance for an employee's children, the allowance will be included in the employee's income.
- If an employer pays the tuition for a course that is directly related to the recipient's employment, it is not considered a taxable benefit.
- If an employer pays the tuition for a course that is related to general business, it is not considered to be a taxable benefit.
- If an employer pays the tuition for a course that is of personal interest to the employee, it is considered to be a taxable benefit.
- If an employer provides free or reduced tuition to a member of an employee's family, it will generally be included in the family member's income, rather than the income of the employee.

Gifts, Awards and Long-Service Awards   Cash and near cash gifts and rewards are always taxable benefits. Non-cash gifts and non-cash awards to an arm's length employee, regardless of number, will not be taxable to the extent that the total aggregate value of all non-cash gifts and awards to that employee is less than $500 annually. The total value in excess of $500 annually will be taxable.

Gift certificates are considered near cash awards and taxable. In addition, gifts with an immaterial value e.g., a coffee mug, can be ignored.

A separate non-cash long service/anniversary award, to the extent its total value is $500 or less, will not be considered a taxable benefit. The value in excess of $500 will be taxable. In order to qualify, the anniversary award cannot be for less than 5 years of service, or for 5 years since the last long service award had been provided to the employee.

In contrast, a performance related award is considered to be a reward and a taxable benefit.

Insurance   Because of the many issues involved with various types of insurance, coverage of insurance requires a separate section in this Chapter which begins at Paragraph 3-143.

Employee Loans   The complications associated with employee loans requires a separate section in this Chapter which begins at Paragraph 3-149.

Loyalty And Other Points Programs   Loyalty points (e.g., Aeroplan points) that were earned through employment activity are not considered to be a taxable benefit provided:

- the points are not converted to cash;
- the plan is not an alternative form of remuneration; and
- the plan is not for tax avoidance purposes.

Meals   In general, reimbursing employees for meals consumed when they are required to work overtime does not create a taxable benefit.

If an employer provides subsidized meals to employees, their value is not considered to be a taxable benefit, provided the employee pays a reasonable amount for the benefit.

Medical Expenses   When an employer pays for an employee's medical expenses, it is considered to be a taxable benefit.

Moving Expenses Employer payments for most types of employee moving expenses does not create a taxable benefit. This subject is discussed more completely in Chapter 9 of this text.

Parking Employer provided parking is, in general considered to be a taxable benefit. Exceptions to this include:

- Parking for employees with disabilities.
- Parking for employees who regularly require a car to carry out their employment duties.
- Scramble parking (e.g., parking at a site where there are significantly fewer spaces than the number of employees who use them).

Pooled Registered Pension Plans Employer contributions to these plans are not considered to be a taxable benefit.

Premiums For Provincial Health Care If an employer pays these premiums for an employee, the payments are considered to be a taxable benefit.

Premiums For Private Health Care Employer payment of such premiums does not create a taxable benefit.

Professional Membership Dues If the employer is the primary beneficiary of the dues, there is no taxable benefit (e.g., membership in the organization is a condition of employment). If the employee is the primary beneficiary, the payment of such dues creates a taxable benefit.

Recreational Facilities And Club Dues Employer payment of these items does not result in a taxable benefit in the following situations:

- Provision of an in-house facility that is available to all employees.
- An arrangement where an employer contracts with a facility and then makes it available to all employees.
- The employer provides individual employees with memberships to a facility and the employer is the primary beneficiary of its use.

Otherwise, payments for these items creates a taxable benefit. A complicating factor in tax planning for this benefit is discussed beginning in Paragraph 3-70.

Stock Options Because of the complexity related to these benefits, this Chapter contains a separate section dealing with employee stock options beginning at Paragraph 3-160.

Social Events Employer provided social events are not a taxable benefit provided:

- they are available to all employees; and
- they cost less than $100 per person.

If the cost is more than $100 person, the full cost, including the first $100 becomes a taxable benefit.

Spousal Travel Expenses Employer payment of these costs creates a taxable benefit unless:

- the spouse was along at the employer's request; and
- the spouse was mostly engaged in business activities during the trip.

Tax-Free Savings Accounts (TFSAs) If an employer makes a contribution to an employee's tax-free savings account, it is a taxable benefit.

Tickets To Events   In general, the value of employer provided tickets to events is considered a taxable benefit unless there is a business reason for the employee to attend the event.

Tool Reimbursement   If an employer reimburses an employee for tools used in his employment activities, it is considered a taxable benefit.

Transit Passes   In general, the provision of transit passes to employees creates a taxable benefit. An exception to this would be transit passes to employees of a transit company.

Travel Allowances   Because of the complexity related to allowances, this Chapter contains a separate section dealing with these benefits. It begins at Paragraph 3-125.

Uniforms Or Special Clothing   The provision of uniforms or special clothing does not create a taxable benefit provided:

- the employer supplies the employee with a distinctive uniform that must be worn while carrying out employment duties; or
- the employer provides the employee with special clothing to protect him from hazards associated with carrying out employment duties.

Exercise Three - 2

Subject: Gifts To Employees

During the current year, Jeffrey's employer provides him with a number of gifts and awards. Describe the tax consequences for Jeffrey that result from each of the following gifts and awards.

Gift	Fair Market Value
T-shirt with employer logo	$ 15
Birthday gift (gift certificate at The Bay)	75
Reward for exceeding sales targets	400
10 year anniversary award (Seiko watch)	275
Wedding gift (crystal vase)	300
Weight loss award (tickets to sporting event)	250
Holiday season gift (gourmet food basket)	150

Exercise Three - 3

Subject: Employee Benefits

John Nilson is an employee of a high end furniture store. During the current year, John receives a number of benefits from his employer. Describe the tax consequences for John that result from receiving each of the following benefits.

- A 35 percent discount on merchandise with a total value of $10,000.
- Reimbursement of $2,000 in tuition fees for a course in creative writing.
- Business clothing with a value of $8,500 to be worn during working hours. (John's employer felt he needed a better image in dealing with clients.)
- A set of china on the occasion of John's wedding anniversary costing $450, including taxes.
- A private health care plan for John and his family. The employer pays an annual premium of $780 for this plan.

SOLUTIONS available in print and online Study Guide.

Tax Planning Considerations

Salary The Benchmark

3-64.   As previously discussed, some of the benefits provided to employees are fully taxable while other benefits can be extended without creating a taxable benefit. This has important implications in planning employee compensation.

3-65.   As the bulk of compensation for most employees is in the form of wages or salaries, such payments provide the benchmark against which other types of compensation must be evaluated. From an income tax point of view, these benchmark payments are fully deductible to the employer in the year in which they are accrued and fully taxable to the employee in the year in which they are received. There is no valid tax reason for using a type of fringe benefit that has these same characteristics.

3-66.   For example, if an employer rewards a valued employee with a holiday trip for achieving a sales goal, the cost of the trip will be fully deductible to the employer. Further, the trip's cost will be fully taxable to the employee on the same basis as if the amount had been paid in the form of additional salary. This means that, while there may be a motivational reason for using a holiday trip as a form of compensation, there is no significant income tax advantage in doing so.

Tax Avoidance

3-67.   The most attractive form of non-salary compensation involves benefits that are deductible to the employer, but are received tax free by the employee. For example, as private health care benefits are not taxable, an employer can provide employees with a dental plan without creating any additional tax liability for the employee.

3-68.   From a tax point of view, this type of compensation should be used whenever practical, provided it is desirable from the point of view of the employee. For example, although providing a dental plan to an employee is a tax free benefit, if the employee's spouse has already been provided with an identical family dental plan by her employer, this benefit is of no value to the employee.

Tax Deferral

3-69.   Also attractive are those benefits that allow the employer to deduct the cost currently, with taxation of the employee deferred until a later period. We have already considered an example of this involving the use of bonus arrangements. A further important example of this would be contributions to a registered pension plan. The employer can deduct the contributions in the period in which they are made, while the employee will not be taxed until the benefits are received in the form of pension income. This will usually involve a significant deferral of taxation for the employee.

Recreational Facilities And Club Dues

3-70.   In the preceding cases, the tax planning considerations are very clear. There are no tax advantages associated with benefits that are fully and currently taxable to the employee. In contrast, advantages clearly arise when there is no taxation of the benefit, or when the taxation of the employee is deferred until a later point in time.

3-71.   There is, however, a complicating factor in the case of certain employer provided recreational facilities or employer payment of club dues. While in some cases, such benefits are not taxable to the employee, the employer is not allowed to deduct the cost of providing such benefits (see Chapter 6 for a more detailed description of these rules). This means that the advantage of no taxes on the employee benefit is offset by the employer's loss of deductibility.

3-72.   Whether this type of benefit is tax advantageous has to be evaluated on the basis of whether the tax savings to the employee are sufficient to offset the extra tax cost to the employer of providing a non-deductible benefit. The decision will generally be based on the relative tax rates applicable to the employee and the employer. If the employee's tax rate is higher than the employer's, this form of compensation may be advantageous from a tax point of view. There are also other non-tax factors that may be important, such as employee loyalty.

Two Problem Benefits - Automobiles and Loans

3-73.   Before leaving this general discussion of tax planning considerations related to employee benefits, we would note that two important types of benefits present significant difficulties with respect to determining their desirability. These two benefits are employer provided automobiles and loans to employees.

3-74.   The basic problem in both cases is that the benefit to the employee is not based on the cost to the employer. In the case of the employee benefit associated with having the use of an employer supplied car, it is partially based on an arbitrary formula, under which the cumulative assessed benefit can exceed the cost of the car. In the case of employee loans, the taxable benefit is assessed using the prescribed rate of interest, not the cost of the funds to the employer.

3-75.   Because of this lack of reciprocity in the measurement of the cost and benefit, a case-by-case analysis is required. In each situation, it must be determined whether the cost to the employer is greater than, or less than, the benefit to the employee. If the cost is greater, the employer may wish to consider some alternative, and more tax effective, form of compensation. This makes these benefits considerably more difficult to administer.

3-76.   The taxable benefits associated with both employer provided automobiles and employer provided loans are discussed in detail at a later point in this chapter.

Exercise Three - 4

Subject: Planning Employee Benefits

As part of her compensation package, Jill Tyler is offered the choice of: a dental plan for her family, an annual vacation trip for her family, or an annual birthday gift of season's tickets to the ballet for her and her spouse. The alternative benefits are each worth about $4,000 per year. Indicate which benefit would be best for Jill from a tax point of view and explain your conclusion.

SOLUTION available in print and online Study Guide.

Inclusions - GST/HST/PST On Taxable Benefits

3-77.   Many benefits included in employment income are goods and services on which an employee would have to pay GST, HST, or PST if he personally acquired the item or service. For example, if an employer provides a free domestic airline ticket to reward an Ontario employee for outstanding service, this is an item on which the employee would have to pay 13 percent HST if he purchased the ticket on his own. This means that the taxable benefit should also include an HST component as the employee has received a benefit with a real value that includes both the price of the ticket and the related HST.

3-78.   Given this situation, ITA 6(7) requires the calculation of employee benefits on a basis that includes any GST/HST/PST that was paid by the employer on goods or services that are included in the benefit. In situations where the employer is exempt from these taxes, a notional amount is added to the benefit on the basis of the amounts that would have been paid had the employer not been exempt.

Exercise Three - 5

Subject: GST On Taxable Benefits

Ms. Vicki Correli, as the result of an outstanding sales achievement within her organization, is awarded a two week vacation in the Bahamas. Her Alberta employer pays a travel agent $4,500, plus GST of $225 for the trip. What is the amount of Ms. Correli's taxable benefit?

SOLUTION available in print and online Study Guide.

Inclusions - Automobile Benefits

Employees And Automobiles

Influence On Employment Income

3-79.   Automobiles have an influence on the determination of an individual's employment income in three different situations. These situations can be described as follows:

Employer Provided Automobiles   It is fairly common for a business to provide an automobile to an employee in order to assist the individual in carrying out his employment duties. In most cases, the employee will be able to make some personal use of the vehicle that is provided. If this is the case, the employee will have a taxable benefit which must be added to his employment income.

Allowances   As an alternative to providing an employee with an automobile, some employers pay an allowance to the employee for employment related use of his personally owned automobile. This allowance may be included in employment income and, when this is the case, the employee will be able to deduct some portion of the automobile's costs against such inclusions.

Deductible Travel Costs   Under certain circumstances, employees can deduct various travel costs. If the employee uses his personally owned automobile for travel related to his employment, a portion of the costs associated with this vehicle can be deducted in the determination of employment income.

3-80.   In this Chapter, we will give detailed attention to the benefit resulting from employer provided automobiles, as well as to the appropriate treatment of allowances for automobile costs. With respect to automobile related travel costs, the rules for these deductions are the same for both employees and businesses. Because of this, we will defer some of our coverage of this subject to Chapter 6 which deals with business income.

Tax Benefit - Employer Provided Automobile

3-81.   There are two types of costs that can be associated with ownership of an automobile. First, there is a fixed cost that accrues from simply owning the vehicle over time. As you are all aware, if you own a car, its value will decline, even if you do not drive the vehicle a single kilometer. For an average vehicle, this "depreciation" takes place on something close to a 25 percent declining balance basis.

3-82.   In addition to this fixed cost or annual depreciation, there will be costs associated with operating the vehicle. These costs will tend to have a direct relationship to the number of kilometers driven. However, the per kilometer amount will vary significantly, depending on the type and age of the vehicle that is being driven.

3-83.   Tax legislation reflects this economic analysis. The two benefits that can be assessed to an employee who is provided with an employer owned or leased automobile can be described as follows:

Standby Charge   This benefit is assessed under ITA 6(1)(e). This benefit reflects the fixed cost of owning an automobile. However, we will find that the amount assessed can vary with the amount of personal, non-employment usage of the vehicle.

Operating Cost Benefit   This benefit is assessed under ITA 6(1)(k) and, as the name implies, it reflects the costs of operating the vehicle. You should note, however, that it is not based on the employer's actual costs. It is assessed at a fixed rate for each kilometer that the employee drives for personal or non-employment usage.

3-84.   As discussed in Paragraph 3-77, a GST/HST/PST component must be included when taxable benefits provided to employees involve goods or services that would normally be subject to the GST, PST, or HST. Personal use of an automobile falls into this category. Both the standby charge benefit and the operating cost benefit that are discussed in the following material are calculated in a manner that includes a GST/HST/PST component.

Allowances And Deductible Travel Costs
3-85.   Both allowances and deductible travel costs involve the determination of amounts that can be deducted by an employee who owns or leases his own automobile. As you may be aware, tax legislation places limits on the amounts that can be deducted for automobile costs, e.g., for 2017, lease payments in excess of $800 per month before taxes are not deductible. In addition, tax depreciation (capital cost allowance or CCA) cannot be deducted on automobile costs in excess of $30,000 before taxes. As these limits are the same for an employee who owns or leases a vehicle that is used in employment activities, and for a business that owns or leases a vehicle that is used in business activities, they are given detailed coverage in Chapter 6 on business income, after we have covered CCA in Chapter 5.

3-86.   However, it is important to note here that the limits that are placed on the deductibility of automobile costs have no influence on the amount of the taxable benefit that will be assessed to an employee who is provided with a vehicle by his employer. The taxable benefit to the employee will be the same, without regard to whether the employer can deduct the full costs of owning or leasing the vehicle. This means that if an employer provides an employee with an automobile that costs $150,000, the employee's benefits will be based on the full $150,000, despite the fact that the employer will be able to deduct capital cost allowance on only $30,000.

Taxable Benefits - Standby Charge
Employer Owned Vehicles
3-87.   While ITA 6(1)(e) requires the inclusion of a standby charge in income, ITA 6(2) provides the formulas for calculating this amount. If the employer owns the automobile, the basic standby charge is determined by the following formula:

$$[(2\%)(\text{Cost Of Car})(\text{Periods Of Availability})]$$

3-88.   The components of this formula require some additional explanation:

Cost Of Car   The cost of the car is the amount paid, without regard to the list price of the car. It includes all related GST/PST/HST amounts.

Periods Of Availability   Periods of availability is roughly equal to months of availability. However, it is determined by dividing the number of days the automobile is "made available" by 30 and rounding to the nearest whole number. Oddly, a ".5" amount is rounded down rather than up.

Made Available   One would think that if an employee simply returned the automobile and its keys to an employer's premises it would not be considered "available for use". For example, if an employee was traveling out of the country for 2 months, you might assume that, if he left the vehicle and keys with his employer during this period, it would not be considered available for his use. However, this is not the case. In a 2011 Income Tax Ruling (#040922), the CRA has indicated that the employee must be "required" to return the vehicle to the employer's premises to avoid the accrual of a taxable benefit. This means that it is not sufficient to voluntarily return the vehicle. It must be the policy of the employer to require this return.

3-89.   If we assume that a vehicle was available throughout the year and cost $33,900, including $3,900 in HST, the standby charge would be $8,136 [(2%)($33,900)(12)]. If the vehicle continues to be available to the employee throughout the year for subsequent years, the benefit would be the same each year, without regard to the age of the car.

3-90.   You should note that the application of this formula can result in a situation where the cumulative standby charge will exceed the cost of the automobile.

EXAMPLE   An employee has use of an automobile that cost $56,500, including HST. This availability continues for five years (60 months).

ANALYSIS   The taxable benefit resulting from the standby charge calculation would be $67,800 [(2%)($56,500)(60)]. This taxable benefit is 20 percent larger than the cost of the car to the employer.

Employer Leased Vehicles

3-91.   In those cases where the employer leases the automobile, the basic standby charge is determined by the following formula:

[(2/3)(Lease Payments For The Year Excluding Insurance)(Availability Factor)]

3-92.   As was the case with the formula for employer owned vehicles, the components of this formula require additional explanation:

Lease Payments   The amount to be included here is the total lease payments for the year, including any relevant GST/PST/HST. This total would be reduced by any amounts that have been included for insuring the vehicle. The insurance costs are excluded as the CRA considers them to be part of the operating cost benefit.

Availability Factor   This is a fraction in which the numerator is the number of days during the year the vehicle is available to the employee and the denominator is the number of days during the year for which lease payments were made. If the employee had the use of the vehicle throughout the lease period, the value of this fraction would be 1. When the car is owned by the employer, the *Act* clearly requires the availability period to be based on the days of availability, rounded to the nearest number of 30 day periods. In contrast, when the car is leased, a strict reading of the *Act* requires the availability period to be based on the days available as a fraction of the days in the lease period. However, the *Employers' Guide: Taxable Benefits And Allowances* (T4130), uses the 30 day rounding rule for both purchase and lease situations. We will be using this latter approach in our examples and problems.

3-93.   An example will illustrate these procedures:

EXAMPLE   A vehicle is leased for 3 months at a rate of $750 per month, including HST. The $750 includes a monthly insurance payment of $75 per month. An employee has use of the vehicle for 85 of the 92 days in the lease term.

ANALYSIS   Since both (85 ÷ 30) and (92 ÷ 30) would round to 3, the standby charge would be $1,350 [(2/3)(3)($750 - $75)(3 ÷ 3)]. If the calculation in the *Act* was strictly followed, the benefit would be $1,247 [(2/3)(3)($750 - $75)(85 ÷ 92)].

3-94.   Unlike the situation with an employer owned vehicle, it is unlikely that the taxable benefit associated with a leased vehicle will exceed the value of the automobile. While we have seen no comprehensive analysis to support this view, it seems clear to us that, in most normal leasing situations, the taxable benefit on a leased vehicle will be significantly less than would be the case if the employer purchased the same vehicle.

EXAMPLE   In the real world, a $55,000 (HST inclusive) vehicle could be leased for 48 months with a lease payment of $800 per month (HST inclusive).

ANALYSIS - Vehicle Purchased   If the car is purchased, the standby charge will be $13,200 per year [(2%)($55,000)(12)].

ANALYSIS - Vehicle Leased   If the vehicle is leased, the standby charge will be $6,400 per year [(2/3)(12)($800)(12 ÷ 12)].

3-95.   This example illustrates what we believe to be a fairly general result. For a given automobile, the taxable benefit for the employee will be lower in situations where the employer leases the vehicle, rather than purchasing the vehicle. It is our opinion that the only exceptions to this would occur when the lease has a very short term.

Reduced Standby Charge

3-96.   When an employer provides an automobile to an employee, it is usually used by that employee for a combination of personal activities and employment related activities. Among different employees, there are significant variations in the mix of these activities. Employees of some organizations may use the car almost exclusively in carrying out employment related activities. In other situations, particularly when the employer and the employee are not at arm's length (e.g., the employee is related to the owner of the business), the car may be used almost exclusively for personal travel.

3-97.   This would suggest that there should be some modification of the basic standby charge in situations where there is only limited personal use of the automobile. This, in fact, is the case. The ITA 6(2) standby charge formula provides for a reduction based on the amount of personal usage of the vehicle.

3-98.   The reduction involves multiplying the regular standby charge for either an employer owned or an employer leased vehicle by the following fraction:

$$\frac{\text{Non - Employment Kilometres (Cannot Exceed Denominator)}}{\text{1,667 Kilometres Per Month Of Availability *}}$$

*The number of months of availability is calculated by dividing the number of days that the automobile is available by 30, and rounding to the nearest whole number.

3-99.   In applying this formula, the numerator is based on the number of kilometers driven for personal or non-employment activities. To prevent the fraction from having a value in excess of one, the numerator is limited to the value in the denominator. The denominator is based on the idea that, if the employee uses the automobile for as much as 1,667 kilometers of personal activities in a month (20,004 kilometers per year), the vehicle has fully replaced the need for a personally owned vehicle.

3-100.   This fraction can be used to reduce the basic standby charge provided two conditions are met:

- The employee is required by the employer to use the automobile in his employment duties.

- The use of the automobile is "primarily" employment related. In general, "primarily" is interpreted by the CRA to mean more than 50 percent. Note that this standby charge reduction formula is not completely fair to everyone, in that it fails to distinguish between an employee who uses the employer's automobile 49 percent for employment related activity from an employee who uses the automobile exclusively for personal travel. Despite the significant difference in personal usage, they would each be assessed the same standby charge on a given vehicle.

3-101.   While the fraction is still applicable when personal use is more than 1,667 kilometers per month (20,004 kilometers for the year), it will be equal to 1 (20,004 ÷ 20,004) and will not provide for any reduction in the basic standby charge.

Operating Cost Benefit
Basic Calculation
3-102. In those cases where the employer pays the operating costs for an automobile that is available to an employee, that employee is clearly receiving a benefit related to the portion of these costs that are associated with his personal use of the automobile. An obvious approach to assessing an operating cost benefit would be to simply pro rate operating costs paid by the employer between personal and employment related usage. The problem with this, however, is that the employer would be required to keep detailed cost and mileage records for each employee. This approach is further complicated by the fact that some operating costs incur GST or HST (e.g., gasoline), while other operating costs are exempt from GST or HST (e.g., insurance and licenses).

3-103. Given these problems, ITA 6(1)(k) has provided an administratively simple solution. The operating cost benefit is determined by multiplying a prescribed amount by the number of personal kilometers driven. For 2017, this prescribed amount is $0.25. This amount includes a notional GST or HST component and, as a consequence, no further GST or HST benefit has to be added to this amount.

3-104. Note that this amount is applicable without regard to the level of the actual operating costs, resulting in favourable treatment for employees driving cars with high operating costs and unfavourable treatment for employees using vehicles with low operating costs.

Alternative Calculation
3-105. There is an alternative calculation of the operating cost benefit. Employees who use an employer provided automobile "primarily" (i.e., more than 50 percent) for employment related activities can elect to have the operating cost benefit calculated as one-half of the standby charge by notifying their employer. This alternative calculation does not have to be used and, in many situations, it will not be a desirable alternative as it will produce a higher figure for the operating cost benefit.

Parking
3-106. It should be noted that ITA 6(1.1) specifically excludes any benefit related to employer provided parking from the automobile operating cost benefit. This does not mean that employer provided parking is not a taxable benefit. While parking is not considered to be a component of the automobile benefit calculation, the Employers' Guide makes it clear that, in general, it is a taxable benefit. The logic of this is that parking may be provided to employees who are not provided with an automobile and, as a consequence, it should be accounted for separately from the automobile benefit calculation.

3-107. As noted in Paragraph 3-63, there are exceptions to the requirement to record parking as a taxable benefit. Parking is not considered to be a taxable benefit in the following situations:

- Parking for employees with disabilities.
- Parking for employees who regularly require a car to carry out their employment duties.
- Scramble parking.

Payments By Employee For Automobile Use
3-108. Under ITA 6(1)(e), the standby charge benefit can be reduced by payments made by the employee to the employer for the personal use of the automobile. In corresponding fashion under ITA 6(1)(k), the operating cost benefit can also be reduced by such payments.

3-109. Note, however, that if the employee pays part of the operating costs (e.g., the employee personally pays for gasoline), it does not reduce the basic $0.25 per kilometer benefit. This is not a desirable result and, if the employee is going to be required to pay a portion of the operating expenses, the employer should pay for all of the costs and have the employee reimburse the employer for the appropriate portion. Under this approach, the payments will reduce the operating cost benefit.

Figure 3 - 2   Summary Of Automobile Benefit Calculations

The **full** standby charge calculation on an employer owned or leased vehicle is:

Owned $[(2\%)(\text{Cost Of Car}^*)(\text{Days Available} \div 30 \text{ Rounded})]$

Leased $\left[\left(\dfrac{2}{3} \right) \left(\begin{array}{c} \text{Lease Payments} \\ \text{For The Year}^* \end{array} \right) \left(\dfrac{\text{Days Available} \div 30 \text{ Rounded}}{\text{Days Leased} \div 30 \text{ Rounded}} \right) \right]$

* Including GST/HST/PST, but excluding any insurance in lease payment

---

A **reduced** standby charge is available if employment related usage is greater than 50%. The calculation is as follows:

$$\left[\left(\begin{array}{c} \text{Full Standby} \\ \text{Charge} \end{array} \right) \left(\dfrac{\text{Personal Use Kilometres (Cannot Exceed Denominator)}}{1{,}667 \text{ Kilometres Per Month Of Availability}} \right) \right]$$

The **regular** operating cost benefit for 2017 is $0.25 per personal use kilometer.

An **alternative** operating cost benefit calculation is available if employment related usage is greater than 50%. It is $[(1/2)(\text{Standby Charge, reduced if applicable})]$.

Summary Of Automobile Benefit Calculations

3-110.   Figure 3-2 summarizes the calculations that relate to the taxable benefit arising from employer provided automobiles.

Example - Employer Owned Automobile

3-111.   The following data will be used to illustrate the calculation of the taxable benefit where an employee is provided with a vehicle owned by an employer in 2017.

Cost Of The Automobile ($30,000 + $3,900 HST)	$33,900
Days Available For Use	310
Months Owned By The Employer	12
Total Kilometers Driven	30,000
Personal Kilometers Driven	16,000

3-112.   The 310 days of availability would be rounded to 10 months (310 ÷ 30 rounded). The basic standby charge benefit to be included in employment income would be calculated as follows:

Standby Charge $= [(2\%)(\$33{,}900)(10)] = \underline{\$6{,}780}$

3-113.   As less than 50 percent [(30,000 - 16,000) ÷ 30,000 = 46.7%] of the driving was related to the employer's business, no reduction in the basic standby charge is available. Also note that the cost figure used in the preceding calculation includes the HST.

3-114.   The operating cost benefit to be included in employment income is as follows:

Operating Cost Benefit $= [(\$0.25)(16{,}000)] = \underline{\$4{,}000}$

3-115.   As the employment related use of the car was less than 50 percent, there is no alternative calculation of the operating cost benefit.

3-116.   As the employee does not make any payments to the employer for the personal use of the automobile, the total taxable benefit included in employment income is as follows:

Total Taxable Benefit $= (\$6{,}780 + \$4{,}000) = \underline{\$10{,}780}$

Exercise Three - 6

Subject: Taxable Benefits - Employer Owned Automobile

Mrs. Tanya Lee is provided with an automobile by her employer. The employer acquired the automobile in 2016 for $25,000, plus $1,250 GST and $2,000 PST. During 2017, Ms. Lee drives the automobile a total of 28,000 kilometers, 16,000 of which were related to employment duties. The automobile is available to Mrs. Lee throughout the year. Calculate Mrs. Lee's minimum 2017 taxable benefit for the use of the automobile.

SOLUTION available in print and online Study Guide.

Example - Employer Leased Vehicle

3-117.   To provide a direct comparison between the employer owned and employer leased cases, this example will be based on the same general facts that were used in the ownership example. If the employer was to lease a $30,000 car with a 36 month lease term, the lease payment, calculated using normal lease terms, would be approximately $822 per month, including HST (this $822 value cannot be calculated with the information given). With the exception of the fact that the car is leased rather than purchased by the employer, all of the other facts are the same as in the Paragraph 3-111 example. The standby charge benefit would be calculated as follows:

$$\text{Standby Charge} = [(2/3)(\$822)(10^*)] = \underline{\$5,480}$$

* The availability factor of 10 is calculated as (310 ÷ 30 rounded).

A Note On Calculations   The ITA 6(2) formula (as described in Figure 3-2) requires the total lease payments made for the year be multiplied by a ratio that has months available divided by the months leased. As lease payments are generally given on a monthly basis, the literal use of this formula would result in the following calculation:

$$\text{Standby Charge (ITA Calculation)} = [(2/3)(12)(\$822)(10/12^*)] = \underline{\$5,480}$$

* The availability factor is calculated as [(310 ÷ 30 rounded)/(365 ÷ 30 rounded)].

Many of our users were previously confused by the fact we first multiplied by the 12 months in the lease period and then divided by the same 12 months. As they pointed out, this double calculation is not relevant to the final result. Given this, in our calculations and problem material, we use the simpler calculation shown in the first equation in which the factor of 2/3 is multiplied by the total lease payments for the period of availability. *Income Tax Act* purists are likely to be offended. However, our focus is on helping users understand the difficult material that is found throughout this text.

3-118.   As was the case when the car was owned by the employer, there is no reduction for actual employment related kilometers driven because the car was driven less than 50 percent for employment related purposes. Also note that the benefit is based on the lease payment including HST.

3-119.   The operating cost benefit is the same as the employer owned case and is as follows:

$$\text{Operating Cost Benefit} = [(\$0.25)(16,000)] = \underline{\$4,000}$$

3-120.   As in the case where the employer owned the car, with the employment related use of the car at less than 50 percent, there is no alternative calculation of the operating cost benefit.

3-121.   Since the employee does not make any payments to the employer for the personal use of the automobile, the total taxable benefit is as follows:

Total Taxable Benefit = ($5,480 + $4,000) = <u>$9,480</u>

3-122.   Note that the total benefit is significantly less ($9,480 as compared with $10,780) when the employer leases the car as opposed to purchasing it. As indicated in our earlier discussion in Paragraph 3-95, this would be the anticipated result.

Exercise Three - 7

Subject: Taxable Benefits - Employer Leased Automobile

Mr. Michael Forthwith is provided with a car that is leased by his employer. The monthly lease payments for 2017 are $525, plus $68 HST. During 2017, he drives the automobile a total of 40,000 kilometers, of which 37,000 kilometers are employment related. The automobile is used by him for 325 days during the year. His employer paid a total of $11,250 in operating costs. When he is not using the automobile, company policy requires that it be returned to their premises. Calculate Mr. Forthwith's minimum 2017 taxable benefit for the use of the automobile.

SOLUTION available in print and online Study Guide.

Employer Provided Cars And Tax Planning

3-123.   Providing employees with cars is not a clearly desirable course of action. As is discussed in more detail in Chapter 6, there are limits on the ability of the employer to deduct the costs of owning or leasing the vehicle (e.g., leasing costs in excess of $800 per month before taxes are not deductible). Further, the taxable benefit calculations are such that they may produce a taxable benefit that exceeds the value to the employee of having the car.

3-124.   This means that a decision by an employer to provide an employee with a car requires a careful analysis of all of the relevant factors. While a complete analysis of all of these issues goes beyond the scope of this material on employment income, some general tax planning points can be made.

Require The Car Be Returned   In many situations, there will be periods of time when an employee does not use an employer provided vehicle. Examples would include vacation periods, extensive periods of travel for work, or confinement because of illness. During such periods, the vehicle will be considered available for use unless the employer **REQUIRES** it to be returned to their premises. Given this, the employer should have a policy of requiring vehicles to be returned during periods of non-use by the employee.

Record Keeping   In the absence of detailed records, an employee can be charged with the full standby charge and 100 percent personal usage. To avoid this, it is essential that records be kept of both employment related and personal kilometers driven.

Leasing Vs. Buying   As was previously noted, in most cases, a lower taxable benefit will result when the employer leases the car rather than purchases it. One adverse aspect of leasing arrangements should be noted. Lease payments are made up of a combination of both interest and principal payments on the car. As the taxable benefit is based on the total lease payment, the interest portion becomes, in effect, a part of the taxable benefit.

Minimizing The Standby Charge   This can be accomplished in a variety of ways including longer lease terms, lower trade-in values for old vehicles in purchase situations, larger deposits on leases, and the use of higher residual values in leasing arrangements. However, this minimization process is not without limits. As is explained in Chapter 6, refundable deposits in excess of $1,000 on leases can reduce the deductible portion of lease costs.

Cars Costing More Than $30,000   With the taxable benefit to the employee based on the full cost of the car and any portion of the cost in excess of $30,000 not being deductible to the employer (this limit on the deductibility of automobile expenses is discussed in Chapter 6), it is difficult to imagine situations in which it would make economic sense for a profit oriented employer to provide any employee with a luxury car. As the taxable benefit to the employee is based on the actual cost of the car, while the deductible amount is limited to $30,000, a situation is created in which the employee is paying taxes on an amount which can be significantly larger than the amount that is deductible to the employer. For example, the standby charge on a $150,000 Mercedes-Benz is $36,000 per year [(2%)($150,000)(12)], an amount that may be fully taxable to the employee. In contrast, the employer's deduction for capital cost allowance (tax depreciation) in the first year of ownership is limited to only $4,500 [($30,000)(30%)(1/2)]. The winner in this type of situation is the CRA.

Consider The Alternative   The alternative to the employer provided automobile is to have the employer compensate the employee for using his own automobile. In many cases this may be preferable to providing an automobile. For example, in those situations where employment related use is less than 50 percent, the provision of an automobile to an employee will result in a benefit assessment for the full standby charge. If employment related use was 45 percent, for example, it is almost certain that the amount assessed will exceed the actual benefit associated with 55 percent personal use of the vehicle. If, alternatively, the employee is reasonably compensated for using his own personal vehicle, there is no taxable benefit.

We suggest you work Self Study Problems Three-3, 4 and 5 at this point.

Inclusions - Allowances

Allowance Vs. Reimbursement

3-125.   A reimbursement is an amount paid to an employee to compensate that individual for amounts that he has disbursed in carrying out his employment duties. An example would be an employee who purchases an airline ticket for travel on behalf of his employer. The employee will present the receipt to the employer who reimburses the employee for the amount shown on the receipt. In general, such reimbursements have no tax consequences for the employee. As noted in Paragraph 3-63, an exception to this is when an employer reimburses an employee for tools used in his work. Reflecting the fact that employees cannot, in general, deduct the cost of their tools, this reimbursement must be treated as a taxable benefit.

3-126.   The situation is more complex with allowances. These are amounts that are paid, usually to provide a general level of compensation, for costs that an employee incurs as part of his employment activities. However, as there is no direct, dollar-for-dollar relationship with the actual costs incurred, the tax treatment of these items is more complicated. These complexities are dealt with in the material that follows.

General Rules

3-127.   The term allowance is used to refer to amounts received by employees from an employer other than salaries, wages, benefits, and reimbursements. In practice, allowances generally involve payments to employees as compensation for travel costs, use of their own automobile, or other costs that have been incurred by employees as part of their efforts on behalf of the employer. A mileage allowance for a traveling salesperson or a technician who does service calls would be typical examples of such an allowance.

3-128.   ITA 6(1)(b) provides a general rule which requires that allowances for personal or living expenses must be included in an employee's income. However, many of the items for which employees receive allowances are costs that an employee can deduct against employment income under ITA 8. (See the discussion of deductions later in this Chapter for a full explanation of these amounts.) Examples of such deductible items are as follows:

- ITA 8(1)(f)   salesperson's expenses
- ITA 8(1)(h)   traveling expenses other than motor vehicle expenses
- ITA 8(1)(h.1)   motor vehicle traveling expenses
- ITA 8(1)(i)   professional dues, office rent, salaries, and supply costs
- ITA 8(1)(j)   motor vehicle capital costs (interest and capital cost allowance)

3-129.   If allowances for these items are included in the employee's income, a circular process is involved in which they are added under ITA 6(1)(b) and then subtracted under ITA 8. In view of this, ITA 6(1)(b) indicates that there are exceptions to the rule that allowances must be included in income. While there is a fairly long list of such items, the most important of these exceptions involve allowances paid for the types of costs that would be deductible under ITA 8. Specifically, the following allowances are among those that do not have to be included in an employee's income:

- ITA 6(1)(b)(v) - Reasonable allowances for traveling expenses paid during a period in which the employee was a salesperson (includes allowances for the use of a motor vehicle).

- ITA 6(1)(b)(vii) - Reasonable allowances for traveling expenses for employees other than salespersons, not including allowances for the use of a motor vehicle.

- ITA 6(1)(b)(vii.1) - Reasonable allowances for the use of a motor vehicle for employees other than salespersons.

Taxable Vs. Non-Taxable Allowances

3-130.   The preceding general rules mean that there are two possible treatments of allowances paid to employees for travel and motor vehicle costs.

Non-Taxable Allowances   If a reasonable allowance is paid to an employee, it will not be included in the employee's income records (T4 Information Return). However, when such allowances are not included in income, the employee will not be able to deduct his actual costs. For example, if an individual received $150 per day of travel to cover hotel costs, this would probably be considered reasonable and not included in his income. If the employee chose to stay at a luxury hotel for $400 per day, he would not be able to deduct the additional cost associated with this choice. Alternatively, if he chose to stay at a hostel for $50 per day, he would pocket the excess allowance on a tax free basis.

Taxable Allowances   If an allowance is not considered to be reasonable, it will be included in the employee's T4 Information Return for the period. To the extent the employee can qualify for the deduction of employment related travel or commission salespersons expenses, related expenses incurred by the employee can be deducted in the determination of his net employment income. If the employee's actual costs exceed the allowance, having the allowance included in his income will be advantageous. Conversely, if his actual costs are less than the allowance, the result will be a net inclusion in employment income.

3-131.   It is not clear what constitutes a reasonable amount in the case of the general costs of travel. It appears that, as long as an allowance appears to be in line with actual costs for food, lodging, and miscellaneous costs, the allowance that is provided is likely to be viewed as reasonable.

3-132.   However, if a junior employee was given $30,000 a month for food and lodging and he was known to be staying at budget motels and eating fast food, it is likely that the allowance would have to be included in income and reduced, to the extent possible, by actual costs incurred (while this example sounds unrealistic, it might be attempted in an owner-managed business where the employee was not dealing at arm's length with the employer).

3-133.   Although it may be more difficult to administer and more costly for the employer, reimbursement of actual costs is less likely to cause this type of tax problem for employees than providing an arbitrarily determined general allowance to cover all possible costs.

Reasonable Allowances For Motor Vehicles

3-134.   In Paragraph 3-129, we noted that ITA 6(1)(b)(v) and 6(1)(b)(vii.1) indicate that "reasonable allowances" for an employee's use of a motor vehicle do not have to be included in the employee's income. While the *Act* is not specific as to what constitutes a reasonable allowance for the use of a motor vehicle, it does point out that an allowance will be deemed not to be reasonable:

- if it is not based solely on the number of kilometers for which the vehicle is used in employment duties [ITA 6(1)(b)(x)]; or

- if the employee, in addition to the allowance, is reimbursed for all or part of the expenses of using the vehicle [(ITA 6(1)(b)(xi)].

3-135.   With respect to the first of these conditions, it is clear that an allowance of $200 per month would have to be included in the employee's income. Any allowance that is not specifically based on kilometers is deemed to be unreasonable. This, however, does not answer the question as to what constitutes a reasonable allowance.

3-136.   On the upper end, the CRA has indicated that if a per kilometer allowance exceeds the prescribed amount that is deductible for a business, it will be considered unreasonable, resulting in its inclusion in the employee's income. For 2017, the relevant amounts are $0.54 per kilometer for the first 5,000 kilometers driven by a given employee, and $0.48 for each additional kilometer.

3-137.   While it is clear that an allowance that is not based on kilometers would be viewed as unreasonable by the CRA, the possibility remains that an allowance could be considered unreasonable based on its size. There has been one case (Brunet vs. H.M.Q) in which an employee was allowed to include a $0.15 per kilometer allowance and deduct actual cost. However, it is unlikely that very many employees would wish to purse this approach.

Exercise Three - 8

Subject: Deductible Automobile Costs

Ms. Lauren Giacomo is required by her employer to use her own automobile in her work. To compensate her, she is paid an annual allowance of $3,600. During the current year, she drove her automobile a total of 24,000 kilometers, of which 6,500 kilometers were employment related. Her total automobile costs for the year, including lease costs, are $7,150. What amounts should Ms. Giacomo include and deduct in determining net employment income for the current year?

Exercise Three - 9

Subject: Automobile Allowances

During the current year, Jacob Lorenz leases an automobile for $450 per month, a total for the year of $5,400. He drives a total of 60,000 kilometers, of which 35,000 are employment related. His total operating costs for the year are $15,000. His employer pays him $0.10 for each employment related kilometer driven, a total of $3,500. What amounts should Mr. Lorenz include and deduct in determining net employment income for the current year?

SOLUTIONS available in print and online Study Guide.

Employer's Perspective Of Allowances

3-138.   From the point of view of the employer, paying taxable allowances is the easiest solution.   All amounts paid will be included in the income of the employees and, as a consequence, there is no necessity for the employer to maintain detailed records of actual costs. It is up to the employee to keep these records and to claim the relevant deductible costs against the allowances included in their T4 Information Return.

3-139.   Somewhat more onerous is an approach which uses direct reimbursements of the employee's actual costs. Some efficiencies are available here in that the CRA will generally accept a modest per diem for food without requiring detailed documentation from either the employer or the employee.   However, for more substantial costs, the reimbursement approach involves more detailed record keeping than is the case with the use of taxable allowances.

3-140.   In the case of employee owned automobile costs, the use of non-taxable allowances is particularly complex. As we have noted, the 2017 amounts that can be deducted by an employer for automobile costs are generally limited to $0.54 per kilometer for the first 5,000 kilometers driven by a given employee, and $0.48 for each additional kilometer. If a non-taxable allowance is based on these rates, the employer will have to keep detailed employee-by-employee mileage records to support the deduction of automobile costs.

Employee's Perspective Of Allowances

3-141.   From the employee's point of view, the receipt of a non-taxable allowance represents a very simple solution to the problem. While records may have to be kept for the information needs of the employer, the employee has the advantage of simply ignoring the allowance and the related costs when it comes time to file a tax return.

3-142.   In real economic terms, however, the non-taxable allowance approach may or may not be advantageous. If the employee's actual deductible costs exceed the allowance, the non-inclusion of the allowance in income eliminates the deductibility of the additional costs. Alternatively, if the actual costs are less than the allowance, the employee has, in effect, received a tax free benefit.

Exercise Three - 10

Subject: Travel Allowances

Sandra Ohm travels extensively for her employer. Her employer provides an allowance of $200 per day to cover hotel costs. In addition, she is paid $0.41 per kilometer when she is required to use her automobile for travel. For her work, during the current year, she traveled a total of 82 days and drove 9,400 kilometers.

Her employer paid her $16,400 for lodging [(82)($200)], as well as $3,854 dollars for mileage [(9,400)($0.41)]. Her actual lodging costs were $18,300, while her total automobile costs were $7,200, including monthly lease payments. Her total mileage on the car during the year was 23,500 kilometers.

What amounts should Ms. Ohm include and deduct in determining net employment income for the current year?

SOLUTION available in print and online Study Guide.

Inclusions - Employee Insurance Benefits

Life Insurance

3-143. The cost of providing life insurance benefits to employees is a taxable benefit under ITA 6(4). This means that any premiums paid on a life insurance policy by the employer must be included in employment income. In the event of the employee's death, the benefit payment received by his estate would not be taxable. No GST (or HST) amount would be included in this benefit as insurance services are exempt from GST (see Chapter 21).

Disability Insurance
(a.k.a. Group Sickness Or Accident Insurance Plan)

3-144. The basic rules for group disability insurance plans are as follows:

Contributions By Employee Contributions made by an employee are not deductible by the employee against employment income. However, they can be offset against disability benefits received.

Contributions By Employer Employer contributions do not create a taxable benefit to the employee as long as the plan benefits received by an employee are taxable. Under ITA 6(1)(f), benefits are taxable to an employee provided they are (1) paid on a periodic basis, and (2) paid to compensate the individual for loss of employment income. If plan benefits do not meet both of these criteria (such as benefits for accidental death), they are not taxable and the employer contributions will be considered a taxable benefit to the employee.

Benefits Received (Employer Makes No Contributions) In the unusual situation where the employee makes all of the contributions to the plan, benefits will be received tax free.

Benefits Received (Employer Makes Any Part Of The Contributions) If the employer makes any part of the contributions, the benefits received by an employee will be taxable. However, the employee can offset the income inclusion by the amount of contributions that he has made to the plan prior to receiving the benefits and during the year he received the benefits. If plan benefits are not taxable, the employer's contribution will be treated as a taxable benefit.

3-145. These rules give rise to three possible situations:

Employee Pay All Plans If the employee makes 100 percent of the contributions to the plan, the contributions will not be deductible and any benefits received will not be taxed.

Employer Contributes - Benefits Not Taxed If the employer makes all or part of the contributions to the plan and benefits received are not taxed (because they are not periodic or do not replace employment income), the employer contributions to the plan will be treated as a taxable benefit to the employee. Any employee contributions to the plan are not deductible.

Employer Contributes - Benefits Taxed If the employer makes all or part of the contributions to the plan and benefits received by the employee are taxed, the employer's contributions do not create a taxable benefit. Any employee contributions to the plan are not deductible by the employee. However, the cumulative amount of contributions made prior to receiving benefits and those made during the year the benefits are received can be used to offset the benefits received.

3-146. The most common of these situations is the last one in which the employer makes contributions that do not create a taxable benefit for the employee, with any benefits received being taxed in the hands of the employee. Most of our examples and problems will be based on this type of situation.

3-147.   You should note that these rules only apply to group disability plans. If the plan is not a group plan, any contributions made by an employer will be treated as a taxable benefit to the employee.

> **EXAMPLE**   Jane Forthy's employer sponsors a group disability insurance plan which provides periodic benefits to compensate for lost employment income. During the period January 1 through April 1 of the current year, Jane's contributions to the plan totaled $1,200. On April 1 of the current year she was involved in a car accident which prevented her from working during the remainder of the year. During this period from April 1 through December 31, she received disability benefits of $16,000. In the previous year, the first year she participated in the plan, Jane contributed a total of $3,600 in premiums to this plan.
>
> **ANALYSIS**   Jane's income inclusion for the current year would be $11,200 [$16,000 - $1,200 - $3,600].

3-148.   As noted in the previous section on life insurance, insurance services are exempt from GST/HST, and no GST/HST amount is associated with taxable benefits related to disability insurance.

Exercise Three - 11

Subject: Disability Insurance Benefits

Mr. Lance Bardwell is a member of a group disability plan sponsored by his employer. The plan provides periodic benefits to compensate for lost employment income. During 2017, his employer's share of the annual premium was $1,800. During 2016, Mr. Bardwell was required to contribute $300 to this plan. During the last 6 weeks of 2017, Mr. Barwell became incapacitated and, as a consequence, received $5,250 in benefits from the disability plan. Because of this period of disability, his 2017 contribution to the disability plan was only $225. What amount will Mr. Bardwell include in his 2017 employment income?

SOLUTION available in print and online Study Guide.

Loans To Employees

General Rules

3-149.   If an employer extends a loan to an employee that is either interest free or has a rate that is below the going market rate, the employee is clearly receiving a benefit that should be taxed. This view is reflected in ITA 6(9), which requires the assessment of a taxable benefit on all interest free or low interest loans to employees. This provision applies whether the loan is made as a consequence of prior, current, or future employment.

3-150.   As specified in ITA 80.4(1), which describes how this benefit is calculated, the taxable benefit would equal imputed interest calculated at a rate specified in the *Income Tax Regulations*. This rate, as determined by ITR 4301, is referred to as the prescribed rate (note that this rate was discussed in more detail in Chapter 2). It is established for each calendar quarter on the basis of Government Of Canada Treasury Bill yields. In general, the taxable benefit is calculated using the prescribed rate that is applicable to each calendar quarter. The amount of the benefit is reduced by any interest paid on the loan by the employee during the year or within 30 days of the end of the year.

> **EXAMPLE** On January 1 of the current year, Ms. Brooks Arden borrows $50,000 from her employer at an annual rate of 1 percent. Assume that during this year, the prescribed rate is 3 percent during the first two quarters, and 4 percent during the last two quarters. Ms. Arden pays the required 1 percent interest on December 31.

ANALYSIS   The taxable benefit to be included in Ms. Arden's net employment income would be calculated as follows:

Imputed Interest:	
Quarters 1 and 2 [(3%)($50,000)(2/4)]	$ 750
Quarters 3 and 4 [(4%)($50,000)(2/4)]	1,000
Total Imputed Interest	$1,750
Interest Paid [(1%)($50,000)]	(500)
Taxable Benefit	**$1,250**

In general, interest calculations that are made for tax purposes are based on the number of days the principal is outstanding. However, IT-421R2, in its illustration of employee loan interest calculation, uses calendar quarters and treats each calendar quarter as one-quarter of the year. In situations where full calendar quarters are involved we will use this approach in our text and problem material.

3-151.   Several additional points should be made with respect to these loans:

• If the rate negotiated with the employer is at least equal to (or greater than) the rate that the employee could have negotiated himself with a commercial lender, then under ITA 80.4(3), no benefit will be assessed to the employee regardless of subsequent changes to the prescribed rate. However, this is rarely applicable as the prescribed rate is consistently lower than rates available on loans to individuals from commercial lenders.

• ITA 80.4(2) contains a different set of rules that is applicable to loans made to certain shareholders of a company. The different rules that are applicable to shareholders are described in Chapter 15, "Corporate Taxation And Management Decisions".

• Proceeds from a loan to an employee could be used to invest in assets that produce business or property income. In general, interest paid on loans to finance investments is deductible against the income produced. ITA 80.5 clearly states that an imputed interest benefit assessed under ITA 80.4(1) or 80.4(2) is deemed to be interest paid for the purposes of determining net business or property income. Referring to the example in Paragraph 3-150, if Ms. Arden had invested the $50,000 loan proceeds in income producing assets, her deductible interest would total $1,750, the $500 that she paid, plus the assessed $1,250 taxable benefit.

• When the purpose of the loan is to assist an employee with a home purchase or home relocation (see Paragraph 3-152), ITA 80.4(4) indicates that the annual amount of interest used in the benefit calculations cannot exceed the annual amount determined using the prescribed rate in effect when the loan was extended. Note that this rule is applied on an annual basis, not on a quarter by quarter basis.

This provides a ceiling for the benefit and, at the same time, allows the taxpayer to benefit if the prescribed rate becomes lower. This ceiling on the benefit is only available for the first five years such loans are outstanding. ITA 80.4(6) indicates that, after this period of time, the loan will be deemed to be a new loan, making the calculation of the benefit subject to the prescribed rate in effect at this point in time. This new rate will again serve as a ceiling for the amount of the benefit for the next five years.

EXAMPLE   On January 1 of the current year, an employee receives a $200,000, interest free home purchase loan from his employer. Assume that the prescribed rate is 4 percent for the first quarter, 3 percent during the second and third quarters and 7 percent in the fourth quarter.

ANALYSIS   If interest is calculated on a quarterly basis, the benefit would be $8,500 [($200,000)(4%)(1/4) + ($200,000)(3%)(2/4) + ($200,000)(7%)(1/4)]. Alternatively, using the prescribed rate in effect at the time the loan was made, the amount is $8,000 [($200,000)(4%)]. As this is lower, the taxable benefit would be $8,000.

Home Relocation Loans

> **BYRD/CHEN NOTE**   For 2018 and subsequent years, the home relocation provision has been repealed.

3-152.   If an employer provides a home purchase loan when an employee moves to a new work location, it is referred to as a home relocation loan if certain conditions are met. If this is an interest free or low interest loan, the ITA 80.4(1) rules apply as outlined in the preceding section. However, in the case of a home relocation loan, there is an offsetting deduction.

3-153.   This deduction is equal to the benefit associated with an interest free home relocation loan of up to $25,000. Note, however, the deduction is applied in the calculation of Taxable Income. This being the case, the usual ITA 80.4(1) imputed interest benefit will be included in net employment income, a figure that will not be changed by the home relocation loan deduction. The deduction will be applied after net employment income has been added to other sources in the determination of Net Income For Tax Purposes. The details of this deduction from Taxable Income are covered in Chapter 4.

3-154.   There is no GST benefit on imputed interest on a low or no interest loan. This reflects the fact that no GST is charged on financial services (see Chapter 21).

Exercise Three - 12

Subject: Housing Loan

On January 1, 2017, Mrs. Caldwell receives a $100,000 loan from her employer to assist her in purchasing a home. The loan requires annual interest at a rate of 1 percent, which she pays on December 31, 2017. Assume that the relevant prescribed rate is 2 percent during the first quarter of 2017, 3 percent during the second quarter, and 1 percent during the remainder of the year. Calculate Mrs. Caldwell's taxable benefit on this loan for the year (1) assuming that the loan qualifies as a home relocation loan and (2) assuming that it does not qualify as a home relocation loan.

SOLUTION available in print and online Study Guide.

Tax Planning For Interest Free Loans
General Approach

3-155.   Tax rules result in a taxable benefit to the employee if the interest rate on the loan is lower than the prescribed rate. Given this, the question arises as to whether the use of employee loans is a tax effective form of providing employee benefits. As with other types of benefits, the question is whether it is better that the employer supplies the benefit or, alternatively, provides sufficient additional salary to allow the employee to acquire the benefit directly. In the case of loans, this additional salary would have to be sufficient to allow the employee to carry a similar loan at commercial rates.

3-156.   To determine whether a loan is an effective form of employee compensation, several factors have to be considered:

- the employer's rate of return on alternative uses for the funds
- the employer's tax rate
- the employee's tax rate
- the prescribed rate
- the rate available to the employee on a similar arm's length loan

3-157.   In analyzing the use of loans to employees, we begin with the assumption that we would like to provide a requested benefit to one or more employees and we are looking for the most cost effective way of providing the benefit. As noted, the alternative to providing an employee with a loan is to provide that employee with sufficient after tax income to carry an equivalent loan at commercial rates of interest.

3-158.   It then becomes a question of comparing the cash flows associated with the employer providing the loan (this would have to include sufficient additional income to pay the taxes on any loan benefit that will be assessed), with the cash flows required for the employer to provide the employee with sufficient income to carry an equivalent loan acquired from a commercial lender.

Example Of Interest Free Loan Benefit

3-159.   The following example illustrates the calculations required to determine whether the use of a low or no interest loan is a tax effective form of employee compensation.

EXAMPLE A key executive asks for a $100,000 interest free housing loan. The loan does not qualify as a home relocation loan. At this time, the employer has an investment opportunity that is expected to provide a rate of return of 12 percent before taxes. Assume the prescribed rate for the period is 2 percent, while the rate for home mortgages is 5 percent. The employee is subject to a marginal tax rate, the tax rate applicable to additional income, of 45 percent, while the employer pays corporate taxes at a marginal rate of 28 percent.

Alternative 1 - Provide Additional Salary In the absence of the interest free loan, the employee would borrow $100,000 at 5 percent, requiring an annual interest payment of $5,000. In determining the amount of salary required to carry this loan, consideration has to be given to the fact that additional salary will be taxed at 45 percent. In terms of the algebra that is involved, we need to solve the following equation for X:

$$\$5,000 = [(X)(1 - 0.45)]$$

You will recall that this type of equation is solved by dividing both sides by (1 - 0.45), resulting in a required salary of $9,091:

$$X = [\$5,000 \div (1 - 0.45)] = \$9,091$$

Using this figure, the employer's after tax cash flow required to provide sufficient additional salary for the employee to carry a conventional $100,000 mortgage would be calculated as follows:

Required Salary [$5,000 ÷ (1 - 0.45)]	$9,091
Tax Savings From Deducting Salary [($9,091)(28%)]	(2,545)
Employer's After Tax Cash Flow - Additional Salary	**$6,546**

Alternative 2 - Provide The Loan If the loan is provided, the employee will have a taxable benefit of $2,000 [(2% - Nil)($100,000)], resulting in additional taxes payable of $900 [(45%)($2,000)]. To make this situation comparable to the straight salary alternative, the employer will have to provide the executive with both the loan amount and sufficient additional salary to pay the $900 in taxes on the benefit that will be assessed. The required amount would be $1,636 [$900 ÷ (1 - 0.45)].

The employer's cash flow associated with the after tax cost of providing the additional salary as well as the after tax lost earnings on the $100,000 loan amount would be calculated as follows:

Required Salary [$900 ÷ (1 - 0.45)]	$1,636
Tax Savings From Deducting Salary [($1,636)(28%)]	(458)
After Tax Cost Of Salary To Cover Taxes On Benefit	$1,178
Employer's Lost Earnings [(12%)(1 - 0.28)($100,000)]	8,640
Employer's After Tax Cash Flow - Loan	**$9,818**

Conclusion Given these results, payment of additional salary appears to be the better alternative. However, the preceding simple example is not a complete analysis of the situation. Other factors, such as the employee's ability to borrow at going rates and the employer's ability to grant this salary increase in the context of overall salary policies, would also have to be considered.

Exercise Three - 13

Subject: Loans To Employees - Tax Planning

A key executive asks for a $125,000 interest free housing loan that does not qualify as a home relocation loan. At this time, the employer has investment opportunities involving a rate of return of 7 percent before taxes. Assume that for the period, the relevant prescribed rate is 2 percent, while the market rate for home mortgages is 5 percent. The employee's tax rate on additional income (i.e., his marginal tax rate), is 42 percent, while the employer's marginal tax rate is 26 percent. Should the employer grant the loan or, alternatively, provide sufficient salary to carry an equivalent loan from a commercial lender? Explain your conclusion.

SOLUTION available in print and online Study Guide.

We suggest you work Self Study Problem Three-6 at this point.

Inclusions - Stock Option Benefits

The Economics Of Stock Option Arrangements

3-160.   Stock options allow, but do not require, the holder to purchase a specified number of shares for a specified period of time at a specified acquisition price. Because of tax considerations, at the time of granting, the option price is usually at or above the market price of the shares. For example, options might be issued to acquire shares at a price of $10 at a time when the shares are trading at that same $10 value.

3-161.   At first glance, such an option would appear to have no value as it simply allows the holder to acquire a share for $10, at a time when that share is only worth that amount. In reality, however, this option could have significant value, in that it allows the holder to participate in any upward price movement in the shares without any obligation to exercise the option if the price stays at, or falls below, $10. Stated alternatively, the option provides full participation in gains on the option shares, with no downside risk. Further, for an employee receiving such options, they provide this participation with no real investment cost until such time as the options are exercised.

EXAMPLE   Because of his excellent work, Andrew Chang is given options to buy 1,000 shares of his employer's stock at a price of $10 per share. At this time, the shares are trading at $10 per share. One year later, he exercises the options and immediately sells the acquired shares for $12 per share.

ANALYSIS   Andrew has enjoyed a gain of $2,000 [(1,000)($12 - $10)] with no initial investment. This clearly illustrates why the options have a value, even when they are not issued "in-the-money". The expression "in-the-money" refers to situations where the option price ($10 in this example) is below current market value. In this example, the options are in-the-money when the market value is greater than $10.

3-162.   Stock options are granted to employees in the belief that, by giving an employee an interest in the stock of the company, he has an incentive to make a greater effort on behalf of the enterprise. In some companies, use of this form of compensation is restricted to senior executives. In contrast, other corporations make options available to larger groups of employees.

3-163. At one point in time, a very significant advantage to the use of stock options was that the cost of issuing such options was not recorded in the financial statements of the issuing corporation. Because of an inability of accountants to agree on the appropriate value for options that were not "in-the-money", corporations were able to issue huge quantities of stock options without recording any compensation expense at all.

3-164. However, this is not the current situation. GAAP requires the recognition of a compensation expense when stock options are issued.

3-165. In contrast to the accounting treatment under GAAP, the issuance of stock options has no tax consequences at the time of issue, either for the issuer or the recipient. The issuer cannot deduct any amount to reflect the economic value of the issued options. Further, the recipient does not have any income inclusion when the options are issued.

Overview Of The Tax Rules

3-166. This is a difficult subject to present in that it involves several different areas of tax legislation. In addition to issues related to employment income, stock options influence the determination of Taxable Income and the calculation of taxable capital gains. While it would be possible to present this material on a piecemeal basis, we have found this to be confusing to our readers. An alternative would be to defer any discussion of this issue until Chapter 8 when all of the relevant material has been covered.

3-167. However, this fails to reflect the fact that stock option issues relate most directly to employment income. As a consequence, most of our material on stock options will be presented in this Chapter. As this involves some material that will not be covered until later Chapters, an overview of the stock option material that will be presented in this Chapter is useful. The basic points here are as follows:

Value At Issue As noted previously, the tax rules give no recognition to the fact that stock options have a positive value at the time of issue. The issuing employer can make no deduction and the recipient employee has no income inclusion. As some of you are aware, this is not consistent with accounting procedures in this area. After many years of controversy, accounting procedures were finally modified to recognize some value for stock options when they are issued. The accounting approach better reflects the economic reality associated with these financial instruments.

Employment Income Inclusion - Measurement The employment income inclusion will be measured on the date that the options are exercised. The amount will be equal to the excess of the per share fair market value on the exercise date over the option price, with the difference multiplied by the number of shares acquired. This amount will be nil or positive as the employee would not normally exercise the options unless the value of the shares is equal to, or exceeds, the option price.

Employment Income Inclusion - Recognition While the employment income inclusion will always be measured at the time the options are exercised, it may not be recognized until the shares are sold. Whether the inclusion will be recognized at the time of exercise or at the time of sale will depend on the type of corporation that is issuing the stock options. Note that when the appropriate event triggers recognition of this income inclusion, it will be classified as employment income, even if the taxpayer is no longer an employee of the organization that issued the options.

Taxable Income Deduction As many of you are aware, gains on dispositions of securities are considered to be capital gains, subject to taxation on only one-half of their total amount. In the absence of some mitigating provision, the full amount of the employment income inclusion that arises on the exercise of options would be subject to tax. As this would not be an equitable situation, tax legislation permits a deduction in the calculation of Taxable Income equal to one-half of the employment income inclusion. While general coverage of Taxable Income is found in Chapters 4 and 11, this deduction will be covered here as part of our discussion of stock options. Note, however, this deduction does not influence the calculation of Net Employment

Income. This means that, if you are solving a problem that requires the calculation of Net Employment Income, you will **NOT** include this deduction in your calculation.

Capital Gains   With the difference between fair market value at the exercise date and the option price being treated as an employment income inclusion, fairness requires that the adjusted cost base of the acquired shares be based on their fair market value at the exercise date, not the actual cost to the employee. This means that, when the shares are eventually sold, there will be a capital gain or loss based on the difference between the sale price and the fair market value of the shares at the time of exercise. As is discussed more fully in Chapter 8, only one-half of capital gains are subject to tax (the "taxable capital gain"). One-half of capital losses are deductible (the "allowable capital loss"), but only to the extent that there are taxable capital gains in the year.

3-168.   A simple example will serve to illustrate the relevant calculations:

EXAMPLE An executive receives options to acquire 1,000 of his employer's common shares at an option price of $25 per share. At this time, the common shares are trading at $25 per share. He exercises the options when the shares are trading at $40 per share. In the following year, he sells the shares for $50 per share.

ANALYSIS   Assuming that the employment income inclusion must be recognized when the options are exercised, the tax consequences for the year of exercise would be as follows:

Employment Income [(1,000)($40 - $25)]	$15,000
Taxable Income Deduction (One-Half)	(7,500)
Taxable Income In Year Of Exercise	$ 7,500

When the shares are sold, the additional tax consequences to the employee would be as follows:

Proceeds Of Disposition [(1,000)($50)]	$50,000
Adjusted Cost Base [(1,000)($40)]	(40,000)
Capital Gain	$10,000
Inclusion Rate	1/2
Taxable Capital Gain In Year Of Sale	$ 5,000

3-169.   Several points should be made with respect to this example:

- The employment income inclusion will always be measured at the time the options are exercised. However, its recognition for tax purposes may be deferred until the acquired shares are sold. This will be discussed in more detail in the material that follows.
- The $7,500 deduction is from Net Income For Tax Purposes in the calculation of Taxable Income, not from employment income. The net employment income that will be included in the executive's current or future Net Income For Tax Purposes, as well as his Earned Income inclusion for RRSP purposes (see Chapter 10), is $15,000.
- The availability of the $7,500 deduction requires that certain conditions be met. These conditions will be discussed in detail in the material that follows.
- As we have noted, when the $15 per share employment income benefit is included in employment income, this amount will be added to the adjusted cost base of the shares, increasing their value to $40 per share ($25 + $15). This inclusion is provided for under ITA 53(1)(j).

CCPCs Vs. Public Companies

3-170.   As is discussed more fully in Chapter 12, "Taxable Income And Tax Payable For Corporations", a Canadian controlled private corporation (CCPC) is generally a corporation that is controlled by Canadian residents and does not have its shares traded on a prescribed stock exchange. This is an important distinction in many areas of tax work. However, our concern here is with the difference between the tax treatment of stock options issued by public companies and the tax treatment of stock options issued by CCPCs.

3-171.   In very simplified terms, for options issued by public companies, the general rule is that the employment income inclusion will be taxed when the options are exercised. In contrast, for options issued by Canadian controlled private corporations, the employment income inclusion is still measured when the options are exercised, but the benefit is not taxed until the acquired shares are sold.

3-172.   This clearly places individuals receiving stock options to acquire shares of public companies at a disadvantage. They are required to pay taxes on an unrealized amount of income, sometimes resulting in a need to dispose of some portion of the acquired shares. The main reason for the difference in the treatment of stock options for public companies and CCPCs is that, unlike public company shares, CCPC shares are usually difficult to convert to cash as there is no established market for private company shares. If the stock option benefit was taxed for CCPCs when the options are exercised (like for public companies), there would be no way the employee could sell a portion of the shares to pay the tax liability.

Rules For Public Companies

3-173.   Under ITA 7(1)(a), when options to acquire the shares of a publicly traded company are exercised, there is an employment income inclusion equal to the excess of the fair market value of shares acquired over the price paid to acquire them. A deduction from Taxable Income, equal to one-half of the employment income that is included under ITA 7(1)(a), can be taken under ITA 110(1)(d).

3-174.   Note, however, this ITA 110(1)(d) deduction in the calculation of Taxable Income is only available if, at the time the options are issued, the option price was equal to, or greater than, the fair market value of the shares at the option grant date. If the option price is less than the fair market value of the shares at the time of issue, the deduction will not be available and the individual will be subject to tax on the full amount of the employment income inclusion.

> **EXAMPLE** On December 31, 2015, John Due receives options to buy 10,000 shares of his employer's common stock at a price of $25 per share. The employer is a publicly traded company and the options are exercisable as of their issue date. At this time, the shares are trading at $25 per share. On July 31, 2017, the shares are trading at $43 per share and Mr. Due exercises all of these options. On September 30, 2018, Mr. Due sells all of his shares for $45 per share.
>
> **ANALYSIS** The tax consequences of the events and transactions are as follows:
>
> - **Issue Date** (December 31, 2015)   Despite the fact that the options clearly have a positive value at this point in time, there are no tax consequences resulting from the issuance of the options.
>
> - **Exercise Date = Measurement and Recognition Date** (July 31, 2017)   As the option price was equal to the fair market value of the shares at the option grant date, Mr. Due can use the ITA 110(1)(d) deduction in calculating his Taxable Income. The tax consequences resulting from the exercise of the options would be as follows:

Fair Market Value Of Shares Acquired [(10,000)($43)]	$430,000
Cost Of Shares [(10,000)($25)]	(250,000)
ITA 7(1)(a) Employment Income Inclusion = **Increase In Net Income For Tax Purposes**	**$180,000**
ITA 110(1)(d) Deduction [(1/2)($180,000)]	(90,000)
Increase In Taxable Income	**$ 90,000**

- **Disposition Date** (September 30, 2018)   The tax consequences resulting from the sale of the shares would be as follows:

Proceeds Of Disposition [(10,000)($45)]	$450,000
Adjusted Cost Base [(10,000)($43)]	(430,000)
Capital Gain	$ 20,000
Inclusion Rate	1/2
Taxable Capital Gain	$ 10,000

Note that, in the 2018 calculation, the adjusted cost base of the shares has been bumped up to the value of the shares at the time of exercise, reflecting the fact that the difference between the $43 per share value on that date and the $25 option price has already been included in the taxpayer's Net Income For Tax Purposes.

Also note that, if the taxpayer had sold the shares in 2018 for less than the $43 value that was established at the time of exercise in 2017, the result would be a capital loss. If this was the case, the taxpayer would not be able to deduct the loss in 2018, unless he had capital gains from some other source. This creates a situation that could be viewed as unfair in that the taxpayer has had to include gains up to the $43 value, but might not be able to deduct the loss resulting from a subsequent decline in value. Note that he cannot carry back the capital loss against the 2017 gain because that amount was classified as employment income, not as a capital gain.

Exercise Three - 14

Subject: Stock Options - Public Company

During 2015, Mr. Gordon Guise was granted options to buy 2,500 of his employer's shares at a price of $23.00 per share. At this time, the shares are trading at $20.00 per share. His employer is a large publicly traded company. During July, 2017, he exercises all of the options when the shares are trading at $31.50 per share. In September, 2017, the shares are sold for $28.00 per share. What is the effect of the exercise of the options and the sale of the shares on Mr. Guise's 2017 Net Income For Tax Purposes and on his Taxable Income? Identify these two amounts separately.

SOLUTION available in print and online Study Guide.

Rules For Canadian Controlled Private Corporations (CCPCs)

3-175.   The basic public company rules that we have just described require the recognition of a taxable benefit when the options are exercised, prior to the realization in cash of any benefit from the options granted. This may not be an insurmountable problem for employees of publicly traded companies, in that they can sell some of the shares or use them as loan collateral if they need to raise the cash to pay the taxes on the benefit.

3-176.   However, for employees of a Canadian controlled private corporation (CCPC), a requirement to pay taxes at the time an option is exercised could create severe cash flow problems since the shares are not publicly traded. As a consequence, a different treatment is permitted for stock options issued by CCPCs. The employment income inclusion is still measured at the time the options are exercised, but it is not taxed until the shares are sold.

3-177.   For CCPCs, the employment income inclusion is determined under ITA 7(1)(a) and 7(1.1). The ITA 110(1)(d) deduction from Taxable Income is also available to CCPCs provided the option price was equal to, or more than, the fair market value of the shares at the option grant date. However, if this condition is not met, an additional provision under ITA 110(1)(d.1) allows the taxpayer to deduct one-half of the employment income inclusion, provided the shares are held for at least two years after their acquisition.

3-178.   Using the same information that is contained in the example in Paragraph 3-174, altered only so that the employer is a CCPC, the tax consequences would be as follows:

Analysis For CCPC Example

- **Issue Date** (December 31, 2015)   Despite the fact that the options clearly have a positive value at this point in time, there are no tax consequences resulting from the issuance of the options.

- **Exercise Date = Measurement Date Only** (July 31, 2017)   While the amount of the employment income inclusion would be measured on this date, it would not be included in income at this point. Based on the increase in share value from $25 to $43 per share, the benefit would be measured as $180,000 [($43 - $25)(10,000 Shares)]. This benefit, along with the related $90,000 Taxable Income deduction, would be deferred until such time as the shares are sold.

- **Disposition Date** = Recognition Date (September 30, 2018)   The tax consequences resulting from the sale of the shares would be as follows:

Deferred Employment Income [($43 - $25)(10,000)]		$180,000
Proceeds Of Disposition [(10,000)($45)]	$450,000	
Adjusted Cost Base [(10,000)($43)]	(430,000)	
Capital Gain	$ 20,000	
Inclusion Rate	1/2	10,000
Increase In Net Income For Tax Purposes		**$190,000**
ITA 110(1)(d) Deduction [(1/2)($180,000)]		(90,000)
Increase In Taxable Income		**$100,000**

3-179.   Note that this is the total increase in Taxable Income that would have resulted from simply purchasing the shares at $25 and later selling them for $45 [(10,000)(1/2)($45 - $25) = $100,000]. The structuring of this increase is different and, in some circumstances, the difference could be significant. For example, the fact that the $180,000 increase in value has been classified as employment income rather than capital gains means that it is not eligible for the lifetime capital gains deduction (see Chapter 11), but it will increase Earned Income for RRSP purposes (see Chapter 10). Although the timing is different, the $100,000 total increase in Taxable Income is the same as in the public company example in Paragraph 3-174.

Exercise Three - 15

Subject: Stock Options - CCPC

In 2015, Ms. Milli Van was granted options to buy 1,800 of her employer's shares at a price of $42.50 per share. At this time, the shares have a fair market value of $45.00 per share. Her employer is a Canadian controlled private corporation. In June, 2016, when the shares have a fair market value of $75.00 per share, she exercises all of her options. In September, 2017, Ms. Van sells her shares for $88,200 ($49.00 per share). What is the effect of the exercise of the options and the sale of the shares on Ms. Van's 2016 and 2017 Net Income For Tax Purposes and her Taxable Income? Identify these two amounts separately.

SOLUTION available in print and online Study Guide.

We suggest you work Self Study Problems Three-7, 8 and 9 at this point.

Other Inclusions

Payments By Employer To Employee

3-180.   As noted in Paragraph 3-58, ITA 6(3) deals with employment related payments made prior to, or subsequent to, the employment period. This includes payments for accepting employment, as well as contractually arranged payments for work to be completed subsequent to the termination of employment. ITA 6(3) requires that all such amounts be included in employment income.

Forgiveness Of Employee Loans

3-181.   There may be circumstances in which an employer decides to forgive a loan that has been extended to an employee. As noted in Paragraph 3-58, ITA 6(15) requires that the forgiven amount be included in the income of the employee in the year in which the forgiveness occurs. The forgiven amount is simply the amount due, less any payments that have been made by the employee.

Housing Loss Reimbursement

3-182.   When an employee is required to move, employers often provide various types of financial assistance. As is discussed in detail in Chapter 9, an employer can pay for the usual costs of moving (e.g., shipping company costs) without tax consequences to the employee. In recent years, particularly when an employee is moved from an area with a weak housing market, it has become more common for employers to reimburse individuals for losses incurred in the disposition of their principal residence.

3-183.   The current rules limit the amount of housing loss that can be reimbursed without tax consequences. This is accomplished in ITA 6(19) by indicating that amounts paid to employees for housing losses, except for amounts related to "eligible housing losses", must be included in income.

3-184.   ITA 6(22) defines an "eligible housing loss" as a loss that is related to a move that qualifies for the deduction of moving expenses. While this issue is discussed in more detail in Chapter 9, we would note here that an employee is generally allowed to deduct moving expenses when he moves at least 40 kilometers closer to a new work location.

3-185.   ITA 6(20) limits the amount of housing loss reimbursement that can be received by indicating that one-half of any amount received in excess of $15,000 as an eligible housing loss must be included in the employee's income as a taxable benefit. Stated alternatively, the tax free amount of housing loss reimbursement is limited to the first $15,000, plus one-half of any amount paid in excess of $15,000.

Discounts On Employer's Merchandise

3-186.   As noted in Paragraph 3-63, when an employee is allowed to purchase merchandise which is ordinarily sold by an employer, any discount given to the employee is not generally considered to be a taxable benefit. If discounts are extended by a group of employers, or if an employer only extends the discounts to a particular group of employees, a taxable benefit may arise. In addition, this administrative position is not intended to apply to big-ticket items (e.g., a contractor giving an employee a discount on a new home).

3-187.   A further interesting note is that the CRA has indicated that, in the case of airline employees, a benefit is assessed if the employee travels on a space confirmed basis and pays less than 50 percent of the economy fare. The benefit is the difference between 50 percent of the economy fare and the amount paid.

3-188.   When a benefit must be included in income as the result of merchandise discounts, it will include any GST/HST that is applicable to these amounts.

Specific Deductions

Overview

3-189.   The provisions covering deductions that can be made against employment income are found in ITA 8. In addition, ITA 8(2) contains a general limitation statement that makes it clear that unless an item is listed in ITA 8, it cannot be deducted in the calculation of employment income.

3-190.   We have noted previously that the ITA 8 list of deductions is very limited, particularly in comparison with the list of deductions available to self-employed individuals earning business income. Despite the shortness of its list, the application of ITA 8 is fairly complex. This results from the fact that there are restrictions on the type of employee that can deduct certain items, on the items that can be deducted, and on the simultaneous use of some of the statutory provisions. Given this complexity, a listing and brief description of the more significant deductions available is a useful introduction to this material.

ITA 8(1)(b) Legal Expenses allows an employee to deduct any legal costs paid to collect or establish the right to salary or wages owed by an employer or former employer. Also deductible are legal costs incurred to recover benefits, such as health insurance, that are not paid by an employer or former employer, but that are required to be included in employment income when received.

ITA 8(1)(f) Sales Expenses covers the deductions available to individuals who earn commission income. It covers travel expenses, motor vehicle expenses, and other types of expenses associated with earning commissions (e.g., licenses required by real estate salespersons).

ITA 8(1)(h) Travel Expenses covers deductions available to all employees for travel expenses, other than motor vehicle expenses. An employee earning commissions can deduct travel costs under ITA 8(1)(f) or ITA 8(1)(h), but cannot use both provisions simultaneously.

ITA 8(1)(h.1) Motor Vehicle Travel Expenses covers deductions available to all employees for motor vehicle expenses. An employee earning commissions can deduct motor vehicle costs under ITA 8(1)(f) or ITA 8(1)(h.1), but cannot use both provisions simultaneously.

ITA 8(1)(i) Dues And Other Expenses Of Performing Duties covers a variety of deductions available to all employees. Included here would be professional dues, office rent paid or costs of maintaining a work space in the home, salaries to an assistant, and the cost of supplies used in employment related activities.

ITA 8(1)(j) Motor Vehicle And Aircraft Costs In general, employees cannot deduct capital costs. This includes tax depreciation (capital cost allowance or CCA) and interest on funds borrowed to acquire capital assets. This Paragraph creates an exception for motor vehicles and aircraft used in employment activities. Both CCA and financing costs on these assets can be deducted under this provision.

ITA 8(1)(p)   Musical Instruments This is a second exception to the general rule that employees cannot deduct capital costs. This Paragraph allows the deduction of CCA on musical instruments required by employment activities. Unlike the provision for motor vehicle and aircraft costs, this provision does not allow the deduction of interest related to the financing of such instruments.

ITA 8(1)(m) Employee's Registered Pension Plan (RPP) Contributions As was noted previously, ITA 6(1)(a) excludes employer's contributions to an RPP from treatment as a taxable benefit. Adding to the attractiveness of these arrangements is the fact that ITA 8(1)(m) provides for the employee's contributions to be treated as a deduction. This deduction is given detailed attention in Chapter 10 which provides comprehensive coverage of the various retirement savings arrangements.

ITA 8(1)(r) **Apprentice Mechanic's Tool Costs** provides for the deduction of tools that are required by an apprentice mechanic. This is a very complex provision that allows for a deduction of costs in excess of an annual threshold amount. The threshold is the lesser of $500 plus the Canada employment credit amount (see Chapter 4), and 5 percent of an adjusted income figure.

ITA 8(1)(s) **Tradesperson's Tool Expenses** provides for the deduction of up to $500 for tools that are required by a tradesperson. Only costs in excess of $1,178 can be deducted. As noted in Chapter 4, this amount is also the base for the Canada Employment Tax Credit.

ITA 8(4) Meals Both ITA 8(1)(f) and ITA 8(1)(h) refer to travel costs. As such costs could include meals, ITA 8(4) specifies when meals can be considered a part of travel costs. This Subsection notes that, for meals to be deductible as travel costs under ITA 8(1)(f) or ITA 8(1)(h), the meal must be consumed when the taxpayer is required, by his employment duties, to be away from the municipality or metropolitan area where his employer's establishment is located for at least 12 hours. Some sources disagree with this travel limitation on the deductibility of meals against employment income. However, it is likely that these sources are confusing meals paid for by an employee out of his own funds, and meals that are reimbursed by an employer. In the latter case, the 12 hour limitation does not apply as the employer is deducting the meals against business income.

We would also note here that ITA 67.1(1) limits the deductibility of food and entertainment costs to 50 percent of the amount paid. This limitation applies without regard to whether the individual is working as an employee, or as a self-employed individual earning business income.

ITA 8(13) **Work Space In Home** provides rules for an employee deducting the costs of a work space in his home (a.k.a. home office costs).

3-191. Most of these provisions will be given more detailed attention in the material in this Chapter. The Employee and Partner GST Rebate available on deductible expenses is covered in Chapter 21. Other, less commonly used Paragraphs such as ITA 8(1)(e) which allows the deduction of certain expenses of railway employees, will not be given coverage.

Salesperson's Expenses Under ITA 8(1)(f)

3-192. Individual employees who are involved with the selling of property or the negotiating of contracts are permitted to deduct all expenses that can be considered necessary to the performance of their duties. As stated in ITA 8(1)(f), to be eligible to deduct salesperson's expenses, all of the following conditions must be met:

1. The salesperson must be required to pay his own expenses. The employer must sign Form T2200 certifying that this is the case. While the form does not have to be filed, it must be available if requested by the CRA.

2. The salesperson must be ordinarily required to carry on his duties away from the employer's place of business.

3. The salesperson must not be in receipt of a travel allowance that was not included in income.

4. The salesperson must receive at least part of his remuneration in the form of commissions or by reference to the volume of sales.

3-193. Items that can be deducted under ITA 8(1)(f) include:

- advertising and promotion
- meals with clients while traveling and client entertainment (subject to the previously noted 50 percent limit)
- lodging
- motor vehicle costs (other than CCA and interest)
- parking (which is not considered a motor vehicle expense)
- work space in the home costs (see the discussion in Paragraph 3-210).

- training costs
- transportation costs
- licences (e.g., for real estate sales)
- bonding and liability insurance premiums
- computers and office equipment (leased only - see following Paragraph)

3-194.   Except in the case of an automobile or aircraft, an employee who is a salesperson cannot deduct CCA or interest on funds borrowed to acquire capital assets. This means that if a salesperson purchases a computer to maintain customer records, he will not be able to deduct CCA on it. Alternatively, if the computer is leased, the lease payments are deductible.

3-195.   In order to deduct 50 percent of the cost of meals, the salesperson must be away from the municipality or metropolitan area where the employer's establishment is located for at least 12 hours. As is the case in the determination of business income, no deduction is permitted for membership fees for clubs or recreational facilities. A salesperson is permitted to deduct motor vehicle costs, supplies, salaries to an assistant, office rent and the cost of maintaining an office in his home. However, these costs can also be deducted by other types of employees and, as a consequence, will be dealt with later in this Chapter.

3-196.   The amount of qualifying expenses that can be deducted under ITA 8(1)(f) is limited to the commissions or other sales related revenues received during the year. This limitation does not, however, apply to CCA or interest on a motor vehicle or aircraft. These costs are deductible under ITA 8(1)(j) (see Paragraph 3-207). The deduction under ITA 8(1)(j) is not limited to commission income and, because it can be used in conjunction with ITA 8(1)(f), the salesperson's total deductions can exceed commission income.

Travel Expenses And Motor Vehicle Costs Under ITA 8(1)(h) and 8(1)(h.1)

3-197.   The conditions for deducting expenses under ITA 8(1)(h) and (h.1) are similar to those for deductions under ITA 8(1)(f), except that there is no requirement that some part of the employee's remuneration be in the form of commissions. The conditions are as follows:

1. The person must be required to pay his own travel and motor vehicle costs. As was the case with commission salespersons, the employee must have Form T2200, signed by the employer, certifying that this is the case.

2. The person must be ordinarily required to carry on his duties away from the employer's place of business.

3. The person must not be in receipt of an allowance for travel costs that was not included in income.

3-198.   There is one further condition that will be discussed more fully beginning at Paragraph 3-202. Both ITA 8(1)(h) and (h.1) state that, if a deduction is made as a salesperson under ITA 8(1)(f), no deduction can be made under either ITA 8(1)(h) or 8(1)(h.1).

3-199.   ITA 8(1)(h) provides for the deduction of travel costs such as accommodation, airline or rail tickets, taxi fares, and meals. As was the case with salespersons' expenses, only 50 percent of the cost of meals is deductible. Here again, the deductibility of meals is conditional on being away from the municipality or metropolitan area in which the employer's establishment is located for at least 12 hours.

3-200.   ITA 8(1)(h.1) provides for the deduction of motor vehicle costs, other than CCA and financing costs, when an employee uses his own vehicle to carry out employment duties. Note that these are the same costs that could be deducted by a salesperson under ITA 8(1)(f).

3-201.   These deductions can be claimed by any employee who meets the specified criteria. Further, they are not limited by employment income. The deductions can be used to create a net employment loss which, if not usable against other types of income in the current year, is subject to the carry forward provisions that are discussed in Chapter 11.

The Salesperson's Dilemma

3-202.   All of the travel and motor vehicle costs that a salesperson could deduct under ITA 8(1)(h) and (h.1) could also be deducted using ITA 8(1)(f). However, the use of ITA 8(1)(f) involves both good news and bad news:

- **Good News** The good news is that, if the salesperson uses ITA 8(1)(f), he can deduct expenses related to sales activity that are not deductible under any other provision (e.g., advertising and promotion).

- **Bad News** The bad news is that, if a salesperson uses ITA 8(1)(f), the amount that he can deduct is limited to the amount of commission income.

3-203.   At first glance, the logical course of action here would be to use ITA 8(1)(h) and (h.1) for the travel and motor vehicle costs (this deduction would not be limited by commission income), and to then use ITA 8(1)(f) to deduct the maximum amount of other items that are available under this latter Paragraph (subject to the commission income limitation). However, this cannot be done — the *Income Tax Act* prohibits the use of ITA 8(1)(h) or (h.1), if a deduction is made under ITA 8(1)(f).

3-204.   The result is, in situations where potential deductions under ITA 8(1)(f) exceed commission income, the salesperson must undertake an additional calculation to determine whether the total travel costs under ITA 8(1)(h) and (h.1) would be greater than the commission limited amount of deductions under ITA 8(1)(f). Should this be the case, the salesperson would deduct the larger amount that is available under ITA 8(1)(h) and (h.1). It is difficult to understand the tax policy goal that is achieved through this complexity.

3-205.   Note that this choice does not influence the amount of other deductions available to the salesperson. The amounts deducted under other ITA 8(1) Paragraphs will be unchanged by whether the salesperson uses ITA 8(1)(f) or the combination of ITA 8(1)(h) and (h.1).

Exercise Three - 16

Subject: Commission Salesperson Expenses

Mr. Morton McMaster is a commission salesperson. During 2017, his gross salary was $82,000 and he received $12,200 in commissions. During the year he had advertising costs of $8,000 and expenditures for entertainment of clients of $12,000. His travel costs for the year totaled $13,100. He is required to pay his own expenses and does not receive any allowance from his employer. What is Mr. McMaster's maximum expense deduction for 2017?

SOLUTION available in print and online Study Guide.

Other Expenses Of Performing Duties Under ITA 8(1)(i)

3-206.   ITA 8(1)(i) contains a list of other items that can be deducted in the determination of employment income by all employees. The major items included here are as follows (see IT-352R2 for more detailed coverage):

- Annual professional membership dues, if their payment was necessary to maintain a professional status recognized by statute.

- Union dues that are paid pursuant to the provisions of a collective agreement.

   In order to deduct the following amounts, the employee must be required to incur the costs under a contract of employment. This must be supported by Form T2200, signed by the employer and certifying that the requirement exists.

  - Office rent, including in the case of work space in the home, an appropriate portion of the rent paid for the taxpayer's residence (see Paragraph 3-210).

- Salary paid to an assistant or a substitute.

- The cost of supplies consumed in the performance of employment duties. Supplies in this context include stationery, long distance telephone calls and cell phone airtime, but not the basic monthly charge for a telephone or amounts paid to connect or license a cell phone. Note that IT-352R2 indicates that the term supplies includes maintenance and operating costs associated with a work space in the home.

Automobile And Aircraft Expenses Under ITA 8(1)(j)

3-207.   Under either ITA 8(1)(f) or ITA 8(1)(h.1) an employee can deduct the operating costs of an automobile used in employment duties. With respect to operating costs, this would include an appropriate share (based on the proportion the employment related kilometers are of the total kilometers driven) of such costs as fuel, maintenance, normal repair costs, insurance, and licensing fees.

3-208.   In addition, under ITA 8(1)(j), an employee can deduct CCA and interest costs on an automobile or an aircraft that is used in employment related activities. The deductible amounts for CCA are calculated in the same manner as they would be for a business. CCA would be calculated on a 30 percent declining balance basis on automobiles and a 25 percent declining balance basis on aircraft, while deductible interest would be based on actual amounts paid or payable. (See Chapter 5 for complete coverage of CCA calculations.) With respect to interest calculations, there is a difference in that, while a business can deduct accrued interest, an employee can only deduct interest that has been paid.

3-209.   However, there are limits on the amounts that can be deducted here for business purposes, and these limits are equally applicable to the calculation of employment income deductions. While these limits are discussed more completely in Chapter 6 on Business Income, we would note that for 2017 there is no deduction for CCA on the cost of an automobile in excess of $30,000 (before GST/HST/PST), that deductible interest is limited to $300 per month, and that deductible lease payments are limited to $800 per month (before GST/HST/PST). With respect to employees, their deduction would be based on the fraction of these costs, subject to the preceding limits, that reflects the portion of employment related kilometers included in the total kilometers driven.

Work Space In The Home Costs For Employees

3-210.   We have noted previously that any employee who is required by his employment contract to maintain a work space in the home can deduct a portion of the costs of maintaining or renting his home. Because of the obvious potential for abuse in this area, ITA 8(13) establishes fairly restrictive conditions with respect to the availability of this deduction. Costs of a work space in the home for an employee are only deductible when the work space is either:

- the place where the individual principally performs the duties of the office or employment, or

- used exclusively during the period in respect of which the amount relates for the purpose of earning income from the office or employment and used on a regular and continuous basis for meeting customers or other persons in the ordinary course of performing the duties of the office or employment.

3-211.   Once it is established that work space in the home costs are deductible, it becomes necessary to determine what kind of costs can be deducted. We have noted previously that, for employees, the only assets on which CCA and interest can be deducted are automobiles and aircraft (CCA only can be deducted on musical instruments). This means that no employee can deduct CCA or mortgage interest related to an office that is maintained in their residence. (Chapter 6 contains a comparison of deductible home office costs for employees and for self-employed contractors.)

3-212.   With respect to other costs, IT-352R2 indicates that under ITA 8(1)(i) an employee can deduct an appropriate portion (based on floor space used for the work space) of maintenance costs such as fuel and electricity, light bulbs, cleaning materials, and minor repairs. The cost of telephone and internet service are considered to be supplies and do not relate to the work space. Employees cannot deduct the monthly basic cost of a home telephone or the cost of fees for home internet service. Long distance charges that reasonably relate to employment income are deductible.

3-213.   For commissioned salespersons who can deduct work space in the home costs, IT-352R2 indicates that, in addition to the items listed in the preceding paragraph, an appropriate portion of property taxes and house insurance premiums can be deducted under ITA 8(1)(f). This means that, for commissioned salespersons, the deduction for work space in the home costs is split between ITA 8(1)(i) and (f). The insurance and property tax components could be limited by commission income as they can only be deducted under ITA 8(1)(f).

3-214.   If the home office is in rented property, the percentage of rent and any maintenance costs paid related to the work space are deductible.

3-215.   The amount deductible for work space in the home costs is limited to employment income after the deduction of all other employment expenses. Stated alternatively, work space in the home costs cannot be used to create or increase an employment loss. Any work space in the home costs that are not deductible in a year can be carried forward to the following year. In effect, there is an indefinite carry forward of these costs as they are rolled forward and become part of the work space in the home costs for the following year. This continues until there is sufficient employment income from the same employer to deduct them.

> **We suggest you work Self Study Problems Three-10 through 14 at this point.**

> **Additional Supplementary Self Study Problems Are Available Online.**

Key Terms Used In This Chapter

3-216.   The following is a list of the key terms used in this Chapter. These terms, and their meanings, are compiled in the Glossary located at the back of the Study Guide.

Allowance	Operating Cost Benefit
Bonus Arrangement	Prescribed Rate
Canadian Controlled Private Corporation	Public Corporation
Employee	Salary
Employer/Employee Relationship	Self-Employed Individual
Employment Income	Standby Charge
Fringe Benefits	Stock Option
Home Relocation Loan	Taxable Allowance
Imputed Interest	Taxable Benefit
In-The-Money	

References

3-217.   For more detailed study of the material in this Chapter, we would refer you to the following:

ITA 5	Income From Office Or Employment
ITA 6	Amounts To Be Included As Income From Office Or Employment
ITA 7	Agreement To Issue Securities To Employees
ITA 8	Deductions Allowed
ITA 80.4	Loans
ITA 80.5	Deemed Interest
ITR 4301	Interest Rates [Prescribed Rate Of Interest]
S2-F1-C1	Health And Welfare Trusts For Employees
S2-F3-C1	Payments from Employer to Employee
S2-F3-C2	Benefits And Allowances Received From Employment
S4-F2-C2	Business Use Of Home Expenses
IC 73-21R9	Claims for Meals and Lodging Expenses of Transport Employees
IT-63R5	Benefits, Including Standby Charge For An Automobile, From The Personal Use Of A Motor Vehicle Supplied By An Employer - After 1992
IT-91R4	Employment At Special Or Remote Work Locations
IT-99R5	Legal And Accounting Fees (Consolidated)
IT-103R	Dues Paid To A Union Or To A Parity Or Advisory Committee
IT-113R4	Benefits To Employees - Stock Options
IT-158R2	Employees' Professional Membership Dues
IT-202R2	Employees' Or Workers' Compensation
IT-352R2	Employee's Expenses, Including Work Space in Home Expenses
IT-421R2	Benefits To Individuals, Corporations And Shareholders From Loans Or Debt
IT-428	Wage Loss Replacement Plans
IT-504R2	Visual Artists And Writers (Consolidated)
IT-518R	Food, Beverages And Entertainment Expenses
IT-522R	Vehicle, Travel and Sales Expenses of Employees
IT-525R	Performing Artists
RC4110	CRA Guide - Employee Or Self-Employed?
T4044	Employment Expenses
T4130	Employers' Guide – Taxable Benefits and Allowances

Problems For Self Study (Online)

To provide practice in problem solving, there are Self Study and Supplementary Self Study problems available on the Companion Website.

Within the text we have provided an indication of when it would be appropriate to work each Self Study problem. The detailed solutions for Self Study problems can be found in the print and online Study Guide.

We provide the Supplementary Self Study problems for those who would like additional practice in problem solving. The detailed solutions for the Supplementary Self Study problems are available online, not in the Study Guide.

The .PDF file "Self Study Problems for Volume 1" on the Companion Website contains the following for Chapter 3:

- 14 Self Study problems,
- 5 Supplementary Self Study problems, and
- detailed solutions for the Supplementary Self Study problems.

Assignment Problems

(The solutions for these problems are only available in
the solutions manual that has been provided to your instructor.)

Assignment Problem Three - 1

(Bonus Arrangements)

Marques Ltd. is a Canadian public company with a taxation year that ends on November 30. Its shares are widely held. However, its senior management is made up of the four Marques brothers. As the year ending November 30, 2017 has been very successful for the Company, it is declaring a bonus to each of the four senior executives. All of the bonuses are declared on November 29, 2017. The details of these arrangements are as follows:

Cheeco Marques   Cheeco is the CEO of the Company. Because of his conservative lifestyle, he has little current need for funds. Given this, his bonus will be paid on March 31, 2023, his expected retirement date.

Zeppo Marques   Zeppo is the Vice President of Finance of the Company. While he is not pressed for current income, he would like to defer the personal payment of tax for as long as possible. Given this, his bonus will be paid on January 1, 2018.

Groucho Marques   Groucho is the Vice President of Human Resources of the Company. Unfortunately Groucho has been married and divorced six times, a fact that may be related to his hiring criteria for female associates. As a consequence, he is constantly in need of funds to maintain his required support payments. Based on this need, his bonus will be paid on December 1, 2017.

Harpo Marques   Harpo, who is in charge of information technology for the company, plans to leave the company in mid-2018. It has always been his dream to pursue a musical career and, to that end, he will need funds to carry him through the early stages of that endeavour. Given this, his bonus will be paid on September 1, 2018.

Required: For each of these brothers, indicate the taxation year in which the Company can deduct the bonus, as well as the taxation year in which the recipient will include it in his tax return.

Assignment Problem Three - 2
(Employee Vs. Self-Employed)

The Alberta Motor Association (the Payor) carried on a business of training and providing instruction to individuals who wanted to obtain vehicle operator's licenses. Mr. Bourne (the Appellant) had an arrangement with the Payor to provide such instruction.

The Payor had treated Mr. Bourne as an independent contractor from 2015 to 2017. Mr. Bourne was claiming that he was an employee of the Alberta Motor Association in 2017.

The facts in this case are as follows:

- the Payor operated as a membership based association; (admitted)
- the Payor had clients who wanted to obtain motor vehicle operator's licences; (admitted)
- the Appellant was hired as a driving instructor; (admitted)
- the Appellant entered into a written contract with the Payor which stated that the Appellant was a contractor and not an employee;
- the Appellant had been under contract with the Payor since 2015;
- the Appellant earned a set fee of $26 per hour;
- the Appellant also received fees for new bookings, student home pickups and a fuel subsidy;
- the Appellant invoiced the Payor;
- the Appellant did not receive any employee benefits such as health, dental or vacation pay;
- the Payor did not guarantee the Appellant a minimum amount of pay;
- the Payor's hours of operation were from 8:00AM to 5:00PM, Monday to Saturday;
- the Appellant set his own schedule of hours and days of work;
- the Appellant could work anytime between 8:00AM and 10:00PM, Monday to Sunday;
- the Appellant did not have a set minimum number of hours of work required;
- the Appellant kept a record of his hours worked;
- the Payor provided the Appellant with the names of the students;
- the Appellant contacted the students and scheduled the road instruction;
- the Payor provided the Appellant with an in-vehicle lesson guide;
- the Appellant chose the routes for the lessons;
- the Appellant was able to hire his own helper for administrative tasks;
- the Appellant provided the major tool which was the vehicle;
- the Payor provided vehicle signage, mirrors, traffic cones and an emergency brake;
- the Appellant paid for the installation and removal of the emergency brake provided by the Payor;
- the Appellant incurred operating expenses including vehicle expenses, liability insurance and a driver training endorsement;
- the Appellant's vehicle expenses included insurance, maintenance and fuel;
- the Payor's intention was that the Appellant was a contractor and not an employee;
- the Appellant had a GST number;
- the Appellant charged the Payor GST;
- the Appellant had operated his own taxi business since 1999;
- the Appellant maintained his own business books and records;
- the Appellant declared business income and business expenses on his 2015, 2016 and 2017 income tax returns.

Required: Should Mr. Bourne be viewed as an employee of the Alberta Motor Association or, alternatively, an independent contractor? List all of the factors that should be considered in reaching a conclusion.

Assignment Problem Three - 3
(Employer Provided Vs. Employee Owned Car)

Jerry Field was hired by Larson Wholesalers at the end of 2016 to fill an executive position in the company. He is scheduled to begin work on January 2, 2017. Larson Wholesalers plans to transfer him to their Hong Kong office after two years.

As part of his compensation package, Jerry has considered having the Company provide him with a car for his personal use. He does not require the vehicle for his employment duties and, as a consequence, it will be used for personal activities only.

Jerry anticipates that he will drive the car about 80,000 kilometers in both 2017 and 2018.

He is considering two different cars and has collected the following information on them:

	Lexus ES	Lexus LS
Purchase Price	$45,000	$100,000
Estimated Operating Costs Per Kilometer	$0.30	$0.40
Estimated Trade In At The End Of 2 Years	$20,000	$40,000

The Company has agreed to provide an additional $100,000 in compensation and they offer Jerry the following alternatives.

Option 1   They will purchase either car and allow Jerry to use it for the calendar years 2017 and 2018. If Jerry prefers the Lexus ES, the Company will provide a signing bonus of $55,000, the difference in the cost of the two cars. The bonus will be paid when the car is delivered on January 2, 2017.

Option 2   They will provide Jerry with a $100,000 signing bonus. This bonus will be paid on January 2, 2017. He will use the funds to purchase one of the cars personally.

If the Company buys either car, Jerry will pay his own operating costs and the Company will take possession of the car after the 2 years.

Jerry's combined federal/provincial marginal tax rate is expected to be 48 percent in both 2017 and 2018.

Assume that the prescribed operating cost benefit will be $0.25 per kilometer for both 2017 and 2018.

Required: Advise Jerry as to which option he should choose if decides that he wants:

A. the Lexus ES.
B. the Lexus LS.

In both parts of this question your advice should be based on undiscounted cash outflows. Ignore GST and HST considerations in your solution.

Assignment Problem Three - 4
(Taxable Automobile Benefits)

Ms. Sharon Herzog works for a large, publicly traded employer. As she is required to travel in her work for that employer, the company provides her with an automobile.

Sharon is allowed to use the vehicle for personal activities. However, there are some periods during the year when she does not need the car for employment related activities. During these periods she is required to return the car to her employer's premises.

The car that she will use was purchased by her employer in 2015 for $45,200, including $5,200 in HST. During the years 2015 and 2016, the company deducted maximum CCA.

During 2017, Sharon drove the car a total of 37,000 kilometers. The company pays all of her operating costs which, during 2017 totaled $11,340.

Required: Indicate the minimum taxable benefit that would be allocated to Sharon in each of the following independent Cases:

Case 1 Sharon has use of the car for 9 months of the year. Personal use during the year totals 6,000 kilometers.

Case 2 Sharon has use of the car for 11 months of the year. Personal use during the year totals 28,000 kilometers.

Case 3 Sharon has use of the car for 7 months of the year. Employment use during the year totals 18,600 kilometers.

Assignment Problem Three - 5
(Taxable Automobile Benefits)

It is the policy of Dorsey Ltd. to provide automobiles to four of their senior executives. The cars may be used for both employment related activities, as well as personal travel. When it is not being used by the employee, the Company requires the cars to be returned to the Company's garage.

For the current year, the details regarding the use of these cars is as follows:

Ms. Marianne Dorsey Marianne is the president of the Company. She is provided with a Bentley Flying Spur Sedan. The Company paid $185,000 for this car two years ago. During the current year, the car was driven 53,000 kilometers, of which 18,000 could be considered to be employment related travel. Operating costs, all of which were paid by the Company, totaled $27,500 for the year. The car was available to Marianne for 11 months of the year.

Mr. John Dorsey John is the vice president in charge of finance. His car is a BMW 528 purchased by the Company for $71,500. During the 10 months that the car was available to John during the current year, he drove a total of 93,000 kilometers, of which 22,000 involved personal travel. Operating costs, all of which were paid by the Company, total $18,600.

Ms. Misty Dorsey Misty is the vice president in charge of design. She is provided with an Infiniti Q60 IPL which the Company leases for $620 per month. This amount includes a $100 per month payment for insurance. The car is available to Misty throughout the current year, during which she drives a total of 51,000 kilometers. Of this total, only 14,000 kilometers involve employment travel. Operating costs, all of which were paid by the Company, total $11,300. Because of her extensive personal use of the vehicle, Misty pays the Company $200 per month.

Mr. Saul Dorsey Saul is the vice president in charge of marketing for the Company. He is provided with a Tesla Model S which the Company leases for $1,200 per month. No insurance is provided for through this payment. During the current year, Saul drives the car a total of 31,200 kilometers, of which 29,500 are employment related. The operating costs average $0.25 per kilometer and are paid for by the Company. The car is available to Jean for 8 months during the current year.

Required: Calculate the minimum taxable benefit that will accrue to each of these executives as the result of having the cars supplied by the Company. Ignore all GST/PST/HST implications.

Assignment Problem Three - 6
(Loans To Employees)

Fred Ethridge is a valued employee of a large Canadian company. He is in the process of negotiating a new compensation package for the coming year. As he is looking to purchase a new residence, one of the alternatives that is being considered is an interest free loan that would be used to purchase this property.

Fred needs $350,000 to comfortably finance this purchase. As he has an excellent credit rating, the Royal Bank is prepared to extend the $350,000 on a 5 year, closed mortgage at a rate of 4.75 percent.

The company has indicated that they will extend a $350,000, 5 year, interest free loan. However, they will only do so if the cost of providing the loan has the same after tax cost as providing additional salary.

The Company is subject to tax at a combined federal/provincial rate of 29 percent. When funds are available, the Company has alternative investment opportunities that earn a pre-tax rate of 10 percent. Because of Fred's current high salary, any additional compensation will be taxed at a combined federal/provincial rate of 49 percent.

Assume that the prescribed rate for the current year is 2 percent.

Required:

A. Determine the tax consequences to Fred and the cost to the Company, in terms of lost after-tax earnings, of providing Fred with a $350,000 interest free loan for the first year of the loan.

B. Determine the amount of additional salary that could be provided to Fred for the same after tax cost to the Company that you calculated in Part A.

C. Which alternative would you recommend that Fred accept? Explain your conclusion.

Assignment Problem Three - 7
(Loans To Employees)

Ms. Teresa Monson is employed by Elmwood Inc. She has asked the employer for a $300,000 interest free loan that will be used to acquire a summer cottage in Huntsville, Ontario. The cottage will be used exclusively as a recreational property. As she is a highly valued employee, Elmwood Inc. is considering her request.

Ms. Monson can acquire a regular mortgage at a rate of 4.5 percent. Assume that the relevant prescribed rate is 2 percent for all periods that the employee loan will be outstanding.

Ms. Monson's tax rate on any additional income is 46 percent. Elmwood Inc. has alternative investment opportunities that earn a before tax rate of 7 percent. Elmwood Inc. is subject to a tax rate of 28 percent on additional amounts of income.

Required: Evaluate Ms. Monson's suggestion of providing her with an interest free loan in lieu of salary from the point of view of the cost to Elmwood Inc.

Assignment Problem Three - 8
(Employee Stock Options)

Floretta Sutphin has worked for several years as an employee of a Canadian public company. In 2015, Floretta was granted options to acquire 2,000 of the company's shares at a price of $19 per share. At that time, the shares were trading at $17 per share.

In February, 2016, with the shares trading at $27 per share, Floretta exercises 1,000 of the options. During the remainder of the year, the shares continue to increase in value, reaching a value of $32 per share in December. At this time, Floretta exercises the remaining 1,000 options.

In the second quarter of 2017, reflecting poor earnings results during the first quarter of the year, the value of the shares declines to $30 per share. At this point, Floretta sells all 2,000 of her shares at this price.

Required:

A. Indicate the tax effect of the transactions that took place during each of the years 2015, 2016, and 2017. Your answer should include the effect on both Net Income For Tax Purposes and Taxable Income. Where relevant, identify these effects separately.

B. How would your answer change if the shares had been trading at $22 per share at the time that the options were issued in 2015?

C. How would your answers to both Part A and Part B change if Floretta's employer was a Canadian controlled private company?

Assignment Problem Three - 9
(Employee Stock Options)

Opting Inc. has a very generous stock option plan that allows all of their long term employees to participate. Sandra has worked for the Company for over 10 years and has participated in this plan on a regular basis. With regards to the last options granted to her, the following information is relevant:

• On January 1, 2015, Sandra was granted options to acquire 275 of the Company's shares at a price of $15.00 per share.

• At a later point in time, when Sandra exercises these options, the Company's shares have a fair market value of $17.50 per share.

• On December 1, 2017, all of the shares acquired with the options are sold.

Required: Indicate the tax effect on Sandra of the transactions that took place during 2015, 2016, and 2017 under each of the following independent Cases. Your answer should include the effect on both Net Income For Tax Purposes and Taxable Income. Where relevant, identify these effects separately.

Case A   Opting is a Canadian controlled private company. At the time the options were granted, the Company's shares had a fair market value of $16.00 per share. The options are exercised on February 28, 2015. When the shares are sold, the proceeds of disposition are $20.25 per share.

Case B   Opting is a Canadian public company. At the time the options were granted, the Company's shares were trading at $16.00 per share. The options are exercised on February 28, 2015. When the shares are sold, the proceeds of disposition are $16.00 per share.

Case C   Opting is a Canadian public company. At the time the options were granted, the Company's shares were trading at $14.00 per share. The options are exercised on

July 1, 2016. When the shares are sold, the proceeds of disposition are $19.75 per share.

Case D   Opting is a Canadian controlled private company. At the time the options were granted, the Company's shares had a fair market value of $14.00 per share. The options are exercised on July 1, 2016. When the shares are sold, the proceeds of disposition are $21.50 per share.

Assignment Problem Three - 10
(Employment Income)

On January 2, 2017, Ms. Shirley Kantor moves from London, Ontario, to Thunder Bay, Ontario, in order to begin employment with Northern Enterprises Ltd. (NEL). Her salary for the year was $142,000. NEL withheld the following amounts from her earnings:

Federal And Provincial Income Tax	$32,500
Registered Pension Plan Contributions	
(NEL Makes A Matching Contribution)	3,200
EI Premiums	836
CPP Contributions	2,564
United Way Donations	450
Professional Association Dues	1,250

Other Information:

1. Shirley's moving expenses total $6,800. NEL reimbursed Shirley for 100 percent of these costs.

2. For the year ending December 31, 2017, Shirley was awarded a bonus of $32,000. Of this total, $25,000 was paid during 2017, with the remainder payable in January, 2018.

3. NEL provided Shirley with a car to be used in her employment activities and paid the operating costs for the year that totalled $8,100. The cost of the car was $39,550, including HST of $4,550. The car was available to Shirley throughout 2017. She drove a total of 63,000 kilometers. This included 8,000 kilometers of personal use.

4. In negotiating her new position with NEL, Shirley had asked for a $50,000 interest free loan as one of her benefits. NEL's human resources department indicated that the CEO would not approve any employee loans. However, they agreed to advance $50,000 of her 2018 salary as of November 1, 2017.

5. In her employment related travels, Shirley has accumulated over 100,000 Aeroplan points. During 2017, she and her partner Diane used 50,000 of these points for a weekend flight to New York City. If she had purchased them, the tickets would have cost a total of $940.

6. NEL provided Shirley with the following additional benefits:

Allowance For Acquiring Business Clothing	$4,800
Squash Club Membership (No Employment Related Usage)	2,800
Financial Advisor Fees	1,200

7. Shirley's previous employer was a Canadian controlled private corporation. In 2016, she was granted options to buy 500 of the company's shares at $20 per share. This option price was higher than the estimated fair market value of the company's shares at the time the options were granted. On January 2, 2017, Shirley exercised these options. At this time the fair market value of the shares was $28 per share. Shirley immediately sells the shares for $28 per share.

8. Shirley was required by her employer to acquire a laptop computer to be used in her employment duties. At the beginning of 2017, she purchased a computer at a cost of $1,356, including HST of $256. During 2017, her expenditures for computer related supplies totalled $150.

Required   Determine Shirley's net employment income for the year ending December 31, 2017.

Assignment Problem Three - 11

(Commission Income And Work Space In Home)

Jerald Gilreath is an employee of a Canadian publicly traded company. He works in their Calgary office and lives downtown in a high-rise condominium. In addition to his 2017 base salary of $175,000, he earns commissions of $21,460.

Other employment related information is as follows:

1. Jerald's employer requires him to pay all of his employment related expenses, as well as provide his own office space. Jerald has the required Form T2200 from his employer.

2. Jerald's travel costs for 2017, largely airline tickets, food, and lodging, total $26,900. This includes $11,300 spent on meals while traveling for his employer. This meal total includes meals with clients of $4,300.

3. Jerald is a member of his employer's registered pension plan. During 2017, $4,100 was withheld from his salary as a contribution to this plan. His employer made a matching contribution of $4,100.

4. During 2017, Jerald pays dues to his professional association of $422.

5. During 2017, Jerald was billed a total of $10,500 by his golf club in Calgary. Of this amount, $2,850 was the annual membership fee, with the remaining amount for meals and drinks with clients. He uses the club only when he is with clients.

6. For his employment related travel, Jerald drives a car that he purchased on January 1, 2017 for $42,000, including GST. During 2017, he drives 52,000 kilometers, of which 43,000 are employment related. Jerald had financed the car with a loan from a local bank and, during 2017, he had paid interest of $2,750.

   The costs of operating the car during 2017 were $10,920. He has been advised by his accountant that, if the car were used 100 percent for employment related activities, the maximum CCA for 2017 would be $4,500.

7. Jerald uses 25 percent of his personal residence as an office. During 2017, the costs associated with his home were as follows:

Interest Payments On Mortgage	$ 9,100
Property Taxes	3,750
Utilities	1,925
Insurance	1,060
Furnace, Wiring And Foundation Repairs	4,200
Total	$20,035

8. At the beginning of 2017, Jerald's employer grants him options to buy 500 of the Company's shares at a price of $17.50 per share. This was the market price of the shares at the time the options were granted. During July, 2017, when the shares are trading at $19.75 per share, he exercises all of these options. In order to buy Christmas gifts for his family, he sells 100 of these shares in early December, 2017. The proceeds are $20.50 per share.

9. His employer has a policy of giving all employees gifts to promote employee loyalty and help local businesses. During 2017, Jerald received the following gifts:

    - A weekend for him and his wife at a local hotel. The value of this gift was $425.
    - A $400 gift certificate at a local electronics/hardware store.
    - A basket of fruit, nuts, and cheeses, with a value of $225.

10. During 2017, Jerald purchased tickets to Calgary Flames games for $1,920. He used these tickets to attend the games with key personnel from important clients. He also purchased tickets to a Montreal Canadiens game in Montreal for $864. He used these tickets to attend the game with a prospective client located in Montreal.

Required: Calculate Jerald's minimum net employment income for the 2017 taxation year. Ignore GST and PST considerations.

Assignment Problem Three - 12
(Employment Income - No Commissions)

Mr. Jason Bond has been employed for many years as a graphic illustrator in Kamloops, British Columbia. His employer is a large publicly traded Canadian company. During 2017, his gross salary was $82,500. In addition, he was awarded a $20,000 bonus to reflect his outstanding performance during the year. As he was in no immediate need of additional income, he arranged with his employer that none of this bonus would be paid until 2022, the year of his expected retirement.

Other Information:

For the 2017 taxation year, the following items were relevant.

1. Mr. Bond's employer withheld the following amounts from his income:

Federal Income Tax	$16,000
Employment Insurance Premiums	836
Canada Pension Plan Contributions	2,564
United Way Donations	2,000
Registered Pension Plan Contributions	3,200
Payments For Personal Use Of Company Car	3,600

2. During the year, Mr. Bond is provided with an automobile owned by his employer. The cost of the automobile was $47,500. Mr. Bond drove the car a total of 10,000 kilometers during the year, of which only 4,000 kilometers were related to the business of his employer. The automobile was used by Mr. Bond for ten months of the year. During the other two months, he was out of the country he was required to leave the automobile with one of the other employees of the corporation.

3. During the year, the corporation paid Mega Financial Planners a total of $1,500 for providing counseling services to Mr. Bond with respect to his personal financial situation.

4. In order to assist Mr. Bond in purchasing a ski chalet, the corporation provided him with a five year loan of $150,000. The loan was granted on October 1 at an interest rate of 1 percent. Mr. Bond paid the corporation a total of $375 in interest for 2017 on January 20, 2018. Assume that, at the time the loan was granted and throughout the remainder of the year, the relevant prescribed rate was 2 percent.

5. Mr. Bond was required to pay professional dues of $1,800 during the year.

6. On June 6, 2017, when Mr. Bond exercised his stock options to buy 1,000 shares of his employer's common stock at a price of $15 per share, the shares were trading at $18 per share. When the options were issued, the shares were trading at $12 per share. During December, 2017, the shares were sold for $20 per share.

Required: Calculate Mr. Bond's minimum net employment income for the year ending December 31, 2017. Provide reasons for omitting items that you have not included in your calculations. Ignore GST and PST considerations.

Assignment Problem Three - 13
(Alternative Employment Offers)

For several years, Alexandra Blanco has represented several companies as an independent sales representative. As she has been very effective for her clients, two of these companies, Mega Inc. and Tetra Ltd., are interested in hiring her as a full time employee. Both of the employment offers would require Alexandra to begin service as of January, 2017. However, the offers from the two corporations differ significantly in the form and content of their proposed compensation.

MEGA INC. OFFER The offer from Mega Inc. contains the following provisions:

- She would be paid a salary of $280,000 per year. No commissions would be paid on her sales.
- Mega will provide an allowance of $35,000 per year to cover hotel, meals while travelling, and airline costs. The employer believes that the CRA will consider this allowance to be reasonable in the circumstances.
- No allowance or reimbursement will be provided for advertising and promotion expenses.
- Mega will provide her with an automobile for 12 months of the year which they would purchase for $45,000. The employer will pay all of the operating costs for the automobile.
- Mega will provide Alexandra with a $250,000 interest free loan for a period of 5 years. Alexandra will be investing all of these funds in publicly traded securities.
- Mega will provide Alexandra with a group disability insurance plan for which the company will pay all of the premiums. The plan provides periodic benefits that compensate for lost employment income. This will cost Mega $4,500 per year.
- Mega will provide Alexandra with a $800,000 face value life insurance policy. All of the premiums, which will total $2,900 per year, will be paid by Mega.

TETRA LTD. OFFER The offer from Tetra Ltd. contains the following provisions:

- She would be paid a salary of $190,000, plus a commission on all of her sales. Alexandra estimates that these commissions will total $90,000 during 2017.
- Tetra will reimburse all of her hotel, meal while travelling, and airline costs.
- No allowance or reimbursement will be provided for advertising and promotion expenses.
- While Tetra will not provide Alexandra with an automobile, it will provide an allowance of $1,800 per month to use her own automobile for her employment activities. Alexandra bought her car last year for $30,000. She estimates that the total cost of using her automobile for both personal and employment activities during 2017 will be as follows:

Operating Costs	$16,800
Capital Cost Allowance (Tax Depreciation) (100%)	4,500
Financing Costs	2,200
Total	$23,500

- Tetra will provide Alexandra with a group disability insurance plan for which the company will pay all of the premiums. The plan provides periodic benefits that compensate for lost employment income. This will cost Tetra $5,000 per year.
- Tetra will provide Alexandra with a $1,500,000 face value life insurance policy. All of the premiums, which will total $4,200 per year, will be paid by Tetra.

Other Information

The following information is applicable to either of the alternative offers.

1. Alexandra estimates that her employment related expenses during 2017 would be as follows:

Travel Costs (Hotel And Airline Costs)	$24,000
Travel Costs (Meals)	10,500
Advertising And Promotion	26,000

2. Whether it is the employer's automobile or her own personal vehicle, she would use the car throughout 2017. She expects to drive this vehicle a total of 48,000 kilometers during 2017, with 32,000 of these kilometers required by her employment activities.

3. Assume that the prescribed rate is 2 percent throughout 2017.

Required:

A. Based on the estimates made by Alexandra, calculate Alexandra's minimum 2017 net employment income for each of the two offers. Ignore PST and GST considerations.

B. Discuss the factors that Alexandra should consider in deciding between the two alternatives.

Assignment Problem Three - 14
(Comprehensive Employment Income)

Ms. Matilda Bracken is a Certified Financial Planner (CFP) with many years of successful experience. In 2016, she decided that she was not adequately appreciated in her current position with a large financial institution in Windsor, Ontario. Given this, she resigned on November 1, 2016.

After several months of investigation, she decided to take a position with Retirement Planners Ltd. (RPL), a Canadian controlled private corporation located in London, Ontario. She commenced working for RPL on May 1, 2017.

She owned a home in Windsor which she had acquired several years ago for $375,000. Because of the depressed real estate market in this area, she was eventually forced to sell the property for $275,000 in October, 2017, resulting in a $100,000 loss on this property.

Because of the uncertainty surrounding the sale of her Windsor property, she moved into an apartment when she arrived in London on May 1, 2017. The apartment was rented on a monthly basis until November 30, 2017. After she accepts an offer to purchase her Windsor house, she finds a home in London that she purchases on November 1, 2017 for $420,000. She moves into this new home on December 1, 2017.

Other Information:

Other information relevant to 2017 is as follows:
1. Because of her strong professional reputation, RPL paid her a signing bonus of $12,000. The signing bonus was paid on June 1, 2017.

2. During the period May 1, 2017 through December 31, 2017, Matilda earned salary of $124,000. Of these earnings, $120,125 was paid during this period with the remainder paid in the first pay period of 2018. The Company withheld the following amounts from her salary:

Income Taxes	$18,650
CPP	2,564
EI	836
RPP Contributions	3,700
Payment For Personal Use Of Automobile	880

3. RPL contributed $3,500 on Matilda's behalf to the Company's RPP.

4. RPL provides group medical coverage to all of its employees. The private health plan premiums paid by RPL on Matilda's behalf cost $562 for the year.

5. On December 12, 2017, a bonus of $10,600 was accrued for Matilda. Matilda received $5,300 of this bonus on December 29, 2017, with the remainder being paid on January 17, 2018.

6. During the year, Matilda received two non-cash gifts, a birthday gift worth $350 and a Christmas gift worth $300.

7. Because of the need to invest some of her additional income, RPL provided Matilda with financial counseling services. The value of these services was $1,200.

8. In order to assist her move, RPL agreed to compensate her for one-half of the $100,000 loss on the sale of her Windsor home. The $50,000 payment was made on December 1, 2017.

9. In order to help Matilda with financing her new London residence, RPL provided her with a $220,000 interest free housing loan. The funds are provided to Matilda on November 1, 2017. Assume that the prescribed rate for all of 2017 is 2 percent.

10. RPL has a stock option plan for its employees. Under this plan, employees are permitted to acquire a limited number of option shares at 10 percent below their fair market value on December 1 of each year. The company hires valuators to determine the fair market value at each of those dates. Matilda acquires 200 shares on December 1, 2017 for cash of $7,200. On December 15, she sells 100 of these shares for $4,100.

11. Matilda paid $1,600 in CFP dues in 2017. RPL's policy is to reimburse 50 percent of such professional dues. RPL reimbursed her $800 in December, 2017.

12. RPL provides its professional employees with a membership in the London Curling Club. They believe this is a useful venue for entertaining clients of the Company. The cost of this annual membership was $1,300.

13. RPL provides Matilda with a vehicle that was purchased in 2017 for $45,200, including HST. The vehicle was used by Matilda for all months during the period May 1, 2017 through December 31, 2017. During this period, she drove the vehicle a total of 52,000 kilometers, of which 40,000 were related to her employment duties. RPL pays all operating and maintenance costs, a total of $8,900 during the period that Matilda used the car. RPL withheld $110 per month from her salary to pay for her personal use of the vehicle.

14. Matilda's new job requires her to meet with clients outside of regular office hours throughout the week. RPL will sign form T2200 stating that she is required to pay for certain employment expenses without reimbursement and use a portion of her home for work.

    Matilda has set aside a separate room in her apartment to be used exclusively to meet with clients. She used this office space between May 1 and November 30, 2017. This home office occupied 150 square feet of the 1,250 square feet available in her apartment. The home office in the residence she moved into on December 1, 2017 will not be available for use until 2018. RPL has agreed to let Matilda use head office space as needed during December.

Home office related costs are as follows:

Monthly Rent	$2,200
Office Furniture	3,400
Computer Purchase	896
Stationery And Office Supplies Purchased	147
Monthly Phone Line Charge (For 7 Months)	210
Employment Related Long Distance Calls (For 7 Months)	110
Electricity Charge (For 7 Months)	350
Paint For Apartment	165
Property Insurance (7 Months)	175

15. Matilda received an allowance of $325 per month for 7 months to cover the costs of maintaining a workspace in her home.

Required: Determine Matilda's net employment income for 2017.

CHAPTER 4

Taxable Income And Tax Payable For Individuals

Budget Changes For 2017

The federal government delivered its 2017 budget on March 22, 2017. It has been referred to as the "stay the course" budget in that it did not contain any major new tax initiatives, either on the revenue or the deductions side.

It did, however, contain a fairly large number of what might be referred to as "tweaks" to the existing tax rules. Several of these are related to the tax credits that are discussed in this Chapter. Prior to the current Liberal government, the Conservative government had made extensive use of tax credits for what many believed to be political purposes. Every budget seemed to introduce one or two new credits, resulting in credits for volunteer firemen, volunteer search and rescue workers, as well as a textbook credit that had nothing to do with the purchase of textbooks.

The 2016 budget, the current government's first, started the process of changing this focus on tax credits for individuals. The 2016 budget provided for the elimination of the education and textbook credits, as well as the children's fitness credit and the children's arts credit. The process continued in the 2017 budget with the elimination of the infirm dependant over 17 credit, as well as the family caregiver credit.

In a move we applaud, the government has replaced the regular caregiver credit with a much more rational and easy to understand provision which incorporates the previous version of the caregiver credit, along the repealed family caregiver and infirm dependant over 17 credits. Anyone who has struggled with the interrelationships between the replaced credits would be aware that this was a situation that was likely incomprehensible to many of the people who were supposed to benefit from the credits. The new Canada caregiver credit, with its single income threshold, represents a major improvement in tax legislation. Detailed attention will be given to this change in this Chapter.

In addition to the changes with respect to tax credits, the government has also eliminated the home relocation loan deduction. However, this change does not come into effect until 2018. As a consequence, it will have not impact on the content of this Chapter and the related problem material.

Introduction

4-1. As discussed in Chapter 1, Taxable Income is Net Income For Tax Purposes, less a group of deductions that are specified in Division C of Part I of the *Income Tax Act*. Also noted in the Chapter 1 material was the fact that Net Income For Tax Purposes is made up of several different income components. These components are employment income, business and property income, taxable capital gains, other sources, and other deductions.

4-2. Some tax texts defer any coverage of Taxable Income and Tax Payable until all of the income components that make up Net Income For Tax Purposes have been given detailed consideration. Despite the fact that the only component of Taxable Income that we have covered to this point is employment income, we decided to introduce material on Taxable Income and Tax Payable for individuals at this point in the text.

Major Reason The major reason for this approach is that it allows us to introduce the many tax credits that go into the calculation of Tax Payable at an earlier stage in the text. We believe that this enhances the presentation of the material in subsequent Chapters on business income, property income, and taxable capital gains. For example, in our discussion of property income, we can deal with after tax rates of return, as well as provide a meaningful discussion of the economics of the dividend gross up/tax credit procedures.

Other Reasons Other reasons for this organization of the material are more peda-gogical in nature.

- Leaving the coverage of tax credits until after the completion of the material on all of the components of Taxable Income places this complex subject in the last weeks of most one semester tax courses. This can create significant difficulties for students.

- By introducing Taxable Income and Tax Payable at this earlier stage in the text, instructors who wish to do so can make more extensive use of the tax software programs provided with the text.

4-3. Since a significant portion of the material on Taxable Income and Tax Payable can be best understood after covering the other types of income that make up Net Income For Tax Purposes, we require a second Chapter dealing with the subject of Taxable Income and Tax Payable. In addition, a few of the credits that are available in the calculation of Tax Payable require an understanding of additional aspects of business income, property income, and taxable capital gains. Given this, Chapter 11 is devoted to completing the necessary coverage of Taxable Income and Tax Payable for individuals. The determination of Taxable Income and Tax Payable for corporations is covered in Chapters 12 and 13. The determination of Taxable Income and Tax Payable for trusts is covered in Chapter 19.

Taxable Income Of Individuals

Available Deductions

4-4. The deductions that are available in calculating the Taxable Income of an individual can be found in Division C of Part I of the *Income Tax Act*. As indicated in the introduction to this Chapter, some of these deductions will be dealt with in this Chapter. However, coverage of the more complex items is deferred until Chapter 11. The available deductions, along with a description of their coverage in this text, are as follows:

ITA 110(1)(d), (d.01), and (d.1) - Employee Stock Options Our basic coverage of stock options and stock option deductions is included in Chapter 3. This coverage will not be repeated here.

ITA 110(1)(f) - Deductions For Payments This deduction, which is available for social assistance and workers' compensation received, is covered beginning in Para-graph 4-6.

ITA 110(1)(j) - Home Relocation Loan   We refer to this deduction in Chapter 3 as it is related to a taxable benefit that is included in employment income. However, more detailed coverage is found in this Chapter beginning in Paragraph 4-9. Note that this deduction is repealed for 2018 and subsequent years.

ITA 110.2 - Lump Sum Payments   ITA 110.2 provides a deduction for certain lump-sum payments (e.g., an amount received as a court-ordered termination benefit and included in employment income). It provides the basis for taxing this amount as though it were received over several taxation years (i.e., income averaging). Because of its limited applicability, no additional coverage is given to this provision.

ITA 110.6 - Lifetime Capital Gains Deduction   The provisions related to this deduction are very complex and require a fairly complete understanding of capital gains. As a consequence, this deduction is covered in Chapter 11.

ITA 110.7 - Residing In Prescribed Zone (Northern Residents Deductions)   These deductions, which are limited to individuals living in prescribed regions of northern Canada, are covered in Paragraph 4-13.

ITA 111 - Losses Deductible   This is a group of deductions that is available for carrying forward or carrying back various types of losses. The application of these provisions can be complex and requires a fairly complete understanding of business income, property income, and capital gains. Coverage of this material is deferred until Chapter 11. Additional coverage of corporate loss carry overs is found in Chapter 12.

Ordering Of Deductions

4-5.   ITA 111.1 specifies, to some degree, the order in which individuals must subtract the various deductions that may be available in the calculation of Taxable Income. As our coverage of these deductions is not complete in this Chapter, we will defer coverage of this ordering provision until Chapter 11.

Deductions For Payments - ITA 110(1)(f)

4-6.   ITA 110(1)(f) provides for the deduction of certain amounts that have been included in the calculation of Net Income For Tax Purposes. The items listed here are:

- amounts that are exempt from tax in Canada by virtue of a provision in a tax treaty or agreement with another country;

- workers' compensation payments received as a result of injury or death;

- income from employment with a prescribed international organization; and

- social assistance payments made on the basis of a means, needs, or income test and included in the taxpayer's income.

4-7.   At first glance, this seems to be a fairly inefficient way of not taxing these items. For example, if the government does not intend to tax social assistance payments, why go to the trouble of including them in Net Income For Tax Purposes, then deducting an equivalent amount in the calculation of Taxable Income?

4-8.   There is, however, a reason for this. There are a number of items that influence an individual's tax obligation that are altered on the basis of the individual's Net Income For Tax Purposes. For example, we will find later in this Chapter that the amount of the age tax credit is reduced by the individual's Net Income For Tax Purposes in excess of a specified amount (a.k.a., the threshold amount or the income threshold). In order to ensure that income tests of this type are applied on an equitable basis, amounts are included in Net Income For Tax Purposes, even in situations where the ultimate intent is not to assess tax on these amounts.

Home Relocation Loan - ITA 110(1)(j)

> **BYRD/CHEN NOTE** As indicated in our note on the 2017 budget, this deduction from Taxable Income will not be available after 2017.

4-9. As discussed in Chapter 3, if an employer provides an employee with a loan on which interest is payable at a rate that is less than the prescribed rate, a taxable benefit must be included in the employee's income. Under ITA 80.4(1), the benefit will be measured as the difference between the interest that would have been paid on the loan at the prescribed rate and the amount of interest that was actually paid. This taxable benefit must be included in income, even in situations where the loan qualifies as a "home relocation loan".

4-10. A home relocation loan is defined in ITA 248(1) as a loan made by an employer to an employee in order to assist him in acquiring a dwelling. This dwelling acquisition must be related to employment at a new work location, and the new dwelling must be at least 40 kilometres closer to the new work location. As is discussed more completely in Chapter 9, the distance is the same 40 kilometre test that is used in determining whether or not an individual can deduct moving expenses.

4-11. Provided the loan qualifies as a home relocation loan, ITA 110(1)(j) provides a deduction in the calculation of the individual's Taxable Income equal to the lesser of:

- **The Benefit Included In Income Under ITA 80.4(1)** As presented in detail in Chapter 3, the benefit on employer provided loans is determined by applying the prescribed rate to the principal amount of the loan on a quarterly basis. The amount of the benefit is then reduced by any interest payments made by the employee for that year which are paid in the year, or within 30 days of the year end. When the loan is a home purchase loan or a home relocation loan, ITA 80.4(4) limits the benefit to the amount that would be determined by applying the prescribed rate that was applicable when the loan was made to the principal amount on an annual basis. This limit is in place for the first five years the loan is outstanding.

- **The Amount That Would Have Been Calculated Under ITA 80.4(1) On A $25,000 Loan** This deduction is calculated using the same rules that are applicable to housing loans in general, except for the fact that:

  (1) it is based on $25,000 rather than the actual amount of the loan, and
  (2) the amount is not reduced by interest payments made by the employee.

  By not deducting interest payments made by the employee, this effectively bases the calculation of the amount on an interest free loan of $25,000. If this calculation is larger than the benefit included in income, the deduction will equal the taxable benefit and the net effect on Taxable Income will be nil.

4-12. This deduction is available for a period of up to 5 years. However, as the deduction is designed to offset a benefit that is included in employment income, the deduction will not be available after the loan has been paid off and there is no longer an employment income inclusion. While the calculation of the benefit and the deduction can be based on the number of days in each quarter, an example in IT-421R2, Benefits to Individuals, Corporations and Shareholders from Loans or Debt, makes it clear that treating each calendar quarter as one-quarter of a year is an acceptable procedure.

> **EXAMPLE** On July 1, 2017, Janice Brock receives an interest free loan from her employer that is provided to assist her with acquiring a home in a new work location. The amount of the loan is $150,000 and it must be repaid on June 30, 2019. Assume the prescribed rate throughout 2017 is 1 percent.
>
> **ANALYSIS** Janice will have a taxable benefit of $750 [(2/4)(1%)($150,000)], an amount that will be included in her Net Income For Tax Purposes. She will have an offsetting deduction of $125 [(2/4)(1%)($25,000)] in the determination of 2017 Taxable Income. This amount is the lesser of this $125 and the taxable benefit of $750. This deduction will not be available after 2017.

Exercise Four - 1

Subject: Home Relocation Loan

On January 1, 2017, in order to facilitate an employee's relocation, Lee Ltd. provides her with a 5 year, $82,000 loan. The employee pays 2 percent annual interest on the loan on December 31 of each year. Assume that at the time the loan is granted the prescribed rate is 4 percent and that the rate is increased to 5 percent for the third and fourth quarters of 2017. What is the effect of this loan on the employee's Taxable Income for 2017?

SOLUTION available in print and online Study Guide.

Northern Residents Deductions - ITA 110.7

4-13.   Residents of Labrador, the Territories, as well as parts of some of the provinces, are eligible for deductions under ITA 110.7. To qualify for these deductions, the taxpayer must be resident in these prescribed regions for a continuous period of six months beginning or ending in the taxation year. The amount of the deductions involves fairly complex calculations that go beyond the scope of this text. The purpose of these deductions is to compensate individuals for the high costs that are associated with living in such prescribed northern zones.

Calculation Of Tax Payable

Federal Tax Payable Before Credits

4-14.   The calculation of federal Tax Payable for individuals requires the application of a group of progressive rates to marginal increments in Taxable Income. The rates are progressive, starting at a low rate of 15 percent and increasing to a high of 33 percent as the individual's Taxable Income increases. In order to maintain fairness, the brackets (i.e., income segments) to which these rates apply are indexed to reflect changes in the Consumer Price Index. Without such indexation, taxpayers could find themselves effectively subject to higher rates without having an increased level of real, inflation adjusted income.

4-15.   For 2017, the brackets to which these five rates apply are as follows:

Taxable Income In Excess Of	Federal Tax	Marginal Rate On Excess
$ -0-	$ -0-	15.0%
45,916	6,887	20.5%
91,831	16,300	26.0%
142,353	29,436	29.0%
202,800	46,966	33.0%

4-16.   Note that the average rate for an individual just entering the 20.5 percent bracket is 15 percent ($6,887 ÷ $45,916). For an individual just entering the highest 33 percent bracket, the average rate is 23.2 percent ($46,966 ÷ $202,800).

4-17.   There is a common misconception that once Taxable Income reaches the next tax bracket, all income is taxed at a higher rate. This is not the case as each rate is a marginal rate. For example, if Taxable Income is $202,801 ($202,800 + $1), only $1 is taxed at 33 percent.

4-18.   The preceding table suggests that individuals are taxed on their first dollar of income. While the 15 percent rate is, in fact, applied to all of the first $45,916 of Taxable Income, a portion of this amount is not really subject to taxes. As will be discussed later in this Chapter, every individual resident in Canada is entitled to a personal tax credit. For 2017, this tax credit is $1,745 [(15%)($11,635)]. In effect, this means that no taxes will be paid on at least the first $11,635 of an individual's Taxable Income. The amount that could be earned tax free would be even higher for individuals with additional tax credits (e.g., the age credit).

4-19.   As an example of the calculation of federal Tax Payable before credits and the resulting average rate of taxation, consider an individual with Taxable Income of $95,300. The calculation would be as follows:

Tax On First $91,831	$16,300
Tax On Next $3,469 ($95,300 - $91,831) At 26%	902
Federal Tax Payable Before Credits	**$17,202**

Average Rate Of Tax ($17,202 ÷ $95,300)	18.1%

4-20.   A surtax is an additional tax calculated on the basis of the regular Tax Payable calculation. While such additional taxes are not assessed at the federal level, they are used in two provinces, most notably in Ontario. For 2017, Ontario has a surtax of 56 percent on amounts of Ontario Tax Payable in excess of $5,831. This significantly increases the highest rate in Ontario from the stated 13.16 percent to 20.53 [(13.16%)(156%)] percent.

Provincial Tax Payable Before Credits

Provincial Rates

4-21.   As is the case at the federal level, provincial Tax Payable is calculated by multiplying Taxable Income by either a single tax rate or a group of progressive rates. In general, the provinces other than Quebec use the same Taxable Income figure that is used at the federal level.

4-22.   Prior to 2016, Alberta was unique in that it used a single flat rate of 10 percent applied to all levels of income. However, Alberta joined the progressive rates club in 2016. All provinces use anywhere from 3 to 6 different tax rates applied to various levels of income. In general, the applicable income levels differ from those used in the federal brackets.

4-23.   To give you some idea of the range of provincial rates, the 2017 minimum and maximum rates for provinces other than Quebec are as found in the following table. The maximum rates include surtaxes where applicable. These rates are correct as of January 1, 2017. You may see other rates after this point in time as provincial budgets are introduced.

As Of January 1, 2017 Province	Minimum 2017 Tax Rate	Maximum 2017 Tax Rate
Alberta	10.00%	15.00%
British Columbia	5.06%	14.70%
Manitoba	10.80%	17.40%
New Brunswick	9.68%	20.30%
Newfoundland and Labrador	8.70%	18.30%
Nova Scotia	8.79%	21.00%
Ontario (including 56% surtax)	5.05%	20.53%
Prince Edward Island (including 10% surtax)	9.80%	16.70%
Saskatchewan	11.00%	15.00%

4-24.   You should note the significant differences in rates between the provinces. The maximum rate ranges from 14.7 percent in British Columbia to 21 percent in Nova Scotia. This difference amounts to extra provincial taxes of $6,300 per year on each additional $100,000 of income. This can make provincial tax differences a major consideration when an individual decides where he should establish provincial residency.

4-25.   When these provincial rates are combined with the federal rate schedule, the minimum combined rate varies from a low of 20.05 percent in Ontario (15 percent federal, plus 5.05 percent provincial), to a high of 26 percent in Saskatchewan (15 percent federal, plus 11 percent provincial).

4-26.   Maximum combined rates are lowest in British Columbia where the rate is 47.7 percent (33 percent federal, plus 14.7 percent provincial). They are highest in Nova Scotia where the combined rate is 54 percent (33 percent federal, plus 21 percent provincial). Because the calculations are completely different, we have not included Quebec in this list of rates. We would note however, the overall rate in Quebec ranges from a low of 28.53 percent to a high of 53.31 percent.

Exercise Four - 2

Subject: Calculation Of Tax Payable Before Credits

During 2017, Joan Matel is a resident of Ontario and has calculated her Taxable Income to be $56,700. Assume that Ontario's rates are 5.05 percent on Taxable Income up to $45,916 and 9.15 percent on the next $45,916. Calculate her 2017 federal and provincial Tax Payable before consideration of credits, and her average rate of tax.

SOLUTION available in print and online Study Guide.

Provincial Residence
4-27. Given the significant differences in provincial tax rates on individuals, it is somewhat surprising that the rules related to where an individual will pay provincial taxes are fairly simple. With respect to an individual's income other than business income, it is subject to tax in the province in which he resides on the last day of the taxation year. This means that, if an individual moves to Ontario from Nova Scotia on December 30 of the current year, any income for the entire year, other than business income, will be taxed in Ontario.

Types Of Income
4-28. In terms of the effective tax rates, the income accruing to Canadian individuals can be divided into three basic categories:

Ordinary Income This would include employment income, business income, property income other than dividends, and other sources of income. In general, the effective tax rates on this category are those presented in the preceding tables. For example, the marginal rate for an individual living in Alberta and earning more than $350,000, would be 48 percent (33 percent federal, plus 15 percent provincial).

Capital Gains As will be discussed in detail in Chapter 8, capital gains arise on the disposition of capital property. Only one-half of such gains are included in Net Income For Tax Purposes and Taxable Income. This means that the effective tax rate on this category of income is only one-half of the rates presented in the preceding tables. Returning to our Alberta resident who is earning more than $350,000, his effective marginal rate on capital gains would be 24 percent [(1/2)(33% + 15%)].

Dividends As will be explained in Chapter 7, dividends from taxable Canadian companies are subject to a gross up and tax credit procedure which reduces the effective tax rate on this type of income. Also in that Chapter, we explain the difference between eligible dividends and non-eligible dividends. Continuing with our Alberta example, maximum federal/provincial tax rates on dividends are as follows:

Eligible Dividends	31.71%
Non-Eligible Dividends	41.24%

4-29. A more complete discussion of the different effective tax rates mentioned here is provided in Chapter 7 (dividends) and Chapter 8 (capital gains).

Taxes On Income Not Earned In A Province
4-30. As will be discussed in Chapter 20, International Issues In Taxation, it is possible for an individual to be considered a resident of Canada for tax purposes, without being a resident of

a particular province or territory. This would be the case, for example, for members of the Canadian Armed Forces who are stationed outside of Canada.

4-31.   Income that is not subject to provincial or territorial tax is subject to additional taxation at the federal level. This additional tax is a surtax of 48 percent on federal tax payable. This gives a maximum rate of 48.84 percent [(33%)(148%)]. This additional tax is paid to the federal government.

Calculating Tax Credits

Federal Amounts

4-32.   The most direct way of applying a tax credit system is to simply specify the amount of each tax credit available. In 2017, for example, the basic personal tax credit could have been specified to be $1,745. However, the Canadian tax system is based on a less direct approach. Rather than specifying the amount of each credit, a base amount is provided, to which the minimum federal tax rate (15 percent) is applied. This means that, for 2017, the basic personal tax credit is calculated by taking 15 percent of $11,635 (we will refer to this number as the tax credit base), resulting in a credit against Tax Payable in the amount of $1,745.

4-33.   Note that the legislation is such that, if the minimum federal tax rate of 15 percent is changed, the new rate will be used in determining individual tax credits. In our tax credit calculations, we will usually calculate the sum of the tax credit bases and apply the 15 percent rate to the total. This approach (rather than applying 15 percent to each credit base) makes relationships between the various credit bases easier to see and reduces calculation errors.

4-34.   As was the case with the tax rate brackets, in order to avoid having these credits decline in value in terms of real dollars, the base for the tax credits needs to be adjusted for changing prices. While it is not a common occurrence, there may be adjustments to tax credit bases for amounts that do not simply reflect the rate of inflation. For example, in 2009, the base for the basic personal credit was increased to $10,320, $220 more than would have been required by a simple inflation adjustment.

4-35.   A technical problem in calculating credits will arise in the year a person becomes a Canadian resident, or ceases to be a Canadian resident. As discussed in Chapter 20, such individuals will only be subject to Canadian taxation for a part of the year. Given this, it would not be appropriate for them to receive the same credits as an individual who is subject to Canadian taxation for the full year. This view is reflected in ITA 118.91, which requires a pro rata calculation for personal tax credits, the disability tax credit and tax credits transferred from a spouse or a person supported by the taxpayer. Other tax credits, for example the tax credits for charitable donations and adoption expenses, are not reduced because of part year residence. This is because these credits reflect actual amounts paid or costs incurred during the period of Canadian residency.

Provincial Amounts

4-36.   In determining provincial tax credits, the provinces use the same approach as that used at the federal level. That is, the minimum provincial rate is applied to a base that is indexed each year. In most cases, the base used is different from the base used at the federal level. For 2017, the basic personal tax credit at the federal level is $1,745 [(15%)($11,635)]. Comparative 2017 figures for selected provinces are as follows:

Province	Base	Rate	Credit
Alberta	$18,690	10.00%	$1,869
British Columbia	10,208	5.06%	517
Newfoundland And Labrador	8,978	8.20%	**781**
Ontario	10,171	5.05%	514

Personal Tax Credits - ITA 118(1)

Individuals With A Spouse Or Common-Law Partner - ITA 118(1)(a)

Basic Personal Credit Plus Spousal Credit

4-37.   For individuals with a spouse or common-law partner, ITA 118(1)(a) provides for two tax credits — one for the individual (sometimes referred to as the basic personal credit which is the term we use in our material) and one for his or her spouse or common-law partner. This latter credit is sometimes referred to as the spousal credit which is the term we use in our material. The spousal credit is applicable to common-law partners, but to include that in the title would be awkward. For 2017, the **basic personal credit is $1,745** [(15%)($11,635)].

Calculation Of Spousal Credit

4-38.   If the individual's spouse is not dependent because of a mental or physical infirmity, the spousal credit is calculated using the same base as the basic personal credit. However, it must be reduced by the spouse or common-law partner's Net Income For Tax Purposes.

4-39.   In those cases where the spouse or common-law partner is dependent on the individual by reason of a mental or physical infirmity, ITA 118(1)(a) adds, for 2017, an additional $2,150. We will discuss in detail the meaning of mental or physical infirmity in our coverage of the Canada caregiver credit beginning in Paragraph 4-53.

4-40.   The two possible calculations of the spousal credit are as follows:

Spousal Credit - Spouse Is Not Infirm
[(15%)($11,635 - Spouse Or Common-Law Partner's Net Income)]

Spousal Credit - Spouse Is Mentally Or Physically Infirm
[(15%)($11,635 + $2,150 - Spouse Or Common-Law Partner's Net Income)]
When the spouse is mentally or physically infirm, the maximum value for the credit is [(15%)($13,785)].

4-41.   As an example, consider an individual with a spouse who had Net Income For Tax Purposes of $5,200. The total personal credits under ITA 118(1)(a) if the spouse (1) was not mentally or physically infirm and (2) was dependent because of a mental or physical infirmity:

Spouse	Not Infirm	Infirm
Basic Personal Amount (For Taxpayer)	$ 11,635	$ 11,635
Spousal Amount ($11,635 - $5,200)	6,435	
Spousal Amount ($11,635 + $2,150 - $5,200)		8,585
Credit Base	$18,070	$20,220
Rate	15%	15%
Personal Tax Credits (Taxpayer And Spouse)	$ 2,711	$ 3,033

4-42.   There are several other points to be made with respect to the credits for an individual with a spouse or common-law partner:

Spouse Or Common-Law Partner's Income   The income figure used for limiting the spousal amount is Net Income For Tax Purposes, with no adjustments of any sort.

Applicability To Either Spouse Or Common-Law Partner   The ITA 118(1)(a) provision is applicable to both spouses and, while each is eligible to claim the basic amount of $11,635, IT-513R specifies that only one spouse or common-law partner may claim the spousal amount. IT-513R indicates that the spouse making the claim should be the one that supports the other (support is defined in Appendix A of IT-513R).

Eligibility   The spousal credit can be claimed for either a spouse or a common-law partner. There is no definition of spouse in the *Income Tax Act*, so it would appear that the usual dictionary definition would apply.   That is, a spouse is one of a pair of persons who are legally married.   With respect to common-law partner, ITA 248(1) defines such an individual as a person who cohabits with the taxpayer in a conjugal relationship and:

- has so cohabited for a continuous period of at least one year; or
- is the parent of a child of whom the taxpayer is also a parent.

There is no requirement in the income tax legislation that either a spouse or a common-law partner be a person of the opposite sex. One can, however, assume that they must be of the same species (e.g., you can't claim your dog).

Multiple Relationships   Based on these definitions, it would be possible for an individual to have both a spouse and a common-law partner. ITA 118(4)(a) makes it clear that, if this is the case, a credit can only be claimed for one of these individuals. In such cases, determining your tax credits may be the least of your problems.

Year Of Separation Or Divorce   In general, ITA 118(5) does not allow a tax credit based on the spousal amount in situations where the individual is making a deduction for the support of a spouse or common-law partner (spousal support is covered in Chapter 9).   However, IT-513R indicates that, in the year of separation or divorce, an individual can choose to deduct amounts paid for spousal support, or claim the additional tax credit for a spouse.

Exercise Four - 3

Subject: Spousal Tax Credit

Johan Sprinkle is married and has 2017 Net Income For Tax Purposes of $35,450. His spouse has 2017 Net Income For Tax Purposes of $2,600. Johan has no tax credits other than the basic personal credits for his spouse and himself. Assuming that Johan's spouse does not have a mental or physical infirmity, determine Johan's federal tax credits for 2017. How would your answer differ if Johan's spouse was dependent because of a mental or physical infirmity?

SOLUTION available in print and online Study Guide.

We suggest you work Self Study Problem Four-1 at this point.

Individuals Supporting A Dependent Person - ITA 118(1)(b)
Basic Personal Credit Plus Eligible Dependant Credit
4-43.   Like ITA 118(1)(a), ITA 118(1)(b) provides for two tax credits. The first is the basic personal credit for the individual based on a 2017 base amount of $11,635. The second credit, based on the same amount, is for a qualifying eligible dependant. With respect to this second credit, if the eligible dependant is physically or mentally impaired, an additional amount of $2,150 is added to the $11,635. As was the case when this amount was added to the spousal credit, we will discuss in detail the meaning of mental or physical infirmity in our coverage of the Canada caregiver credit beginning in Paragraph 4-53.

Eligibility And Eligible Dependant Defined
4-44.   The eligible dependant credit is available to an individual who is not claiming the spousal credit and who supports a wholly dependent person who lives with them in a self-contained domestic establishment (we will refer to this person as an eligible dependant). To qualify for this credit, the individual taxpayer must be:

- unmarried;
- not living in a common-law partnership; or
- a person who is married or has a common-law partner but neither supports nor lives with that spouse or common-law partner.

4-45.   To claim this credit, the eligible dependant must be "related" to the individual making the claim and "wholly dependent". ITA 251(2) defines related individuals as those who are related by blood, marriage, common-law partnership, or adoption. Income Tax Folio S1-F5-C1, *Related Persons And Dealing At Arm's Length*, indicates that this would exclude aunts, uncles, nieces, nephews, and cousins. To be "wholly dependent" would mean that the taxpayer provides all means of support (food, clothing, shelter), as well as all financial support. For example, a young child would normally be wholly dependent on a parent. Also note that the death of a spouse or common-law partner severs all marriage and common-law relationships. For example, an individual is not related to his deceased wife's mother.

4-46.   In view of today's less stable family arrangements, the question of exactly who is considered a child for tax purposes requires some elaboration. As explained in IT-513R, the credit may be taken for natural children, children who have been formally adopted, as well as for natural and adopted children of a spouse or common-law partner.

Application

4-47.   This credit is most commonly claimed by single parents who are supporting a minor child. More generally, this credit is available to individual taxpayers who are single, widowed, divorced, or separated, and supporting a dependant who is:

- related to the individual by blood, marriage, adoption or common-law relationship;
- wholly dependent on the individual for support;
- under 18 at any time during the year, or mentally or physically infirm, or the individual's parent or grandparent;
- living with the individual in a home that the individual maintains (this would not disqualify a child who moves away during the school year to attend an educational institution as long as the home remains the child's home); and
- residing in Canada (this requirement is not applicable to an individual's child as long as they are living with the individual).

4-48.   The eligible dependant credit cannot be claimed by an individual:

- if the individual is claiming the spousal credit;
- if the individual is living with, supporting, or being supported by a spouse (the claim is only available for individuals who are either single, or living separately from their spouse);
- for more than one person;
- if the dependant's Net Income exceeds $11,635 or $13,785 ($11,635 + $2,150) if they are mentally or physically infirm;
- if someone other than the individual is making this claim for the same individual; or
- for the individual's child, if the individual is required to make child support payments to another individual, for that child. As is noted in Chapter 9, when child support is being paid, only the recipient of such payments can claim this tax credit.

Calculation Of Eligible Dependant Tax Credit

4-49.   As we have noted, the base for the eligible dependant credit is $11,635, the same value that is used for the basic personal credit and the spousal credit. As was the case with the spousal credit, if the eligible dependant is dependent because of a mental or physical infirmity, an additional $2,150 is added to the 2017 base, bringing the total to $13,785. The amount of the base is reduced by the eligible dependant's Net Income For Tax Purposes for the year. As was the case with the spousal credit, the infirmity does not have to be severe enough to qualify for the disability tax credit. For 2017, the calculation of the eligible dependant credit is as follows:

Eligible Dependant Credit - Is Not Infirm
[(15%)($11,635 - Eligible Dependant's Net Income)]

Eligible Dependant Credit - Is Mentally Or Physically Infirm
[(15%)($11,635 + $2,150 - Eligible Dependant's Net Income)]

4-50.   As an example, consider an unmarried person supporting a parent who has Net Income For Tax Purposes of $5,200. The total personal credits under ITA 118(1)(b) if the (1) was not mentally or physically infirm and (2) was dependent because of a mental or physical infirmity, would be calculated as follows:

Eligible Dependant	Not Infirm	Infirm
Basic Personal Amount (For Taxpayer)	$ 11,635	$ 11,635
Eligible Dependant Amount ($11,635 - $5,200)	6,435	
Eligible Dependant Amount ($11,635 + $2,150 - $5,200)		8,585
Credit Base	$18,070	$20,220
Rate	15%	15%
Personal Tax Credits (Taxpayer And Eligible Dependant)	$ 2,711	$ 3,033

4-51.   Note that this credit provides for the same total credits that would be available to an individual with a spouse who had Net Income For Tax Purposes of $5,200 (see Paragraph 4-41). For this reason, it is sometimes referred to as the equivalent to married tax credit.

Canada Caregiver Amount For Child - ITA 118(1)(b.1)

4-52.   There is no general tax credit available for a child who is under 18 at the end of the taxation year. However, in those cases where an under 18 year old child has a mental or physical infirmity, ITA 118(1)(b.1) provides a credit based on a 2017 base amount of $2,150. We will discuss in detail the meaning of mental or physical infirmity in our coverage of the Canada caregiver credit beginning in Paragraph 4-53.

EXAMPLE   Mr. and Mrs. Barton have a 7 year old child who has a physical infirmity.

ANALYSIS   Either Mr. Barton or Mrs. Barton can claim a credit against Tax Payable of $323 [(15%)($2,150)].

Single Persons (Basic Personal Tax Credit) - ITA 118(1)(c)

4-53.   Individuals living with a spouse, common-law partner or eligible dependant receive a credit for themselves and their spouse or common-law partner under ITA 118(1)(a), or themselves and their eligible dependant under ITA 118(1)(b). For individuals who do not have a spouse, common-law partner or eligible dependant, a basic personal tax credit is received under ITA 118(1)(c). For 2017, the credit is equal to $1,745 [(15%)($11,635)].

EXAMPLE   Jason Broad is 35 years old, single, is not involved in a relationship with a common-law partner (though he has been known to fool around from time to time), and has no dependants.

ANALYSIS   Jason can claim a credit against Tax Payable of $1,745 [(15%)($11,635)].

Canada Caregiver Tax Credit - ITA 118(1)(d)
Background

4-54.   An important issue in Canada is the fact that many individuals are responsible for taking care of, and/or supporting some related individual because of that individual's mental or physical infirmity. For some time, the federal government has dealt with this problem by providing some amount of monetary relief through the use of tax credits.

4-55.   Prior to 2017, this tax relief was provided through three separate tax credits:

- the family caregiver credit
- the caregiver credit
- the infirm dependant over 17 credit

4-56.   The application of these credits, particularly in dealing with the interplay between them, proved to be very confusing to most taxpayers. Reflecting this, the March 22, 2017 budget has repealed these credits and replaced them with a single Canada caregiver credit.

4-57.   While this new approach will produce the same or similar results as were produced by the now repealed credits, it will be far easier for taxpayers to understand and implement. We would note that our focus will be on the new Canada caregiver credit. We will not attempt to provide a comparison of this credit with the credits that it replaced.

Mental Or Physical Impairment/Infirmity

4-58.   In our presentation on the spousal and eligible dependant credits, we noted that an extra base amount is available when the spouse or eligible dependant is mentally or physically impaired. In addition, this is a requirement for eligibility for the Canada caregiver credit. Given this, it is important to have some understanding of this concept.

4-59.   Later in this Chapter, we will discuss the disability tax credit. This fairly substantial credit is available to an individual having one or more severe and prolonged impairments in physical or mental functions. For example, the disability tax credit would be available to an individual who could not dress or feed herself.

4-60.   It is clear that an individual who qualifies for the disability tax credit would also qualify for the Canada caregiver amount and for the extra base amount that can be added to the spousal and eligible dependant amounts. It is also clear that an individual with a less severe impairment could qualify for these amounts.

4-61.   While there have been a number of court cases which have discussed the meaning of mental or physical impairment, no consistent definition has emerged. For our purposes in this material, the following description will be used:

> The term mental or physical infirmity is not defined in the the *Income Tax Act* and, therefore, it should be applied using its ordinary meaning. In most dictionaries and infirmity is described as a physical or mental weakness or ailment. In terms of the application of the term infirmity in tax work, it does not refer to a temporary weakness or ailment. In addition, the infirmity must be such that it requires the person to be dependent on the individual for a considerable period of time.

Calculation Of The Canada Caregiver Credit

4-62.   As described in the budget papers, the Canada caregiver amounts for 2017 will be:

- An indexed amount of $6,883 for infirm dependants who are parents, grandparents, brothers, sisters, aunts, uncles, nieces, nephews, and children of the claimant or his spouse or common-law partner who are over 17. (We refer to this amount as the regular Canada caregiver amount.)

- An indexed amount of $2,150 for:

  - An infirm dependent spouse or common-law partner in respect of whom the individual claims the spouse or common-law partner credit.
  - An infirm dependant for whom the individual claims the eligible dependant credit.
  - An infirm child who is under 18 at the end of the year.

These amounts will be reduced on a dollar for dollar basis by the dependant's Net Income For Tax Purposes in excess of $16,163 (an indexed value).

BYRD/CHEN NOTE   In terms of the actual legislation, only the $6,883 amount is referred to in ITA 118(1)(d). The $2,150 amounts for a spouse or eligible dependant are included under ITA 118(1)(a) and 118(1)(b). In those provisions, the $2,150 amount is not referred to as a caregiver amount. To prevent double counting for a spouse or an eligible dependant, ITA 118(4)(c) indicates that, if an individual is entitled to a credit for an infirm spouse or eligible dependant under ITA 118(1)(a) or ITA 118(1)(b), they cannot make any claim under ITA 118(1)(d). You will note, however, the simplified approach described in Paragraph 4-61 that was included in the budget papers is easier to understand.

4-63.   Several other points are relevant here:

- Only one Canada caregiver credit will be available for each infirm dependant. If there is more than one caregiver, the credit must be shared.

- An individual will not be able to claim the Canada caregiver credit for a particular person if the individual is required to pay a support amount for that person to their former spouse or common law partner.

- There is no requirement that the infirm dependant live in the caregiver's home in order to claim the Canada caregiver credit.

- Except in the case of children or grandchildren, to qualify for the Canada caregiver credit, the infirm dependant must be a resident of Canada.

Exercise Four - 4

Subject: Canada Caregiver Tax Credit

Joan Barton lives with her husband whose Net Income For Tax Purposes is $5,000. Two years ago her father and mother moved in with her. The father, who is 69 years old is still very active. However, her 67 year old mother is dependent because of a physical infirmity, but the infirmity is not severe enough to qualify for the disability tax credit. Her father's 2017 Net Income For Tax Purposes is $25,300. The corresponding amount for her mother is $21,400. Determine the amount of Joan's Canada caregiver tax credit, if any, for 2017.

Exercise Four - 5

Subject: Infirm Spouse And Infirm Adult Child

Marcia Flood is married to Josh Flood. Josh has a mental infirmity. They have a 20 year son who has a physical infirmity. Neither infirmity is severe enough to qualify for the disability tax credit. Josh has 2017 Net Income For Tax Purposes of $5,600. Their son has no 2017 income. Determine the amount of any 2017 tax credits that Marcia will have related to her spouse and son.

Exercise Four - 6

Subject: Infirm Eligible Dependant Who Is Child Under 18

Darcy Gates is a single father who takes care of his 9 year old daughter, Janice. Janice has a physical infirmity, but the infirmity is not severe enough to qualify for the disability tax credit. Janice has no 2017 income of her own. Determine the amount of any 2017 tax credits that Darcy will have related to his daughter.

SOLUTIONS available in print and online Study Guide.

Canada Caregiver Credit - Additional Amount

4-64.   There is a problem in those cases where the $2,150 amount is provided through either the spousal tax credit or the eligible dependant tax credit. The base for both of these credits is reduced, on a dollar-for-dollar basis, by the dependant's Net Income For Tax Purposes. While the usual Canada caregiver amount is not eroded until the dependant's Net Income For Tax Purposes is greater than $16,163, the spousal and eligible dependant credits would be completely eliminated once income reaches $13,785 ($11,635 + $2,150). In effect, this would result in the caregiver for an infirm spouse or an infirm eligible dependant getting no benefit from the Canada caregiver credit provisions.

4-65.   Under ITA 118(1)(e), when an individual has an infirm spouse or infirm eligible dependant, they are entitled to an additional amount of credit base in those situations where their claim for the spousal or eligible dependant amount is less than the regular Canada caregiver amount. The additional amount is the amount that would be required to bring the claimant's credit up to the amount that would have been the regular caregiver amount.

> **EXAMPLE**   Mark Stucky has an infirm spouse. Assume her 2017 Net Income For Tax Purposes is (1) $15,000 and (2) $8,000.
>
> **ANALYSIS - $15,000**   The base for Mark's spousal credit would be nil ($11,635 + $2,150 - $15,000). Given this, the additional amount would be $6,883 ($6,883 - nil). When this additional amount is added to the base for the spousal credit of nil, the total is $6,883, the 2017 base for the Canada caregiver credit.
>
> **ANALYSIS - $8,000**   The base for Mark's spousal credit would $5,785 ($11,635 + $2,150 - $8,000). Given this, the additional amount would be $1,098 ($6,883 - $5,785). When this additional amount is added to the base for the spousal credit, the total is $6,883, the 2017 base for the Canada caregiver credit.

Exercise Four - 7

Subject: Canada Caregiver Tax Credit - Additional Amount

Sandy Hill is single and lives with her 63 year old mother, Ariel. Ariel has a physical infirmity, but the infirmity is not severe enough to qualify for the disability tax credit. Ariel has 2017 Net Income For Tax Purposes of $18,000. Determine the amount of any 2017 tax credits that Sandy will have related to her mother.

SOLUTION available in print and online Study Guide.

Other Tax Credits For Individuals

Age Tax Credit - ITA 118(2)

4-66.   For individuals who attain the age of 65 prior to the end of the year, ITA 118(2) provides an additional tax credit of $1,084 [(15%)($7,225)]. However, the base for this credit is reduced by **15 percent** of the individual's Net Income For Tax Purposes in excess of $36,430. This means that, at an income level of $84,597 [($7,225 ÷ 15%) + $36,430], the reduction will be equal to $7,225 and the individual will not receive an age credit. Note that the reduction is only 15% of the income above the threshold, not a dollar for dollar reduction.

> **EXAMPLE**   A 67 year old individual has 2017 Net Income For Tax Purposes of $38,000.
>
> **ANALYSIS**   An age credit of $1,048 {[15%][$7,225 - (15%)($38,000 - $36,430)]} will be available to this individual.

4-67. As we shall see when we consider the transfer of credits to a spouse, if an individual does not have sufficient Tax Payable to use this credit, it can be transferred to a spouse.

Exercise Four - 8

Subject: Age Tax Credit

Joshua Smythe is 72 years old and has 2017 Net Income For Tax Purposes of $51,500. Determine Mr. Smythe's age credit for 2017.

SOLUTION available in print and online Study Guide.

Pension Income Tax Credit - ITA 118(3)

General Rules

4-68. The pension income credit is equal to 15 percent of the first $2,000 of eligible pension income. This results in a maximum value of $300 [(15%)($2,000)]. The base for this credit is not indexed for inflation and has been $2,000 since 2006.

4-69. The credit is only available with respect to "eligible pension income". Specifically excluded from this definition are:

- payments under the Old Age Security Act or Canada Pension Plan;
- payments under certain provincial pension plans;
- payments under salary deferral arrangements;
- payments under retirement compensation arrangements;
- payments under an employee benefit plan; and
- death benefits.

4-70. Like the age credit, if an individual does not have sufficient Tax Payable to use this credit, it can be transferred to a spouse.

Individuals 65 Or Over

4-71. For an individual who has reached age 65 before the end of the year, this credit is available on "pension income" as defined in ITA 118(7). This includes payments that are:

- periodic (not lump sum) payments from a registered pension plan (RPP);
- an annuity payment out of a Registered Retirement Savings Plan (RRSP);
- a payment out of a Registered Retirement Income Fund (RRIF);
- an annuity payment from a Deferred Profit Sharing Plan (DPSP); and
- the interest component of other annuities.

Individuals Under 65

4-72. For an individual who has not reached age 65 during the year, the credit is based on "qualified pension income", also defined in ITA 118(7). In general, this only includes the periodic payments from a registered pension plan. However, if the other types of pension income described in Paragraph 4-71 are received as a consequence of the death of a spouse or common-law partner, these amounts are also qualified, regardless of the age of the recipient.

Canada Employment Tax Credit - ITA 118(10)

4-73. This credit is available to all individuals who have employment income. From a conceptual point of view, it is designed to provide limited recognition of the fact that there are costs associated with earning employment income. As only limited deductions are available against employment income, this would appear to be an appropriate form of relief.

4-74.   For 2017, the amount of the credit is equal to 15 percent of the lesser of:

- $1,178; and

- the individual's Net Employment Income, calculated without the deduction of any employment related expenses.

4-75.   For most employed individuals, this will produce a credit of $177 [(15%)($1,178)].

Adoption Expenses Tax Credit - ITA 118.01

4-76.   The adoption expenses tax credit is available to a taxpayer who adopts an "eligible child". As defined in ITA 118.01(1), an eligible child means a child who has not attained the age of 18 years at the time that an adoption order is issued or recognized by a government in Canada in respect of the adoption of that child. For 2017, the indexed base for this credit is up to $15,670 of eligible adoption expenses. This provides a maximum credit of $2,351.

4-77.   The expenses can only be claimed in the year in which the adoption is finalized. The total amount of eligible expenses is reduced by any assistance that is received and not included in that taxpayer's income. Normally, if an employer reimburses any portion of an employee's adoption expenses, this amount will be treated as a taxable benefit. Given this, such amounts will not be deducted from the adoption expenses that form the basis for this credit as they will be taxed as employment income.

4-78.   Eligible adoption expenses must be incurred during the "adoption period" (see next Paragraph) and, as defined in ITA 118.01(1), include:

(a) fees paid to an adoption agency licensed by a provincial government;
(b) court costs and legal and administrative expenses related to an adoption order in respect of that child;
(c) reasonable and necessary travel and living expenses of the child and the adoptive parents;
(d) document translation fees;
(e) mandatory fees paid to a foreign institution;
(f) mandatory expenses paid in respect of the immigration of the child; and
(g) any other reasonable expenses related to the adoption required by a provincial government or an adoption agency licensed by a provincial government.

4-79.   An "adoption period" is also defined in ITA 118.01(1) as follows:

It begins at the earlier of:

- the time that an application is made for registration with a provincial ministry responsible for adoption (or with an adoption agency licensed by a provincial government); and
- time, if any, that an application related to the adoption is made to a Canadian court; and

It ends at the later of:

- the time an adoption order is issued by, or recognized by, a government in Canada in respect of that child, and
- the time that the child first begins to reside permanently with the individual.

4-80.   In the usual situation, a child will be adopted by a couple, either legally married or co-habiting on a common-law basis. The legislation points out that, while both parties are eligible for this credit, the $15,670 limit must be shared by the couple. The claim can be made by either party or split at their discretion.

Exercise Four - 9

Subject: Adoption Expenses Tax Credit

Ary Kapit and his spouse have adopted an infant Chinese orphan. The adoption process began in June, 2016 when they applied to an adoption agency licensed by the provincial government. Later that year they traveled to China to discuss the adoption and view available children. The cost of this trip was $4,250. Their provincial government opens the adoption file on February 13, 2017, and the adoption order is issued on August 27, 2017. In September, the couple returns to China to pick up their new daughter. The happy family returns to Canada on September 18, 2017. The cost of this trip is $6,420.

Additional expenses paid during the first week of September, 2017 were $1,600 paid to the Chinese orphanage and $3,200 paid to a Canadian adoption agency. Legal fees incurred during the adoption period were $2,700. After arrival in Canada, an additional $2,500 in medical expenses were incurred for the child prior to the end of 2017. Mr. Kapit's employer has a policy of providing reimbursement for up to $5,000 in adoption expenses eligible for the adoption expenses tax credit. This amount is received in September, 2017 and will be considered a taxable benefit to Mr. Kapit. What is the maximum adoption expenses tax credit that can be claimed by the couple?

SOLUTION available in print and online Study Guide.

Public Transit Passes Tax Credit - ITA 118.02

BYRD/CHEN NOTE   The March 22, 2017 Federal budget repealed this provision as of July 1, 2017. Expenditures made on or after that date will no longer qualify for a tax credit.

4-81.   This credit is equal to 15 percent of the cost of eligible public transit passes attributable to the use of an individual, his spouse or common-law partner, and his children who have not attained the age of 19 during the year. Either spouse can claim this credit.

4-82.   Eligible public transit passes are defined as follows:

• Passes that provide for unlimited travel for an uninterrupted period of at least 28 days (monthly passes).

• Passes that provide for unlimited travel for an uninterrupted period of at least 5 days, provided a sufficient number of such passes are acquired that at least 20 days will be covered in a period of 28 days (a group of weekly passes).

4-83.   The credit is also available with respect to the costs of "eligible electronic payment cards". These must provide for at least 32 one-way trips during an uninterrupted period that does not exceed 31 days.

4-84.   The passes must be for use on "public commuter transit services" which means services offered to the general public, ordinarily for a period of at least 5 days per week, of transporting individuals, from a place in Canada to another place in Canada, by means of bus, ferry, subway, train or tram, and in respect of which it can reasonably be expected that those individuals would return daily to the place of their departure.

4-85.   As was the case with adoption expenses, the costs that are eligible for the credit must be reduced by any amounts that are reimbursed and not included in the taxpayer's income. Note, however, that employer reimbursements are generally included in an employee's income as a taxable benefit and, as a consequence, would not reduce the base for this credit.

Home Accessibility Tax Credit - ITA 118.041
Described

4-86.   Beginning in 2016, the government is providing a non-refundable tax credit for renovations that will allow seniors and persons with disabilities to live more independently at home. The base for the credit is equal to the lesser of $10,000 and the amount of qualifying expenditures for the year. The means that the maximum credit is $1,500 [(15%)($10,000)]. It does not appear that the $10,000 limit will be indexed.

4-87.   The credit is available to a **qualifying individual** or an **eligible individual** for **qualifying expenditures** on an **eligible dwelling**.

4-88.   As is often the case with income tax legislation, this basic provision contains a number of technical terms (in **bold** in Paragraph 4-87) which require further explanation.   These explanations follow.

Qualifying And Eligible Individuals

4-89.   A qualifying individual is an individual who is 65 years of age or older, or who is eligible to claim the disability tax credit.

4-90.   An eligible individual is a qualifying individual's spouse or common-law partner, or an individual who has claimed, or could have claimed under certain conditions, the eligible dependant, caregiver or infirm dependant over 17 credit for the qualifying individual.   It would normally be a relative who ordinarily inhabits the same dwelling as the qualifying individual.

Eligible Dwelling

4-91.   To begin, an eligible dwelling is a housing unit located in Canada. It must be owned by the qualifying individual or by an eligible individual. While it will usually be the principal residence of the individual, this is not a requirement. It can be a house, cottage or condominium, but it cannot be a rented dwelling.

4-92.   If more than one individual is eligible to claim the credit in relation to the same eligible dwelling, the $10,000 limit applies to the total amount claimed for that dwelling in the year. If there is more than one qualifying individual for an eligible dwelling, the total qualifying expenses cannot exceed $10,000 for the dwelling. If the qualifying individual has more than one principal residence in a tax year, the $10,000 limit applies to the total cost of qualifying expenses for both residences, not for each residence.

Qualifying Renovations And Expenditures

4-93.   To be considered a qualifying expenditure in a qualifying renovation, the renovation or alteration must be made to allow the qualifying individual to gain access to, or to be more mobile or functional within the dwelling, or to reduce the risk of harm to the qualifying individual either when gaining access to the home or within the dwelling itself. The improvements must be of an enduring nature and be considered integral to the eligible dwelling. As a general rule, if the item purchased will not become a permanent part of the dwelling, it is not eligible.

4-94.   Qualifying expenses can include materials, fixtures, labour or professional services. The credit will only apply to work performed and paid for and/or goods acquired in that particular tax year. Any expenses claimed for the home accessibility tax credit must be supported by receipts. This is expected to help the CRA battle the underground cash economy as receipts will be needed for qualifying labour in order to claim the credit.

4-95.   Although the CRA website does not provide a list of qualifying expenditures, it does provide a list of some of the expenses that are not eligible for the credit such as outdoor maintenance services and electronic home entertainment devices. Some renovations that would clearly qualify would be wheelchair ramps or lifts, walk-in bathtubs and wheel-in showers.

4-96.   Note that some expenditures would qualify for both this credit and the medical expenses tax credit (see Paragraph 4-119). For example, the cost of installing a ramp for a qualifying individual who is in a wheelchair would be a qualifying expenditure for both credits. Interestingly, the legislation is clear that, in cases such as this, the expenditures can be used in determining the base for both of these credits. This, in effect, results in a double credit for the same expenditure.

Exercise Four - 10

Subject: Home Accessibility Tax Credit

Della and Marcus Jacobs are married and they are both aged 68. They jointly own the house they live in. Because a recent automobile accident damaged his back, Marcus has limited mobility and has great difficulty climbing stairs. During 2017, they spent $8,500 installing a ramp to replace the steps to the front door and $2,000 for a snow removal contract as Marcus was no longer able to shovel the snow. What is the maximum home accessibility credit that can be claimed for the 2017 taxation year and who should claim it?

SOLUTION available in print and online Study Guide.

First Time Home Buyer's Tax Credit - ITA 118.05

4-97.   A tax credit is available for first-time home buyers who acquire a qualifying home in Canada. The credit is equal to 15 percent of the first $5,000 of the cost of a qualifying home, resulting in a maximum credit of $750. This amount is not indexed. To be eligible for the credit, the buyer must intend to occupy the home no later than one year after its acquisition.

4-98.   An individual will be considered a first-time home buyer if neither the individual nor the individual's spouse or common-law partner, owned and lived in another home in the calendar year of the home purchase, or in any of the 4 preceding calendar years.

4-99.   The credit may be claimed by the individual who acquires the home or by that individual's spouse or common-law partner. For the purpose of this credit, a home is considered to be acquired by an individual only if the individual's interest in the home is registered in accordance with the applicable land registration system.

Volunteer Firefighters And Volunteer Search And Rescue Workers Tax Credits - ITA 118.06 And 118.07

4-100.   A credit is made available for both volunteer firefighters and volunteer search and rescue workers. The required services are defined in the *Income Tax Act* as follows:

Volunteer Firefighters Services   In this Section 118.06 and in Section 118.07, "eligible volunteer firefighting services" means services provided by an individual in the individual's capacity as a volunteer firefighter to a fire department that consist primarily of responding to and being on call for firefighting and related emergency calls, attending meetings held by the fire department and participating in required training related to the prevention or suppression of fires, but does not include services provided to a particular fire department if the individual provides firefighting services to the department otherwise than as a volunteer.

Volunteer Search And Rescue Workers Services means services, other than eligible volunteer firefighting services, provided by an individual in the individual's capacity as a volunteer to an eligible search and rescue organization that consist primarily of responding to and being on call for search and rescue and related emergency calls, attending meetings held by the organization and participating in required training related to search and rescue services, but does not include services provided to an organization if the individual provides search and rescue services to the organization otherwise than as a volunteer.

4-101.   As you can see, except for the type of services rendered, the conditions of service for the two types of credits are very similar.

4-102.   For either type of volunteer, if they perform at least 200 hours of volunteer services during a taxation year, they are eligible for the relevant credit. It would appear that the required 200 hours can be solely one type of volunteer service or, alternatively, a combination of both types of services. The base for the non-refundable credit is $3,000, resulting in a credit of $450 [(15%)($3,000)]. This amount is not indexed.

4-103.   Other relevant considerations are as follows:

- An individual meeting the 200 hour requirement can take either credit. However, they cannot take both, regardless of the number of hours of volunteer services.

- Under ITA 81(4), there is an exemption from inclusion in Net Income For Tax Purposes for up to $1,000 in compensation received for these types of volunteer work. This exemption is not available to individuals who claim either of these tax credits. Stated alternatively, an individual cannot have both the exemption and the tax credits.

Charitable Donations Tax Credit - ITA 118.1
Extent Of Coverage In This Chapter
4-104.   For tax purposes, donations, even in the form of cash, are segregated into categories, each with a different set of rules. Additional complications arise when non-cash donations are made. To be able to deal with gifts of depreciable capital property, a full understanding of capital gains and CCA procedures is required. Given these complications, a comprehensive treatment of charitable gifts is deferred until we revisit Taxable Income and Tax Payable in Chapter 11. However, there is limited coverage of charitable donations in this Chapter including the First-Time Donor's Super Credit (FDSC).

Eligible Gifts
4-105.   In our coverage of donations in this Chapter, we will deal only with gifts of cash or monetary assets. Donations of other types of property are covered in Chapter 11.

4-106.   In this Chapter, our coverage will be limited to what is referred to in ITA 118.1 as total charitable gifts. These include amounts donated to entities such as:

- a registered charity;
- a registered Canadian amateur athletic association;
- a Canadian municipality;
- the Canadian government;
- a university outside of Canada which normally enrolls Canadian students; and
- a charitable organization outside of Canada to which the Canadian government made a gift in the current or preceding taxation year. In addition, a provision exists that allows the federal government to provide a limited 24 month registration for foreign charities that are involved in relief and humanitarian aid, provided the activities are in the national interest of Canada.

Limits On Amount Claimed
4-107.   It is the policy of the government to limit the amount of charitable donations that are eligible for the tax credit to a portion of a taxpayer's Net Income For Tax Purposes. Note that, while corporations deduct their donations from Taxable Income as opposed to receiving a credit against Tax Payable, the limits on the amount of eligible donations are the same for corporations as they are for individuals.

4-108.   The general limit on eligible amounts of charitable gifts is 75 percent of Net Income For Tax Purposes. For individuals, this limit is increased to 100 percent of Net Income For Tax Purposes in the year of death and the preceding year.

Calculating The Credit (Without The First-Time Donor's Super Credit)

4-109.   All of the credits that we have discussed to this point apply the lowest federal bracket of 15 percent to some defined base. In contrast, this credit has always used a combination, with 15 percent being applied to the first $200 of eligible gifts and the highest bracket (29 percent prior to 2016) to eligible gifts in excess of $200. The use of this higher rate reflects the belief that, without the use of this higher rate, high income individuals would not have an adequate monetary incentive to make charitable donations.

4-110.   The fact that, in 2016, the maximum rate was increased from 29 percent to 33 percent resulted in a change to the charitable donations calculation in that year. While under the previous system, the 29 percent credit rate was applied to income that was taxed at lower rates, policy makers decided that they did not want the new highest rate of 33 percent to be available for this tax credit except to the extent that the taxpayer's income was being taxed at that rate. Given this, the calculation of this credit became more complex. More specifically, the credit is determined using the following formula:

$$[(15\%)(A)] + [(33\%)(B)] + [(29\%)(C)], \text{ where}$$

A = The first $200 of eligible gifts.

B = The lesser of:
- The amount by which total eligible gifts exceed $200; and
- The amount, if any, by which the individual's Taxable Income for the year exceeds $202,800 (i.e., the amount of income taxed at 33 percent)

C = The amount, if any, by which the individual's total gifts exceed the sum of $200 plus the amount determined in B.

Note If the taxpayer's Taxable Income does not exceed $202,800, the lesser amount of component B will be nil. This means that none of the credit is based on the 33 percent rate as no income is taxed at that rate. In these situations, the credit calculation is simply 15 percent of the first $200 of eligible gifts, plus 29 percent of any eligible gifts in excess of $200.

4-111.   The following example will serve to illustrate the application of this formula:

EXAMPLE For 2017, Doyle McLaughlin has Net Income For Tax Purposes of $620,000 and Taxable Income of $600,000. During the year, Doyle makes eligible gifts of $300,000. He is not eligible for the first-time donor's super credit.

ANALYSIS The maximum base for his charitable donations credit would be $465,000 [(75%)($620,000)]. Doyle's charitable donations tax credit would be calculated as follows (note that Taxable Income is used in the following calculation):

A = $200
B = The Lesser Of:
  • $300,000 - $200 = $299,800
  • $600,000 - $202,800 = $397,200 = the income taxed at 33 percent
C = Nil [$300,000 - ($200 + $299,800)]

The charitable donation credit would be equal to $98,964, calculated as [(15%)($200)] + [(33%)($299,800)] + [(29%)(Nil)]. As you would expect with Doyle's Taxable Income exceeding $202,800 by more than the amount of his eligible gifts, none of his credit is based on 29 percent.

Exercise Four - 11

Subject: Charitable Donations Tax Credit

For 2017, Travis Hoffman has Net Income For Tax Purposes of $350,000 and Taxable Income of $325,000. During the year, he makes eligible charitable gifts of $225,000.

He is not eligible for the first-time donor's super credit. Determine Mr. Hoffman's 2017 charitable donations tax credit.

SOLUTION available in print and online Study Guide.

4-112.   For couples, the CRA's administrative practices permit either spouse or common-law partner to claim some or all of the donations made by the couple. If neither individual has income taxed at 33 percent, combining the donations is advantageous given the 15 percent rate on the first $200 of donations. It would also be advantageous if one individual has sufficiently low income that not all of the couple's donations can be claimed, or if only one individual has income that is taxed at 33 percent. If both individuals have income that will be taxed at 33 percent, but neither can claim all the donations at that rate, the analysis is more complicated as splitting the donations could result in a higher combined donations credit.

Carry Forward Of Charitable Donations

4-113.   With the limit set at 75 percent of Net Income, individuals will normally be able to claim all of the donations that they make in a year. However, if their donations exceed the 75 percent limit, or they choose not to claim all of the donations that year, any unused amounts can be carried forward. The carry forward is generally 5 years. However, for ecological gifts, the period has been extended to 10 years.

4-114.   A further point here is that this limit is based on Net Income For Tax Purposes. This means that an individual could have eligible donations in excess of Taxable Income. This could occur, for example, if the individual deducted a large loss carry forward from a previous year. In situations such as this, it is important to recognize that the charitable donations tax credit is non-refundable. Given this, only the amount of donations required to reduce Tax Payable to nil should be claimed. Any additional amounts should be carried forward to future periods. Any claim that does not serve to reduce Tax Payable will simply be lost.

> **EXAMPLE**   Barry Mann has Net Income For Tax Purposes of $80,000. This is reduced to a Taxable Income of $20,000 because of a large business loss carry forward from a previous year. Because of a fortuitous lottery win, he chooses to make a charitable donation of $100,000.

> **ANALYSIS**   The potential base for Barry's charitable donations tax credit is $60,000 [(75%)($80,000)]. However, if he were to claim this amount, the credit of $17,372 [(15%)($200) + (29%)($59,800)] would be far in excess of the Tax Payable on only $20,000 of Taxable Income. Claiming the maximum amount would result in simply losing the greater part of the available credit. The preferable alternative would be to claim only enough to reduce his Tax Payable to nil and carry the remainder forward.

4-115.   Determining the specific amounts to be used and carried forward will be discussed in Chapter 11.

First-Time Donor's Super Credit (FDSC) - ITA 118.1(3.1)

4-116.   In a move designed to encourage charitable giving by new donors, especially young new donors, the 2013 budget introduced a temporary, First-Time Donor's Super Credit (FDSC) to supplement the existing regular charitable donations credit. An individual is considered a first-time donor if neither the individual nor the individual's spouse or common-law partner has claimed a charitable donations tax credit since 2008. Note that the restriction is on donations that have been claimed. Unclaimed donations do not count.

4-117.   The rules related to this supplement to the charitable donations credit are, unfortunately, relatively complicated. It can only be claimed once in the 2013 to 2017 taxation years. The last year to claim the FDSC is 2017. It is also limited to cash donations. This credit, which is added to the regular donations tax credit, provides an additional 25 percent credit on up to $1,000 in eligible donations. The FDSC may be shared by first-time donor couples, but couples must share the $1,000 limit.

4-118.   Since 2017 is the last year for the FDSC, any carried forward eligible donations must be claimed in 2017 to take advantage of the FDSC.

Exercise Four - 12

Subject: Charitable Donations Tax Credit (FDSC)

For 2017, Travis Hoffman has Net Income For Tax Purposes of $350,000 and Taxable Income of $250,000. During the year, he makes eligible charitable gifts of $225,000. He is eligible for the first-time donor's super credit. Determine Mr. Hoffman's 2017 charitable donations tax credit.

SOLUTION available in print and online Study Guide.

Medical Expense Tax Credit - ITA 118.2
Qualifying Medical Expenses

4-119.   There are many types of medical expenses which qualify for the credit under ITA 118.2. (For more detailed information, see Income Tax Folio S1-F1-C1, *Medical Expense Tax Credit*.) The current list of qualifying medical expenses includes amounts paid for:

- the services of authorized medical practitioners, dentists and registered nurses,
- prescribed drugs, medicaments and other preparations or substances,
- prescription eyeglasses or contact lenses,
- preventive, diagnostic and other laboratory work,
- dentures,
- premiums to private health services plans,
- the costs of home modifications for those with severe mobility restrictions, and to allow individuals confined to a wheelchair to be mobile within their home (see also the related home accessibility credit coverage beginning in Paragraph 4-86),
- guide and hearing-ear dogs and other specially trained animals, such as service animals trained to help an individual manage severe diabetes,
- artificial limbs, aids and other devices and equipment,
- products required because of incontinence,
- oxygen tents,
- the cost of rehabilitative therapy to adjust for speech or hearing loss,
- devices and equipment listed in ITR 5700 and prescribed by a medical practitioner,
- amounts paid for the design of an individualized therapy plan in situations where the cost of the therapy would be eligible for the medical expense tax credit.

4-120.   Although payments for attendants, nursing home care, and care in an institution are qualifying medical expenses, there are many complications with claiming these expenses. They will be briefly covered after we have dealt with the disability tax credit.

4-121.   Costs incurred for purely cosmetic reasons do not qualify for the medical expense tax credit. Examples of non-qualifying procedures include liposuction, hair replacement procedures, Botox injections and teeth whitening. Cosmetic procedures do qualify if they are required for medical or reconstructive purposes (e.g., facial surgery required due to a car accident). Perhaps wisely, the CRA refused to deal with the question of whether male infant circumcision was, or was not, cosmetic.

4-122.   An important qualifying factor here is the fact that the provinces control the identification of authorized medical practitioners for the purposes of this credit. The CRA website contains a current list of these authorized medical practitioners by province. For example, acupuncturists are considered authorized in Alberta, British Columbia, Newfoundland, Ontario and Quebec, but not in other provinces. Homeopaths are currently authorized medical practitioners only in Ontario. This means that there is considerable variation between the provinces in the types of costs that qualify for the medical expense tax credit.

Determining The Credit

4-123.   Qualifying medical expenses of an individual do not include any expense for which the individual has been, or is entitled to be, reimbursed unless the amount is required to be included in income. An amount reimbursed under a public or private medical, dental or hospitalization plan would not qualify for purposes of the medical expense tax credit.

4-124.   The medical expense tax credit is determined by the following formula:

$$A \ [(B - C) + D], \text{ where:}$$

A   is the appropriate percentage for the taxation year (15 percent).

B   is the total of an individual's medical expenses for himself, his spouse or common-law partner, and any of his children who have not reached 18 years of age at the end of the year.

C   is the lesser of 3 percent of the individual's Net Income For Tax Purposes and $2,268 (2017 figure). Note that the B - C total cannot be negative.

D   is the total of all amounts each of which is, in respect of a dependant of the individual (other than a child of the individual who has not attained the age of 18 years before the end of the taxation year), the amount determined by the formula

$$E - F, \text{ where:}$$

E   is the total of the dependant's medical expenses

F   is the lesser of 3 percent of the dependant's Net Income For Tax Purposes and $2,268 (2017 figure).

4-125.   If the taxpayer has no dependants who are 18 years of age or older, components D, E and F in the formula are not relevant. In this case, the B component is equal to the total of the qualifying medical expenses of the taxpayer, his spouse or common-law partner, and his minor children. This balance is reduced by the C component, the lesser of 3 percent of the taxpayer's income and an indexed figure which for 2017 is equal to $2,268. This latter figure is the limiting factor if an individual's 2017 Net Income For Tax Purposes is $75,600 ($2,268 ÷ 3%) or higher.

4-126.   If the taxpayer has dependants who are 18 years of age or older, a separate credit base calculation is required for each of these dependants. This credit base is equal to the dependant's qualifying medical expenses, reduced by the lesser of 3 percent of the dependant's Net Income For Tax Purposes and $2,268 (E and F in the formula). The taxpayer adds the total of these amounts to the credit base calculated for the taxpayer, his spouse or common-law partner and his minor children.

4-127.   A further point here relates to who actually pays for medical expenses. Interestingly, there is a conflict between legislation and administrative practice in this area. Both ITA 118.2 and Income Tax Folio S1-F1-C1 clearly state that medical expenses can only be deducted by the individual who paid for them. However, in the T1 Guide, this rule is contradicted for couples. According to this Guide, either spouse can claim the medical expense credit, without regard to who actually paid for the expenses. This administrative position is used in practice. The T1 Guide even includes a Tax Tip which suggests that since the credit can be claimed by either spouse, a comparison should be made to choose the better result.

Twelve Month Period

4-128.   Medical expenses can be claimed for any period of 12 months that ends in the taxation year. This provision is extended to 24 months in the year of death. The ability to claim expenses for a 12 month period ending in the year is advantageous for individuals with large medical expenses in a 12 month period other than a calendar year.

EXAMPLE   Alex Lau has Net Income For Tax Purposes of $60,000 in both 2016 and 2017. In July, 2016, he began a year long (and very painful) corrective dental surgery program. During July to December, 2016 he paid $10,000 in dental fees. During January to June, 2017 he paid $12,000 in dental fees.

ANALYSIS   The 2016 claim could be deferred and the $22,000 total could be claimed in full in the 2017 taxation year. The advantage of doing this is that the threshold amount reduction would be applied only once in 2017. If medical expenses had to be claimed in the year in which they were incurred, Mr. Lau would have to apply the threshold reduction of $1,800 [(3%)($60,000)] in both years. If the full amount is claimed in 2017, federal tax savings would total $270 [(15%)($1,800)].

Example Of Medical Expense Tax Credit Calculation

4-129.   The following example will illustrate the medical expense tax credit formula:

EXAMPLE   Sam Jonas and his dependent family members had the following Net Income For Tax Purposes and medical expenses for 2017. Sam paid for all of the medical expenses.

Individual	Net Income	Medical Expenses
Sam Jonas	$100,000	$ 5,000
Kelly (Sam's Wife)	12,000	4,400
Sue (Sam's 16 Year Old Daughter)	8,500	4,100
Sharon (Sam's 69 Year Old Mother)	6,000	16,500
Martin (Sam's 70 Year Old Father)	12,000	200
Total Medical Expenses		$30,200

ANALYSIS   Sam's 2017 medical expense tax credit, using the formula in Paragraph 4-124, would be calculated as follows:

Amount B Qualifying Expenses ($5,000 + $4,400 + $4,100)		$13,500
Amount C - Lesser Of:		
• [(3%)($100,000)] = $3,000		
• 2017 Threshold Amount = $2,268		(2,268)
Subtotal		$11,232
Amount D		
Sharon's Medical Expenses	$16,500	
Reduced By The Lesser Of:		
• $2,268		
• [(3%)($6,000)] = $180	(180)	16,320
Martin's Medical Expenses	$ 200	
Reduced By The Lesser Of:		
• $2,268		
• [(3%)($12,000)] = $360	(360)	Nil*
Allowable Amount Of Medical Expenses		$27,552
Amount A The Appropriate Rate (Minimum Rate)		15%
Medical Expense Tax Credit		$ 4,133

* Medical expenses can only be reduced to nil, the net result cannot be negative in this calculation.

Exercise Four - 13

Subject: Medical Expense Tax Credit

Ms. Maxine Davies and her spouse, Lance Davies, have 2017 medical expenses which total $4,330. While Ms. Davies has 2017 Net Income For Tax Purposes of $150,000, Lance's only income is $360 in savings account interest. They have three children. Mandy is 12, has 2017 medical expenses of $4,600 and no Net Income For Tax Purposes. Max is 21, has 2017 medical expenses of $8,425 and Net Income For Tax Purposes of $8,250. Matt is 23, has 2017 medical expenses of $120 and Net Income For Tax Purposes of $6,000. Ms. Davies pays all of the medical expenses. Determine Ms. Davies' medical expense tax credit for 2017.

SOLUTION available in print and online Study Guide.

Disability Tax Credit - ITA 118.3
Calculation
4-130.   The disability tax credit is available under ITA 118.3 and, for 2017, it is equal to $1,217 [(15%)($8,113)]. In addition, there is a supplement to this amount for a disabled child who is under the age of 18 at the end of the year. For 2017, the base for the supplement is $4,733, providing a total maximum credit for a disabled minor of $1,927 [(15%)($8,113 + $4,733)]. Note, however, that the supplement amount of $4,733 is reduced by the total of amounts paid for attendant care or supervision in excess of $2,772 that are deducted as child care costs, deducted as a disability support amount, or claimed as a medical expense in calculating the medical expense tax credit. This means that once such costs reach $7,505 ($4,733 + $2,772) for the year, the supplement for a child is completely eliminated.

4-131.   To qualify for the disability credit, the impairment must be such that there is a "marked" restriction of the activities of daily living or a "significant" restriction in more than one activity (while both terms are undefined, it appears that significant is less severe than marked). In addition, it must have lasted, or be expected to last, for at least 12 months.

4-132.   In general, a medical doctor, nurse practitioner (this group was added by the 2017 federal budget), or optometrist, must certify on Form T2201 that a severe physical or mental impairment exists. In the case of restrictions on the ability to walk, a physiotherapist can make the required certification.

4-133.   ITA 118.4(1) tries to make the conditions for qualifying for this credit as clear as possible. This Subsection points out that an individual clearly qualifies if they are blind. They also qualify if 90 percent of the time they cannot perform, or take an inordinate amount of time to perform, a basic activity of daily living. The following are listed as basic activities:

- mental functions necessary for everyday life;
- feeding oneself or dressing oneself;
- speaking such that the individual can be understood in a quiet setting by someone familiar with the individual;
- hearing such that the individual can, in a quiet setting, understand someone familiar with the individual;
- bowel or bladder functions; or
- walking.

Disability Credit Transfer To A Supporting Person
4-134.   In many cases, an individual who is sufficiently infirm to qualify for the disability credit will not have sufficient Tax Payable to use it. In this situation, all or part of the credit may be transferred to a spouse, or a supporting person who claimed the disabled individual as:

- a dependant under the eligible dependant provision [ITA 118(1)(b)];
- a dependant for purposes of the caregiver tax credit [ITA 118(1)(c.1)]; or
- a disabled dependant over 17 [ITA 118(1)(d)].

4-135.   In order to make the disability credit transfer available in situations where there is a disabled dependant who does not qualify for one of these credits, the transfer is extended by a somewhat awkward measure to situations in which the supporting person:

- could have claimed the eligible dependant credit, if the supporting person was not married; or

- could have claimed the disabled dependant over 17, or the caregiver credit, if the dependant had been 18 years of age or older and had no income.

4-136.   The credit amount that can be transferred is the same $1,217 that could be claimed by the disabled individual. However, if the disabled individual has Tax Payable in excess of credits under ITA 118 (personal credits), 118.01 to 118.07 (various credits including public transit passes) and 118.7 (CPP and EI credits), the credit must first be applied to reduce the disabled individual's Tax Payable to nil. If a balance remains after all Tax Payable has been eliminated, it can then be transferred to the supporting person.

4-137.   Income Tax Folio S1-F1-C2, *Disability Tax Credit* provides detailed guidance on the disability tax credit, including its transfer to a supporting person.

Exercise Four - 14

Subject: Disability Tax Credit

John Leslie lives with his wife and 21 year old blind son, Keith, who qualifies for the disability tax credit. Keith has no income of his own. During 2017, John paid medical expenses of $16,240 for Keith. None of these expenses involve attendant care. John's Taxable Income for 2017 was $100,000. Determine the total amount of tax credits related to Keith that will be available to John.

SOLUTION available in print and online Study Guide.

Other Credits And Deductions Related To Disabilities

4-138.   Disabled individuals, or a supporting person, may have paid significant medical expenses involving attendant care and/or nursing home care. The availability of the medical expense tax credit for these costs is limited by the following considerations:

- Neither the individual, nor a supporting person, can claim the disability credit if a medical expense credit is claimed for a full time attendant, or for full time care in a nursing home. However, the individual or supporting person can claim either of the two amounts.

- The disability credit can be claimed if a medical expense credit is claimed for a part-time attendant. Part-time is defined as expenses claimed of less than $10,000 for the year ($20,000 in the year of death). Note that part-time attendant care can only be claimed as a medical expense credit if no part of that care is claimed as child care costs or for attendant care required to produce income.

4-139.   For disabled individuals who work, or who attend a designated educational institution or secondary school, the disability supports deduction provides tax relief for a number of medical expenses, including attendant care, which would assist a disabled person to work or go to school. (See Chapter 9, Other Income, Other Deductions And Other Issues for coverage of this deduction.)

4-140.   There are complications and restrictions related to claiming these and many other types of medical expenses. Complete coverage of all the relevant rules goes beyond the scope of this text. For those interested in this subject, we refer you to the Income Tax Folio 1, "*Health and Medical"*. There are currently three Chapters (as of January, 2017) that provide detailed guidance on the medical expense tax credit, (S1-F1-C1), disability tax credit (S1-F1-C2) and disability supports deduction (S1-F1-C3).

Education Related Tax Credits

Tuition Fees Tax Credit - ITA 118.5(1) To ITA 118.5(4)

4-141.   Under ITA 118.5, individuals receive a credit against Tax Payable equal to 15 percent of qualifying tuition fees paid with respect to the calendar year, regardless of the year in which they are actually paid. The fees must total at least $100, but there is no upper limit on this credit. The following tuition fees qualify:

- Tuition fees paid to a university, college, or other institution for post-secondary courses located in Canada.

- Tuition fees paid to an institution certified by the Minister of Employment and Social Development for a course that developed or improved skills in an occupation (the individual must be 16 or older).

- Tuition fees paid to a university outside Canada. To qualify the course must have a minimum duration of 3 weeks.

- For individuals who live near the U.S. border and commute, tuition fees paid to a U.S. college or university for part-time studies.

4-142.   The March 22, 2017 Federal budget expanded the availability of the tuition tax credit to include fees paid for occupational skills courses offered by a university, college or other post-secondary institution and that are not at the post-secondary level. To qualify, the course must be taken for the purposes of providing the individual with skills in an occupation and the individual must have attained the age of 16 before the end of the year.

4-143.   It is not uncommon for employers to reimburse employees for amounts of tuition paid, particularly if the relevant course is related to the employer's business. If the reimbursement is included in the employee's income, the student can claim a credit for the tuition paid. However, if amounts reimbursed are not included in the student's income, the tuition credit is not available.

Ancillary And Examination Fees Included In Tuition Fees Tax Credit

4-144.   It has been noted that universities are relying more heavily on ancillary fees for such items as health services, athletics, and various other services including examinations. To the extent that such fees are required for all full time students (if the student is attending full time) or all part time students (if the student is attending part time), these fees are eligible for inclusion in the base for the tuition fees tax credit. The general provision of ancillary fees is found in ITA 118.5(3), while the provision for ancillary examination fees is found in ITA 118.5(4).

4-145.   If such fees are not required of all full time or part time students, ITA 118.5(3) allows up to $250 in such ancillary fees to be added to the total, even if they do not meet the condition of being required for all full or part time students.

4-146.   In addition, ITA 118.5(4) allows up to $250 in ancillary examination fees to be added to the total if they are not required to be paid by all students taking the examination. To be eligible, the fees must exceed $100.

4-147.   Eligible fees include amounts for items such as the cost of examination materials or required identification cards. It does not, however, include fees for examinations required for entrance to professional programs.

Interest On Student Loans Tax Credit - ITA 118.62

4-148.   There is a credit available under ITA 118.62 if a student or a related person has paid interest on student loans. The credit for the student is equal to 15 percent of interest paid in the year, or in any of the five preceding years. The interest paid must be on a loan under the

Canada Student Loans Act, the *Canada Student Financial Assistance Act*, the *Apprentice Loans Act*, or a provincial statute governing the granting of financial assistance to students at the post-secondary school level.

Exercise Four - 15

Subject: Education Related Tax Credits

During 2017, Sarah Bright attends university for 4 months of full time study and 2 months of part-time study. Her total tuition for the year, including all ancillary fees, is $3,200 of which she prepaid $1,000 in 2016. The amount paid in 2017 includes $400 in fees that are only charged to students in her geology program. Interest paid for the year on her student loan was $325. Determine the total amount of education related tax credits that would be available for Ms. Bright for 2017.

SOLUTION available in print and online Study Guide.

Carry Forward Of Tuition, Education, And Textbook Credits - ITA 118.61

> **Byrd/Chen Note**   Prior to 2017, education and textbook credits were available for students. As these two credits were repealed for 2017 and subsequent years, we have not covered them and will not include them in any of the problem material. However, to the extent that such credits have not been used in years prior to 2017, they can be carried forward and used in years after 2016. This is why the carry forward provision (ITA 118.61) still refers to these credits. We will not include such carry forwards in any of our problem material.

4-149.   There are situations in which a student does not have sufficient Tax Payable to use their tuition credit and, in addition, has not transferred it to a spouse, common-law partner, parent, or grandparent (see Paragraph 4-154). To deal with this type of situation, ITA 118.61 allows a carry forward of unused tuition credits. There is no time limit on this carry forward. In addition, ITA 118.62 provides for a 5 year carry forward of unused interest on student loans.

4-150.   Unfortunately, the calculation of the amount that is carried forward can be complex. Although the *Income Tax Act* uses Tax Payable and credit amounts to calculate carry forwards and transfers, Schedule 11 in the personal tax return uses Taxable Income and credit base amounts in its calculations. We will explain and illustrate both approaches in the example in Paragraph 4-158.

4-151.   To carry amounts forward, the total available credits must be reduced by the student's Tax Payable, calculated using the following credits (note the medical expense tax credit is not included in the list):

- ITA 118 (Personal)
- ITA 118.01 Through ITA 118.07 (Various credits)
- ITA 118.3 (Disability)
- ITA 118.7 (CPP And EI)

4-152.   The available amount is also reduced by transfers to other individuals. The resulting balance can be carried forward and is available for the student's personal use in any subsequent year. However, once it is carried forward, it cannot be transferred to another individual.

4-153.   As indicated in the **Byrd/Chen Note**, while the legislation that provides for the education credit and textbook credit was eliminated for 2017 and subsequent taxation years, amounts that are unused at the end of 2016 can be carried forward to years after 2017.

Transfer Of Tuition Credit - ITA 118.9

4-154.   ITA 118.9 provides for a transfer of this tax credit to a parent or grandparent. ITA 118.8 provides for a transfer of this credit (plus several others), to a spouse or common-law partner. ITA 118.81 limits the total amount of the tuition credit that can be transferred under either of these provisions. The transfer is at the discretion of the student and the legislation states that he must indicate in writing the amount that he is willing to transfer.

4-155.   The maximum transfer for an individual student is the lesser of the available credit and $5,000, multiplied by the tax rate for the minimum tax bracket (referred to as the "appropriate percentage"). This amount is $750 [(15%)($5,000)].

4-156.   This $750 maximum amount must be reduced by the student's Tax Payable calculated after the same credits used to calculate the carry forward of education related credits. As described in Paragraph 4-151, these are the credits available under ITA 118 through ITA 118.07, 118.3 and 118.7. If these credits reduce the student's Tax Payable to nil, the full $750 is available for transfer.

4-157.   The $750 limit is on a per student basis. A parent or grandparent could have $750 transfers from any number of children or grandchildren. For obvious reasons, transfers from more than one spouse would not be acceptable for tax purposes (even if having more than one spouse could be acceptable for other purposes). If the student is married, the supporting parent or grandparent can make the claim only if the student's spouse did not claim the spousal credit, or any unused credits transferred by the student (see Paragraph 4-166).

4-158. An example will serve to illustrate both the ITA 118.9 transfer, as well as the ITA 118.81 limits on this transfer.

> **EXAMPLE**   Megan Doxy has 2017 Taxable Income of $13,000, all of which is rental income. She attends university full time for 8 months of the year, paying a total amount for tuition of $8,000. Other than her tuition credit, her only other tax credit is her personal amount of $1,745 [(15%)($11,635)]. She would like to transfer the maximum credits to her father.
>
> **ANALYSIS - Income Tax Act Approach**   Megan's tuition credit is $1,200 [(15%)($8,000)], well in excess of the maximum transfer of $750. However, this maximum of $750 would have to be reduced by Megan's Tax Payable after the deduction of her personal amount. This amount would be $205 [(15%)($13,000 - $11,635)], leaving a maximum transfer of $545 ($750 - $205). This would leave Megan with remaining unused credits of $450 ($1,200 - $205 - $545) which can be carried forward to future years, but only for her own use. These calculations are the result of using the approach presented in the *Income Tax Act*.
>
> **ANALYSIS - Tax Return Approach**   The alternative calculation approach that is used in the tax return begins with the total tuition amount of $8,000. The maximum transfer amount in this approach is $5,000. This would be reduced by $1,365 ($13,000 - $11,635), the excess of Megan's Taxable Income over her basic personal amount. This results in a maximum transfer of $3,635 ($5,000 - $1,365). Megan's carry forward amount is $3,000 ($8,000 - $1,365 - $3,635). Multiplying these amounts by 15 percent gives the same $545 [(15%)($3,635)] transfer and $450 [(15%)($3,000)] of unused credits as the preceding *Income Tax Act* approach.

Exercise Four - 16

Subject: Transfer And Carry Forward Of Tuition Tax Credits

Jerry Fall has 2017 Taxable Income of $12,250. He attends an American university on a full time basis for 11 months of the year, paying a total amount for tuition of $23,500 (Canadian dollars). His only tax credits, other than the tuition credit, are his basic personal credit and a medical expense credit of $233 [(15%)($1,555)]. Determine Jerry's total tuition tax credit and indicate how much of this total could be transferred to a parent and how much would be carried forward.

SOLUTION available in print and online Study Guide.

Employment Insurance (EI) And Canada Pension Plan (CPP) Tax Credits - ITA 118.7

4-159.   ITA 118.7 provides a tax credit equal to 15 percent of the Employment Insurance (EI) premiums paid by an individual, all of the Canada Pension Plan (CPP) contributions paid on employment income, and half of the CPP contributions paid on self-employed income.

4-160.   For 2017, an employee's CPP contributions are based on maximum pensionable earnings of $55,300, less a basic exemption of $3,500. The rate for 2017 is 4.95 percent, resulting in a maximum contribution of $2,564 [(4.95%)($55,300 - $3,500)]. This provides for a maximum 2017 credit against federal Tax Payable of $385 [(15%)($2,564)]. The employer matches the contributions made by the employee. However, this matching payment has no tax consequences for the employee.

4-161.   A self-employed individual earning business income must make a matching CPP contribution for himself, effectively paying twice the amount he would as an employee. As discussed in Chapter 9, the matching contribution is a deduction from Net Income For Tax Purposes under ITA 60(e) (a Division B, Subdivision e deduction). This treatment for the matching CPP contribution as a deduction is analogous to the treatment used by employers. This means that a self-employed individual will have a tax credit equal to one-half of his CPP contributions for self-employed income, and a deduction for the remaining one-half.

4-162.   For 2017, EI premiums are based on maximum insurable earnings of $51,300. The employee's rate is 1.63 percent, resulting in a maximum annual premium of $836. This results in a maximum credit against federal Tax Payable of $125 [(15%)($836)].

4-163.   Employers are also required to pay EI premiums, the amount being 1.4 times the premiums paid by the employee. However, these employer paid premiums have no tax consequences for the employee. While self-employed individuals can elect to participate in the EI program, unlike for the CPP, they do not have to remit the employer share. Their premiums will be limited to the same $836 that is applicable to employees.

Overpayment Of EI Premiums And CPP Contributions

4-164.   It is not uncommon for employers to withhold EI and CPP amounts that are in excess of the amounts required. This can happen through an error on the part of the employer's payroll system. Even in the absence of errors, overpayments can arise when an individual changes employers. We would note that the CRA's form T2204 is designed to assist taxpayers in calculating any overpayment of EI. Schedule 8 of the T1 provides similar assistance in calculating any CPP overpayment.

4-165.   A refund of these excess amounts is available when an individual files his tax return. While any CPP or EI overpayment is not part of the base for the tax credit, it will increase the refund available or decrease the tax liability that is calculated in the return.

EXAMPLE   Jerry Weist changed employers during 2017 and, as a consequence, the total amount of EI premiums withheld during the year was $933. In a similar fashion, the total amount of CPP contributions withheld by the two employers was $2,613. His employment income was well in excess of the maximum insurable and pensionable earnings.

ANALYSIS   In filing his 2017 tax return, Jerry will claim a refund of $146, calculated as follows:

EI Premiums Withheld	$933	
2017 Maximum	(836)	$ 97
CPP Contributions Withheld	$2,613	
2017 Maximum	(2,564)	49
Refund		$146

Transfers To A Spouse Or Common-Law Partner - ITA 118.8

4-166.   In the preceding material, we have covered several tax credits that can be claimed by either spouse, such as the charitable donations credit. There are also four tax credits that can be transferred to a spouse or common-law partner under ITA 118.8. They are:

- the age tax credit (see Paragraph 4-66),
- the pension income tax credit (see Paragraph 4-68),
- the disability tax credit (see Paragraph 4-130), and
- the tuition tax credit to a maximum of $750 (see material beginning in Paragraph 4-154).

4-167.   The maximum amount that can be transferred is based on the sum of the preceding credits, reduced by a modified calculation of the spouse or common-law partner's Tax Payable.   While the legislation is based on Tax Payable, the T1 tax return uses a simplified approach based on Taxable Income, much like the alternative calculation for the tuition credit transfer. This approach starts with the sum of the base for all of the preceding credits. From this amount is subtracted the spouse's taxable income, reduced by the bases of:

- the basic personal credit,
- the Canada employment credit, CPP and EI credits,
- the credits under ITA 118.01 through ITA 118.07 (various credits including public transit fees credit and adoption expenses credit),
- the tuition credit.

4-168.   The resulting remainder, if any, is the amount that can be transferred to a spouse or common-law partner.

Exercise Four - 17

Subject: Transfer Of Credits From A Spouse

Mr. Martin Levee is 68 years old and has Net Income For Tax Purposes of $42,000. Of this total, $24,000 was from a life annuity that he purchased with funds in his RRSP. His spouse is 66 years old and blind. She has no income of her own (she is ineligible for OAS), and is attending university on a full time basis. Her tuition fees for the year were $2,200 and she was in full time attendance for 4 months of the year. Determine Mr. Levee's maximum tax credits for 2017. Ignore the possibility of splitting his pension income with his spouse.

SOLUTION available in print and online Study Guide.

We suggest you work Self Study Problems Four-2 and 3 at this point.

Political Contributions Tax Credits - ITA 127(3)
Federal Accountability Act

4-169.   While no changes have been made in the *Income Tax Act*, the *Federal Accountability Act* limits the ability to make political contributions to individuals only. More specifically, this *Act* contains the following provisions:

- There is a total ban on contributions by corporations, trade unions and unincorporated associations.

- For 2017, the amount that can be contributed by an individual:

    - to each registered party,
    - in total to all the registered associations, nomination contestants and candidates of each registered party,
    - in total to all leadership contestants in a particular contest, and
    - to each independent candidate

    is limited to $1,550 for the year. The limits increase by $25 on January 1 in each subsequent year.

Income Tax Rules

4-170.   A federal tax credit is available on monetary political contributions made to a registered federal political party, or to candidates at the time of a federal general election or by-election. The maximum value is $650 and it is available to both individuals and corporations.

4-171.   However, as discussed in the preceding Paragraph, the *Federal Accountability Act* totally bans contributions by corporations. The credit is calculated as follows:

	Contributions	Credit Rate	Tax Credit
First	$ 400	3/4	$300
Next	350	1/2	175
Next	525	1/3	175
Maximum Credit	$1,275		$650

4-172.   The $650 credit is achieved when contributions total $1,275. Contributions in excess of this amount do not generate additional credits. Also note that most provinces have a similar credit against provincial Tax Payable. There is a difference, however, in that the eligible contributions must be made to a registered provincial political party.

Exercise Four - 18

Subject: Political Contributions Tax Credit

Ms. Vivacia Unger contributes $785 to the Liberal New Conservative Democratic Party, a registered federal political party. Determine the amount of her federal political contributions tax credit.

SOLUTION available in print and online Study Guide.

Labour Sponsored Venture Capital Corporations Credit - ITA 127.4

4-173.   Labour Sponsored Venture Capital Corporations (LSVCCs) are a form of mutual fund corporation, sponsored by an eligible labour organization, and mandated to provide venture capital to small and medium sized businesses.

4-174. There is a 15 percent federal tax credit for provincially registered LSVCCs prescribed under the ITA. The maximum credit available is $750 [(15%)($5,000 net cost of shares)]. To be eligible for the federal credit, the provincially registered LSVCC would need to:

- be eligible for a provincial tax credit of at least 15 percent of the cost of an individual's shares;
- be sponsored by an eligible labour body; and
- mandate that at least 60 percent of the LSVCC's shareholders' equity be investments in small and medium sized enterprises.

Dividend Tax Credit
4-175. The dividend tax credit is covered in Chapter 7 as part of our discussion of property income.

Foreign Tax Credits
4-176. The credits that are available for taxes paid in foreign jurisdictions are covered in Chapters 7 and 11.

Investment Tax Credits
4-177. When taxpayers make certain types of expenditures, they become eligible for investment tax credits. These credits reduce federal Tax Payable. While these credits can be claimed by individuals as well as corporations, they are much more commonly used by corporations and, as a consequence, we cover investment tax credits in Chapter 14.

We suggest you work Self Study Problems Four-4 and Four-5 at this point.

Refundable Credits

Introduction
4-178. The credits that we have encountered to this point can be described as non-refundable. This means that, unless the taxpayer has Tax Payable for the current taxation year, there is no benefit from the credit. Further, with the exception of the charitable donations credit and education related credits, there is no carry forward of these non-refundable credits to subsequent taxation years. This means that, if the credits are not used in the current year, they are permanently lost.

4-179. In contrast, refundable credits are paid to the taxpayer, without regard to whether that individual has a Tax Payable balance. In this section we will describe four of these refundable credits:

- the GST/HST tax credit;
- the refundable medical expense supplement;
- the working income tax benefit (WITB); and
- the refundable teacher and early childhood educator school supply tax credit.

4-180. With respect to the GST/HST credit, our coverage will be limited. This reflects the fact that, unlike the other three refundable credits, taxpayers do not calculate the GST/HST credit in their tax returns. Rather, the CRA calculates the credit from the tax returns that the taxpayer has filed in previous years and pays the amount to the eligible taxpayers. Given this, there is no need to provide coverage of the detailed calculation of this credit.

GST/HST Credit - ITA 122.5
4-181. One of the major problems with the goods and services tax (GST) is the fact that it is a regressive tax (see discussion in Chapter 1). In order to provide some relief from the impact of the GST on low income families, there is a refundable GST credit available under ITA 122.5.

4-182.   The GST/HST credit is determined by the CRA on the basis of eligibility information supplied in the individual's tax returns for previous years. Because of this, it is only paid to individuals who file tax returns.

4-183.   For the payments made between July, 2016 through June, 2017 (the most current amounts available at the time of writing), the GST/HST credit is calculated as follows:

- $280 for the "eligible individual". An eligible individual includes a Canadian resident who is 19 years of age or over during the current taxation year, or is married or living common-law, or is a parent who resides with their child. In the case of a married couple, only one spouse can be an eligible individual.

- $280 for a "qualified relation". A qualified relation is defined as a cohabiting spouse or common-law partner. If the eligible individual does not have a qualified relation, he is entitled to an additional credit that is the lesser of $147 and 2 percent of the individual's Net Income For Tax Purposes in excess of $9,073.

- $280 for a dependant eligible for the eligible dependant tax credit.

- $147 for each "qualified dependant". A "qualified dependant" is defined as a person who is the individual's child or is dependent on the individual or the individual's cohabiting spouse or common-law partner for support. In addition, the child or dependent person must be under 19 years of age, reside with the individual, have never had a spouse or common-law partner, and have never been a parent of a child he has resided with.

4-184.   The total of these amounts must be reduced by 5 percent of the excess of the individual's 2015 "adjusted income" over an indexed threshold amount of $36,429. The system uses information provided on the 2015 tax return, since this return is normally filed by early 2016. "Adjusted Income" is defined as total income of the individual and his qualified relation, if any.

4-185.   The GST/HST credit is available to all eligible individuals, without regard to whether they have Tax Payable. The amount of the credit is calculated by the CRA on the basis of information included in the individual's tax return for a particular year, and the amounts are automatically paid to the taxpayer in subsequent years.

Refundable Medical Expense Supplement - ITA 122.51

4-186.   The calculation of the GST/HST credit is not included in the tax return. The three other refundable credits, including the refundable medical expense supplement, are included in the tax return.

4-187.   To be eligible for the 2017 medical expense supplement, the individual must be 18 or over at the end of the year, and must have earned income (employment or business) of at least $3,514. The credit is the lesser of $1,203 and 25/15 of the medical expense tax credit that can be claimed for the year. This can also be described as 25 percent of the expenses eligible for the medical expense tax credit plus 25 percent of the disability supports deduction (see Paragraph 4-153).

4-188.   The lesser amount is reduced by 5 percent of "family net income" in excess of an indexed threshold amount. Family net income is the sum of the income of the taxpayer and his spouse or common-law partner, but not that of an eligible dependant. For 2017, the income threshold is $26,644 and the credit is completely eliminated when family net income reaches $50,704 [($1,203 ÷ 5%) + $26,644]. A simple example will serve to illustrate this provision:

EXAMPLE   For 2017, Mr. Larry Futon and his spouse have medical expenses that total $4,650. His Net Income For Tax Purposes is $26,900, all of which qualifies as earned income. His spouse has Net Income For Tax Purposes of $500. Mr. Futon claims the caregiver tax credit for his mother who has Net Income of $8,000. She is not mentally or physically infirm. He has no tax credits other than personal and medical credits.

ANALYSIS   Mr. Futon's allowable medical expenses for tax credit purposes would be $3,843 [$4,650 - (3%)($26,900)], resulting in a tax credit of $576 [(15%)($3,843)]. Given this, 25/15 of the credit, or alternatively, 25 percent of the allowable medical expenses, would equal $961. Since this is less than the maximum of $1,203, his refundable credit would be $961 less a reduction of $38 [(5%)($26,900 + $500 - $26,644)], leaving a balance of $923 ($961 - $38).

4-189.   The receipt of this refundable credit does not affect an individual's ability to claim a tax credit for the same medical expenses that are used to calculate the refundable credit. In the preceding example, Mr. Futon's basic personal, spousal, caregiver, and medical expense credit bases total $31,345 [$11,635 + ($11,635 - $500) + $4,732 + $3,843]. This is more than his Taxable Income of $26,900 which results in his federal Tax Payable being nil. This means that he will be able to claim the entire $923 as a refund.

Exercise Four - 19

Subject: Refundable Medical Expense Supplement

During 2017, Ms. Lara Brunt and her common-law partner, Sara, have medical expenses that total $6,250. Her Net Income For Tax Purposes is $27,400, all of which qualifies as earned income. Sara has no income of her own. Determine Lara's minimum Tax Payable for 2017. Ignore any credits other than the basic, spousal and medical expense related credits.

SOLUTION available in print and online Study Guide.

Working Income Tax Benefit - ITA 122.7
The Welfare Wall

4-190.   Despite the rantings of ostensibly virtuous individuals of a right-wing persuasion, many individuals who are receiving various types of social assistance are not necessarily lazy or lacking in motivation. The simple fact is that, given the types of wages such individuals receive, they are often better off economically if they do not work. The types of wages that such individuals can earn are typically at the legal "minimum" (e.g., the minimum wage ranges from $10.65 in Nova Scotia to $13.60 per hour in Alberta). The amounts earned at this wage are typically offset by reductions in social assistance payments. Additional negative effects flow from loss of subsidized housing, prescription drug assistance, and other benefits that are available to individuals with little or no income.

4-191.   It has been demonstrated that, if such individuals find employment, the result can be a reduction in their real income. Instead of rewarding their efforts, our current system can actually punish individuals who make an effort to improve their economic status. This is commonly referred to as the welfare wall.

Calculation Of The Basic Working Income Tax Benefit (WITB)

4-192.   To deal with this problem, the *Income Tax Act* provides a refundable credit for individuals over the age of 19 and have working income in excess of $3,000. Working income is defined as gross employment income (i.e., no employment expenses deducted), business income, scholarships, and research grants. The amount of the benefit will depend on whether the individual is single or, alternatively, has a spouse or an eligible dependant. For this purpose, an eligible dependant is a child who lives with the individual and who is under the age of 19 at the end of the year.

4-193.   Unfortunately, the calculation of this benefit is fairly complex and, in addition, there is a significant lag in the availability of relevant parameters for the current year. Given this, we have decided not to include detailed coverage of the calculation of this refundable credit. We have, however, provided sufficient information about the general nature of the benefit that users of this material will be aware of when the refundable credit might be available.

Refundable Teacher And Early Childhood Educator School Supply Tax Credit - ITA 122.9

4-194.   The government has observed that early childhood educators often use their own funds to acquire supplies for the purpose of teaching or enhancing students' learning. In recognition of this situation, the 2016 federal budget introduced a measure that allows an employee who is an eligible educator to claim a 15 percent tax credit for up to $1,000 of eligible expenditures. While it is unlikely that employed teachers will not have sufficient Tax Payable to claim the credit, the credit is refundable.

4-195.   The definitions relevant to this credit are as follows:

Eligible Educator   To be eligible for this credit, a teacher will need to have a teacher's certificate that is valid in the province where they are employed. Early childhood educators qualify if they hold either a teacher's certificate or a diploma in early childhood education that is recognized by the province in which they are employed.

Eligible Supplies   Eligible supplies will include the following durable goods:

- games and puzzles;
- supplementary books for classrooms;
- educational support software;
- or containers such as plastic boxes for themes and kits.

Eligible supplies will also include consumable goods such as:

- construction paper for activities, flashcards, or activity centres;
- items for science experiments, such as seeds, potting soil, vinegar, and stir sticks;
- art supplies, such as paper, glue, and paint; and
- various stationery items, such as pens, pencils, posters, and charts.

4-196.   For the cost of supplies to qualify for this credit, employers will be required to certify that the supplies were purchased for the purpose of teaching or otherwise enhancing learning in a classroom or learning environment. Claimants will be required to retain their receipts for eligible purchases.

Social Benefits Repayment (OAS And EI)

Basic Concepts

Clawbacks

4-197.   Many Canadian tax credits and benefits are available on a universal basis, without regard to the income level of the recipient. However, both Old Age Security payments (OAS) and Employment Insurance payments (EI) are reduced for higher income individuals.

4-198.   With respect to OAS payments, the government assesses a Part I.2 tax on OAS benefits received by individuals with an adjusted Net Income above a threshold amount. In similar fashion, the *Employment Insurance Act* requires that individuals with an adjusted Net Income above a specified threshold amount repay a portion of any Employment Insurance (EI) benefits received. These required repayments are commonly referred to as "clawbacks".

Treatment In Net And Taxable Income

4-199.   Both OAS payments received and EI payments received must be included in an individual's Net Income For Tax Purposes. However, in situations where part or all of these amounts must be repaid, it would not be equitable to have the full amounts received flow through to Taxable Income and be fully taxed.

4-200.   This problem is dealt with by providing a deduction for amounts repaid. You may recall from Chapter 1 that one of the components of Net Income For Tax Purposes was Other Deductions (subdivision e of the *Income Tax Act*). While we will not provide detailed coverage of this subdivision until Chapter 9, we need to note here that ITA 60(v.1) provides a deduction for repayments of EI, and ITA 60(w) provides a deduction for repayment of OAS amounts received.

4-201.   As both the EI and OAS repayments are calculated on the basis of the individual's income in excess of a threshold amount, the question arises as to whether these tests should be applied using income figures which include the full amount received or, alternatively, income figures from which the repayments have been deducted. The solution to this problem will be discussed in the two sections which follow.

Employment Insurance (EI) Benefits Clawback

4-202.   The *Employment Insurance Act* requires the partial repayment of benefits received if the recipient's threshold income is greater than $64,125 (1.25 times the 2017 maximum insurable earnings of $51,300). This $64,125 income figure includes all of the components of Net Income For Tax Purposes except the deductions for repayment of EI benefits [ITA 60(v.1)] and the deduction for the repayment of OAS benefits [ITA 60(w)]. As the EI clawback is deducted from the threshold income used for determining the OAS clawback, the EI clawback must be determined prior to calculating any amount of OAS clawback.

4-203.   Once the amount of threshold income over $64,125 is determined, it must be compared to the EI benefits included in the current year's Net Income For Tax Purposes. The lesser of these two amounts is multiplied by 30 percent and this becomes the amount that must be repaid for the year as a social benefits repayment. This amount can then be deducted under ITA 60(v.1) in the determination of Net Income For Tax Purposes for the year.

Old Age Security (OAS) Benefits Clawback

4-204.   The OAS clawback is the lesser of the OAS payments included in income and 15 percent of the taxpayer's income in excess of the $74,788 income threshold. For this purpose, income is equal to Net Income For Tax Purposes computed after any EI clawback, but before consideration of the deduction for the OAS clawback.

4-205.   For the first quarter of 2017, the OAS benefit is $578.53 per month. If this rate did not change during the coming year, the 2017 total would be $6,942.36. Based on this figure, the benefit would disappear at an income level of $121,070.

4-206.   For higher income seniors, OAS benefits are clawed back on a regular basis, with some individuals never receiving benefits during their lifetime. Given this, the government has an administrative procedure under which they withhold payments that they expect to be clawed back. Expectations are based on tax returns filed in the two previous years.

> **EXAMPLE**   In her tax returns for both 2015 and 2016, Sally Leung has reported Taxable Income in excess of $200,000 per year. Despite the fact that Sally is 70 years of age, she would receive no OAS payments in 2017.

4-207.   Interestingly, once an individual has applied for OAS, the government will issue an information slip [T4A(OAS)] indicating that they have received the full benefit, even in cases where no OAS was paid and the full amount has been withheld. The information slip will show any amount that is clawed back. This means the full benefit must be included in income, accompanied by a deduction for the amount "repaid". For an individual who reaches age 65 with the expectation that they will have very high income for the foreseeable future, this process can be avoided by not applying for OAS.

Exercise Four - 20

Subject: EI and OAS Clawbacks

For 2017, Ms. Marilyn Jacobi has net employment income of $60,000, receives EI payments of $10,000, and receives $7,000 in Old Age Security (OAS) payments. No amount was withheld from the OAS payments because she had very low income in the previous two years due to large rental losses. Determine Ms. Jacobi's Net Income For Tax Purposes for 2017.

SOLUTION available in print and online Study Guide.

Comprehensive Example

4-208.   While this Chapter has provided a reasonably detailed description of the determination of Tax Payable for individuals, including small examples of some of the issues that arise in this process, a more comprehensive example is appropriate at this point. To focus on the federal tax calculations, we have ignored provincial income taxes and income tax withholdings on employment income. In the Study Guide, there is an additional example containing a completed tax return which includes provincial income taxes.

Basic Data

Mr. Thomas Baxter is 66 years of age and his 2017 income is made up of net employment income of $73,800 and Old Age Security benefits of $7,000 (because of large business losses during the previous two years, no amount was withheld from these payments). For 2017, Mr. Baxter's employer withheld maximum CPP and EI contributions. Other information pertaining to 2017 is as follows:

1. Mr. Baxter's spouse is 49 years old and qualifies for the disability tax credit. Her income for the year totalled $5,000.

2. Mr. and Mrs. Baxter have two daughters, Kim, aged 14 and Lori, aged 17. Kim had income of $2,700 for the year while Lori had net income of $2,000. In September, 2017, Lori began full time attendance at a Canadian university. Mr. Baxter paid her tuition fees of $5,000, of which $2,500 was for the fall, 2017 semester. Lori is willing to transfer her tuition credit to her father.

3. The family medical expenses for the year, all of which were paid by Mr. Baxter, totalled $2,843. Of this amount, $300 was paid for Kim and $900 for Lori.

4. During the year, Mr. Baxter made cash donations to registered Canadian charities in the amount of $3,000. As he has made donations every year for the last 10 years, he is not eligible for the first time super donor tax credit.

5. During the year, Mr. Baxter made contributions to federal political parties totalling $800.

Net And Taxable Income

Net Employment Income	$73,800
OAS Benefits	7,000
Net Income Before Clawback	$80,800
OAS Clawback (Note One)	(902)
Net Income For Tax Purposes And Taxable Income	$79,898

Note One   The required repayment of OAS is the lesser of:

- $7,000, the OAS payments included in income, and
- $902 [(15%)($80,800 - $74,788)].

Tax Payable/Federal Balance Owing

The federal tax payable and balance owing is calculated as follows:

Federal Tax On First $45,916		$ 6,887
Federal Tax On Next $33,982 ($79,898 - $45,916) At 20.5%		6,966
Gross Tax		$13,853
Tax Credits:		
Basic Personal Amount	($11,635)	
Spousal Including Infirm Amount		
($11,635 + $2,150 - $5,000)	(8,785)	
Additional Caregiver Amount (Note Two)	Nil	
EI Premiums (Maximum)	(836)	
CPP Contributions (Maximum)	(2,564)	
Canada Employment	(1,178)	
Age [$7,225 - (15%)($79,898 - $36,430)]	(705)	
Medical Expenses (Note Three)	(575)	
Mrs. Baxter's Disability Transferred	(8,113)	
Lori's Tuition For 2017 Transferred		
($5,000 - $2,500) (Note Four)	(2,500)	
Total	($36,891)	
Rate	15%	(5,534)
Charitable Donations (Note Five)		
{[(15%)($200)] + [(33%)(Nil)]+ [(29%)($3,000 - $200)]}		(842)
Political Contributions Tax Credit		
[($400)(3/4) + ($350)(1/2) + ($50)(1/3)]		(492)
Federal Tax Payable		$ 6,985
Social Benefits Repayment (Note One)		902
Federal Balance Owing		$ 7,887

Note Two   As the spousal amount is larger than the Canada caregiver amount of $6,883, there is no additional Canada caregiver amount.

Note Three   Since both daughters are under 18 at the end of the year, their expenses can be aggregated with those of Mr. Baxter for the purposes of this calculation.

Total Medical Expenses		$2,843
Lesser Of:		
• [(3%)($79,898)] = $2,397		
• 2017 Threshold Amount = $2,268		(2,268)
Allowable Amount Of Medical Expenses		$ 575

Note Four   Since Lori has no Tax Payable before consideration of her tuition credit, it can be all be transferred to her supporting parent as it totals less than the $5,000 transfer limit. Alternatively, she could have chosen to carry forward these credits to apply against her own Tax Payable in a subsequent year.

Note Five   Since none of Mr. Baxter's income is taxed at 33 percent, this rate is not used to calculate the charitable donations credit.

We suggest you work Self Study Problems Four-6 to Four-8 at this point.

Additional Supplementary Self Study Problems Are Available Online.

Key Terms Used In This Chapter

4-209.   The following is a list of the key terms used in this Chapter. These terms, and their meanings, are compiled in the Glossary located at the back of the Study Guide.

Adoption Expenses Tax Credit
Age Tax Credit
Canada Caregiver Amount For Child
Canada Caregiver Tax Credit
Canada Employment Credit
Canada Pension Plan (CPP)
Canada Pension Plan Tax Credit
Charitable Donations Tax Credit
Charitable Gifts
Clawback
Common-Law Partner
Dependant
Disability Tax Credit
Disability Tax Credit Supplement
Eligible Dependant Tax Credit
Employment Insurance (EI)
Employment Insurance Tax Credit
First Time Home Buyer's Tax Credit
First Time Donor's Super Tax Credit
GST Tax Credit
Home Accessibility Tax Credit
Home Relocation Loan
Indexation
Labour Sponsored Funds Tax Credit
Medical Expense Tax Credit

Non-Refundable Tax Credit
Northern Residents Deductions
OAS Clawback
Old Age Security (OAS) Benefits
Pension Income Tax Credit
Personal Tax Credits
Political Contributions Tax Credit
Progressive Tax System
Public Transit Pass Tax Credit
Refundable Medical Expense Supplement
Refundable Tax Credit
Regressive Tax System
Social Benefits Repayment
Spousal Tax Credit
Spouse
Student Loan Interest Tax Credit
Tax Credit
Taxable Income
Teacher School Supply Tax Credit
Tuition Fees Tax Credit
Volunteer Firefighters Tax Credit
Volunteer Search And Rescue Tax Credit
Wholly Dependent Person
Working Income Tax Benefit

References

4-210.   For more detailed study of the material in this Chapter, we would refer you to:

ITA 110	Deductions Permitted
ITA 111.1	Order Of Applying Provisions
ITA 117	Individual Taxes Payable
ITA 117.1	Annual Adjustment (Indexation)
ITA 118(1)	Personal Credits
ITA 118(2)	Age Credit
ITA 118(3)	Pension Credit
ITA 118(10)	Canada Employment Credit
ITA 118.01	Adoption Expense Credit

ITA 118.02	Public Transit Pass Credit
ITA 118.041	Home Accessibility Tax Credit
ITA 118.05	First-Time Home Buyers' Credit
ITA 118.06	Volunteer Firefighters Tax Credit
ITA 118.07	Volunteer Search And Rescue Workers Tax Credit
ITA 118.1	Definitions (Charitable Gifts)
ITA 118.2	Medical Expense Credit
ITA 118.3	Credit For Mental Or Physical Impairment
ITA 118.5	Tuition And Other Education Related Credits
ITA 118.61	Unused Tuition, Textbook And Education Tax Credits
ITA 118.62	Credit For Interest On Student Loan
ITA 118.7	Credit For EI And QPIP Premiums And CPP Contributions
ITA 118.8	Transfer Of Unused Credits To Spouse Or Common-Law Partner
ITA 118.81	Tuition Tax Credit Transferred
ITA 118.9	Transfer To Parent Or Grandparent
ITA 122.5	Definitions (GST Credit)
ITA 122.51	Definitions (Refundable Medical Expense Supplement
ITA 122.7	Working Income Tax Benefit
ITA 127(3)	Federal Political Contributions Tax Credit
ITA 127.4	Labour Sponsored Venture Capital Corporations Credit
ITA 180.2	OAS Clawback
ITR 5700	Prescribed Device Or Equipment
IC 75-2R9	Contributions To A Registered Political Party Or To A Candidate At A Federal Election
IC 75-23	Tuition Fees And Charitable Donations Paid To Privately Supported Secular and Religious Schools

S1-F1-C1	Medical Expense Tax Credit
S1-F1-C2	Disability Tax Credit
S1-F1-C3	Disability Supports Deduction
S1-F2-C1	Education And Textbook Tax Credits
S1-F2-C2	Tuition Tax Credit
S1-F2-C3	Scholarships, Research Grants, And Other Education Assistance
S1-F4-C1	Basic Personal And Dependant Tax Credits
S1-F5-C1	Related Persons And Dealing At Arm's Length
S7-F1-C1	Split-receipting and Deemed Fair Market Value

IT-113R4	Benefits To Employees — Stock Options
IT-226R	Gift To A Charity Of A Residual Interest In Real Property Or An Equitable Interest In A Trust
IT-244R3	Gifts By Individuals Of Life Insurance Policies As Charitable Donations
IT-407R4	Dispositions Of Cultural Property To Designated Canadian Institutions
IT-421R2	Benefits to Individuals, Corporations and Shareholders from Loans or Debt
IT-513R	Personal Tax Credits
IT-523	Order Of Provisions Applicable In Computing An Individual's Taxable Income And Tax Payable

Sample Tax Return And Tax Software SS Problem

The Chapter 4 Sample Tax Return and the Tax Software Self Study Problem for Chapter 4 can be found in the print and online Study Guide,

Problems For Self Study (Online)

To provide practice in problem solving, there are Self Study and Supplementary Self Study problems available on the Companion Website.

Within the text we have provided an indication of when it would be appropriate to work each Self Study problem. The detailed solutions for Self Study problems can be found in the print and online Study Guide.

We provide the Supplementary Self Study problems for those who would like additional practice in problem solving. The detailed solutions for the Supplementary Self Study problems are available online, not in the Study Guide.

The .PDF file "Self Study Problems for Volume 1" on the Companion Website contains the following for Chapter 4:

- 8 Self Study problems,
- 3 Supplementary Self Study problems, and
- detailed solutions for the Supplementary Self Study problems.

Assignment Problems

(The solutions for these problems are only available in
the solutions manual that has been provided to your instructor.)

Assignment Problem Four - 1
(Personal Tax Credits - 5 Cases)

In each of the following independent Cases, determine the maximum amount of 2017 personal tax credits, including transfers from a spouse or dependant, that can be applied against federal Tax Payable by the taxpayer. In all Cases, the taxpayer's Net Income For Tax Purposes is equal to their Taxable Income. Ignore, where relevant, the possibility of pension income splitting.

A calculation of Tax Payable is **NOT** required, only the applicable credits.

1. Cammy Tarbell has Net Income For Tax Purposes of $96,500, all of which is employment income. Her employer has withheld maximum EI and CPP contributions. She is married to Bob Tarbell who has Net Income For Tax Purposes of $8,650. They have four children ages 3, 5, 7, and 9. All of the children are in good health and none of them have any income during the current year.

2. Scotty Severa has been divorced for a number of years. Because his former wife is an airline pilot who travels extensively, he has been awarded custody of their three children. The children are aged 7, 10, and 15 and they are all in good health. Scotty's Net Income For Tax Purposes is $71,400, all of which is spousal support payments. The two younger children have no income of their own. The 15 year old has income from part time jobs of $8,640.

3. Donald Preble has Net Income For Tax Purposes of $126,325, all of which is rental income. His spouse Donna has Net Income For Tax Purposes $6,340. Their daughter Diane is 26 years old and has a mental disability. While the disability is not severe enough to qualify for the disability tax credit, she has no income during the current year and continues to live with Donald and Donna.

4. Bibi Spillman is 68 years old. Her Net Income For Tax Purposes totals $65,420 and is made up of OAS payments of $7,000 and pension income from a former employer. Her spouse is 62 years old and has Net Income For Tax Purposes of $6,250.

5. Clarice McBryde has Net Income For Tax Purposes of $132,400, all of which is employment income. Her employer has withheld the maximum EI and CPP contributions. She and her husband Moishe have two children aged 11 and 13. Moishe and the children have no income of their own during the current year.

   The 13 year old child was severely injured in a car accident two years ago and qualifies for the disability tax credit. No amount was paid for attendant care for this child during the current year.

   Clarice spent $12,500 installing wheelchair ramps to improve access to various parts of the family residence. She also spent the following on dental fees and fees for various medical practitioners:

Clarice	$ 4,420
Moishe	2,620
11 Year Old Child	1,875
13 Year Old Child	14,250
Total Medical Fees Paid	$23,165
Reimbursement From Company Medical Plan	
- Plan's Annual Maximum	(11,000)
Net Medical Fees Paid	$12,165

Assignment Problem Four - 2

(Individual Tax Payable - 7 Cases)

There are seven independent cases which follow. Each case involves various assumptions as to the amount and type of income earned by John Moss during 2017, as well as to other information that is relevant to the determination of his 2017 Tax Payable. John's Net Income For Tax Purposes is equal to his Taxable Income in all Cases.

In those cases where we have assumed that the income was from employment, the employer withheld the maximum EI premium and CPP contribution.

Case 1 John is 58 years old and has employment income of $87,600. His common-law partner is 48 years old and has income of $8,260. They have an adopted child who is 19 years old and lives at home. John and his partner have medical expenses of $4,600. Medical expenses for the son total $10,300. The son has Net Income For Tax Purposes of $4,300.

Case 2 John is 46 years old and has employment income of $143,000. His wife Mary is 41 years old and has Net Income For Tax Purposes of $6,100. They have a 20 year old son who lives at home. He is dependent because of a physical infirmity, but it is not severe enough to qualify him for the disability tax credit. However, he is able to attend university on a full time basis for 8 months during 2017. John pays his tuition fees of $9,400, as well as $720 for the textbooks that he requires in his program. The son has Net Income For Tax Purposes of $8,350. The son agrees to transfer the maximum of his tuition fee amount to John.

Case 3 John and his wife Beverly are both 67 years of age. Beverly is sufficiently disabled that she qualifies for the disability tax credit. The components of income earned by John and Beverly are as follows:

Assignment Problems

	John	Beverly
Interest	$ 1,300	$ 720
Canada Pension Plan Benefits	11,400	Nil
Old Age Security Benefits	7,000	7,000
Income From Registered Pension Plan	36,200	840
Total Net Income	$55,900	$8,560

Case 4   John is 45 years old and has employment income of $92,100. His wife Marcia is 37 years old and has Net Income For Tax Purposes of $8,600. They have no children. However, they provide in home care for Marcia's father who is 61 years old, dependent because of a physical infirmity, and has no income of his own.   His disability is not severe enough to qualify for the disability tax credit. Also living with them is John's 67 year old father and 63 year old mother. They are both in good physical and mental health. John's father has Net Income For Tax Purposes of $23,200 and his mother has Net Income For Tax Purposes of $11,700.

Case 5   John is 31 years old, has employment income of $83,000, and makes contributions of $3,000 to registered charities. John qualifies for the first-time donor's super credit. He is not married and has no dependants.

Case 6   John is 58 years old and has net rental income of $114,000. He is divorced and has been awarded custody of his 21 year old disabled son. The son qualifies for the disability tax credit and has Net Income For Tax Purposes of $8,430.   He is dependent on his father for support.

Case 7   John is 43 years old and has net rental income of $92,300. His wife died last year and he is a single parent of two children. Mack is 16 and is physically infirm, but does not qualify for the disability tax credit. He has income from part time work as a student counselor of $4,800. His daughter, Serena, is 10 and is in good health.

Required: In each Case, calculate the minimum 2017 federal Tax Payable for John Moss. Indicate any carry forwards available to him and his dependants and the carry forward provisions. Ignore any amounts John might have had withheld for taxes or paid in tax instalments and the possibility of pension splitting.

Assignment Problem Four - 3
(Individual Tax Payable - 7 Cases)

The following seven independent Cases make varying assumptions with respect to Roger Blaine and his 2017 tax status. In all Cases, where Roger earned employment income, his employer withheld the maximum EI premium and CPP contribution.

Case A   Roger Blaine is 48 years of age and has employment income of $65,000. During the year, Roger makes contributions to federal political parties in the amount of $1,000. Roger is not married and has no dependants.

Case B   Roger Blaine is 48 years of age and has employment income of $65,000. His wife, Martha, is 43 years of age and has Net Income For Tax Purposes of $4,650. They have one child, Eileen, who is 11 years of age and has income of $3,000. During the year, the family had eligible medical expenses of $1,050 for Roger, $1,800 for Martha, and $300 for Eileen.

Case C   Roger Blaine is 48 years old and his wife, Martha, is 43. Roger has rental income of $65,000 and Martha has investment income of $9,400. They have a 19 year old disabled son, Albert, who lives with them. His disability qualifies him for the disability tax credit and he has no income of his own. During the year, Roger and Martha have medical expenses of $1,250. Medical expenses for Albert during the year total $8,350.

Case D   Roger Blaine is 48 years of age and his wife, Martha, is 43. They have no children. Roger has employment income of $65,000. Martha has employment income of $12,000. Martha's 68 year old father, Ahmed, and her 70 year old aunt, Jaleh, live with them. Both are in good health. Ahmed's Net Income For Tax Purposes is $9,200 and Jaleh's Net Income For Tax Purposes is $11,000. Roger paid $375 in interest related to his student loan during the year.

Case E   Roger Blaine is 48 years of age and his common-law partner Bob is 43. Roger has employment income of $65,000. Bob has Net Income For Tax Purposes of $4,500. They have two adopted children, Barry aged 8 and Don aged 10. After living in rented premises for the last 7 years, Roger and Bob decide to purchase a residence. They acquire a 3 bedroom house in the suburbs at a cost of $245,000 and move into the house during the year.

Case F   Roger Blaine is 48 years of age and his wife, Martha, is 43. Roger has employment income of $65,000. Martha has Net Income For Tax Purposes of $5,050. They have a son, Albert, who is 19 years old and lives at home. He attends university on a full time basis during 8 months of the year. Roger pays $5,400 for Albert's tuition for two semesters during the 2017 calendar year and $525 for required textbooks. Albert had employment income of $3,000 that he earned during the summer. He agrees to transfer the maximum of his tuition fee amount to his father.

Case G   Roger Blaine is 67 and his wife Martha is 68. Martha has been completely disabled for a number of years and the extent of her disability qualifies her for the disability tax credit. Their son, Albert, is 38 years old, in good health and lives with them to help care for Martha. Albert has $10,000 of income from spousal support. The components of Roger and Martha's income are as follows:

	Roger	Martha
Interest	$ 300	$ 50
Canada Pension Plan Benefits	4,400	200
Old Age Security Benefits	7,000	7,000
Income From Registered Pension Plan	31,150	450
Total Net Income	$42,850	$7,700

Required: In each Case, calculate Roger Blaine's minimum federal Tax Payable for 2017. Indicate any carry forwards available to him and his dependants and the carry forward provisions. Ignore any amounts Roger might have had withheld or paid in instalments and the possibility of pension income splitting.

Assignment Problem Four - 4
(Personal Tax Credits - 6 Cases)
In each of the following independent Cases, determine the maximum amount of 2017 personal tax credits, including transfers from a spouse or dependant, that can be applied against federal Tax Payable by the taxpayer.

A calculation of Tax Payable is **NOT** required, only the applicable credits.

1. Ms. Jones is married and has Net Income For Tax Purposes of $123,000, none of which is employment income or income from self-employment. Her husband is currently unemployed, but has interest income from investments of $3,750. Her 20 year old dependent son attends university and lives at home. Her son has Net Income For Tax Purposes of $4,800 and does not agree to transfer his tuition credit to her.

Assignment Problems

2. Ms. Martin is 66 years old and has Net Income For Tax Purposes of $28,350. This total is made up of OAS of $7,000, plus pension income of $21,350 from a former employer. Her husband is 51 years old and blind. He has no income of his own. Ignore the possibility that Ms. Martin would split her pension income with her husband.

3. Mr. Sharp has Net Income For Tax Purposes of $72,350, none of which is employment income or income from self-employment. He lives with his common-law partner and her three children from a previous relationship. The children are aged 13, 15, and 20. The 20 year child is dependent because of a physical disability. However, the disability is not sufficiently severe to qualify for the disability tax credit. Neither the common-law partner nor any of the children have any source of income.

4. Mr. Barton was divorced two years ago and maintains a residence separate from his former spouse. He has custody of the three children of the marriage, aged 8, 9, and 10 and receives $2,500 per month in child support payments. Mr. Barton has Net Income For Tax Purposes of $62,300, none of which is employment income or income from self-employment. None of the children have any income of their own.

5. Ms. Cole has Net Income For Tax Purposes of $175,000, all of which is employment income. Her employer has withheld and remitted the required EI and CPP amounts. She was married on December 1, 2017. Her new husband is an accounting student with a large firm. His salary for the period January 1 through November 30, 2017 was $33,000. For the month of December, 2017, his salary was $3,000.

6. Mr. Smead has Net Income For Tax Purposes of $85,000, none of which is employment income or income from self-employment. He lives in a residence that he has owned for many years. He does not currently have a spouse or common-law partner. However, he has custody of his 10 year old son who lives with him. Also living with him is his 68 year old, widowed mother. She has a physical infirmity. However, it is not sufficiently severe for her to qualify for the disability tax credit. Mr. Smead's son had no income during the year. His mother had OAS benefits and pension income which totaled $18,500 during the year.

Assignment Problem Four - 5
(Comprehensive Tax Payable)

Ms. Tanja Umstead is 46 years old and lives in Richmond, British Columbia. She is in good health and works in the sales department of a large publicly traded company.

Tanja's Personal Information

1. She is divorced from her husband and has custody of her 11 year old daughter, Cynthia. The daughter is sufficiently disabled that she qualifies for the disability tax credit. The daughter has 2017 Net Income For Tax Purposes of $6,425, largely made of interest on bonds purchased from an inheritance.

2. Tanja's 68 year old mother lives with her and provides care for Cynthia on a full time basis. As she receives no compensation for this work, Tanja has no child care costs during 2017. The mother's 2017 Net Income For Tax Purposes is $13,460.

3. Because of a 2017 decrease in Cynthia's mobility, Tanja has had to install access ramps in several locations in her home. The cost of these ramps was $14,600.

4. During 2017, Tanja worked nearly 300 hours as a volunteer search and rescue volunteer. She received $200 in compensation for this work.

5. Tanja's 2017 medical expenses are as follows:

Various Prescription Drugs Including	
Medical Marijuana (Tanja And Cynthia)	$ 3,465
Various Medical Specialist Treatments For Cynthia	10,490
Prescription Sunglasses For Tanja And Cynthia	875
Liposuction For Tanja To Reduce Fat On Her Thighs	2,463
Dentist Fees For Tanja's Mother	3,300
Dentures For Tanja's Mother	1,325

6. During 2017, Tanja contributes $3,500 to Unplanned Parenthood, a registered Canadian charity. Tanja is eligible for the first time donor's super credit.

Employment Information

1. Tanja's salary compensation for 2017 is $93,500. In addition, she was awarded a year-end bonus of $12,000, all of which is payable in January 2018.

2. Tanja's employer sponsors a defined benefit registered pension plan. During 2017, Tanja and her employer each contribute $4,150 to the plan. In addition, her employer withheld maximum EI contributions of $836 and maximum CPP contributions of $2,564.

3. Her employer offers to pay the tuition for employees taking foreign language courses. Tanja is taking an intensive course in spoken Chinese at a British Columbia university. The tuition fee for the course is $3,600, all of which is paid for by her employer. The tuition payment is to be included in her employment income as a taxable benefit. The duration of the course is 8 months and Tanja must purchase her own textbooks for $150.

4. Tanja is provided with disability insurance by an employer sponsored plan. During 2017, as a consequence of an automobile accident, she was unable to go to work for one month and receives benefits of $6,500. Starting in 2015, Tanja has been contributing $340 per year for the plan's coverage. Her employer makes a matching contribution in each year.

5. Tanja's employer provides her with an automobile that was purchased several years ago at a cost of $39,500. During 2017, the car is driven 41,000 kilometers, 34,000 of which were for employment related travel. Tanja is required to pay her own operating costs, which for 2017 totaled $7,240. Except for the one month that she was off from work, the car was available to Tanja throughout the year. During the one month that she was off, the car was left in her employer's garage.

6. Tanja's employer provides all of its employees with financial counseling services. The cost to the company of the services provided to Tanja was $450.

7. As a result of winning a sales contest, Tanja received a one week trip to Las Vegas. The value of this trip in Canadian dollars was $5,620.

8. Several years ago, Tanja received options to acquire 250 shares of her employer's common stock at a price of $25 per share. When the options were granted, the shares were trading at $25 per share. During 2017, Tanja exercises all of these options. On the exercise date, the shares are trading at $32 per share. Tanja is still holding the shares at the end of the year.

Required: Calculate, for the 2017 taxation year, Tanja's minimum Taxable Income and federal Tax Payable. Ignore GST and PST considerations.

Assignment Problem Four - 6
(Comprehensive Tax Payable)

Phil Cousteau is an accountant. Phil is 47 years old and is married to Claire who is 45 years old and blind. She has Net Income For Tax Purposes in 2017 of $9,000, all of which is interest on investments she inherited from her mother.

Phil and Claire have two children, a 15 year old daughter, Haley, and a 19 year old son, Manny. Both Haley and Manny live at home. Haley earned $800 during 2017 baby-sitting.

Manny has a disability that is not severe enough for his doctor to sign off on the T2201 form. Manny inherited investments from his grandmother and received $15,000 in interest income from them during 2017.

Phil's brother, Cameron, lives in the basement of Phil's Toronto home. Cameron is 50 years old and his only income for 2017 was EI benefit payments totaling $3,000. Phil also supports his 85 year old father, Jay, who is physically infirm and lives in a retirement home. Jay had Net Income For Tax Purposes of $9,000 for 2017. His income consisted of OAS, investment income and payments from a registered pension plan of $1,000.

Phil works for ModFam Company and was paid a salary of $70,000 in 2017. He also earned a bonus of $5,000 in 2017, with one-fifth of the bonus to be paid each year from 2017 to 2021.

During 2017 he received a briefcase worth $800 as an award for being the "employee of the year" and a Christmas basket from the company worth $600. All of the Company's employees received a similar basket.

ModFam transferred Phil from their Toronto office to their Vancouver office in 2017. On April 1, Phil moved his family out of the house they had rented in Toronto for the last 10 years and into a brand new house in Vancouver that cost $800,000. Although Jay was to stay at the retirement home in Toronto, Cameron moved with the family to Vancouver. Phil was reimbursed by his employer for all of his moving costs. As a consequence, he has no deductible moving costs.

To help finance the new house, ModFam Company lent Phil $500,000 on April 1 at 1 percent interest. Phil would have paid 5 percent interest on a similar loan from the bank.

ModFam provides Phil with a company car. While he was at the Toronto office, he had a Toyota Highlander that the company leased for $875 per month ($50 of which was for insurance). The company paid $1,600 for the Highlander's other operating costs from January 1 to March 31. During that period, Phil drove the car 9,000 kilometers of which 6,000 kilometers were employment related.

On April 1, the Vancouver office gave Phil the keys to a Toyota Camry Hybrid that was purchased for $31,300. The company paid $4,500 for the Camry's operating costs from April 1 to December 31. During that period, Phil drove the car 24,000 kilometers of which 10,000 kilometers were employment related.

During 2017, the following amounts were deducted from Phil's pay:

Federal Income Tax	$8,500
CPP	2,564
EI	836
Group Life Insurance Premiums	600
Registered Pension Plan	1,200
United Way Donations	1,500

The company matched the life insurance and RPP amounts.

During 2017, Phil paid the following amounts of eligible medical expenses:

Himself	$ 650
Claire	1,940
Haley	860
Manny	1,250
Cameron	480
Jay	990

Phil paid $900 for his 2017 professional association dues. Claire made a $500 donation to their church during 2017. Because both Phil and Clair contribute to charities on a regular basis, they do not qualify for the first-time donor's super tax credit.

Assume that the prescribed interest rates for 2017 were 2 percent for the first and fourth quarter and 3 percent for the second and third quarter.

Required: For the 2017 taxation year, calculate Mr. Cousteau's minimum:

1. Net Income For Tax Purposes,
2. Taxable Income,
3. Federal Tax Owing.

In determining these amounts, ignore GST, PST and HST considerations.

Assignment Problem Four - 7
(Comprehensive Tax Payable)

Lydia Hines is a translator who works for a consulting firm in Ottawa. Her 2017 salary is $73,500, from which her employer, a Canadian controlled private company, deducts maximum CPP and EI contributions. Also deducted is an RPP contribution of $2,600. The employer makes a matching contribution. Her employment compensation does not include any commission income.

Lydia's husband, Mark is the beneficiary of a trust. Mark's mother was extremely wealthy and when she died, she left her assets to a trust for her children and her grandchildren. Mark will eventually inherit much of the estate. As a result, he no longer works for pay and devotes much of his time to volunteer work. His 2017 Net Income For Tax Purposes is $8,600. All of this income is from the trust.

The couple have three children aged 15, 20, and 22 who live with them. The 15 year old, Barry, is in good health and has 2017 Net Income For Tax Purposes of $9,400 from the trust.

The 20 year old, Mary, is dependent on her family because of mental health issues. However, she does not qualify for the disability tax credit. Her 2017 Net Income For Tax Purposes of $3,100 is from the trust.

The 22 year old, Harry, attends university on a full time basis in Vancouver for 8 months of the year. Lydia pays his tuition of $11,300, his textbook costs of $1,250 and his residence fees of $8,000. Harry's 2017 Net Income For Tax Purposes of $14,100 is from the trust. He has agreed to transfer the maximum tuition amount to Lydia.

Other Information:

1. To reward Lydia for her outstanding work, and as an incentive to stay with the company, her employer has awarded her a bonus of $10,000. Of this total, $4,000 will be paid in 2018, with the remaining $6,000 payable in 2021.

2. Lydia received options to purchase 200 shares of her employer's stock at a price of $72 per share last year. At the time the options were granted, the fair market value of the shares was $74 per share. During May, 2017, when the shares had a fair market value of $90 per share, Lydia exercises all of these options. She is still holding these shares at the end of the year.

3. Lydia is provided with an automobile by her employer. The automobile was leased on February 1, 2017 at a monthly rate of $565, a figure which includes a payment for insurance of $75 per month. The automobile is driven a total of 36,000 kilometers, 32,000 of which were employment related. It was available to her from February 1 to the end of the year. The employer did not provide an automobile during the month of January.

4. During 2017, Lydia spent $5,600 on employment related meals and entertainment with clients of her employer. Her employer reimbursed $3,200 of these costs.

5. During 2017, Lydia receives several gifts from her employer:

   - As is the case for all of the company's employees, Lydia receives a $150 gift certificate that can be used for merchandise at a local department store.

   - In recognition of her 10 years of service, Lydia receives a Visconti fountain pen she has been coveting. The retail value of this pen is $1,000.

• At Christmas, all of the company's employees receive a gift basket of holiday treats. The retail value of these gift baskets is $200.

6. After years of accumulating savings and living in rental units, Lydia and Mark purchase a residence. The cost of the house is $380,000 and, to assist with the purchase, Lydia's employer provides a $100,000 interest free loan. The loan was granted on May 1, 2017 and will have to be repaid on April 30, 2022. It is not a home relocation loan. Assume the prescribed rate is 2 percent throughout the year 2017.

7. Because of the nature of her employment, Lydia is required to pay annual professional dues of $350.

8. During 2017, Lydia makes her annual contribution of $2,000 to a registered charity, The No Hope Of Salvation Army. (Lydia is an atheist.)

9. Lydia's employer provides all employees with a health care plan. It reimburses employees for 50 percent of all prescriptions, dental and vision fees for the employee, the employee's spouse and all children under 18 years of age. The family's 2017 medical expenses, all of which were paid by Lydia, were as follows:

Lydia - Prescriptions	$2,500
Lydia - Botox treatments	1,400
Mark - Dentist's fees for root canals (3)	7,200
Mark - Hair replacement procedures	3,700
Barry - Dentist's fees, including $1,000 for a tooth replacement	2,100
Mary - Doctor's fees for treatment for depression	8,400
Mary - Prescriptions	3,900
Mary - Liposuction treatment for her upper arms	4,200
Harry - Physiotherapy	1,500
Harry - Fees for prescription glasses and contact lenses	2,200

Required:

A. Determine Lydia's minimum Net Income For Tax Purposes for the 2017 taxation year.

B. Determine Lydia's minimum Taxable Income for the 2017 taxation year.

C. Based on your answer in Part B, determine Lydia's federal Tax Payable for the 2017 taxation year.

Assignment Problem Four - 8

(Comprehensive Tax Payable)

Ezra Pinnock is 73 years old and is an engineering professor at a major Canadian University. He is in good health and lives in Toronto in a large house he inherited from his mother.

Employment Information

1. Ezra's salary received for 2017 is $163,000. As the result of a negotiations by his union, he is entitled to receive an additional $8,000 in salary related to his work during 2017. However, this adjustment will not be received until January, 2018.

2. During 2017, Ezra's employer deducts EI contributions of $836. Because of his age and the fact that he is collecting CPP benefits, Ezra no longer has to make CPP contributions.

3. Ezra's employer sponsors a defined benefit pension plan. Because of his age, Ezra no longer contributes to this plan. However, when he reached age 69, he was required to start receiving a pension. During 2017, he received benefits from this plan of $26,000.

4. As much of Ezra's work involves distance education, he is required by his employer to maintain an office in his home. This home office occupies 18 percent of the space in his residence and is viewed as his principal place of business. The 2017 costs associated with this residence are as follows:

Electricity	$ 4,680
Property Taxes	19,200
Interest On Mortgage	12,000
Insurance	3,450
Repairs To Roof	4,970
Lawn Maintenance	863
Snow Removal	647
Total	$45,810

5. As Ezra is one of his university's more charismatic professors, he does an extensive amount of travel promoting the university's programs. He receives an allowance of $1,000 per month ($12,000 in total) to cover his travel costs. The actual costs for 2017 are as follows:

Hotels	$4,200
Meals While Travelling	1,650
Airline Tickets	2,150

In addition to these costs, Ezra uses his personal automobile for some of the travel. During 2017, the milage on the car totaled 32,000 kilometers, with 16,000 of these kilometers related to his travel for the university. Operating costs for the year totaled $3,200. His accountant has advised him that CCA for the year (100 percent basis) would be $4,500.

6. In 2017, having accumulated 10 years of service with his current employer, Ezra receives a cash award of $350 and a very fancy plaque. In addition, all of the university employees receive a basket of gourmet food at Christmas. The value of this basket is $325.

7. The university provides Ezra with $500,000 in life insurance coverage, as well as a supplemental accident and sickness insurance plan. The 2017 cost to the university for the life insurance coverage is $675, while the cost for the accident and sickness plan is $472. The accident and sickness plan would pay cash benefits due to injury or illness, it would not pay periodic benefits to replace salary if Ezra was unable to work. Ezra does not contribute to the accident and sickness plan.

8. After he was hit by a speeding bicyclist and injured, Ezra receives benefits under the accident and sickness plan of $1,245 during the year.

Other Income
Having worked for several other universities prior to joining his present employer, Ezra has 2017 receipts from the registered pension plans sponsored by these universities of $35,000. In addition, he receives Canada Pension Plan benefits of $13,000. Since he knows his income will remain quite high for the foreseeable future, Ezra has not applied for OAS.

Personal Information
1. Ezra has been married to Laurie Pinnock for over 40 years. Laurie is 64 years old and, because of a terrible skiing accident 3 years ago, she is sufficiently disabled that she qualifies for the disability tax credit. She has 2017 Net Income of $8,420 which includes $2,500 from a registered pension plan.

2. Ezra and Laurie have a 25 year old son named Martin. As the result of significant substance abuse, he continues to live at home. He is currently unemployed and his only income is $3,400 in employment insurance benefits.

3. Laurie's father Ezekial is 92 years old. Two years ago, on a senior's trip to Las Vegas, he met a retired pole dancer named Blaze. They hit it off immediately and Blaze returned to Canada with Ezekial. She is 77 years old and has established Canadian residency. They have both been living with Ezra and Laurie in the basement granny suite, presumably in a conjugal relationship, since that time. Ezekial has a physical infirmity and has income from various sources of $17,300. Blaze has no infirmity and no income in 2017. She is not eligible for OAS.

4. During 2017, Ezra spent $11,400 for home modifications required to deal with the mobility restrictions caused by Laurie's disability. Since Ezekial has very poor night vision, he also spent $1,200 on installing motion activated external lights for his safety.

5. During 2017, the family had medical expenses, all of which were paid for by Ezra, as follows:

Ezra	$2,850
Laurie	3,420
Martin	2,470
Ezekial	685
Blaze*	1,432

*All of Blaze's expenses were for the reversal of a breast enhancement operation. Although the spectacular results of her operation were very helpful to her career, she now feels the enhancement is not in keeping with her post-retirement lifestyle.

6. During 2017, Laurie wins $200,000 in a lottery. She donates cash of $50,000 to the Safe Skiing Research Fund, a registered Canadian charity. Laurie has been a regular donor since her accident.

Required: For the 2017 taxation year, calculate Ezra's minimum:

1. Net Income For Tax Purposes,
2. Taxable Income,
3. Federal Tax Owing.

In determining these amounts, ignore GST/HST considerations and the possibility of pension income splitting.

Tax Software Assignment Problems

(The solutions for these problems are only available in
the solutions manual that has been provided to your instructor.)

Tax Software Assignment Problem Four - 1

This problem is continued in Chapter 11.

DISCLAIMER: All characters appearing in this problem are fictitious. Any resemblance to real persons, living or dead, is purely coincidental.

Mr. Buddy Musician (SIN 527-000-061) was born in Vancouver on August 28, 1949. He has spent most of his working life as a pianist and song writer. He and his family live at 111 WWW Street, Vancouver, B.C. V4H 3W4, phone (604) 111-1111.

Mr. Musician's wife, Natasha (SIN 527-000-129), was born on June 6, 1991. She and Mr. Musician have four children. Each child was born on April 1 of the following years, Linda; 2011, Larry; 2012, Donna; 2013, and Donald; 2014. Natasha's only income during 2016 is $3,840 [(4)($160)(6 months)] in universal child care benefits.

Buddy and Natasha Musician have two adopted children. Richard (SIN 527-000-285) was born on March 15, 1999 and has income of $2,800 for the year. Due to his accelerated schooling, he started full time attendance at university in September of 2016 at the age of 17. His first semester tuition fee is $3,000 and he requires books with a total cost of $375. These amounts are paid by Mr. Musician.

The other adopted child, Sarah, was born on September 2, 1996, and is in full time attendance at university for all of 2016 (including a four month summer session). Her tuition is $9,600 and she requires textbooks which cost $750. These amounts are also paid by Mr. Musician. Sarah has no income during the year.

Neither Richard nor Sarah will have any income in the next three years. They both have agreed that the maximum education related amount should be transferred to their father.

Mr. Musician's mother, Eunice, was born on April 10, 1929 and his father, Earl, was born on November 16, 1927. They both live with Mr. Musician and his wife. While his father has some mobility issues, he is not infirm. His mother is legally blind. Eunice Musician had income of $9,500 for the year, while Earl Musician had income of $7,500.

Other information concerning Mr. Musician and his family for 2016 is as follows:

1. Mr. Musician earned $16,500 for work as the house pianist at the Loose Moose Pub. His T4 showed that his employer withheld $500 for income taxes and $310.20 for EI. No CPP was withheld as he has previously filed an election to stop contributing to the CPP.

2. During the year, Mr. Musician made his annual $3,000 donation to Planned Parenthood Of Canada, a registered Canadian charity. He has made this donation for the last 5 years.

3. Mr. Musician has been married before to Lori Musician (SIN 527-000-319). Lori is 52 years old and lives in Fort Erie, Ontario.

4. Mr. Musician has two additional children who live with their mother, Ms. Dolly Nurse (SIN 527-000-582), in Burnaby, British Columbia. The children are Megan Nurse, aged 12 and Andrew Nurse, aged 14. Neither child has any income during 2016. While Ms. Nurse and Mr. Musician were never married, Mr. Musician acknowledges that he is the father of both children. Although Buddy has provided limited financial aid by paying their dental and medical expenses, the children are not dependent on Buddy for support.

5. Mr. Musician wishes to claim all his medical expenses on a calendar year basis. On December 2, 2016, Mr. Musician paid dental expenses to Canada Wide Dental Clinics for the following individuals:

Himself	$1,200
Natasha (wife)	700
Richard (adopted son)	800
Sarah (adopted daughter)	300
Linda (daughter)	100
Earl (father)	1,050
Lori (ex-wife)	300
Dolly Nurse (mother of two of his children)	675
Megan Nurse (daughter of Dolly Nurse)	550
Total	$5,675

6. Mr. Musician signed a contract with Fred Nesbitt on January 13, 2016 to do permanent modifications to his house. The contract was for the installation of ramps with sturdy hand railings outside his front and back doors to give his parents easier access to the house and modifications to their bathroom so they would be less likely to fall when using the shower. The contract price was $5,800. As neither of his parents has a severe and prolonged mobility impairment, these expenditures are not eligible medical expenses.

7. Mr. Musician paid four quarterly instalments of $1,000 each (total of $4,000) for 2016, as requested on his Instalment Reminders from the CRA. He paid each instalment on the due date.

8. Assume that Mr. Musician has not applied to receive either OAS or CPP benefits.

Required: With the objective of minimizing Mr. Musician's Tax Payable, prepare Mr. Musician's 2016 income tax return using the ProFile tax software program assuming Natasha does not file a tax return. List any assumptions you have made, and any notes and tax planning issues you feel should be placed in the file.

Tax Software Assignment Problem Four - 2

This problem is continued in Chapter 11.

DISCLAIMER: All characters appearing in this problem are fictitious. Any resemblance to real persons, living or dead, is purely coincidental.

George Pharmacy is a pharmaceutical salesman who has been very successful at his job in the last few years. Unfortunately, his family life has not been very happy. Three years ago, his only child, Anna, was driving a car that was hit by a drunk driver. She and her husband were killed and their 14 year old son, Kevin, was blinded in the accident. He also suffered extensive injuries to his jaw that have required major and prolonged dental work.

George and his wife, Valerie, adopted Kevin. Valerie quit her part-time job to care for him. She also cares for her mother, Joan Drugstore who lives with them. Joan suffers from dementia, Parkinson's and severe depression. The family doctor has signed a letter stating that she is dependent on George and Valerie because of her impairments. Joan does not meet the residency requirements necessary to qualify for Canadian Old Age Security payments.

Valerie's parents separated two years ago in Scotland after her father, David Drugstore, suffered enormous losses in the stock market. They were forced to sell their home and David moved to Chile. David phones periodically to request that money be deposited in his on-line bank account.

George's brother, Martin, completed an alcohol rehabilitation program after being fired for drinking on the job. He is also living with George and Valerie while he is enrolled as a full time student at Western University. George is paying his tuition and Martin has agreed to transfer any available education related amounts to George. Although Martin plans to file his 2016 tax return, he has not done so yet.

Kevin is taking several undergraduate psychology courses at Western University. After hearing a talk given by an expert blind echolocator, i.e., one who uses sound to locate objects, his goal is to become a researcher at the Brain and Mind Institute and study the use of echolocation.

Other information concerning George for 2016 is given on the following pages.

Required: With the objective of minimizing George's Tax Payable, prepare the 2016 income tax return of George Pharmacy using the ProFile tax software program assuming Valerie does not file a tax return. List any assumptions you have made, and any notes and tax planning issues you feel should be placed in the file. Ignore HST implications in your solution by assuming that George does not qualify for the GST/HST rebate.

Personal Information	Taxpayer
Title	Mr.
First Name	George
Last Name	Pharmacy
SIN	527-000-509
Date of birth (Y/M/D)	1952-07-02
Marital Status	Married
Canadian citizen?	Yes
Provide information to Elections Canada?	Yes
Own foreign property of more than $100,000 Canadian?	No

Taxpayer's Address	
123 ZZZ Street, London, Ontario N0Z 0Z0	
Phone number (519) 111-1111	

Family Members	Spouse	Child	Mother-In-Law
First Name	Valerie	Kevin	Joan
Last Name	Pharmacy	Pharmacy	Drugstore
SIN	527-000-483	527-000-517	None
Date of birth (Y/M/D)	1951-12-30	2000-10-17	1931-02-24
Net income	$6,520 in CPP	Nil	$500

Family Members	Father-In-Law	Brother
First Name	David	Martin
Last Name	Drugstore	Pharmacy
SIN	None	527-000-533
Date of birth (Y/M/D)	1932-01-12	1969-06-02
Net income	Nil	$8,300

During September, David was arrested in Chile. Valerie had to spend three weeks in Chile and $2,000 in bribes before she could get him released from jail. George had to pay Nannies On Call $3,500 for in-home help to take care of Kevin while she was gone.

T2202A (Martin)	Box	Amount
Tuition fees - for Martin Pharmacy (brother)	A	8,000
Number of months in school - part-time	B	0
Number of months in school - full-time	C	8

T2202A (Kevin)	Box	Amount
Tuition fees - for Kevin	A	3,600
Number of months in school - part-time	B	8
Number of months in school - full-time	C	0

Donor	Charitable Donation Receipts	Am't
Valerie	Mothers Against Drunk Drivers (MADD)	1,000
George	Canadian Institute For The Blind (CNIB)	3,000

George is not eligible for the first time super donor tax credit.

Tax Software Assignment Problems

T4	Box	Amount
Issuer - Mega Pharma Inc.		
Employment income	14	378,000.00
Employee's CPP contributions	16	2,544.30
Employee's EI premiums	18	955.04
Income tax deducted	22	114,000.00
Employment commissions	42	82,000.00
Charitable donations	46	400.00

During 2016, Mega reimbursed George $3,788 for meals and entertainment with clients, $2,268 for hotels and $4,925 for airline tickets.

In addition to George's salary, he also earns commissions. His employer requires him to have an office in his home and has signed the form T2200 each year to this effect.

During 2016, George purchased a new computer and software that will be used solely in his home office for employment related uses. The computer cost $3,600 and the various software programs cost $1,250.

House Costs	
Area of home used for home office (square feet)	650
Total area of home (square feet)	5,000
Telephone line including high speed internet connection	620
Hydro	3,200
Insurance - House	4,000
Maintenance and repairs	3,800
Mortgage interest	6,200
Mortgage life insurance premiums	400
Property taxes	6,700

(Y/M/D)	Patient	Medical Expenses	Description	Am't
2016-12-31	George	Johnson Inc.	Out of Canada insurance	731.00
2016-08-31	George	Dr. Smith	Dental fees	155.40
2016-09-19	George	Optician	Prescription glasses	109.00
2016-11-07	Valerie	Pharmacy	Prescription	66.84
2016-06-07	Joan	Dr. Wong	Psychiatric counseling	2,050.00
2016-03-22	David	Tropical Disease Centre	Prescription	390.00
2016-12-20	Martin	Dr. Walker	Group therapy	6,000.00
2016-10-01	Kevin	Dr. Takarabe	Orthodontics and Dental	30,000.00

George paid $800 for the care and feeding of Kevin's seeing eye dog, Isis, during 2016.

Tax Software Assignment Problem Four - 3

This problem is continued in Chapter 11.

DISCLAIMER: All characters appearing in all versions of this problem are fictitious. Any resemblance to real persons, living or dead, is purely coincidental.

Seymour Career and Mary Career are your tax clients. They have been married for two years. Mary has progressed quickly in MoreCorp, the large, publicly traded firm she is working for due to her strong tax and accounting background. Her firm has an excellent health and dental plan that reimburses 100 percent of all medical and dental expenses.

Although Seymour has been working, his increasing ill health makes it likely that he will not be able to continue to work in 2017. He is contemplating a return to university as a student of music.

In order to estimate her possible financial position in 2017, she would like you to prepare her 2016 tax return assuming that Seymour has no income for 2016. As she is expecting a promotion and the choice of working in any of MoreCorp's offices across Canada, she would also like you to compare her 2016 tax liability in all the different provinces and territories except Quebec assuming Seymour has no income except for Universal Child Care Benefits for 2016.

Personal Information	Taxpayer	Spouse
Title	Ms.	Mr.
First Name	Mary	Seymour
Last Name	Career	Career
SIN	527-000-129	527-000-079
Date of birth (Y/M/D)	1978-12-08	1957-01-29
Marital status	Married	Married
Canadian citizen?	Yes	Yes
Provide information to Elections Canada?	Yes	Yes
Own foreign property of more than $100,000 Cdn?	No	No

Taxpayer's Address
123 ABC Street, Saint John, N.B.   E0E 0E0
Phone number (506) 111-1111
Spouse's address same as taxpayer? Yes

Dependant	Child
First Name	William
Last Name	Career
SIN	527-000-319
Date of Birth (Y/M/D)	2009-02-24
Net Income	Nil
UCCB received for William	$360

Tax Software Assignment Problems

T4 - Mary	Box	Amount
Issuer - MoreCorp		
Employment Income	14	152,866.08
Employee's CPP Contributions	16	2,544.30
Employee's EI Premiums	18	955.04
RPP Contributions	20	Nil
Income Tax Deducted	22	48,665.11
Charitable Donations	46	1,000.00

Donor	Charitable Donation Receipts	Amount
Seymour	Canadian Cancer Foundation (annual donation)	500
Seymour	Salvation Army (annual donation)	250

Required: With the objective of minimizing Mary's Tax Payable, prepare her 2016 income tax return using the ProFile tax software program assuming Seymour does not file a tax return. Assume that Seymour has no income other than UCCB in 2016.   List any other assumptions you have made and provide any explanatory notes and tax planning issues you feel should be placed in the files.

CHAPTER 5

Capital Cost Allowance

Note On Changes For 2017

What you will find in this Chapter is a detailed presentation of the rules related to the tax treatment of depreciable assets. For those of you familiar with the accounting procedures for dealing with these assets, this material will be somewhat familiar. There are differences, perhaps the most important of which is the fact that for tax purposes assets are grouped into classes rather than being treated individually. The two approaches share the same goal, allocating the cost of these assets over some period of time.

There is one particular group of assets that has caused significant difficulties for both accounting standard setters and tax legislators. In somewhat simplified terms, this group is made up of two types of assets:

- Goodwill, sometimes thought of as an asset that cannot be identified with a particular property.

- Identifiable intangible assets with unlimited lives, e.g. an unlimited life government license.

After struggling with the issues associated with these assets for many years, accountants concluded that they should not be amortized or depreciated. Rather they are tested for impairment on a periodic basis and, if impairment is present, they are written down. If there is no impairment, no amount is written off.

Prior to 2017, in tax legislation, these assets were designated as "Eligible Capital Expenditures (ECE)" and collected in a balance referred to as "Cumulative Eligible Capital (CEC)". While the treatment of this balance was similar to that accorded to other depreciable assets, there were significant differences. For example, only a fraction (three-quarters) of the cost of these CEC assets was added to the CEC balance.

For a number of years, most authorities believed that the special treatment given to CEC balances should be eliminated, subjecting these assets to procedures that were the same as those that applied to other depreciable assets. This view was implemented as of December 31, 2016. As of that date, the CEC legislation was eliminated and, in simplified terms, the December 31, 2016 CEC balance became the January 1, 2017 balance in a new depreciable asset group called Class 14.1.

While our focus will be on the current procedures associated with Class 14.1, you will need to be aware of some of the history to understand the effect of this change. Given this, we will contrast the CEC procedures with the Class 14.1 procedures in the various sections of this Chapter dealing with additions, write offs, and dispositions.

As is the case with any change of this magnitude, there are a number of fairly complex transitional rules. Complete coverage of these rules could occupy an entire Chapter and would not be appropriate. This reflects the fact that these transitional rules are of limited interest to many of our users and will become less important over time. Based on this view, these rules will be given limited coverage at the end of this Chapter. There we will also provide some coverage of the economic impact of this change. In certain situations, it will be significant.

Capital Cost Allowance System

General Rules

5-1.   In Chapter 6, we will give consideration to the calculation of business income as described in Subdivision b of the *Income Tax Act*. As was the case with employment income, business income is based on a group of inclusions and deductions that are combined to arrive at a net income or loss for the taxation year.

5-2.   In Subdivision b, ITA 18(1) lays out a group of general limitations with respect to what can be deducted in the determination of net business income. In Paragraph 18(1)(b), it is noted that a taxpayer cannot deduct capital expenditures except as expressly permitted in the *Act*. In this same Subdivision b, ITA 20(1) provides a list of specific items that can be deducted in the determination of net business income. Paragraph 20(1)(a) notes that taxpayers can deduct such part of the capital cost of property "as is allowed by regulation". Taken together, these two Paragraphs provide the basis for the deduction of the tax equivalent of what financial accountants refer to as either depreciation or amortization. This tax "depreciation" is referred to as capital cost allowance (CCA).

5-3.   While ITA 20(1)(a) provides the legislative basis for deducting CCA, all of the detailed rules for determining the amounts to be deducted are found in the *Income Tax Regulations* (ITR). More specifically, ITR Part XI lists the items to be included in the various CCA classes, while ITR Schedules II through VI provide the rates for each of these classes.

Tax And Accounting Procedures Compared

Introduction

5-4.   There are many similarities between the capital cost allowance system that is used for tax purposes and the amortization procedures that are used by financial accountants. In fact, the general goal of both sets of procedures is to allocate the cost of a depreciable asset to the expenses (deductions) of periods subsequent to its acquisition. However, there are a number of differences that are described in the material which follows.

Terminology

5-5.   The two sets of procedures use different terms to describe items that are analogous. While the amounts involved will be different, the underlying concepts are the same. For example, both Undepreciated Capital Cost (UCC) and Net Book Value refer to the original cost of a depreciable asset, less amounts that have been deducted in the calculation of income. A general comparison of these analogous terms is found in Figure 5-1 (on facing page).

5-6.   However, one technical difference in the use of the terms is that where Net Book Value at the end of the year is reduced by the amortization expense for the year, UCC is reduced by CCA deducted in preceding years only. In other words, the December 31, 2017 UCC is not reduced by the 2017 CCA. The 2017 CCA is deducted in the calculation of the January 1, 2018 UCC.

Figure 5 - 1
Comparison Of Accounting And Tax Terminology

Taxation Term		Accounting Term
Capital Cost	⟷	Acquisition Cost
Capital Cost Allowance (CCA)	⟷	Amortization Or Depreciation Expense*
Undepreciated Capital Cost (UCC)	⟷	Net Book Value (NBV)

*While these two terms are used interchangeably in most tax literature, for accounting purposes, their use is more prescribed. In the *Handbook* for Canadian private enterprises, the term depreciation is not used. The write off of all types of business assets is consistently referred to as amortization.

In contrast, under International Financial Reporting Standards, the term depreciation is used for tangible business assets and the term amortization is reserved for intangible business assets.

Both terms are used in tax literature without being attached to particular types of assets. This is the approach that is used in this text.

5-7.   With respect to dispositions of depreciable assets, the accounting and tax procedures are very different and, as a result, the related terminology cannot be directly compared. For accounting purposes, a disposition will simply result in a gain or loss. For tax purposes, a disposition could result in no tax effect, a capital gain and recapture of CCA, recapture of CCA only, or a terminal loss. There is no real equivalency between these two sets of terminology.

Acquisitions

5-8.   The accounting and tax procedures for acquisitions can be described as follows:

Accounting   In general, accountants record an acquisition cost for each material asset acquired. The acquisition cost that will be recorded in individual asset records is the amount of consideration given up to acquire the asset. This would include all costs directly attributable to the acquisition, including installing it at the relevant location and in the condition necessary for its intended use.

Tax   In general, the capital cost of acquired assets will be allocated to what is referred to as a class. These classes are, in most cases, broadly defined (e.g., Class 10 contains most types of vehicles acquired by an enterprise).

In general, the amount of capital cost to be recorded is the same number that would be recorded as the acquisition cost in the accounting records. A difference can arise, however, when non-arm's length transactions are involved. In accounting, the acquired asset will consistently be recorded at the fair value of the consideration given up. This is not always the case when tax procedures are applied to non-arm's length transactions as will be discussed in Chapter 9, Other Income, Other Deductions and Other Issues.

In general, there is no need to keep track of individual assets for purposes of calculating CCA. However, the procedures applicable to dispositions require that we know the capital cost of each individual asset. Given this, it will be necessary, in the tax records, to track this information.

Dispositions

5-9.   The accounting and tax procedures for dispositions can be described as follows:

Accounting   For accounting purposes, the Net Book Value of the asset disposed of is subtracted from the proceeds from that disposition. If the result is positive, a gain is recorded. Alternatively, if the result is negative, a loss is recorded. For a disposition to result in no income item for accounting purposes, the proceeds of disposition would have to be equal to the net book value of the individual asset. This would be a fairly rare event.

Tax   Tax procedures require that the lesser of the proceeds of disposition and the capital cost of the specific asset be deducted from the UCC balance of its class. While this procedure will often have no tax consequences in the current year (other than decreasing future CCA), there are several other possibilities. There may be a capital gain, a capital gain and recapture of CCA, recapture of CCA only, or a terminal loss. These more complex concepts will be explained at a later point in this Chapter.   As noted, while CCA calculations are based on classes of assets, to deal with the disposition of assets, the capital cost of each individual asset must be available.

Amortization And Capital Cost Allowance

5-10.   The accounting and tax procedures for allocating the cost of depreciable assets to income can be described as follows:

Accounting   Accounting amortization is based on the consistent application of generally accepted accounting principles (GAAP). While these principles would encompass a wide variety of methods, including those used for calculating the maximum CCA for tax purposes, the straight-line method is by far the most widely used method for accounting purposes.

Once a method is chosen, it is generally applied to individual assets. The adopted method must be applied consistently, with the full amount that results from its application being charged as an expense in the determination of accounting Net Income for the current period.

Tax   The *Income Tax Regulations* specify the method that must be applied to each class. Two methods are used for this purpose — the straight-line method and the declining balance method. The required method will be applied to calculate a maximum deduction for the taxation year.

While taxpayers will usually wish to deduct this maximum amount, they are not required to do so. They can deduct all of the maximum amount, none of it, or any value in between. While the regulations specify consistency in the calculation method used, there is no requirement for year-to-year consistency in the portion of the maximum amount deducted. This is in sharp contrast to the accounting requirement that the full amount of amortization be deducted in each year.

5-11.   As previously noted, most companies use straight-line amortization for accounting purposes. In contrast, the *Income Tax Regulations* require the use of declining balance procedures on the majority of important CCA classes. Given that the declining balance method provides a faster write off than the straight-line method, and the fact that most enterprises will deduct the maximum amount of CCA under this method, the amount of CCA deducted is usually larger than the amount of accounting amortization charged to expense. Because of this, most companies will have accounting values for their depreciable assets that are significantly larger than the corresponding tax values. These differences are referred to as temporary differences and, as many of you are aware, GAAP requires the recording of a Future Income Tax Liability to reflect such differences.

Additions To Capital Cost

Determination Of Amounts

General Rules

5-12.   To be added to a CCA class, an asset must be owned by the taxpayer and, in addition, it must be used for the purpose of producing income from business, property, or in certain limited circumstances, employment. Stated alternatively, the asset must be a capital asset rather than inventory. This means that whether an asset should be added to a CCA class depends on the nature of the business. A drill press is a capital asset for a taxpayer using it in a manufacturing process. However, it would be treated as inventory by a taxpayer in the business of selling that type of equipment.

5-13.   Capital cost means the full cost to the taxpayer of acquiring the property and would include all freight, installation costs, duties, non-refundable provincial sales taxes, legal, accounting, appraisal, engineering, or other fees incurred to acquire the property. Note that any refundable GST or HST would not be added to the capital cost (see Paragraph 5-21).

5-14.   In the case of property constructed by the taxpayer for use in producing income, it would include material, labour, and an appropriate allocation of overhead. If the property is paid for in a foreign currency, the Canadian dollar capital cost would be determined using the exchange rate on the date of acquisition.

Repeal Of CEC Legislation

5-15.   In our introductory note at the beginning of this Chapter, we explained that, as of January 1, 2017, assets that were considered eligible capital expenditures are allocated to Class 14.1, rather than the now-repealed CEC balance of the business. Under the old CEC regime, only three-quarters of the cost of an eligible capital expenditure was added to the CEC balance. The new Class 14.1 follows normal CCA procedures where 100 percent of the cost of an asset is added to the Class.

> **EXAMPLE**   A business acquires an unlimited life franchise at a cost of $100,000.

> **ANALYSIS**   Prior to January 1, 2017, only $75,000 [(3/4)($100,000)] of this cost would have been added to the CEC balance. In contrast, if this transaction occurs after December 31, 2016, the full $100,000 cost is added to the new Class 14.1.

Capitalization Of Interest

5-16.   In addition to the direct costs described in the two preceding Paragraphs, ITA 21(1) allows a taxpayer to elect to add the cost of money borrowed to acquire depreciable property to its capital cost. This election is in lieu of deducting the interest in the current taxation year and will usually be an undesirable choice.

5-17.   However, if the deduction of the interest in the current year would result in a non-capital loss, this election may be desirable. By adding the interest to the capital cost of the asset, the amount can be deducted as part of the CCA on the asset's class for an unlimited number of future years. Alternatively, if it serves to increase the non-capital loss for the year, it would become part of the loss carry forward or loss carry back for the year. It would then be subject to the business and property loss carry over time limits of 3 years back and 20 years forward.

Government Assistance

5-18.   Another consideration in determining the capital cost of an addition to a CCA class is government assistance. Under ITA 13(7.1), any amounts received or receivable from any level of government for the purpose of acquiring depreciable assets must be deducted from the capital cost of those assets. This would include grants, subsidies, forgivable loans, tax deductions, and investment tax credits.

5-19.   This tax requirement is consistent with the requirements of IAS 20, *Accounting For Government Grants And Disclosure Of Government Assistance*, which, in general, requires government assistance, including investment tax credits, to be deducted from the cost of assets for accounting purposes.

Non-Arm's Length Acquisitions

5-20.   If transfers of depreciable property between persons not dealing at arm's length are not made at fair market value or as a gift, they are subject to very unfavourable tax treatment. This may result in the capital cost of the asset not being equal to the amount of consideration given for the asset. This point is discussed in more detail in Chapter 9.

GST, HST And PST Considerations

5-21. GST, PST (Provincial Sales Tax), or HST (Harmonized Sales Tax) is usually paid on depreciable asset acquisitions. While we will not provide detailed coverage of GST/HST until Chapter 21, you should be aware of the following:

- GST paid by businesses on the acquisition of assets will, in general, be refunded as input tax credits. Note that there are many complications related to this rule and they will be discussed in Chapter 21.
- HST is the term used to refer to the combined GST and PST amounts that are collected in Ontario and all of the Atlantic provinces. In general, HST paid on the acquisition of depreciable assets is refunded as input tax credits.
- The Quebec PST is integrated with the GST system and, as a consequence, these amounts are refunded on much the same basis as GST.
- The PST that is paid in other provinces, such as Manitoba and British Columbia, is not refunded and, as a consequence, it is included in the capital cost of acquired assets.

5-22. From a technical point of view, all amounts of GST/HST/PST are, at least initially, included in the capital cost of depreciable assets. However, to the extent that these amounts are refunded as input tax credits, they are defined in ITA 248(16) as a form of government assistance and, as a consequence, the refunds are deducted from the capital cost of depreciable assets in the same manner as other government assistance. In somewhat simplified terms, GST/HST/PST amounts that are refunded are not included in the capital cost of depreciable assets.

> **EXAMPLE** An enterprise acquires a depreciable asset in Manitoba at a cost of $11,300. The cost is determined as follows:
>
> | | |
> |---|---:|
> | Cost Before Tax | $10,000 |
> | Federal GST At 5 Percent | 500 |
> | Manitoba's 8 Percent Provincial Retail Sales Tax | 800 |
> | Total Cost | $11,300 |
>
> **ANALYSIS** Provided the enterprise is a GST registrant and the asset is used in delivering GST taxable supplies, the $500 federal GST will be refunded as an input tax credit. However, there will be no refund of the $800 paid to Manitoba. This means that the CCA base for this asset is the amount of $10,800 ($10,000 + $800).

Expenditures On Assets - Expense Or Improvement?

5-23. When a business owns assets with extended useful lives (e.g., buildings or certain types of machinery), it is likely that, over the lives of these types of assets, the enterprise will incur additional costs. When this occurs, a question arises as to whether the costs should be added to the capital cost of the asset or, alternatively, deducted as a current expense.

5-24. Unfortunately, there is no simple answer to this question, resulting in relatively frequent conflicts between the CRA and the taxpayer making such expenditures. To avoid such conflicts, the CRA's website provides some criteria to be used in making such decisions. Although the web page relates to rental income, the criteria are generally applicable and are as follows:

1. Does the expense provide a lasting benefit?
   - The CRA notes that painting the exterior of a wooden building would not provide a lasting benefit and should be charged to current expense.
   - In contrast, putting vinyl or metal siding on a wooden building would be a lasting improvement and should be added to the capital cost of the building.

2. Does the expense maintain or improve the property?
   - If a business repairs an existing set of wooden steps, the repair costs would be viewed as a current expense.
   - In contrast, if the wooden steps are replaced with concrete steps, this would improve the property and should be added to the capital cost of the property.

3. Is the expense for a part of the property or is it a separate asset?
  - The CRA notes that the replacement of existing wiring in a building would normally be an expense, provided it does not improve the property.
  - In contrast, buying a compressor for use in a business would be treated as a separate addition to the appropriate class.

5-25. If a decision cannot be made on the basis of the three preceding factors, the CRA notes that the amount of the expenditure relative to the value of the property should be considered. If the expenditure is large relative to the value of the property, this would suggest that it should be added to the capital cost, rather than treated as an expense. The CRA also notes that the question of whether an expenditure improves the market value of an asset is not a relevant consideration in this matter.

Summary

5-26. In reviewing the detailed tax rules applicable to depreciable asset acquisitions, it is clear that these rules will produce capital costs for depreciable assets that are almost always identical to the acquisition costs produced when GAAP is applied. While differences between amortization amounts and the corresponding CCA deductions will cause these values to diverge significantly as the assets are used, the initial amounts recorded for depreciable assets will normally be the same for both accounting and tax purposes.

Available For Use Rules

5-27. For many types of assets, the available for use rules do not present a problem. Most acquired assets are put into use immediately and the acquirer is allowed to deduct CCA in the year of acquisition. For other assets, the rules can make CCA calculations quite complicated. Real estate assets, especially those that require several years to develop, can be particularly hard hit by the fact that there can be a deferral of the right to deduct CCA for two years, or until the structure is considered available for its income producing use.

5-28. The basic rules are found in ITA 13(26) through 13(32). In simplified terms, properties are considered to be available for use, and thereby eligible for CCA deductions, at the earliest of the following times:

- For properties other than buildings, when the property is first used by the taxpayer for the purpose of earning income.
- For buildings, including rental buildings, when substantially all (usually 90% or more) of the building is used for the purpose for which it was acquired.
- The second taxation year after the year in which the property is acquired. This maximum two year deferral rule is also referred to as the rolling start rule.
- For public companies, the year in which amortization is first recorded on the property under generally accepted accounting principles.
- In the case of motor vehicles and other transport equipment that require certificates or licences, when such certificates or licences are obtained.

5-29. The preceding is a very incomplete description of the available for use rules. There are other special rules for particular assets, as well as significant complications in the area of rental properties. Detailed coverage of these rules goes beyond the scope of this text.

Segregation Into Classes

General Rules

5-30. Part XI and Schedules II through VI of the *Income Tax Regulations* provide a detailed listing of classes and rates for the determination of CCA. There are over 40 classes that vary from extremely narrow (Class 26 which contains only property that is a catalyst or deuterium enriched water) to extremely broad (Class 8 refers to property that is a tangible capital asset and not included in another class). As the applicable rates vary from a low of 4 percent to a high of 100 percent, the appropriate classification can have a significant impact on the amount of CCA that can be taken in future years. This, in turn, has an impact on Taxable Income and Tax Payable.

5-31.   In general, assets do not belong in a class unless they are specifically included in the ITR description of that class. While there are a large number of classes and, as we have noted, Class 8 contains a provision for tangible property not listed elsewhere, some assets are specifically excluded from depreciable property status by ITR 1102. Most importantly, inventories and land cannot be added to any CCA Class. This means, in dealing with real property, the land component of the total cost must be separated from the building component.

5-32.   For your convenience in working with CCA problems, the Appendix to this Chapter provides an alphabetical list of common assets, indicating the appropriate CCA class as well as the rate applicable to that class.

Separate Classes

5-33.   The general rule is that all of the assets that belong in a particular class are allocated to that class, resulting in a single class containing all of the assets of a particular type. There are, however, a number of exceptions to this general rule that are specified in ITR 1101. Some of these exceptions, for instance the requirement of a separate Class 30 for each telecommunication spacecraft, are not of general importance. However, some of the other exceptions are applicable to a large number of taxpayers. These important exceptions are as follows:

Separate Businesses An individual may be involved in more than one unincorporated business. While the income of all of these businesses will be reported in the tax return of the individual, separate CCA classes will have to be maintained for each business. For example, an individual might own both an accounting practice and a coin laundry. Both of these unincorporated businesses would likely have Class 8 assets. However, a separate Class 8 would have to be maintained for each business. In contrast, if an individual owned three separate shopping malls, these could be viewed as a single business and, as a consequence, have combined classes for the three operations. Note, however, that if each mall was incorporated separately, the group could not be viewed as a single business.

Rental Properties Of particular significance in the tax planning process is the requirement that each rental property acquired after 1971 at a cost of $50,000 or more be placed in a separate CCA class. When the property is sold, the lesser of the proceeds of disposition and the cost of the asset will be removed from the particular class. This will commonly result in a negative balance in the class and this amount will have to be taken into income by the taxpayer (see later discussion of recapture of CCA). If it were not for the separate class requirement, this result could be avoided by adding other properties to a single rental property class.

Luxury Cars The separate class rules apply to passenger vehicles that have a cost in excess of a prescribed amount. While this prescribed amount was expected to be changed periodically, it has been $30,000 from 2001 through 2017.

Elections For the assets described in the preceding three paragraphs, separate classes must be used. The taxpayer has no choice in the matter. There are other situations where a taxpayer is allowed to elect having a separate class. One of these situations involves non-residential buildings where the election to use a separate class can result in an additional amount of CCA (see Paragraph 5-37). Another situation involves assets subject to high rates of technological obsolescence (e.g., photocopiers). In this case a separate class election can provide for the recognition of terminal losses. This election is discussed later in this Chapter.

Capital Cost Allowances

General Overview

Methods

5-34.   Once capital assets have been allocated to appropriate classes, these amounts form the base for the calculation of CCA. The maximum CCA is determined by applying a rate that is specified in the Regulations to either the original capital cost of the assets in the class (straight-line classes) or, more commonly, to the end of the period UCC for the class (declining balance classes). The following example will illustrate this difference:

> **EXAMPLE**   A particular CCA class contains assets with a capital cost of $780,000 and an end of the period UCC balance of $460,000. There have been no additions to the class during the year. The rate for the class is 10 percent.
>
> **Declining Balance Class**   If we assume that this is a declining balance class, the rate would be applied to the $460,000 end of the period UCC balance. This would result in a maximum CCA for this class of $46,000 [(10%)($460,000)].
>
> **Straight-Line Class**   If we assume that this is a straight-line class, the rate would be applied to the $780,000 original cost of the assets. This would result in a maximum CCA for this class of $78,000 [(10%)($780,000)].

5-35.   This basic process is fairly simple and straightforward. However, it is complicated by a number of other considerations.

> **Half-Year (a.k.a. First Year) Rules**   For most classes, one-half of any excess of additions for acquisitions over deductions for dispositions to a class for the year must be subtracted prior to the application of the appropriate CCA rate.
>
> **Short Fiscal Periods**   There are several situations in which a business will have a short fiscal period (e.g., a new unincorporated business that starts in July and has a December 31 year end). In these situations, maximum CCA must be reduced to an appropriate fraction of a full year.

5-36.   Each of these complications will be given separate treatment in this section on the calculation of CCA. A further complication arises from the fact that, in general, taxpayers are not permitted to create or increase a net rental loss by claiming CCA on rental properties. Coverage of this topic will be deferred until Chapter 7 where we give detailed attention to the issues related to the taxation of property income.

Rates For Commonly Used CCA Classes

5-37.   The following is a brief description of the more commonly used CCA classes, including the items to be added, the applicable rates, and the method to be used:

> **Class 1 - Buildings (4%, 6%, or 10%)**   In general, Class 1 is a 4 percent declining balance class, applicable to buildings acquired after 1987. This class also includes bridges, canals, culverts, subways, tunnels, and certain railway roadbeds.
>
> Each rental building with a cost of $50,000 or more must be allocated to a separate Class 1.
>
> If a new building, acquired after March 18, 2007 is allocated to a separate Class 1, the general 4 percent rate is increased as follows:
>
> - to 10 percent if it is used 90 percent or more for manufacturing and processing,
> - to 6 percent if it does not qualify for the manufacturing and processing rate, but is used 90 percent or more for non-residential purposes.
>
> Note that these enhanced rates only apply to new buildings, not buildings that have been previously used.
>
> **Class 3 - Buildings Pre-1988 (5%)**   Class 3 is a 5 percent declining balance class. It contains most buildings acquired before 1988. As is the case for Class 1 rental properties, separate classes were required for each rental building with a cost of $50,000 or more. This class also includes breakwaters, docks, trestles, windmills, wharfs, jetties, and telephone poles.

Class 8 - Various Machinery, Equipment, and Furniture (20%)   Class 8 is a 20 percent declining balance class. It includes most machinery, equipment, structures such as kilns, tanks and vats, electrical generating equipment, advertising posters, bulletin boards, and furniture not specifically included in another class. As will be discussed at a later point in the Chapter, individual photocopiers, fax machines, and pieces of telephone equipment purchased for $1,000 or more can be allocated to a separate Class 8 at the election of the taxpayer.

Class 10 - Vehicles (30%)   Class 10 is a 30 percent declining balance class. It includes most vehicles (excluding certain passenger vehicles that are allocated to Class 10.1), automotive equipment, trailers, wagons, contractors' movable equipment, mine railway equipment, various mining and logging equipment, and TV channel converters and decoders acquired by a cable distribution system.

Class 10.1 - Luxury Cars (30%)   Class 10.1 is a class established for passenger vehicles with a cost in excess of an amount prescribed in ITR 7307(1)(b). For cars acquired in 2001 through 2017, the prescribed amount is $30,000. Like Class 10, where most other vehicles remain, it is a 30 percent declining balance class. However, each vehicle must be allocated to a separate Class 10.1. Also important is that the amount of the addition to the separate class is limited to the prescribed amount of $30,000. This, in turn, limits the base for CCA to this same amount.

On the positive side, in the year in which the vehicle is retired, one-half of the normal CCA for the year can be deducted, despite the fact that there will be no balance in the class at the end of the year. A further difference from the regular Class 10 is that, in the year of retirement, neither recapture nor terminal losses are recognized for tax purposes.

Class 12 - Computer Software and Small Assets (100%)   Class 12 includes computer software that is not systems software, books in a lending library, dishes, cutlery, jigs, dies, patterns, uniforms and costumes, linen, motion picture films, and videotapes. Dental and medical instruments, kitchen utensils, and tools are included, provided they cost less than $500. This class is subject to a 100 percent write-off in the year of acquisition. As will be discussed later, we will find that the half-year rule must be applied to some Class 12 assets. When this rule is applicable, the relevant Class 12 assets are effectively subject to a 2 year write off at 50 percent per year.

Class 13 - Leasehold Improvements (Straight-Line)   In general, only assets that are owned by the taxpayer are eligible for CCA deductions. However, an exception to this is leasehold improvements which are allocated to Class 13. For Class 13, the Regulations specify that CCA must be calculated on a straight-line basis for each capital expenditure incurred. The maximum deduction will be the lesser of:

- one-fifth of the capital cost of the improvement; and
- the capital cost of the lease improvement, divided by the lease term (including the first renewal option, if any).

The lease term is calculated by taking the number of full 12 month periods from the beginning of the taxation year in which the particular leasehold improvement is made until the termination of the lease. For purposes of this calculation, the lease term is limited to 40 years. Note that, in the case of such straight-line classes, the application of the half-year rules (see later discussion) will mean that the maximum CCA in the first and last years will be based on one-half of the straight-line rate.

Class 14 - Limited Life Intangible Assets (Straight-Line, No Half-Year Rules)   Class 14 covers the cost of intangible assets with a limited life. These assets are subject to straight-line amortization over their legal life. IT-477 indicates that CCA should be calculated on a pro rata per diem basis. Because of this, neither the half-year rule nor the short fiscal period rule applies to Class 14. In both the first and last years of the asset's life, the per diem approach would be used. Note, however, if there is a disposition of Class 14 assets, the usual recapture and terminal loss procedures would apply.

Class 14.1 - Goodwill And Other Intangible Assets   Class 14.1 is a new CCA Class as of January 1, 2017. The rate for any post-2016 additions to this Class is 5 percent applied to a declining balance and the half year rule is applied. In general terms, the items that are added to this Class 14.1 are:

- Goodwill.
- Intangible assets that do not belong in any other Class. While this is something of a simplification, this category will largely be intangible assets that do not have a limited life. Intangible assets with limited lives are allocated to Class 14 or 44.
- Amounts included in CEC balances that were present on December 31, 2016.

There are a number of complications associated with this Class, including the fact that old CEC balances were transferred into this Class. Given this, we will provide a more extensive discussion of Class 14.1 beginning at Paragraph 5-48.

Class 44 - Patents (25%)   At one point in time, patents were allocated to Class 14 where they were amortized over their legal life of 20 years. This approach failed to recognize that the economic life of this type of asset was usually a much shorter period. To correct this problem, patents are now allocated to Class 44, where they are subject to write-off at a 25 percent declining balance rate. Note, however, that a taxpayer can elect to have these assets allocated to Class 14. This would be a useful alternative if a patent was acquired near the end of its legal life. For example, if a patent only had two years remaining in its legal life, allocating its acquisition to Class 14 would result in the business being able to write off the asset over two years at a 50 percent rate.

Class 50 - Computer Hardware And Systems Software   For computer hardware and systems software acquired after January 31, 2011, the required allocation is to Class 50. CCA on this Class is calculated on a declining balance basis, using a 55 percent rate. The half-year rules are applicable.

The CRA has issued an interpretation that iPhones are "general purpose electronic data processing equipment", i.e., Class 50 assets. Although there is no specific reference to them, it would be logical to assume that tablets and other smartphones would also qualify. Basic cell phones (that are not smart enough to be smartphones) would be Class 8 assets as they are communications equipment.

If an expenditure of this type had a short life that is expected to be less than a year, e.g., a disposable cell phone, it would not normally meet the definition of capital property and would be considered a current expense, not a depreciable capital asset.

Classes 53, 29 and 43 - Manufacturing and Processing Assets   The situation here has been complicated by changes in the designated class for manufacturing and processing assets. Unfortunately, at this point in time, there may be balances in all of the classes that have been used. The relevant information is as follows:

- **Class 53**   Beginning in 2016, manufacturing and processing assets are allocated to Class 53. This Class has a 50 percent rate applied to a declining balance.

- **Class 29**   Manufacturing and processing assets acquired after March 18, 2007 and before 2016 are allocated to Class 29 where CCA is calculated on a 50 percent straight-line (not declining balance) basis.

- **Class 43**   Manufacturing and processing assets acquired before March 19, 2007 are included in Class 43 where the rate is 30 percent applied to a declining balance.

With all three of these Classes, the half-year rule is relevant.

This treatment of manufacturing and processing assets illustrates the procedures often used when the government wishes to change the rate applicable to certain types of assets. While they could accomplish this by simply changing the rate applicable to the relevant Class, this would, in effect, change the rules for asset purchase decisions made in previous years. Given this, they normally implement a decision to change rates by allocating newly acquired assets to a new or different class. This means that the new rate is only applicable to new asset acquisitions. This does, however, complicate matters in that the same type of asset may be found in more than one class, depending on when it was acquired. This is illustrated here where it would be possible to have the same type of equipment found in three different CCA classes and subject to three different calculations.

Exercise Five - 1

Subject: Segregation Into CCA Classes

For each of the following depreciable assets, indicate the appropriate CCA Class. (The Appendix to this Chapter contains a listing of CCA classes.)

- Taxicab
- Manufacturing and processing equipment acquired in 2017
- Franchise with a limited life
- Automobile (i.e., passenger vehicle) with a cost of $120,000
- Government licence with an unlimited life acquired in 2017
- Water storage tank
- Photocopy machine
- Leasehold improvements
- Residential rental property acquired for $200,000. The purchase price was allocated $150,000 to the building and $50,000 to the land.

SOLUTION available in print and online Study Guide.

Half-Year Rules (a.k.a. First Year Rules)
General Rules
5-38.   At one time, a taxpayer was permitted to take a full year's CCA on any asset acquired during a taxation year. This was true even if the asset was acquired on the last day of the year. This was not an equitable situation and the most obvious solution would have been to base CCA calculations on the proportion of a taxation year that the asset was used. Despite the fact that this pro rata approach is widely used for accounting purposes, the government decided that this would be too difficult to implement and an alternative approach was chosen.

5-39.   The approach adopted is based on the arbitrary assumption that assets acquired during a particular taxation year were in use for one-half of that year. Stated simply, in determining the end of period UCC for the calculation of maximum CCA, one-half of the excess, if any, of the additions to UCC for acquisitions over the deductions from UCC for dispositions is removed. As established by the use of the phrase "if any", this adjustment is only made when the net amount is positive.

5-40.   The following example is a simple illustration of the half-year adjustment for additions to most CCA classes. It has not been complicated by the presence of capital gains, recapture of CCA, or terminal losses.

EXAMPLE Radmore Ltd., with a taxation year that ends on December 31, has a Class 10 (30 percent) UCC balance on January 1, 2017 of $950,000. During 2017, it acquires 15 cars at a cost of $20,000 each, for a total addition of $300,000, and disposes of 18 cars for total proceeds of $144,000. In no case did the proceeds of disposition exceed the capital cost of the vehicle being disposed of. The maximum CCA for 2017 and the January 1, 2018 UCC balance are calculated as follows:

January 1, 2017 UCC Balance		$ 950,000
Add: Acquisitions During The Year	$300,000	
Deduct: Dispositions During The Year	(144,000)	156,000
Deduct: One-Half Net Additions [(1/2)($156,000)]		(78,000)
Base Amount For CCA Claim		$1,028,000
Deduct: 2017 CCA [(30%)($1,028,000)]		(308,400)
Add: One-Half Net Additions		78,000
January 1, 2018 UCC Balance*		$ 797,600

*Note the December 31, 2017 UCC is equal to $1,106,000 ($1,028,000 + $78,000).

Exceptions To Half-Year Rules

5-41. There are some classes, or parts of classes, to which the half-year rules do not apply. For the classes that we have described in this Chapter, the exceptions are as follows:

• All assets included in Class 14 (limited life intangible assets).

• Some Class 12 assets such as medical or dental instruments and tools costing less than $500, uniforms, and chinaware. Other Class 12 assets such as certified Canadian films, computer software, and rental video cassettes, are subject to the half-year rules.

5-42. A further exception is available for some property transferred in non-arm's length transactions. Specifically, depreciable property acquired in non-arm's length transactions is generally exempt from the half-year rule if, prior to the transfer, the property was depreciable property that was owned for at least one year and was used to produce business or property income. The property remains in the CCA class that it was in prior to its transfer. This prevents the double application of this rule in situations where there is no real change in the ownership of the property.

EXAMPLE Amber Bailey has an unincorporated business that owns Class 8 assets with capital cost of $200,000 and a UCC of $75,000. The assets are sold to her sister for their fair market value of $250,000. Her sister plans to continue operating the unincorporated business.

ANALYSIS This is a non-arm's length transfer and, both before and after the transfer, the Class 8 assets will be used to produce business income. In this situation, the half-year rule would not be applicable. As the half-year rule was applicable when Ms. Bailey acquired the assets, this exception prevents a double application of this rule to the same assets.

Exercise Five - 2

Subject: CCA Error

During the taxation year ending December 31, 2017, your company acquired a depreciable asset for $326,000 and you included this asset in Class 1 for the year (it was not allocated to a separate Class 1). Early in 2018, you discover that the asset should have been allocated to Class 10. What was the impact of this error on your company's 2017 deductions from business income?

SOLUTION available in print and online Study Guide.

Exercise Five - 3

Subject: Class 13 And Half-Year Rule

Vachon Ltd. has a December 31 year end. The Company leases its office space under a lease that was signed on January 1, 2012. The lease term is 10 years, with an option to renew at an increased rent for an additional five years. In 2012, the Company spent $52,000 renovating the premises. In 2017, changing needs require the Company to spend another $31,000 renovating the space. Determine the maximum amount of Class 13 CCA that the Company can deduct for 2017.

Exercise Five - 4

Subject: Class 8 And Half-Year Rule

Justin Enterprises, an unincorporated business with a December 31 year end, has a Class 8 UCC balance on January 1, 2017 of $212,000. During 2017, it acquires additional Class 8 assets at a cost of $37,400. Also during 2017, it deducts $18,300 from the UCC balance for dispositions. Determine the maximum CCA for 2017 and the January 1, 2018 UCC balance.

Exercise Five - 5

Subject: Class 14 - No Half-Year Rule

Arnot Ltd. has a December 31 year end. On April 1, 2017, Arnot pays $375,000 to enter a franchise agreement. The life of the franchise is 10 years. Determine the maximum CCA for 2017 and the January 1, 2018 UCC balance.

SOLUTIONS available in print and online Study Guide.

Short Fiscal Periods

5-43.   The previous material noted that a half-year assumption has been built into the capital cost allowance system to deal with assets that are acquired or disposed of during a given taxation year. In contrast to this somewhat arbitrary provision for dealing with part year ownership, a more precise rule has been included in the Regulations for dealing with short fiscal periods.

5-44.   In the first or last years of operation of a business, or in certain other types of situations that will be covered in later chapters, a taxation year with less than 365 days may occur. Under these circumstances, the maximum CCA deduction for most classes must be calculated using a proration based on the relationship between the days in the actual fiscal year and 365 days.

5-45.   For example, assume that a business with a taxation year that ends on December 31 begins operations on November 1. On December 1, $100,000 of Class 8 assets (20 percent declining balance) are purchased. There are no further additions or dispositions in December. The maximum CCA for the first fiscal year, taking into consideration the half-year rules, would be calculated as follows:

$$[(1/2)(20\%)(\$100,000)(61/365)] = \underline{\$1,671}$$

5-46.   As is illustrated in the preceding calculation, the half-year rules also apply in these short fiscal period situations. Note it is the length of the taxation year for the business, not the period of ownership of the asset, which determines the proration. If the asset in the preceding example had been acquired on December 31, the amount of maximum CCA for the year would be unchanged.

5-47. Two additional points are relevant here:

- As noted previously, Class 14 assets are subject to pro rata CCA calculations, based on the number of days of ownership in the year. This eliminates the need for the application of the short fiscal period rules.

- When an individual uses assets to produce property income (e.g., rental income), the full calendar year is considered to be the taxation year of the individual. This means that the short fiscal period rules are not applicable in these situations.

Exercise Five - 6

Subject: Short Fiscal Periods

Olander Inc. is incorporated on August 1, 2017. On September 15, 2017, the Company acquires $115,000 in Class 8 assets. The Company has a December 31 year end and no other depreciable assets are acquired before December 31, 2017. Determine the maximum CCA for the year ending December 31, 2017.

SOLUTION available in print and online Study Guide.

Class 14.1 And The Repeal Of The CEC Regime
Additions To The Class

5-48. One of the changes that resulted from moving eligible capital expenditures to the new Class 14.1 was the portion of the cost added to the relevant balances. Under the CEC rules, only three-quarters of the cost of these expenditures was added to the CEC balance. In contrast, 100 percent of such expenditures are added to Class 14.1.

5-49. While the amounts are different, the items that are added to Class 14.1 appear to be the same as those that were added to the CEC balance. These were:

Goodwill   We will give additional attention to this asset in that its treatment under the Class 14.1 rules is somewhat different than its earlier treatment under the CEC regime.

Intangible Assets Other Than Goodwill   This classification only includes intangible assets with unlimited lives. Those intangible assets with limited lives are allocated to Class 14. The following are examples of items that were added to the old CEC balance and are now added to Class 14.1:

- Customer lists purchased and not otherwise deductible.
- The cost of trademarks, patents, licences, and franchises with unlimited lives. (In general, if these expenditures have limited lives they are Class 14 or Class 44 assets.)
- Expenses of incorporation (now only amounts over $3,000 as explained in Paragraph 5-54), reorganization, or amalgamation.
- The costs of government rights.
- Appraisal costs associated with valuing intangible assets, such as a government right, and on an anticipated property purchase that does not take place.
- Initiation or admission fees to professional or other organizations for which the annual maintenance fees are deductible.
- Some payments made under non-competition agreements.

5-50. In addition to the items listed in the preceding paragraph, there will be a further one-time addition to Class 14.1 consisting of:

December 31, 2016 CEC Balances   With the repeal of the CEC legislation, there was a need to deal with CEC balances that were present at the repeal date. As you would anticipate, this resulted in a number of fairly complex transitional provisions.

These will be given attention at the end of this Chapter. At this point we would note that, in very simple terms, the CEC balance that was present on December 31, 2016 was added to the Class 14.1 balance as of January 1, 2017.

It is important to note that, in adding these balances to Class 14.1, they were not adjusted to 100 percent values. Rather they were transferred at the 75 percent values that were used under the CEC rules. This complicates CCA calculations and results in the need for some adjustment in the CCA rate, as well as adjustments related to dispositions (see transitional rules at end of Chapter).

Rates

5-51.   The CCA rate for the new Class 14.1 is 5 percent, applied to a declining balance. This replaces the CEC rate of 7 percent, applied to a declining balance. However, this higher rate was applied to a smaller balance. When this is taken into consideration, the resulting reduction in the effective rate is very small:

Effective Rate - CEC [(7%)(75%)]		5.25 Percent
Effective Rate - Class 14.1 [(5%)(100%)]		5.00 Percent

5-52.   As noted in Paragraph 5-50, the CEC balances that are transferred to Class 14.1 are not adjusted to 100 percent values. As they are still based on 75 percent amounts, it would not be entirely appropriate to apply the new 5 percent rate to these balances. This is reflected in the transitional rules which allow the old 7 percent rate to be applied to CEC balances that are carried forward from December 31, 2016. This higher rate can be applied for 10 years subsequent to 2016, at which point it is likely that most of these balances will have been reduced to insignificant amounts. The relief for small corporations provisions that are discussed in the following paragraphs will assist with this.

Relief For Small Corporations

5-53.   For small corporations, additions to the CEC balance were usually very limited. There would always be an addition for the costs associated with incorporating. However, for many of these new corporations, this would be the only addition. While it was normally a small balance, under the application of declining balance amortization, it would remain on the books as long as the corporation existed.

5-54.   To provide relief in this area, the change in legislation was accompanied by the addition of ITA 20(1)(b) which allows new corporations to deduct the first $3,000 of incorporation costs. While amounts in excess of $3,000 must be added to Class 14.1, in many cases, the $3,000 figure will cover all of the costs of incorporation and eliminate the need to establish a Class 14.1.

> **EXAMPLE**   Artone Inc. is incorporated on February 24, 2017. The costs associated with the incorporation are $2,700.

> **ANALYSIS**   In the absence of the new ITA 20(1)(b), the $2,700 would be added to Class 14.1 and amortized at the rate of 5 percent applied to a declining balance. In contrast, ITA20(1)(b) allows this full amount to be deducted in 2017, with no amount added to Class 14.1.

5-55.   A further problem for small corporations was the December 31, 2016 carry forward of unamortized CEC balances to Class 14.1. As the balance likely reflected incorporation costs, the amounts involved would usually be small. Further, under the declining balance CCA procedures they would have to be dealt with for a considerable period of time. To provide relief in this area, the new Class 14.1 legislation allows for the deduction of a minimum CCA amount of $500 per year with respect to pre-2017 CEC balances carried forward.

> **EXAMPLE**   On December 31, 2016, Pharly Ltd. has a CEC balance of $750.

> **ANALYSIS**   The $750 CEC balance will become the January 1, 2017 UCC balance for Class 14.1. In the absence of a special provision, this balance would be subject to declining balance depreciation at a rate of 7 percent for the next ten years. However,

with the ability to deduct a minimum CCA of $500 per year on this balance, it will be eliminated in two years, a $500 deduction in 2017, followed by a $250 deduction in 2018.

Goodwill

5-56.   The general concept of goodwill is that it reflects the value of a business that is in excess of the sum of the assets of a business that can be specifically identified. It reflects the fact that, if an organization puts a group of assets together in an effective manner, the resulting business can have a value that exceeds the current fair market value of the combined assets. As the source of this value cannot be identified, it is excluded from the concept of identifiable assets. Note that the concept of identifiable assets includes both tangible and intangible assets (e.g., while a patent is an intangible asset, its value can be "identified" as resulting from legal rights specific to that asset).

5-57.   Under both accounting rules and the now repealed CEC legislation, goodwill was only recognized when a business was acquired at a cost in excess of the sum of its identifiable assets. Under the new legislation related to Class 14.1, there are two components to goodwill:

- The conventional component based on the excess of cost of a business acquisition over the fair market values of its identifiable assets.
- Expenditures made by a business that do not relate to a specific property.

5-58.   Unfortunately, the Department Of Finance has not provided guidance on the meaning of this latter concept. It would appear that it would include incorporation costs, as well as various types of reorganization costs. However, it is not clear what else might fall into this category.

5-59.   This situation is further complicated by the Department's decision to allow the deduction of the first $3,000 of incorporation costs in the determination of net business income under ITA 20(1)(b). Only amounts in excess of $3,000 are added to Class 14.1.

5-60.   The other important feature here is that a business will only have one goodwill account. Even if there are multiple transactions resulting in goodwill, all such costs will be accumulated in a single capital cost for goodwill. While this is not important in terms of amounts added to Class 14.1 or the amount of CCA that will be taken on Class 14.1 balances, it will become important if there are disposals of goodwill. As will be discussed in the section titled "Dispositions Of Depreciable Assets", the fact that there is only one capital cost amount for the goodwill balance influences the results of such transactions.

5-61.   A further point here requires some understanding of the legal forms through which business acquisitions can be implemented. While a specific business can have only one balance for its goodwill, ITR 1100(1) requires that when a taxpayer owns properties of the same CCA Class that are used in separate businesses, these assets must be segregated into separates CCA Classes. The consequences of this rule are as follows:

- If a business acquires goodwill as part of a business acquisition and continues to operate that business as a separate business, the acquired goodwill will be allocated to a separate Class 14.1 along with any other Class 14.1 assets for that separate business.

- If a business acquires goodwill as part of a business acquisition and absorbs that business into its other operations, the cost of the acquired goodwill will be added to the single goodwill balance of the acquiring business and included with any other amounts that are already in this balance.

5-62.   This analysis is further complicated by the various legal forms that can be used for business organizations. Without going into detail, we would note that, if a corporation acquires another corporation and operates it as a subsidiary, any goodwill that was part of that transaction will not be recognized in the tax records of the parent company. While such goodwill would show up in the consolidated financial statements that the parent company would prepare under GAAP, Canadian tax legislation does not permit such consolidated statements. The parent and subsidiary would maintain separate tax records and file separate tax returns and the goodwill would not be present in the single entity tax records.

Tax Planning Considerations For CCA

5-63.   As previously noted, the rules for CCA are expressed in terms of maximum amounts that can be deducted. There is, however, no minimum amount that must be deducted, and this leaves considerable discretion as to the amount of CCA to be taken in a particular year. In fact, under certain circumstances, a taxpayer is allowed to revise the CCA for a previous taxation year. The guidelines for this type of amendment are found in IC 84-1. Note, however, that a revision of CCA for a previous year is only permitted if there is no change in the Tax Payable of any year.

5-64.   If the taxpayer has Taxable Income and does not anticipate a significant change in tax rates in future years, tax planning for CCA is very straightforward. The optimum strategy will generally be to take the maximum CCA allowed to minimize Taxable Income and Tax Payable.

5-65.   The situation becomes more complex in a loss year. If a taxpayer wishes to minimize a loss for tax purposes, one approach is to reduce the amount of CCA taken for the year (whether or not the taxpayer will wish to minimize a loss is affected by the loss carry over provisions that are discussed in Chapter 11). In these circumstances, it is necessary to decide on which class or classes the CCA reduction should be applied.

5-66.   The general rule is that CCA should be reduced (i.e., not taken or taken in less than maximum amounts) on classes with the highest rates, while taking full CCA on those classes with the lowest rates.   There could be exceptions to this general rule under certain circumstances such as if an asset is to be sold with recapture resulting, or if it is in Class 10.1 which does not allow recapture or terminal losses.

EXAMPLE   A taxpayer has a $100,000 loss he would like to eliminate by reducing his CCA by $100,000. The UCC of Class 1 (4 percent) is $2,500,000 and the UCC of Class 10 (30 percent) is $333,333. Both classes would have maximum CCA of $100,000.

ANALYSIS   If $100,000 in CCA is taken on Class 1, the following year's maximum CCA will be reduced by only $4,000, from $100,000 [(4%)($2,500,000)] to $96,000 [(4%)($2,400,000)]. In contrast, taking the $100,000 CCA on Class 10 would reduce the following year's maximum CCA by $30,000, from $100,000 [(30%)($333,333)] to $70,000 [(30%)($233,333)]. It would clearly be preferable to take the CCA on Class 1, so that the taxpayer has the option of taking higher CCA in the following year.

5-67.   Similar opportunities arise when current tax rates are below those expected in the future. For example, some provinces institute periodic tax holidays for certain types of businesses. As taxes will be applied in future years, it may be advantageous to stop taking CCA in order to maximize Taxable Income during the years of tax exemption.

Exercise Five - 7

Subject: CCA And Tax Planning

Monlin Ltd. has determined that, for the current year, it has Taxable Income before the deduction of CCA of $45,000. It is the policy of the Company to limit CCA deductions to an amount that would reduce Taxable Income to nil. At the end of the year, before the deduction of CCA, the following UCC balances are present:

Class 1 (4%)	$426,000
Class 8 (20%)	126,000
Class 10 (30%)	89,000
Class 10.1 (30%)	21,000

There have been no additions to these classes during the year. Which class(es) should be charged for the $45,000 of CCA that will be required to reduce Taxable Income to nil? Explain your conclusion.

SOLUTION available in print and online Study Guide.

Dispositions Of Depreciable Assets

Overview Of Procedures

Basic Rule

5-68.   The basic rule for dealing with dispositions of capital assets is as follows:

Basic Rule For Dispositions   When there is a disposition of a depreciable property, an amount will be deducted from the UCC balance in the relevant CCA Class. The deduction will be equal to the lesser of:

- The proceeds of disposition.
- The capital cost of the individual asset.

5-69.   Note that, while we do not need the value of individual assets for purposes of determining maximum CCA, it is necessary to track the value of individual assets in order to apply this basic disposition rule. It is important to understand this in order to deal with the transition of CEC balances to the new Class 14.1. The reason for this, which will be discussed in more detail later in this section, is that under the old CEC regime, it was not necessary to know the capital cost of individual assets.

Dispositions With No Immediate Tax Consequences

5-70.   In the majority of cases, the proceeds of disposition for a depreciable asset will be less than its capital cost. In applying the basic rule, this means that the proceeds of disposition will be subtracted from the balance in the relevant CCA Class.

5-71.   Given the broadly based nature of most CCA Classes, it is likely that a business would have additional assets in the Class subsequent to the disposition. Further, it is also likely that a balance will remain in the Class after the proceeds of disposition have been deducted. In such situations, there are no immediate tax consequences associated with the disposition. While the balance in the Class will be reduced and this will result in smaller CCA deductions in current and future years, the disposition does not give rise to any immediate income inclusion or deduction.

5-72.   For students who are used to working with accounting procedures, this tends to be an uncomfortable result. The accounting procedures for dispositions require that we compare the proceeds of disposition for the individual asset with the net book value of that asset. It would be very unusual for these procedures not to result in either a gain (the proceeds exceed the net book value) or a loss (the proceeds are less than the net book value). In contrast, many, perhaps a majority, of depreciable asset dispositions have no immediate tax consequences.

EXAMPLE   A business owns 20 vehicles, each with a cost of $25,000. All of these vehicles are in Class 10. On January 1, 2017, this Class has a UCC balance of $297,500. During 2017, one of these vehicles is sold for $15,000. The business has a December 31 year end. There are no further acquisitions or dispositions during the year ending December 31, 2017.

ANALYSIS   The lesser of the vehicle's capital cost ($25,000) and the proceeds of disposition ($15,000) would be $15,000. This amount would be subtracted from the January 1, 2017 UCC, leaving a balance of $282,500 ($297,500 - $15,000). As there are additional assets in the class and the end of year balance is positive, the disposition would have no immediate tax consequences. Maximum Class 10 CCA for the year would $84,750 [(30%)($282,500)], leaving a January 1, 2018 UCC of $197,750.

For accounting purposes, the gain or loss on this sale cannot be calculated without having the net book value of the vehicle sold. Unless the net book value was exactly $15,000, a somewhat unlikely value, there would be an accounting gain or loss on this sale.

Dispositions With Tax Consequences

5-73.   As noted in the previous section, the disposition of a depreciable asset will have no immediate tax consequences, provided that:

- The proceeds of disposition are less than the capital cost of the asset.
- There are additional assets in the CCA Class.
- There is a positive balance in the CCA Class, subsequent to the subtraction of the proceeds of disposition. Even if the balance is negative at the time of the disposition, there will still be no tax consequences, provided additions to the Class prior to the end of the year leave a positive balance.

5-74.   While many dispositions meet these conditions, there will also be situations where one or more of these conditions are not present. When this happens, immediate tax consequences will arise. While we will discuss each of these results in more detail, in general terms the various possible consequences can be described as follows:

Capital Gain   A capital gain will arise on the disposition of a depreciable asset if the proceeds of disposition exceed the capital cost of the asset.

Recapture Of CCA   Subtraction of either the proceeds of disposition or the capital cost from the UCC may result in the creation of a negative balance in the class. This can occur whether or not there are any assets left in the class. If this negative balance is not eliminated by new acquisitions prior to the end of the taxation year, this negative amount must be included in income as recapture of CCA. The amount will also be added to the UCC for the class, thereby setting the balance to nil for the beginning of the next year.

Terminal Loss   This occurs only when there are no assets left in the class at the end of the year. If, when the proceeds from the disposition of the last asset(s) are deducted from the UCC for the class, a positive balance remains, this balance can be deducted as a terminal loss. Note that it is not a capital loss. A terminal loss is 100 percent deductible against any other income. The amount of the terminal loss will also be deducted from the UCC for the class, thereby leaving the balance at nil.

No Capital Losses Possible   It is important to note that there is no possibility of a capital loss arising on the disposition of a depreciable asset. When a depreciable asset is acquired for use in a business, there is an expectation that it will decline in value as it is used to produce income. This is reflected in the fact that its tax value will be written down by taking fully deductible CCA. Given this, it would not be equitable to record a capital loss, only one-half of which would be deductible. The only type of loss that can arise on the disposition of a depreciable asset is a fully deductible terminal loss.

Capital Gains

5-75.   The tax rules related to capital gains are fairly complex and will be covered in detail in Chapter 8. However, in order to fully understand the tax procedures related to dispositions of depreciable assets, some understanding of this component of Net Income For Tax Purposes is required. The basic idea is that, if a depreciable capital asset is sold for more than its capital cost, the excess of the proceeds of disposition over the capital cost of the asset is a capital gain. As many of you are aware, only one-half of this gain will be included in the taxpayer's Net Income For Tax Purposes. As we have noted, this one-half of the capital gain is referred to as the taxable capital gain.

5-76.   An important point to remember when calculating CCA is that this excess amount will not be deducted from the UCC. When the proceeds of disposition exceed the capital cost of the asset, the amount deducted from the UCC on the disposition is limited to its capital cost. This is reflected in the basic rule for dispositions that was presented in Paragraph 5-68.

Exercise Five - 8

Subject: Capital Gains On Depreciable Assets

Vaughn Ltd. has a Class 8 balance of $275,000. During the current year, an asset with a capital cost of $18,000 is sold for $23,000. There are no other dispositions during the year and there are over 100 assets left in Class 8. What are the tax consequences of this disposition?

SOLUTION available in print and online Study Guide.

Recapture Of Capital Cost Allowance

Procedures - Negative UCC Balance At Year End

5-77.   Recapture of capital cost allowance refers to situations in which a particular class contains a negative balance at the end of the taxation year. As previously described, the UCC ending balance for a particular class is calculated by starting with the opening balance of the class, adding the cost of acquisitions, and subtracting the lesser of the proceeds of disposition and the capital cost of any assets sold (CCA is subtracted at the beginning of the following taxation year). If the disposal subtraction exceeds the balance in the class, a negative balance will arise.

5-78.   Note, however, that a disposition that creates a temporary negative balance at some point during the year does not create recapture. If additions to the class that are made later in the year eliminate this negative balance prior to year end, no recapture will have to be included in income.

5-79.   It is important to note that acquiring additional assets of a particular class will not eliminate negative balances in those situations where each individual asset has to be allocated to a separate class (e.g., rental buildings costing $50,000 or more). As was intended by policy makers, when individual assets must be allocated to separate classes, a disposition that creates a negative balance at any time during the taxation year will result in recapture. This result cannot be eliminated as no subsequent acquisitions can be added to this separate class.

Economic Analysis

5-80.   Recapture of CCA arises when deductions from the class exceed additions and this generally means that the proceeds of the dispositions, when combined with the CCA taken, exceed the cost of the assets added to the class. In effect, recapture is an indication that CCA has been deducted in excess of the real economic burden of using the assets (cost minus proceeds of disposition). As a reflection of this situation, ITA 13(1) requires that the recaptured CCA be added back to income. The recapture amount is also added to the UCC balance, leaving a balance of nil at the beginning of the next taxation year.

Exercise Five - 9

Subject: Recapture of CCA

At the beginning of 2017, Codlin Inc. has two assets in Class 8. The cost of each asset was $27,000 and the Class 8 UCC balance was $24,883. On June 30, 2017, one of the assets was sold for $28,500. There are no other additions or dispositions prior to the Company's December 31, 2017 year end. What is the effect of the disposition on the Company's 2017 net business income? In addition, determine the January 1, 2018 UCC balance.

SOLUTION available in print and online Study Guide.

Terminal Losses

Procedures - Positive Year End UCC Balance With No Remaining Assets

5-81.   When there is a disposition of the last asset in a CCA class, or the disposition of the only asset when a separate class is used, the resulting balance may be positive or negative. As discussed in the previous section, a negative balance will have to be included in income as recapture. If a positive balance remains, this balance is referred to as a terminal loss.

5-82.   A terminal loss occurs only when there are no assets in the class at the end of the year. In contrast, recapture will occur whether or not there are assets in the class at the end of the year, as long as the balance is negative. (The belief that recapture will only occur if there are no assets in the class is a common misconception.) Similar to recapture, if there is a positive balance in the class at some point during the year, but no assets in the class, there is no terminal loss if additional assets are acquired prior to the end of the year.

5-83.   Terminal losses are fully deductible in the determination of business or property income. In addition, the amount of the loss is subtracted from the CCA class, leaving a nil balance at the beginning of the following year.

5-84.   An additional point here relates to employment income. While employees can deduct CCA on automobiles and aircraft and are subject to the usual rules with respect to recapture, IT-478R2 indicates that terminal losses cannot be deducted on such assets. The reason for this position is that ITA 8(2) indicates that employees can only deduct items that are listed in ITA 8. As terminal losses are not covered by this Section, no deduction is available. Note, however, that any recapture realized by an employee would be included in employment income.

Economic Analysis

5-85.   The presence of a positive balance subsequent to the sale of the last asset in the class is an indication that the taxpayer has deducted less than the full cost of using the assets in this class. Under these circumstances, ITA 20(16) allows this terminal loss to be deducted in full. As we have previously noted, this is not a capital loss. While it is possible to have capital gains on assets that are subject to CCA, it is not possible to have a capital loss on the disposition of a depreciable asset.

Exercise Five - 10

Subject: Terminal Losses

At the beginning of 2017, Codlin Inc. has two assets in Class 8. The cost of each asset was $27,000 and the Class 8 UCC balance was $24,883. On June 30, 2017, both of these assets are sold for a total of $18,000. There are no other additions or dispositions prior to the Company's December 31, 2017 year end. What is the effect of the disposition on the Company's 2017 net business income? In addition, determine the January 1, 2018 UCC balance.

Exercise Five - 11

Subject: Depreciable Asset Dispositions

Norky Ltd. disposes of a Class 8 asset for proceeds of $126,000. The capital cost of this asset was $97,000 and it had a net book value of $43,500. The Company's Class 8 contains a number of other assets and the balance for the Class prior to this disposition was $2,462,000. Describe briefly the accounting and tax treatments of this disposition.

SOLUTIONS available in print and online Study Guide.

Dispositions Of Class 14.1 - Differences From Other Classes

CEC Dispositions

5-86. In order to understand the transitional rules that are presented at the end of this Chapter, you need to be aware of how, during the years prior to 2017, the treatment of CEC dispositions differed from other depreciable asset dispositions.

> **EXAMPLE** On January 1, 2016, Fortco Inc. had a CEC balance of $260,000. During 2016, the Company disposes of an unlimited life franchise for proceeds of $130,000. The capital cost of this franchise was $30,000.
>
> **ANALYSIS** With this being a CEC situation, three-quarters of the proceeds of disposition would be subtracted from the CEC balance, without consideration of the capital cost of the franchise that is being sold. The CEC balance would be reduced to $162,500 [$260,000 - (3/4)($130,000)]. No capital gain would be recognized.
>
> In contrast, if this had been a regular CCA Class, the lesser of the proceeds of disposition of $130,000 and the capital cost of $30,000 would be subtracted from the UCC balance, leaving a UCC of $230,000 ($260,000 - $30,000). In addition, a taxable capital gain of $50,000 [(1/2)($130,000 - $30,000)] would be recognized.

5-87. With eligible capital expenditures now being added to a regular CCA Class, the need to subtract the lesser of the proceeds of disposition and the capital cost will clearly result in capital gains being recognized on a more regular basis. We will return to this fact when we consider the economic impact of the replacement of the CEC regime with regular CCA procedures at the end of this Chapter.

Class 14.1 Anomalies

5-88. The tax policy goal with respect to eligible capital expenditures was to eliminate the old CEC legislation which, in effect, provided a unique tax treatment for these expenditures, and to begin treating these items in a manner consistent with other depreciable assets. That is, eligible capital expenditures would be allocated to a CCA Class and be subjected to the same rules that applied to other depreciable assets as follows:

- 100 percent of the cost of eligible capital expenditures would be allocated to a Class;
- the balance would be written off using either straight-line or declining balance amortization; and
- when a disposition occurs, the lesser of the capital cost or the proceeds of disposition would be subtracted from the UCC of the Class.

5-89. While this desired change was largely implemented, two anomalies remain:

- ITA 13(34) deems that every business will have a single goodwill property. Unlike the situation with other assets added to Class 14.1, where a separate capital cost will be tracked for each asset, there will be only one capital cost for goodwill, regardless of the number of goodwill acquisitions that have been added to the Class.
- ITA 20(16.1) does not permit terminal losses on Class 14.1 assets as long as the business continues to operate.

5-90. We will give individual attention to each of these differences. You should note, however, that these differences do not alter the calculation of maximum CCA for the current year. They only become relevant when there is a disposition of Class 14.1 assets.

Single Goodwill Account

5-91. As we have noted, each business will have only one goodwill property for each business. This means that we will not keep track of individual capital costs for each acquisition of goodwill. We are accustomed to the fact that a given CCA Class has only one UCC balance. However, as we pointed out in our general discussion of dispositions, each individual asset has a separate capital cost that is used to determine whether there is a capital gain on a disposition. This general rule applies equally well to additions to Class 14.1 other than goodwill. In contrast, even if we had a dozen additions to goodwill, there would be a single capital cost which sums these additions.

EXAMPLE   During 2017, Brasco Ltd. acquires two businesses. The acquisition of Business 1 includes a payment for goodwill of $125,000, while the acquisition of Business 2 includes a payment for goodwill of $180,000. Neither of these businesses will be carried on as a separate business. This is important in that, if Brasco continued to operate these businesses separately, a separate Class 14.1 would be established for each business.

In December, 2018, a portion of Brasco's business is sold at a price that includes goodwill of $140,000. Brasco had no Class 14.1 balance as of January 1, 2017, and there were no other Class 14.1 transactions during 2017 or 2018.

ANALYSIS   CCA on Class 14.1 for 2017 would be calculated as follows:

January 1, 2017 Balance	Nil
2017 Additions ($125,000 + $180,000)	$305,000
One-Half Net Additions [(1/2)($305,000)]	(152,500)
CCA Base	$152,500
2017 CCA [(5%)($152,500)]	(7,625)
One-Half Net Additions	152,500
January 1, 2018 UCC	$297,375

When a portion of Brasco's business is sold with a payment for goodwill of $140,000, we would subtract from the UCC balance the lesser of:

- the proceeds of disposition of $140,000; and
- the cost of the single goodwill property of $305,000.

There would be no immediate tax consequences resulting from the disposition and the new UCC figure for Class 14.1 would be $157,375 ($297,375 - $140,000).

5-92.   You should note how this result would differ if Brasco had continued to operate either of the acquired businesses as a separate business. To illustrate this possibility, consider this modified version of the example from Paragraph 5-91.

EXAMPLE   During 2017, Brasco Ltd. acquires two businesses. The acquisition of Business 1 includes a payment for goodwill of $125,000, while the acquisition of Business 2 includes a payment for goodwill of $180,000. Both of these businesses will be operated as separately managed businesses within the Brasco organization. Given this, there will be a separate Class 14.1 balance for each business.

In December, 2018, Business 1 is sold at a price that includes goodwill of $140,000. Brasco had no Class 14.1 balance as of January 1, 2017, and there were no other Class 14.1 transactions during 2017 or 2018.

ANALYSIS   CCA on Class 14.1 for 2017 would be calculated as follows:

	Business 1	Business 2
January 1, 2017 Balance	Nil	Nil
2017 Additions	$125,000	$180,000
[(1/2)($125,000)]	(62,500)	
[(1/2)($180,000)]		(90,000)
CCA Base	$ 62,500	$ 90,000
2017 CCA		
[(5%)($62,500)]	(3,125)	
[(5%)($90,000)]		(4,500)
One-Half Net Additions	62,500	90,000
January 1, 2018 UCC (Total = $297,375)	$121,875	$175,500

In 2018, the sale of the Business 1 would result in recapture as follows:

January 1, 2018 UCC Of Business 1 - Class 14.1	$121,875
Disposition - Lesser Of:	
Proceeds Of Disposition = $140,000	
Capital Cost = $125,000	(125,000)
Negative Ending Balance = Recapture Of CCA	($ 3,125)

In addition, there would be a taxable capital gain of $7,500 [(1/2)($140,000 - $125,000)].

Exercise Five - 12

Subject: Disposition Of Goodwill

During 2017, Dextrin Inc. acquires two businesses. The cost of the first acquisition includes a payment for goodwill of $85,000, while the cost of the second includes a payment for goodwill of $105,000. Neither of these businesses will be operated as a separate business entity. Dextrin Inc. had no Class 14.1 balance as of January 1, 2017, and there were no other Class 14.1 transactions during the year. In December 2018, two portions of Dextrin's business activities are sold. The first results in a goodwill receipt of $65,000, while the second results in a goodwill receipt of $115,000. Dextrin always claims maximum CCA. Determine the January 1, 2018 UCC balance and describe the tax effect of the dispositions.

SOLUTION available in print and online Study Guide.

No Terminal Losses

5-93. As we have noted, a Class 14.1 disposition can only result in a terminal loss in those situations where the business as a whole is being terminated. A simple example will serve to illustrate this difference:

EXAMPLE On January 1, 2017, there is no balance in Roper Inc.'s Class 14.1. Later that month, the Company expands its business by acquiring an unlimited life franchise at a cost of $200,000. During February, 2018, the franchise is sold for $150,000. Roper Inc. continues its operations into 2019.

ANALYSIS The relevant calculations for 2017 and 2018 are as follows:

Class 14.1 Balance - January 1, 2017	Nil
2017 Addition	$200,000
One-Half Net Additions	(100,000)
CCA Base	$100,000
2017 CCA [(5%)($100,000)]	(5,000)
One-Half Net Additions	100,000
January 1, 2018 UCC	$195,000
Disposition - Lesser Of:	
Proceeds Of Disposition = $150,000	
Capital Cost = $200,000	(150,000)
December 31, 2018 UCC*	$ 45,000
2018 CCA [(5%)($45,000)]	(2,250)
January 1, 2019 UCC	$ 42,750

*You might note that this $45,000 balance reflects the $50,000 loss on the asset reduced by the CCA of $5,000 already claimed in 2017.

5-94.   If we were not dealing with a Class 14.1 asset, the $45,000 would have been deducted as a terminal loss, subtracted from the Class balance, and no CCA would have been taken. The only asset that was added to the Class was sold and a positive balance remains. In contrast, with Class 14.1, the $45,000 balance is left in the Class and the Company continues to deduct CCA in future periods.

5-95.   There are a couple of possible reasons for this difference. First, it is consistent with the old CEC rules. Under this previous legislation, no deduction could be made for losses on CEC dispositions unless the business was being terminated. A second reason is more conceptual. We have noted that ITA 13(34) deems every business to have a goodwill property. That being the case, there will always be an asset left in the Class. That is, as long as a business is operating, there can be no situation in which no assets are left in Class 14.1. Given this, it would not be appropriate to deduct a terminal loss.

Summary Of Disposition Tax Consequences

5-96.   Figure 5-2 provides a summary of the various tax consequences that can result from dispositions of depreciable assets, along with a description of the conditions that lead to each possible consequence.

Figure 5 - 2	
Dispositions Of Depreciable Assets - Summary of Tax Consequences	
Result	**Conditions**
Capital Gain	If the proceeds of disposition exceed the capital cost of the asset. A capital gain will normally be accompanied by recapture of CCA. An exception to this is Class 10.1 where capital gains are not recognized.
Recapture Of CCA	If a deduction resulting from a disposition exceeds the balance in the CCA Class and a **negative** balance remains at the **end** of the taxation year. An exception to this is Class 10.1 where recapture of CCA is not recognized. Note that recapture can occur even if there are still assets in the Class.
Terminal Loss	If the **last asset** in a CCA Class is disposed of and a **positive** balance remains in the Class at the **end** of the taxation year. The exceptions to this are Class 10.1 and Class 14.1 where terminal losses are not recognized.
No Immediate Tax Consequences	If all the following conditions are present: • the proceeds of disposition are less than the capital cost of the asset (no capital gain), • the disposition does not leave a negative balance in the CCA Class at the end of the taxation year (no recapture), and • there are assets left in the CCA Class at the end of the taxation year (no terminal loss).

CCA Schedule

5-97.   At this point, it is useful to summarize the CCA calculations in a schedule.   A commonly used format is illustrated in the following example.

> **EXAMPLE**   The fiscal year end of Blue Sky Rentals Ltd. is December 31. On January 1, 2017, the UCC balance for Class 8 is $155,000. During the year ending December 31, 2017, $27,000 was spent to acquire Class 8 assets. During the same period, a used Class 8 asset was sold for $35,000. The capital cost of this asset was $22,000.

UCC Of The Class At The Beginning Of The Year		$155,000
Add: Acquisitions During The Year	$27,000	
Deduct: Dispositions During The Year - Lesser Of:		
• Capital Cost = $22,000		
• Proceeds Of Disposition = $35,000	(22,000)	5,000
Deduct: One-Half Net Additions [(1/2)($5,000)]*		(2,500)
Amount Subject To CCA		$157,500
Deduct: CCA For The Year [(20%)($157,500)]		(31,500)
Add: One-Half Net Additions		2,500
UCC Of The Class At The Beginning Of The Subsequent Year		$128,500

> *This adjustment for one-half of the excess of additions over disposal deductions is only made when the net amount is positive (e.g., the cost of acquisitions, if any, exceeds the amounts deducted for dispositions).

5-98.   While this schedule is not designed to show this value, there is also a taxable capital gain of $6,500 [(1/2)($35,000 - $22,000)] resulting from the sale of the asset.

> **We suggest you work Self Study Problems Five-1, 2, 3, 4, and 5 at this point.**

CCA Determination - Special Situations

Separate Class Election

The Problem

5-99.   In our discussion of CCA procedures we noted that, in general, all assets of a particular type must be allocated to a single CCA class. However, we also noted that there were a number of exceptions to this general approach. For example, the *Income Tax Regulations* require that a separate class be used for each rental property with a cost in excess of $50,000.

5-100.   As a further point, we noted that for certain other types of assets, the taxpayer could elect to use a separate CCA class for each individual asset. Now that you have an understanding of the procedures associated with dispositions of depreciable assets, we can meaningfully discuss the reasons for making such an election for certain types of assets.

5-101.   Consider a $25,000 high volume colour photocopier that would normally be allocated to Class 8. After two years, the UCC balance would be calculated as follows:

Capital Cost	$25,000
CCA Year One [(20%)(1/2)($25,000)]	(2,500)
CCA Year Two [(20%)($25,000 - $2,500)]	(4,500)
UCC - Beginning Of Year Three	$18,000

5-102.   Given the rate of technological change in this area, it is possible that this photocopier would be replaced after two years. Further, the value of the old photocopier would likely be relatively small. If, for example, the photocopier was disposed of for proceeds of $5,000, there would be a terminal loss equal to $13,000 ($18,000 - $5,000).

5-103.   There are two problems with this analysis:

- Most businesses will have more than one asset in Class 8. This disposition would leave other assets in the Class and no terminal loss could be recognized.

- Even if the photocopier is the only Class 8 asset, if the photocopier is replaced, the replacement would likely be acquired within the same taxation year, again resulting in a situation where no terminal loss could be recognized because there are remaining assets in the Class.

5-104.   The election to allocate this photocopier to a separate Class 8 balance alleviates these problems. When the photocopier is disposed of, a terminal loss can be recognized, even if the business replaces it prior to year end or has other Class 8 assets.

Eligible Assets (Rapidly Depreciating Electronic Equipment)

5-105.   There are a number of high tech or electronic products that are normally included in Class 8 (20 percent declining balance) that have actual service lives that are significantly shorter than the rates applicable to that Class would imply. ITR 1101(5p) lists the following specific types of Class 8 assets that are eligible for separate class treatment, provided they have a capital cost of $1,000 or more:

- photocopiers (Class 8)
- electronic communications equipment, such as telephone equipment (Class 8)
- computer software (only if included in Class 8 rather than Class 12 or 50)

5-106.   As noted in our earlier discussion, the purpose of this separate class election is to provide for the recognition of terminal losses on the disposition of certain short-lived assets. Under the usual single class procedures, such recognition is not usually possible, either because there are assets remaining in the particular CCA class, or because the retired assets are being replaced on a regular and ongoing basis. Note that there are many types of rapidly depreciating electronic equipment currently available that are not listed, such as 3D printers.

Exercise Five - 13

Subject: Separate Class Election

In January, 2017, Edverness Inc. acquires ten photocopiers at a cost of $20,000 each. In December, 2017, two of these photocopiers are traded in on faster machines with more features. The new photocopiers cost $22,000 each, and the Company receives a trade-in allowance for each old machine of $3,000. Indicate the amount(s) that would be deducted from 2017 business income if no election is made to put each photocopier in a separate class. Contrast this with the deduction(s) that would be available if the separate class election is used.

SOLUTION available in print and online Study Guide.

Non-Residential Buildings

5-107.   As noted in Paragraph 5-37, for Class 1 new non-residential buildings, there are enhanced CCA rates. The regular 4 percent rate is increased to 10 percent if more than 90 percent of the building is used for manufacturing and processing. If the building does not meet the manufacturing and processing test, but is used more than 90 percent for non-residential purposes in general, the rate is 6 percent.

5-108.   The availability of these special rates is conditional on the taxpayer allocating each eligible building to a separate class. While this election allows for higher CCA rates, there is a possible downside to this alternative. With the higher rates, the building can be written off faster, resulting in a lower UCC. This means that, if the building is sold, there will likely be recapture of CCA. If the building had not been put in a separate class, this could be avoided by replacing the building before the end of the taxation year.

Change In Use For Automobiles

5-109.   In general, when there is a change in the use of a capital asset, the *Income Tax Act* requires that the change be treated as a deemed disposition/re-acquisition, a requirement that can result in tax consequences such as capital gains or recapture. To fully understand this requirement requires a fairly complete understanding of capital gains taxation. Given this, we have deferred our detailed coverage of this subject to Chapter 8.

5-110.   However, in the problem material found in this Chapter and in the following Chapter 6 on Business Income, there are number of situations where an individual uses an automobile for both personal and business usage. In most of these situations, the amount of personal vs. business use will vary each year.

5-111.   For example, assume that Sally Rand uses her automobile 20 percent for business in 2016 and 30 percent for business in 2017. Technically, such a change represents a change in use and, if no special provisions were available, Sally would have a deemed disposition/re-acquisition in 2017, resulting in a need to deal with the resulting tax consequences.

5-112.   Fortunately, an alternative approach appears to be acceptable to the CRA. A CCA amount is calculated each year on the assumption that the car is used 100 percent for business or employment activities. Using this figure, the deductible amount is determined by multiplying the 100 percent use figure by the portion of the use that was business or employment related during the current year. This procedure avoids the complications associated with determining market values and recording annual deemed dispositions/re-acquisitions.

> **EXAMPLE**   Joan Stream acquires an automobile for $25,000. It will be used for both business and personal activities. During 2016, business milage is 40 percent of the total driven. In 2017, business usage increases to 60 percent of the total usage.
>
> **ANALYSIS**   Maximum CCA for 2016 would be $3,750 [(1/2)(30%)($25,000)]. This amount would be deducted from the UCC without regard to personal usage. The CCA deductible from business income for Joan would be $1,500 [(40%)($3,750)].
>
> In calculating CCA for 2017, the 100 percent figure would be $6,375 [(30%)($25,000 - $3,750)] and the deductible amount would be $3,825 [(60%)($6,375)].

Other Special Situations

5-113.   There are a number of other situations which involve special rules that are applicable to real and deemed dispositions of depreciable assets. While all of the following special situations require an understanding of the concepts introduced in this Chapter 5, they also require a sound understanding of the taxation of capital gains and losses. Given this situation, we will defer our coverage of these situations to Chapter 8, Capital Gains And Losses.

5-114.   Briefly described, these special situations are as follows:

Changes In Use   While we have covered the special rules for changes in the use of an automobile, the basic rules for these transactions require a more complete understanding of capital gains. Given this, additional coverage will be required.

Sale Of Real Properties (Land And Buildings)   When real properties are sold, it is not uncommon that the result is a capital gain on the land, combined with a terminal loss on the building. Given that the loss is fully deductible, while only one-half of the capital gain is subject to tax, it is not surprising that special rules are applicable.

Replacement Properties   When an involuntary disposition (a disposition resulting from events such as fire or expropriation) occurs, it may result in large capital gains and recapture of CCA. Similarly, when there is a voluntary disposition (e.g., a business sells its assets to move to a new location), such taxable amounts may also arise. In such situations, the *Income Tax Act* has provisions that provide relief, provided the assets are replaced within a specified period of time. For example, these rules could mitigate the tax effect of the recapture arising in the situation described in Paragraph 5-108 where the taxpayer has elected to allocate a building to a separate class.

CEC To Class 14.1 - Transitional Rules

Approach

5-115.   As we have noted, when the new Class 14.1 rules came into effect, existing CEC balances did not simply disappear. As a result, there was a need for rules to deal with the transition from the old CEC rules to the new Class 14.1 procedures. Given the magnitude of this change, it is not surprising to find that these rules are fairly complex. As an indication of this, the Department Of Finance explanatory notes related to these changes run to nearly 15 pages.

5-116.   Providing detailed coverage of these rules in a general text such as this would clearly not be appropriate. This view is reinforced by the fact that, over time, the importance of these rules declines. We suspect that five years from now, we will no longer provide any coverage of these rules.

5-117.   That being said, it would be equally inappropriate to provide no coverage of these transitional rules. Substantial CEC balances exist in the real world and are present in the problem material provided with this text. Given this, we will provide coverage of those transitional rules that we view as necessary to understanding the changes. Specifically, we will deal with the following issues.

Conversion Of CEC Balances To Class 14.1   CEC balances that existed on December 31, 2016 were converted to a January 1, 2017 Class 14.1 balance. If there have been numerous additions to and disposals from the CEC account, this can be somewhat complex. However, we will confine our presentation to situations where there have been a limited number of eligible capital expenditures and no disposals of CEC assets.

Disposition Of Pre-2017 Asset   When there is a post-2016 disposal of a CEC asset acquired prior to January 1, 2017, the transitional rules require some adjustments to the normal disposal procedures for depreciable assets. We will provide coverage of these adjustments.

5-118.   We would note that we will not provide coverage of the transitional rules related to:

• Taxation years that straddle the introduction of the new Class 14.1 rules.

• Rules designed to prevent the use of non-arm's length transfers to take advantage of the transition from the CEC regime to the new Class 14.1 rules.

Basic CEC Procedures

5-119.   In order to understand the transitional provisions related to this change, some understanding of the old CEC procedures is required. While we have made earlier references to parts of these procedures in various sections of the Chapter, a more complete presentation will facilitate your understanding of the transitional rules.

5-120.   The basic CEC procedures can be described as follows:

Additions   Only three-quarters of the cost of eligible capital expenditures was added to the CEC balance, unlike the normal CCA procedures for Class 14.1 (100 percent of additions). No half-year rule was applicable to CEC additions. The half-year rule is applicable to Class 14.1.

Amortization   A rate of 7 percent was applied to the end-of-period CEC balance.

Dispositions   Three-quarters of the proceeds of disposition were subtracted from the CEC balance. As we have noted, there was no comparison with the capital cost of the disposed asset. This is very different than the normal CCA procedures where the lesser of the proceeds of disposition and the capital cost of the asset is subtracted from the UCC balance. Also as noted, this difference will, in many situations, result in an income inclusion that would not have occurred under the old CEC procedures.

When the proceeds of disposition were subtracted from the CEC balance, there were two possible results:

- In most cases, a positive balance of CEC remained. In this case, there would have been no immediate tax consequences related to the disposal.

- If the result was a negative balance, the result was an income inclusion. Without becoming involved in the details applicable to this situation, we would note that the inclusion resembled recapture, or a taxable capital gain, or some combination of the two.

5-121. A simple example will serve to illustrate these procedures.

EXAMPLE A corporation begins operations on March 1, 2014 and acquires goodwill for $40,000 on May 24, 2014. In July, 2016, the goodwill is sold for $46,000. The company's fiscal year ends on December 31.

ANALYSIS The analysis of the cumulative eligible capital account would be as follows:

	CEC Balance	CEC Deductions
Addition, May, 2014 [(3/4)($40,000)]	$30,000	
CEC Amount [($30,000)(7%)(306/365)]	(1,761)	$1,761
Balance, January 1, 2015	$28,239	
CEC Amount [($28,239)(7%)]	(1,977)	1,977
Balance, January 1, 2016	$26,262	
Proceeds Of Sale [(3/4)($46,000)]	(34,500)	
Balance After Sale	($ 8,238)	$3,738

An amount of $3,738 that represents recapture of previous CEC deductions would be added to income in full.

The $4,500 excess ($8,238 - $3,738) would be multiplied by two-thirds to arrive at an income inclusion of $3,000. The logic behind this approach becomes clear when you recognize that $3,000 is one-half of the $6,000 ($46,000 - $40,000) gain on the sale of the goodwill, demonstrating that these procedures give capital gains treatment to gains on the disposition of CEC balances.

5-122. It is important to note that while the $3,000 represents one-half of the gain on the disposition of goodwill, a result that is like a taxable capital gain in terms of the amount, it is not a capital gain. It is of significance, as will be explained later in this section, that this $3,000 is business income. This is in contrast to the results that will occur with Class 14.1 dispositions where such amounts will be treated as taxable capital gains.

5-123. There were other special rules related to CEC, as well as an election to provide a different treatment of dispositions. However, coverage of these extra rules is not required to understand the transition to the new Class 14.1 procedures.

Conversion Of CEC Balances

5-124. The basic conversion process does not involve any real complications. The transitional rules indicate that the CEC balance that is present on December 31, 2016 becomes the Class 14.1 UCC balance on January 1, 2017. While the basic rate for Class 14.1 is 5 percent, until 2027, an additional 2 percent of CCA is available on these carry forward amounts. In effect, the rate on these carry forward amounts is 7 percent (the old rate for CEC) for a period of 10 years.

5-125. As previously noted, in order to eliminate the need to deal with small amounts of these carry forward balances, the minimum CCA amount is $500 per year with respect to pre-2017 CEC balances carried forward.

EXAMPLE   Cognor Ltd. has a December 31, 2016 CEC balance of $157,420.

ANALYSIS   The $157,240 will become the January 1, 2017 balance of Class 14.1. If there are no other Class 14.1 transactions during 2017, maximum Class 14.1 CCA is equal to $11,019 [(7%)($157,420)]. Note that the half-year rule is not applicable to this addition to Class 14.1.

Exercise Five - 14

Subject: Conversion Of CEC Balances

On December 31, 2016, Farmo Inc. has a CEC balance $149,610. During 2017, Farmo acquires an unlimited life franchise at a cost of $89,000. What is the maximum amount of Class 14.1 CCA that can be deducted for 2017?

SOLUTION available in print and online Study Guide.

5-126.   While there are complications related to determining the capital costs of the former CEC assets, these only become relevant when there is a disposition. Given this, we will deal with these issues in the next section which covers post-2016 dispositions of pre-2017 CEC assets.

Dispositions Of Pre-2017 CEC Assets
Determination Of Total Capital Cost

5-127.   With the application of the usual depreciable asset procedures to pre-2017 CEC assets, it will be necessary to determine the capital cost of the items that were included in this balance. This reflects the fact that, under the usual depreciable asset rules, a disposition is recorded by subtracting the lesser of the proceeds of disposition for the asset and its capital cost. This is in contrast to the CEC procedures under which proceeds of disposition were subtracted, without regard to whether this value was higher or lower than the capital cost of the asset.

5-128.   We would remind you that, with respect to the goodwill component of Class 14.1, each business will have a single goodwill account, without regard to the number of items that have been added to or subtracted from this account. It follows that there will be only one capital cost for all of the goodwill items that are included in Class 14.1. This is in contrast to other Class 14.1 assets where individual capital costs will be determined for each addition to the account.

5-129.   In somewhat simplified terms, the capital cost for the December 31, 2016 CEC balance, is calculated as follows:

$$[(4/3)(A + B)], \text{ where}$$

> **A** = The CEC balance at the beginning of the day on January 1, 2017.
>
> **B** = The total amount of CEC deductions taken prior to January 1, 2017 that have not been recaptured.

5-130.   A simple example will serve to illustrate this definition.

EXAMPLE   The balance in Dupor Inc.'s CEC account on December 31, 2016 is $97,301. This is the unamortized balance of an unlimited life franchise that was acquired in 2015 for $150,000. The amount added to the CEC balance was $112,500 [(3/4)($150,000)].

ANALYSIS   The capital cost of the franchise would be calculated as follows:

[(4/3)($97,301)]	$129,735
[(4/3)($112,500 - $97,301)]	20,265
Capital Cost - Unlimited Life Franchise	$150,000

Exercise Five - 15

Subject: Determination Of Capital Cost

Falar Ltd.'s CEC balance on December 31, 2016 was $120,654. This is the unamortized balance of two unlimited life franchises that were acquired in 2014. The first was acquired for $120,000. The second for $80,000. What is the total capital cost of the two unlimited life franchises on January 1, 2017?

SOLUTION available in print and online Study Guide.

Allocation Of Capital Cost To Individual Items

5-131.   If there have been no dispositions of CEC assets prior to December 31, 2016, this is a very simple process.

> **EXAMPLE (No Pre-2017 CEC Disposition)**   During 2016, Cybor Inc. acquires two unlimited life franchises, the first on January 1, 2016 for $100,000, the second on July 1, 2016 at a cost of $150,000. The Company deducts maximum amortization for 2016.
>
> **ANALYSIS**   The addition to the CEC balance for these acquisitions would be $187,500 [(3/4)($100,000 + $150,000)]. The deduction for amortization of these amounts would be $13,125 [(7%)($187,500)]. This would leave a CEC balance on December 31, 2016 of $174,375 ($187,500 - $13,215). This would then become the Class 14.1 UCC as of January 1, 2017.
>
> The total capital cost for the Class 14.1 assets would be calculated as follows:
>
> | | |
> |---|---:|
> | [(4/3)($174,375)] | $232,500 |
> | [(4/3)($13,125)] | 17,500 |
> | January 1, 2017 Capital Cost | $250,000 |
>
> As the total is simply the sum of the costs of the two CEC assets, $100,000 would be allocated to the first franchise and $150,000 would be allocated to the second franchise.

5-132.   Unfortunately, the situation becomes more complex when there were CEC dispositions prior to December 31, 2016. This problem arises from the fact that, under the CEC rules, a disposition resulted in a deduction from the CEC balance equal to the proceeds of disposition, without regard to whether this was higher or lower than the capital cost of the asset being sold. To illustrate this problem, consider this modified version of the example from 5-131.

> **EXAMPLE (With Pre-2017 CEC Disposition)**   During 2016, Cybor Inc. acquires two unlimited life franchises, the first on January 1, 2016 for $100,000, the second on July 1, 2016 at a cost of $150,000. On November 1, 2016, the first franchise that was acquired is sold for $120,000. The Company deducts maximum amortization for 2016.
>
> **ANALYSIS**   The relevant calculations are as follows:
>
> | | |
> |---|---:|
> | Additions To CEC [(3/4)($100,000 + $150,000)] | $187,500 |
> | Disposition [(3/4)($120,000)] | (90,000) |
> | CEC Deduction Base | $ 97,500 |
> | CEC Deduction [(7%)($97,500)] | (6,825) |
> | December 31, 2016 CEC Balance | $ 90,675 |

The total capital cost for the Class 14.1 assets would be calculated as follows:

[(4/3)($90,675)]	$120,900
[(4/3)($6,825)]	9,100
January 1, 2017 Capital Cost	$130,000

5-133.   At this point, a transitional rule is required. In somewhat simplified terms, the rule indicates that the capital cost of individual assets is equal to the lesser of:

- the total capital cost; and
- the expenditure that was made to acquire the CEC asset.

5-134.   In our example, the capital cost of the second franchise would be $130,000, the lesser of the $150,000 expenditure to acquire this asset and the CEC balance of $130,000.

5-135.   The economics of this simple example are not difficult to understand. When the first franchise was sold, $90,000 was subtracted from the CEC balance. This was $15,000 more than the $75,000 that was put into the balance when the franchise was acquired. This results in a reduction in the amount of capital cost allocated to the other CEC asset of $20,000 [(4/3)($15,000)]. This is reflected in the fact that the capital cost allocated to the second franchise is $20,000 ($150,000 - $130,000) less than its cost.

Exercise Five - 16

Subject: Allocation Of Capital Cost

During January, 2016, Corvex Ltd. acquired three unlimited life franchises. The first cost $126,000, the second $185,000, and the third, $94,000. To raise funds to pay their accountant's fees, the first and second of these franchises were sold during November, 2016. The first was sold for $142,000 and the second for $220,000. Corvex claims the maximum CEC deduction for 2016. Determine the total capital cost of the third franchise as of January 1, 2017.

SOLUTION available in print and online Study Guide.

CEC Dispositions After January 1, 2017 - Excess Recapture

5-136.   To this point we have covered only dispositions that occurred prior to January 1, 2017. In this context, we have provided examples of the calculation of both the initial UCC balance of the new Class 14.1, as well as the determination of the capital cost of the assets that are present when the new regime is initiated.

5-137.   There is a problem, however, when one of the assets in the initial Class 14.1 balance is disposed of subsequent to January 1, 2017. A simple example will illustrate this problem:

EXAMPLE   On July 1, 2016, Tabor Ltd. acquires an unlimited life franchise for $200,000. On July 1, 2017, this franchise is sold for $225,000. There was no balance in Tabor's CEC account on January 1, 2016 and no other CEC transactions during 2016.

ANALYSIS   The relevant 2016 calculations are as follows:

January 1, 2016 CEC	Nil
2016 Addition [(3/4)($200,000)]	$150,000
CEC Deduction [(7%)($150,000)]	(10,500)
December 31, 2016 CEC	$139,500

5-138.   The December 31, 2016 CEC balance will become the January 1, 2017 UCC for Class 14.1. The capital cost of the franchise will be:

[(4/3)($139,500)]	$186,000
[(4/3)($10,500)]	14,000
January 1, 2017 Capital Cost	$200,000

5-139.   If we followed the usual rule for dispositions of depreciable property, we would subtract the lesser of the $200,000 capital cost and the $225,000 proceeds of disposition from the Class 14.1 balance of $139,500. The result would be recapture of $60,500 ($200,000 - $139,500).   There would also be a taxable capital gain of $12,500 [(1/2)($225,000 - $200,000)].

5-140.   The recapture figure is clearly unreasonable. The $60,500 figure is far in excess of the $10,500 CEC deduction that was actually taken. The source of this problem is the fact that we are deducting a 100 percent figure from a balance that only reflects 75 percent of the capital cost of the asset.

5-141.   To deal with this problem, when there is a disposition, ITA 13(39) deems the taxpayer to have acquired an addition to Class 14.1 UCC equal to 25 percent of the lesser of the proceeds of disposition and the capital cost of the particular property. The calculation for the 2017 disposition, incorporating this rule, is as follows:

January 1, 2017 UCC	$139,500
Deemed Acquisition - Lesser Of:	
25% Of Proceeds Of Disposition	
= [(25%)($250,000)] = $62,500	
25% Of Capital Cost = [(25%)($200,000)] = $50,000	50,000
Adjusted Balance	$189,500
Disposition - Lesser Of:	
Proceeds Of Disposition = $250,000	
Capital Cost = $200,000	(200,000)
Negative Ending UCC Balance = Recapture	($ 10,500)

5-142.   As the $10,500 of recapture is equal to the CEC deduction actually taken, this is clearly a reasonable result.

CEC Dispositions After January 1, 2017 - No Terminal Loss

5-143.   The preceding example illustrates how the ITA 13(39) deeming rules solve the problem of excess recapture. However, it does not illustrate the application of this rule when the proceeds of disposition are less than the capital cost of the relevant asset. We will use a modified version of the Paragraph 5-137 example to illustrate this situation.

EXAMPLE   On July 1, 2016, Tabor Ltd. acquires an unlimited life franchise for $200,000. On July 1, 2017, this franchise is sold for $160,000. There was no balance in Tabor's CEC account on January 1, 2016 and no other CEC transactions during 2016.

ANALYSIS   Without going through the calculations again, the January 1, 2017 balance in the Class 14.1 UCC would be $139,500 and the capital cost of the asset would be $200,000. Using this information, the relevant calculation for the disposition would be as follows:

January 1, 2017 UCC	$139,500
Deemed Acquisition - Lesser Of:	
25% Of Proceeds Of Disposition	
= [(25%)($160,000)] = $40,000	
25% Of Capital Cost = [(25%)($200,000)] = $50,000	40,000
Adjusted Balance	$179,500
Disposition - Lesser Of:	
Proceeds Of Disposition = $160,000	
Capital Cost = $200,000	(160,000)
December 31, 2017 UCC	$ 19,500
CCA [(7%)($19,500)]	(1,365)
January 1, 2018 UCC	$ 18,135

5-144.   Several points are relevant here:

- There was a $40,000 ($200,000 - $160,000) loss on the sale, three-quarters of which would be $30,000. In terms of the economics involved, the loss is reduced by the $10,500 CEC deduction in 2016 and results in the $19,500 ($30,000 - $10,500) UCC balance remaining subsequent to the disposition.

- Under normal CCA procedures, the $19,500 would be treated as a terminal loss. However, with respect to Class 14.1 dispositions, a terminal loss in Class 14.1 can only arise when the business ceases to operate.

We suggest you work Self Study Problems Five-6. 7, and 8 at this point.

Additional Supplementary Self Study Problems Are Available Online.

Economic Impact Of These Changes

5-145.   The conversion of CEC balances to a regular CCA Class is a long overdue change. There was always something about the CEC procedures that was both odd and inconsistent with the treatment of other depreciable assets. However, while this change can easily be defended on conceptual grounds, it will have economic results that are largely unfavourable to most taxpayers.

5-146.   To begin, in many cases, more income will have to be recognized. Under the old CEC regime, a disposition only resulted in income when it created a negative CEC balance. This was the case even when the proceeds of disposition were greater than the capital cost of the asset.

5-147.   This is no longer the situation. As previously indicated, if a Class 14.1 asset is sold at a price in excess of its capital cost, a capital gain will be included in income. As is the case with other depreciable assets, there is no possibility of a capital loss on Class 14.1 dispositions.

5-148.   A further problem involves the type of income that arises under these new rules. As shown in our basic example (see Paragraph 5-121), it was possible for a capital gains like figure to arise under the CEC procedures. While the amount of this inclusion was based on one-half of a gain, it was treated as business income, not as a capital gain. This is an important difference for Canadian controlled private companies in that capital gains are subject to combined tax rates as high as 54 percent (see Chapter 13). In contrast, the active business income of these companies could be taxed at a rate as low as 12.5 percent. While some of the higher taxes paid on capital gains can be refunded when the income is paid out of the corporation as dividends, the deferral of taxes that is available on active business income is lost.

    Byrd/Chen Note   Do not be concerned if you don't fully understand the preceding paragraph in that such understanding requires a knowledge of corporate taxation which is not presented until Chapters 12 and 13.

5-149.   As mentioned previously, another negative result from this change is a reduction in the write-off rate for these assets. The effective rate under the CEC regime was 5.25 percent [(7%)(75%)]. This was slightly higher than the new Class 14.1 rate of 5 percent.

Key Terms Used In This Chapter

5-150.   The following is a list of the key terms used in this Chapter. These terms, and their meanings, are compiled in the Glossary located at the back of the Study Guide.

Capital Cost	Goodwill
Capital Cost Allowance (CCA)	Half-Year Rules (a.k.a. First Year Rules)
Capital Gain	Non-Depreciable Capital Property
Class	Recapture Of CCA
Cumulative Eligible Capital (CEC)	Separate Class Rules
Declining Balance Method	Short Fiscal Year
Depreciable Capital Property	Straight-Line Method
Disposition	Taxable Capital Gain
Eligible Capital Expenditure	Terminal Loss
First Year Rules	Undepreciated Capital Cost (UCC)

References

5-151.   For more detailed study of the material in this Chapter, we would refer you to the following:

ITA 13(1)	Recaptured Depreciation
ITA 13(7.1)	Deemed Capital Cost Of Certain Property
ITA 13(26) to	
ITA 13(32)	Available For Use Rules
ITA 13(34)	Goodwill
ITA 13(35)	Outlays Not Relating To Property
ITA 13(36)	Receipts Not Relating To Property
ITA 13(37) to	
ITA 13(41)	Class 14.1 - Transitional Rules
ITA 14(1.01)	Election Re Capital Gain
ITA 20(1)(a)	Capital Cost Of Property
ITA 20(1)(b)	Incorporation Costs
ITA 20(16)	Terminal Loss
ITA 20(16.1)	Non-Application Of ITA 20(16)
ITR Part XI	Capital Cost Allowances
ITR II-VI	Capital Cost Allowances
IC-84-1	Revision Of Capital Cost Allowance Claims And Other Permissive Deductions
IT-79R3	Capital Cost Allowance - Buildings Or Other Structures
IT-128R	Capital Cost Allowance - Depreciable Property
IT-143R3	Meaning Of Eligible Capital Expenditure
IT-190R2	Capital Cost Allowance - Transferred And Misclassified Property
IT-195R4	Rental Property - Capital Cost Allowance Restrictions
IT-206R	Separate Businesses
IT-220R2	Capital Cost Allowance - Proceeds Of Disposition Of Depreciable Property
IT-285R2	Capital Cost Allowance - General Comments
IT-418	Capital Cost Allowance - Partial Dispositions Of Property
IT-472	Capital Cost Allowance - Class 8 Property
IT-478R2	Capital Cost Allowance - Recapture And Terminal Loss

Appendix - CCA Rates For Selected Assets

> Note that for your convenience, this Appendix of common CCA rates, as well as the 2017 rates, credits and other data, is available online as a .PDF file.

This Appendix lists the CCA Class and rate for assets commonly used in business. Restrictions and transitional rules may apply in certain situations. ITR Part XI contains detailed descriptions of the CCA Classes.

Asset	Class	Rate
Aircraft (including components)	**9**	**25%**
Airplane runways	17	8%
Automobiles, passenger		
• Cost < or = Prescribed amount ($30,000 in 2017)	10	30%
• Cost > Prescribed amount	10.1	30%
Automotive equipment	10	30%
Bar code scanners	**8**	**20%**
Billboards	8	20%
Boats, canoes and other vessels	7	15%
Bridges, canals, culverts and dams	1	4%
Buildings Acquired Before 1988	3	5%
Buildings Acquired After 1987 - No Separate Class	1	4%
Buildings (New Only) Acquired After March 18, 2007:		
• Manufacturing and Processing In Separate Class 1	1	10%
• Non-Residential In Separate Class 1	1	6%
Buses	10	30%
Calculators	**8**	**20%**
Cash registers	8	20%
China, cutlery and tableware	12	100%
Communications equipment		
(including cellphones too dumb to be smartphones)	8	20%
Computer hardware and systems software,		
(including smartphones and tablets)		
acquired after March 18, 2007	50	55%
Computer software (applications)	12	100%
Copyrights	14	Straight-line
Data network infrastructure equipment		
acquired after March 22, 2004	46	30%
Dies, jigs, patterns, and molds	12	100%
Docks, breakwaters and trestles	3	5%
Electrical advertising billboards	**8**	**20%**
Electronic point-of-sale equipment	8	20%
Equipment (not specifically listed elsewhere)	8	20%
Fences	**6**	**10%**
Films	10	30%
Franchises (limited life)	14	Straight-line
Franchises (unlimited life)	14.1	5%
Furniture and fixtures		
(not specifically listed elsewhere)	8	20%
Goodwill	**14.1**	**5%**

Asset	Class	Rate
Instruments, dental or medical (See Tools)		
Kitchen utensils (See Tools)		
Land	**N/A**	**N/A**
Landscaping	N/A	Deductible
Leasehold improvements	13	Straight-line
Licences (limited life)	14	Straight-line
Licences (unlimited life)	14.1	5%
Linen	12	100%
Machinery and equipment		
(not specifically listed elsewhere)	**8**	**20%**
Manufacturing and processing equipment		
• acquired before March 19, 2007	43	30%
• acquired after March 18, 2007 and before 2016	29	50% Straight-Line
• acquired after 2015	53	50%
Office equipment (not specifically listed elsewhere)	**8**	**20%**
Outdoor advertising billboards	8	20%
Parking area and similar surfaces	**17**	**8%**
Patents (limited life)	44	25%
Patents (unlimited life)	14.1	5%
Photocopy machines	8	20%
Portable buildings and equipment used in a construction business	10	30%
Power operated movable equipment	38	30%
Radio communication equipment	**8**	**20%**
Railway cars		
• acquired after February 27, 2000	7	15%
• acquired before February 28, 2000	35	7%
Roads	17	8%
Sidewalks	**17**	**8%**
Software (applications)	12	100%
Software (systems)	10	30%
Storage area	17	8%
Storage tanks, oil or water	6	10%
Tangible Capital Assets		
(not specifically listed elsewhere)	**8**	**20%**
Taxicabs	16	40%
Telephone systems	8	20%
Television commercials	12	100%
Tools		
• acquired after May 1, 2006 (under $500)	12	100%
• acquired after May 1, 2006 ($500 or over)	8	20%
Trailers	10	30%
Trucks and tractors for hauling freight	16	40%
Trucks (automotive), tractors and vans	10	30%
Uniforms	**12**	**100%**
Video games (coin operated)	**16**	**40%**
Video tapes	10	30%
Video tapes for renting	12	100%
Wagons	**10**	**30%**

Problems For Self Study (Online)

To provide practice in problem solving, there are Self Study and Supplementary Self Study problems available on the Companion Website.

Within the text we have provided an indication of when it would be appropriate to work each Self Study problem. The detailed solutions for Self Study problems can be found in the print and online Study Guide.

We provide the Supplementary Self Study problems for those who would like additional practice in problem solving. The detailed solutions for the Supplementary Self Study problems are available online, not in the Study Guide.

The .PDF file "Self Study Problems for Volume 1" on the Companion Website contains the following for Chapter 5:

- 8 Self Study problems,
- 2 Supplementary Self Study problems, and
- detailed solutions for the Supplementary Self Study problems.

Assignment Problems

(The solutions for these problems are only available in
the solutions manual that has been provided to your instructor.)

Assignment Problem Five - 1
(CCA And Tax Planning)

For its taxation year ending December 31, 2017, Martin's Enterprises has determined that its Net Income For Tax Purposes before any deduction for CCA amounts to $53,000. The Company does not have any Division C deductions, so whatever amount is determined as Net Income For Tax Purposes will also be the amount of Taxable Income for the taxation year.

On January 1, 2017, the Company has the following UCC balances:

Class 1 (Building Acquired in 2004)	$876,000
Class 8	220,000
Class 10	95,000
Class 10.1 (Porsche - Cost $110,000)	25,500
Class 10.1 (Cadillac - Cost $45,000)	25,500

During 2017, the cost of additions to Class 10 amounted to $122,000, while the proceeds from dispositions in this class totaled $87,000. The capital cost of the assets retired totaled $118,000. None of the individual assets sold had proceeds of disposition that exceeded their individual capital cost. There were still assets in Class 10 on December 31, 2017.

There were no acquisitions or dispositions in Class 1, 8 or 10.1 during 2017. The Company plans to sell the Porsche in January, 2018 and expects to receive about $75,000.

During the preceding three taxation years, the Company reported Taxable Income totalling $39,000 for the three years.

Required:

A. Calculate the maximum CCA that could be taken by Martin's Enterprises for the taxation year ending December 31, 2017. Your answer should include the maximum that can be deducted for each CCA class.

B. As Martin's Enterprises' tax advisor, indicate how much CCA you would advise the Company to take for the 2017 taxation year, and the specific classes from which it should be deducted. Provide a brief explanation of the reasons for your recommendation. In determining your solution, ignore the possibility that 2017 losses can be carried forward to subsequent taxation years.

Assignment Problem Five - 2
(CCA Calculations)

The following information relates to Bodlink Manufacturing's depreciable assets.

1. During 2017, a new factory building was acquired at a cost of $1,656,000. The estimated value of the land included in the purchase price is $450,000. The building will be used 100 percent for manufacturing and processing activity. It will be allocated to a separate Class.

2. The January 1, 2017 balance in Class 3 was $936,000. During 2017, one of the buildings in this Class burned to the ground. It had a capital cost of $723,000. The insurance proceeds totaled $972,000.

3. The January 1, 2017 balance in Class 8 was $476,000. During 2017, the Company acquired Class 8 assets at a cost of $163,000. Class 8 assets with a capital cost of $105,000 were sold for proceeds of $86,000. None of the individual assets sold had proceeds that exceeded their individual capital cost.

4. The January 1, 2017 balance in Class 10 was $876,000. During 2017, 3 passenger vehicles were acquired at a cost of $26,000 each. In addition, a delivery van with a capital cost of $37,000 was sold for $16,000.

5. The January 1, 2017 balance in Class 10.1 was $25,500. The only asset in this Class was the CEO's $510,000 Rolls Royce. Because of public relations concerns with such an extravagant vehicle, the car was sold during 2017 for $385,000.

6. The January 1, 2017 balance in Class 13 was $149,500, reflecting improvements that were made in 2015, the year in which the lease commenced. These improvements were made on a property leased as office space for the Company's executives. The basic lease term is for 6 years, with an option to renew for a period of 2 years. Additional improvements, costing $75,000, were made during 2017.

7. The January 1, 2017 balance in Class 50 was $47,000. During 2017, there were additions to this Class with a capital cost of $23,500.

8. The January 1, 2017 balance in Class 53 was $645,000. During 2017, the Company acquired additional manufacturing and processing equipment at a cost of $232,000.

Bodlink Manufacturing always takes maximum CCA on each Class of depreciable assets.

Required: Calculate the maximum CCA that can be taken by Bodlink Manufacturing on each class of assets for the year ending December 31, 2017 and calculate the UCC for each class of assets on January 1, 2018. In addition, determine the amount of any capital gain, recapture, or terminal loss that arises. Ignore GST/HST/PST considerations and the replacement property rules that are covered in Chapter 8.

Assignment Problem Five - 3
(CCA Calculations Over 4 Years)

Giovanni Bertoluccia believes that his grandmother's recipe makes the best pizza crust that he has ever tasted. Given this belief, he has decided to open an Italian restaurant in Toronto that will feature pizzas that use his grandmother's closely guarded secret recipe. Reflecting the unique color of the pizza crusts that are produced using this recipe, the restaurant will be called Giovanni's Golden Crust. Its advertising will feature a portrait of his kindly looking grandmother dressed in clothing typical of her native Sicily, her current home.

Assignment Problems

While the restaurant will have seating for 85 guests, he will also offer a take out and delivery service. He eventually hopes to develop a chain of such restaurants, at which time he intends to incorporate the business. However, for the first years of operation, the business will be a proprietorship.

The business begins operations on September 1, 2014. By that date Giovanni has acquired or arranged for the use of the following assets for the business:

- **Building**   He has leased a building for a period of 5 years, with an option to renew for an additional 5 years. In order to upgrade the dining room and use the property for takeout and delivery, he has made $175,000 in leasehold improvements.

- **Furniture, Fixtures And Kitchen Equipment**   Since the building had housed a pizzeria whose owner had retired, he has acquired the furnishings and equipment of the restaurant for a cost of $124,000. His accountant has placed all of these assets in Class 8.

- **Vehicles**   In order to make deliveries, he has acquired 8 vehicles at a cost of $25,000 each.

Events related to these depreciable assets during the years 2015 through 2017 are as follows:

2015   As the delivery operations are very successful, 5 additional vehicles are acquired at a cost of $27,000 each in January. Because of their high mileage, 4 of the original 8 vehicles acquired in 2014 are retired in December. The 4 vehicles are sold for total proceeds of $81,000. The amount received for each vehicle was less than its capital cost.

2016   Because of the continuing success of the sit down operation, additional leasehold improvements are made at a cost of $98,000 and new furniture and fixtures are purchased at a cost of $62,000. Giovanni gives some of the most damaged old furniture to the nearby Sicilian Club. He estimates his cost for this furniture was $5,000. On the advice of his accountant, he decides to lease delivery vehicles, rather than continuing to own his delivery fleet. The remaining 9 vehicles are sold for total proceeds of $185,000. The amount received for each vehicle was less than its capital cost.

2017   After discovering that one of Giovanni's hiring criteria for his waitresses was a willingness to sleep with him, his wife, Sophia Bertoluccia is suing him for divorce. Given the great success of Giovanni's business, Sophia writes to his grandmother, informing her of his use of her recipe and image, as well as his reprehensible hiring practices. As Sophia suspected, his grandmother was not even aware of Giovanni's business, much less that her image and recipe were being used.

Sophia assists the grandmother in locating a Canadian lawyer who plans to sue Giovanni for the unauthorized use of his grandmother's recipe and image. Giovanni's lawyer advises him that his grandmother is very likely to win a large settlement that will force him into bankruptcy. Anticipating this, Giovanni sells his business to his friend, Salvatorio, and goes into hiding. The proceeds are as follows for the business:

- **Leasehold Improvements**   As Salvatorio is assuming the remainder of the lease, he has paid Giovanni $112,000 for leaving the leasehold improvements in place.

- **Furniture, Fixtures And Kitchen Equipment**   Salvatorio pays Giovanni $50,000 for all of the Class 8 assets.

- **Goodwill**   While the business will suffer as a result of the lawsuit, Salvatorio is confident that the business will continue to be very profitable. He plans to immediately begin the use of his own grandmother's image and secret pizza crust recipe with her blessing. Salvatorio's wife will be in charge of hiring staff for the business. Given this, he pays an additional $100,000 for the goodwill of the business.

Required: For each of the taxation years 2014 through 2017, calculate the maximum available CCA deduction for Giovanni's Golden Crust. In addition, determine the amount of any other tax consequences that arises on any of the transactions that occurred during these years. Ignore GST/HST/PST considerations.

Assignment Problem Five - 4
(CCA And CEC Calculations Over 3 Years)

Park Manufacturing began operations on January 1, 2015 and chose to have a December 31 taxation year end. The costs of incorporation were $25,000.

The Company leased the building in which it will operate for a monthly lease payment of $5,000. The term of the lease is 5 years, with three renewal options, each for a period of 5 years. In order to fit the building to its needs, the Company spends $150,000 on leasehold improvements.

The Company's products are manufactured under a 5 year franchise agreement. The cost of this agreement was $220,000. It was signed on January 1, 2015.

Other capital expenditures during 2015 are as follows:

Manufacturing Equipment	$262,000
Furniture And Fixtures	87,000
Small Tools (All Under $500 Each)	12,000
Delivery Vans (5 At $32,000)	160,000

In addition to these assets, the Company purchased a $95,000 BMW in 2015 for use by Martin Park, the CEO and only shareholder of the Company.

The Company earned substantial profits during 2015 and 2016 and took maximum CCA and CEC deductions in both years. On January 3, 2017, Martin Park was killed in an automobile accident when his smartphone exploded while he was returning from a very long and enjoyable New Year's party. He was driving the Company BMW which was totally destroyed. The insurance proceeds for the car were $65,000, all of which was received in 2017.

Early in 2017 an individual was found to assume the lease obligation on the building. He also paid $75,000 to the estate to retain the leasehold improvements in the building, $200,000 for the continued use of the manufacturing franchise (it was transferable), and $50,000 for the customer lists accumulated by the Company.

The Company did not acquire any additional assets during 2017 and had disposed of all assets by the end of the year. The proceeds resulting from the other asset sales during 2017 were as follows:

Manufacturing Equipment	$186,000
Furniture And Fixtures	23,000
Small Tools	5,000
Delivery Vans	85,000

The executors of Mr. Park's estate found that the accounting and tax records had not been well maintained. Winding up the Company could not be completed until December 30, 2017.

Required: Determine the maximum CCA and CEC deductions for the years 2015 and 2016 and the UCC and CEC balances on January 1, 2017. In addition, determine any Net Income For Tax Purposes inclusions or deductions resulting from the asset dispositions during 2017.

Assignment Problem Five - 5
(CCA Calculations Over 3 Years)

Bob's Buttons is an unincorporated business that began operations on September 1, 2015. The owner/operator is Bob Pope and his business is selling decorative and promotional buttons to various clients throughout the city of Toronto and online. Clients include political parties, retail and online stores, sports teams, and various religious organizations.

When he began operations in 2015, he acquired the following assets:

- A building to house his operations. The total cost of the building was $862,000, including an estimated $220,000 for the land. The building is used exclusively for his business, with 92 percent of the space being used for manufacturing the buttons. The building is allocated to a separate Class 1.

- Furniture and fixtures with a cost of $120,000.

- Two customized delivery vehicles at a cost of $36,000 each.

Bob's business policy is to take maximum CCA. During 2016, the following transaction involving capital assets take place:

- As the business has enjoyed early success, on April 1, Bob purchases a $110,000 Lexus. He has large logos of the business painted on both sides of the vehicle. Since Bob inherited a Jeep, a Ferrari and a BMW motorcycle, he drives the Lexus 100 percent for business purposes.

- The business acquires four new delivery vehicles at a cost of $38,000 each. As part of this purchase, the two vehicles acquired in 2015 are traded in. An allowance of $21,000 is received for each vehicle.

As Bob believes in free speech and has been told repeatedly by his family that he has a very twisted sense of humour, some of his favourite buttons have created social media firestorms. After Bob receives death threats, he decides to terminate his business in 2017 and start a new home security business in Alberta. By December 31, 2017 all of the assets are sold. The proceeds are as follows:

Building   The building is sold for $903,000, with $220,000 of this value allocated to the land on which the building is situated.

Furniture And Fixtures   These assets are sold for $53,000.

Delivery Vehicles   The four delivery vehicles are sold for $34,000 each.

Lexus   The Lexus is sold for $62,000.

Required: Determine the maximum CCA that can be taken in each of the years 2015 through 2017. In your calculations, include and identify the UCC balances for January 1, 2016, January 1, 2017, and January 1, 2018.

In addition, indicate any tax effects resulting from the 2016 and 2017 dispositions. Ignore GST/HST considerations.

Assignment Problem Five - 6
(Purchase And Sale Of Goodwill)

Mortex is a Canadian public company with a taxation year that ends on December 31. It is the policy of Mortex Ltd. to claim maximum CCA for all Classes. On January 1, 2017, Mortex had no balance in its Class 14.1.

The following five independent cases involve payments for goodwill and receipts for goodwill. In each case assume that Mortex has no other transactions during 2017 or 2018 that involve Class 14.1.

Case One   During 2017, Mortex acquires two businesses. With the acquisition of Business 1, a payment of $86,000 is made for goodwill. With the acquisition of Business 2, a payment of $75,000 is made for goodwill. Both businesses are absorbed into Mortex's other operations.

During 2018, Mortex sells a portion of its business and, as a consequence, receives a payment for goodwill of $90,000.

Case Two   Using the same information as in Case One, assume that Mortex continues to operate both of the 2017 acquisitions as separate businesses and that the $90,000 receipt for goodwill results from the sale of the first business acquired.

Case Three   During 2017, Mortex acquires a business. The cost of this business includes a payment for goodwill of $96,000. The business is absorbed into Mortex's other operations and is not operated separately. Also during 2017, Mortex acquires an unlimited life franchise at a cost of $113,000.

During 2018, Mortex sells a portion of its business and, as a consequence, receives a payment for goodwill of $102,000.

Case Four   Using the same information as in Case Three, assume that, instead of selling a portion of its business for an amount that includes goodwill of $102,000, the unlimited life franchise is sold for $102,000.

Case Five   Using the same information as in Case Three, assume that, instead of selling a portion of its business for an amount that includes goodwill of $102,000, the unlimited life franchise is sold for $135,000.

Required: Determine the tax consequences for the years 2017 and 2018 in each of these five cases. Your answer should include the January 1, 2019 UCC balance for Class 14.1.

Assignment Problem Five - 7
(Asset Retirements And Goodwill Sale - Includes Capital Gain)

Vance Enterprises closes its books on December 31 of each year.   On January 1, 2017, the following information on the CCA classes of the business was contained in its records:

Type Of Asset	Undepreciated Capital Cost	Original Capital Cost	Date Of Acquisition
Equipment (Class 8)	$ 2,100	$ 26,000	January, 2010
Buildings (Class 1)	205,000	250,000	January, 2005
Automobile (Class 10)	10,200	20,500	June, 2013

During the 2017 fiscal year, the following transactions occur:

Sale Of Equipment - As the result of an extensive analysis, it is decided that it would be better to sell the existing equipment and to replace it with improved equipment that will be leased. The equipment is sold for $21,000.

Sale Of Buildings - A similar decision is made with respect to the buildings. They are sold for $342,000 and replaced with leased premises. Of the $342,000 received, $80,000 is for the land on which the buildings are situated. The adjusted cost base of the land was equal to the $80,000 proceeds of disposition. The lease term is for four years with no options for renewal. However, a total of $39,000 is spent on leasehold improvements to make the buildings more suitable for the business.

Sale Of Automobile - The automobile is used by Ms. Vance for both business and personal matters. It is sold during the current year and replaced with a leased vehicle. The sale proceeds are $8,900.

Sale Of Goodwill - In order to further streamline her operations, Ms. Vance sells off a portion of her operations to another individual. No depreciable or capital assets were disposed of. However, an amount of $110,000 was received for the goodwill of this portion of the business.

Required: For the taxation year ending December 31, 2017 calculate the maximum CCA that can be deducted by Vance Enterprises for each CCA class.   In addition, calculate the January 1, 2018 UCC balances and indicate any other tax consequences that would result from the described transactions.

Assignment Problem Five - 8
(Cumulative Eligible Capital)

On January 1, 2015, MDI had a cumulative eligible capital balance of nil. During 2015, Moxy Distributors Inc. (MDI) acquired three unincorporated operations. These acquisitions required the following amounts to be paid for goodwill:

Operation	Goodwill Acquired
A	$150,000
B	225,000
C	180,000

Moxy absorbed all of these operations into its regular operations. MDI's corporate policy is to make the maximum CEC deductions available each year.

During the taxation year ending December 31, 2016, a portion of Moxy's operations was sold, with the Company receiving a payment for goodwill of $82,000.

During the taxation year ending December 31, 2017, Moxy divested itself of an additional portion of its operations, resulting in a payment for goodwill of $493,000

Required: Determine the tax consequences resulting from the preceding transactions for the year ending December 31, 2017.

Assignment Problem Five - 9
(CCA And CEC Calculations)

Microhard Ltd. has a December 31 year end. As of January 1, 2017, Microhard had the following UCC balances for its various tangible assets:

Class 1	$606,929
Class 8	347,291
Class 10	142,800
Class 13	175,500

Other information related to the Company's tangible assets is as follows:

Class 1   The January 1, 2017 balance in Class 1 reflected a single building that was acquired in 2013 for $900,000. Of this total, $200,000 was allocated to the land on which the building was situated. On February 1, 2017, this building and the land was sold for $800,000. At this time, the value of the land was unchanged at $200,000.

A new building was purchased on November 15, 2017 at a cost of $950,000, with $150,000 of this total being allocated to the land on which the building was situated. The new building is used 50 percent for manufacturing and processing and 50 percent for office space. It is allocated to a separate Class 1.

Class 8   On March 1, 2017, the Company acquired Class 8 assets for $111,256. As a result of trading in older Class 8 assets, the Company received a trade in allowance of $20,000, resulting in a net cost for the new assets of $91,256. The capital cost of the assets traded in was $58,425.

Class 10   The January 1, 2017 balance in Class 10 reflects 8 vehicles that were being used by the Company's sales staff. Their original cost totaled $240,000. The Company decided it would be more economical to provide their sales staff with leased vehicles. To this end, the 8 vehicles were sold for proceeds of $150,000 on October 31, 2017. The amount received for each vehicle was less than its capital cost.

On August 1, 2017, the Company acquires a BMW 750 for the use of the Company's president. The cost of this vehicle was $142,000. The president drives it 65,000 kilometers during the 2017 fiscal year, with only 10,000 kilometers involving employment duties. The president is not a shareholder of Microhard.

Class 13   Some of the Company's business is conducted out of a building that is leased. The lease, which had an initial term of 6 years, can be renewed for 2 additional years at the end of the initial term. Immediately after the lease was signed on January 1, 2015, Microhard spent $216,000 on leasehold improvements. During April, 2017, an additional $42,000 was spent upgrading this property.

On May 1, 2015, the Company purchased an unlimited life franchise for $124,000. This franchise was sold December 1, 2017 for $136,000.

It is the policy of the Company to deduct maximum CCA and the maximum write-off of cumulative eligible capital allowable in each year of operation.

Required: Calculate the maximum CCA for the year ending December 31, 2017. Your answer should include the maximum that can be deducted for each CCA class. In addition, indicate the amount of any recapture, terminal loss or taxable capital gain that results from dispositions during 2017.

CHAPTER 6

Income Or Loss From A Business

Overview

Net Income For Tax Purposes

Where We Are At

6-1. In Chapter 1, we indicated that much of this volume would be devoted to the concepts and procedures associated with determining Net Income For Tax Purposes. In terms of the *Income Tax Act*, this subject is covered in Part I, Division B. This Division, titled Computation Of Income, contains 11 Subdivisions, with the first three dealing with specific types of income. They are as follows:

Subdivision a   Income Or Loss From An Office Or Employment

Subdivision b   Income Or Loss From A Business Or Property

Subdivision c   Taxable Capital Gains And Allowable Capital Losses

6-2. At this point, we have provided fairly comprehensive coverage of the first of these Subdivisions. In Chapter 3, we discussed in detail the inclusions and deductions that go into the calculation of employment income or loss.

6-3. While we could have followed the discussion of employment income with coverage of the other components of Net Income For Tax Purposes, we chose to devote Chapter 4 to an introduction to Taxable Income and Tax Payable for individuals. While most texts leave this subject until the end of their coverage of all components of Net Income For Tax Purposes, we provided this introduction so that we could include comprehensive problems at an early stage in the text.

6-4. Again in contrast to some other texts, we introduced CCA calculations in Chapter 5, prior to our coverage of business income. As you are now aware, this is a very technical subject which involves what is often one of the most important deductions in the determination of business income. It was included prior to our coverage of business income in order to facilitate the presentation of complete examples of the determination of business income.

Where We Are Going

6-5. Chapters 6, 7, and 8 will provide coverage of the remaining specific types of income that go into the determination of Net Income For Tax Purposes. While business income and property income are dealt with in a single Subdivision of the *Income Tax Act*, these two types of income are subject to somewhat different rules. In addition, in some circumstances, they are subject to significantly different rates of tax. Given this, we will deal with Subdivision b in two separate Chapters. This Chapter 6 will cover business income, with Chapter 7 dealing with property income.

6-6.   The final major component of Net Income For Tax Purposes, taxable capital gains and allowable capital losses, will be dealt with in Chapter 8.

Classification Of Income
A Net Determination
6-7.   We have then, four basic types of income:

- employment income;
- business income;
- property income; and
- capital gains.

6-8.   Each of these basic types is determined on a net basis. That is, each amount that is to be included in Net Income For Tax Purposes is based on a specific group of inclusions that will usually be reduced by a specific group of deductions.

6-9.   In general, the deductions applicable to one type of income cannot be deducted against the inclusions in a different type. However, if a loss is created in a particular year by an excess of deductions over inclusions, that loss can generally be applied against other types of income. The exception to this is a current year net capital loss. While such losses can be carried back or forward to other taxation years, they cannot be applied against other types of income that have been recognized during the current year. In fact, even in carry over years, allowable capital losses can only be deducted to the extent that taxable capital gains are present.

Applicable Taxpayers
6-10.   Employment income is unique in that only individuals can earn this type of income. In contrast, business income, property income, and capital gains can be recognized by all taxpayers. This would include individuals, corporations, and trusts.

Classification And The Use Of Property
6-11.   Business income, property income, and capital gains generally involve the use of property. Further, it is usually the manner in which the property is being used that determines the classification of the resulting income. Because of this, it is important to understand the use of this term in the *Income Tax Act*.

6-12.   Property is defined very broadly in ITA 248(1) as "property of any kind whatever whether real or personal or corporeal or incorporeal". This would include both depreciable and non-depreciable property. The definition also encompasses both tangible and intangible property.

6-13.   In terms of classifying the various types of income, it is useful to identify four categories of property on the basis of the manner in which they are used.

Property Acquired For Use In A Business   These are assets acquired to be used in a business. Examples would be factory and store buildings, the land underlying such buildings, furniture and fixtures in a retail store, and equipment used in manufacturing. While these assets are held, the income produced will be classified as business income. If the taxpayer disposes of such assets, classification of the income that is produced will depend on the type of asset.

Non-Depreciable Capital Assets   A disposition will result in a capital gain or a capital loss.

Depreciable Capital Assets   A disposition may result in recapture, a capital gain and recapture, a terminal loss, or no immediate tax consequences (we would remind you that capital losses cannot arise on the disposition of depreciable assets). As noted in Chapter 5, both recapture and terminal losses are components of business income when the asset is used in the business.

Property Acquired And Held As An Investment These assets are acquired to be held while they produce income. They are distinguished from business assets in that they produce income with little or no effort on the part of the acquirer. Examples would be holdings of debt securities, holdings of equity securities, and ownership of rental properties. While they are held, these investment assets produce property income. As was the case with assets acquired for use in a business, the classification of income that results from a disposition of such assets will depend on whether the asset is depreciable or non-depreciable.

>   **Non-Depreciable Capital Assets** A disposition will result in a capital gain or a capital loss.

>   **Depreciable Capital Assets** A disposition may result in recapture, a capital gain and recapture, a terminal loss, or no immediate tax consequences. Both recapture and terminal losses are components of property income when the asset is used to produce property income.

Property Acquired For Resale At A Profit These assets are acquired with the objective of reselling them at a profit. Examples would be the typical inventory balances that are held by many businesses. Any gain or loss that arises on their disposition will be treated as a business income or loss, not as a capital gain or loss. In most cases, such assets will not produce income while they are held.

Property Acquired By Individuals For Personal Use These are assets acquired by individuals for personal use. Examples would be personal use automobiles, personal use boats, and real property that is not held to produce income. While these assets are held they do not produce income. However, if they are sold at a value in excess of their adjusted cost base, the excess will be subject to tax as a capital gain. Alternatively, if they are sold for less than their adjusted cost base, the resulting loss will generally not be deductible (see the discussion of personal use property in Chapter 8).

6-14.   As you can see, this categorization of the various ways a property can be used serves to outline how the various types of income are classified. The types of income produced by the various categories of property are summarized in Figure 6-1.

Figure 6-1 - Classification Of Income		
Use Of Property	**Income While Held**	**Income At Disposition**
Used In Business		
Depreciable	Business Income	Capital Gain, Recapture, Terminal Loss, Or No Income
Non-Depreciable	Business Income	Capital Gain (Loss)
Acquired As Investment		
Depreciable	Property Income	Capital Gain, Recapture, Terminal Loss, Or No Income
Non-Depreciable	Property Income	Capital Gain (Loss)
Acquired For Resale	Generally None	Business Income (Loss)
Acquired For Personal Use	None	Capital Gain (In general, losses are not deductible)

Areas Of Controversy

6-15.   In many situations, classification presents no problems.

- An individual being paid an hourly rate on the General Motors assembly line is clearly earning employment income.

- An individual operating a Second Cup franchise is clearly earning business income.

- An investor receiving interest on Canada Savings Bonds is clearly earning property income.

6-16.   However, this is not always the case. As the manner in which income is classified can have significant tax consequences, it is not surprising that classification is a controversial issue in some situations. In general terms, there are three types of problems that can arise:

Business Income Vs. Employment Income   For some individuals, it is not clear whether they are working as an employee or, alternatively, as an independent contractor earning business income (a.k.a., self-employed individual). The tax consequences and classification guidelines related to this issue were discussed, in detail, in Chapter 3.

Business Income Vs. Property Income   While income producing assets are being held, there may be a question as to whether they are producing business income or, alternatively, property income. The tax consequences and classification guidelines related to this issue will be discussed in this Chapter.

Business Income Vs. Capital Gains   On dispositions of property, it is sometimes difficult to establish whether the resulting gain is business income or, alternatively, a capital gain. The tax consequences and classification guidelines related to this issue will also be discussed in this Chapter.

Business Income Vs. Property Income

Tax Consequences Of Classification

Rates

6-17.   For individuals, both business income and property income will generally be subject to tax at the rates that were discussed in Chapter 4. This will require the application of a progressive rate structure, beginning at the low federal rate of 15 percent and increasing to the maximum federal rate of 33 percent. In terms of applicable rates, the business vs. property classification is not a significant issue for individuals.

6-18.   This is not the case for corporations. If a corporation is Canadian controlled and its shares are not publicly traded, the first $500,000 (federal amount) of its business income may be eligible for a small business deduction that, in effect, can lower the corporate tax rate by up to 15 percentage points. Property income earned by such corporations is not eligible for this deduction and, as a result, will be much more heavily taxed. This makes the business vs. property classification a very important consideration for Canadian controlled private corporations.

Other Considerations

6-19.   Other tax considerations related to the business vs. property income classification are as follows:

- **CCA Calculations**   When property income is being earned, the deduction of capital cost allowance (CCA) generally cannot be used to create or increase a net loss for the period. In addition, when property income is being earned by individuals, there is no requirement for a pro rata CCA reduction to reflect a short fiscal period. If business income is being earned, CCA can be used to create a loss. However, CCA deductions must generally be prorated for short fiscal periods.

- **Attribution Rules**   When property income is being earned, the income attribution rules (see Chapter 9) are applicable. This is not the case when business income is being earned.

- **Earned Income Calculations**   Property income is generally not included in the determination of earned income, either with respect to RRSP contributions or the limit on child care cost deductions. Business income is included in these figures.

- **Expense Deductions**   Certain expenses can be deducted against business income, but not property income. These include write-offs of goodwill and most travel expenses. In contrast, for individuals, there is a deduction for foreign taxes on property income in excess of 15 percent that is not available against foreign business income.

Business Income Defined

General Rules

6-20.   ITA 9 indicates a taxpayer's business income is his profit from a business. While profit is not defined in the *Act*, it is generally understood that it is a net amount resulting from the application of generally accepted accounting principles, modified by the rules found in Subdivision B. Business is defined in the *Act* as follows:

> **ITA 248(1)**   Business includes a profession, calling, trade, manufacture or undertaking of any kind whatever and, except for the purposes of paragraph ..., an adventure or concern in the nature of trade ...

6-21.   While this definition lists some of the things that might be considered to be a business, it does not provide a description of the characteristics that identify these activities as a business. A more useful definition can be found in Abstract No. 124 from the CICA's Emerging Issues Committee (now withdrawn):

> A business is a self-sustaining integrated set of activities and assets conducted and managed for the purpose of providing a return to investors. A business consists of (a) inputs, (b) processes applied to those inputs, and (c) resulting outputs that are used to generate revenues.

6-22.   Some of the other principles involved in making the distinction between business and property income are as follows:

- Whether income is from a business or property is a question of fact. The fact that property is used to earn income is not determinative.

- Where funds are employed and risked by a business and the investment of these funds is necessary for the taxpayer to conduct its business, the income from this investment activity will likely be considered income from a business.

- Income from property does not require active and extensive business-like intervention to produce it; it is passive income resulting from the mere ownership of property, without a significant commitment of time, labour, or attention.

- Income from business requires organization, systematic effort, and a certain degree of activity.

Adventure Or Concern In The Nature Of Trade

6-23.   When a person habitually does a thing that is capable of producing a profit, then he is carrying on a trade or business, notwithstanding that these activities may be quite separate and apart from his or ordinary occupation. An example of this would be a dentist who habitually buys and sells real estate.

6-24.   Where such a thing is done only infrequently, or possibly only once, it still is possible to hold that the person has engaged in a business transaction if it can be shown that he has engaged in "an adventure or concern in the nature of trade". If this is the case, the ITA 248(1) definition of a business makes it clear that any income that is produced will be considered business income. In addition, any gain or loss arising on the disposition of any property acquired as part of this adventure or concern will be considered business income, rather than a capital gain or loss.

6-25.   As described in IT-459, "Adventure Or Concern In The Nature Of Trade", factors that would identify a transaction as an adventure or concern in the nature of trade are as follows:

Taxpayer's Conduct   If the taxpayer's actions in regard to the property in question were essentially what would be expected of a dealer in such a property, it would be considered to be an adventure or concern in the nature of trade.

Nature Of The Asset   If the asset in question was not capable of producing income, this would indicate an adventure or concern in the nature of trade.

Taxpayer's Intention   If the taxpayer acquired the asset with an intention to sell, this would be evidence of an adventure or concern in the nature of trade.

Property Income Defined

6-26.   While the *Income Tax Act* does not define income from property, it can be thought of as the return on invested capital in situations where little or no effort is required by the investor to produce the return. Falling into this category would be rents, interest, dividends, and royalties earned for the right to use property.   In terms of tax legislation, capital gains are not treated as a component of property income, even in cases where they arise on investments being held to produce property income (e.g., capital gains on dividend paying shares).

6-27.   In cases where a great deal of time and effort is directed at producing interest or rents, such returns can be considered business income. For example, while rent is generally viewed as a type of property income, the rents earned by a large real estate holding company would be treated as a component of business income.

Exercise Six - 1

Subject: Business Vs. Property Income

Joan Bullato, because of her great fondness for his music, has purchased the rights to one of the songs written by John Clapton. She estimates that the royalties from the song will total about $35,000 per year for the next few years. She has no plans to buy any additional song rights. Explain whether the royalties she receives would be treated as business income or property income. In addition, indicate how any gain or loss on a disposition of the rights would be taxed.

SOLUTION available in print and online Study Guide.

Business Income Vs. Capital Gains

Tax Consequences Of Classification

6-28.   The tax consequences associated with the classification of a disposition as a capital transaction vs. a business income transaction can be described as follows:

- Only one-half of a capital gain is taxed and only one-half of a capital loss is deductible. If a gain transaction can be classified as capital in nature, the savings to the taxpayer is very significant. Alternatively, if a loss is involved, classification as a capital transaction reduces the value of this loss by one-half.

- Allowable capital losses (i.e., the deductible one-half) can only be deducted against taxable capital gains (i.e., the taxable one-half). This can be of great importance, particularly to individual taxpayers and smaller business enterprises. It may be years before such taxpayers realize taxable capital gains, resulting in a situation where there is significant deferral of the tax benefits associated with allowable capital losses.

6-29. These are, of course, very significant tax consequences. Not surprisingly, this has resulted in thousands of disputes related to this classification, many of which wind up in the various levels of our court system.

Capital Gains Defined

6-30. The business income vs. property income issue arises while an asset is being held. Using the criteria discussed in the previous section, during the period of ownership the taxpayer must determine whether the income that is produced by the asset is business income or, alternatively property income.

6-31. In contrast, the business income vs. capital gains issue is only applicable when there is a disposition of an asset. If the disposition is of a non-depreciable capital asset, the result will be a capital gain or loss. If the asset is a depreciable capital asset, no capital loss can occur and there may be other outcomes such as recapture of CCA or a terminal loss. If the disposition is of an asset that is not a capital or personal in nature, the result will be business income or loss.

6-32. The basic concept is a simple one — capital assets are acquired and held to produce income through their use. If an asset is acquired not to be held but, rather, to be resold for a profit, it is not a capital asset.

6-33. As a simple example, consider the assets of a retail store. These will include inventories of purchased merchandise that are being held for resale. Such assets are not part of the capital assets of the business, and any income related to their sale would be classified as business income. However, the building in which the merchandise is being offered for sale, as well as the furniture and fixtures necessary to the operation of the business, are capital assets. This would mean that if the operation were to sell these assets for more than their capital cost, any resulting gain would be capital in nature.

6-34. In a general manner, capital assets are somewhat analogous to the accounting classification of non-current assets, while non-capital assets are somewhat analogous to the accounting classification of inventories.

6-35. An additional analogy, sometimes applied in court cases, is with a fruit bearing tree. The tree itself is a capital asset and its sale would result in a capital gain or loss. In contrast, the sale of the fruit from the tree would generate business income.

6-36. The actual use of the asset often determines the appropriate classification. A particular type of asset can be classified as capital by one business and as inventory by another. Consider a piece of equipment such as a backhoe. For a construction company using this asset for excavating construction sites, it would clearly be a capital asset. Alternatively, if it were held for sale by a dealer in construction equipment, it would be classified as inventory, with any gain on its sale being taxed as business income.

6-37. It should be noted that you cannot always equate capital property with income producing property. Consider a real estate developer who is holding an inventory of properties for sale. If he chooses to rent some of these properties on a short term basis, they would be producing income. However, this would not alter the fact that the developer's primary intent is to sell these properties, making inventory the appropriate classification.

Criteria For Identifying Capital Gains
Primary And Secondary Intention

6-38. As implied in the previous discussion, the determination of whether a property is a capital property is based on the intent of the taxpayer when the asset was acquired. If his primary intention was to use the property to produce income it is a capital property and its disposition will result in a capital gain or capital loss. If the intent was to resell the property as quickly as possible, its disposition will result in business income.

6-39.   There may be situations where a property is originally acquired for income producing purposes but is sold because the acquirer's primary goal cannot be met. It is possible to argue that the taxpayer's secondary intention was to sell in the event his primary intention was frustrated.

6-40.   Unfortunately, only the taxpayer has unequivocal knowledge of his intention at the time a property is acquired. Because of this, other, more objectively measurable factors have to be considered in making this determination.

Other Considerations

6-41.   Other factors that have been considered in attempting to establish whether an asset should be considered capital property include the following:

Length Of The Ownership Period   The longer the period of ownership, the more likely it is that the taxpayer's intent was to hold the asset to produce income.

Number And Frequency Of Transactions   A large number of closely spaced transactions in a given period of time would be an indication that the investor was in the business of dealing in this type of asset, not holding it to produce income.

Relationship To The Taxpayer's Business   If the transaction is related to the taxpayer's business, this may be sufficient to disqualify any gain or loss from capital gains treatment. For example, a gain on a mortgage transaction might be considered business income to a real estate broker.

Supplemental Work On The Property   Additional work on the property, directed at enhancing its value or marketability, would indicate an adventure in the nature of trade resulting in business income.

Nature Of The Assets   The conventional accounting distinction between fixed assets and working capital has been used in some cases to determine whether income was business or capital in nature. Also, whether the asset is capable of producing income would be a consideration.

6-42.   For more specific guidance with respect to transactions in securities, IT-479R, "Transactions In Securities" provides a list of factors that the courts have considered in making the capital gains/business income distinction. A similar list for the classification of real estate transactions can be found in IT-218R, "Profit, Capital Gains And Losses From The Sale of Real Estate, Including Farmland And Inherited Land And Conversion Of Real Estate From Capital Property To Inventory And Vice Versa".

Exercise Six - 2

Subject: Business Income Vs. Capital Gain

During 2017, Sandra Von Arb acquired a four unit apartment building for $230,000. While it was her intention to operate the building as a rental property, one month after her purchase she received an unsolicited offer to purchase the building for $280,000. She accepts the offer. Should the $50,000 be treated as a capital gain or as business income? Justify your conclusion.

SOLUTION available in print and online Study Guide.

Business Income And GAAP

6-43.   Financial statements requiring audit opinions must be prepared in accordance with generally accepted accounting principles, or GAAP. These principles have had a significant influence on the development of the tax concept of business income. This is reflected in the fact that, for tax purposes, business income is usually an accrual, rather than a cash based calculation. Further, it is a net rather than a gross concept. In addition, GAAP continues to be influential in that income as computed under these principles is usually required for tax purposes, unless a particular provision of the *Act* specifies alternative requirements.

6-44.   This means that business income under the *Income Tax Act* will not be totally unfamiliar to anyone who has had experience in applying GAAP. However, there are a number of differences between GAAP based Net Income and net business income for tax purposes. While many of these will become apparent as we cover specific provisions of the *Act*, it is useful to note some of the more important differences at this point. They are as follows:

Amortization (Depreciation)   As was noted in Chapter 5, the *Income Tax Regulations* provide the methods and rates to be used in determining the maximum CCA that can be deducted in a given taxation year. However, there is no requirement that this maximum amount be deducted, nor is there any requirement that a consistent policy be followed as long as the annual amount involved is no greater than the maximum amount specified in the *Act*. In contrast, GAAP allows management to choose from a variety of amortization methods. However, once a method is adopted, it must be used consistently each year to deduct the full amount as calculated by that method.

Because of these different approaches, CCA deducted will be different and usually larger, than the corresponding amortization expense under GAAP. This is the most common and, for most enterprises, the largest difference between accounting Net Income and Net Income For Tax Purposes.

Other Allocations   There are other items, similar to amortization charges, where the total cost to be deducted will be the same for tax and accounting purposes. However, they will be deducted using different allocation patterns. Examples would be pension costs (funding payments are deducted for tax purposes) and warranty costs (cash payments are deducted for tax purposes).

Permanent Differences   There are some differences between tax and accounting income that are permanent in nature. For example, 100 percent of capital gains are included in accounting Net Income, while only one-half of this income is included in Net Income For Tax Purposes. Other examples of this type of difference would be the non-deductible 50 percent of business meals and entertainment and the non-deductible portion of automobile lease payments (see discussion later in this Chapter).

Unreasonable Expenses   In applying GAAP, accountants are generally not required to distinguish between expenses that are reasonable and those that are not. If assets were used up in the production of revenues of the period, they are expenses of that period. This is not the case for tax purposes. ITA 67 indicates that only those expenditures that may be considered reasonable in the circumstances may be deducted in the computation of Net Income For Tax Purposes. If, for example, a large salary was paid to a spouse or to a child that could not be justified on the basis of the services provided, the deduction of the amount involved could be disallowed under ITA 67. The fact that this salary could be deducted in the determination of accounting Net Income would not alter this conclusion.

Non-Arm's Length Transactions   ITA 69 deals with situations involving transactions between non-arm's length parties and provides special rules when such non-arm's length transactions take place at values other than fair market value (see Chapter 9 for a complete discussion of these rules). For example, if a taxpayer acquired an asset with a fair market value of $2,000 from a related party for $2,500 (a value in excess of its fair market value), the transferee is deemed to have acquired it at its fair market value of $2,000, while the transferor is taxed on the basis of the $2,500 consideration received. If the transferee was a business, no similar adjustment would be required under GAAP. Note, however, there are requirements under GAAP for disclosing related party transactions.

6-45. As many of you are aware, the financial reporting rules applicable to accounting for taxes focus on temporary differences. GAAP defines these differences with reference to Balance Sheet items. However, in determining business income (for tax purposes), the normal approach is to reconcile accounting Net Income with Net Income For Tax Purposes. As a consequence, individuals working in the tax area focus on Income Statement differences, as opposed to Balance Sheet differences.

Business Income - Inclusions (Revenues)

Inclusions In Business Income - Income Tax Act Provisions

ITA 12

6-46. In subdivision b of the *Income Tax Act*, inclusions in business and property income are covered in Sections 12 through 17.1. The focus in this Chapter will be on Section 12 where we find the tax treatment of most of the items that we commonly think of as operating revenues for a business.

6-47. We would note, however, that ITA 12(1)(c) deals with interest income and ITA 12(1)(j) and (k) deal with dividends received. As these inclusions most commonly relate to property income, they will be discussed in Chapter 7, Income From Property.

6-48. In addition, ITA 12(1)(l) requires the inclusion of business and property income from a partnership, and ITA 12(1)(m) requires the inclusion of benefits from trusts. These inclusions will be dealt with in Chapters 18 and 19 which deal, respectively, with partnerships and trusts.

ITA 13 Through 17

6-49. Sections 13 and 14, which deal with recapture of CCA and CEC inclusions, were largely covered in Chapter 5. Section 15, which deals with benefits conferred on shareholders of corporations, will be covered in Chapter 15, Corporate Taxation And Management Decisions. Sections 16 and 17 deal with specialized issues that will not be covered in this text.

Amounts Received And Receivable

6-50. The most important inclusion in business income is found in ITA 12(1)(b) which requires the inclusion of amounts that have become receivable during the year for property sold or services rendered. This provision clearly establishes that, in general, business income is determined on an accrual basis.

6-51. ITA 12(1)(b) also notes that amounts generally become receivable on the day on which the services were rendered. You will note that this is consistent with the accountant's point of sale approach to revenue recognition.

6-52. However, in a departure from the usual GAAP definition of revenue, ITA 12(1)(a) requires the inclusion of amounts received for goods to be delivered in the future. Under GAAP such advances from customers are treated as a liability, rather than as a revenue. While this would appear to create a difference between accounting Net Income and business income for tax purposes, we will find that this difference is eliminated through the use of a reserve for undelivered goods.

6-53. In the following material we will examine how reserves are used to modify the amount of revenues recorded under ITA 12(1)(a) and (b). While, at first glance, these procedures are somewhat different than those used under GAAP, they will generally result in a final inclusion that is identical to the amount of revenue that is recognized under GAAP.

Reserves
The General System

6-54.   In tax work, the term "reserve" is used to refer to a group of specific items that can be deducted in the determination of net business income. Unlike most deductions that relate either to cash outflows or the incurrence of liabilities, these items are modifications of amounts received (reserve for undelivered goods) or amounts receivable (reserve for doubtful debts and reserve for unpaid amounts).

6-55.   With respect to the use of such reserves, the basic rules are as follows:

Deductible Reserves   ITA 18(1)(e) indicates that a particular reserve cannot be deducted unless it is specifically provided for in the *Act*. This means that, for example, when estimated warranty costs are deducted as an accounting expense in the year in which the related product is sold, no reserve can be deducted for tax purposes, as a reserve for estimated warranty costs is not specified in the *Act*. Note that while ITA 20(1)(m.1) does refer to a manufacturer's warranty reserve, careful reading shows that amounts can only be deducted under this provision when they are for an extended warranty covered by an insurance contract.

Addition To Income   When a reserve is deducted in a particular taxation year, it must be added back to income in the immediately following year. These additions are required under various Paragraphs in ITA 12 [e.g., ITA 12(1)(d) requires the addition of reserves deducted for doubtful debts in the preceding year].

6-56.   The most common reserves that are specified in the *Income Tax Act* as deductions from business income are as follows:

- ITA 20(1)(l) - **Reserve For Doubtful Debts (Bad Debts)**

- ITA 20(1)(m) - **Reserve For Undelivered Goods And Services**

- ITA 20(1)(n) - **Reserve For Unpaid Amounts**

6-57.   The details of these reserves will be covered in the following material.

Reserve For Doubtful Debts - ITA 20(1)(l)

6-58.   While specific tax procedures for dealing with bad debts differ from those used under GAAP, these alternative procedures will normally produce identical results. The required tax procedures are as follows:

- Under ITA 20(1)(l), a year end deduction is permitted for an estimate of the bad debts that will be realized subsequent to the current year.

- During the subsequent year, actual bad debts may be deducted under ITA 20(1)(p).

- At the end of this subsequent year, the old reserve must be included in business income under ITA 12(1)(d). A new reserve is established under ITA 20(1)(l).

EXAMPLE   On December 31, 2016, at the end of its first year of operations, Ken's Print Shop estimates that $5,500 of its ending Accounts Receivable will be uncollectible. For 2016, an Allowance For Bad Debts is established for this amount for accounting purposes (by debiting Bad Debt Expense and crediting Allowance For Bad Debts). In addition, a reserve of $5,500 is deducted under ITA 20(1)(l). During the year ending December 31, 2017, $6,800 in accounts receivable are written off. At December 31, 2017, estimated uncollectible accounts total $4,800.

6-59.   For accounting purposes, the 2016 estimate of bad debts would be charged to expense and credited to an Allowance For Bad Debts (a contra account to Accounts Receivable). For tax purposes, the same amount would be deducted from net business income as a Reserve For Doubtful Debts.

6-60.   During 2017, the accountant for Ken's Print Shop would credit Accounts Receivable and debit Allowance For Bad Debts for the actual write offs of $6,800. This would leave a debit (negative) balance in this account of $1,300 ($5,500 - $6,800), indicating that the 2016 estimate was too low. This error would be corrected by adding the $1,300 to the Bad Debt Expense for 2017. The total expense for 2017 would be as follows:

2017 Estimate Of Future Bad Debts (Credit Allowance)	$4,800
Increase In Expense To Eliminate Debit Balance In Allowance	1,300
2017 Bad Debt Expense For Accounting Purposes	$6,100

6-61.   For tax purposes, the total Bad Debt Expense would be the same $6,100. However, the calculation follows a different pattern:

Add: 2016 Reserve For Tax Purposes		$ 5,500
Deduct:		
2017 Actual Write-Offs	($6,800)	
2017 Reserve For Tax Purposes	(4,800)	(11,600)
2017 Net Deduction For Tax Purposes		($ 6,100)

Exercise Six - 3

Subject: Bad Debts And Reserve For Doubtful Accounts

On December 31, 2016, Norman's Flowers estimates that $16,000 of its ending Accounts Receivable will be uncollectible. A reserve for this amount is deducted for tax purposes. During the year ending December 31, 2017, $17,200 in bad accounts are written off. At December 31, 2017, estimated uncollectible accounts total $18,400. What is the 2017 Bad Debt Expense for accounting purposes? By what amount will the 2017 net business income (for tax purposes) of Norman's Flowers be increased or decreased by the preceding information with respect to bad debts?

SOLUTION available in print and online Study Guide.

Reserve For Undelivered Goods And Services - ITA 20(1)(m)

6-62.   It was previously noted that, unlike the situation under GAAP, amounts received for goods or services to be delivered in the future must be included in the calculation of revenues for tax purposes. However, this difference is offset by the ability to deduct, under ITA 20(1)(m), a reserve for goods and services to be delivered in the future. This means that, while the procedures are somewhat different, the treatment of amounts received for undelivered goods and services is the same under both the *Income Tax Act* and GAAP.

> **EXAMPLE**   During the taxation year ending December 31, 2017, Donna's Auto Parts has receipts of $275,000. Of this amount, $25,000 is a prepayment for goods that will not be delivered until 2018.

> **ANALYSIS**   While the $275,000 will be considered an inclusion in 2017 net business income, Donna will be able to deduct a reserve of $25,000 under ITA 20(1)(m). This $25,000 amount will be added back to her 2018 net business income, reflecting the fact that the goods have been delivered and the revenue realized.

Exercise Six - 4

Subject: Reserve For Doubtful Accounts And Undelivered Services

As an unincorporated business, Barbra's Graphic Design keeps its records on a cash basis. During 2017, its first year of operation, the business has cash sales of $53,400. At the end of the year, an additional $26,300 of revenues was receivable. Of the amounts received, $5,600 was for services that will be delivered during 2018. Barbra estimates that $425 of the end of year receivable amounts will be uncollectible. By what amount will the 2017 net business income of Barbra's Graphic Design be increased by the preceding information?

SOLUTION available in print and online Study Guide.

Reserve For Unpaid Amounts - ITA 20(1)(n)

6-63.　If a business sells goods with the amount being receivable over an extended period (i.e., instalment sales), ITA 20(1)(n) permits the deduction of a reasonable reserve in very specific circumstances. The calculation of the reserve is based on the gross profit on the sale. Note that this reserve is only available on business income and should not be confused with capital gains reserves which are covered in Chapter 8. While this appears to provide for the recognition of revenue on a cash basis, there are two significant constraints:

ITA 20(1)(n) indicates that no reserve can be deducted unless at least some part of the proceeds will not be received until at least two years after the date the property is sold (this two year requirement does not apply to sales of real property inventory).

ITA 20(8) specifies that no reserve can be deducted in a year, for any type of property, if the sale took place more than 36 months before the end of that year (i.e., the reserve is limited to a maximum of 3 years). In addition, the reserve is not available if the purchaser is a corporation controlled by the seller, or a partnership in which the seller has a majority interest.

Exercise Six - 5

Subject:　Reserve For Unpaid Amounts

During November, 2017, Martine's Jewels Ltd. sells a necklace for $120,000. The cost of this necklace was $55,000, resulting in a gross profit of $65,000. The $120,000 sales price is to be paid in four equal annual instalments on December 31 in each of the years 2018 through 2021. Martine's Jewels Ltd. has a December 31 year end. Indicate the amount of the reserve that can be deducted, and the net business income, for each of the years 2017 through 2021.

SOLUTION available in print and online Study Guide.

We suggest you work Self Study Problems Six-1 and Six-2 at this point.

Other Inclusions

6-64.　There are a number of other inclusions in business income. While some are of limited interest in a text such as this [e.g., ITA 12(1)(z.4) requires the inclusion of eligible funeral arrangements], some of these inclusions warrant additional comment. Income Tax Folio S3-F9-C1, *Lottery Winnings, Miscellaneous Receipts, and Income (and Losses) from Crime* provide some coverage of the following, as well as coverage of other miscellaneous receipts:

Crowdfunding　Crowdfunding is the collection of funds from a large number of small contributors, usually online by means of a web platform. This is a relatively new source of funds that has been successfully used for a variety of purposes, including developing a new product. In a technical Interpretation 2013-0484941E5, the CRA has indicated that non-equity funds derived from a crowdfunding campaign are generally taxable as business income under ITA 9(1). Given this, the costs of mounting the crowdfunding campaign would be deductible against the income derived.

Income Tax Folio S3-F9-C1 includes this conclusion in an example under the section "Gifts and other voluntary payments". It is likely that there will be more consideration of this issue, particularly in situations where equity shares are issued to the crowdfunding contributors.

Profits From Gambling   Profits derived from bookmaking or from the operation of any legal or illegal gambling establishment constitute income from a business.   An individual's gambling activities, if extensive enough, could constitute a business (e.g., a professional poker player). In this case such income would be taxable and it would suggest that losses would be fully deductible.

Lottery Schemes   In general, the amount or value of a prize received by a taxpayer from a lottery scheme is not taxable as either a capital gain or income.

Profits From An Illegal Business   Many people are aware that the famous American gangster Al Capone was sent to jail, not for his illegal activities involving alleged robbery and murder, but rather for his failure to pay taxes on the resulting profits. As illegal revenues must be included in business income, related expenses are generally deductible. This can lead to interesting conclusions as evidenced by a publication of the New Zealand Inland Revenue Department. This publication provided a detailed list of items that could be deducted by what was referred to as "sex workers". Without going into detail, we would note that see-through garments and whips were on the list, provided they were used in delivering services to a client.

6-65.   Other inclusions in business income that are not covered in IT Folio S3-F9-C1 include the following:

Damage Payments Received   Damages are usually received as the result of non-performance of a contractual arrangement. Their tax treatment depends on what the damage award is intended to replace. If it replaces revenue that would have been included in income, then the award is income. If it is compensation for damages to reputation, organization, or structure, it may be considered a tax free capital receipt.

Debt Forgiveness   Situations arise in which outstanding debt is forgiven, often by a related taxpayer. When this happens, ITA 80 contains a complex set of rules that apply when the debtor has been able to deduct the interest expense on the forgiven debt. These rules may require the amount of debt forgiven to be applied to reduce loss carry over balances, the tax cost of certain properties and, in some situations, to be included in income in the year of forgiveness. The details of these rules are beyond the scope of this text.

Government Assistance   Whether or not government assistance will be included in current income depends on the nature of the assistance. The tax rules here largely reflect the accounting rules that are found in GAAP. That is, assistance related to current revenues and expenses will be included in current income while, in contrast, assistance related to the acquisition of capital assets will be deducted from the cost of these assets.

Inducement Receipts Businesses may receive payments that induce them to undertake some activity. An example of this would be a payment received by a lessor to induce him to undertake improvements to the leased property. The taxpayer has several alternatives here. The amount received can be included in current income, used to reduce the cost of any related assets, or used to reduce any required expenses. These are the same alternatives that are available under GAAP.

Restrictive Covenant Receipts A restrictive covenant is an agreement entered into, an undertaking made, or a waiver of an advantage or right by a taxpayer. ITA 56.4 would, in general, require that these payments be included in income. There are a limited number of exceptions, one of which would allow the receipt to be allocated to cumulative eligible capital.

Limitations On Deductions From Business And Property Income

General Approach - Restrictions In ITA 18 Through ITA 19.1

6-66.   It would be extremely difficult to provide a detailed list of all of the items that might possibly be considered a business expense. While ITA 20 spells out many such items, it is often necessary to have more general guidance when new types of items arise. ITA 18 through ITA 19.1 gives this guidance in a somewhat backwards fashion by providing guidelines on what should not be deducted in computing business income. However, this negative guidance frequently provides assistance in determining what should be deducted in computing business income.

6-67.   Note, however, that if an item is specifically listed in the *Act* as a deduction, the specific listing overrides the general limitation. For example, Section 18 prohibits the deduction of capital costs, thereby preventing the immediate write-off of a capital asset. The fact that ITA 20(1)(aa) permits the deduction of landscaping costs, some of which would be capital expenditures, overrides the general prohibition found in Section 18.

6-68.   The restrictions contained in ITA 18 through ITA 19.1 apply only to deductions from business and property income. There are other restrictions, for example the cost of business meals and entertainment, which apply to deductions from both business and property income, as well as to deductions from employment income. Most of these more general restrictions are found in Subdivision f, "Rules Relating To Computation Of Income", and are discussed later in this Chapter.

Specific Limiting Items Under ITA 18

Incurred To Produce Income

6-69.   One of the most important of the limiting provisions is as follows:

> **ITA 18(1)(a)**   No deduction shall be made in respect of an outlay or expense except to the extent that it was made or incurred by the taxpayer for the purpose of gaining or producing income from the business or property.

6-70.   When there is a question as to the deductibility of an item not covered by a particular provision of the *Act*, it is usually this general limitation provision that provides the basis for an answer. As a consequence, there are many Interpretation Bulletins dealing with such matters as motor vehicle expenses (IT-521R). IT Folio S4-F2-C1, *Deductibility Of Fines Or Penalties* and S4-F2-C2, *Business Use of Home Expenses* also deal with this issue. In addition, there have been hundreds of court cases dealing with particular items. For example, with respect to insurance costs, there have been cases in the following areas:

- Damage insurance on business assets (deductible)
- Life insurance when required by creditor (deductible, if interest on loan is deductible)
- Life insurance in general (not deductible)
- Insurance against competition (deductible)

6-71.   As can be seen from the preceding list, this is a complex area of tax. If there is doubt about a particular item's deductibility, it will sometimes be necessary to do considerable research to establish whether it is dealt with in an Interpretation Bulletin or a court case.

6-72.   In applying this provision, it is not necessary to demonstrate that the expenditure actually produced income. It is generally sufficient to demonstrate that it was incurred as part of an income earning process or activity.

Capital Expenditures

6-73.   ITA 18(1)(b) prohibits the deduction of any expenditure that is designated as a capital expenditure. However, deductions are permitted under ITA 20(1)(a) for capital cost allowances. The limitations on this deduction were discussed in detail in Chapter 5.

Exempt Income Expenditures

6-74.   ITA 18(1)(c) prohibits the deduction of any expenditures that were incurred to produce income that is exempt from taxation. For a business, this would have limited applicability as few sources of business income are tax exempt.

Personal And Living Expenses

6-75.   ITA 18(1)(h) prohibits the deduction of an expenditure that is a personal or living expense of the taxpayer. This means that if, for example, a corporation pays for the personal travel of a shareholder, the corporation cannot deduct the costs. Note, however, if a corporation pays for the personal travel of an arm's length employee, this provision is not applicable and the costs would be deductible.

6-76.   This can create a very unfortunate tax situation in that, not only will the costs of such travel be non-deductible to the business, the shareholder will have to include the value of the trip in their income as a shareholder benefit. Clearly, it would be preferable to simply pay additional salary equal to the value of the trip. Using this alternative, the tax consequences to the employee or owner would be the same. However, the business would benefit from being able to deduct the amount paid.

6-77.   Somewhat indirectly, ITA 18(1)(h) introduces an additional rule with respect to the deductibility of costs. The ITA 248(1) definition of "personal or living expenses" indicates that the expenses of properties maintained for the use of an individual or persons related to that individual are personal unless the properties maintained are connected to a business that is either profitable, or has a reasonable expectation of being profitable. This could result in some deductions being denied for a cottage that was rented during the year, but was used by the taxpayer for a part of that year.

Deferred Income Plans

6-78.   ITA 18(1)(i) restricts the deductibility of contributions under supplementary unemployment benefit plans to the amount specified in ITA 145. ITA 18(1)(j) and 18(1)(k) provide similar limitations for contributions to deferred profit sharing plans and profit sharing plans. ITA 18(1)(o) prohibits the deduction of contributions to an employee benefit plan. Finally, under ITA 18(1)(o.1) and (o.2), limits are placed on the deductibility of amounts paid to salary deferral arrangements and retirement compensation arrangements. These amounts are only deductible as specified under ITA 20(1)(r) and (oo). All of these provisions are discussed in detail in Chapter 10, Retirement Savings And Other Special Income Arrangements.

Recreational Facilities And Club Dues

6-79.   ITA 18(1)(l) prohibits the deduction of amounts that have been incurred to maintain a yacht, camp, lodge, golf course or facility, unless the taxpayer is in the business of providing such property for hire. Because of the fairly specific wording of this provision, it would appear that the costs of providing other types of recreational benefits would be deductible. For example, a corporation could deduct the costs of providing a general fitness center for their employees, provided it was made available to all employees.

6-80.   A similar prohibition is made against the deduction of membership fees or dues to dining, sporting, or recreational facilities. Note, however, that there is no prohibition against deducting the cost of legitimate entertainment expenses incurred in such facilities, subject to the 50 percent limitation that will be described shortly.

Political Contributions

6-81.   ITA 18(1)(n) prohibits the deduction of political contributions in the determination of business or property income. Given the restrictions on making of political contributions that are found in the *Federal Accountability Act*, this is not a costly provision for business. As covered in Chapter 4, this *Act* limits individual contributions to an annual amount of $1,550 (for 2017) for a party or contestant and completely prohibits contributions by corporations.

Expenses Of A Personal Services Business

6-82.   A personal services business is a corporation that has been set up by an individual to provide personal services that are, in effect, employment services. ITA 18(1)(p) restricts the deductible expenses of such a corporation to those that would normally be deductible against employment income.   Chapter 12, Taxable Income And Tax Payable For Corporations, provides coverage of this subject.

Automobile Mileage Payments

6-83.   As is discussed in Chapter 3, a business may pay its employees or shareholders a per kilometer fee for having them use their own automobile on behalf of the business.   The amount of such payments that can be deducted by a business is limited by ITA 18(1)(r) to an amount prescribed in ITR 7306. For both 2016 and 2017, this amount is 54 cents for the first 5,000 kilometers and 48 cents for additional kilometers driven by an employee.

6-84.   Amounts paid in excess of these limits will only be deductible to the payer to the extent that they are included in the income of the recipient.

Interest And Property Taxes On Land

6-85.   Many businesses pay interest and property taxes on land. If the primary purpose of holding this land is to produce income, these payments clearly represent amounts that can be deducted as part of the costs of carrying the land while it is producing income.

6-86.   In contrast, when vacant land is generating insignificant amounts of income, ITA 18(2) restricts the deduction for property taxes and interest to the amount of net revenues produced by the land. For example, if a parcel of land that is being held as a future plant site is generating some revenue by being rented for storage, interest and property taxes on the land can only be deducted to the extent of the net revenues from the rent. ITA 53(1)(h) allows the undeducted interest and property taxes to be added to the adjusted cost base of the property, thereby reducing any future capital gain resulting from the disposition of the property. This addition to the adjusted cost base is only available if the primary purpose of holding the land is to produce income.   There is, however, no requirement that income be produced in a given year.

6-87.   In the case of land that is being held as inventory, ITA 10(1.1) permits the non-deductible interest and property taxes to be added to the cost of the land.

6-88.   The preceding general rules could be viewed as too restrictive for those companies whose "principal business is the leasing, rental or sale, or the development for lease, rental or sale, of real property". As a consequence, these real estate companies are allowed to deduct interest and property tax payments to the extent of net revenues from the property, plus a "base level deduction".

6-89.   This base level deduction is defined in ITA 18(2.2) as the amount that would be the amount of interest, computed at the prescribed rate, for the year, in respect of a loan of $1,000,000 outstanding throughout the year. This means that, if the prescribed rate for the year was 2 percent, real estate companies could deduct interest and property taxes on the land that they are carrying to the extent of net revenues from the land, plus an additional $20,000 [(2%)($1,000,000)].

Soft Costs

6-90.   Costs that are attributable to the period of construction, renovation, or alteration of a building, or in respect of the ownership of the related land, are referred to as soft costs. These costs could include interest, legal and accounting fees, insurance, and property taxes. In general, ITA 18(3.1) indicates that such costs are not deductible and must be added to the cost of the property.

Appraisal Costs

6-91.   While these costs are not covered in ITA 18, there are limitations on their deductibility that are discussed in IT-143R3, *Meaning Of Eligible Capital Expenditures*. As discussed in that Bulletin, the treatment of appraisal costs on capital property will depend on the reason for their incurrence:

- If they are incurred on a capital property for the purpose of its acquisition or disposition, they are generally added to the cost of the property.
- If they are incurred with respect to a proposed acquisition that does not take place, they should be treated as eligible capital expenditures (see Byrd/Chen Note).
- If they are incurred for the purpose of gaining or producing income from a business (e.g., the cost of an appraisal required for insurance purposes), they are deductible in computing income for the year.

> **BYRD/CHEN NOTE**   While items that were previously viewed as eligible capital expenditures are now allocated to Class 14.1, a regular CCA Class, IT-143R3 is still in effect. This means that the preceding guidance on the treatment of appraisal costs would still be appropriate. The only difference is with respect to the second bullet. Appraisal costs that are incurred with respect to a proposed acquisition that does not take place will now be treated as an addition to Class 14.1.

Interest In Thin Capitalization Situations

6-92.   In general, interest paid on debt is deductible to a business, whereas dividends paid on outstanding shares are not. Given this, there is an incentive for a non-resident owner of a Canadian resident corporation to take back debt rather than equity for the financing that he provides to the corporation. This could result in a situation where the payment of the interest is deductible in Canada and, at the same time, is not taxable to the non-resident recipient due to an international tax treaty (see Chapter 20).

6-93.   To prevent this from happening, ITA 18(4) through 18(6) limit the deductibility of interest paid in such "thin capitalization" situations. Interest paid or payable to the non-resident specified shareholder is disallowed if it is paid on amounts of debt in excess of 1.5 times the sum of the shareholder's share of contributed capital, plus 100 percent of the corporation's Retained Earnings at the beginning of the year. In conjunction with this, ITA 214(16) re-characterizes the interest as a non-deductible dividend (as discussed in Chapter 20, this will result in Canadian taxes being withheld from the distribution to the non-resident). For this purpose, a specified shareholder is defined in ITA 18(5) as a person who holds shares that give him 25 percent or more of the votes that would be cast at the annual meeting of the shareholders, or 25 percent or more of the fair market value of all issued and outstanding shares. A simple example will serve to clarify these rules:

> **EXAMPLE**   Throughout 2017, Mr. Lane, a resident of the U.S., owns 45 percent of the shares and holds $3,000,000 of the long-term debt securities of Thinly Ltd. The capital structure of Thinly Ltd. throughout the year is as follows:

> | | |
> |---|---|
> | Long-Term Debt (11% Rate) | $5,000,000 |
> | Common Stock | 200,000 |
> | Retained Earnings | 300,000 |
> | Total Capital | $5,500,000 |

> **ANALYSIS** Mr. Lane is clearly a specified shareholder as he holds 45 percent of the corporation's shares. His relevant equity balance is $390,000 [(45%)($200,000) + (100%)($300,000)]. His debt holding is clearly greater than 1.5 times this relevant equity balance. As a consequence, there would be disallowed interest of $265,650 calculated as follows:

Limitations On Deductions From Business And Property Income

Total Interest Paid To Mr. Lane [(11%)($3,000,000)]	$330,000
Maximum Deductible Interest [(11%)(1.5)($390,000)]	(64,350)
Disallowed Interest (Re-Characterized As A Dividend)	$265,650

Exercise Six - 6

Subject: Interest In Thin Capitalizations

On January 1, 2016, a new Canadian corporation is formed with the issuance of $8,600,000 in debt securities and $2,400,000 in common shares. On this date, Ms. Sally Johnson, who is a resident of Mexico, acquires $4,500,000 of the debt securities and 30 percent of the common shares. The debt securities pay interest at 9 percent. The company has a December 31 year end. On January 1, 2017, the Retained Earnings balance of the company is $900,000. How much, if any, of the interest paid on Ms. Johnson's holding of debt securities during 2017 would be disallowed under the thin capitalization rules in ITA 18(4)?

SOLUTION available in print and online Study Guide.

Prepaid Expenses
6-94.   ITA 18(9) prevents the deduction of amounts that have been paid for goods or services that will be delivered after the end of the taxation year. This Subsection also prohibits the deduction of interest or rents that relate to a subsequent taxation year. As a result, the tax treatment of these items is the same as their treatment under GAAP.

Business Use Of Home Expenses (Work Space In The Home Costs)
6-95.   The rules related to the use of a home office to earn business income are found in ITA 18(12). Guidance for the application of these rules is found in IT Folio S4-F2-C2, *Business Use Of Home Expenses*. As was the case when a home office was used for earning employment income, the deductibility of related expenses is limited to situations where:

- the work space is the individual's principal place of business; or
- the work space is used exclusively for the purpose of earning income from business and is used on a regular and continuous basis for meeting clients, customers, or patients of the individual.

6-96.   If an individual qualifies for this deduction because it is his principal place of business, the space does not have to be used exclusively for business purposes. If, for example, a dining room table is used to run a mail order business and that room qualifies as the principal place of business for the operation, work space in the home costs can be deducted for the dining room space. Note, however, that in determining the appropriate amount of costs, consideration would have to be given to any personal use of that space.

6-97.   If the work space is not the principal place of business, it must be used exclusively for the purpose of earning income. This requires that some part of the home must be designated as the home work space and not be used for any other purpose. In addition, this second provision requires that the space be used on a regular and continuous basis for meeting clients, customers, or patients. IT Folio S4-F2-C2 indicates that a work space for a business that normally requires infrequent meetings, or frequent meetings at irregular intervals, would not meet this requirement.

6-98.   When the conditions for deductibility are met, expenses must generally be apportioned between business and non-business use in a reasonable manner, usually on the basis of floor space used. Maintenance or repair expenses that relate directly to the area being used for business can be deducted in full. Figure 6-2 (following page) compares the deductibility of work space in the home costs for an employee with no commission income, an employee with commission income and a self-employed individual earning business income.

Limitations On Deductions From Business And Property Income

Figure 6 - 2
Deductibility Of Work Space In The Home Costs

	Employee - No Commissions	Employee - With Commissions	Self-Employed Business Income
Rent (if tenant)	Yes	Yes	Yes
Utilities	Yes	Yes	Yes
Repairs, Maintenance	Yes	Yes	Yes
Telephone (Supply)*	NO/Yes	NO/Yes	Yes
Internet (Supply)*	NO	NO	Yes
Property Taxes	NO	Yes	Yes
Home Insurance	NO	Yes	Yes
Mortgage Interest	NO	NO	Yes
CCA On House	NO	NO	Yes

*Employees cannot deduct the monthly basic cost of a home telephone or the cost of fees for home internet service. Long distance charges that reasonably relate to employment income are deductible. In contrast, to the extent that telephone and internet service at an individual's home is used for both business and personal purposes, the business portion of the expense are deductible. A reasonable basis of proration should be used.

6-99.   You will note in Figure 6-2 that individuals earning business income can deduct CCA on their home. While this deduction would result in a lower Taxable Income for the current year, tax professionals generally advise people not to make this deduction. The reason for this relates to the fact that gains on an individual's principal residence can generally be received on a tax free basis (see Chapter 8 for a full discussion of the principal residence exemption). If an individual deducts CCA on this property as a self-employed individual, the result can be that part of the gain on the sale of the residence will be taxable. This assumes that relevant real estate prices are increasing.

6-100.   Regardless of the types of costs deducted, work space in the home costs cannot create or increase a business (or employment) loss. As a result, the total deduction will be limited to the amount of net business income calculated without reference to the work space in the home costs. Any expenses that are not deductible in a given year because they exceed the business income in that year can be carried forward and deducted in a subsequent year against income generated from the same business. In effect, there is an indefinite carry forward of unused work space in the home costs. This carry forward is conditional on the work space continuing to meet the test for deductibility in future years.

Exercise Six - 7

Subject: Work Space In The Home Costs

During the current year, Jobul Krist has the following costs:

Utilities	$2,400
Maintenance And Repairs	4,600
Property Taxes	5,200
House Insurance	2,300
Interest On Mortgage	7,800
Repainting And Rewiring The Work Space In The Home	1,000
Home Internet Service Fees	960
Home Telephone:	
Monthly Charge	600
Employment/Business Related Long Distance Charges	390

Limitations On Deductions From Business, Property, And Employment Income

Mr. Krist is a workaholic with no family, friends, pets or personal interests. He estimates that he uses 25 percent of his residence and 95 percent of his home phone and home internet service for employment/business related purposes. Maximum CCA on 100 percent of the house would be $12,000. Determine the maximum deduction that would be available to Mr. Krist assuming:

A. He is an employee with $50,000 in income (no commissions).
B. He is an employee with $50,000 in commission income.
C. He is self-employed and earns $50,000 in business income.

SOLUTION available in print and online Study Guide.

We suggest you work Self Study Problem Six-3 at this point.

Foreign Media Advertising - ITA 19 And 19.1

6-101. In order to provide some protection to Canadian media, the *Income Tax Act* places limitations on the deductibility of advertising expenditures in foreign media. For print media, this limitation is found in ITA 19, with ITA 19.1 containing a corresponding provision for broadcast media. In general, these provisions deny a deduction for expenditures made in foreign print or foreign broadcast media in those cases where the advertising message is directed primarily at the Canadian market. It does not apply where such foreign media expenditures are focused on non-Canadian markets.

6-102. ITA 19.01 modifies the general non-deductibility rule by exempting certain foreign periodicals. Canadian businesses can deduct 100 percent of advertising costs in these publications, without regard to whether it is directed at the Canadian market, provided 80 percent or more of its non-advertising content is "original editorial content". Original editorial content is defined as non-advertising content:

- the author of which is a Canadian citizen or a permanent resident of Canada and, for this purpose, "author" includes a writer, a journalist, an illustrator and a photographer; or

- that is created for the Canadian market and has not been published in any other edition of that issue of the periodical published outside Canada.

6-103. If the periodical cannot meet the 80 percent criteria, only 50 percent of such advertising costs will be deductible. Note that ITA 19.01 applies to periodicals only, and not to other foreign media.

Limitations On Deductions From Business, Property, And Employment Income

Introduction

6-104. The restrictions that are found in ITA 18 through ITA 19.1 are applicable only to business and property income. For the most part, they involve expenses that would only be deductible against this type of income and so the restriction has no influence on the determination of other types of income. The exception to this is work space in the home costs, which can be deducted in the calculation of either employment or business income. Note, however, that in this case, different ITA Sections are applicable to each type of income.

6-105. Other types of expenses, for example business meals and entertainment, can be deducted against either employment or business income. The restrictions on deductions of these more general types of expenses are applicable to business, property, or employment income and, as a consequence, they are found in other Sections of the *Act*. More specifically, Division B's Subdivision f, "Deductions In Computing Income", covers these restrictions.

Reasonableness

6-106.   Subdivision f begins with a broad, general rule which limits deductible expenses to those that are "reasonable in the circumstances". This general limitation, which is applicable to the determination of business, property, or employment income, is as follows:

> **ITA 67**   In computing income, no deduction shall be made in respect of an outlay or expense in respect of which any amount is otherwise deductible under this Act, except to the extent that the outlay or expense was reasonable in the circumstances.

6-107.   This general rule is most commonly applied in non-arm's length situations. For example, it is fairly common for the sole owner of a small private company to make salary payments to a spouse and/or children. While there is a considerable amount of latitude for the amount of such payments, the owner should be able to demonstrate that the individual who received the payment provided services that had a value that could reasonably be associated with the amount received.

> **EXAMPLE**   The sole shareholder of a private corporation appoints his 6 month old daughter as vice president of the corporation and pays her a salary of $100,000. (While this sounds absurd, similar arrangements have been attempted.)

> **ANALYSIS**   As the services of a 6 month old are extremely unlikely to have any business value, the $100,000 would be disallowed on the grounds of being unreasonable in the circumstances.

Meals And Entertainment
General Rules - ITA 67.1

6-108.   It can be argued that business expenditures for food, beverages, or entertainment involve an element of personal living costs and, to the extent that this is true, such amounts should not be deductible in calculating Net Income For Tax Purposes. This idea is embodied in ITA 67.1(1) which restricts the amount that can be deducted for the human consumption of food or beverages, or the enjoyment of entertainment. The amount of these costs that can be deducted is equal to 50 percent of the actual costs. The Subsection makes it clear that this limit does not apply to meals related to moving costs, child care costs, amounts eligible for the medical expense tax credit or amounts eligible for the adoption expenses tax credit. Further exceptions to this general rule are described in the next section of this Chapter.

Exceptions

6-109.   ITA 67.1(1.1) provides an exception to the 50 percent for meal costs incurred by long-haul truck drivers during eligible travel periods (i.e., away from home for at least 24 continuous hours). Individuals who are long-haul truck drivers and their employers can deduct 80 percent of the cost of eligible meals.

6-110.   ITA 67.1(2) provides a number of additional exceptions for food and entertainment. Situations where the 50 percent rule does not apply include:

- Hotels, restaurants, and airlines provide food, beverages, and entertainment in return for compensation from their customers. The costs incurred by these organizations in providing these goods and services continue to be deductible. However, when the employees of these organizations travel or entertain clients, their costs are subject to the 50 percent limitation.

- Meals and entertainment expenses relating to a fund raising event for a registered charity are fully deductible.

- Where the taxpayer is compensated by someone else for the cost of food, beverages, or entertainment and the amount is separately identified in writing. Such amounts will be fully deductible against this compensation. For example, if Mr. Spinner was a management consultant and was reimbursed by his client for separately billed meals and entertainment, he could deduct 100 percent of these costs. However, his client

Limitations On Deductions From Business, Property, And Employment Income

would only be able to deduct 50 percent of the reimbursements.

- When amounts are paid for meals or entertainment for employees and, either the payments create a taxable benefit for the employee, or the amounts do not create a taxable benefit because they are being provided at a remote work location, the amounts are fully deductible to the employer.

- When amounts are incurred by an employer for food, beverages, or entertainment at a special event that is generally available to all individuals employed by the taxpayer, the amounts are fully deductible. Note, however, this exception applies to no more than six special events held by an employer during a calendar year.

6-111. In addition to the preceding exceptions, ITA 67.1(3) provides a special rule for meals that are included in conference or convention fees. When the amount included in the fee for meals and entertainment is not specified, the Subsection deems the amount to be $50 per day. In these circumstances, it is this $50 per day that is subject to the 50 percent limitation.

6-112. Airline, bus, and rail tickets can include meals in their price. It appears that the government views the value of such meals as being fairly immaterial (those of you who have consumed airline food would likely agree with this conclusion on the value of such meals). This is reflected in the fact that ITA 67.1(4) deems the food component of the ticket cost to be nil.

"Luxury" Automobile Costs

6-113. When a business provides an automobile to an employee or shareholder, it is clear that these individuals have received a taxable benefit to the extent that they make any personal use of the vehicle. This fact, along with the methods used to calculate the benefit, was covered in detail in Chapter 3. As you will recall, the amount of the benefit is based on the cost of cars purchased or, alternatively, the lease payments made on cars that are leased.

6-114. A different issue relates to the costs that can be deducted by a business in the determination of its net business income, or by any employee in the determination of net employment income. For many years, it has been the policy of the government to discourage the deduction of costs related to the use of what is perceived to be luxury automobiles. This has been accomplished by limiting the amounts that can be deducted for:

- CCA on cars owned by the taxpayer;
- interest costs on cars owned by the taxpayer and financed with debt; and
- lease payments on cars that are leased by the taxpayer.

6-115. Before describing these limitations, we would again remind you that the taxable benefit that results from a business providing an automobile to an employee or shareholder is calculated without regard to restrictions on the deductibility of its costs. For example, if an employee has the exclusive personal use of a passenger vehicle that has been acquired by his employer for $150,000, his basic standby charge for each year would be $36,000 [(2%)(12)($150,000)]. The calculation of this amount will not be affected by the fact that the employer's deduction for CCA on this automobile is based on only $30,000.

Automobiles Owned By The Taxpayer
Limits On CCA - ITA 13(7)(g)
6-116. With respect to cars that are owned by a business, ITA 13(7)(g) limits the deductibility of capital costs to a prescribed amount. From 2001 through 2017, this prescribed amount has been unchanged at $30,000, plus GST/HST and PST. This amount would be reduced by any GST/HST and PST that was recoverable as input tax credits.

Limits On Interest - ITA 67.2
6-117. When the automobile is owned by the business, there may be interest costs associated with related financing. If this is the case, ITA 67.2 restricts the amount of interest that can be deducted to an amount determined by the following formula:

Limitations On Deductions From Business, Property, And Employment Income

$(A \div 30)(B)$, where

A   is a prescribed amount ($300 from 2001 through 2017)
B   is the number of days in the period during which interest is paid or payable

6-118.   While the popular press sometimes describes this limit as $300 per month, you can see from the formula that this is not correct. For 2017, the correct limit is $10 per day.

Exercise Six - 8

Subject: Deductible Automobile Costs (Business Owns Automobile)

On October 1, 2017, Ms. Vanessa Lord purchased an automobile to be used exclusively in her newly formed unincorporated business that commenced operations on September 15, 2017. The cost of the automobile was $45,000, before GST and PST. She finances a part of the purchase price and, as a consequence, has financing charges for the period October 1 to December 31, 2017 of $1,200. In calculating her net business income for 2017, how much can Ms. Lord deduct with respect to this acquisition? Ignore GST and PST considerations.

SOLUTION available in print and online Study Guide.

Automobile Leasing Costs - ITA 67.3
Basic Formula (Cumulative)
6-119.   When a business leases a passenger vehicle, ITA 67.3 restricts the deductibility of the lease payments to a prescribed amount. The basic formula that is used to implement this limitation is as follows:

$$\text{Basic Cumulative Formula} = \left[A \times \frac{B}{30} \right] - C - D - E, \text{ where}$$

A   is a prescribed amount ($800 for vehicles leased in 2001 through 2017);
B   is the number of days from the beginning of the term of the lease to the end of the taxation year (or end of the lease if that occurs during the current year);
C   is the total of all amounts deducted in previous years for leasing the vehicle;
D   is a notional amount of interest since the inception of the lease, calculated at the prescribed rate on refundable amounts paid by the lessee in excess of $1,000;
E   is the total of all reimbursements that became receivable before the end of the year by the taxpayer in respect of the lease.

6-120.   In simplified language, this Section restricts, for leases entered into in the years 2001 through 2017, the deductibility of lease payments to $800 (Item A) plus GST/HST and PST, for each 30 day period from the inception of the lease through the end of the current taxation year. Note that this is a cumulative amount over the entire lease term and this means that the prescribed amount for the year in which the lease is signed is applicable throughout the lease term. That is, if the $800 limit was increased after 2017, the change would have no effect on the leasing cost limit calculations for leases entered into in 2017.

6-121.   The formula also contains components that:

• remove lease payments that were deducted in previous taxation years (Item C);
• require the deduction of imputed interest on refundable deposits that could be used by the lessee to reduce the basic lease payments (Item D);
• remove reimbursements that are receivable by the taxpayer during the year (Item E).

6-122.   In applying this formula, it is important to note that all of the components are cumulative from the inception of the lease.

Limitations On Deductions From Business, Property, And Employment Income

Anti-Avoidance Formula

6-123. While the basic concept of limiting the deductible amount to a prescribed figure is fairly straightforward, it would be very easy to avoid the intended purpose of the preceding formula. Almost any vehicle can be leased for less than $800 per 30 day period through such measures as extending the lease term, or including a required purchase by the lessee at the end of the lease term at an inflated value. Because of this, a second formula is required and is based on the manufacturer's suggested list price for the vehicle and is as follows:

$$\text{Anti-Avoidance Formula} = \left[A \ X \ \frac{B}{.85 \ C} \right] - D - E, \ \text{where}$$

A   is the total of the actual lease charges paid or payable in the year;

B   is a prescribed amount ($30,000 for vehicles leased in 2001 through 2017);

C   is the greater of a prescribed amount ($35,294 for vehicles leased in 2001 through 2017) and the manufacturer's list price for the vehicle (note that this is the original value, even when a used vehicle is leased);

D   is a notional amount of interest for the current year, calculated at the prescribed rate on refundable amounts paid by the lessee in excess of $1,000;

E   is the total of all reimbursements that became receivable during the year by the taxpayer in respect of the lease.

6-124. Note that, unlike the calculations in the basic cumulative formula, the components of this formula are for the current year only. Also note that the .85 in the denominator is based on the assumption of a standard 15 percent discount off the manufacturers' list price. When the list price is $35,294, 85 percent of this amount is $30,000, leaving the (B ÷ .85C) component equal to one. This means that this component only kicks in when the list price exceeds $35,294, a vehicle that the formula assumes has been acquired for $30,000.

Deductible Amount

6-125. ITA 67.3 indicates that, when lease payments are being deducted, the amount cannot exceed the lesser of the two formula based amounts. This means that the deductible amount is the least of:

• the actual amount of the lease payments;
• the amount determined using the basic cumulative formula; and
• the amount determined using the anti-avoidance formula.

Example

6-126. The following example will serve to illustrate the application of these rules.

EXAMPLE A car with a manufacturer's list price of $60,000 is leased on December 1, 2016 by a company for $1,612 per month, payable on the first day of each month. The term of the lease is 24 months and a refundable deposit of $10,000 is made at the inception of the lease. In addition, the employee who drives the car pays the company $200 per month for personal use. Assume that the prescribed rate is 2 percent per annum for all periods under consideration. Ignoring GST and PST implications, determine the maximum deductible lease payments for 2016 and 2017.

ANALYSIS - 2016 For 2016, the D component in both of the ITA 67.3 formulae is $15 [(2%)($10,000 - $1,000)(31/365)]. The E component is $200 [($200)(1)]. The maximum deduction for 2016 is $612, the least of the following amounts:

• [($1,612)(1)] = $1,612

• $\left[\$800 \times \dfrac{31}{30} \right] - \$0 - \$15 - \$200 = \$612$ (Basic cumulative formula)

• $\left[\$1,612 \times \dfrac{\$30,000}{(85\%)(\$60,000)} \right] - \$15 - \$200 = \$733$ (Anti-avoidance formula)

ANALYSIS - 2017   Because the lease was entered into during 2016, the 2016 limit of $800 applies for the life of the lease. For 2017, the D components in the ITA 67.3 formula are $195 [(2%)($10,000 - $1,000)(396/365)] in the basic formula and $180 [(2%)($10,000 - $1,000)(365/365)] in the anti-avoidance formula.

The 2017 E components are $2,600 [($200)(13)] in the basic formula, and $2,400 [($200)(12)] in the anti-avoidance formula.

The maximum deduction for 2017 is $7,153, the least of the following amounts:

- $[(\$1,612)(12)] = \underline{\underline{\$19,344}}$

- $\left[\$800 \times \dfrac{396}{30}\right] - \$612 - \$195 - \$2,600 = \underline{\underline{\$7,153}}$ (Basic cumulative formula)

- $\left[\$19,344 \times \dfrac{\$30,000}{(85\%)(\$60,000)}\right] - \$180 - \$2,400 = \underline{\underline{\$8,799}}$ (Anti-avoidance formula)

Exercise Six - 9

Subject: Deductible Automobile Costs (Business Leases Automobile)

On August 1, 2017, Mr. Sadim Humiz leases an automobile to be used 100 percent of the time in his unincorporated business. The lease cost is $985 per month. The manufacturer's suggested list price for the automobile is $78,000. Mr. Humiz makes no down payment and no refundable deposits. Determine his maximum deduction for lease payments for 2017. Ignore GST and PST considerations.

SOLUTION available in print and online Study Guide.

We suggest you work Self Study Problems Six-4, 5 and 6 at this point.

Leasing Property

6-127.   While, from a legal perspective, leasing a property is a distinctly different transaction than purchasing the same property, the economic substance of many long-term leases is that they are arrangements to finance the acquisition of assets. This fact has long been recognized by accounting standard setters, both in Canada and internationally. Accounting standards for leases require that, when a leasing arrangement transfers the usual risks and rewards of ownership to a lessee, the lease must be treated as a sale by the lessor and a purchase by the lessee.

6-128.   In general, this view is not recognized by the CRA. For tax purposes, a lease is always treated as a lease. The actual lease payments will be included in the income of the lessor and deducted from the income of the lessee. However, there is a provision under ITA 16.1 which allows the lessee and lessor to elect to treat the lease in the same manner that it is treated under accounting rules.

6-129.   This will often create a significant difference between the accounting and tax rules for dealing with leases. For accounting purposes, when a lease transfers the usual risks and rewards of ownership, the lessee will record an asset and an obligation, while the lessor will record either a sale of an asset or a lease receivable. The expenses and revenues related to this approach will often be significantly different from the lease payments and receipts recorded for tax purposes.

Exercise Six - 10

Subject: Leases: Tax vs. GAAP Treatment

Markit Ltd. signs a 10 year lease for an asset with an economic life of 11 years. The lease payments are $23,000 per year. Compare the tax treatment of the lease with its treatment under GAAP.

SOLUTION available in print and online Study Guide.

Illegal Payments, Fines And Penalties - ITA 67.5 And 67.6

6-130.   Under ITA 67.5, "Non-Deductibility Of Illegal Payments", payments made to Canadian or foreign government officials that constitute an offence under certain provisions of either the *Corruption of Public Foreign Officials Act* or Canada's *Criminal Code* are not deductible. This would be the case, even if the related income was taxable.

6-131.   It is not uncommon for fines and penalties to be incurred in the process of carrying on business activity (e.g., the driver for a courier company receives a parking ticket while making a delivery). ITA 67.6, "Non-Deductibility Of Fines And Penalties" states that no deduction can be made for any fine or penalty imposed under a law of a country or of a political subdivision of a country.

6-132.   You can find a more detailed discussion of the issues related to fines and penalties in IT Folio S4-F2-C1, *Deductibility Of Fines And Penalties*.

Business Income - Specific Deductions

Inventory Valuation (Cost Of Sales)
General Procedures
6-133.   IT-473R points out that ITA 10 and ITR 1801 allow two alternative methods of inventory valuation. They are:

- valuation at lower of cost or fair market value for each item (or class of items if specific items are not readily distinguishable) in the inventory;
- valuation of the entire inventory at fair market value.

6-134.   The selected method must be applied consistently from year to year, and cannot normally be changed. IT-473R indicates that, in exceptional circumstances, the CRA will allow a change, provided it can be shown that the new method is more appropriate, it is used consistently in future periods, and the new method is used for financial statement purposes.

6-135.   IT-473R indicates that fair market value can mean either replacement cost or net realizable value. The Bulletin also notes that the method used in determining "fair market value" for income tax purposes should normally be the same as the method used to determine "market" for financial statement purposes.

6-136.   IT-473R indicates that cost can be determined through specific identification, an average cost assumption, a First In, First Out (FIFO) assumption, or through the use of the retail method. However, the Bulletin specifically prohibits the use of a Last In, First Out (LIFO) assumption for the determination of inventory costs. Since GAAP does not allow LIFO for accounting purposes, it cannot be used for either tax or accounting purposes.

Overhead Absorption
6-137.   While not discussed in ITA 10, IT-473R indicates that, in the case of the work in process and finished goods inventories of manufacturing enterprises, an applicable share of overhead should be included. The CRA will accept either direct costing, in which only variable overhead is allocated to inventories, or absorption costing, in which both variable and fixed overhead is added to inventories. The Bulletin does indicate, however, that the method used should be the one that gives the truer picture of the taxpayer's income.

6-138.   Under absorption costing, amortization will generally be a component of the overhead included in beginning and ending inventories. In calculating net business income, the amounts recorded as accounting amortization will be replaced by amounts available as CCA deductions. This process will require adjustments reflecting any amounts of amortization included in beginning and ending inventories. While these adjustments go beyond the scope of this text, interested readers will find that they are illustrated in an Appendix to IT-473R.

Tax Vs. GAAP

6-139.   GAAP rules for inventories (both the *International Financial Reporting Standard* and the *Accounting Standard For Private Enterprises*) can be compared to tax rules as follows:

Inventory Valuation   For tax purposes, inventories can be valued at either lower of cost and fair market value, or at fair market value. The accounting rules require that inventories be valued at the lower of cost and net realizable value.

Determination Of Market   For tax purposes, market can be determined using either replacement cost or net realizable value. The accounting rules require the use of net realizable value.

Determination Of Cost   For tax purposes, cost can be determined using specific identification, a First In, First Out (FIFO) or average cost assumption, or through the use of the retail method. The accounting rules permit the use of the same methods, but is more prescriptive with respect to when each method must be used.

Use Of Direct Costing   The use of direct costing is not permitted for accounting purposes. We have noted that, with respect to this issue, IT-473R does permit the use of direct costing provided it is the method that gives a "truer picture" of the taxpayer's income. However, with the accounting rules prohibiting the use of direct costing, it would be difficult to argue that this method provides such a picture.

6-140.   While there are some differences between the tax rules and the accounting requirements, the two sets of rules are largely the same. Differences can arise, however, in situations where depreciation (CCA) is included in the determination of inventory values.

Special Rule For Artists

6-141.   When artists are required to apply normal inventory valuation procedures, it prevents them from writing off the cost of their various works until they are sold. Given the periods of time that such works are sometimes available for sale, this can result in hardship for some artists. As a consequence, ITA 10(6) allows artists to value their ending inventories at nil, thereby writing off the costs of producing a work prior to its actual sale.

Exercise Six - 11

Subject: Inventory Valuation

Brandon Works sells a single product which it buys from various manufacturers. It has a December 31 year end. During 2017, purchases of this item were as follows:

Date	Quantity	Price
February 1	50,000	$2.50
May 23	35,000	2.85
August 18	62,000	2.95
October 28	84,000	3.05

On December 31, 2017, 102,000 of these items are on hand. Their replacement cost on this date is $3.10 and they are being sold for $4.50. It is estimated that selling costs average 10 percent of the sales price. It is not possible to identify the individual items being sold. Calculate all the values that could be used for the 102,000 remaining units for tax purposes, identifying the method you used for each value.

SOLUTION available in print and online Study Guide.

> **We suggest you work Self Study Problem Six-7 at this point.**

Other Deductions

6-142.   Earlier in this Chapter we described some of the many restrictions that the *Income Tax Act* places on the deduction of items in the determination of net business income. In considering these restrictions, it becomes clear that they also serve to provide general guidance on the items that are deductible.

6-143.   In addition to this general guidance, ITA 20 contains a detailed list of specific items that can be deducted in computing net business income. If an item falls clearly into one of ITA 20's deduction categories, it is not subject to the restrictions listed in ITA 18. Some of the more important deductions described in ITA 20 are as follows:

- 20(1)(a) - **Capital Cost Of Property**   This Paragraph provides for the deduction of a portion of the cost of capital assets as capital cost allowances. The detailed provisions related to this deduction are covered in Chapter 5.

- 20(1)(b) - **Incorporation Expenses**   This paragraph provides for the deduction of up to $3,000 in incorporation expenses. Incorporation expenses in excess of this amount are added to Class 14.1.

  BYRD/CHEN NOTE   Prior to 2017, ITA 20(1)(b) provided for the deduction of cumulative eligible capital amounts. With the elimination of the cumulative eligible capital provisions, this was replaced with a provision which allows for the deduction of up to $3,000 in incorporation expenses. It is likely that this was added so that small corporations would not have to deal with writing off a small Class 14.1 balance.

- 20(1)(c) and (d) - **Interest**   These two Paragraphs cover both current and accrued interest, provided the borrowed money was used to earn business or property income. Chapter 7 contains a detailed discussion of some of the problems that arise in this area.

- 20(1)(e) - **Expenses Re Financing**   In general, costs related to the issuance of shares or incurred on the borrowing of funds must be deducted on a straight-line basis over five years. Any undeducted financing costs can be written off if the loan is repaid or the shares redeemed prior to the end of five years.

- 20(1)(f) - **Discount On Certain Obligations**   For tax purposes, bond discount cannot be amortized over the life of the bonds, the normal accounting treatment. This means that only the amount of interest actually paid can be deducted in the determination of business income. It also means that, since the discount balance is not being amortized, it will have to be deducted when the bonds are retired. If the bonds are issued for not less than 97 percent of their maturity amount and, if the effective yield is not more than 4/3 of the coupon rate, the full amount of the discount can be deducted when the bonds are retired. If these conditions are not met, the payment of the discount at maturity is treated in the same manner as a capital loss, with only one-half of the payment being deductible. Note that the tax treatment of bond premiums also differs from the normal accounting treatment. We would note here that, for tax purposes, bond premiums will not normally be amortized over the life of the bond. This issue is discussed in more detail in Chapter 7 which deals with property income.

- 20(1)(j) - **Repayment Of Loan By Shareholder**   As is explained in Chapter 15, if a loan to a shareholder is carried on the Balance Sheet of a corporation for two consecutive year ends, the principal amount must be added to the income of the borrower. This Paragraph provides for a deduction when such loans are repaid.

- 20(1)(l) - **Reserves For Doubtful Debts** See Paragraphs 6-58 to 6-61.

- 20(1)(m) - **Reserves For Goods And Services To Be Delivered In Future Taxation Years** See Paragraph 6-62.

- 20(1)(m.1) - **Reserves For Warranties** This provision only applies to amounts paid to third parties to provide warranty services. It does not apply to so-called "self warranty" situations where the business that sold the warrantied item assumes the risk of providing warranty services.

- 20(1)(n) - **Reserve For Unpaid Amounts** This reserve provides for limited use of cash based revenue recognition in computing net business income. See Paragraph 6-63.

- 20(1)(p) - **Actual Write Offs Of Bad Debts** See Paragraphs 6-58 to 6-61.

- 20(1)(q) - **Employer's Contributions To Registered Pension Plans** This deduction is subject to the limitations described in Chapter 10. At this point we would note that, unlike the accrual approach to pension costs that is used for financial reporting purposes, this deduction is on a cash basis. For tax purposes, the deduction for pension costs is based entirely on funding payments made during the year or within 120 days after the end of the year.

- 20(1)(y) - **Employer's Contributions Under A Deferred Profit Sharing Plan** Only amounts that are paid during the year or within 120 days of the end of the year can be deducted.

- 20(1)(z) and (z.1) - **Costs Of Cancellation Of A Lease** This deduction, in effect, requires amounts paid by a lessor to cancel a lease to be treated as a prepaid expense. Such amounts can be deducted on a pro rata per diem basis over the remaining term of the lease, including all renewal periods. If the property is sold subsequent to the cancellation, the remaining balance can be deducted at that time. If the property is a capital property, only one-half of the remaining balance can be deducted.

- 20(1)(aa) - **Costs For Landscaping Of Grounds** In the absence of this provision, landscaping costs would have to be treated as a capital expenditure. While this provision allows for an immediate deduction, it is based on amounts paid in the year. Costs accrued at the end of the taxation year cannot be deducted.

- 20(1)(cc) - **Expenses Of Representation**

- 20(1)(dd) - **Costs Of Investigation Of A Site To Be Used In The Business**

- 20(1)(oo) - **Amounts Deferred Under A Salary Deferral Arrangement**

- 20(1)(qq) and (rr) - **Disability Related Costs** These two paragraphs allow the costs of disability related building modifications and acquisitions of disability related equipment to be treated as current deductions, rather than as capital assets. Like the similar provision for landscaping costs, the deduction is only available for amounts paid during the year.

- 20(4) - **Uncollectible Portion Of Proceeds From Disposition Of A Depreciable Property**

- 20(10) - **Convention Expenses** This allows the taxpayer to deduct the costs of attending no more than two conventions held during the year, provided they are in a location that is consistent with the territorial scope of the organization.

- 20(11) - **Foreign Taxes On Income From Property Exceeding 15 Percent** This provision is only applicable to individuals and reflects the fact that an individual's credit for foreign taxes paid is limited to 15 percent. This matter is discussed in Chapters 7 and 11.

- 20(16) - **Terminal Losses** This deduction was explained in Chapter 5.

Figure 6 - 3
Conversion Of Accounting Net Income To Net Income For Tax Purposes

Additions To Accounting Income:

- Income tax expense
- Amortization, depreciation, and depletion of tangible and intangible assets (accounting amounts)
- Recapture of CCA
- Tax reserves deducted in the prior year
- Losses on the disposition of capital assets (accounting amounts)
- Pension expense (accounting amounts)
- Scientific research expenditures (accounting amounts)
- Warranty expense (accounting amounts)
- Amortization of discount on long-term debt issued (see discussion in Chapter 7)
- Foreign tax paid (accounting amounts)
- Excess of taxable capital gains over allowable capital losses
- Interest and penalties on income tax assessments
- Non-deductible automobile costs
- 50 percent of business meals and entertainment expenses
- Club dues and cost of recreational facilities
- Non-deductible reserves (accounting amounts)
- Charitable donations
- Asset write-downs including impairment losses on intangibles
- Fines, penalties, and illegal payments

Deductions From Accounting Income:

- Capital cost allowances (CCA)
- Incorporation costs (First $3,000)
- Terminal losses
- Tax reserves claimed for the current year
- Gains on the disposition of capital assets (accounting amounts)
- Pension funding contributions
- Deductible scientific research expenditures
- Deductible warranty expenditures
- Amortization of premium on long-term debt issued
- Foreign non-business tax deduction [ITA 20 (12)]
- Allowable business investment losses
- Landscaping costs

Reconciliation Schedule

6-144.   While it would be possible to calculate net business income starting with a blank page, adding inclusions, and subtracting deductions, this approach is rarely used. Since most businesses have an accounting system that produces an accounting Net Income figure, the normal approach to determining net business income is to start with accounting Net Income, then add and deduct various items that are different for tax purposes. Note, however, that some smaller businesses that do not require audited financial statements base their regular accounting system on tax rules. In such cases, no reconciliation is needed.

6-145.   For those businesses that base their accounting system in whole or part on GAAP, a reconciliation between accounting Net Income and net business income is required. While there are many other items that could require adjustment, the items shown in Figure 6-3 are the common reconciliation items for most taxpayers.

6-146.   In working with this schedule, several general points are relevant:

- Accounting Net Income is an after tax concept. This means that the Tax Expense that is recorded in the accounting records must be added back in this reconciliation schedule. This addition would include both the current tax expense and any future tax expense or benefit recorded under GAAP.

- The amounts deducted in the accounting records for amortization, scientific research, and resource amounts will generally be different from the amounts deducted for tax purposes. While it would be possible to simply deduct the net difference (the tax amount is normally larger than the accounting amount), the traditional practice here is to add back the accounting amount and subtract the tax amount (e.g., we add back accounting amortization and subtract CCA).

- Accounting gains on the disposition of capital assets will be deducted and losses added in this schedule. With these amounts removed, they will be replaced by the relevant tax amounts. As explained in Chapter 5, the disposition of depreciable capital assets can result in capital gains, recapture, or terminal losses. In addition, capital losses can arise on the disposition of non-depreciable capital assets. These amounts are listed separately in Figure 6-3.

- As was noted in Chapter 1, allowable capital losses can only be deducted against taxable capital gains. As a consequence, only the excess of taxable capital gains over allowable capital losses is included in this schedule. If there is an excess of allowable capital losses over taxable capital gains in the current year, the excess can be carried forward or carried back, but it cannot be deducted in the current year. As a consequence, such amounts are not included in this reconciliation schedule.

- You will note that there are no adjustments related to either Sales or Cost Of Sales. With respect to sales, this simply reflects the fact that the tax and accounting rules produce, in the great majority of situations, identical results. With respect to Cost Of Sales, differences between the *Income Tax Act* and GAAP are not common and were covered in Paragraph 6-139.

Business Income - Example

Example Data

6-147. The Markee Company has a December 31 accounting and taxation year end and, for the year ending December 31, 2017, its GAAP determined income before taxes amounted to $1,263,000. You have been asked to calculate the Company's 2017 Net Income For Tax Purposes, and have been provided with the following additional information concerning the 2017 fiscal year:

1. Accounting amortization expense totalled $240,000. For tax purposes, the Company intends to deduct CCA of $280,000.

2. Accounting income includes a gain on the sale of land in the amount of $20,000. For tax purposes, one-half of this amount will be treated as a taxable capital gain.

3. During December, the Company spent $35,000 on landscaping costs. These costs were capitalized in the Company's accounting records. As the expenditure was near the end of the year, no amortization was recorded.

4. The Company's Interest Expense includes $5,000 in bond discount amortization.

5. Financing costs, incurred on January 1, to issue new common stock during the year totaled $60,000. All of these costs were charged to expense in the accounting records.

6. Accounting expenses include $48,000 in business meals and entertainment.

7. During the year, the Company begins selling a product on which it provides a five year warranty. At the end of the year, it recognizes a warranty liability of $20,000.

8. In the accounting records, the Company recognized a Pension Expense of $167,000. Contributions to the pension fund totaled $150,000.

9. The Company leased a car beginning on June 1, 2016 that is used by the sales manager. The lease payments are $750 per month on a car with a manufacturer's suggested list price of $33,000. No refundable deposit was paid.

Example Analysis

6-148. The following points are relevant to the Net Income calculation:

- Item 1 - The accounting amortization has to be added back and replaced with the CCA deduction.

- Item 2 - The accounting gain has to be removed and replaced by the taxable capital gain.

- Item 3 - Despite the fact that landscaping costs are usually capital costs, ITA 20(1)(aa) specifically permits their immediate deduction.

- Item 4 - The bond discount has to be added back to income.

- Item 5 - Financing costs must be amortized over five years on a straight-line basis under ITA 20(1)(e). As a result, only $12,000 is deductible in the current year and $48,000 must be added back to income.

- Item 6 - Only 50 percent of business meals and entertainment can be deducted.

- Item 7 - Warranty costs can only be deducted as incurred.

- Item 8 - Pension costs can only be deducted when they are funded.

- Item 9 - The lease payments are not limited by the restrictions described beginning in Paragraph 6-119. As a result, the payments are fully deductible and no adjustment is needed.

6-149. Based on the preceding analysis, the calculation of 2017 Net Income For Tax Purposes would be as follows:

Accounting Income Before Taxes		$1,263,000
Additions (Identified By Item Number):		
1 - Accounting amortization	$240,000	
2 - Taxable capital gain on land sale [(1/2)($20,000)]	10,000	
4 - Bond discount amortization	5,000	
5 - Financing costs [(80%)($60,000)]	48,000	
6 - Meals and entertainment [(50%)($48,000)]	24,000	
7 - Warranty liability	20,000	
8 - Unfunded pension expense ($167,000 - $150,000)	17,000	364,000
Deductions (Identified By Item Number):		
1 - Capital Cost Allowance (CCA)	($280,000)	
2 - Accounting gain on sale of land	(20,000)	
3 - Landscaping costs	(35,000)	(335,000)
Net Income For Tax Purposes		$1,292,000

We suggest you work Self Study Problems Six-8, 9, and 10 at this point.

Taxation Year

General Rules

6-150. The *Act* defines a taxation year as follows:

ITA 249(1) For the purpose of this Act, a "taxation year" is

(a) in the case of a corporation, a fiscal period, and

(b) in the case of an individual, a calendar year,

and when a taxation year is referred to by reference to a calendar year, the reference is to the taxation year or years coinciding with, or ending in, that year.

6-151.   For corporations, ITA 249.1(1) defines a fiscal period as a period that does not exceed 53 weeks. The 53 week designation provides for situations where a corporation wishes to have a fiscal period that ends in a specified week within a month. For example, if the corporate year end is the last Friday in January, the fiscal year will, in some years, include 53 weeks.

6-152.   A new corporation can select any fiscal year end. However, subsequent changes require the approval of the Minister, unless a specific provision provides for a change (e.g., and amalgamation or change in control). In most situations, corporations will have a fiscal year for tax purposes that coincides with the fiscal period used in their financial statements.

Unincorporated Businesses - Non-Calendar Fiscal Year

6-153.   Unincorporated businesses such as proprietorships and partnerships are not, for income tax purposes, separate taxable entities. The income of such businesses is included in the tax return of the individual proprietor or partner.

6-154.   While unincorporated businesses are not required to file an income tax return, they are required to calculate an annual business income figure to be included in the tax returns of their owners. Given that the individuals who are the owners of proprietorships and partnerships must use a taxation year based on the calendar year, it would seem logical to require that these unincorporated businesses also base their taxation year on a calendar year.

6-155.   This logic is overridden, however, by the fact that there can be important reasons, unrelated to income tax, for the use of a non-calendar fiscal year (e.g., having the year end at a low point in the activity of the business). As a consequence, under ITA 249.1(4), a proprietorship or partnership can elect to have a fiscal year that does not end on December 31.

6-156.   This election is available to any new unincorporated business. However, it must be made on or before the filing date for the individual proprietor or partner. This would be June 15 of the year following the year in which the business commences. The election cannot be made in a subsequent year.

6-157.   If the election is made, ITA 34.1(1) requires taxpayers to include an amount of income for the period between the end of their normal fiscal year and December 31 of that year. This income is referred to as "additional business income" and, in simple terms, it is a pro rata extrapolation of the income earned during the non-calendar fiscal period that ends in the year. It is used to create an estimate of the income that will be earned from the end of the non-calendar fiscal period to the end of the calendar year. A simple example will illustrate this process.

> **EXAMPLE**   Jack Bartowski forms a new business on November 1, 2016. Because of the cyclical nature of his business, he chooses a January 31 year end as it is a slow time in the business. Between November 1, 2016 and January 31, 2017, he has net business income of $25,000. During the fiscal year ending January 31, 2018, the net business income is $80,000.
>
> **ANALYSIS - 2017**   The period November 1, 2016 through January 31, 2017 has 92 days. The period from February 1, 2017 to December 31, 2017 has 334 days. Based on this, the "additional business income" that must be added for 2017 is calculated as follows:
>
> $$[(\$25{,}000)(334 \text{ Days} \div 92 \text{ Days})] = \underline{\$90{,}761}$$
>
> The income that will be reported by Mr. Bartowski in his 2017 personal tax return is calculated as follows:
>
> | | |
> |---|---:|
> | Actual Business Income: | |
> | November 1, 2016 To January 31, 2017 | $ 25,000 |
> | Additional Business Income: | |
> | February 1, 2017 To December 31, 2017 (Estimate) | 90,761 |
> | 2017 Business Income | $115,761 |

Note that he will be taxed on his estimated income for 14 months. There is an election available that would alleviate this situation by allowing him to report the November and December 2016 income in 2016, and not 2017.

ANALYSIS - 2018   The "additional business income" that must be added for 2018 is calculated as follows:

$$[(\$80,000)(334 \text{ Days} \div 365 \text{ Days})] = \underline{\$73,205}$$

The 2018 business income will be calculated by taking the actual figure for February 1, 2017 through January 31, 2018, deducting the additional business income that was included in his 2017 tax return, and adding the new additional business income for the period February 1, 2018 through December 31, 2018. The calculations are as follows:

Actual Business Income - February 1, 2017 To January 31, 2018	$80,000
Additional Business Income:	
Deduction Of Estimated Amount Added In 2017	(90,761)
Addition Of Estimate Of Income for Feb. 1 to Dec. 31, 2018	73,205
2018 Business Income	$62,444

Exercise Six - 12

Subject: Additional Business Income - Non-Calendar Fiscal Year

Mr. Morgan Gelato starts a business on March 1, 2017. Because it will be a slow time of year for him, he intends to have a fiscal year that ends on June 30. During the period March 1, 2017, through June 30, 2017, his business has income of $12,300. What amount of business income will Mr. Gelato report in his personal tax return for the year ending December 31, 2017?

SOLUTION available in print and online Study Guide.

We suggest you work Self Study Problem Six-11 at this point.

Special Business Income Situations

Income For Farmers

Farm Losses

6-158.   For an individual who looks to farming as his chief source of activity and income, farm losses are fully deductible against other types of income. The difficulty with farm losses is that there are various levels of interest in farming activity, ranging from a full time endeavour to produce profits from farming, through situations where an individual acquires a luxury home in a rural setting, allows three chickens to run loose in the backyard, and then tries to deduct all the costs of owning and operating the property as a "farm loss". In the latter case, the ownership of a "farm" is nothing more than a hobby or a means to enhance the individual's lifestyle.

6-159.   For such hobby farmers, engaged in farming activity as merely an attractive addition to a lifestyle and with no serious intent to produce a profit from this type of activity, the costs of farming must be viewed as personal living expenses. This means that no portion of farm losses should be considered deductible by hobby farmers.

Restricted Farm Losses

6-160. The more complex situation is an individual who expects to make a profit from farming but, in addition, has another source of income (e.g., a university professor who grows medicinal marijuana on a part time basis). In such situations, ITA 31 restricts the amount of farm losses that can be deducted.

6-161. This provision indicates that farm losses are subject to limits:

"... if a taxpayer's chief source of income for a taxation year is neither farming nor a combination of farming and some other source of income that is a subordinate source of income for the taxpayer ..."

6-162. Stated alternatively, this provision states that in situations where an individual has both farming income and some other source of income, farm losses will be limited unless the other source of income is less important than the taxpayer's farming source.

6-163. As a result of this legislation, there are three classes of farmers.

- Hobby farmers with no expectation of profit. Such taxpayers cannot deduct any farm losses.
- Farmers whose major source of income is farming. Such taxpayers can deduct all of their losses against other sources of income; and
- Part-time farmers for whom farming income is a secondary source of income. Such farmers would have their losses "restricted" under ITA 31.

6-164. For part-time farmers, the limit on the amount of current year farming losses that can be deducted against other current year sources of income is equal to the first $2,500 of such losses, plus one-half of the next $30,000, for a maximum deduction of $17,500 [$2,500 + (1/2) ($32,500 maximum - $2,500)] on farm losses of $32,500 or greater. Any amount of the farm loss that is not deductible in the current year is commonly referred to as a "restricted farm loss". Such amounts can be carried over to past or future years, but can only be deducted to the extent of farm income in the carry over years (see Chapter 11 for a more complete discussion of loss carry overs).

Exercise Six - 13

Subject: Farm Losses

Ms. Suzanne Morph is a high school teacher. To help finance the annual family vacation, she has been growing zucchinis for sale in a little plot next to her house. Her investment in time and money in this endeavor has been small, but the growing conditions are ideal for zucchinis. Although she has no farming background, in most years she has made a small profit selling at the weekly farmers' market for two months in the summer. However, she incurred a loss in 2017 of $18,700 due to a lawsuit claiming her zucchinis poisoned a customer. How much of this loss is deductible in her 2017 tax return? Calculate any farm loss carry over available to her.

SOLUTION available in print and online Study Guide.

Farming Income And Cash Basis Accounting

6-165. As previously noted in this Chapter, business income is generally computed on the basis of accrual accounting. A major exception to this is permitted in ITA 28 for taxpayers engaged in a farming or fishing business. They can elect to determine income on a cash basis.

6-166. As most farmers will have receivables and inventories in excess of their payables, the ability to calculate income on a cash basis has a general tendency to defer the payment of tax. While it is clear that the original intent of ITA 28 was to provide this form of relief to the farming industry, the government became concerned that taxpayers were using even bona fide farms, in contrast to those described previously as hobby farms, as tax shelters, particularly in years when losses were incurred.

6-167.   The remedy to this problem that has evolved is to require an inventory adjustment in those cases where the use of the cash basis produces a loss. This requires the lesser of the amount of the cash basis loss and the value of purchased inventories to be added back to the cash basis income. The tax rules for farming income can be very complex. There is limited coverage of farm loss carry overs in Chapter 11. However detailed coverage of farming income is beyond the scope of this text.

6-168.   Although the procedures involved are complicated by a number of factors, a simple example will illustrate the basic calculation:

> **EXAMPLE**   Garfield Farms begins operations on January 1, 2017. At this time, it has no Accounts Receivable, Accounts Payable, or Inventories. The Loss on a cash basis for the year ending December 31, 2017 amounted to $600,000. On December 31, 2017, Garfield Farms has the following:
>
> - Accounts Receivable of $2,000,000
> - Inventories that total $1,400,000
> - Accounts Payable of $750,000
>
> **ANALYSIS - Inventory Adjustment**   A mandatory inventory adjustment of $600,000 (lesser of the $600,000 loss and $1,400,000 in inventories) would be added to the cash basis loss of $600,000, resulting in a final income figure for tax purposes of nil.
>
> **ANALYSIS - Accrual Basis Income**   If cash basis accounting was not used, normal accrual basis income for the year ending December 31, 2017 would amount to $2,050,000 (-$600,000 + $2,000,000 + $1,400,000 - $750,000).

Lifetime Capital Gains Deduction Available For Farm Properties

6-169.   One of the most important tax benefits available to Canadian residents is the lifetime capital gains deduction. This deduction can provide for up to $1 million of capital gains on dispositions of qualified farm properties and fishing properties to be received tax free. This complex provision, which can also apply to gains on the shares of qualified small business corporations, is discussed in detail in Chapter 11.

Professional Income (Billed Basis Of Recognition)

> **BYRD/CHEN NOTE**   In the material that follows, we describe a procedure that allows certain professionals to defer taxes on their work in process. Under normal accrual procedures, the revenue associated with work in progress would be included in Net Income For Tax Purposes as the work progressed. In contrast, some professionals were allowed to elect to use a procedure under which work in process was not included in Net Income For Tax Purposes until it was billed, resulting in what could be a significant tax deferral.
>
> The government has concluded that this procedure is no longer appropriate and, in the March 22, 2017 Federal budget, they have indicated that it will be eliminated.
>
> To soften the blow, a transitional provision has been provided. For taxation years that begin on or after the budget day, the billed basis will be available on one-half of the professional's work in process. For subsequent years it will not be available on any of the work in process.
>
> Most of our examples involve calendar taxation years. For such years, the change will have no effect in 2017, will be available on one-half of the work in process for 2018, and will become totally unavailable for 2019.

6-170.   When a business involves the delivery of professional services, clients are billed on a periodic basis, normally after a block of work has been completed. This block of work may be task defined (e.g., billing when a client's tax return is finished), time defined (e.g., billing on a monthly basis), or on some other basis. However, in the majority of professional income situations, billing does not occur until after the work has been completed.

6-171.   If the normal accrual approach was applied to this type of business income, the inclusion in net business income would be recorded at the time work is being done. This would require the inclusion of work in progress (i.e., unbilled receivables) in net business income.

6-172.   However, ITA 34 contains a special rule that is applicable to accountants, dentists, lawyers, medical doctors, veterinarians, and chiropractors. These professionals can elect not to include unbilled work in progress in their income. This so-called "billed basis of income recognition" is not available to other professionals such as architects, engineers, and management consultants.

> **EXAMPLE**   Ms. Shelly Hart begins her new accounting practice on January 1, 2017. During her first year of operation, she records 2,050 billable hours. Her regular billing rate is $100 per hour and, at the end of her first year, she has billed 1,750 hours, or a total of $175,000. Of this amount, $32,300 is uncollected at the end of the year.

> **ANALYSIS**   As Ms. Hart is an accountant, she can elect the use of the billed basis. If she does so, her inclusion in Net Income For Tax Purposes will be $175,000. Alternatively, if she used the normal accrual approach, the inclusion would be $205,000 [($100)(2,050)]. It would clearly be to her advantage to use the billed basis.

Exercise Six - 14

Subject: Professional Income (Billed Basis Of Recognition)

Jack Winters is a lawyer and, at the beginning of the current year, he had unbilled work in process of $35,000, as well as uncollected billings of $57,000. During the year, he bills the remaining work in process and collects all of these new receivables, as well as the uncollected amounts that were present at the beginning of the year. His work during the year totals potential billings of $245,000. Of this amount, $185,000 has been billed and $160,000 of these billings have been collected. Calculate his inclusion in net business income for the year using:

- the cash basis;
- the billed basis; and
- accrual accounting.

SOLUTION available in print and online Study Guide.

We suggest you work Self Study Problems Six-12 and Six-13 at this point.

Sale Of A Business
General Rules

6-173.   ITA 22 through 25 contain a group of provisions that apply when a person sells substantially all of the assets that have been used to carry on a business. The need for special provisions here reflects the fact that, because the business in its entirety is considered to be a capital asset, the gains or losses that result from the sale would be considered to be capital in nature.

6-174.   While this capital gains treatment may be appropriate with respect to many of the assets of a business, gains and losses on the sale of some assets would not be considered capital in nature. In particular, a separate sale of either inventories or accounts receivable would normally result in business income or loss, not a capital gain or loss. Because of this anomaly, there are special provisions with respect to gains and losses on the disposition of these assets when they are sold as part of a business disposition.

Inventories

6-175.   ITA 23 provides that when inventories are included in the sale of a business, the sale will be viewed as being in the ordinary course of carrying on the business. This means that any gain or loss resulting from a sale of inventory will be treated as business income or loss. No election is required to produce this result.

Accounts Receivable - ITA 22 Election

6-176.   In dealing with the sale of accounts receivable as part of the disposition of a business, there are two basic problems. The first is that, if the receivables are worth less than their carrying value, the difference will be considered to be a capital loss. This means that only one-half of the amount of the loss will be deductible, and that the deduction can only be made against taxable capital gains.

6-177.   The second problem is that bad debts cannot be deducted, or a reserve established, unless the receivables have been previously included in income. In the case of the sale of a business, this would create a problem for the purchaser in that the purchased receivables would never have been included in his income.

6-178.   To deal with these two problems, ITA 22 provides for a joint election by the vendor and purchaser of the accounts receivable. The following example illustrates the application of this election.

EXAMPLE   Mr. Whitney agrees to buy Mr. Blackmore's business. As part of the transaction, Mr. Whitney acquires Mr. Blackmore's trade receivables for $25,000. These receivables have a face value of $30,000 and Mr. Blackmore has deducted a $4,000 reserve for doubtful debts with respect to these receivables.

ANALYSIS - Vendor   Whether or not the election is made under ITA 22, Mr. Blackmore will have to include the $4,000 reserve in business income. If no election is made, he will then record an allowable capital loss of $2,500 [(1/2)($30,000 - $25,000)]. Assuming Mr. Blackmore has taxable capital gains against which the $2,500 loss can be deducted, the transaction will result in a net inclusion in income of $1,500 ($4,000 - $2,500).

In contrast, if the ITA 22 election is made, Mr. Blackmore would still have to include the $4,000 reserve in income. However, it will be offset by a business loss of $5,000 on the sale of the receivables, a distinct improvement over the results with no election. Under this approach, there will be a net deduction from income of $1,000.

ANALYSIS - Purchaser   From the point of view of Mr. Whitney, if no election is made, he will record the receivables as a $25,000 capital asset. If more or less than $25,000 is actually collected, the difference will be a capital gain or a capital loss.

If, however, the ITA 22 election is made, he will have to include the $5,000 difference between the face value and the price paid in income, in the year the receivables are acquired. Subsequent to the sale, any difference between the $30,000 face value of the receivables and amounts actually collected will be fully deductible in the calculation of net business income. Mr. Whitney could establish a new reserve for doubtful debts related to the purchased receivables that are still outstanding at the year end. If the amount collected is equal to $25,000, Mr. Whitney will be in exactly the same position, whether or not the election is made. If more than $25,000 is collected, he will be worse off with the election because 100 percent rather than one-half of the excess will be taxable. Correspondingly, if less than $25,000 is collected, he will be better off with the election as the shortfall will be fully deductible.

Exercise Six - 15

Subject: Sale Of Receivables

Mr. Donato Nero is selling his unincorporated business during 2017. Included in his assets are accounts receivable with a face value of $53,450. He and the purchaser of the business, Mr. Labelle, have agreed that the net realizable value of these receivables is $48,200. In 2016, Mr. Nero deducted a reserve for doubtful debts of $3,800. Determine the tax consequences of the sale of these receivables for Mr. Nero and Mr. Labelle, provided that they jointly elect under ITA 22.

SOLUTION available in print and online Study Guide.

We suggest you work Self Study Problems Six-14, 15 and 16 at this point.

Scientific Research And Experimental Development

6-179.   In an effort to encourage expenditures in this area of business activity, special provisions for scientific research and experimental development (SR&ED) expenditures are provided in ITA 37 as well as other Sections of the *Income Tax Act*. As SR&ED expenditures are usually made by corporations, our coverage of them is found in Chapter 14, "Other Issues In Corporate Taxation".

Additional Supplementary Self Study Problems Are Available Online.

Key Terms Used In This Chapter

6-180.   The following is a list of the key terms used in this Chapter. These terms, and their meanings, are compiled in the Glossary located at the back of the Study Guide.

Accrual Basis	Inventory
Allowable Capital Loss	Net Business Income
Billed Basis	Net Income
Business	Property Income
Business Income	Reserve
Capital Asset	Restricted Farm Loss
Capital Gain/Loss	Restrictive Covenant
Cash Basis	Soft Costs
Crowdfunding	Specified Shareholder [ITA 18(5)]
Fiscal Period	Taxable Capital Gain
GAAP	Taxation Year
Hobby Farmer	Thin Capitalization

References

6-181.   For more detailed study of the material in this Chapter, we would refer you to the following:

ITA 9	Income
ITA 10	Valuation Of Inventory
ITA 12	Income Inclusions
ITA 18	General Limitations [On Deductions]
ITA 20	Deductions Permitted In Computing Income From Business Or Property
ITA 22	Sale Of Accounts Receivable
ITA 23	Sale Of Inventory
ITA 24	Ceasing To Carry On Business
ITA 28	Farming Or Fishing Business
ITA 31	Loss From Farming Where Chief Source Of Income Not Farming
ITA 34	Professional Business
ITA 67	General Limitation Re Expenses
ITA 67.1	Expenses For Food
ITA 67.2	Interest On Money Borrowed For Passenger Vehicle
ITA 67.3	Limitation Re Cost Of Leasing Passenger Vehicle
ITA 67.5	Non-Deductibility Of Illegal Payments
ITA 67.6	Non-Deductibility Of Fines And Penalties
S3-F9-C1	Lottery Winnings, Miscellaneous Receipts, and Income (and Losses) from Crime
S4-F2-C1	Deductibility Of Fines Or Penalties
S4-F2-C2	Business Use of Home Expenses
IT-51R2	Supplies On Hand At The End Of A Fiscal Period
IT-99R5	Legal And Accounting Fees (Consolidated)
IT-154R	Special Reserves
IT-188R	Sale Of Accounts Receivable
IT-218R	Profit, Capital Gains And Losses From The Sale Of Real Estate, Including Farmland And Inherited Land And Conversion Of Real Estate From Capital Property To Inventory And Vice Versa
IT-287R2	Sale Of Inventory
IT-322R	Farm Losses
IT-357R2	Expenses Of Training
IT-359R2	Premiums And Other Amounts With Respect To Leases
IT-364	Commencement Of Business Operations
IT-417R2	Prepaid Expenses And Deferred Charges
IT-433R	Farming Or Fishing - Use Of Cash Method
IT-442R	Bad Debts And Reserves For Doubtful Debts
IT-457	Election By Professionals To Exclude Work In Progress From Income
IT-459	Adventure Or Concern In The Nature Of Trade
IT-473R	Inventory Valuation
IT-475	Expenditures On Research And For Business Expansion
IT-479R	Transactions In Securities
IT-487	General Limitation On Deduction of Outlays or Expenses
IT-518R	Food, Beverages And Entertainment Expenses
IT-521R	Motor Vehicle Expenses Claimed By Self-Employed Individuals
IT-525R	Performing Artists (Consolidated)

Problems For Self Study (Online)

To provide practice in problem solving, there are Self Study and Supplementary Self Study problems available on the Companion Website.

Within the text we have provided an indication of when it would be appropriate to work each Self Study problem. The detailed solutions for Self Study problems can be found in the print and online Study Guide.

We provide the Supplementary Self Study problems for those who would like additional practice in problem solving. The detailed solutions for the Supplementary Self Study problems are available online, not in the Study Guide.

The .PDF file "Self Study Problems for Volume 1" on the Companion Website contains the following for Chapter 6:

- 16 Self Study problems,
- 6 Supplementary Self Study problems, and
- detailed solutions for the Supplementary Self Study problems.

Assignment Problems

(The solutions for these problems are only available in
the solutions manual that has been provided to your instructor.)

Assignment Problem Six - 1
(Bad Debts)
Coretta Kirkman is the sole proprietor of an unincorporated business that sells security related products to both retail customers and to building contractors. The business began operations on January 1, 2017. The business will use a December 31 end.

The following information relates to the year ending December 31, 2017:

- Cash sales of delivered merchandise total $375,000.

- Account sales of delivered merchandise total $130,000.

- As of December 31, uncollected Accounts Receivable balances total $55,000. Coretta expects $6,000 of the accounts to become uncollectible.

- Coretta's business receives payments of $36,000 for merchandise to be delivered in 2018.

- During 2017, Coretta's business installs a comprehensive security system in a 462 unit condominium development. The gross profit on this sale was $12,500. Because of the size of the contract, Coretta agrees to accept payment in three instalments as follows:

2017	$23,000
2018	32,000
2019	18,000
Total Contract Price	$73,000

The following information relates to the year ending December 31, 2018:

- A total of $5,800 of accounts receivable were written off during the year.

- All of the merchandise on which 2017 deposits were received was delivered.

- The $32,000 instalment on the condominium project was received.

- Sales of delivered merchandise and services totaled $520,000, with $150,000 of this amount being on account. As of December 31, $52,000 of the account sales had not been collected. Coretta anticipates that $7,500 of these outstanding accounts will not be collectible.

- In addition to sales of delivered merchandise, the business received deposits on orders in the amount of $29,000. This merchandise is scheduled to be delivered in early 2019.

Required: How would the preceding information affect the calculation of Coretta Kirkman's business income for the 2017 and 2018 taxation years? Include the full details of your calculations for each year, not just the net result for each year. Ignore GST/PST implications.

Assignment Problem Six - 2
(Deductible Automobile Costs And Taxable Benefit)

Bob Neat is the sole shareholder and only employee of Bob's Bookkeeping Services Ltd., a Canadian controlled private corporation with a December 31 year end. The Company provides on-site bookkeeping services to a number of clients in the greater Toronto area.

As Bob must travel extensively to service clients, the Company provides him with a vehicle to be used in his work. As Bob does not personally own a vehicle, he also uses the vehicle for personal travel. During 2017, two different vehicles were provided:

Ford Focus   During the period January 1, 2017 through April 30, 2017, Bob had use of a Ford Focus that had been purchased in 2016 for $23,600. As of January 1, 2017, the Class 10 UCC balance was $20,060. During this period, Bob drove the car a total of 31,000 kilometers, 18,000 of which related to his work for the Company. On April 30, 2017, the car was sold for proceeds of $18,200.

Mercedes E-Class Sedan   As the business was becoming very profitable, Bob decided he deserved a better equipped and more comfortable vehicle. On May 1, 2017, the Company acquires a Mercedes E-Class sedan for $52,000. During the period May 1 through December 31, 2017, Bob drives the car a total of 42,000 kilometers, 23,000 of which involved personal activities.

These were the only vehicles owned by Bob's Bookkeeping Services during 2017. Bob had one of these vehicles available to him at all times during 2017.

Throughout 2017, the Company paid for all of the operating costs of both vehicles, a total of $17,460.

Required: Determine the following:

A. The tax consequences to Bob's Bookkeeping Services Ltd. that result from owning and selling the Ford Focus and owning the Mercedes E-Class sedan during 2017.

B. The minimum amount of the taxable benefit that Bob will have to include in his Net Income For Tax Purposes for 2017.

Ignore HST considerations in your solution.

Assignment Problem Six - 3
(Employer Provided Vs. Employee Owned Vehicle)

Jordan Nash has an employment contract with Emmitt Industries, a Canadian public company. The contract commences as of January 1, 2017 and covers the three years ending December 31, 2019. His income is well above the floor of the maximum tax bracket and, given this, the combined federal/provincial tax rate that is effective for any additional income or deductions is 50 percent.

Jordan will require a vehicle for use in his employment duties. Because of the nature of his work, a luxury vehicle is required and he and Emmitt have agreed that a $125,000 BMW 750 would be an appropriate choice. Based on this decision, Emmitt has offered Jordan the following two alternatives. Emmitt is indifferent as to which alternative he chooses.

Alternative 1   The Company will provide the automobile and pay all of the operating costs, including those related to Jordan's personal use of the vehicle. The automobile will be available to Jordan on a full time basis throughout the three year term of his employment contract. It will be returned to the Company at the end of that period.

Alternative 2   The Company will provide Jordan with an interest free loan for $125,000 in order to facilitate the purchase of the vehicle. No payments are required on the loan and it must be repaid in full on December 31, 2019. Jordan will pay all of the operating costs for the vehicle and, to assist with these costs, the Company will provide Jordan with an allowance of $2,000 per month. Jordan will retain ownership of the vehicle at the end of his employment contract.

In order to make a decision on these alternatives, Jordan recognizes the need to make estimates of both operating costs and usage of the automobile. The estimates that he will use in making his decision are as follows:

- He anticipates driving the vehicle 65,000 kilometers each year, with 18,000 of these kilometers being for personal usage.

- If he owns the vehicle, he estimates that his operating costs will average $0.32 per kilometer over the three year term of his employment contract. At the end of the employment contract, he will sell the vehicle and estimates that the proceeds will be $52,000.

Assume that the prescribed rate for the operating cost benefit is $0.25 per kilometer in all of the years 2017 through 2019, and that the prescribed interest rate is 2 percent throughout this period.

Required: Advise Jordan as to which of the alternatives he should accept. Base your decision on the undiscounted cash flows associated with the two alternatives. Ignore GST/HST considerations.

Assignment Problem Six - 4
(Valuation Of Business Inventories)

Alphonse Bona owns and operates an unincorporated business which sells a single product to retail customers. During his first year of operations, his purchases are as follows:

Date	Quantity	Price	Total Cost
January 20	10,300	$2.50	$ 25,750
March 12	11,400	$2.75	31,350
June 15	12,600	$3.15	39,690
October 8	10,200	$3.27	33,354
December 9	8,600	$2.85	24,510
Totals	53,100		$154,654

On December 31, the end of his first year of operation, the inventory on hand amounts to 19,400 units. It is estimated that these units have a replacement cost of $2.90 per unit and a net realizable value of $3.18 per unit.

Required: Calculate the various closing inventory values that could be used to determine business income for tax purposes. Your answer should indicate the valuation method being used, as well as the resulting value.

Assignment Problem Six - 5
(Proprietorship - Reverse Business Income)

Several years ago George Danton, after being laid off, decided he could benefit from his love of flowers and fascination for viewing dead bodies by opening a flower shop. This allowed him to make frequent visits to the various funeral homes in the area. The shop uses a December 31 taxation year. The business has been a great success, both in terms of being profitable and in enhancing George's enjoyment of life (and death).

As George is the sole proprietor of the business, he has had no need to report income figures to anyone. Given this, he has always used tax procedures to calculate the annual income of the business. For the year ending December 31, 2017, using his usual tax procedures, George has calculated his net business income to be $613,300.

Because a very large funeral home has opened in a suburb, George has decided to expand into that area. To do this, he needs a mortgage on the property that will be acquired for operations in the new location. To his dismay, he finds that the lender is insisting on financial statements prepared in accordance with generally accepted accounting principles (GAAP).

As he has no knowledge of GAAP, he has asked you to determine the amount of GAAP based income that Danton's Flowers has earned for the 2017 year.

Other Information:

1. In the net business income calculation based on tax procedures, George deducted $8,450 in business meals and entertainment costs.

2. Because his shop is near the U.S. border, George spent $7,420 advertising on a U.S. television station. The commercials were directed at Canadian resident viewers.

3. Because of a broken window during early December, live flowers costing $6,320 were destroyed.

4. During 2017, George paid a high level Canada Customs official a total of $19,460 in cash. In return, he received priority clearance for all his imports, as well as clearance for live plant imports that should have been restricted. Since this is an illegal payment to a government official, a.k.a., a bribe, it is not deductible for tax purposes.

5. During 2017, the business made $6,300 in contributions to the Hospice Association. This association is a registered charity.

6. For tax purposes, the ending inventories of the business were carried at the market value of $86,300. Their total cost, determined on a FIFO basis, was $73,150.

7. George deducted $51,400, the maximum amount of CCA that was available for the year. You have determined that amortization under GAAP would have been $46,350.

8. While George agreed to spend $6,070 on uniforms for the local men's softball team, the team refused to play if Danton's Flowers was printed on the front of their shirts. George finally accepted the use of the initials DF in a strong, bold font instead. He was influenced by the fact that in recent years the team had experienced numerous injuries requiring hospitalization of players and spectators. This was the result of wild throwing due to poor lighting of the playing field and the periodic 2 for 1 beer sales in the park.

9. George owns a delivery vehicle which cost $29,000. It is the only Class 10 asset of the business and, as of January 1, 2017, the Class had a UCC balance of $8,455. Under GAAP, its net book value at the time of the sale would have been $14,500. During the year, the vehicle is sold for $4,300 and replaced with a leased vehicle. The leasing costs are fully deductible for tax purposes.

10. In December, 2017, George spent $15,200 on landscaping the grounds around his store. Given the late date at which this work was done, no amortization would be required for accounting purposes with respect to these costs for 2017. It is expected that these landscaping improvements will last at least 10 years.

11. During 2017, George sold Class 8 assets for $21,300. These assets had a capital cost of $32,600 and were not the last assets in Class 8. There was a positive balance in Class 8 at the end of the year. If these assets had been subject to GAAP amortization, their net book value would have been $18,300.

12. As the business is unincorporated, no taxes were deducted in calculating Net Income.

Required: Determine the 2017 GAAP based net income for Danton's Flowers. Do not include in your calculations any tax that George will have to pay on this income. If you do not make an adjustment for some of the items included in other information, indicate why this is the case.

Assignment Problem Six - 6

(Partnership - Business Income, Employee vs. Self-Employed)

Richmond Consultants is a partnership with three architects as members. The partnership provides services throughout their local region. The partnership began operations on July 1, of the current year.

While the partners themselves will undertake much of the work required by their various contracts, some smaller projects may be contracted out. These outside contracts will require the architect to undertake a well defined project for a fixed fee, plus related expenses. The partners are uncertain as to the need for source deductions (income tax, EI and CPP contributions) on amounts paid to these individuals.

The partners have hired you to assist them with some of the tax issues that will arise in the operation of the partnership.

Required:

A. Explain to the partners how business income from partnerships is taxed in Canada.

B. Explain to the partners what choice they have in selecting a year end for their business.

C. Advise the partners on whether source deductions will be required on the amounts paid to the outside architects.

Assignment Problem Six - 7

(Proprietorship - Business Income With CCA)

Carol Basque is an experienced lawyer who has not incorporated her professional practice. She doesn't trust accountants as she was married to two of them (not at the same time). She operates her practice out of a building which she purchased several years ago for $725,000. Of this total, it is estimated that $175,000 reflects the value of the land. It was a new building when she acquired it, her practice uses 100 percent of the building, and it was allocated to a separate Class 1. On January 1, 2017, the building has a UCC of $447,831.

As her practice specializes in cases where lack of anger management has caused legal difficulties, she has had to replace her office furniture several times. The latest was during 2017, when the divorcing owners of a martial arts club could not come to a peaceful resolution to an asset split. A registered charity, Ex-Cons R Us, hauled her destroyed furniture away to be used for training purposes and as spare parts in their furniture repair shop.

The old furniture had a capital cost of $53,000 and a January 1, 2017 UCC of $38,160. She acquires new furniture and fixtures at a cost of $78,000.

In January, 2015, Carol acquired a $92,000 Lexus that she uses largely for business purposes. She has concluded that, given the nature of her clientele, this car appears too luxurious. Based on this view, she trades it in on the purchase of a $28,000 Toyota. The January 1, 2017 UCC for the Lexus is $17,850.

Because the vehicle had been badly damaged by an exiting client who lost his case, the trade-in allowance that she receives is only $22,000. During 2017, the Toyota is driven 41,000 kilometers, only 3,000 of which were for personal use. The operating costs for the year were $6,150.

Other asset acquisitions during 2017 are as follows:

New Computer	$ 1,250
Applications Software	1,475
Client List From Retiring Lawyer	32,000

Other 2017 costs of operating her business, determined on an accrual basis, are as follows:

Building Operating Costs	$27,300
Payments To Assistants (Note)	46,100
Miscellaneous Office Costs	13,600
Meals With Clients	15,500

Note   The payments include $25,000 paid to her 17 year old daughter. She works part time during the school year and full time during the summer doing online research for Carol's practice.

During 2017, the revenues of Carol's practice total $297,800.

Required: Calculate the minimum net business income Carol would include in her 2017 personal income tax return. In preparing your solution, ignore GST and PST implications and her CPP liability.

Assignment Problem Six - 8
(Work Space In The Home Costs And CCA)

Olin Packett has decided that he must find a way to earn additional income. While he has a reasonable salary from his current employment, it is not nearly adequate to provide for the luxury items that he feels he really should be enjoying.

After consulting his know-it-all brother, he concludes that a home-based online business which provides premium quality organic nut, fruit and candy products would do well. He opens his website for business on March 1, 2017.

He will operate this business out of his home. This property was acquired during 2016 at a total cost of $467,000, of which $130,000 can be attributed to the value of the land on which the house is situated. The business will have exclusive use of 23 percent of the floor space in Olin's home. Olin does not believe that the value of the property has changed significantly since its acquisition.

Olin was not prepared for the immediate large orders he receives as he thought business would be slow to start. On March 15, 2017, he acquires office, shipping and storage furniture and shelving at a cost of $42,000. Later that month, on March 27, he acquires an all-in-one computer at a cost of $1,940, along with business software at a cost of $467. He also arranges to have a separate phone line installed for the use of the business. As he meets with more suppliers and clients, he purchases a tablet for $400 on June 30 to enable him to operate more efficiently outside his home.

The phone package that he acquires includes the use of a toll-free number for his customers, as well as unlimited long distance calls in Canada.

For the year ending December 31, 2017, costs associated with owning his home are as follows:

Utilities For Home (Heat, Light, And Water)	$ 2,650
Mortgage Interest Paid	14,600
House Insurance	1,300
Property Taxes	7,005
Repairs And Maintenance For Home*	13,400
Total	$38,955

*Of the repair costs, $12,200 represents the cost of replacing the aging cedar siding on the home with metal siding. The remaining $1,200 ($13,400 - $12,200) involves ordinary day to day maintenance (e.g., replacing light bulbs and furnace filters).

During the period March 1, 2017 through December 31, 2017, his sales total $233,000. Costs associated with these sales are as follows:

Cost Of Merchandise Purchased	$116,014
Unsold Merchandise At December 31, 2017	16,327
Packaging Materials	4,206
Shipping Costs	8,354
Office Supplies	3,210
Telephone (Total Charge For The Period)	862
Advertising In Various Canadian Media	6,438
Insurance On Business Inventories	423
Cleaning Services For Office And Shipping Space	3,250
Meals And Entertainment For Suppliers	2,450
Credit Card Fees	2,300
Estimated Bad Debts	1,450

Olin's parents have been helping him by taking orders and packaging product for shipping. They refuse any payment for their work as they are both bored with the retirement life and, unlike their son, feel they have more than adequate income for their modest needs.

Required:

A. Can Olin deduct work space in the home costs? Briefly explain your conclusion.

B. Compute the minimum net business income or loss that Olin must report in his 2017 personal income tax return.

C. Briefly describe any issues that should be discussed with Olin concerning the work space in his home and business costs.

Assignment Problem Six - 9
(Corporate Business Income With CCA)

Angie's Amazing Getups Incorporated is a Canadian controlled private corporation with a head office in London, Ontario. The company is a manufacturer of high end custom costumes and makeup used in movie and theatre productions with sales in Canada and the U.S.

The company started in business in 2014 when the sole shareholder, Angela Q. Snodgrass, was photographed by the paparazzi after a particularly enthusiastic night of partying. When Angela saw herself on the front page of every tabloid newspaper the next day, she knew that fame was not for her. Since Angela was a highly trained clothing designer and makeup artist, she felt she would be able to use those skills to start her own business and keep out of the limelight.

In November, 2017, after discovering that her bookkeeper, Ponzi Madoff, had been defrauding her, Angela fired him and took over the bookkeeping responsibilities herself, despite having a limited knowledge of accounting. She has produced the following Income Statement and miscellaneous financial information for the year ended December 31, 2017 and needs your help.

Angie's Amazing Getups Incorporated
Income Statement
Year Ending December 31, 2017

Sales		$7,578,903
Cost Of Goods Sold		(5,468,752)
Gross profit		$2,110,151
Expenses:		
General And Administrative Expenses	($852,000)	
Amortization Expense	(550,000)	
Interest	(8,500)	(1,410,500)
Operating Income		$ 699,651
Other Income:		
Loss On Disposal Of Limited Life Licence		(17,000)
Interest Income		110,532
Income Before Income Taxes		$ 793,183
Income Taxes		
Current	($182,000)	
Future	(35,000)	(217,000)
Net Income		$ 576,183

During your review of Angela's work and last year's tax return for the corporation, you have made the following notes.

1. In the accounting records, the Allowance For Doubtful Accounts was $25,000 at December 31, 2017, and $20,000 at December 31, 2016. During 2017, the company had actual write-offs of $11,750. As a result, the accounting Bad Debt Expense was $16,750. This amount is included in General and Administrative Expenses on the Income Statement.

    A review of the listing of receivables (for tax purposes), indicates that the actual items that may be uncollectible total $15,000 at December 31, 2017. In 2016, the company deducted a reserve for bad debts of $13,000 for tax purposes.

2. General And Administrative Expenses include:

Donations To Registered Charities	$ 27,000
Accrued Bonuses - Accrued September 1, 2017, Paid June 15, 2018	78,000
Meals And Entertainment Costs:	
$1,000 Per Month For Premium Membership At Golf Club For Angie	12,000
$200 Per Month For Memberships At Golf Club For Salespeople	2,400
$32,000 For Meals While Entertaining Clients	32,000
$5,000 In Food Costs For Angie's Personal Chef For Her Meals At Home	5,000
$6,000 For Annual Summer BBQ For All Staff	6,000
Sponsorship Of Various Theatre Productions That Use Angie's Costumes	100,000
Advertising In A U.S. Theatre Magazine Directed At U.S. Clients	15,000
New Software Purchased October 1, 2017	
($13,000 For Applications And $25,000 For Systems)	38,000
Accounting And Legal Fees For Amended Articles Of Incorporation	6,000
Costs To Attend Annual Convention Of Costume Designers Held In Thailand	17,000

Assignment Problems

3. Interest Expense consists of the following:

Interest Expense - Operations	$5,000
Penalty And Interest For Late And Insufficient Instalment Payments	2,000
Interest On Late Payment Of Municipal Property Taxes	1,500

4. Travel costs (included in General and Administrative costs) include both air travel and travel reimbursement to employees for business travel. The company policy is to reimburse employees $0.58 per kilometer for the business use of their automobiles. During the year, seven employees each drove 4,000 kilometers on employment related activities and one employee drove 7,500 kilometers. None of the kilometer based allowances are required to be included in the income of the employees.

5. Maximum CCA has always been taken on all assets. The undepreciated capital cost balances at January 1, 2017 were as follows:

Class 1 (4%)	$650,000
Class 8	95,000
Class 10.1	17,850
Class 14	68,000
Class 14.1	Nil
Class 44	65,000
Class 53	135,000

6. During 2017, a limited life licence to produce costumes based on an popular theme park was sold for $63,000. The original cost of this licence was $95,000 and its net book value at the time of sale was $80,000. The licence was the only asset in Class 14.

7. Purchases and sales of equipment and other capital assets made during 2017 were as follows (note: some items are discussed in other sections of this problem). All amounts were capitalized for accounting purposes:

    a. The company purchased land and constructed a new building on it during the year. The building will be used 95% for manufacturing and processing. The cost of the land was $350,000, and the building cost $475,000 to construct.
    b. The company purchased a new set of furniture for the reception area for $1,200.
    c. Some outdated desks used by the finance department with a cost of $5,000 were sold for proceeds of $3,500.
    d. Landscaping of the grounds around the new building cost $35,000. This amount was capitalized for accounting purposes.

    e. A company car for use by the president of the company was purchased for $90,000. This car replaced the only other existing company car, which was purchased in 2015 for $95,000. The old car was sold for $60,000.
    f. A fence around the new building, high enough to prevent the paparazzi from taking pictures of Angela while she was at the office cost $52,000.

8. The company sold some shares that had been purchased several years ago. The capital gain on these shares was $152,708. Angela didn't know how to account for this, so she credited the entire amount to retained earnings.

Required: Determine Angie's Amazing Getups Incorporated's minimum Net Income For Tax Purposes for the year ending December 31, 2017. Ignore GST/HST/PST implications.

Assignment Problem Six - 10
(Deductibility Of Business Expenses And CCA)

Lorna Jung is a psychiatrist whose private practice specializes in treating children with psychiatric disorders. Her husband, Alec Jung, was the president of a very successful mental health clinic until it was bought out last year. He is currently creating and testing recipes to be included in his new ground breaking BBQ cookbook.

Over the past two years, Lorna has been investigating the patient benefits of having a therapy dog as part of her practice and has amassed an extensive library of clinical studies that show the effectiveness of this therapy. She is convinced that the use of a therapy dog will be advantageous to many of her patients and will improve the rate of their recovery.

On January 2, 2017, after much research, Lorna purchased a Labradoodle puppy for $2,000 that she named Sigmund. This particular breed was designed to be used as therapy dogs and Sigmund's mother was a well established therapy dog.

Sigmund became an important part of the Jung family. Whenever Sigmund wasn't in training or at Lorna's office, Alec would take Sigmund for walks and to the dog park. As Alec currently has no source of income, he charged Lorna the going rate of $20 per 1 hour (minimum) walk. He plans to report this income on his tax return.

For the month of September, 2017, Sigmund accompanied Lorna to consultations with all her patients except for those few who had a fear of dogs. She saw an immediate improvement in the attitudes of almost all her patients. Some children who refused to speak with her, could describe their feelings when they addressed Sigmund.

As word of Lorna's success with her therapy dog treatments spread, new patients would register only if assured that Sigmund would be present.

On Lorna's website, she had two hourly rates. The one with Sigmund participating was 15 percent higher than the rate without Sigmund. By December 31, 2017, 70 percent of her patients were paying the higher rate with Sigmund.

On July 1, 2017, in anticipation of taking Sigmund to the office and patient's homes on a regular basis, Lorna signed a 3 year lease for a Lexus SUV with sufficient room in the back for a sturdy, well-padded dog crate.

The lease payments were $950 per month. The manufacturer's list price for the vehicle was $65,000. As the Jungs have two other vehicles, this SUV was used only for business purposes.

For the year ending December 31, 2017, Lorna spent the following amounts on Sigmund:

Food, including puppy vitamins and supplements	$2,600
Veterinary fees	800
Therapy dog training course fees	1,400
Dog walking fees paid to Alec	3,280
Car lease for SUV [($950)(6)]	5,700
Operating expenses for SUV	2,950
Purchase of paw protectors (good for one winter)	140
Purchase of custom made protective clothing (estimated life of 3 years)	820
Dog crate	400
Total Dog-Related Expenditures	$18,090

Lorna's tax accountant informed her that Sigmund's original cost could not be written off as there was no specific CCA class for dogs and CCA Class 8, the usual catch-all class, specifically excluded animals.

In 2019, Lorna's parents were in a car accident that left them both severely injured. After much thought, she decided she had to close her practice in order to care for them and help in the long rehabilitation process.

Lorna knew that Sigmund would become depressed without patient interaction, so she sold Sigmund to Dr. Skinner, a psychiatrist she had known for years who already had a therapy dog and was looking to expand his practice. Although Lorna could not sell her patient list to Dr. Skinner due to confidentiality constraints, she e-mailed all her patients that Sigmund would be available at Dr. Skinner's office so he would soon see familiar faces there.

Dr. Skinner paid $8,700 for Sigmund. This included $200 for the protective clothing and the crate. He promised the Jungs unlimited visitation rights.

Due to her high income, Lorna always claims the maximum deductions available each year.

Required:

A. Lorna's accountant does not plan to deduct any dog-related expenditures other than the maximum allowable SUV expenses. Do you agree this is the appropriate course of action? Justify your conclusion.

B. Indicate how much of the preceding expenditures you feel Lorna should deduct in the calculation of business income for 2017.

C. Calculate the amount, if any, that will be included in Lorna's 2019 Net Income For Tax Purposes due to the sale of Sigmund.

Ignore all GST/HST considerations in your solution.

Assignment Problem Six - 11
(ITA 22 Accounts Receivable Election)

Porsha Tortora is the sole proprietor of Tortora's Tarts, an unincorporated business that has been operating successfully for a number of years. Porsha is about to fulfill her life-long dream of marrying into an enormous amount of money. On December 1, 2017, she will wed Grady Barrett, a billionaire Vancouver real estate developer. She met Grady last year at a sky diving course in Kelowna.

Because she is anticipating a future life with few financial constraints, she has decided to sell all of the assets of Tortora's Tarts to Martin Bunn, an unrelated party. Mr. Bunn will continue to operate business and will maintain the same December 31 year end that was used by Ms. Tortora. He does not anticipate incorporating the business, at least for the next few years.

The sale is finalized on June 3, 2017. Information related to the Accounts Receivable of the business at that point in time is as follows:

- Face Value Of The Receivables $346,000
- Estimated Realizable Value $328,000
- Bad Debt Reserve Deducted In 2016 $24,000

Between June 3, 2017 and December 31, 2017, $333,000 of the Accounts Receivable are collected, with the remaining $13,000 being written off as uncollectible.

Both Ms. Tortora and Mr. Bunn have heard of an election under ITA 22 that may have some influence on the tax treatment of the transfer of accounts receivable. They would like to have your advice on this matter. They will both have significant capital gains in 2017.

Required:

A. Indicate the tax effects, for both Ms. Tortora and Mr. Bunn, of the disposition of the accounts receivable and the subsequent 2017 collections and write-offs, assuming:

- that no election is made under ITA 22.
- that they make an election under ITA 22.

B. Indicate, from the point of view of each taxpayer, whether making the election would be a desirable course of action. Would your conclusion for each taxpayer differ if the amount collected had been $321,000, rather than the $333,000 given in the problem?

Assignment Problem Six - 12
(Comprehensive Case Covering Chapters 1 to 6)

Family Information
Dorian Wilde is 42 years old and married to his high school sweetheart, Gloria. Gloria has Net Income For Tax Purposes and Taxable Income of $8,200. The income is from investments that she purchased with funds that she inherited.

Dorian and Gloria have two sons:

Oscar is 15 years old and in good health. He has income from part-time summer jobs of $8,460.

Bart is 21 years old, in good health, and attends university on a full time basis for 10 months of the year. All of his university costs are paid for by Dorian, including tuition of $8,700, textbook costs of $1,350, and residence fees of $9,250. Bart has income from investments of $7,400. The investments were acquired with funds he earned during his high school years. Bart has agreed to transfer his tuition credit to his father.

The family's medical expenses, all of which were paid for by Dorian, were as follows:

Dorian	$ 1,350
Gloria (Note 1)	4,600
Oscar	1,250
Bart	3,125
Total	$10,325

Note 1 Gloria's medical expenses were the result of a liposuction procedure to deal with a cellulite problem that she has had since childhood.

Employment Information
Dorian is employed by a Canadian public company. His annual salary is $92,500, none of which involves commissions. His employer withholds the following amounts from his earnings:

Registered Pension Plan Contributions (Note 2)	$5,600
EI Premiums	836
CPP Contributions	2,564
Contributions To Unplanned Parenthood (Note 3)	3,200

Note 2 Dorian's employer makes a matching contribution of $5,600.

Note 3 Unplanned Parenthood is a registered Canadian charity. Because of contributions in previous years, Dorian and his spouse are not eligible for the charitable donations super credit.

Dorian is provided with an automobile by his employer. The vehicle was purchased in 2015 for $40,000 and, on January 1, 2017, its UCC on the employer's books was $25,500. During 2017, the automobile is driven 51,000 kilometers, 28,000 of which are related to Dorian's employment duties. It was available to Dorian for 11 months during the year and, during the month that he did not use the car, the company required that it be returned to the company's garage.

During the year, Dorian received a travel allowance from his employer of $550 per month, an annual total of $6,600. Dorian's actual travel costs were as follows:

Hotels	$3,200
Meals While Travelling	1,800
Airline Tickets	1,500
Total	$6,500

During 2017, Dorian received the following gifts from his employer:

- A $400 gift certificate for merchandise at a local department store.

- A Christmas gift basket containing various gourmet items. This basket, which has a value of $325, was provided to all of the company's employees.

Dorian is required by his employer to maintain an office in his home. This home office uses 20 percent of the floor space in his home. The cost of the house, excluding the land, was $426,000. It was purchased in 2016 and, during 2017, costs were as follows:

Mortgage Interest	$ 6,200
Property Taxes	4,320
Utilities And Maintenance	1,850
Insurance	1,140
Total	$13,510

Business Information

Because of his interest in antiques, Dorian operates a small, unincorporated retail business. The business uses a taxation year that ends on December 31, and during the year ending December 31, 2017, the business produced an accounting net income of $71,500. As his business is not incorporated, this figure does not include a deduction for income taxes. Other relevant information with respect to his business is as follows:

1. At the beginning of 2017, Dorian owned depreciable assets that were used in the business and their UCC balances are as follows:

	Class 1	Class 8	Class 10
January 1, 2017 UCC	$351,000	$63,400	$25,000

The Class 1 building was acquired in 2013, is used exclusively for retail purposes and is the only building in Class 1.

In March, 2017, Class 8 assets with a cost of $18,000 were sold for $11,300. They were replaced by Class 8 assets with a cost of $21,100.

2. During 2017, the business spent $12,600 landscaping its premises. For accounting purposes, this amount is being amortized over 10 years on a straight line basis.

3. The Net Income figure is after the deduction of Amortization Expense of $31,200 and $11,000 in meals and entertainment with clients of the business. The Amortization Expense includes the amortization of the landscaping costs.

4. Dorian intends to deduct the maximum amount of CCA for the year.

Required: For the taxation year ending December 31, 2017, calculate Dorian's:

A. minimum Net Income For Tax Purposes.

B. minimum Taxable Income.

C. Federal Tax Payable.

Ignore GST/HST/PST considerations in your solution.

Assignment Problem Six - 13
(Comprehensive Case Covering Chapters 1 to 6)

Family Information

Jamine Ramiz is 46 years old. She is married to Raul Ramiz. Raul is 41 years old and has 2017 Net Income For Tax Purposes of $5,650.

The couple have two children:

Diego   Their son, Diego, is 15 years old and has a 2017 Net Income For Tax Purposes of $6,420.

Isabella   Their daughter, Isabella is 20 years old and has no 2017 income of her own. She attends university on a full time basis for 8 months of the year. Jamine pays for all of Isabella's education costs, including $10,200 for tuition and $2,200 for textbooks and supplies. She has agreed to transfer the maximum tuition credit to her mother.

The family's 2017 medical expenses, all paid for by Jamine, are as follows:

Jamine	$ 3,200
Raul*	7,800
Diego	2,450
Isabella	7,235
Total	$20,685

*$4,800 was for hair transplants and the remaining $3,000 was for plastic surgery on his nose as a result of a collision with a tree while bike riding.

During 2017, Jamine makes donations to the United Way Fund of $2,150. In addition, she makes donations to registered federal political parties in the amount of $450. She is not eligible for the first time donor's super credit.

Employment Income

Jamine is employed by Dominion Steel, a large public company, in their human resources department. For 2017, her basic salary is $143,000. In addition, she earned $18,500 in commissions. For the year, her employer withheld the following amounts from her income:

CPP Contributions	$2,564
EI Premiums	836
RPP Contributions*	4,200
Union Dues	625
Payments For Personal Use Of Company Car	1,800

*For 2017, her employer makes a matching contribution to her RPP of $4,200.

Dominion Steel provides Jamine with a car that was purchased in 2015 for $40,000. In the Company's records, this Class 10.1 asset has a January 1, 2017 UCC of $17,850. During 2017, the car was available to Jamine for only 10 months, during which she drove it a total of 42,000 kilometers. Of this total, 15,000 kilometers were for personal use. The Company pays all of the costs of operating the car, a total of $7,560 for the year.

Several years ago, Jamine was granted options to purchase 2,000 shares of her employer's stock. The option price was $25 per share and, at the time the options were granted, the stock was trading at $27 per share. During March, 2017, she exercises all of the options. At this time, the shares are trading at $32 per share and, immediately after exercising the options, she sells 1,000 of the shares at $32 per share. She is still holding the other 1,000 shares at the end of the year when they are trading at $20 per share.

In recognition of her 10 years of service with the Company, Dominion Steel gives Jamine a $600 watch. In addition, all of the Company's employees were given a $300 gift certificate for online purchases at Amazon for Christmas.

Jamine is provided with a travel allowance of $600 per month to cover hotel and meal costs during employment related travel. Her actual costs for 2017 were as follows:

Hotels	$4,200
Meals	2,900

It is the policy of Dominion Steel to reimburse tuition paid by employees when taking college or university courses. During 2017, Jamine received $3,400 in reimbursements for two courses:

- $2,800 was for a two week course in negotiating skills
- $600 was for a weekend course in music appreciation

Business Income

On January 1, 2017, Jamine opened a management consulting business that assists people with making sales contacts.

Information related to this business is as follows:

Office Space   Jamine rents space on the ground floor of the mixed use building in which she lives. This means that, for the activities of this business, she makes no use of the vehicle provided by her employer. The rental agreement with the building's management company has a term of 3 years and there are no options for renewal.

The rent is $750 per month and, in order for the space to suit her needs, she makes improvements at a cost of $18,000.

Revenues   During 2017, Jamine issued invoices for her services totaling $63,450. In addition, she has unbilled work in progress of $5,055.

Capital Expenditures   During 2017, Jamine acquired office furniture and fixtures at a cost of $16,300. In addition, she purchased a computer for $1,230 and application software for $723.

Costs   During 2017, the following costs were incurred in operating the management consulting business:

Part Time Office Help	$6,340
Office Supplies	623
Web Hosting Fee	
(A simple web page for informational purposes only)	240
Cell Phone Plan (For Business Use Only)	462
Meals With Clients And Client Entertainment	4,340

Required: Calculate Jamine's 2017 Net Income For Tax Purposes, her 2017 Taxable Income, and her minimum 2017 federal Tax Payable. Ignore GST and PST considerations and any amounts that were withheld for income taxes by her employer.

CHAPTER 7

Income From Property

Introduction

7-1.   Subdivision b of Division B of the *Income Tax Act* provides simultaneous coverage of both income from business and income from property. The parts of this subdivision relating to business income are covered in Chapter 6, and many of these provisions are equally applicable to income from property. However, there are sufficient features that are unique to income from property that separate coverage of this subject is warranted and is provided in this Chapter. We have also included coverage of some of the basic issues related to interest deductibility in this Chapter.

Property Income: General Concept

7-2.   Income from property is thought of as the return on invested capital in situations where little or no effort is required by the investor to produce the return. Falling into this category would be rents, interest, dividends, and royalties. In terms of tax legislation, capital gains are not treated as a component of property income, even in cases where they arise on investments being held to produce property income (e.g., capital gains on dividend paying shares). This point is made clear in ITA 9(3) which states that "income from a property does not include any capital gain ...".

7-3.   In cases where a great deal of time and effort is directed at producing interest or rents, such returns can be considered business income. For example, the rents earned by a company that owns a number of shopping centers would be treated as a component of business income. As explained in Chapter 12, this is an important distinction for corporations since business income qualifies for the small business deduction, while property income generally does not.

7-4.   The primary characteristic that distinguishes property income from business income is the lack of effort directed towards its production. However, in some circumstances, other factors must also be considered. Some examples of why the correct classification is important are as follows:

- When some types of property income are being earned, the deduction of capital cost allowance (CCA) cannot be used to create or increase a net loss for the period.

- When property income is being earned by individuals, there is no requirement for a pro rata CCA reduction to reflect a short fiscal period.

- When property income is being earned, the income attribution rules (see Chapter 9) are applicable. This is not the case when business income is being earned.

- Certain expenses can be deducted against business income, but not property income. These include travel costs and convention expenses. In contrast, for individuals, there is a deduction for foreign taxes on property income in excess of 15 percent that is not available against foreign business income.

7-5.   A further general point is that the cost of obtaining investment counseling is generally deductible against property income. Although the cost of having a safety deposit box to hold investments was once deductible, it is no longer deductible.

Interest As A Deduction

The Problem

7-6.   There are differing views on the extent to which interest costs should be considered a deductible item for various classes of taxpayers. At one extreme, we have the situation that once existed in the U.S where it was possible for individuals to deduct all interest costs, without regard to the purpose of the borrowing. In contrast, there are other tax regimes where the deductibility of interest is restricted to certain, very specific types of transactions.

7-7.   From a conceptual point of view, it can be argued that interest should only be deductible to the extent it is paid on funds that are borrowed to produce income that is fully taxable in the period in which the interest is paid. The application of this concept would clearly disallow the current deduction of interest when it relates to:

- the acquisition of items for personal consumption;
- the acquisition of assets which produce income that is only partially taxed (e.g., capital gains); or
- the acquisition of assets which produce income that will not be taxed until a subsequent taxation year (e.g., gains on investments in land).

7-8.   To some extent, the preceding view is incorporated into the current legislation. The real problem, however, is that there are such a multitude of provisions related to the special treatment of certain types of income and to the deferral of income, that the application of this fairly straightforward concept becomes very complex.

7-9.   As is noted in Chapter 6, the general provision for the deduction of interest is found in ITA 20(1)(c). This provision provides for the deduction of interest only if it relates to the production of business or property income. This means that, in general, interest cannot be deducted if it relates only to such other sources of income as employment income or capital gains. Note, however, that if this production of income criteria is met, the deduction is available to all types of taxpayers, including corporations, individuals, and trusts.

7-10.   As a final general point here, you will recall that when an employee receives an interest free or low interest loan from an employer, imputed interest on the loan will be included in employment income as a taxable benefit. Under ITA 80.5, this imputed interest is deemed to be interest paid and, if the loan from the employer is used to produce business or property income, the amount that was included in the employee's income will be deductible under ITA 20(1)(c).

IT Folio S3-F6-C1 "Interest Deductibility"

7-11.   The rules for interest deductibility are largely found in IT Folio S3-F6-C1, *Interest Deductibility*. We will give fairly detailed attention to the content of this Folio in the material which follows.

What Is Interest?

7-12.   In order to be considered interest for tax purposes, IT Folio S3-F6-C1 indicates that the amount has to satisfy three criteria:

- It must be calculated on a day-to-day accrual basis.
- It must be calculated on a principal sum or the right to a principal sum.
- It must be compensation for the use of the principal sum or the right to the principal sum.

7-13.   IT Folio S3-F6-C1 notes that, in general, participating payments (e.g., payments based on earnings) are not considered to be interest. However, if there is an upper limit on the applicable rate and that upper limit reflects prevailing market conditions, such payments may qualify as interest. Payments that are contingent on some future event would not generally be considered interest.

7-14.   IT Folio S3-F6-C1 also notes that in some situations where a contract does not explicitly identify any amount as interest, amounts that can reasonably be regarded as interest will be deemed to be interest for income and expense purposes.

Legislation

7-15.   The basic provision for interest deductibility is found in ITA 20(1)(c). It indicates that an amount paid or payable in a year can be deducted if:

- it is interest on borrowed money used for the purpose of earning income from a business or property, other than exempt income; or
- it is interest on an amount payable for property acquired for the purpose of gaining or producing income, other than exempt income.

7-16.   The basic idea here is that you can deduct interest if it is paid to earn non-exempt income. While this basic concept sounds very simple and straightforward, its application has proved to be extremely contentious. Many issues related to this concept have found their way into all levels of the Canadian court system, including a number of cases that have been heard at the Supreme Court level. Of these hundreds of court cases, some have involved substantial sums of money. IT Folio S3-F6-C1 was issued to provide assistance in dealing with the issues that have arisen over recent years.

Borrowed To Produce Income

7-17.   For money to be borrowed, a relationship between a borrower and a lender is required. There is a distinction between "borrowed money" and "an amount payable for property". However, in either situation, interest can be deductible and need not concern us in the context of this introductory text.

7-18.   The more complex issue here is whether the interest relates to the production of income. The relevant test is whether, considering all the circumstances, the taxpayer had a reasonable expectation of income from the investments that were made with the borrowed funds. Note that there does not have to be a profit generated. This requirement simply means that as a result of the borrowing, there will be an amount that would be included in the determination of the taxpayer's Net Income For Tax Purposes, should the investment prove to be profitable.

Direct Or Indirect Use

The Singleton And Ludco Cases

7-19.   A number of court cases have dealt with this issue, thereby establishing the principle that it is the direct use of the funds that establishes deductibility. This was, perhaps, most clearly established in the Singleton case (The Queen vs. Singleton; 2001 DTC 5533). This case involved a lawyer who made a withdrawal of funds from his capital account in the law firm where he worked. These funds were used to purchase a residence for his personal use. Immediately after, he borrowed sufficient funds to replace the capital balance that he had withdrawn from his firm and then proceeded to deduct the interest on these borrowings. Mr. Singleton argued that the money borrowed was directly used to invest in the partnership and, because this was an income producing purpose, the interest should be deductible.

7-20.   The CRA denied this deduction on the basis that the real purpose of the borrowings was to finance the purchase of his residence, a view that was supported by the Tax Court of

Canada. However, both the Federal Court of Appeal and the Supreme Court of Canada disagreed. In making this decision, the Supreme Court noted that, in the absence of a sham or a specific provision in the *Act* to the contrary, the economic realities of a transaction cannot be used to recharacterize a clearly established legal relationship.

7-21.   The facts in the Ludco case (Ludco Enterprises Ltd. vs. The Queen; 2001 DTC 5505) involved the Company borrowing $7.5 million which was used to finance investments in two offshore companies. During the period that these investments were held, Ludco paid $6 million in interest on the borrowings and received $600,000 in dividends on the shares held. When the shares were ultimately redeemed, Ludco realized a $9.2 million capital gain.

7-22.   The CRA denied the deduction of the interest on the grounds that the shares were acquired for the purpose of earning a capital gain, not for the purpose of earning property income. While the Federal Court of Appeal agreed with the CRA, the Supreme Court of Canada did not. They concluded that an investment can have multiple purposes and, as long as one of these was the earning of property income, the condition that borrowing must be for the purpose of earning income was satisfied. That provision does not require either a quantitative determination of income or a judicial assessment of the sufficiency of income in order to satisfy its requirements.

Examples Of Direct Use Approach

7-23.   IT Folio S3-F6-C1 provides several examples designed to illustrate the implementation of the direct use concept:

EXAMPLE 1 - Restructured Borrowings   Ms. A owns 1,000 shares of X Corporation, a corporation listed on the TSX. Ms. A also owns a personal use condominium that was financed with borrowed money. At this point, the direct use of the borrowed money was to acquire the condominium. Ms. A may choose to sell the 1,000 shares of X Corp., use the proceeds to pay down the mortgage, and subsequently obtain additional borrowed money to acquire another 1,000 shares of X Corp. At this point, the additional borrowed money is directly used to acquire 1,000 shares of X Corporation.

EXAMPLE 2 - Cash Damming   Cash damming is a procedure that involves segregating funds received from borrowed money from those received from other sources. B Corporation establishes two accounts with its financial institution. The only deposits to account X are those consisting of borrowed money. All other deposits (e.g., funds from operations) are made to account Y.   B Corporation ensures that all payments from account X are for expenditures for which the conditions for interest deductibility are clearly met (e.g., capital expenditures). Account Y is used for other expenditures.

Examples 3 to 6 are examples of tracing/linking borrowed money to its current use.

EXAMPLE 3 - Replacement With Single Property   Mr. A acquired income producing Property X with $100,000 of borrowed money, the entire amount of which remains outstanding. Mr. A subsequently disposed of Property X for $100,000 and used the proceeds of disposition to acquire income producing Property Y for $100,000. As the current use of the borrowed money is with respect to Property Y, the interest on the original loan would continue to be deductible.

EXAMPLE 4 - Replacement With Multiple Properties   Ms. A acquired income producing Property X with $100,000 of borrowed money, the entire amount of which remains outstanding. Ms. A subsequently disposed of Property X for $100,000 and used the proceeds of disposition to acquire income producing Property Y for $60,000 and income producing Property Z for $40,000. The borrowed money would be allocated 60 percent ($60,000/$100,000) to Property Y and 40 percent to Property Z. The interest on the original loan would continue to be deductible.

EXAMPLE 5 - Flexible Approach To Linking   B Corp. acquired income producing Property X with $1,000,000 of borrowed money, the entire amount of which remains outstanding. B Corp. subsequently disposed of Property X for $1,500,000 and used the proceeds of disposition to acquire income producing Property Y for $1,200,000 and income producing Property Z for $300,000. B Corp. has flexibility in choosing the allocation of the current use of the borrowed money. Since the value of Property Y exceeds the $1,000,000 amount of the borrowings, it could be entirely allocated to Property Y. Alternatively, B Corp. could choose to allocate $300,000 of the current use of the borrowed money to Property Z, allocating the remaining $700,000 to Property Y. In either case, interest on the $1,000,000 would continue to be deductible.

EXAMPLE 6 - Replacement Properties Less Than Borrowed Money   Assume the same facts as in Example 5, except that Property X was sold for $800,000. The proceeds of disposition were used to acquire income producing Property Y for $600,000 and income producing Property Z for $200,000. The current use of the borrowed money would have to be pro-rated between the two new properties, with 75 percent ($600,000/$800,000) to Property Y and 25 percent ($200,000/$800,000) to Property Z. Interest on the $1,000,000 would continue to be deductible.

EXAMPLE 7 - Disappearing Source Rule   Mr. A borrows $100,000 to purchase an income-earning property. The entire amount of the loan remains outstanding and interest on the loan is deductible. Mr. A subsequently disposes of the property for its fair market value, now down to $60,000. He uses the $60,000 to reduce the outstanding loan. Under ITA 20.1, the remaining loan balance of $40,000 will be deemed to be used for the purpose of earning income and interest on this remaining amount will continue to be deductible.

Exceptions To The Direct Use Approach

7-24.   While direct use is the general rule, IT Folio S3-F6-C1 does indicate, however, that there are exceptions to this rule. These exceptions include:

Filling The Hole   IT Folio S3-F6-C1 uses the term "filling the hole" to describe situations where money is borrowed to pay dividends, to redeem shares, or to return capital of a corporation or partnership. The basic idea here is that the new debt replaces other forms of capital that were invested in income producing assets. In the case of dividends, this seems to be a bit of a stretch. However, the argument is that the borrowings replace the retained earnings that are being distributed in the form of dividends.

Interest-Free Loans   In general, interest on money borrowed to make interest-free loans would not be deductible as the purpose of the borrowing is not to produce income. However, it can be argued that an interest-free loan to a wholly owned subsidiary has been made with a view to helping the subsidiary produce income which can ultimately be used to pay dividends. IT Folio S3-F6-C1 indicates that the interest on borrowings to make interest-free loans of this type would be deductible.

A further exception is when money is borrowed to make interest-free loans to employees. The argument here is that the interest-free loan is a form of employee compensation, the purpose of which is to encourage the employees to help the employer produce income.

Interest Deductibility On Investments In Common Shares

7-25.   IT Folio S3-F6-C1 deals with a number of other issues associated with interest deductibility. Its guidance on dealing with premium and discount on the issuance of debt is discussed later in this Chapter. Most of the other issues covered are sufficiently specialized that they go beyond the scope of this text. There is, however, one other issue here of general importance.

7-26.   This is the question of whether interest on funds used to invest in common shares should be considered deductible. The problem is that common shares generally do not carry a stated interest or dividend rate and, in some cases, simply do not pay dividends, either currently or for the foreseeable future. While capital gains may ultimately make such investments profitable, there are many cases where investments in common shares could be viewed as not producing property income.

7-27.   Fortunately, IT Folio S3-F6-C1 indicates that in most circumstances the CRA will consider interest on funds borrowed to invest in common shares to be deductible. This is on the basis of a reasonable expectation, at the time the shares are acquired, that the holder will at some time in the future receive dividends. They do, however, give an example of a situation where this expectation is not viable:

> **EXAMPLE**   X Corp. is an investment vehicle designed to provide only a capital return to the investors in its common shares. The corporate policy with respect to X Corp. is that dividends will not be paid, that corporate earnings will be reinvested to increase the value of the shares and that shareholders are required to sell their shares to a third-party purchaser in a fixed number of years in order to realize their value. In this situation, it is not reasonable to expect income from such shareholdings and any interest expense on money borrowed to acquire X Corp. shares would not be deductible.

7-28.   An example is also provided of a situation in which interest would be deductible:

> **EXAMPLE**   Y Corp. is raising capital by issuing common shares. Its business plans indicate that its cash flow will be required to be reinvested for the foreseeable future. Y Corp. discloses to shareholders that dividends will only be paid when operational circumstances permit (that is, when cash flow exceeds requirements) or when it believes that shareholders could make better use of the cash. In this situation, the purpose of earning income test will generally be met and any interest on borrowed money used to acquire Y Corp. shares would be deductible.

We suggest you work Self Study Problem Seven-1 at this point.

Discount And Premium On Long-Term Issued Debt

Economic Background

7-29.   When a debt security is issued with an interest rate below the current rate, investors will react by offering a price that is less than the maturity value of the security. Such securities are said to sell at a discount and, in economic terms, this discount generally represents an additional interest charge to be recognized over the life of the security.

7-30.   For example, a 10 year bond with a maturity value of $100,000 and a 10 percent stated interest rate, would sell for $88,700 to investors expecting a 12 percent interest rate. The discount of $11,300 ($100,000 - $88,700) would then be added to interest expense at the rate of $1,130 per year for the ten year period. Note that, in order simplify the presentation of this material, we are using the straight-line amortization of discount and premium. This approach is acceptable under GAAP for private enterprises. However, under international accounting standards, the effective rate method must be used.

7-31.   In a corresponding fashion, a debt security that offered an interest rate above that currently expected by investors would command a premium. Such a premium would then be treated as a reduction in interest expense over the remaining life of the debt security.

7-32.   The procedures described in the preceding Paragraph are, of course, well known to anyone familiar with normal accounting procedures. Surprisingly, the tax rules for dealing with bond premium and discount do not reflect these well established principles.

7-33.   The required tax procedures are completely different from the accounting procedures, are inconsistent in the treatment of premium and discount, and have no conceptual basis of support. Despite this, IT Folio S3-F6-C1, *Interest Deductibility,* makes it clear that these somewhat bizarre procedures reflect the intent of the government.

Tax Procedures - Issuers Of Discount Bonds

7-34.   From the point of view of the issuer of a discount bond, the tax deductible amount of interest will be based on the stated, or coupon, rate without consideration of the difference between the proceeds received from the sale of the bonds and the larger amount that must be paid when the bonds mature. This excess will be treated as a loss on the retirement of the debt (i.e., a liability is being extinguished by paying more than its carrying value for tax purposes). You may recall from Chapter 6 that, under ITA 20(1)(f), this loss will be considered a fully deductible amount, provided:

- the bonds are issued for not less than 97 percent of their maturity value; and
- the effective yield on the bonds is not more than 4/3 of the stated, or coupon, rate.

7-35.   If these conditions are not met, only one-half of the loss will be deductible. This, in effect, treats the loss in the same manner as a capital loss. It would appear that the goal here is to prevent the use of deep discount bonds which, because of the failure of tax legislation to deal appropriately with bond discount, results in the investor having a part of his interest income being converted to a capital gain. A more logical solution to this problem would be to revise the relevant tax legislation to better reflect the economic substance of bond discount.

Exercise Seven - 1

Subject: Discount Bonds

On January 1, 2017, Moreau Ltd. issues bonds with a maturity value of $1,000,000 and a maturity date of December 31, 2019. The bonds pay interest on December 31 of each year at an annual coupon rate of 4 percent. They are sold for proceeds of $985,000 for an effective yield of 4.6 percent. The maturity amount is paid on December 31, 2019. What are the tax consequences related to this bond issue for Moreau Ltd. in each of the years 2017, 2018, and 2019? How would these tax consequences differ from the information included in Moreau's GAAP based financial statements? Moreau uses the straight-line method to amortize the discount on the bonds for accounting purposes.

SOLUTION available in print and online Study Guide.

Tax Procedures - Issuers Of Premium Bonds

7-36.   IT Folio S3-F6-C1 makes it clear that premium situations are not treated in a manner that is analogous with the treatment of discounts. IT Folio S3-F6-C1 indicates that, depending on the situation, three different possible approaches may be used by debt issuers for dealing with bond premium. These alternatives can be described as follows:

Money Lenders   IT Folio S3-F6-C1 indicates that, in situations where the borrowed money constitutes stock-in-trade for a taxpayer that is in the financing business, premium on the debt must be taken into income immediately. IT Folio S3-F6-C1 also makes it clear that this amount would not be given capital gains treatment and, as a consequence, would be 100 percent taxable. Given this treatment of the premium, the deductible amount of interest would be equal to the stated, or coupon, rate.

Other Taxpayers   In what constitutes something of a windfall for taxpayers issuing debt at a premium, IT Folio S3-F6-C1 indicates that the amount of premium received at the time of issue would be considered a non-taxable capital receipt. While IT Folio S3-F6-C1 is not clear on this issue, it appears that there will be no further tax consequences related to the premium when the bonds are retired. Unlike the case with bond discount, where there is a specific ITA Paragraph which provides for the deduction of this amount at the maturity of the bonds, there is no corresponding provision that requires the premium to be treated as a gain when the bonds are retired.

Deliberate Creation Of A Premium   IT Folio S3-F6-C1 introduces a third approach based on the very fuzzy concept of a "premium which arises because the debt was deliberately priced to give rise to a premium". There appears to be concern here that an enterprise might create additional tax deductions by setting an unrealistically high rate of interest on the issuance of debt. While it is not clear how "unrealistically high" will be measured, the tax consequence is that the contractual amount of interest paid will be viewed as unreasonable and will be reduced to a reasonable amount over the life of the debt. As this appears to be consistent with the premium amortization approach used in accounting, it seems the CRA's position is that only in unreasonable circumstances is it appropriate to use a reasonable approach to dealing with bond premium.

7-37.   With most conventional debt issuances, the second approach would be applicable. It is interesting to note that, in comparison with the applicable accounting procedures, this approach produces a larger interest deduction and this enhanced deduction is not offset by a gain when the bonds are retired. This permanent difference between accounting and tax income should make taxpayers who issue premium bonds very happy.

Exercise Seven - 2

Subject: Premium Bonds

On January 1 of the current year, Cannon Inc. issues 10 year bonds payable with a maturity value of $1,000,000. The bonds have a coupon rate of 18 percent, pay interest on January 1 of each year, and are sold for $1,400,000. The Company has a December 31 year end. Determine the current year tax consequences under each of the following assumptions:

- Cannon is in the business of lending money.
- Cannon is not in the business of lending money and did not make a deliberate effort to create a premium on the issuance of the bonds.
- Cannon is not in the business of lending money and made a deliberate effort to create a premium on the issuance of the bonds.

SOLUTION available in print and online Study Guide.

Interest Income

General Provision

7-38.   ITA 12(1) lists inclusions in business and property income. Paragraph (c) of this Subsection is as follows:

Interest ... any amount received or receivable by the taxpayer in the year (depending on the method regularly followed by the taxpayer in computing the taxpayer's income) as, on account of, in lieu of payment of or in satisfaction of, interest to the extent that the interest was not included in computing the taxpayer's income for a preceding taxation year.

7-39.   The wording of ITA 12(1)(c) suggests that taxpayers can use the cash basis to recognize interest income (amounts received or receivable). This is not the case. ITA 12(3) and 12(4) require the use of an accrual approach by all taxpayers. As is discussed in the following material, the accrual approach used by individuals differs from that used by corporations and partnerships.

Corporations And Partnerships - Accrual Method

7-40.   ITA 12(3) requires that corporations, partnerships, and some trusts use accrual accounting. The concept of accrual accounting that is applied to these taxpayers is the conventional one in which interest income is recorded as a direct function of the passage of time. IT-396R indicates that this calculation will generally be based on the number of days a principal amount is outstanding.

> **EXAMPLE** A corporation acquires a $5,000 debt instrument on August 15th of the current year. The instrument pays interest at an annual rate of 8 percent.
>
> **ANALYSIS** Interest for the current year would be calculated as follows:
>
> $$[(\$5,000)(8\%)(139 \div 365)] = \$152.33$$

7-41. For corporations and partnerships, interest income for tax purposes is, generally speaking, identical to that required under the application of generally accepted accounting principles. However, as will be explained later in this Chapter, an exception to this is interest income on bonds that have been purchased at a premium or a discount.

Individuals - Modified Accrual Method

7-42. While ITA 12(3) requires conventional accrual accounting for corporations and partnerships, ITA 12(4) provides for a less familiar version of this concept for individuals. Under this modified version of accrual accounting, interest is not accrued on a continuous basis. Rather, ITA 12(4) requires the accrual of interest on each anniversary date of an investment contract.

7-43. ITA 12(11) defines "investment contracts" to include most debt securities and "anniversary date" to be that date that is one year after the day before the date of issue of the security, and every successive one year interval. This would mean that, for a five year contract issued on July 1, 2017, the anniversary dates would be June 30 of each of the five years 2018 through 2022. If the holder of the investment contract disposes of it prior to its maturity, the disposal date is also considered to be an anniversary date from the point of view of that particular taxpayer.

7-44. To the extent that the income accrued on the anniversary date has not been previously included in income, it must then be included in the individual's income, regardless of whether the amount has been received or is receivable.

> **EXAMPLE** An investment contract with a maturity value of $100,000 and an annual interest rate of 10 percent is issued on July 1, 2017. The $100,000 maturity amount is due on June 30, 2022. An interest payment for the first 2.5 years of interest ($25,000) is due on December 31, 2020. The remaining interest ($25,000) is due with the principal payment on June 30, 2022. The contract is purchased by an individual at the time that it is issued.
>
> **ANALYSIS** As no interest has been received in calendar year 2017 and no anniversary date has occurred during the year, no interest would have to be included in the individual's tax return for that year. As compared to the use of the full accrual method, this provides a one year deferral of $5,000 [(10%)($100,000)(1/2)] of interest.
>
> Annual interest of $10,000 would have to be accrued on the first two anniversary dates of the contract, June 30, 2018 and June 30, 2019. This means that $10,000 would be included in Net Income For Tax Purposes for each of these two years. When the $25,000 payment is received on December 31, 2019, an additional $5,000 would be subject to taxation for that year because it has been received, and not previously accrued. This results in taxation of $15,000 in 2019. At this point, the cumulative results are identical to those that would result from the application of the full accrual approach.
>
> For 2020, the June 30, 2020 anniversary date would require the accrual of $10,000. However, as $5,000 of this amount was already included in income during 2019, only $5,000 of this amount would be subject to taxation in 2020. There would be a further accrual of $10,000 on the anniversary date in 2021. In 2022, an interest payment of $25,000 will be received. As $15,000 ($5,000 + $10,000) of the amount received has been included in 2020 and 2021 income, the total for 2022 will be $10,000 ($25,000 - $15,000).

Under the modified accrual method, the total interest of $50,000 would be recognized as follows:

2017	$ Nil
2018	10,000
2019	15,000
2020	5,000
2021	10,000
2022	10,000
Total	$50,000

7-45.   Note that the anniversary date is established by the date on which the investment contract is issued. It is not influenced by the date on which the individual investor acquires the contract. If this contract had been sold to another individual, for example on January 1, 2021, the required interest accruals would have been the same for the seller. There would, however, be an adjustment for accrued or recognized interest at transfer as discussed in Paragraph 7-48.

Exercise Seven - 3

Subject: Annual Accrual Rules

On October 1, 2017, Ms. Diane Dumont acquires a newly issued debt instrument with a maturity value of $60,000. It matures on September 30, 2023 and pays interest at an annual rate of 8 percent. Payment for the first three and one-quarter years of interest is due on December 31, 2020, with interest for the remaining two and three-quarters years payable on the maturity date. What amount of interest will Ms. Dumont have to include in her tax returns for each of the years 2017 through 2023?

SOLUTION available in print and online Study Guide.

Discount And Premium On Long-Term Debt Holdings

7-46.   Tax legislation takes the view that the taxable amount of interest is based on the accrual of the stated, or coupon, rate, without consideration of the fact that, in the case of bonds sold at a discount or premium, the investor will receive an amount at maturity that is larger or smaller than the amount that was paid for the bonds. Because tax procedures do not provide for the usual amortization of this discount or premium, it will be treated as a gain or loss at maturity by the investor.

7-47.   If the bonds are acquired at a discount, the additional amount that will be received at maturity (the discount) will be treated as a capital gain, only one-half of which will be taxable. In similar fashion, if the bonds are acquired at a premium, the receipt of just the face value at maturity will result in the premium being treated as a capital loss, only one-half of which will be deductible.

Accrued Interest At Transfer

7-48.   Publicly traded debt securities are bought and sold on a day-to-day basis, without regard to the specific date on which interest payments are due. To accommodate this situation, accrued interest from the date of the last interest payment date will be added to the purchase price of the security.

7-49.   Consider, for example, a 10 percent coupon, $1,000 maturity value bond, with semi-annual interest payments of $50 on June 30 and December 31 of each year. If we assume that the market value of the bond is equal to its maturity value and it is purchased on October 1, 2017, the price would be $1,025, including $25 [($50)(92/184 days)] of interest for the period from July 1, 2017 through October 1, 2017.

7-50.   In the absence of a special provision dealing with this situation, the $25 would have to be included in the income of the purchaser when it is received as part of the $50 December 31, 2017 interest payment. Further, the extra $25 received by the seller would receive favourable treatment as a capital gain. To prevent this result, ITA 20(14) indicates that the seller must include the accrued interest in income and the purchaser can deduct a corresponding amount from the interest received on the bonds.

Exercise Seven - 4

Subject: Accrued Interest At Transfer

On May 1, 2017, Mr. Milford Lay purchases bonds with a maturity value of $50,000 at par. These bonds pay semi-annual interest of $3,000 on June 30 and December 31 of each year. He purchases the bonds for $51,989, including interest accrued to the purchase date. He holds the bonds for the remainder of the year, receiving both the June 30 and December 31 interest payments. What amount of interest will be included in Mr. Lay's 2017 tax return?

SOLUTION available in print and online Study Guide.

Payments Based On Production Or Use (Royalties)

7-51.   The relevant *Income Tax Act* Paragraph here reads as follows:

ITA 12(1)(g) Payments based on production or use — any amount received by the taxpayer in the year that was dependent on the use of or production from property whether or not that amount was an instalment of the sale price of the property, except that an instalment of the sale price of agricultural land is not included by virtue of this paragraph.

7-52.   While ITA 12(1)(g), by referring only to amounts received, suggests the use of cash basis revenue recognition, this has limited application. ITA 12(2.01) indicates that ITA 12(1)(g) cannot be used to defer the inclusion of any item that would normally be included in the determination of business income. This would require the use of an accrual approach.

7-53.   ITA 12(1)(g) also requires that, except in the case of agricultural land, payments that represent instalments on the sale price of the property must also be included if their payment is related to production or use. An example will serve to illustrate this provision:

EXAMPLE   The owner of a mineral deposit sells the asset with the proceeds to be paid on the basis of $2 per ton of ore removed. The total amount to be paid is not fixed by the sales agreement.

ANALYSIS   In this situation, the owner would have to include in income the full amount received in each subsequent year, even though a portion of the payment may be of a capital nature.

Rental Income

General Rules

7-54.   Rental income is not specifically mentioned in the ITA Sections that deal with income from property. There is some merit in the view that rental receipts fall into the category of payments for production or use. However, rents are generally payable without regard to whether or not the property is used and, as a consequence, this view may not be appropriate. In any case, it is clear that rental receipts must be included in income and, given this fact, income from property would appear to be the most logical classification.

7-55.   With respect to the recognition methods to be used for rental income, the CRA's Guide, "Rental Income" (T4036) provides the following guidance:

> In most cases, you calculate your rental income using the accrual method. With this method, you:
>
> - include rents in income for the year in which they are due, whether or not you receive them in that year; and
> - deduct your expenses in the year you incur them, no matter when you pay them.
>
> However, if you have practically no amounts receivable and no expenses outstanding at the end of the year, you can use the cash method. With this method, you:
>
> - include rents in income in the year you receive them; and
> - deduct expenses in the year you pay them.
>
> You can use the cash method only if your net rental income or loss would be practically the same if you were using the accrual method.

7-56.   Once the rental revenues are included in income, a variety of expenses become deductible against them. These would include utilities (such as heat, electricity and water), repairs, maintenance, interest, insurance, property taxes, management fees, and fees to rental agents for locating tenants. CCA can also be deducted. However, as discussed in the next section, this deduction is subject to several special rules.

Capital Cost Allowances
General Rules

7-57.   As noted, CCA on rental properties can be claimed. In the year of acquisition, the half-year rule is applied when calculating the maximum available amount. For individuals, the calendar year is considered the fiscal year for property income purposes. As a consequence, there is no adjustment for a short fiscal period in the year of acquisition.

7-58.   Buildings acquired after 1987 will generally fall into Class 1, where they are eligible for CCA calculated on a declining balance basis at a rate of 4 percent. However, as was noted in Chapter 5, if:

- a new building is acquired after March 18, 2007;
- it is used more than 90 percent for non-residential activities by the taxpayer or a lessee; and
- it is allocated to a separate Class 1;

> it will be eligible for the enhanced CCA rates that were discussed in Chapter 5. You may recall that if the usage is 90 percent or more for manufacturing and processing, the rate is 10 percent. If this test is not met, but the building is used 90 percent or more for non-residential activity, the rate is 6 percent.

7-59.   As mentioned in Chapter 5, buildings acquired prior to 1988 were allocated to Class 3, where the rate was 5 percent. This rate is still available on buildings that were allocated to Class 3 prior to 1988.

7-60.   Without regard to the CCA class to which a building is allocated, the rate is applied only to the cost of the building, exclusive of land. This means that usually, the total cost of a real property must be segregated into land and building components. The land, of course, is not eligible for CCA deductions.

Special Rules

7-61.   There are two special rules that apply to CCA calculations on rental properties. These rules, along with a brief explanation of the reason that each was introduced, are as follows:

> **Separate CCA Classes**   Each rental building that is acquired after 1971 at a cost of $50,000 or more must be placed in a separate class for calculating CCA, recapture, and terminal losses. In most real world situations, the amount of CCA that can be

deducted on a rental property exceeds any decline in the value of the building. In fact, it is not uncommon for the value of such properties to increase over time. This means that, if an investor is required to account for each rental property as a separate item, a disposition is likely to result in recapture of CCA and an increase in Tax Payable.

In the absence of this special rule, all rental properties could be allocated to a single class. This would mean that the investor could avoid recapture for long periods of time by simply adding new properties to the class. This separate class rule prevents this from happening.

Rental Property CCA Restriction In general, taxpayers are not permitted to create or increase a net rental loss by claiming CCA on rental properties. For this purpose, rental income is the total rental income or loss from all properties owned by the taxpayer. This amount includes any recapture, as well as any terminal losses. The reason for this restriction is a desire to limit the use of rental losses for purposes of sheltering other types of income (e.g., applying rental losses against employment income).

The fact that CCA is the only restricted deduction is probably based on the fact that, unlike most depreciable assets, the value of many rental properties does not decline over time. This restriction does not apply to a corporation or a corporate partnership whose principal business throughout the year is the rental or sale of real property. There are similar restrictions on CCA with respect to leasing properties other than real estate.

7-62. Without question, these special rules make real estate less attractive as an investment. However, a number of advantages remain:

- taxation on a positive cash flow can be eliminated through the use of CCA;
- some part of the capital cost of an asset can be deducted despite the fact that real estate assets are generally not decreasing in value;
- increases in the value of the property are not taxed until the property is sold; and
- any gain resulting from a sale is taxed as a capital gain, only one-half of which is taxable.

7-63. These factors continue to make the tax features of investments in rental properties attractive to many individuals.

Rental Income Example

7-64. An example will serve to illustrate the basic features involved in determining net rental income.

EXAMPLE On January 1, 2017, Mr. Bratton owns the following two rental properties:

- Property A was acquired in 1987 at a cost of $120,000, of which $20,000 was allocated to land. It has a UCC of $68,000.

- Property B was acquired in 2010 at a cost of $120,000, of which $30,000 is allocated to land. It has a UCC of $74,200. On August 28, 2017, Property B is sold for $155,000. At this time, the value of the land is unchanged at $30,000.

On December 1, 2017, Mr. Bratton acquires Property C at a cost of $200,000, of which $50,000 is allocated to land. The property is used exclusively for residential purposes.

Rents on all of the properties totaled $35,000 during 2017 and the cost of maintenance, property taxes, and mortgage interest totaled $45,400.

Net Rental Income Calculation The maximum available CCA on the three properties would be as follows:

- Property A (Class 3) = $3,400 [(5%)($68,000)]
- Property B (Class 1) = Nil (The property was sold during the year.)
- Property C (Class 1) = $3,000 [($150,000)(1/2)(4%)]

Since a rental loss cannot be created by claiming CCA, the net rental income would be calculated as follows:

Gross Rents	$35,000
Recapture Of CCA On Property B ($90,000 - $74,200)	15,800
Expenses Other Than CCA	(45,400)
Rental Income Before CCA	$ 5,400
CCA Class 1 (Maximum)	(3,000)
CCA Class 3 (Limited)	(2,400)
Net Rental Income	Nil

7-65.   The maximum CCA was taken on Class 1, the 4 percent class, leaving the limited amount CCA deduction for Class 3 which has the higher rate of 5 percent. This follows the general tax planning rule that suggests that, when less than the maximum allowable CCA is taken, the CCA that is deducted should be taken from the classes with the lowest rates. However, if there had been Class 8 rental assets such as appliances, it could have been more tax advantageous to take CCA on those assets first as there is little likelihood of recapture on them.   Note that the taxable capital gain of $17,500 [(1/2)($125,000 - $90,000) + (1/2)($30,000 - $30,000)] on the sale of Property B is not part of the rental income or loss calculation.

Exercise Seven - 5

Subject: Rental Income

Ms. Sheela Horne acquires a residential rental property in September, 2017 at a total cost of $185,000. Of this total, $42,000 can be allocated to the value of the land. She immediately spends $35,000 to make major improvements to the property. Rents for the year total $7,200, while rental expenses other than CCA total $5,100. This is the only rental property owned by Ms. Horne. Determine the maximum CCA that is available for 2017 and Ms. Horne's minimum net rental income for the year.

SOLUTION available in print and online Study Guide.

We suggest you work Self Study Problem Seven-2 at this point.

Cash Dividends From Taxable Canadian Corporations

The Concept Of Integration

7-66.   While this concept will be given much more detailed attention in the Chapters dealing with corporate taxation, it is virtually impossible to understand the tax procedures associated with dividends received from taxable Canadian corporations without some elementary understanding of the concept of integration. It is fundamental, both to the procedures associated with the taxation of dividends, as well as to many other provisions related to the taxation of corporations.

7-67.   An individual who owns an unincorporated business or, alternatively, holds investments that earn property income, can choose to transfer these assets to a corporation. The various reasons for doing this will be given detailed consideration in Chapter 15. At this point,

Cash Dividends From Taxable Canadian Corporations

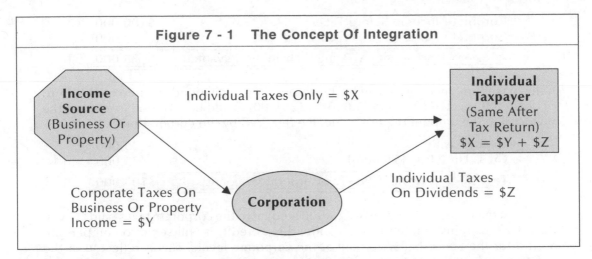

Figure 7 - 1   The Concept Of Integration

however, our concern is with the fact that, in making such a transfer, the taxpayer creates an additional taxable entity. As depicted in Figure 7-1, if the individual incorporates his source of business or property income, the corporation will be taxed on the resulting income. In addition, the individual will pay taxes on the dividends which the corporation will distribute from the corporation's after tax income.

7-68.   As is also depicted in Figure 7-1, the goal of integration is to ensure that the use of a corporation does not alter the total amount of taxes that will be paid on a given stream of business or property income. Stated alternatively, the procedures associated with integration are directed at equating the total amount of taxes paid by an individual who does not incorporate an income source and pays taxes only at the individual level, with the amount of taxes that would be paid if the relevant assets were transferred to a corporation and taxed at both the corporate level and at the individual level on distribution of the after tax corporate income.

7-69.   As we will find in the various chapters dealing with corporate taxation, there are a number of procedures associated with achieving this goal. However, from the point of view of individual taxpayers, the dividend gross up and tax credit procedures are the primary tools used in building a system which integrates corporate and individual tax amounts.

Implementing Integration
Gross Up And Tax Credit Procedures
7-70.   The primary tool for implementing integration in the Canadian tax system involves two procedures:

Dividend Gross Up   Dividends received by individuals from taxable Canadian corporations are "grossed up" (i.e. increased) by an amount that reflects the tax paid at the corporate level. This grossed up amount then represents the amount of income that was received by the corporation prior to the payment of corporate taxes.

Dividend Tax Credit   After the individual calculates his regular Tax Payable on the grossed up amount, a credit is provided against this Tax Payable that makes up for the taxes that were paid at the corporate level.

7-71.   A simple example will serve to illustrate how this works. Note that this is a conceptual example and does not reflect the rates that are built into the actual tax legislation.

EXAMPLE   Martin Tall has an income source which produces $100,000 of net business income each year. As Martin is in the 45 percent tax bracket, in the absence of a corporation he would pay taxes on this income of $45,000, resulting in after tax retention of $55,000. If he transfers this income source to a corporation, the corporation would pay taxes at a rate of 25 percent.

ANALYSIS   Results at the corporate level would be as follows:

Cash Dividends From Taxable Canadian Corporations

Corporate Income Before Taxes	$100,000
Corporate Taxes At 25 Percent	(25,000)
After Tax Income And Maximum Dividend Payable	**$ 75,000**

If the maximum dividend is paid by the corporation, a dividend gross up of one-third of dividends received [(1/3)($75,000) = $25,000] would be required to convert the dividend to the amount of pre-tax income received by the corporation:

Dividends Received	$ 75,000
Gross Up [(1/3)($75,000)]	25,000
Taxable Dividends = Pre-Tax Corporate Income	**$100,000**

Note that the required gross up of $25,000 is equal to the corporate taxes paid. Given this, if we use this amount as the dividend tax credit, it will serve to compensate Martin for the taxes that were paid at the corporate level. This is reflected in the following calculation of Martin's Tax Payable:

Taxable Dividends (After Gross Up)	$100,000
Martin's Tax Rate	45%
Tax Payable Before Dividend Tax Credit	$ 45,000
Dividend Tax Credit (Equal To Gross Up)	(25,000)
Martin's Tax Payable	**$ 20,000**

Based on the preceding calculation of Tax Payable, Martin's after tax retention would be calculated as follows:

Dividends Received	$75,000
Tax Payable	(20,000)
After Tax Retention - Use Of Corporation	**$55,000**

7-72.   You will note that this is exactly the same $55,000 of after tax retention that would result from Martin receiving the $100,000 in income directly and being taxed on it at 45 percent. This means that, in this example, the gross up and tax credit procedures have produced perfect integration. That is, Martin has retained exactly the same amount of after tax income, without regard to whether the pre-tax income is received directly or, alternatively, is channeled through a corporation.

The Problem

7-73.   Thoughtful readers of the preceding example will recognize that the reason integration works is that the gross up and the resulting tax credit are exactly equal to the corporate taxes paid. For integration to work perfectly in the real world one of two sets of conditions would have to be present:

Uniform Corporate Tax Rates   If every taxable Canadian corporation was taxed at the same rate, integration would work using a single gross up factor. For example, if all corporations were taxed at the 25 percent rate that was used in our illustration, a gross up of one-third would always produce perfect integration. While we haven't dealt with corporate taxation at this point, you are likely aware that there are literally dozens of different corporate tax rates in use. There are different rates for different types of income, as well as different corporate rates for each of the provinces and territories. This creates unavoidable imperfections in the integration system.

Variable Gross Up Factors   It would still be possible to implement perfect integration in the presence of varying corporate tax rates if we had a system in which specific gross up factors were used for each corporation, with the factor being used reflecting the corporate tax rate applicable to that particular corporation. However, this would create many complications and has never been considered as a practical alternative.

The Solution - Eligible And Non-Eligible Dividends

7-74.   With the presence of different corporate tax rates, the use of a single gross up factor must result in imperfections in the integration system. While this problem could be solved by having individualized gross up factors for each corporation, our taxation system uses a more practical approach based on two categories of corporations, Canadian controlled private companies and other corporations, consisting primarily of Canadian public companies.

> **Eligible Dividends**   Public companies are taxed at combined federal/provincial rates that range from 26 percent to 31 percent (for 2016). Dividends paid by these companies are referred to as "eligible" dividends. As will be explained later, they are eligible for the enhanced gross up and tax credit procedures. These procedures applied to eligible dividends reflect an assumed corporate tax rate of 27.536 (a rounded figure) percent. This is within the range of the rates that are applicable to these companies. However, integration imperfections will still exist.

> **Non-Eligible Dividends**   For 2016, Canadian controlled private companies that pay dividends out of income eligible for the small business deduction are taxed at combined federal/provincial rates that range from 10.5 percent to 18.5 percent. Dividends paid by these companies are referred to as non-eligible dividends. The gross up and tax credit procedures applied to these dividends reflect an assumed corporate tax rate of 14.530 (a rounded figure) percent. This is within the range of the rates that are applicable to these companies. However, integration imperfections will still exist.

> **BYRD/CHEN NOTE**   We have retained the 2016 corporate rates, as well as the 2016 dividend tax credit rates (see Paragraph 7-81) as the provincial dividend tax credit rates are not established until each province has issued a budget. This is likely to be too late for inclusion in this text. We would note that provincial rates do not usually change dramatically from year to year,

A Note Of Caution

7-75.   The preceding material on gross up and tax credit procedures is greatly simplified and, given that we have not yet covered any material on corporate taxation, may be difficult to understand. However, we believe the preceding explanation of integration concepts must be understood in order to comprehend the material on dividends which follows.

Gross Up And Tax Credit Procedures - Eligible Dividends

Definition Of Eligible Dividends

7-76.   ITA 89(1) defines "eligible dividends" as a taxable dividend that has been designated as such by the paying corporation. Prior to our more detailed coverage of corporate taxation, we will think of such designated dividends as those paid by Canadian public companies. While this is generally true, this simplification ignores the fact that:

- some dividends paid by Canadian public companies cannot be designated as eligible; and
- some dividends paid by Canadian controlled private companies can be designated as eligible.

Eligible Dividend Gross Up Procedure

7-77.   When an individual receives eligible dividends, the amount received is grossed up by 38 percent. This rate reflects an assumed corporate tax rate of 27.53623 percent. As illustrated in the following example, given this corporate tax rate, a 38 percent gross up will create taxable dividends that reflect the amount of pre-tax corporate income received:

> **EXAMPLE**   Marin Ltd. is subject to a combined federal/provincial tax rate of 27.53623 percent. During 2017, the company has Taxable Income of $100,000. All of the Company's after tax income is paid to Mr. Marin, its only shareholder, as a dividend.

Cash Dividends From Taxable Canadian Corporations

ANALYSIS The results at the corporate and individual levels are as follows:

Corporate Taxable Income	$100,000.00
Corporate Tax At 27.53623 Percent	(27,536.23)
Corporate After Tax Income And Eligible Dividends Paid	$ 72,463.77
38 Percent Gross Up [(38%)($72,463.77)]	27,536.23
Mr. Marin's Taxable Eligible Dividends	$100,000.00

7-78.   You should note that the 38 percent gross up only works in situations where the corporation is taxed at a 27.53623 percent rate. (We have used 5 decimal places in these examples to eliminate the need for rounding.) If the corporate tax rate was higher, the taxable dividends would be less than the pre-tax corporate income. Correspondingly, if the tax rate was lower, the taxable dividends would be greater than the pre-tax corporate income.

Eligible Dividend Tax Credit Procedure

7-79.   The federal dividend tax credit for eligible dividends is equal to 6/11 (54.5455%) of the dividend gross up. This could also be expressed as 15.0198% of the grossed up dividends or 20.7273% of dividends received. In the Paragraph 7-77 example, this amount would be $15,019.80 which can be expressed as:

- 6/11 of the gross up = [(6/11)($27,536.23)], the calculation we will use in most of our examples, or;
- 15.0198% of grossed up dividends = [(15.0198%)($100,000)], or;
- 20.7273% of dividends received = [(20.7273%)($72,463.77)].

Note   The popular press often refers to the dividend tax credit as either a percent of grossed up dividends or, alternatively, a percent of dividends received. In this text and related problem material, we will follow the tax legislation and express the dividend tax credit as a fraction of the gross up.

7-80.   The 6/11 factor is the federal dividend tax credit. There is also an additional dividend tax credit available in each of the provinces and territories. For integration to be perfect, the combined federal/provincial dividend tax credit must be equal to the corporate taxes paid. As the gross up is designed to reflect corporate taxes paid, this means that the combined federal/provincial dividend tax credit must equal the gross up. This requires a provincial dividend tax credit of 5/11 or 45.4545 percent (6/11 + 5/11 = 54.5455% + 45.4545% = 100%).

7-81.   The following table shows the actual lowest and highest dividend tax credit rates for 2016, as well as the average rate for the 10 provinces (see Note to Paragraph 7-74).

Eligible Dividends - 2016	Lowest	Highest	Average
Provincial Dividend Tax Credit			
As Percentage Of 38% Gross Up	19.6%	43.6%	35.4%
Federal + Provincial Dividend Tax Credit	74.1%	98.1%	89.9%

7-82. You should note that, in all provinces, the combined federal/provincial dividend tax credit rate is below 100 percent, the rate required for perfect integration.

7-83.   A further point that should be made here is that the 27.54 (rounded) percent corporate rate that is assumed in the gross up of eligible dividends is higher than the combined federal/provincial tax rate on low income individuals in any of the provinces. A typical combined individual rate would be 23 percent (15 percent federal and 8 percent provincial). In this situation, integration will not work because, at this rate, the credit cannot compensate for the corporate taxes paid. This is illustrated by Mr. Plummer in the following example.

Example Of Eligible Dividends

7-84.   The following example illustrates how integration works when the dividend gross up is 38 percent and the federal dividend tax credit is equal to 6/11 of the gross up. We have noted that, for integration to work perfectly for eligible dividends, the corporate tax rate must be 27.53623 percent and the provincial dividend tax credit equal to 5/11 of the gross up.

EXAMPLE During 2017, Mr. Plummer and Ms. Black each have a business that produces $10,000 in Taxable Income. While they both live in the same province, Mr. Plummer's income is subject to a 15 percent federal tax rate and an 8 percent provincial tax rate. In contrast, Ms. Black's income is subject to a 33 percent federal tax rate and an 18 percent provincial tax rate. The provincial dividend tax credit is equal to 5/11 of the gross up and the combined federal/provincial tax rate on corporations is 27.54 percent.

ANALYSIS - Direct Receipt Of Income If Mr. Plummer and Ms. Black received the business income directly, the taxes paid and the after tax retention of the income would be as follows:

	Mr. Plummer	Ms. Black
Taxable Income	$10,000	$10,000
Total Individual Tax Payable:		
At 23 Percent (15% + 8%)	(2,300)	
At 51 Percent (33% + 18%)		(5,100)
After Tax Retention - Direct Receipt	$ 7,700	$ 4,900

ANALYSIS - Incorporation Of Income If the businesses were incorporated, and all of the corporate after tax income is paid out as dividends, the taxes paid and the after tax retention of the income would be as follows:

	Mr. Plummer	Ms. Black
Corporate Taxable Income	$10,000	$10,000
Corporate Taxes At 27.54 Percent	(2,754)	(2,754)
Eligible Dividends Paid	$ 7,246	$ 7,246
Eligible Dividends Received	$ 7,246	$ 7,246
Gross Up At 38 Percent [(38%)($7,246)]	2,754	2,754
Taxable Dividends (= Corporate Income)	$10,000	$10,000
Individual Tax Before Dividend Tax Credit:		
At 23 Percent (15% + 8%)	$2,300	
At 51 Percent (33% + 18%)		$5,100
Less: Dividend Tax Credit		
(= Corporate Taxes Paid)		
[(6/11+ 5/11)($2,754)]	(2,754)	(2,754)
Total Individual Tax Payable	Nil	$2,346
Eligible Dividends Received	$7,246	$7,246
Total Individual Tax Payable	(Nil)	(2,346)
After Tax Retention - Use Of Corporation	$7,246	$4,900
After Tax Retention - Direct Receipt	$7,700	$4,900

7-85. The rates in this example are those that are built into the gross up and tax credit procedures applicable to eligible dividends. That is, the corporate tax rate is 27.54 (rounded) percent and the provincial dividend tax credit is equal to 5/11 of the gross up. You will note that, while Ms. Black's $4,900 of after tax retention is not changed by the use of a corporation, Mr. Plummer's after tax eligible dividends are $7,246, $454 less than the $7,700 that he would have retained on the direct receipt of the business income. This reflects the fact that

Cash Dividends From Taxable Canadian Corporations

the assumed corporate tax rate of 27.54 percent is 4.54 percent higher than his personal tax rate of 23 percent, a situation that cannot be corrected by a non-refundable credit against his tax payable. Note, however, if Mr. Plummer had other sources of income, this excess would offset the taxes on that income.

Exercise Seven - 6

Subject: Dividend Income - Eligible Dividends

During 2017, Ms. Ellen Holt receives $15,000 in eligible dividends from taxable Canadian corporations. Her income is such that all additional amounts will be taxed at a 29 percent federal rate and a 14.5 percent provincial rate. Her provincial dividend tax credit for eligible dividends is equal to 30 percent of the gross up. Determine the total federal and provincial tax that will be payable on these dividends and her after tax retention.

SOLUTION available in print and online Study Guide.

Gross Up And Tax Credit Procedures - Non-Eligible Dividends
Non-Eligible Dividend Gross Up Procedure
7-86.   For non-eligible dividends received in 2017, the gross up is 17 percent. As noted in Paragraph 7-74, this factor is based on an assumed combined federal/provincial corporate tax rate of 14.530 percent. As illustrated in the following example, this corporate tax rate will create taxable dividends that reflect the amount of pre-tax corporate income received.

EXAMPLE Marin Ltd. is subject to a combined federal/provincial tax rate of 14.530 percent. During 2017, the company has Taxable Income of $100,000. All of the Company's after tax income is paid to Mr. Marin, its only shareholder, as a dividend.

ANALYSIS The results at the corporate and individual levels are as follows:

Corporate Taxable Income	$100,000
Corporate Tax At 14.530 Percent	(14,530)
Corporate After Tax Income And Non-Eligible Dividends Paid	$ 85,470
17 Percent Gross Up [(17%)($85,470)]	14,530
Mr. Marin's Taxable Non-Eligible Dividends	$100,000

7-87.   As demonstrated in the preceding calculation, the 17 percent gross up has resulted in a taxable dividend that is equal to the $100,000 pre-tax corporate income that is required to pay the dividend. This is also the amount of income that Mr. Marin would have received directly had he chosen not to incorporate his source of income. Similar to the case with eligible dividends, the 17 percent gross up for non-eligible dividends only works with one corporate tax rate. It must be exactly 14.530 percent. If the corporate tax rate was higher, the taxable dividends would be less than the pre-tax corporate income. Correspondingly, if the tax rate was lower, the taxable dividends would be greater than the pre-tax corporate income.

Non-Eligible Dividend Tax Credit Procedure
7-88.   Provided the corporate tax rate is 14.530 percent, the gross up procedure has served to increase Mr. Marin's Taxable Income to the $100,000 amount of corporate Taxable Income on which the non-eligible dividend payment was based. What is now required is a credit against Mr. Marin's Tax Payable to make up for the $14,530 in taxes that were paid at the corporate level. As we found with eligible dividends, to accomplish this goal, the combined federal/provincial tax credit has to be equal to 100 percent of the gross up.

7-89.   With respect to the federal component, under ITA 121, the individual will receive a credit against federal Tax Payable that is equal to 21/29 (72.4138 percent) of the gross up on non-eligible dividends. This credit can also be expressed as 10.5217 percent of taxable (i.e., grossed up) dividends or as 12.3104 percent of dividends received. In the example in Paragraph 7-86, this amount would be $10,522 which could be calculated as:

- 21/29 of the gross up = [(21/29)($14,530)], the calculation we will use in most of our examples as it follows tax legislation, or;
- 10.5217% of grossed up dividends = [(10.5217%)($100,000)], or;
- 12.3104% of dividends received = [(12.3104%)($85,470)].

7-90.   In order for the combined federal/provincial dividend tax credit to equal 100 percent of the gross up, the provincial credit has to equal 8/29 or 27.5862 percent. The following table shows the actual lowest and highest rates for 2016, as well as the average rate for the 10 provinces (see Note to Paragraph 7-74).

Non-Eligible Dividends - 2016	Lowest	Highest	Average
Provincial Dividend Tax Credit			
As Percentage Of 17% Gross Up	5.7%	48.5%	24.4%
Federal + Provincial Dividend Tax Credit	78.1%	120.9%	96.9%

7-91.   Unlike the situation with eligible dividends, provincial credits for non-eligible dividends, for some provinces, create a combined dividend tax credit that is in excess of the 100 percent that is required for perfect integration.

Example Of Non-Eligible Dividends

7-92.   We have noted that, for non-eligible dividends, integration works perfectly, provided the corporate tax rate is 14.530 percent and the provincial dividend tax credit is equal to 8/29 of the gross up. The following illustration of this point uses the same two scenarios that were used in Paragraph 7-84 to illustrate the taxation of eligible dividends.

EXAMPLE   During 2017, Mr. Plummer and Ms. Black each have a business that produces $10,000 in Taxable Income. While they both live in the same province, Mr. Plummer's income is subject to a 15 percent federal tax rate and an 8 percent provincial tax rate. In contrast, Ms. Black's income is subject to a 33 percent federal tax rate and an 18 percent provincial tax rate. The provincial dividend tax credit is equal to 8/29 of the gross up and the combined federal/provincial tax rate on corporations is 14.530 percent.

ANALYSIS - Direct Receipt Of Income   If Mr. Plummer and Ms. Black received the business income directly, the taxes paid and the after tax retention of the income would be as follows:

	Mr. Plummer	Ms. Black
Taxable Income	$10,000	$10,000
Total Individual Tax Payable:		
At 23 Percent (15% + 8%)	(2,300)	
At 51 Percent (33% + 18%)		(5,100)
After Tax Retention - Direct Receipt	$ 7,700	$ 4,900

ANALYSIS - Incorporation Of Income   If the businesses were incorporated, and all of the corporate after tax income is paid out as dividends, the taxes paid and the after tax retention of the income would be as follows:

Cash Dividends From Taxable Canadian Corporations

	Mr. Plummer	Ms. Black
Corporate Taxable Income	$10,000	$10,000
Corporate Taxes At 14.530 Percent	(1,453)	(1,453)
Non-Eligible Dividends Paid	$ 8,547	$ 8,547
Non-Eligible Dividends Received	$ 8,547	$ 8,547
Gross Up At 17 Percent [(17%)($8,547)]	1,453	1,453
Taxable Non-Eligible Dividends	$10,000	$10,000

	Mr. Plummer	Ms. Black
Individual Tax Before Dividend Tax Credit:		
At 23 Percent (15% + 8%)	$2,300	
At 51 Percent (33% + 18%)		$5,100
Less: Dividend Tax Credit		
(= Corporate Taxes Paid)		
[(21/29 + 8/29)($1,453)]	(1,453)	(1,453)
Total Individual Tax Payable	$ 847	$3,647
Non-Eligible Dividends Received	$8,547	$8,547
Total Individual Tax Payable	(847)	(3,647)
After Tax Retention - Use Of Corporation	$7,700	$4,900
After Tax Retention - Direct Receipt	$7,700	$4,900

7-93.   The rates in this example are those that are built into the gross up and tax credit procedures applicable to non-eligible dividends. That is, the corporate tax rate is 14.530 percent and the provincial dividend tax credit is equal to 8/29 of the gross up. As you would expect with the assumed corporate rate of 14.530 percent below the individual tax rates applicable to the two individuals, the after tax retention is the same, without regard to whether the $10,000 of income is received directly by the taxpayers or, alternatively, received indirectly after being flowed through a corporation. This is in contrast to the eligible dividend case. In that case (Paragraph 7-84), Mr. Plummer did not have sufficient Tax Payable to use all of the available dividend tax credit, resulting in Mr. Plummer being worse off when the income source was flowed through a corporation.

Exercise Seven - 7

Subject: Dividend Income - Non-Eligible Dividends

During 2017, Mr. John Johns receives $17,000 in non-eligible dividends from a taxable Canadian corporation. His income is such that all additional amounts will be taxed at a 29 percent federal rate and a 12 percent provincial rate. His provincial dividend tax credit for non-eligible dividends is equal to 30 percent of the gross up. Determine the total federal and provincial tax that will be payable on these dividends and his after tax cash retention.

SOLUTION available in print and online Study Guide.

Comparison Of Investment Returns

7-94.   The table which follows shows, for an individual in the maximum tax bracket applicable in the stated province, the tax rates on various types of investment income. As you will note, the rates vary significantly, both between provinces and with the type of investment income.

Maximum 2017 Tax Rates For Individuals
By Type Of Investment Income In Selected Provinces

	Interest Income	Capital Gains*	Non-Eligible Dividends	Eligible Dividends
Alberta	48.0%	24.0%	40.2%	31.7%
British Columbia	47.7%	23.9%	40.6%	31.3%
New Brunswick	53.3%	26.7%	45.4%	36.3%
Ontario	53.5%	26.8%	45.3%	39.3%
Quebec	53.3%	26.7%	43.8%	39.8%

*Only one-half of capital gains are included in Taxable Income.

7-95.   As only one-half of any capital gains are subject to tax, such gains are clearly the most favourable type of investment income. While the tax rates on dividends are not as attractive as those on capital gains, these rates are clearly better than the rates applied to interest income. The fact that eligible dividends are taxed at lower rates than is the case with non-eligible dividends reflects the fact that corporations that pay these dividends are generally subject to higher corporate rates than those applicable to corporations paying non-eligible dividends.

We suggest you work Self Study Problems Seven-3, 4, 5, and 6 at this point.

Income Trusts

How Do Trusts Work?

7-96.   While this subject is covered in detail in Chapter 19, Trusts And Estate Planning, it is impossible to discuss the taxation of income trusts without an understanding of the basic nature of trusts. Trusts are essentially flow-through entities. What this means is that, if the income earned by a trust is distributed immediately to its beneficiaries, the trust will pay no taxes. Consistent with this, the beneficiaries of the trusts will pay taxes on that income as though they had received it directly from its source. If a trust earns $100,000 in interest and distributes the full amount to the beneficiaries, the trust will pay no income taxes and the beneficiaries will be taxed on the $100,000 of interest income.

7-97.   The other important characteristic of trusts, including publicly traded income trusts, is that certain types of income retain their character as they flow through the trust. Although ITA 108(5) states that income distributed from a trust should be treated as income from property, there are specific exceptions that allow for flow through treatment. Most types of income that receive favourable tax treatment are included in the list of exceptions. For example, capital gains, taxable dividends and capital dividends that are earned in a trust are distributed to beneficiaries as capital gains, taxable dividends and capital dividends, thereby receiving the favourable treatment that these types of income have when they are received directly. Although there are other exceptions on the list, these are the important ones and the ones we will use in our material. Since business income is not on the exceptions list, business income earned in a trust is distributed to beneficiaries as property income.

Investments In Publicly Traded Trusts

Comparison Of Tax Consequences

7-98.   The use of trusts has been common for many years for both estate planning (e.g., a

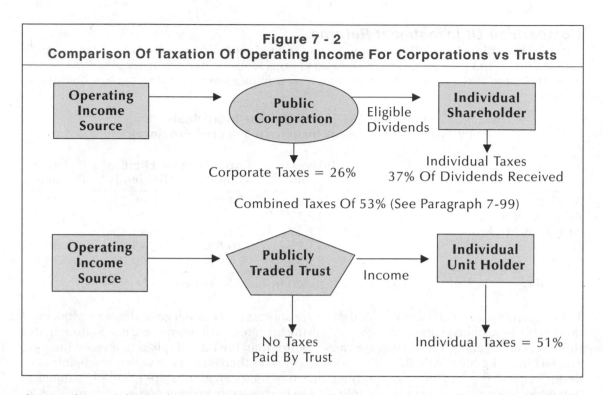

Figure 7 - 2
Comparison Of Taxation Of Operating Income For Corporations vs Trusts

deceased parent leaves his assets in a trust for his children) and for retirement savings (e.g., RRSPs are trusts). What is different here is that these trusts were created to raise financing through the public sale of their units, with the funds used to acquire various types of businesses.

> **EXAMPLE** The Zorin Real Estate Income Trust sells 1,000,000 units at a price of $50 per unit. The $50 million that was raised is used to acquire the assets and operations of Zorin Ltd., a Canadian public company. The trust is committed to distributing 100 percent of the Taxable Income from the Zorin operations to its unitholders.

Prior to the transfer of assets to the income trust, Zorin Ltd.'s income was subject to a combined federal/provincial corporate tax rate of 26 percent. Its shareholders were subject to a combined federal/provincial rate on dividends received of 37 percent. Unit holders of the Zorin Income Trust will be subject to a combined federal/provincial rate of 51 percent on distributions from the income trust.

7-99. The tax consequences of this transaction are illustrated in Figure 7-2.

- Prior to the existence of the trust, the income from the Zorin operations was subject to a corporate tax rate of 26 percent. The after tax income could then be distributed to shareholders as dividends. In the Example, these dividends were taxed at a combined federal/provincial rate of 37 percent. The resulting overall tax rate on the income stream channeled through Zorin Ltd. was 53 percent [26% + (37%)(1 - 26%)].

- In contrast, the Zorin Trust will pay no taxes if it distributes all of its income. However, the distributions to its unit holders will be taxed as ordinary income. In the Example, that would be at a rate of 51 percent. Unlike the situation when the income from the Zorin operations was subject to corporate taxes, there will be no dividend gross up and tax credit benefits.

7-100. This example illustrates that, in situations where normal provincial rates and dividend tax credits prevail, income that is flowed through an income trust will be subject to lower taxes than would be the case if the same stream of income was flowed through a public corporation. While the amount of the advantage may be more or less in individual provinces, results will generally favour the use of income trusts.

SIFT Trusts And REITs

7-101. It is not surprising that income trusts became an extremely popular investment vehicle since:

- They often provided an overall tax savings as illustrated in the preceding example.

- They had to distribute all of their earnings to unit holders in order to avoid taxes at the trust level.

- Most income trusts were committed to paying out 100 percent of the cash flows from the acquired operations. As these cash flows would typically exceed both accounting and tax income, a part of the distribution was received as a tax free return of capital.

7-102. However, they provided a significant problem in terms of tax policy. As shown in Figure 7-2, there was an assumption that amounts distributed to unit holders would be subject to tax. Over time, it became clear to the government that this was not always the case. Specifically:

Non-Resident Investors If the income trust units are held by a non-resident investor, they may not be subject to any Canadian taxes. At most, the taxes will be at the low Part XIII rates. (See Chapter 20, Issues In International Income.)

Tax Exempt Entities (e.g., RPPs, RRSPs, Other Tax Exempt Entities) If the income trust units are held inside a tax exempt entity, the distributions will not be subject to tax at the time they are received from the income trust. While they will eventually be subject to tax when they are withdrawn from the registered plan, this taxation could be deferred for 30 to 40 years. (See Chapter 10 which covers retirement savings.)

7-103. Because of these situations, the government concluded that it would no longer allow such a major leakage of tax revenues. Legislation was introduced under which most income trusts were designated as Specified Investment Flow Through (SIFT) trusts. Under this legislation most SIFT trusts are taxed at roughly the combined federal/provincial rate applicable to public corporations. This has the effect of removing most of the available tax advantage. As a consequence, the income trusts that were subject to this legislation converted to a conventional corporate structure.

7-104. For a variety of reasons, income trusts that were involved in owning real estate were exempted from this legislation. These real estate investment trusts (REITs) continue to enjoy the previously cited advantages associated with the income trust structure. Because of this, REITs continue to provide investors with very attractive yields, making them an important and popular choice for many investors. Given this popularity, we are providing coverage of the basic tax procedures associated with REITs.

Taxation Of Real Estate Investment Trusts (REITs)

Distributions

7-105. Most income trusts are committed to distributing their net cash flow to unit holders. As you are aware from your accounting courses, this amount will not be equal to accounting income as determined under GAAP. In most cases, because of non-cash deductions for amortization, the net cash flow will exceed accounting net income. This means that trust distributions will, in general, consist of an income distribution, combined with an additional distribution that represents a return of capital (i.e., the return of amounts invested).

7-106. To the extent that distributions reflect income that has been earned in the trust, they will be taxed in the hands of individual investors at the usual federal and provincial rates. As discussed in Paragraph 7-97, if the trust earned capital gains or dividends (eligible, non-eligible or capital), the distribution of these amounts will be treated as capital gains or dividends (eligible, non-eligible or capital) by the recipient of the distributions. On the other hand, business income will be distributed to unit holders as property income.

7-107. To the extent that the trust distribution exceeds the trust's income, the excess will be treated as a return of capital. These distributions will be received by individual investors on a tax free basis.

Adjusted Cost Base

7-108. The determination of the adjusted cost base for income trust units is complicated by the fact that some part of its distributions may be a tax free return of capital. While such distributions are not taxed currently, they do reduce the adjusted cost base of the units held by an investor. This means that the adjusted cost base of an investment in income trust units is equal to the cost of the units to the investor, less any amounts of capital returned as part of the trust's distributions.

7-109. A further complication relates to the fact that many income trusts have distribution reinvestment plans (DRIPs). To the extent an investor chooses to have his distributions reinvested, the amount reinvested will be an addition to the adjusted cost base of the units held. This will be accompanied by an increase in the number of units held. Note that, if the investor disposes of a part of his holding, the adjusted cost base of the units sold will be based on the average cost of all units held (see Chapter 8 on identical properties).

EXAMPLE On January 1, 2017, Joan Arden acquires 1,000 units of the Newcor Income Trust at a total cost of $100,000 or $100 per unit. On December 15, 2017, the trust distributes $6 per unit, $2 of which is a return of capital and $4 of which is business income earned in the trust that is distributed as property income. At this time, the trust has a purchase price of $110 per unit.

ANALYSIS Regardless of whether or not Ms. Arden reinvests the distribution, she will include $4,000 [($4)(1,000 units)] in her 2017 Net Income For Tax Purposes. If Ms. Arden chooses not to reinvest the distribution, she would have received $6,000 [(1,000)($6)] in cash, her Net Income would be increased by $4,000 and her 1,000 units would have an adjusted cost base, after the $2,000 [($2)(1,000)] return of capital, of $98 per unit [($100,000 - $2,000) ÷ 1,000].

If the $6,000 distribution is reinvested in additional trust units at a cost of $110 per unit, her holding increases to 1,054.55 [1,000 + ($6,000 ÷ $110)] units. Her adjusted cost base would be calculated as follows:

	Adjusted Cost Base	No. Of Units
Original Investment	$100,000	1,000.00
Reinvestment Of Distribution	6,000	54.55
Tax Free Return Of Capital	(2,000)	N/A
Adjusted Cost Base/Number Of Units	$104,000	1,054.55

This will result in an average cost for her units of $98.62 ($104,000 ÷ 1,054.55).

Exercise Seven - 8

Subject: Income Trust Distributions

On January 1, 2017, John Dore acquires 2,000 units of Xeron Income Trust at $55 per unit, a total cost of $110,000. During 2017, the trust distributes $5.00 per unit, $1.50 of which is a return of capital and $3.50 of which is a business income distribution. John has asked the trust to reinvest all distributions. The $5.00 per unit distribution was reinvested at a cost of $57 per additional unit. What are the tax consequences to John of the 2017 distribution and its reinvestment? What will be his adjusted cost base per unit after the reinvestment?

SOLUTION available in print and online Study Guide.

Mutual Funds

Objective

7-110.   Mutual funds are organized to provide investment management, largely for individual taxpayers. The basic idea is that investors provide funds to these organizations which they, in turn, use to make direct investments in stocks, bonds, and other types of investment property. As will be discussed in the following material, mutual funds can be organized as either trusts or as corporations.

Organization

Mutual Fund Trusts

7-111.   In Canada, most mutual funds are organized as trusts. As was discussed in Paragraph 7-96, trusts are flow-through entities. This means that, if all of the income earned in the trust is distributed to beneficiaries, no taxes will be paid at the trust level.

7-112.   Mutual fund trusts are generally structured to make use of this flow-through feature. In most cases, the by-laws will require that the trust distribute, to the unit holders of the trust, all of the income it earns during a taxation year. This will free the mutual fund trust from any obligation to pay taxes on income earned during the year.

Mutual Fund Corporations

7-113.   Mutual fund corporations are less common than mutual fund trusts. In this case, the mutual fund will be taxed at regular corporate tax rates on the investment income that it earns. As the investors will be shareholders rather than trust unit holders, in general, their distributions will be treated as dividends subject to the usual gross up and tax credit procedures. Note, however, ITA 131 provides an election that allows the dividends of mutual fund corporations to be treated as capital gains in the hands of shareholders. Like mutual fund trusts, mutual fund corporations are usually committed to distributing all of the after tax income earned during a taxation year to their shareholders.

7-114.   There are other complications here involving capital dividends and refundable taxes on investment income that go beyond the scope of the material in this Chapter.

Distributions

Mutual Fund Trusts

7-115.   As noted in our discussion of income trusts in Paragraph 7-96, an important feature of the trust legal form is that certain types of income can retain their tax characteristics as they flow through the trust. For example, if the mutual fund trust has a capital gain, it will be distributed to investors as a capital gain. This means that, when a mutual fund provides an investor with an information return (a T3, if the fund is organized as a trust), it will indicate the various types of income that are included in its distributions. These types will commonly include:

- **Eligible Dividends**   These amounts will be subject to the gross up and tax credit procedures that were previously discussed in this Chapter. Eligible dividends received by the trust will be distributed as eligible dividends to the trust unit holders.

- **Canadian Interest Income**   These amounts will be taxed as ordinary interest income.

- **Capital Gains**   As with capital gains earned directly by the individual, only one-half of these amounts will be subject to taxes (this type of income is discussed in Chapter 8).

- **Foreign Non-Business (Interest And Dividend) Income**   These amounts are taxable on the same basis as Canadian interest income. As will be discussed in a later section of this Chapter, the gross amount of this income will be included in income, with amounts withheld at the foreign source being eligible for tax credit treatment.

- **Capital Distributions**   A fund can make distributions that exceed its income for the year. These are identified as a return of capital and are received tax free. They do, however, reduce the adjusted cost base of the investment.

Mutual Fund Corporations

7-116.   Shareholders in mutual fund corporations receive dividends from the after tax income earned by the corporation's investments. Unlike the situation with mutual fund trusts, the investment income earned by the mutual fund corporation does not retain its tax features when distributed to shareholders. Without regard to whether the income of the mutual fund corporation was interest, dividends, or capital gains, it is paid out as taxable dividends.

7-117.   Dividends paid by mutual fund corporations will usually be eligible dividends and these eligible dividends will qualify for the usual gross up and tax credit procedures. As was discussed earlier in this Chapter, this provides the recipient with a reduced rate of taxation.

Adjusted Cost Base

Mutual Fund Trusts

7-118.   Determining the adjusted cost base of a mutual fund trust unit uses procedures that are similar to those used in determining the adjusted cost base of an income trust unit. Any distributions that are reinvested in the fund increase the adjusted cost base of the units of a mutual fund trust. The balance is reduced by any amounts that represent a tax free return of capital. Amounts of income that are distributed to investors do not alter the adjusted cost base of the investment.

> **EXAMPLE**   On October 15, 2017, Martin Diaz purchases 1,000 units of CIC Growth Fund for $7.30 per unit. On December 1, 2017, the fund has an interest income distribution of $.50 per unit. At this time, the fund has a purchase price of $6 per unit.

> **ANALYSIS**   Regardless of whether or not Mr. Diaz reinvests the distribution, he will include $500 [($0.50)(1,000 units)] in his 2017 Net Income For Tax Purposes. If Mr. Diaz chooses not to reinvest the distribution, he will receive $500 in cash. He would then have 1,000 units with his original adjusted cost base of $7.30 per unit. Alternatively, if the distribution is reinvested, he will receive 83.33 ($500 ÷ $6) additional units. This will leave him with a holding of 1,083.33 units with an adjusted cost base of $7,800 ($7,300 + $500), or $7.20 ($7,800 ÷ 1,083.33) per unit.

Mutual Fund Corporations

7-119.   In general, the adjusted cost base of a mutual fund corporation will not be altered by distributions that are made by the corporation. The exception to this would be a situation where the corporation distributed a return of capital. This, however, would rarely occur. In addition, coverage of this type of situation goes beyond the material covered in this Chapter (see Chapter 14).

7-120.   If the holder of the shares decides to reinvest the amounts distributed, the cost of the additional shares is added to the adjusted cost of the original shares. Such reinvestments are less common with mutual fund corporations than they are with mutual fund trusts.

Exercise Seven - 9

Subject: Mutual Fund Distributions

Ms. Marissa Tiompkins owns 3,500 units of the RB Small Cap Fund, a mutual fund trust. These units were purchased at a price of $11.25 per unit, for a total value of $39,375. There have been no changes in her adjusted cost base prior to the current year. On September 1 of the current year, the Fund has an income distribution of $0.30 per unit, a total of $1,050 for Ms. Tiompkins. She reinvests this amount to acquire additional fund units at $13.00 per unit. What will be her adjusted cost base per unit after the reinvestment?

SOLUTION available in print and online Study Guide.

> **We suggest you work Self Study Problem Seven-7 at this point.**

Other Types Of Dividends

Capital Dividends

7-121.   When a corporation has a capital gain, only one-half of this amount will be taxable. However, the full amount of the proceeds of disposition is still held by the corporation. In the absence of a special provision, this full amount would be taxed if it were distributed to a shareholder as a dividend. In order to avoid this result for private companies only, one-half of the capital gain will be allocated to a balance referred to as a "capital dividend account" (as you will find in Chapter 14, several other items are allocated to this account).

7-122.   When the amounts allocated to this capital dividend account are paid out to shareholders of private companies, they will be received by Canadian resident investors on a totally tax free basis. Also to be noted here is that, for Canadian residents, such capital dividends do not have to be deducted from the adjusted cost base of the investor's shares.

Stock Dividends

7-123.   A stock dividend involves a pro rata distribution of additional shares to the existing shareholders of a company. For example, if the XYZ Company had 1,000,000 shares outstanding and it declared a 10 percent stock dividend, the Company would be distributing 100,000 new shares to its present shareholders on the basis of one new share for each ten of the old shares held.

7-124.   While there is no real change in anyone's financial position as a result of this transaction, in the accounting records it is accompanied by a transfer from the Company's Retained Earnings to contributed capital or paid up capital. The amount of this transfer is normally the fair market value of the shares to be issued, determined on the dividend declaration date.

7-125.   For tax purposes, stock dividends are dealt with in the same manner as cash dividends. The value of the dividend is based on the amount of the increase in the paid up capital of the issuer. In some cases, provincial legislation requires that this amount be equal to the fair market value of the shares issued. In other provinces, the increase can be established at the discretion of the directors. Whatever the amount, it is treated as a cash dividend and subject to the eligible or non-eligible gross up and tax credit procedures. As this amount has been subject to tax, it is added to the adjusted cost base of all of the shares owned by the investor.

7-126.   This approach places the investor in the position of having to pay taxes on an amount of dividends that has not been received in cash, an unfavourable situation with respect to the investor's cash flows. As a consequence, public companies make little use of stock dividends. However, they are often used in the tax planning arrangements of private companies.

Exercise Seven - 10

Subject: Stock Dividends

Morgna Inc. has 2,000,000 common shares outstanding. John Morgna acquired 10 percent of these shares at a cost of $12 per share. During the current year, when the shares are trading at $15 per share, the Company declares a 10 percent stock dividend which it designates as eligible. The Company transfers the amount of the stock dividend to paid up capital. What are the tax consequences to John Morgna of this transaction? Your answer should include the adjusted cost base per share of his holding.

SOLUTION available in print and online Study Guide.

Foreign Source Income

General Rules

7-127.   As Canadian taxation is based on residency, income that has a foreign source must be included in full in the calculation of Net Income For Tax Purposes of any Canadian resident. This is complicated by the fact that many foreign jurisdictions levy some form of withholding tax on such income.

7-128.   The general approach to this situation is to require Canadian residents to include 100 percent of any foreign income earned in their Net Income For Tax Purposes. They then receive a credit against Tax Payable for taxes withheld in the foreign jurisdiction. The basic idea behind this approach is to have the combined foreign and Canadian tax on this income be the same as that which would be levied on the same amount of income earned in Canada.

> **EXAMPLE**   An individual earned $1,000 in a foreign jurisdiction. As the authorities in that jurisdiction withhold $100, his net receipt is $900. The individual's marginal tax rate is 45 percent.
>
> **ANALYSIS**   The Canadian Tax Payable on the amount received would be calculated as follows:
>
> | | |
> |---|---:|
> | Amount Received | $ 900 |
> | Foreign Tax Withheld | 100 |
> | Increase In Taxable Income | $1,000 |
> | Rate | 45% |
> | Tax Payable Before Credit | $ 450 |
> | Foreign Tax Credit (Equal To Withholding) | (100) |
> | Canadian Tax Payable | $ 350 |

Note that the combined foreign and Canadian tax equal $450 ($350 + $100), the same amount that the individual would have paid on the domestic receipt of $1,000 of income.

Foreign Non-Business (Property) Income

7-129.   Following the general rule, 100 percent of foreign source non-business income is included in Net Income For Tax Purposes. However, for individuals, the credit against Tax Payable that is provided under ITA 126(1) is limited to a maximum of 15 percent of the foreign source non-business income. If the withheld amounts exceed 15 percent, the excess can be deducted under ITA 20(11).

Foreign Business Income

7-130.   In the case of foreign source business income, there is no direct limitation on the use of the amounts withheld as a credit against Tax Payable and, correspondingly, no deduction in the calculation of Net Income For Tax Purposes for any part of the amount withheld by the foreign jurisdiction. The following example compares the difference in the treatment of tax withheld on foreign non-business income and foreign business income.

> **EXAMPLE**   Mr. Grant, a taxpayer with a marginal tax rate of 45 percent, earns foreign source income of $1,000. The foreign government withholds 40 percent ($400) and he receives $600.
>
> **ANALYSIS**   The Canadian Tax Payable on the amount received assuming it is foreign non-business income or business income would be calculated as follows:

	Non-Business Income	Business Income
Amount Received	$ 600.00	$ 600.00
Foreign Tax Withheld	400.00	400.00
Inclusion For Foreign Income	$1,000.00	$1,000.00
Deduction Of Excess Withholding [$400 - (15%)($1,000)]	(250.00)	N/A
Increase In Taxable Income	$ 750.00	$1,000.00
Rate	45%	45%
Tax Payable Before Credit	$ 337.50	$ 450.00
Foreign Tax Credit [(15%)($1,000)]	(150.00)	
Foreign Tax Credit (Amount Withheld)		(400.00)
Canadian Tax Payable	$ 187.50	$ 50.00

ANALYSIS - Foreign Non-Business Income   Income of $750 will be included in Net Income For Tax Purposes. Foreign and Canadian taxes combined would be $587.50 ($400 + $187.50), well in excess of the $450 he would have paid on $1,000 of Canadian source income. This illustrates that the availability of the deduction does not make up for the fact that the tax credit is limited to 15 percent. The value of a $1 tax credit is $1, whereas the value of a $1 deduction to Mr. Grant is only $0.45 [($1)(45%)].

ANALYSIS - Foreign Business Income   The gross income of $1,000 will be included in Net Income For Tax Purposes. The full $400 of withholding will be used to calculate a credit against his Canadian Tax Payable of $450 [(45%)($1,000)]. This leaves $50 in Canadian Tax Payable and a total tax of $450 ($400 + $50). This is the same amount that he would have paid on the receipt of $1,000 in Canadian source income.

Exercise Seven - 11

Subject: Foreign Source Income

Norah Johns has foreign source income of $30,000 during the current year. As the foreign jurisdiction withholds 25 percent of such income, she only receives $22,500. She has other income such that this foreign source income will be taxed at a marginal federal tax rate of 29 percent. Determine the amount by which this foreign income would increase Norah's Taxable Income and federal Tax Payable, assuming that the foreign source income (1) is non-business income and (2) is business income.

SOLUTION available in print and online Study Guide.

Shareholder Benefits

7-131.   Shareholders sometimes receive benefits from a corporation that are directly related to their investment in the shares of that corporation. Examples would include:

- A corporation providing a shareholder with an automobile for personal use.
- A corporation building a swimming pool at a shareholder's personal residence.
- A corporation providing a shareholder with an interest free loan.

7-132.   Such benefits are taxable as property income, largely under ITA 15(1) of the *Income Tax Act*. Further, in almost all cases, the corporation is not able to deduct the cost of providing the benefit. The following simple example illustrates some of the potential tax problems related to shareholder benefits.

EXAMPLE   A corporation provides a shareholder with a $10,000 holiday trip to Italy.

ANALYSIS   ITA 15(1) requires the inclusion of the $10,000 cost of the trip in the income of the shareholder. Despite the fact that this amount is now being taxed in the hands of the shareholder, the corporation cannot deduct the cost of the trip.

7-133.   There are a number of complications that result from shareholder benefits, particularly those associated with low or interest free loans. These complications will be given detailed coverage in Chapter 15, Corporate Taxation And Management Decisions.

Tax Credits Revisited

Dividend Tax Credits

7-134.   Most of the credits that are available to individuals in determining their Tax Payable are discussed in Chapter 4. However, because an understanding of some amount of additional material was required, it was appropriate to defer coverage of a few of these credits to later Chapters. Given the content of this Chapter, we have added two additional credits.

7-135.   The first of these was the dividend tax credit and there are two different versions of this credit:

Eligible Dividends   For eligible dividends received from taxable Canadian corporations, the federal dividend tax credit is equal to 6/11 of a 38 percent gross up. It can also be calculated as 15.0198 percent of the grossed up amount of dividends or, alternatively, as 20.7273 percent of dividends received.

Non-Eligible Dividends   For non-eligible dividends received from taxable Canadian corporations, the federal dividend tax credit is equal to 21/29 of a 17 percent gross up. It can also be calculated as 10.5217 percent of the grossed up amount of dividends or, alternatively, as 12.3104 percent of dividends received.

Foreign Income Tax Credits

7-136.   The other tax credit that was introduced in this Chapter was the credit for foreign taxes paid on foreign source income. For the purposes of this Chapter, we have indicated that this credit is equal to the amount of foreign taxes withheld, subject to the limitation that, in the case of foreign source non-business income earned by individuals, the credit is limited to 15 percent of the foreign source income.

7-137.   This, however, is not the end of the story. For both foreign source non-business income and foreign source business income, the amount of the credit may be limited by the total amount of taxes paid by the individual. This limit is based on an equation that requires an understanding of loss carry overs. As this material has not been covered at this point, we will have to return to coverage of the credits for foreign taxes paid when we revisit Taxable Income and Tax Payable For Individuals in Chapter 11.

We suggest you work Self Study Problems Seven-8 and 9 at this point.

Additional Supplementary Self Study Problems Are Available Online.

Key Terms Used In This Chapter

7-138.   The following is a list of the key terms used in this Chapter. These terms, and their meanings, are compiled in the Glossary located at the back of the Study Guide.

Accrual Basis	Eligible Dividends
Business Income	Foreign Taxes Paid Credit
Capital Dividend	Income Trust
Capital Dividend Account	Interest Income
Cash Basis	Mutual Fund
Cash Damming	Net Business Income
Disappearing Source Rules	Net Property Income
Dividend Gross Up	Non-Eligible Dividends
Dividend Tax Credit	Property Income
Dividends	Stock Dividend

References

7-139.   For more detailed study of the material in this Chapter, we refer you to the following:

ITA 12(1)(c)	Interest
ITA 12(1)(g)	Payments Based On Production Or Use
ITA 12(3)	Interest Income
ITA 12(4)	Interest From Investment Contract
ITA 12(11)	Definitions (Investment Contract)
ITA 15	Benefits Conferred On Shareholder
ITA 20(1)(c)	Interest
ITA 20(1)(f)	Discount On Certain Obligations
ITA 20(14)	Accrued Bond Interest
ITA 20.1	Borrowed Money Used To Earn Income From Property
ITA 82(1)(b)	Taxable Dividends Received
ITA 121	Deduction For Taxable Dividends
ITA 126	Foreign Tax Deduction
S3-F6-C1	Interest Deductibility
S5-F2-C1	Foreign Tax Credit
IT-67R3	Taxable Dividends From Corporations Resident In Canada
IT-195R4	Rental Property - Capital Cost Allowance Restrictions
IT-295R4	Taxable Dividends Received After 1987 By A Spouse
IT-396R	Interest Income
IT-434R	Rental Of Real Property By Individual
IT-443	Leasing Property - Capital Cost Allowance Restrictions
IT-462	Payments Based On Production Or Use
IT-506	Foreign Income Taxes As A Deduction from Income
T4036	Rental Income Guide

Problems For Self Study (Online)

To provide practice in problem solving, there are Self Study and Supplementary Self Study problems available on the Companion Website.

Within the text we have provided an indication of when it would be appropriate to work each Self Study problem. The detailed solutions for Self Study problems can be found in the print and online Study Guide.

We provide the Supplementary Self Study problems for those who would like additional practice in problem solving. The detailed solutions for the Supplementary Self Study problems are available online, not in the Study Guide.

The .PDF file "Self Study Problems for Volume 1" on the Companion Website contains the following for Chapter 7:

- 9 Self Study problems,
- 6 Supplementary Self Study problems, and
- detailed solutions for the Supplementary Self Study problems.

Assignment Problems

(The solutions for these problems are only available in
the solutions manual that has been provided to your instructor.)

Assignment Problem Seven - 1
(Interest Deductibility - 4 Cases)

Each of the following independent Cases involves the payment of interest and the issue of whether the interest will be deductible for tax purposes.

Case A Thomas Sanjuan finances the acquisition of an income producing property. The cost of the property is $435,000 and Thomas finances 100 percent of the purchase. The investment proves successful, with the property being sold for $610,000. He uses the proceeds of the sale to acquire two properties with costs of $495,000 and $115,000 respectively. Explain how the original $435,000 proceeds from the loan can be allocated to the two properties.

Case B Tamara Sherrell has a trading account which holds equity securities with a current fair market value of $1,500,000. She would like to purchase a new Bentley for $325,000. Her bank will finance her purchase with a $325,000 loan that requires interest to be paid at a rate of 8.3 percent. However, as her equity securities are in a margin account, she can use her margin balance to borrow the $325,000 at a rate of 3.25 percent. She chooses the latter approach.

During the year, she pays interest on this loan of $10,500. Also during the year, the securities in her trading account pay total dividends of $75,000. Can she deduct the $10,500 of interest against the dividend income generated by the securities in her trading account? Explain your conclusion.

Case C Manuel Pettie takes out a mortgage on his house for $500,000 and immediately transfers the entire amount to his brokerage account to invest in publicly traded securities. Relying solely on company names that come to him in his dreams, he makes some very bad investment choices. As a result, after one year, his securities are worth only $240,000. Feeling very discouraged, he sells all of the securities and uses the proceeds to reduce the loan balance. He will not have the resources to pay off the remaining $260,000 until he receives $500,000 from his trust fund in 2 years. Is the interest on the mortgage deductible before he sells the shares? If so, does this change after he sells the shares? Explain your conclusion.

Case D   Bo Godina borrows $220,000 in order to purchase an income producing property for that same amount. The results from this investment are not promising and, as a result, he sells the investment for $150,000. He uses these funds to buy two properties. The first property costs $35,000, while the second costs $115,000. How will the $220,000 in borrowing be linked to the two properties?

Assignment Problem Seven - 2
(Rental Income)

During 2017, Ms. Jessica Roberts owns four residential rental properties. Information on these properties is as follows:

	124 Glengarry Avenue	4251 Oak Street	1322 Curry Avenue	436 Rankin Avenue
CCA Class	3	1	1	1
Capital Cost Of Building	$827,000	$456,000	$246,000	$947,000
January 1, 2017 UCC	$563,086	$411,845	$213,018	Nil

Rental receipts and expenses, not including CCA, for year ending December 31, 2017 are as follows:

	124 Glengarry Avenue	4251 Oak Street	1322 Curry Avenue	436 Rankin Avenue
Rental Receipts	$50,400	$37,200	$12,800	$63,600
Property Taxes	(12,400)	(6,840)	(9,690)	(14,205)
Interest Charges	(24,000)	(10,200)	(4,200)	(41,300)
Other Expenses (Not Including CCA)	(5,400)	(8,400)	(1,100)	(3,600)
Net Rental Income (Loss) Before CCA	**$ 8,600**	**$11,760**	**($ 2,190)**	**$ 4,495**

Other Information:

1. During 2017, Ms. Roberts spent $63,000 on improvements to the property at 124 Glengarry Avenue. While none of the changes were required, the tenant insisted on the changes before he was prepared to renew his lease. These improvements will also enhance the value of this property.

2. The building at 4251 Oak Street was sold during 2017 for $523,000.

3. The building at 1322 Curry Avenue was sold during 2017 for $185,000.

    Ms. Roberts had furnished this property several years ago at a cost of $23,000. The UCC for these Class 8 assets was $3,598 on January 1, 2017. Given the condition of the furnishings, they were simply given to the former tenants who agreed to take them when they moved out.

4. The property at 436 Rankin Avenue was acquired during 2017 for $947,000.

Required: Calculate Ms. Robert's minimum net rental income for 2017. You should provide a separate CCA calculation for each property and specify how much CCA should be taken for each building. Include in your solution any tax consequences associated with the sale of the two buildings and the disposition of the furniture.

Assignment Problem Seven - 3
(Rental Income)

Mr. Beau Truett has always believed that real estate was a better investment than equity securities. While real estate has a downside in its lack of liquidity, it has three major advantages:

- Current taxation can be avoided through the deduction of CCA. In fact, if properties are heavily financed, there can be current losses on real estate that can shelter other types of income from taxation.
- Over long periods of time, gains can be enormous. Further, as these gains are, in general, capital gains, only one-half will be subject to taxation.
- Taxation of any increase in value of a property can be deferred until that property is sold.

Based on these views, Beau has, for many years, actively invested in rental properties. At the beginning of 2017, he owns four such properties. Relevant information on these properties for the year ending December 31, 2017, is as follows:

13 Jane   The cost of this property was $825,000, of which $650,000 was allocated to the building and $175,000 was allocated to the land on which it was situated. It is in a separate Class 1 with a January 1, 2017 UCC balance of $531,044. During 2017, its net rental income, before the deduction of CCA, was calculated as follows:

Rents		$42,000
Property Taxes	($ 7,000)	
Mortgage Interest	(16,250)	
Other Expenses (Other Than CCA)	(8,600)	(31,850)
Net Rental Income (Before CCA)		$10,150

146 Bronsen   This property has been held for many years and had an original cost of $48,000. This was divided into $36,000 for the building and $12,000 for the land. It is included in a single Class 3, along with 27 Front (see next property). The UCC balance in this Class on January 1, 2017 is $21,000. During 2017, the property was sold for $146,000, with $110,000 being allocated to the building and $36,000 to the land. Prior to its sale, net rental income was recorded as follows:

Rents		$13,500
Property Taxes	($1,500)	
Mortgage Interest	(1,400)	
Other Expenses (Other Than CCA)	(1,100)	(4,000)
Net Rental Income (Before CCA)		$ 9,500

27 Front   This property had an original cost of $58,000, allocated $42,000 to the building and $16,000 to the land. It is included in the Class 3 balance with 146 Bronsen. For 2017, the property had net rental income, before the deduction of CCA, calculated as follows:

Rents		$16,700
Property Taxes	($ 1,800)	
Mortgage Interest	(2,600)	
Other Expenses (Other Than CCA)	(2,100)	(6,500)
Net Rental Income (Before CCA)		$10,200

4826 Jarvus   This property had an original cost of $750,000, allocated $600,000 to the building and $150,000 to the land. It is included in a separate Class 1 with a January 1, 2017 UCC balance of $479,439. During 2017, its net rental income, before the deduction of CCA, was calculated as follows:

Rents		$ 8,400
Property Taxes	($ 6,200)	
Mortgage Interest	(15,250)	
Other Expenses (Other Than CCA)	(7,400)	(28,850)
Net Rental Income (Loss) (Before CCA)		($20,450)

Unlike the other properties, this property was rented fully furnished. However, when this unit became empty early in 2017, Beau had great difficulty finding a new tenant. Finally, in October, he decided to replace the aging furnishings and appliances and repaint the property. With the improvement in appearance, he was able to rent the property in late November.

The old furnishings and appliances, all Class 8 assets, were acquired at a cost of $46,000. The January 1, 2017 UCC balance was $21,197. During 2017, all of these assets were replaced at a cost of $51,000. A generous trade-in allowance (considering the condition of the assets) of $5,000 was received for the old assets.

Beau has received an unsolicited offer for 4826 Jarvus that would result in a substantial capital gain. Although he has not made up his mind, he thinks he could use the funds to purchase real estate that would give him a better return.

Required: Determine the tax consequences for the year ending December 31, 2017 of the operation of these rental properties, the sale of 146 Bronsen, and replacement of the furnishings in 4826 Jarvus. Your answer should include Beau's net rental income for the year and the January 1, 2018 UCC balances for the rental assets.

Assignment Problem Seven - 4
(Dividend vs. Interest Income)

Betty, Barbra, and Becky Larson are sisters who live in the same city. Due to disparate life choices, they have experienced varying degrees of economic success. Because of this, their additional income will be taxed at different rates as follows:

	Betty	Barbra	Becky
Federal Marginal Tax Rate	15%	20.5%	33%
Provincial Marginal Tax Rate	8%	12%	20%

In 2016, the three sisters bought a block of lottery tickets and agreed to an equal sharing of any winnings. One of the tickets turned out to be a winner, and they shared a $60,000 prize.

They each intend to invest their $20,000 on January 1, 2017 and are considering the following alternatives:

Corporate Bonds Corporate bonds that provide a 5 percent coupon rate. These bonds can be purchased at their maturity value. They mature in 20 years.

Preferred Stock Preferred shares are available at a price of $25 per share. These shares pay a non-cumulative dividend of $1.50 per share.

The income from these investments would not move any of the three sisters to a higher federal or provincial tax bracket. The provincial dividend tax credit on eligible dividends is equal to 27 percent of the dividend gross up. Each sister has sufficient income to use all of her available tax credits.

Required: Advise each of the Larson sisters as to which investment they should make. As part of your recommendation, calculate the after tax income that would be generated for each of the sisters, assuming that they invested their $20,000 in:

A. The corporate bonds.
B. The preferred stock.

Assignment Problem Seven - 5

(Investments In Income Trusts And Common Stock)

On January 1, 2017, Carolyn Jackson received a $200,000 inheritance from her mother. While she has no plans to use any of these funds during 2017, she and her three sisters plan to open a bed and breakfast in a year and she will need the funds to purchase her share of the business on January 1, 2018.

In the meantime, she would like to invest the $200,000 for a one year period. She is considering the following investments and would like your advice on the appropriate choice:

Reel Estate Income Trust   On January 1, 2017, this trust is selling for $25 per unit. It makes a distribution of $0.10 per unit per month. This distribution includes a return of capital of $0.01 per month, with the balance of the distribution being property income. Carolyn will sell the units at the end of 2017. She anticipates that these units will be selling for at least $26 per unit at that time.

Ventex Inc. Common Stock   On January 1, 2017, the shares of this public company are selling for $80 per share. The Company pays an annual eligible dividend of $3.00 per share. Carolyn anticipates that these shares will be selling for at least $85.00 per share on December 31, 2017.

During 2017, Carolyn will continue to work at her present job. Her employment income is such that any additional income will be taxed at a combined federal/provincial rate of 32 percent. Carolyn lives in a province where the provincial dividend tax credit for eligible dividends is equal to 30 percent of the gross up.

Required: Write a brief memorandum providing investment advice to Carolyn.

Assignment Problem Seven - 6

(Business Income And Income Trusts)

Ms. Janee Borel is a very successful lawyer who specializes in real estate transactions. She practices in British Columbia's lower mainland.

Relevant information on her practice for the taxation year ending December 31, 2017, is as follows:

January 1 Unbilled Work In Progress	$ 33,500
Billable Hours (1,840 Hours At $300)	552,000
December 31 Unbilled Work In Progress	27,600
Office Supplies And Office Expenses	31,462
Rent For Office And Equipment	72,000
Business Meals And Entertainment	24,650

While she rents all of her office equipment, including computer equipment, she owns the furniture and fixtures in her office. At the beginning of the year the Class 8 UCC balance was $27,648. During the year she replaces items that had an original capital cost of $18,000. The new items cost $31,500. She received a trade in allowance of $5,000 for the replaced items.

In addition to her professional income, Ms. Borel owns 4,100 units of Dundor Income Trust. These units were acquired on December 31, 2016 at a cost of $27 per unit. During 2017, she received a distribution of $2.75 per unit, of which $1.20 was a return of capital and the remainder was property income. The entire distribution was reinvested at a price of $28.50 per unit.

On December 31, 2017, all the trust units are sold for proceeds of $127,341.

For tax purposes, Ms. Borel uses the billed basis of revenue recognition. She also has a policy of deducting maximum CCA in each year.

Required: Determine Ms. Borel's minimum Net Income For Tax Purposes for the year ending December 31, 2017. Ignore GST/HST/PST considerations and the need to make CPP contributions by Ms. Borel.

Assignment Problem Seven - 7
(Foreign Property Income, Income Trusts And Mutual Funds)

As a result of receiving a large inheritance, Ms. Belinda Ho invests in five different financial instruments in 2016. The investments, along with their results during the year ending December 31, 2017, are as follows:

Public Company Shares She acquires 5,000 shares of Avator Inc. at a cost of $20 per share. During 2017, the shares pay eligible dividends of $1.10 per share. On December 31, 2017, the shares are sold for $22 per share.

CCPC Shares She acquires 1,250 shares in her father's Canadian controlled private company at a price of $80 per share. During 2017, these shares pay non-eligible dividends of $5.00 per share. She is still holding these shares at the end of 2017.

Income Trust Units She acquires 12,500 units of the RioKan income trust at a cost of $8 per unit. During 2017, the trust makes a distribution of $0.90 per unit. Of this total, $0.40 represents a return of capital, with the balance being property income. The proceeds of this distribution are invested in additional RioKan units at a cost of $8.75 per unit. She is still holding these shares at the end of 2017.

Mutual Fund Units She acquires 4,000 units of Fidel Large Cap, a mutual fund trust, at a price of $25 per unit. During 2017, the trust makes a distribution of $1.75 per unit. The composition of this distribution is as follows:

Capital Gains	$0.60
Eligible Dividends	0.80
Interest	0.35
Total Per Unit	$1.75

Belinda reinvests this distribution in new Fidel Large Cap units at $26.50 per unit. She is still holding these shares at the end of 2017.

Foreign Term Deposit On January 1, 2017, she acquires a Euro (€) term deposit with a maturity value of €80,000 at a Canadian dollar cost of $100,000. On December 31, 2017, the principal amount of the term deposit is paid, along with interest of €8,000. Foreign tax authorities withhold 20 percent of the interest. Assume that throughout 2017, €1.00 = $1.45.

Belinda has other income that places her in the 29 percent federal tax bracket and 16 percent provincial tax bracket for any additional income. Taxes on that income are sufficient to use all of her available tax credits before considering the effects of the investments purchased with her inheritance. She lives in a province where the dividend tax credit on eligible dividends is 30 percent of the gross up, and on non-eligible dividends is 25 percent of the gross up.

Required: Calculate the amount of Taxable Income and Tax Payable that will result from the dispositions and distributions of her investments. In addition, indicate the per unit adjusted cost base for each of the two trust units on December 31, 2017. Ignore any tax implications resulting from international tax treaties.

Assignment Problem Seven - 8
(Comprehensive Case Covering Chapters 1 to 7)

Family Information

Christopher Dunn is 37 years old. He has been married to Kathy Dunn for 12 years. During 2017, Kathy has Net Income For Tax Purposes of $8,200. The remainder of her income is from investments that were left to her by her deceased mother. During 2017, Christopher works 275 hours as a volunteer firefighter in his local community. He did not receive any compensation for this work.

After many years of renting, on February 1, 2017, Christopher and Kathy purchase a new residence for $432,000. They get a $200,000 mortgage at 2.5 percent per annum to finance the purchase.

Christopher and Kathy's only surviving parent is her father, Jason. He is 66 years old and, while he is dependent on Christopher and Kathy because of a physical infirmity requiring the use of a wheelchair, his condition is not severe enough for him to qualify for the disability tax credit. His 2017 Net Income For Tax Purposes is equal to $9,400. This includes OAS payments and a small pension from a former employer.

During 2017, Christopher spent $12,000 modifying their new home to accommodate Jason's wheelchair. The work was enduring in nature and will allow Jason to be much more mobile within the home.

During 2017 Christopher paid the following:

Root Canal Fee For Christopher	$1,525
Hair Replacement Fees For Christopher	4,300
Prescription Glasses And Contact Lenses For Kathy	1,342
Teeth Whitening Fees For Kathy	2,000
Psychologist Consulting Fees For Mark	2,450
Electric Wheelchair For Jason	3,300
Physiotherapy Fees For Jason	3,420

Employment Information

Christopher works for a large Canadian public company. His salary is $67,460, none of which involves commissions. His employer withholds the following amounts during 2017:

Registered Pension Plan Contributions (Note 1)	$4,200
EI Premiums	836
CPP Contributions	2,564
Contributions To The Canadian Cancer Society (Note 2)	3,200

Note 1   Christopher's employer makes a matching contribution of $4,200.

Note 2   The Canadian Cancer Society is a registered Canadian charity. Because of contributions in previous years, Christopher is not eligible for the First-Time Donor's Super Credit.

Christopher is required to travel fairly extensively by his employer. He uses his own automobile for this travel. His current automobile was acquired on January 1, 2017 at a cost of $42,000. During 2017, the automobile is driven 32,000 kilometers, 25,600 of which were employment related. Operating costs for the year totaled $4,900.

At the time he purchased this automobile, his employer provided him with an interest free loan of $20,000 to assist in the car purchase. None of this loan will be repaid until 2018. Assume that the relevant prescribed rate of interest throughout 2017 was 1 percent.

In addition to his automobile costs, his other 2017 travel costs were as follows:

Hotels	$2,700
Food While Travelling For Employer	1,800

His employer provides him with the following allowances for his travel:

Hotels And Food	$4,800
Use Of Personal Automobile ($100 Per Week)	5,200

Investment Information

Early in 2017, Christopher's father died of cancer and left him a very large inheritance which Christopher invested to create a substantial investment portfolio. Christopher paid off his mortgage on September 25, 2017 with funds from his inheritance. On October 1, 2017, he used his house as collateral for a new $200,000 mortgage at the same 2.5 percent per annum rate. He immediately invested the funds in shares of Canadian public companies.

The 2017 results for his investments are as follows:

Canadian Public Companies   During the year he receives $23,000 in eligible dividends from his holdings of Canadian public companies.

Canadian Controlled Private Company   He has invested in a local company founded by a close friend that has developed a revolutionary new product. As the product is becoming successful, the Company pays Christopher non-eligible dividends of $15,000 during the year.

Foreign Preferred Shares   In 2017 he purchased US$25,000 in preferred shares of U.S. based public companies. At the time he purchased these shares, the exchange rate was US$1.00 = C$1.40. During 2017, these shares pay dividends of US$1,800. Ten percent of this amount was withheld by U.S. tax authorities. The average exchange rate for 2017 was US$1.00 = C$1.35.

Mutual Fund Trusts   During the year, Christopher's holdings of mutual fund trusts distribute a total of $34,250. The breakdown of these distributions is as follows:

Capital Gains	$20,000
Eligible Dividends	9,000
Interest Income	5,250
Total	$34,250

Required: Ignore GST/HST/PST considerations in your solution, as well as the provisions of the U.S./Canada international tax treaty.

A. Determine Christopher's 2017 Net Income For Tax Purposes

B. Determine Christopher's 2017 Taxable Income

C. Determine Christopher's 2017 Federal Tax Payable.

Assignment Problem Seven - 9
(Comprehensive Case Covering Chapters 1 to 7)
Family Information

John Davis is 66 years old. He has been married to Martha Davis for over 40 years. Martha is 72 years old and has Net Income For Tax Purposes or $10,100. This total is made up of OAS payments of $7,000, plus a $3,100 withdrawal from her RRIF.

John and Martha have two children. Their 28 year old son, Brian has been blind since birth. He is totally dependant on John and Martha, lives with them, and has no 2017 income of his own.

Their daughter, Nadine Spence is 33 years old and was recently divorced. Her only income is $38,400 in child support that she receives under the provisions of the divorce decree. She and her two children live with John and Martha. Neither Nadine nor her children have any income during 2017.

In order to establish a new life, Nadine is attending university on a full time basis. Her tuition for 2017 was $11,300, all of which was paid by John. Nadine has agreed to transfer any unused tuition credit to her father.

The family's medical expenses, all of which have been paid by John, are as follows:

John	$ 900
Martha*	2,100
Brian	11,600
Nadine	2,450
Nadine's Children	700
Total Medical Expenses	**$17,750**

*Martha's medical expenses consisted of a $1,000 charge for teeth whitening and $1,100 in charges for 3 pairs of prescription eyeglasses, including prescription sunglasses.

Employment And Pension Income

While John is over 65 and receives a significant pension from a former employer's RPP, he is a full time employee of Larson Enterprises Ltd. During 2017, his gross wages were $71,500. Larson withheld the following amounts from these wages:

RPP Contributions	$3,890
EI Premiums	836
CPP Contributions	2,564
Union Dues	633
United Way Contributions	2,200

During 2017, his pension receipts from his former employer totaled $51,000. He has not applied for OAS as he knows that all of it will be clawed back. Further, he has not applied for CPP as he is aware that deferring this application will result in larger benefits.

Property Income

During 2017, John received the following dividends (all amounts in Canadian dollars):

Eligible Dividends From Taxable Canadian Corporations	$13,200
Non-Eligible Dividends On Shares In His Sister's CCPC	4,100
Dividends On Foreign Shares - Net Of 15 Percent Withholding	11,900
Total Dividends Received	**$29,200**

In addition to dividends, John had 2017 interest income of $2,843.

Business Income

Because of the project management skills that he has acquired over the years, John started a management consulting business in 2014. In that year he acquired a new building to be used as an office for his business. The building cost $523,000 of which $123,000 was the estimated value of the land. On January 1, 2017, the UCC of the building is $342,847.

The building contains office furniture and fixtures that were acquired in 2014 at a cost of $51,000. On January 1, 2017, they have a UCC of $29,376.

During 2017, he spends $37,000 on improving and upgrading the building. In addition, he sells the old furniture and fixtures for $21,300 and acquires replacement furniture and fixtures for $58,000.

As John has no reason to keep detailed accounting records, he records business income on a cash basis. For 2017, his net cash flow from operations was $146,300. Relevant figures for the beginning and end of 2017 are as follows:

	January 1	December 31
Billed Receivables	$14,100	$19,100
Unbilled Work In Process	18,300	22,300
Accounts Payable	9,200	10,400

Since the inception of the business, John has owned a car that is used 100 percent for business activity. The car that he acquired in 2014 was sold in 2016. He acquired a new car on January 1, 2017 at a cost of $56,200. He financed the car through his bank and, during 2017, he made payments on the loan of $12,600. All of this amount was deducted in determining his net cash flow from operations. Of the total, $4,610 represented payments for interest. John paid car operating costs totaling $8,600 during 2017.

Required: Calculate John's 2017 minimum Net Income For Tax Purposes, his 2017 minimum Taxable Income, and his 2017 minimum federal Tax Payable. Ignore GST/HST/PST considerations and the possibility of pension income splitting.

CHAPTER 8

Capital Gains And Capital Losses

Economic Background

Capital Assets And Income Taxation Policy

8-1. Capital gains and losses result from the disposition of assets that are being, or have been, used to produce business or property income. As such, they are viewed as a separate category of income. They are not included in the determination of either business or property income and, in general, these gains and losses will be incidental to the ongoing activities that produce business or property income. Given this, a case can be made for exempting this type of income from taxation.

8-2. This case is reinforced during periods of high inflation. If a business is going to continue operating as a going concern, it will usually have to replace any capital assets that are sold. As gains on the sale of capital assets often reflect nothing more than inflationary price increases, such gains cannot be distributed to the owners of the business as they must be used to finance the replacement of the assets sold.

8-3. Until 1972, Canadian tax legislation did not levy any income tax on capital gains. One of the most significant changes in the 1972 tax reform legislation was the introduction of taxation on capital gains as the government believed that the ability to completely escape taxation on this type of income was creating severe inequities in the taxation system.

8-4. The capital gains taxation that became effective January 1, 1972, represented a compromise between the view that capital gains should be exempt from tax and the position that such freedom from taxation creates serious inequities among various classes of taxpayers. Taxation of capital gains was introduced, but on a basis that was very favourable to the taxpayer.

8-5. In simple terms, the 1972 rules indicated that one-half of a capital gain would be treated as a taxable capital gain and, similarly, one-half of a capital loss would be deductible against capital gains as an allowable capital loss. This meant that for an individual taxpayer in the 45 percent tax bracket, the effective tax rate on capital gains was an attractive 22.5 percent.

Lifetime Capital Gains Deduction

8-6. Even though capital gains taxation was applied in a very favourable manner, there was a continuing view that any taxation of such income was not appropriate. As a reflection of this view, in 1985, the government introduced the lifetime capital gains deduction. The original legislation provided that every Canadian resident could enjoy tax free treatment of up to $500,000 of capital gains on the disposition of any type of capital asset. From its introduction, this provision was heavily criticized as a gift to higher income Canadians, particularly in view of the fact that it was available on any type of capital gain. It was difficult for many analysts to see the economic justification for providing favourable tax treatment of gains on the sale of a wealthy Canadian's Florida condominium.

8-7. As a result of such criticism, a variety of limitations were introduced over subsequent years. Without going through a detailed history of these changes, we would note that, as of 2017, a deduction is available for the taxable part of an $835,716 capital gain resulting from the disposition of shares of a qualified small business corporation. Even more attractive is the availability of a deduction for the taxable component of a $1,000,000 capital gain on the disposition of a qualified farming or fishing property.

8-8. It should be noted here that the provisions related to the lifetime capital gains deduction do not affect any of the material in this Chapter. The lifetime capital gains legislation did not alter the determination of the amount of taxable capital gains to be included in Net Income For Tax Purposes. Rather, the legislation provided for a deduction in the determination of Taxable Income for all or part of the taxable capital gains included in Net Income For Tax Purposes. This material is covered in Chapter 11, Taxable Income And Tax Payable For Individuals Revisited.

Changes In The Inclusion Rate

8-9. For gains and losses on capital assets disposed of subsequent to October 17, 2000, the inclusion rate has been one-half. Prior to that time, the rate was variously set at two-thirds (1988, 1989, and part of 2000) or three-fourths (1990, through February, 2000). There are a very limited number of situations in which these alternative inclusion rates are still relevant. However, we do not believe such situations are of sufficient interest to warrant coverage in a general taxation text.

8-10. Given this situation, very little coverage of these rates will be included in either the text or the related problems.

General Rules

Capital Gains In The *Income Tax Act*

8-11. The material in this Chapter is a continuation of our discussion of the calculation of Net Income For Tax Purposes. In Chapter 3, detailed attention was given to employment income. In terms of the *Income Tax Act*, this discussion was based on Subdivision a of Division B of the *Act*. Chapters 5, 6, and 7 dealt with Subdivision b of Division B and provided a comprehensive consideration of both business and property income. This included detailed coverage of the calculations related to capital cost allowance (CCA), an important deduction in the determination of both business and property income.

8-12. Capital gains and losses are the third major component of Net Income For Tax Purposes. This subject is covered in Subdivision c of Division B, Sections 38 through 55. Sections 38 and 39 define taxable capital gains, allowable capital losses, and other items that relate to the calculation of these amounts. Section 40 provides the general tax rules for computing these amounts. The remaining Sections 41 through 55 deal with more specific matters, such as identical properties (Section 47), adjustments to the cost base (Section 53), and various additional definitions (Section 54).

Capital Gains Defined

Capital Assets

8-13. In general, capital gains can occur when a taxpayer disposes of a capital asset. You will recall that capital assets were described in Chapter 6 as being those assets which are capable of earning income in the form of business profits, interest, dividends, royalties, or rents. This means that the assets must be held for this income producing purpose, rather than for a quick resale at a profit.

8-14. It was also noted in Chapter 6 that, in making the determination as to whether a particular amount of income was capital in nature, the courts would take into consideration the intent and course of the taxpayer's conduct, the number and frequency of transactions involving the type of asset under consideration, the nature of the asset, and the relationship of the asset to the business of the taxpayer.

Capital Gains Election On Canadian Securities

8-15. Despite these guidelines, the fact that capital gains receive favourable income tax treatment has led to much controversy and litigation with respect to the distinction between capital and other assets. In the case of equity securities, it is often difficult to distinguish between those situations where a taxpayer is holding the securities in order to earn dividend income or, alternatively, holding the securities in order to generate a gain on their ultimate disposition. Fortunately, the *Income Tax Act* provides an election which keeps this issue out of the courts.

8-16. ITA 39(4) allows taxpayers, including corporations and trusts, to elect to have all Canadian securities that they own deemed to be capital property, and all sales of such securities deemed to be dispositions of capital property. Once this election is made, it cannot be revoked and it applies to all future dispositions of Canadian securities by the taxpayer, thus assuring the taxpayer that all gains will be treated as favourably taxed capital gains. The downside of this election is that, if a taxpayer experiences a loss on the disposition of securities, it must be treated as a capital loss, only one-half of which is deductible.

8-17. ITA 39(5) indicates that this election is not available to traders or dealers in securities, financial institutions, a corporation in the business of lending money or purchasing debt obligations, or non-residents.

Dispositions

Actual Dispositions

8-18. The definition of "disposition" in ITA 248(1) states that, in general, a disposition is any transaction or event that entitles a taxpayer to "proceeds of disposition" (see Paragraph 8-24 for an explanation of this term). The most obvious such transaction would be a simple sale of property for cash. However, as listed in this definition, there are many other transactions and events that would be considered dispositions for income tax purposes. The more common of those listed would be:

- sales of property;
- redemptions of debt securities or shares;
- cancellations of debt securities or shares;
- expirations of options;
- expropriations of capital property;
- destruction of property through natural or other causes; and
- conversions of debt or shares.

8-19. In general, transfers of capital assets are not considered to involve a disposition unless there is a change in beneficial ownership. For example, a transfer of property between two trusts with identical beneficiaries would not be considered a change in beneficial ownership and, as a result, the transfer would not be treated as a disposition. An exception to this general rule occurs when there is a transfer to an RRSP. Even though there is no change in beneficial ownership, the transfer would be treated as a disposition of the transferred asset.

Gifts

8-20. A gift between taxpayers generally involves a transfer of beneficial ownership. While gifts are not one of the examples listed in the ITA 248(1) description of a disposition, from a legal perspective it is clearly a disposition. In the absence of a special provision, the proceeds of disposition for a gift would be nil. However, in this situation, ITA 69 kicks in, deeming the proceeds of disposition for the gift to be the fair market value of the property transferred.

8-21.   While most gifts are made to non-arm's length taxpayers, the ITA 69 provision cited in the preceding paragraph applies to any gift, without regard to whether the recipient is at arm's length with the person making the gift. This means that any taxpayer that has made a gift will be deemed to have proceeds equal to the fair market value of the gifted property.

8-22.   ITA 69 also indicates that where a taxpayer acquires a property by way of a gift, that taxpayer is deemed to have acquired the property at its fair market value.

Deemed Dispositions

8-23.   In addition to actual dispositions of capital property, there are a number of situations in which a disposition is deemed to have occurred. That is, even though there is no actual disposition, rules in the *Income Tax Act* require that, when certain events occur, the taxpayer must assume that a disposition and immediate re-acquisition of specified capital properties has occurred. In this Chapter we will give consideration to deemed dispositions that result from a change in the use of a property and deemed dispositions that occur when an individual departs from Canada. Deemed dispositions that arise on the death of a taxpayer will be covered in Chapter 9.

Proceeds Of Disposition

Actual Proceeds Of Disposition

8-24.   The term, "proceeds of disposition", is defined in ITA 54 and ITA 13(21). Included in both of these definitions are the following:

- The sale price of property sold.
- Compensation for property unlawfully taken or for property destroyed, including related proceeds from insurance policies.
- Compensation for property that has been appropriated or injuriously affected whether lawfully or unlawfully.
- Compensation for damaged property, including amounts payable under insurance policies.

Deemed Proceeds Of Disposition

8-25.   Deemed proceeds of disposition can arise in two different ways. When there is a deemed rather than an actual disposition, the legislation that requires the deemed disposition will specify how the deemed proceeds of disposition will be determined. For example, when there is a deemed disposition for an individual departing from Canada, the deemed proceeds of disposition will generally be the fair market value of the relevant asset.

8-26.   There are other situations in which there is an actual disposition, with the *Income Tax Act* requiring the use of a deemed proceeds that is different from the actual proceeds. For example, if there is a non-arm's length transfer and the proceeds of disposition are below the fair market value of the relevant assets, ITA 69 deems the proceeds to be fair market value.

Adjusted Cost Base

Definition

8-27.   The adjusted cost base of an asset is defined in ITA 54 as follows:

(i)   where the property is depreciable property of the taxpayer, the capital cost to him of the property as of that time, and

(ii)   in any other case, the cost to the taxpayer of the property adjusted, as of that time, in accordance with Section 53.

8-28.   This definition means that, in general, the adjusted cost base of a capital asset is analogous to the accounting concept of historical cost. As with the GAAP approach to historical cost, it includes the invoice cost, delivery and setup charges, non-refundable provincial sales taxes, non-refundable GST/HST, and any other costs associated with acquiring the asset, or putting it into use.

8-29.   As indicated in the adjusted cost base definition, ITA 53 specifies a number of adjustments to the cost base. Some of the more important of these adjustments can be described as follows:

Government Grants And Assistance   When a taxpayer receives government grants or other types of assistance, these amounts are generally deducted from the adjusted cost base of the related asset. This is consistent with the accounting treatment of government grants under GAAP.

Superficial Losses   A superficial loss occurs when a taxpayer disposes of a property and:

- within the period of 30 days before the disposition or 30 days after the disposition, the taxpayer or his spouse or common-law partner acquires the same property (referred to as the substituted property), and,

- at the end of the period (60 days), the taxpayer or his spouse or common-law partner owns the substituted property.

Any loss on the disposition of the original property is called a superficial loss. Such losses cannot be deducted, but must be added to the adjusted cost base of the substituted property.

As an example, assume that in 2013 Ms. Deffett acquires 100 shares of Norton Limited for $75 per share. On December 27, 2017 the shares are trading at $60 and, because she has realized capital gains in 2017, Ms. Deffett sells the shares on this date in order to realize a loss that can be used to offset the capital gains. One-half of the capital loss of $15 per share on the December 27, 2017 sale would be deductible, provided no Norton Limited shares are purchased between November 27, 2017 and January 26, 2018. If, however, she was to purchase 100 Norton shares on December 15, 2017 or January 15, 2018 for $65 per share, the December, 2017 loss would be disallowed. The disallowed loss would be added to the adjusted cost base of the new shares, giving these shares an adjusted cost base of $80 ($65 + $15) per share. This amount would be appropriate in that it reflects her net cash outlay per share ($75 - $60 + $65).

Stock Option Benefit   When shares are acquired through the exercise of stock options, the adjusted cost base of the shares is increased by the amount of any employment income benefit that is recorded at the time of acquisition. In effect, the adjusted cost base of the shares is written up to their fair market value at the time of exercise. (See Chapter 3, Employment Income, for coverage of stock options.)

Other Adjustments To The Cost Base   Other important adjustments would include the addition of undeducted interest and property taxes on vacant land to the adjusted cost base (only available if the land is used in a business and held primarily to produce income), the addition of subsequent capital contributions by a shareholder to a corporation to the cost base of the shares, and the requirement that under certain circumstances, forgiveness of debts on property must be deducted from the cost base of that property.

8-30.   There are several other such adjustments in ITA 53. You should note, however, that in the case of depreciable property, any deductions taken for CCA do not change the adjusted cost base of the property. Capital gains are determined on the basis of the original capital cost of the asset, not the UCC.

Exercise Eight - 1

Subject: Government Assistance

On January 1 of the current year, Rotan Ltd. acquires a real property at a cost of $5,600,000. Of this amount, $600,000 represents the fair market value of the land. The building is new and will be used 100 percent for non-residential activity, none of which involves manufacturing. Rotan allocates its cost to a separate Class 1. In order to encourage Rotan's move to this location, the local government has given them $1,500,000 to assist in the acquisition of the building. What is the maximum amount of CCA that Rotan can deduct on this building for the current year?

Exercise Eight - 2

Subject: Superficial Loss

Ms. Nadia Kinski owns 1,000 shares of Bord Ltd. They have an adjusted cost base of $23 per share. On August 20, 2017, she sells all of these shares at $14.50 per share. On August 25, 2017, she acquires 600 shares of Bord Ltd. at a cost of $13.75 per share and is still holding the shares at the end of the year. What are the tax consequences of these transactions?

SOLUTIONS available in print and online Study Guide.

Negative Adjusted Cost Base

8-31.   It is possible that sufficient adjustments could be made to an adjusted cost base that its balance will become negative. When this occurs, ITA 40(3) requires that the deficiency be treated as a capital gain and the adjusted cost base of the asset be adjusted to nil. Note that, unlike the situation with recapture of CCA, this would apply even if additions to the cost base prior to the end of the taxation year were sufficient to eliminate the deficit balance.

8-32.   Also note that ITA 40(3) is not applicable to most partnership interests. That is, a negative adjusted cost base for a partnership interest does not automatically trigger a capital gain and can be carried forward indefinitely. However, this exemption from ITA 40(3) does not apply to limited partners or certain inactive partners. For more details on this point, see Chapter 18, Partnerships.

GST/HST/PST Considerations

8-33.   A business will pay GST, HST, or PST on most of the capital assets that it acquires. As is discussed in more detail in Chapter 21, all or part of the amounts paid can be refunded under certain circumstances. From a technical point of view, all amounts of GST/HST/PST are, at least initially, included in the capital cost of depreciable assets. However, to the extent that these amounts are refunded as input tax credits, they are defined in ITA 248(16) as a form of government assistance and, as a consequence, the refunds are deducted from the capital cost of depreciable assets in the same manner as other government assistance. In effect, this means that GST/HST/PST amounts that are refunded are not included in the capital cost of depreciable assets.

Calculating The Capital Gain Or Loss

8-34.   The general formula for determining the amount of a capital gain or loss can be described very simply. The calculation, using assumed data, is as follows:

Proceeds Of Disposition			$4,750
Less - The Aggregate Of:			
Adjusted Cost Base	($3,890)		
Expenses Of Disposition	(560)		(4,450)
Capital Gain (Loss)			$ 300
Inclusion Rate			1/2
Taxable Capital Gain (Allowable Capital Loss)			$ 150

8-35. If, as in the preceding example, there is a capital gain, one-half of the amount will be treated as a taxable capital gain. The adjective "taxable" is consistently used to indicate the portion of the total gain that will be included in income. Similarly, one-half of a negative amount (a capital loss) resulting from the application of the preceding formula would be treated as an allowable capital loss. The adjective "allowable" is consistently used to indicate the deductible portion of the total amount of the loss.

8-36. In Chapter 1 we noted that ITA 3 specifies that Net Income For Tax Purposes includes the amount, if any, by which taxable capital gains exceed allowable capital losses. At that point, we noted that the use of the phrase "if any" establishes the rule that current year allowable capital losses can only be deducted to the extent that there are current year taxable capital gains.

Detailed Application Of The Rules

Identical Properties

8-37. A taxpayer can own a group of identical properties that have been acquired over a period of time at different costs. This would arise most commonly with holdings of securities such as common stock in a particular corporation. If part of such a group of assets is disposed of, ITA 47 requires that the adjusted cost base for the assets being disposed of be based on the average cost of the entire group.

8-38. The following example illustrates the application of the identical property procedures, other than the procedures applicable to shares acquired through stock options:

EXAMPLE An individual has engaged in the following transactions involving the common stock of Gower Company, a Canadian public company:

Acquisition Date Or Sale Date	Shares Purchased (Sold)	Cost Per Share	Total Cost	Average Cost/Share
2003	4,000	$10.00	$ 40,000	
2004	3,000	12.00	36,000	
Subtotal	7,000		$ 76,000	$10.86
2007	(2,000)	$10.86	(21,720)	
Subtotal	5,000		$ 54,280	$10.86
2010	2,500	$11.00	27,500	
2015	3,000	10.00	30,000	
Subtotal	10,500		$111,780	$10.65
2017	(1,500)	$10.65	(15,975)	
End Of Year Balances	9,000		$ 95,805	$10.65

The 2,000 units sold in 2007 were sold for $10 per unit. The 1,500 units sold in 2017 were sold for $13 per unit.

ANALYSIS Using the information from the preceding table, the 2007 allowable capital loss is calculated as follows:

Detailed Application Of The Rules

Proceeds Of Disposition [(2,000)($10)]	$20,000
Adjusted Cost Base [(2,000)($10.86)]	(21,720)
Capital Loss	($ 1,720)
Inclusion Rate	1/2
Allowable Capital Loss	($ 860)

The 2017 taxable capital gain would be calculated as follows:

Proceeds Of Disposition [(1,500)($13)]	$19,500
Adjusted Cost Base [(1,500)($10.65)]	(15,975)
Capital Gain	$ 3,525
Inclusion Rate	1/2
Taxable Capital Gain	$ 1,763

Exercise Eight - 3

Subject: Identical Properties

Ms. Chantal Montrose makes frequent purchases of the common shares of Comco Inc. During 2016, she purchased 650 shares at $23.50 per share on January 15, and 345 shares at $24.25 per share on March 12. She sold 210 shares on September 15, 2016 at $25.50 per share. On February 14, 2017, she purchases an additional 875 shares at $26.75 per share and, on October 1, 2017, she sells 340 shares at $29.50 per share. Determine Ms. Montrose's taxable capital gains for 2016 and 2017.

SOLUTION available in print and online Study Guide.

We suggest you work Self Study Problem Eight-1 at this point.

Partial Dispositions

8-39. In those situations where a taxpayer disposes of part of a property, ITA 43 requires that a portion of the total adjusted cost base be allocated to the disposition on a reasonable basis.

EXAMPLE A 500 hectare tract of land has an adjusted cost base of $6,000,000. During the current year, 200 of these hectares were sold.

ANALYSIS It would appear to be reasonable to allocate $2,400,000, or 40 percent (200 hectares ÷ 500 hectares), of the total adjusted cost base to the land that was sold. If, however, there was some reason that the part of the tract sold had a value that was not proportionate to the total tract, some alternative basis of allocation could be used.

Warranties On Capital Assets

8-40. If a taxpayer disposes of capital property and the proceeds include some payment for a warranty or other contingent obligation, ITA 42 requires that the full proceeds must be used in determining the capital gain. Stated alternatively, no reserve can be established to provide for any future obligations. However, one-half of any outlays related to such contingent obligations that are made in a subsequent year can be deducted as allowable capital losses, but only against taxable capital gains. Any undeducted losses are subject to the carry over provisions described in Chapter 11.

8-41. You will recall that there was some discussion of warranties in Chapter 6, Business Income. More specifically, we noted there that under ITA 20(1)(m.1), it was possible to deduct the cost of warranties provided by arm's length parties from business income.

However, for most product warranties, the situation is similar to the treatment of warranties on capital assets in that the estimated warranty costs can only be deducted when incurred, not deducted from the proceeds of the asset sale. Note, however, there is a difference in that warranty costs related to the sale of a capital asset will create a capital loss when incurred, rather than a 100 percent deductible business loss.

Exercise Eight - 4

Subject: Warranties On Capital Assets

During the taxation year ending December 31, 2016, Vivid Ltd. sells a capital asset with an adjusted cost base of $237,000 for proceeds of $292,000. The Company provides the purchaser with a one year warranty and the Company estimates that it will cost $4,500 to fulfill the warranty provisions. On October 1, 2017, the Company spends $4,800 to fulfill the warranty provisions. Determine the effect of these transactions on Net Income For Tax Purposes for 2016 and 2017.

SOLUTION available in print and online Study Guide.

We suggest that you work Self Study Problem Eight-2 at this point.

Capital Gains Reserves
General Principles

8-42. In some cases, a capital asset disposition may involve debt as a component of the proceeds of disposition. For example, assume Mr. Filoso sold a piece of land for a capital gain and collected only 10 percent of the total proceeds in the year of sale. In such cases, it would seem reasonable to allow him to defer recognition of a part of the capital gain. This deferral can be accomplished through the establishment of a capital gains reserve.

8-43. The general idea is that a reserve can be deducted from the total gain when not all of the proceeds are receivable in the year of the sale. The reserve would reflect the portion of the gain that is contained in the uncollected proceeds. As with other reserves, this amount must be added back to the following year's income, with a new reserve deducted to reflect any remaining uncollected proceeds. Note that the reserve is based solely on the principal amount of the debt. Accrued interest is not included in the reserve calculations.

8-44. In order to use this elective provision, individuals must file Form T2017. Other taxpayers are not required to submit this form and can simply make this election in their return of income.

8-45. At one point in time, the deductible reserve was simply based on the portion of the proceeds of disposition that were not yet received. If a taxpayer collected only 10 percent of the proceeds, the reserve could be equal to 90 percent of the gain. It appears that this provision was being used for what the government viewed as excessive deferrals and, as a consequence, ITA 40(1)(a)(iii) limits the reserve to the lesser of two amounts.

8-46. The first of these two amounts is referred to in the *Act* as a "reasonable amount". While the *Act* does not provide a formula for this "reasonable amount", it refers to amounts that are payable after the end of the taxation year. This can be expressed as follows:

$$\left[\begin{array}{c} \text{Total} \\ \text{Gain} \end{array} \right] \left[\frac{\text{Proceeds Not Receivable Until After End Of Current Taxation Year}}{\text{Total Proceeds Of Disposition}} \right]$$

8-47. The second amount uses a formula that ensures that the maximum reserve will decline by at least 20 percent each year, going from a maximum of 80 percent of the gain in the year of disposition to nil in the fourth year after the disposition. The formula is as follows:

{[Total Gain] [20%] [4 - (Number of preceding taxation years ending after the disposition)]}

8-48.   Under this formula, a minimum of 20 percent of the gain must be recognized in the year of the sale and each of the following four years. This prevents a reserve from being used to defer taxation for longer than 4 years. If the proceeds are collected faster than 20 percent per year, the reserve will be based on the actual uncollected proceeds as per the formula in Paragraph 8-46.

8-49.   While this reserve is similar to the ITA 20(1)(n) reserve for uncollected amounts described in Chapter 6, the circumstances when the reserves can be used differ as follows:

ITA 20(1)(n) Reserve   Used when there is a sale of an inventory item and part of the proceeds are not due until at least two years after the end of the current taxation year. In addition, this provision restricts the reserve to three years. However, there is no restriction on the amount of the reserve during the years that it is available.

ITA 40(1)(a)(iii) Reserve   Used when there is a capital asset disposition and all or part of the proceeds are not due until after the end of the current taxation year. In contrast to the reserve being restricted to three years under the provisions of ITA 20(1)(n), ITA 40(1)(a)(iii) allows the reserve to be used for a maximum of five years.

Example - Outstanding Balance Greater Than Formula Limit

8-50.   Assume that during 2017, Mr. Filoso sold a piece of land with an adjusted cost base of $340,000, for total proceeds of $1,000,000, resulting in a capital gain of $660,000 ($1,000,000 - $340,000) and a taxable capital gain of $330,000 [(1/2)($660,000)]. He received only $100,000 of the total amount in cash in 2017 and accepted a $900,000 note payable for the balance. The note is payable at the rate of $100,000 per year beginning in 2018. Interest charged at 5 percent of the outstanding balance is also paid annually.

8-51.   As he collected only 10 percent of the total proceeds, the reserve would be 90 percent under the "reasonable amount" component of ITA 40(1)(a)(iii). As a result, the maximum reserve will be based on the second component of the formula which limits the reserve in the first year to 80 percent of the gain. The maximum reserve would be $528,000, the lesser of:

- [($660,000)($900,000 ÷ $1,000,000)] $594,000 (Reserve)
- [($660,000)(20%)(4 - 0)] $528,000 (Reserve)

8-52.   Applying this formula, the taxable capital gain that will be recognized in 2017 is $66,000 [(1/2)($660,000 - $528,000)]. Note that, despite the fact that Mr. Filoso has only collected 10 percent of the proceeds ($100,000 ÷ $1,000,000), the application of the formula requires that he recognize 20 percent ($66,000 ÷ $330,000) of the total gain.

8-53.   In 2018, the $528,000 reserve would have to be added back to income. The new reserve for 2018 would be $396,000, the lesser of:

- [($660,000)($800,000 ÷ $1,000,000)] $528,000 (Reserve)
- [($660,000)(20%)(4 - 1)] $396,000 (Reserve)

8-54.   Adding back the previous year's reserve of $528,000, and deducting the new maximum reserve of $396,000, gives a 2018 capital gain of $132,000. This would result in a net addition to 2018 income of $66,000 [(1/2)($528,000 - $396,000)], or 20 percent of the $330,000 taxable capital gain.

8-55.   Based on similar calculations, the maximum reserve in 2019 would be $264,000. This would decline to $132,000 in 2020 and, in 2021, no reserve would be available. This would result in $66,000 [(1/2)($132,000)] being added to income each year. The entire $330,000 of the taxable capital gain will have been included in income by the end of 2021. This is despite the fact that, at the end of this five year period, $500,000 of the initial proceeds remains uncollected.

Example - Outstanding Balance Less Than Formula Limit

8-56. In the preceding example, collections of cash were less than 20 percent in all years under consideration. As a result, the application of ITA 40(1)(a)(iii) resulted in the recognition of 20 percent of the gain in each year.

8-57. Situations in which the uncollected portion of the proceeds is greater than the formula limit will result in more than 20 percent of the gain being taxed in a year. As an illustration of this possibility, assume that in the Paragraph 8-50 example, Mr. Filoso collected $250,000 in the year of the disposition, and that the required payments were $75,000 per year for the following ten years.

8-58. Based on this information, the maximum reserve for 2017 would be $495,000, the lesser of:

- [($660,000)($750,000 ÷ $1,000,000)] $495,000 (Reserve)
- [($660,000)(20%)(4 - 0)] $528,000 (Reserve)

8-59. This means that a taxable capital gain of $82,500 [(1/2)($660,000 - $495,000)] would be recognized in 2017.

8-60. In 2018, the $495,000 reserve would be added back to income. The new reserve for 2018 would be $396,000, the lesser of:

- [($660,000)($675,000 ÷ $1,000,000)] $445,500 (Reserve)
- [($660,000)(20%)(4 - 1)] $396,000 (Reserve)

8-61. This results in the recognition of a $49,500 [(1/2)($495,000 - $396,000)] taxable capital gain in 2018. At this point, the minimum 20 percent per year recognition requirement has become the determining factor in calculating the capital gain to be included in income. As a consequence, the amount to be included in income in the years 2019, 2020, and 2021 would be as presented in Paragraph 8-55.

Exercise Eight - 5

Subject: Capital Gains Reserves

During December 2016, Mr. Gerry Goodson sells a capital property with an adjusted cost base of $293,000 for proceeds of disposition of $382,000. Selling costs total $17,200. In the year of sale, he receives $82,000 in cash, along with the purchaser's note for the balance of the proceeds. The note is to be repaid at the rate of $60,000 per year beginning in 2017. He receives the 2017 payment in full. Assume that Mr. Goodson deducts the maximum capital gains reserves. Determine his taxable capital gain for 2016 and 2017.

SOLUTION available in print and online Study Guide.

We suggest you work Self Study Problems Eight-3 and Eight-4 at this point.

Bad Debts On Sales Of Capital Property

8-62. When an amount receivable results from the disposition of a capital property, the possibility arises that some of the proceeds of disposition will have to be written off as a bad debt. When this occurs, ITA 50(1) allows the seller to elect to have disposed of the receivable and immediately reacquired it at a proceeds and cost of nil. Consider the following:

EXAMPLE   During 2017, a capital property with a cost of $500,000 is sold for $510,000. The proceeds are made up of $360,000 in cash, plus the purchaser's note for $150,000.

8-63.   If the vendor of the capital property does not choose to deduct a capital gains reserve for the uncollected amount, a taxable capital gain of $5,000 [(1/2)($510,000 - $500,000)] would be recognized in 2017. If, during 2017, the note received from the purchaser turns out to be uncollectible, the deemed disposition and reacquisition would result in an allowable capital loss of $75,000 [(1/2)($150,000)], $5,000 of which would offset the $5,000 taxable capital gain on the disposition. The remaining allowable capital loss of $70,000 ($75,000 - $5,000) would first be applied against any other taxable capital gains that are realized in 2017 with any balance carried over. (Loss carry overs are covered in Chapter 11.) If, at a later point in time, some amount of the debt was recovered, any excess over the deemed nil proceeds would be considered a capital gain.

Exercise Eight - 6

Subject: Bad Debts From Dispositions Of Capital Property

During 2016, a capital property with an adjusted cost base of $125,000 is sold for $110,000. The proceeds of disposition are made up of $75,000 in cash, plus the purchaser's one-year note for $35,000. In 2017, the note proves to be uncollectible. What are the tax consequences of these events in 2016 and in 2017?

SOLUTION available in print and online Study Guide.

We suggest you work Self Study Problems Eight-5 and Eight-6 at this point.

Special Rule For Sales Of Real Property
The Problem

8-64.   Real property, a.k.a. real estate, is land and all appurtenances to it, such as buildings (although crops and mineral rights would also be included, coverage of these types of assets is beyond the scope of this material). As only the building component qualifies for CCA deductions, it is always necessary to separate these two components. As separate market prices for the two components do not usually exist, this separation requires the use of estimates. As you are likely aware, estimates involve judgment and can vary significantly from expert to expert.

8-65.   The problem is that when there is a disposal of real property, the amounts of the proceeds that are allocated to the two components have a significant impact on any resulting Taxable Income. Larger amounts allocated to the land will create or increase a capital gain, only one-half of which is taxable. If this results in smaller amounts being allocated to the building, this could result in a fully deductible terminal loss.

EXAMPLE   Martin Ltd. has only one Class 1 building. During 2017, the Company disposes of the building and replaces it with a leased property. The following information relates to this disposition:

Proceeds Of Disposition Allocation	
Land (Estimated Value)	$300,000
Building (Estimated Value)	110,000
Total Proceeds Of Disposition	$410,000

Adjusted Cost Base Of Land	$200,000
Original Cost Of Building	175,000
UCC Class 1	150,000

8-66.   In the absence of a special rule, there would be a $50,000 taxable capital gain on the land [(1/2)($300,000 - $200,000)]. There would also be a $40,000 ($150,000 - $110,000) terminal loss on the building. The inclusion in Net Income For Tax Purposes would be $10,000 ($50,000 - $40,000).

8-67.   If, for example, $30,000 of the proceeds were shifted from the building to the land, the result would be a $15,000 increase in the taxable capital gain, accompanied by a $30,000 increase in the terminal loss on the building. Clearly, there is an incentive to maximize the amount of the proceeds of disposition that is allocated to the land.

The Solution

8-68.   Because of this incentive, ITA 13(21.1)(a) contains a provision that can serve to limit the amount of any terminal loss that might arise on the disposition of real property. Using the example from Paragraph 8-65, this provision requires a deemed proceeds of disposition for the building to be determined as follows:

The Lesser Of:

- The FMV of the land and building $410,000
  Reduced By The Lesser Of:
  - The ACB of the land = $200,000
  - The FMV of the land = $300,000   (200,000) $210,000

- The Greater Of:
  - The FMV of the building = $110,000
  - The Lesser Of:
    The cost of the building = $175,000
    The UCC of the building = $150,000 $150,000

8-69.   In this case, the proceeds that would be allocated to the building would be $150,000, leaving $260,000 ($410,000 - $150,000) to be allocated to the land. The net result is that the $40,000 terminal loss is completely eliminated and the capital gain is reduced by a corresponding amount to $60,000 ($260,000 - $200,000). The taxable amount of $30,000 [($60,000)(1/2)] would be included in the taxpayer's income instead of the $10,000 that would have been recorded in the absence of the special rule in ITA 13(21.1).

8-70.   The effect of ITA 13(21.1)(a) on the results is summarized in the following table:

	Results Without ITA 13(21.1)(a)	Results With ITA 13(21.1)(a)
Taxable Capital Gain	$50,000	$30,000
Terminal Loss	(40,000)	Nil
Net Inclusion	$10,000	$30,000

8-71.   If the potential capital gain had been less than the potential terminal loss, the terminal loss would have been reduced by the amount of the potential capital gain and the capital gain would have been eliminated. You might also note that this special rule only affects the vendor and has no tax consequences for the purchaser.

Exercise Eight - 7

Subject: Building Dispositions

On February 24, 2017, Drucker Ltd. disposed of real property for total proceeds of $1,250,000. Information with respect to this property is as follows:

Original cost of building	$930,000
UCC Class 1 (Building - only asset in class)	615,000
Fair market value of building on February 24, 2017	500,000
Adjusted cost base of land	425,000
Fair market value of land on February 24, 2017	750,000

Determine the tax consequences of this disposition assuming (1) there is no special rule for building dispositions, and (2) the ITA 13(21.1) special rule for building dispositions applies.

SOLUTION available in print and online Study Guide.

Provisions For Special Assets

Principal Residence

Principal Residence Defined

8-72.   For many individuals resident in Canada, one of the most attractive features of our tax system is the fact that, in general, capital gains arising on the disposition of a principal residence can be received free of tax. It is important to note that only one taxpayer in a family unit can designate a property as a principal residence for a particular year. For this purpose, a family unit includes a spouse or common-law partner, as well as children unless they are married or in a common-law partnership, or over 18 during the year.

8-73.   ITA 54 defines a principal residence as any accommodation owned by the taxpayer that was ordinarily inhabited in the year by the taxpayer, his spouse, a former spouse, or a child, and is designated by the taxpayer as a principal residence. The definition notes that this would include land up to a limit of one-half hectare as well as a building. If the property includes additional land, it will be subject to capital gains taxation unless the taxpayer can demonstrate that the additional land was necessary for the use and enjoyment of the property.

8-74.   An individual taxpayer may own more than one property that would meet the definition of a principal residence. A typical example of this would be a family that has both a city home and cottage in the country. Either of these properties could satisfy the definition of a principal residence and, given that a family can have only one property that qualifies for the principal residence exemption, a sale of either property would require a decision as to whether that property should benefit from the exemption. This choice can be clarified by the use of form T2091, *Designation Of A Property As A Principal Residence By An Individual*.

8-75.   Prior to 2016, it was the administrative policy of the CRA not to require reporting of the sale of a principal residence or the filing of form T2091. However, as of January 1, 2016, the reporting related to the sale of a principal residence has been expanded.

8-76.   Relevant points with respect to dispositions after 2015 are as follows:

- If an individual has only one property that qualifies as a principal residence, they must report in their tax return a description of the property sold, when it was acquired, and the proceeds of disposition. Form T2091 is not required.

- The same reporting is required if the individual owns more than one property that qualifies as a principal residence, but is designating only one property sold for all years owned.

- If the individual owns more than one property that qualifies as a principal residence, but does not wish to designate just one property owned for all years that it has been owned, form T2091 is required. This would be in addition to reporting any resulting capital gain in the usual schedule (S3) in their tax return.

8-77. Failure to report the disposition will result in a penalty of $100 per month, to a maximum value of $8,000.

Gain Reduction Formula

8-78. Technically speaking, capital gains on a principal residence are taxable. However, ITA 40(2)(b) provides a formula for reducing such gains. The formula calculates the taxable portion, which is based on the relationship between the number of years since 1971 that the property has been designated a principal residence and the number of years since 1971 that the taxpayer has owned the property. It is as follows:

$$A - \left[A \times \frac{B}{C} \right] - D, \text{ where}$$

A is the total capital gain on the disposition of the principal residence;

B is 1 plus the number of years since 1971 the property is designated as the taxpayer's principal residence (but cannot be greater than the denominator C);

C is the number of years since 1971 that the taxpayer has owned the property;

D relates to the 1994 capital gains election (not of general interest to users of this text).

8-79. The formula in Paragraph 8-78 is applied to any capital gain resulting from the disposition of a principal residence in order to determine the amount that will be subject to taxation. For example, assume a property was purchased in 2009 and was sold in 2017 for an amount that resulted in a capital gain of $100,000. If it was designated as a principal residence for 6 of the 9 years of ownership (not 8 years, a common error being to simply subtract the years without adding 1 for the initial year), the calculation of the taxable portion of the capital gain would be as follows:

$$\left[\$100,000 - (\$100,000)\left(\frac{1+6}{9} \right) \right]\left[\frac{1}{2} \right] = \$11,111$$

8-80. If a taxpayer has only a single property that could qualify as a principal residence, that property can be designated as the principal residence for all years owned. In such situations, the use of this formula will then completely eliminate any capital gains on the disposition of that property.

8-81. When only one residence is involved in each year, the plus one in the B component of the formula is not relevant. However, if a taxpayer sells one home and acquires another in a single year, the plus one becomes important.

EXAMPLE During 2012, Mr. Fodor acquires a principal residence at a cost of $130,000. The residence is sold in 2015 for $150,000. A replacement residence is acquired in 2015 at a cost of $170,000. In 2017, the second residence is sold for $200,000, with Mr. Fodor moving to an apartment.

ANALYSIS During 2015, Mr. Fodor owns two properties, only one of which can be designated as a principal residence for that year. If there was no extra year in the numerator of the reduction formula (component B), Mr. Fodor would be taxed on a portion of one of the gains. For example, assume Mr. Fodor allocates the 3 years 2012 through 2014 to the first property and the 3 years 2015 through 2017 to the second. All of the $30,000 gain on the second property would be eliminated. Since the first property was sold in 2015, the denominator in the reduction formula (component C) is 4 (2012 to 2015). If the plus one was not in the numerator, only three-quarters of the $20,000 gain would be eliminated, leaving a capital gain of $5,000 [$20,000 - ($20,000)(3 ÷ 4)]. However, with the addition of the plus one to the years in the numerator of the reduction formula, the fraction on the first property becomes four-fourths, and there is no taxable capital gain.

Exercise Eight - 8

Subject: Sale Of Principal Residence

Mr. Norm Craft purchases his first home in 2008 at a cost of $89,000. In 2013, this home is sold for $109,500 and a second home is purchased for $152,000. In 2017, this second home is sold for $178,000 and Mr. Craft moves to a rental property. Determine the minimum tax consequences of the two property sales.

Exercise Eight - 9

Subject: Sale Of Principal Residence

Ms. Jan Sadat owns a house in Ottawa, as well as a cottage in Westport. She purchased the house in 2006 for $126,000. The cottage was gifted to her in 2009 by her parents. At the time of the gift, the fair market value of the cottage was $85,000. During June, 2017, both properties are sold, the house for $198,000 and the cottage for $143,500. She has lived in the Ottawa house during the year, but has spent her summers in the Westport cottage. Determine the minimum capital gain that she must report on the 2017 sale of the two properties.

SOLUTIONS available in print and online Study Guide.

We suggest you work Self Study Problem Eight-7 at this point.

Non-Residential Usage Of Principal Residence

8-82.   A complication arises when a taxpayer either begins to rent a part of his principal residence, or begins to use it for non-residential purposes (e.g., a self-employed individual who maintains an office at home). Under the general rules for capital assets, this would be a partial change in use (coverage of change in use begins at Paragraph 8-113), potentially resulting in a capital gain on a partial disposition of the property.

8-83.   However, the CRA has indicated in IT Folio S1-F3-C2, *Principal Residence* and IT Folio S4-F2-C2, *Business Use of Home Expenses* that it will not apply the partial disposition rules so long as the income producing use is ancillary to the main use as a principal residence, there is no structural change to the property, and no capital cost allowance is claimed. Given this, the standard tax planning advice to taxpayers who use a portion of their principal residence for business purposes is not to deduct CCA on this property.

Principal Residence On Farm Properties

8-84.   Many farmers have a principal residence that is a part of their farm property. This means that when the farm is sold, the farmer's principal residence will generally be included in the package that is sold. In this situation, ITA 40(2)(c) identifies two approaches that can be used in this situation.

8-85.   The first approach requires that the land be divided into two components — the portion used for farming and the portion used for the use and enjoyment of the principal residence. Separate capital gains are calculated for each, with the gain on the principal residence portion being eligible for the principal residence reduction. Note that the ITA 54 definition of principal residence indicates that, as a general guideline, the land required for the use and enjoyment of the principal residence is limited to one-half hectare (i.e., 1.25 acres).

8-86.   As an alternative, a farmer can elect to be taxed on the capital gain from the sale of the entire property, reduced by a fixed amount of $1,000, plus an additional $1,000 per year for every year for which the property was a principal residence.

Personal Use Property

Definition

8-87. ITA 54 defines personal use property as any property that is owned by the taxpayer and used primarily for his personal use or enjoyment, or for the personal use or enjoyment of one or more individuals related to the taxpayer. In non-technical terms, we are talking about any significant asset owned by a taxpayer that is not used for earning business or property income. This would include personal use automobiles, principal residences, vacation homes, boats, furniture, and many other items.

Capital Gains And Losses

8-88. In general, gains on the disposition of personal use property are taxed in the same manner as gains on other capital assets. However, there is an important difference with respect to losses. In general, losses on such property are not deductible. The reason for this is that most types of personal use property depreciate over time and to allow capital losses on the property to be deductible would, in effect, permit a write-off of the cost of personal living expenses. As explained later, beginning in Paragraph 8-92, the exception to this general rule is losses on listed personal property that can be deducted on a restricted basis.

8-89. To simplify the enforcement of capital gains taxation on personal use property, ITA 46(1) provides a $1,000 floor rule. In using this rule to calculate capital gains on personal use property, the proceeds are deemed to be the greater of $1,000 and the actual proceeds. In a similar fashion, the adjusted cost base is deemed to be the greater of $1,000 and the actual adjusted cost base. This rule is illustrated in the following example involving dispositions of personal use property in four different cases:

Capital Gains (Losses) On Personal Use Property

	Case A	Case B	Case C	Case D
Proceeds Of Disposition (POD)	$300	$850	$ 500	$1,500
Adjusted Cost Base (ACB)	800	400	1,300	900
Using the $1,000 floor rule results in the following capital gain or loss:				
Greater Of Actual POD Or $1,000	$1,000	$1,000	$1,000	$1,500
Greater Of ACB Or $1,000	(1,000)	(1,000)	(1,300)	(1,000)
Gain (Non-Deductible Loss)	Nil	Nil	($ 300)	$ 500

8-90. In situations where a taxpayer disposes of a part of an item of personal use property while retaining the remainder, the taxpayer must establish the ratio of the adjusted cost base of the part disposed of, to the total adjusted cost base of the property. Then, in applying the $1,000 floor rule, the adjusted cost base is deemed to be the greater of the portion of the adjusted cost base associated with the part disposed of, or the same portion of $1,000. In the same fashion, the proceeds would be deemed to be the greater of the actual proceeds and the appropriate portion of $1,000.

8-91. The government perceived an abuse of this $1,000 floor rule in art donation schemes where individuals would acquire art in bulk for nominal amounts ($10 each) and would then donate them immediately to various educational institutions at values apparently determined by questionable appraisers ($1,000 or less). The capital gains would be exempt because of the $1,000 floor rule, but the individuals would receive charitable donation receipts of $1,000. As a result, ITA 46(5) excludes certain property from the $1,000 rule when it is donated as part of a scheme to receive donation receipts of artificially high value.

Listed Personal Property

8-92. Listed personal property consists of certain specified items of personal use property. The specified items are found in ITA 54 as follows:

    (i)   print, etching, drawing, painting, sculpture, or other similar work of art,
    (ii)   jewelry,
    (iii) rare folio, rare manuscript, or rare book,
    (iv) stamp, or
    (v)   coin.

8-93.   In general, listed personal property is subject to the same capital gains rules as would apply to other personal use property. This would include the applicability of the $1,000 floor rule. However, there is one very important difference. While, in general, losses on personal use property cannot be deducted, allowable capital losses on listed personal property can be deducted subject to a significant restriction.

8-94.   The restriction is that allowable capital losses on listed personal property can only be deducted against taxable capital gains on listed personal property. In the absence of such taxable capital gains, the listed personal property losses cannot be deducted. However, any undeducted losses are subject to the carry over provisions described in Chapter 11.

Exercise Eight - 10

Subject: Personal Use Property

During the current year, Martha Steward disposes of several items. The proceeds of disposition and the adjusted cost base of the various items are as follows:

	Adjusted Cost Base	Proceeds Of Disposition
Sailboat	$43,000	$68,000
Oil Painting	200	25,000
Personal Automobile	33,000	18,000
Diamond Necklace	46,000	18,000

What is the net tax consequence of these dispositions?

SOLUTION available in print and online Study Guide.

We suggest you work Self Study Problem Eight-8 at this point.

Gains And Losses On Foreign Currency
Introduction
8-95.   As foreign currency exchange rates are constantly fluctuating, any taxpayer who engages in foreign currency transactions is certain to experience gains and losses that relate to these fluctuations. With respect to dealing with the tax aspects of foreign currency transactions, there are two basic issues:

    Income Vs. Capital Transactions If a foreign exchange gain or loss arises as the result of an income transaction (i.e., buying or selling goods or services with the amounts denominated in foreign currency), the full amount will be taxable or deductible. In contrast, if a foreign exchange gain or loss arises as the result of a capital transaction (i.e., purchase of, sale of, or financing of, a capital asset), only one-half of the amount will be taxable or deductible.

    Regular Vs. Foreign Currency Capital Gains   The issue here is whether the gain on a particular capital transaction is a regular capital gain as defined in ITA 39(1) or, alternatively, a "capital gain or loss in respect of foreign currencies" as described in ITA 39(1.1). For individuals, under ITA 39(1.1) the first $200 of a foreign currency gain for the year is not subject to tax and the first $200 of a foreign currency loss cannot be claimed. This reduces the need to account for and report small foreign currency gains and losses, i.e., vacationers returning to Canada converting their remaining foreign currency to Canadian dollars.

Foreign Currency Income Transactions

8-96. Foreign currency income transactions usually result in exchange gains and losses. For example, if a business acquires goods in the U.S. for US$5,000 at a point in time when US$1.00 = C$1.40, no gain or loss would arise if the goods were paid for immediately. However, if the goods are paid for at a later point in time when US$1.00 = C$1.42, there would be an exchange loss of C$100 [(US$5,000)(C$1.40 - C$1.42)]. The issue here is whether the loss should be recognized only when the payable is settled or, alternatively, accrued if a Balance Sheet date occurs before the payment.

8-97. IT-95R indicates that, with respect to income transactions, the taxpayer can use any method that is in accordance with generally accepted accounting principles (GAAP). Under GAAP, current payables and receivables must be recorded at current rates of exchange as at each Balance Sheet date. No alternative method is acceptable.

8-98. The resulting changes in value must be recorded as gains or losses at the time they are measured. As this is the only acceptable method under GAAP, it would require that foreign exchange gains and losses on income transactions be taken into income on an accrual basis, rather than waiting until the foreign exchange balance is settled in Canadian dollars.

Capital Transactions Involving Foreign Currency Financing

8-99. Purchases or sales of capital assets may be financed with long-term payables or receivables that are denominated in a foreign currency. In such situations, the foreign exchange gains and losses on the payables or receivables are considered to be capital gains or losses.

8-100. The accounting rules here are consistent with those applicable to income transactions. That is, changes in the value of payables and receivables are recognized and taken into income as of each Balance Sheet date.

8-101. It is somewhat surprising that the CRA does not permit this approach. While it does not address the issue of gains and losses on long-term receivables, Paragraph 13 of IT-95R states that:

> The Department considers that a taxpayer has "made a gain" or "sustained a loss" in a foreign currency ... resulting in the application of subsection 39(2) ...

> (c) at the time of repayment of part or all of a capital debt obligation.

8-102. This means that, if a Canadian company has used long-term foreign currency debt to finance capital assets, no exchange gain or loss will be included in the determination of Net Income For Tax Purposes until the debt matures and is paid off in Canadian dollars. This may result in significant differences between accounting Net Income and Net Income For Tax Purposes.

Foreign Currency Purchase And Sale Of Securities

8-103. Individuals will most commonly encounter foreign exchange gains or losses when they are involved in purchasing or selling securities with settlement amounts denominated in a foreign currency. For purposes of distinguishing between ordinary capital gains and those that can be classified under ITA 39(2) as being in respect of foreign currencies, IT-95R provides the following examples of the time when the Department considers a transaction resulting in the application of ITA 39(2) to have taken place:

(a) At the time of conversion of funds in a foreign currency into another foreign currency or into Canadian dollars.

(b) At the time funds in a foreign currency are used to make a purchase or a payment (in such a case the gain or loss would be the difference between the value of the foreign currency expressed in Canadian dollars when it arose and its value expressed in Canadian dollars when the purchase or payment was made).

8-104. An example will serve to illustrate this approach:

EXAMPLE On August 1, 2014, Mr. Conrad White uses $180,000 to open a British pound (£) account with his broker. Assume that at this time, £1 = $1.80, so that his $180,000 is converted to £100,000.

On December 31, 2014, he uses his entire British pound balance to acquire 10,000 shares in a British company, Underling Ltd. at a cost of £10 per share. At this time, £1 = $1.82. On July 1, 2017, the shares are sold for £21 per share. On this date, £1 = $1.65, and all of the proceeds from the sale are immediately converted into $346,500 [(10,000)(£21)($1.65)] Canadian dollars.

ANALYSIS - Purchase As a result of his December 31, 2014 purchase, he will have an exchange gain of $2,000 [(£100,000)($1.82 - $1.80)]. As this qualifies as an ITA 39(2) foreign currency capital gain (see Paragraph 8-103), Mr. White will only include $900 [(1/2)($2,000 - $200)] of this in his Net Income For Tax Purposes.

ANALYSIS - Sale When he sells the shares for £21 per share, his total capital gain is $164,500 [(£210,000)($1.65) - (£100,000)($1.82)]. This entire amount would be treated as an ITA 39(1) (regular) capital gain and would not be eligible for the $200 exclusion that is available to individuals. This result is not influenced by the conversion of the British currency into Canadian dollars. However, if the £210,000 proceeds were not converted and, at a later point in time, were converted into Canadian dollars at a rate other than £1 = $1.65, an ITA 39(2) foreign currency capital gain or loss would arise.

8-105. Without going into detail, these procedures are not consistent with GAAP or reasonable economic analysis. Under GAAP, no gain would be recognized at the time of the share purchase. Because of this, there would be a gain at the time of sale of $166,500 [(£210,000)($1.65) - (£100,000)($1.80)].

Funds On Deposit

8-106. IT-95R also notes that foreign currency funds on deposit are not considered to be disposed of until they are converted into another currency, or are used to purchase a negotiable instrument or some other asset. This means that foreign funds on deposit may be moved from one form of deposit to another and, as long as such funds can continue to be viewed as "on deposit", no gain or loss will be recognized.

Exercise Eight - 11

Subject: Foreign Currency Gains And Losses

On January 5, 2016, Mr. Michel Pratt purchases 35,000 Trinidad/Tobago dollars (TT$) at a rate of TT$1 = C$0.21. Using TT$30,600 of these funds, on June 5, 2016, he acquires 450 shares of a Trinidadian company, Matim Inc., at a price of TT$68 per share. At this time, TT$1 = C$0.23. During September, 2017, the shares are sold for TT$96 per share. The Trinidad/Tobago dollars are immediately converted into Canadian dollars at a rate of TT$1 = C$0.19. What amounts will be included in Mr. Pratt's 2016 and 2017 Net Income For Tax Purposes as a result of these transactions?

SOLUTION available in print and online Study Guide.

We suggest you work Self Study Problem Eight-9 at this point.

Options

8-107. The term "option" would include stock rights, warrants, options to purchase capital assets, as well as stock options granted to executives and other employees (the special rules related to options granted to employees were covered in Chapter 3). From the point of view of the taxpayer acquiring these options, they are treated as capital property. The tax consequences related to such options will vary depending on future events:

- If they are sold before their expiry date, a capital gain or loss will usually arise.
- If they are exercised, the cost of acquiring the options will be added to the adjusted cost base of the assets acquired.
- If the options expire before they are either sold or exercised, a capital loss equal to the cost of the options will be incurred.

8-108.   From the point of view of the issuer of the option, any proceeds from the sale of the option will usually be treated as a capital gain at the time the option is issued. If the holder decides to exercise the option, the sale price of the option becomes part of the proceeds of disposition to the issuer and the original gain on the sale of the option is eliminated. If the sale of the option occurs in a different taxation year than the exercise of the option, the issuer is permitted to file an amended return for the year of sale.

8-109.   An example will serve to illustrate the preceding rules.

EXAMPLE   John Powers has a capital property with an adjusted cost base of $250,000. During 2017, he sells an option on this property to Sarah Myers for $18,000. This option allows her to acquire the capital property for $300,000 at any time prior to December 31, 2020.

ANALYSIS - Option Expires   Mr. Powers, as a result of selling the option in 2017, will have to record a taxable capital gain of $9,000 [(1/2)($18,000)] in that year. If the option expires, there will be no further tax consequences to Mr. Powers as he has already recognized the $9,000 taxable capital gain in 2017. For Ms. Myers, the expiry of the option will allow her to recognize an allowable capital loss of $9,000.

ANALYSIS - Option Is Exercised   If the option is exercised in 2020, Mr. Powers can file an amended return for 2017, removing the capital gain that was recognized in that year. However, if he does, he will have to include the $18,000 in the proceeds of disposition from the sale of the asset, thereby recording a capital gain of $68,000 ($18,000 + $300,000 - $250,000). Ms. Myers will have acquired the capital property at a cost of $318,000 ($300,000 + $18,000).

8-110.   There are three exceptions to the preceding general rules for vendors of options. The first of these is an exemption from taxation on the proceeds of any options sold on a taxpayer's principal residence.

8-111.   The second involves options sold by a corporation on its capital stock or debt securities. In this situation, the corporation will not be taxed on the proceeds at the time the options are sold. Rather, the proceeds will be treated as part of the consideration for the securities issued if the options are exercised. However, if the options expire without being exercised, the corporation will have a capital gain equal to the amount of the proceeds.

8-112.   The third exception relates to options granted by a trust to acquire units of the trust that are to be issued by the trust.

Deemed Dispositions - Change In Use

General Rules

Deemed Disposition

8-113.   The Glossary to this text (see the Study Guide) defines deeming rules and deemed disposition as follows:

Deeming Rules   Rules that are used to require that an item or event be given a treatment for tax purposes that is not consistent with the actual nature of the item or event.

Deemed Disposition   A requirement to assume that a disposition has taken place when, in fact, a disposition transaction has not occurred.

8-114.   Such rules are fairly common in the *Income Tax Act* and are applied in a wide variety of situations. In this Chapter 8, we will deal with the deemed dispositions that occur when there is a change in use, and the deemed dispositions that occur when a taxpayer departs from Canada. In Chapter 9, we will provide coverage of the deemed dispositions that occur when an individual dies.

8-115.   You should also note that, since no real proceeds of disposition are involved in deemed dispositions, we will also need a deemed proceeds of disposition. The most common situation here is that the proceeds of disposition will be based on fair market values.

Change In Use

8-116.   The basic idea here is that when a property used to produce income is converted to some other purpose or, alternatively, when a property that was acquired for some other purpose becomes an income producing property, ITA 13(7) requires that the change be treated as a deemed disposition combined with a simultaneous deemed reacquisition.

8-117.   Different rules apply, depending on whether the change is from business to personal use or, alternatively, from personal to business use. We will give separate attention to each of these changes. In addition, we will cover some special change in use rules that apply to principal residences and to automobiles that are owned by an individual.

Business To Personal Use

8-118.   This situation is straightforward. If the conversion is from business to personal use, the deemed proceeds will be equal to fair market value, with the transferor recognizing a capital gain, recapture, or terminal loss in the usual manner. The fair market value will also be used as the acquisition cost of the personal use asset.

Personal To Business Use

8-119.   If a personal use asset is converted to an income producing asset, the rules vary depending on the relationship between the fair market value of the asset and its cost.

Fair Market Value Less Than Cost   In this case, the fair market value will serve as both the proceeds of the deemed disposition and as the capital cost of the asset reacquired.

Fair Market Value Greater Than Cost   In this case, the fair market value will serve as the proceeds of the deemed disposition, resulting in the recognition of a capital gain. However, under ITA 13(7)(b), the capital cost of the reacquired asset for CCA purposes will be equal to its cost, plus one-half of the difference between its cost and its fair market value. While this value will be used for determining CCA and recapture amounts, for purposes of determining the capital gain on the deemed disposition, the capital cost will be deemed to be the full fair market value of the asset.

8-120.   There is a reason for this different rule in situations where the fair market value exceeds the cost. It reflects the fact that only one-half of the capital gain that arises on such a deemed disposition will be subject to tax. If the reacquisition was recorded at the full fair market value of the asset, 100 percent of the capital gain amount could be deducted as CCA. A simple example will serve to illustrate this problem.

EXAMPLE Shirley Malone owns a pleasure boat which cost $100,000. She is changing its use to a charter boat and, at the time of the change, the fair market value of the boat is $150,000.

ANALYSIS Shirley's deemed proceeds of disposition will be $150,000, resulting in a capital gain of $50,000. This will increase her Net Income For Tax Purposes by one-half of this amount or $25,000.

The deemed Capital Cost of the boat to the charter operation, for capital gains purposes, will also be $150,000. This value will be used in the determination of any capital gain that might arise on a future disposition of the sailboat. As it is a depreciable asset, there could be no capital loss.

If the $150,000 was also used as the basis for CCA, Shirley would be able to deduct 100 percent of the $50,000 increase in value that occurred while she owned the boat for personal use. This would not be an equitable result as Shirley only paid taxes on $25,000 of this increase.

Given this, in situations where there is a gain on the change in use, the capital cost addition for CCA purposes will be limited to the cost of the asset, plus one-half of the gain (the taxable portion of the capital gain, a.k.a. the bump up). This means that for the purpose of determining CCA or recapture, Shirley's UCC balance will be $125,000 [$100,000 + (1/2)($150,000 - $100,000)].

Example - Change In Use

8-121.   The following example will serve to illustrate the procedures associated with changes in use.

EXAMPLE On January 1, 2016, Ms. Barker, a professional accountant, acquires a building at a cost of $500,000, with $400,000 allocated to the building and $100,000 allocated to the land. During the entire year, 20 percent of the floor space was used for her accounting practice, while the remainder was used as her principal residence.

On January 1, 2017, an additional 30 percent of the total floor space was converted to business use. On this date, the fair market value of the real property had increased to $620,000, with $480,000 allocated to the building and $140,000 allocated to the land.

On January 1, 2018, the entire building was converted to residential use as Ms. Barker's accounting practice had grown to the point where it had to move to more extensive facilities. On this date, the fair market value had increased to $700,000, with $550,000 allocated to the building and $150,000 allocated to the land.

ANALYSIS In using this example, we will focus only on the determination of CCA and any tax consequences associated with the changes in use. We will assume that net rental revenues are adequate to claim maximum CCA.

2016 CCA Calculation The maximum 2016 CCA would be calculated as follows:

January 1, 2016 UCC	Nil
Add: Cost Of Acquiring Business Portion [(20%)($500,000 - $100,000)]	$80,000
Deduct: One-Half Net Additions [(1/2)($80,000)]	(40,000)
Base Amount For CCA Claim	$40,000
Deduct: CCA For The Year [(4%)($40,000)]	(1,600)
Add: One-Half Net Additions	40,000
January 1, 2017 UCC (For 20 Percent Of The Building)	$78,400

2017 Tax Consequences The change in use would trigger capital gains on the land and building as follows:

	Land	Building
Fair Market Value	$140,000	$480,000
Cost	(100,000)	(400,000)
Change In Value	$ 40,000	$ 80,000
Change In Use Percent	30%	30%
Capital Gain	$ 12,000	$ 24,000
Inclusion Rate	1/2	1/2
Taxable Capital Gain	$ 6,000	$ 12,000

It is likely that this capital gain could be eliminated through the use of the principal residence exemption that was discussed earlier in this Chapter.

The calculation of the 2017 CCA deduction would be as follows:

January 1, 2017 UCC (For 20 Percent Of The Building)		$ 78,400
Add: Deemed Cost Of Increase In Business Usage:		
Cost [(30%)($400,000)]	$120,000	
Bump Up [(1/2)(30%)($480,000 - $400,000)]	12,000	132,000
Deduct: One-Half Net Additions* [(1/2)($132,000)]		(66,000)
Base Amount For CCA Claim		$144,400
Deduct: CCA For The Year [(4%)($144,400)]		(5,776)
Add: One-Half Net Additions		66,000
January 1, 2018 UCC (For 50 Percent Of The Building)		**$204,624**

*Non-arm's length transfers are exempt from the half-year rule, provided the transferor used the property as a depreciable property prior to the transfer. The portion of the property being transferred was not previously used as a depreciable property and, as a consequence, the half-year rule is applicable.

2018 Tax Consequences As all of the building has been converted to personal use and is no longer being used for business purposes, there would be no CCA for 2018. However, there would be recapture of CCA as follows:

January 1, 2018 UCC	$204,624
Lesser Of:	
• Cost For CCA Purposes ($80,000 + $132,000) = $212,000	
• Deemed Proceeds Of Disposition	
= [(20% + 30%)($550,000)] = $275,000	(212,000)
Negative Ending UCC Balance = Recapture Of CCA	**($ 7,376)**

Note that the amount of this recapture of CCA is equal to the sum of the CCA ($1,600 + $5,776) that was taken in the two years during which some of the asset was used for business purposes.

The change in use would trigger capital gains on the land and building as follows:

	Land	Building
Fair Market Value	$150,000	$550,000
Change In Use Percent	50%	50%
Deemed Proceeds Of Disposition	$ 75,000	$275,000
Cost Of 2016 Acquisition		
20 Percent Of $100,000 and $400,000	(20,000)	(80,000)
Cost Of 2017 Acquisition		
30 Percent Of $140,000 and $480,000	(42,000)	(144,000)
Capital Gain	$ 13,000	$ 51,000
Inclusion Rate	1/2	1/2
Taxable Capital Gain	**$ 6,500**	**$ 25,500**

Exercise Eight - 12

Subject: Change In Use - Personal Property To Rental Property

During July, 2017, Ms. Lynn Larson decides to use her summer cottage as a rental property. It has an original cost of $43,000 (building = $23,000, land = $20,000) and its current fair market value is $231,000 (building = $111,000, land = $120,000). It has never been designated as her principal residence. Describe the 2017 tax consequences of this change in use, including the capital cost and UCC that will be applicable to the rental property. In addition, indicate the maximum amount of CCA that would be available for 2017.

SOLUTION available in print and online Study Guide.

Special Rules For Principal Residences
Change In Use - Principal Residence To Rental Property

8-122.   As we have previously noted, when the use of a property is changed from personal to business, the *Income Tax Act* requires that this change be treated as a deemed disposition and reacquisition at fair market value. The conversion of a principal residence to a rental property is a common example of this type of situation and, in the absence of any election, the fair market value at the time of the change will become the capital cost of the rental property. As was previously discussed, if the fair market value exceeds the cost, a different value will be used for the calculation of CCA.

8-123.   An alternative to this treatment is provided under ITA 45(2). Under this Subsection, the taxpayer can make an election under which he will be deemed not to have commenced using the property for producing income. Note that there is no required form for this election. It is made in the taxpayer's income tax return.

8-124.   If this election is made, the taxpayer will still include the rents from the property as rental income and deduct all of the expenses associated with the property other than CCA. However, use of the ITA 45(2) election prevents the taxpayer from deducting any amounts for CCA on this property.

8-125.   While this inability to deduct CCA can be viewed as a disadvantage associated with the election, the election does, in fact, have an offsetting advantage. Based on the ITA 54 definition of a principal residence, the property can continue to be designated as a principal residence for up to four years while the election is in effect. This would appear to be the case even in situations where the individual does not return to live in the property.

8-126.   In practical terms, the preceding means that an individual who moves out of a principal residence can retain principal residence treatment for the property, for up to four years. This allows the individual to enjoy any capital gains that accrue on the property during that period on a tax free basis.

8-127.   This would be of particular importance to an individual who moves to a rental property and does not have an alternative principal residence during this period. Even if the individual purchases an alternative residential property, the election can be helpful as it allows a choice as to which property will be designated as the principal residence during the relevant years. If one of the properties experiences a substantially larger capital gain during this period, the use of this election could produce a significant savings in taxes.

8-128.   Also of interest is the fact that the four year election period can be extended. ITA 54.1 specifies that if the following conditions are met either by the taxpayer or the taxpayer's spouse or common-law partner, the election can be extended without limit:

• you leave the residence because your employer requires you to relocate;

• you return to the original residence while still with the same employer, or before the end of the year following the year you leave that employer, or you die before such employment terminates; and

- the original residence is at least 40 kilometers further from your new place of employment than your temporary residence.

Exercise Eight - 13

Subject: Change In Use - Principal Residence To Rental Property

During 2012, Jan Wheatley acquired a new home at a cost of $220,000. On December 31, 2015, she moves from this home into an apartment. At this time, the home is appraised for $210,000. Because she believes that real estate in her area is temporarily undervalued, she decides to rent the property for a period of time and sell it at a later date. During 2016, she receives rents of $21,600 and has expenses, other than CCA, of $12,600. On January 1, 2017, she sells the home to the current tenant for $345,000. Indicate the 2016 and 2017 tax consequences to Ms. Wheatley assuming that, in 2016, she does not elect under ITA 45(2) and deducts CCA. How would these results differ if she made the ITA 45(2) election? In providing your answers, ignore the cost of the land on which the home is located.

SOLUTION available in print and online Study Guide.

Change In Use - Rental Property To Principal Residence

8-129.   Here again, unless an election is made, this change in use will be treated as a deemed disposition at fair market value, with possible results including capital gains, recapture, or terminal loss. When this type of change occurs, ITA 45(3) allows an individual to elect out of the deemed disposition for capital gains purposes as long as no CCA has been taken on the property. To make the election, the taxpayer must notify the Minister in writing. The election must be made by the taxpayer's filing deadline for the year following the disposition (April 30 or June 15).

8-130.   When the ITA 45(3) election is used, it is possible to designate the property as a principal residence for up to four years prior to the time it stopped being used as a rental property. This can be beneficial both to individuals who did not own another residential property during this four year period, and to individuals with an alternative residential property that experiences a capital gain at a lower annual rate, or a loss.

Exercise Eight - 14

Subject: Change In Use - Rental Property To Principal Residence

On January 2, 2016, Lance Ho acquires a small condominium in downtown Toronto for $375,000. When his mother threatens to commit suicide if he ever moves out, he rents the unit to a friend until December 31, 2016. Net rental income, before any deduction for CCA, is $9,800. Mr. Ho's mother is hit by a bus and dies on December 26, 2016. The grieving Mr. Ho moves into the unit on January 1, 2017. At this time, the appraised value of the property is $450,000.

After moving in, he finds that the congested traffic in the downtown area is intolerable and, on December 31, 2017, he sells the unit for $510,000. Indicate the 2016 and 2017 tax consequences to Mr. Ho, assuming that he deducts CCA in 2016 and does not elect under ITA 45(3). How would these results differ had he not taken CCA and made the ITA 45(3) election? In providing your answers, ignore the cost of the land on which the condominium is located.

SOLUTION available in print and online Study Guide.

We suggest you work Self Study Problems Eight-10 and Eight-11 at this point.

Special Rules For Automobiles

8-131. As was illustrated in the example in Paragraph 8-121, the change in use rules generally apply when there is a change in use involving only a part of an asset. If this rule was applied to automobiles used in employment or business activities, there would be a significant problem. As the deductible percentage of usage of usage would change each year, strict application of the rule would result in a deemed disposition/re-acquisition every year. However, as was discussed in Chapter 5 (see material beginning at Paragraph 5-109), an alternative approach is accepted by the CRA. As this alternative approach was illustrated in Chapter 5, it will not be presented again in this Chapter.

Deemed Dispositions - Departures From Canada

Basic Rules

8-132. When a taxpayer leaves Canada, ITA 128.1(4)(b) calls for a deemed disposition of all property owned at the time of departure. The disposition is deemed to occur at fair market value. If the taxpayer is an individual, certain types of property are exempted from this deemed disposition rule. The major categories of exempted property are as follows:

- Real property situated in Canada, Canadian resource properties, and timber resource properties.

- Property of a business carried on in Canada through a permanent establishment. This would include capital property and inventories.

- "Excluded Right or Interest" This concept is defined in ITA 128.1(10). The definition includes right and interests in Registered Pension Plans, Registered Retirement Savings Plans, Deferred Profit Sharing Plans, stock options, death benefits, retiring allowances, as well as other rights of individuals in trusts or other similar arrangements.

Additional Complications

8-133. There are a number of other tax complications associated with both immigration and emigration. These include the ability to elect to have an exempt property taxed at the time of departure and procedures that allow a taxpayer to unwind a deemed disposition. These are given detailed attention in Chapter 20, International Issues In Taxation.

Exercise Eight - 15

Subject: Emigration

John Porker owns publicly traded securities with an adjusted cost base of $920,000 and a fair market value of $1,030,000. On April 21, 2017, he permanently departs from Canada still owning the shares. What would be the tax consequences of his departure, if any, with respect to these securities?

SOLUTION available in print and online Study Guide.

Exercise Eight - 16

Subject: Emigration

Ms. Shari Twain owns a rental property in London, Ontario with a capital cost of $275,000 and a fair market value of $422,000. The land values included in these figures are $75,000 and $122,000, respectively. The UCC of the building is $107,800. On December 31, 2017, Ms. Twain permanently departs from Canada still owning the property. What are the tax consequences of her departure, if any, with respect to this rental property?

SOLUTION available in print and online Study Guide.

We suggest you work Self Study Problem Eight-12 at this point.

Deferral Provisions On Small Business Investments

Basic Provision

8-134.   ITA 44.1 was introduced to provide small businesses, especially start-up companies, with greater access to risk capital. It provides for the deferral of capital gains resulting from the disposition of "eligible small business corporation shares" when sold by an individual. The deferral is conditional on reinvestment of some or all of the proceeds of disposition in other eligible small business corporation shares (replacement shares). As you would expect, the adjusted cost base of these replacement shares will be reduced by the capital gain that is eliminated in the current year. In effect, this defers the gain until such time as the new investment is sold and not reinvested in replacement shares.

Definitions

8-135.   ITA 44.1 is a very technical Section of the *Act* and, as such, requires a number of definitions. Some of the more important definitions are as follows:

Eligible Small Business Corporation   To be eligible for the deferral, the corporations must comply with the definition of an eligible small business corporation. This is a Canadian controlled private corporation that has substantially all (meaning more than 90 percent) of the fair market value of its assets devoted principally to an active business carried on primarily (meaning more than 50 percent) in Canada. The corporation's qualifying assets include its holdings of shares or debt in other eligible small business corporations. To be eligible for the ITA 44.1 provisions, the small business corporation and corporations related to it cannot have assets with a carrying value in excess of $50 million. Shares or debt of related corporations are not counted when determining the $50 million limit on assets.

Qualifying Disposition   To qualify for the deferral, the gain must result from the sale of common shares in an eligible small business corporation that was owned by the investor throughout the 185 day period that preceded the disposition.

Replacement Shares These are common shares of an eligible small business corporation that are acquired within 120 days after the end of the year in which the qualifying disposition took place. They must be designated as replacement shares in the individual's tax return. Note that an individual can establish a deferral that is less than the maximum permitted amount by designating a lesser amount of replacement shares.

Permitted Deferral The deferral is limited to a fraction of the capital gain resulting from the qualifying disposition. The fraction is based on the ratio of the lesser of the cost of the replacement shares and proceeds of disposition, divided by the proceeds of disposition (the value cannot exceed one).

> **EXAMPLE** The common shares of an eligible small business corporation with an adjusted cost base of $2,000,000 are sold for $2,500,000. Within 30 days, $1,800,000 of the proceeds are used to purchase replacement shares.

> **ANALYSIS** The total gain is $500,000 ($2,500,000 - $2,000,000). Of this total, the maximum permitted deferral would be $360,000 [($500,000)($1,800,000 ÷ $2,500,000)].

Adjusted Cost Base Reduction The adjusted cost base of the replacement shares will have to be reduced by the amount of any capital gains deferral. Using the preceding example, the adjusted cost base of the replacement shares would be $1,440,000 ($1,800,000 - $360,000). If there is more than one block of replacement shares, this reduction will be allocated in proportion to their costs.

Example

8-136. The following example illustrates the application of the ITA 44.1 deferral:

EXAMPLE During the current year, an individual makes a qualifying disposition of shares of Corporation A with an adjusted cost base of $3,000,000, for proceeds of disposition of $4,500,000.

Within 120 days after the current year end, the individual purchases replacement shares in Corporation B with a cost of $2,200,000 and in Corporation C with a cost of $2,300,000. Corporations A, B, and C are unrelated.

ANALYSIS As the $4,500,000 proceeds of disposition is equal to the $4,500,000 ($2,200,000 + $2,300,000) cost of the replacement shares, the permitted deferral is equal to $1,500,000 [($1,500,000)($4,500,000 ÷ $4,500,000)], which is the total capital gain on the disposition.

In calculating the adjusted cost base of the new shares, the $1,500,000 reduction would be allocated as follows:

	B Shares	C Shares
Purchase Price	$2,200,000	$2,300,000
Deferral:		
[($1,500,000)($2,200,000/$4,500,000)]	(733,333)	
[($1,500,000)($2,300,000/$4,500,000)]		(766,667)
Adjusted Cost Base	$1,466,667	$1,533,333

The total adjusted cost base is $3,000,000 ($1,466,667 + $1,533,333), which was the adjusted cost base of the Corporation A shares.

Exercise Eight - 17

Subject: Deferral Of Small Business Gains

On January 15, 2017, Jerri Hamilton sells all of her common shares of Hamilton Ltd., an eligible small business corporation. She had owned the shares for 12 years. The adjusted cost base of these shares is $750,000 and they are sold for $1,350,000. On February 15, 2017, $1,200,000 of these proceeds are invested in the common shares of JH Inc., a new eligible small business corporation. How much of the capital gain arising on the sale of the Hamilton Ltd. shares can be deferred by the investment in JH Inc.? If the maximum deferral is elected, what will be the adjusted cost base of the JH Inc. shares?

SOLUTION available in print and online Study Guide.

We suggest you work Self Study Problem Eight-13 at this point.

Deferral Provisions On Replacement Property

The Problem

Potential Taxation

8-137.   The disposition of a capital property can give rise to capital gains and, in the case of depreciable capital property, recapture of CCA. In certain situations, such dispositions are unavoidable, with the related income inclusions creating significant financial problems for the taxpayer.

EXAMPLE   An enterprise has its only Class 1 building completely destroyed by fire. The building has a capital cost of $1,200,000 and a UCC of $450,000. It is insured for its replacement cost of $4,000,000 and this amount is received during the current year.

ANALYSIS   In the absence of any mitigating legislation, these events would result in a taxable capital gain of $1,400,000 [(1/2)($4,000,000 - $1,200,000)] and, if the building is not replaced during the current year, recapture of $750,000. The taxes on this $2,150,000 increase in Taxable Income would be added to the many other problems associated with the fire.

8-138.   A similar problem may arise when a business changes its location. The sale of its old facilities may result in significant capital gains. In addition, if these old facilities are not replaced in the same year as their disposition, there may also be recapture of CCA.

Legislative Relief

8-139.   Given the problems such situations can generate, it is not surprising that the government has provided relief. The relevant provisions are ITA 13(4) which deals with the recapture problem and ITA 44(1), which deals with the capital gains.

8-140.   In somewhat simplified terms, these provisions allow the taxpayer to eliminate or reduce capital gains and recapture that arise on qualifying dispositions. The use of these provisions is conditional on the replacement of the property within a specified period of time. There is a corresponding reduction in the capital cost and UCC of the replacement assets. This, in effect, defers these income inclusions until the replacement assets are sold or used.

8-141.   You should note that the application of these provisions is not required. Both ITA 13(4) and ITA 44(1) are elections that are made in filing the taxpayer's return of income (i.e., there is no prescribed form). They do not apply automatically and, if the taxpayer fails to make the required elections, the result can be a significant increase in Tax Payable in the year of disposition.

Voluntary And Involuntary Dispositions

8-142.   There are two types of situations for which the combination of ITA 13(4) and ITA 44(1) provide relief. They can be described as follows:

Involuntary Dispositions   This description is used to describe dispositions of depreciable property resulting from theft, destruction, or expropriation under statutory authority. In the case of this type of disposition, the relieving provisions cover all types of depreciable property. These provisions are available as long as the replacement occurs within 24 months after the end of the year in which the proceeds of disposition were received.

Voluntary Dispositions   As the name implies, these are voluntary dispositions, usually involving the relocation of a business. As a relocation may involve a disposition, taxpayers undergoing a move may encounter problems similar to those experienced when there is an involuntary disposition. In these voluntary dispositions, the applicability of ITA 13(4) is more limited.

Specifically, this provision only applies to "former business property", a term that is defined in ITA 248(1) to consist of real property or interests in real property. This means that assets other than those specified in the ITA 248 definition (e.g., equipment, furniture and fixtures) will not benefit from this provision. A further difference here is that the replacement must occur within 12 months after the year in which the proceeds of disposition are received.

Timing Considerations

Dispositions

8-143.   Note that, from a technical point of view, a disposition does not take place until the proceeds become receivable. In the case of voluntary dispositions, the proceeds will become receivable at the time of sale. However, in the case of involuntary dispositions, the receipt of insurance or expropriation proceeds may occur in a taxation year subsequent to the theft, destruction, or expropriation of the property. For purposes of determining the 24 month replacement period, the clock will generally start ticking in this later year.

Replacements

8-144.   With respect to capital gains, they will be recognized in the year in which the disposition takes place. They will occur without regard to when the replacement is made. This means that their reduction or elimination will always require the application of ITA 44(1).

8-145.   The situation with recapture is different. You will recall from Chapter 5 that recapture only occurs when there is a negative balance in the class at the end of the period. If the replacement occurs in the same period as the disposition, it is likely that there will be a positive balance in the class at the end of the period. If this is the situation, there is no recapture and the election under ITA 13(4) is not relevant.

8-146.   A further point here is that, if the replacement occurs in a period subsequent to the disposition, the application of ITA 13(4) and ITA 44(1) will have to be implemented via an amended return for the period of disposition. Any capital gain or recapture that occurs at the time of disposition will, in effect, be reversed through the amended return.

Application Of ITA 44(1) To Capital Gains

8-147.   If a qualifying property is disposed of and replaced within the required time frame, ITA 44(1) provides an election that will reduce the capital gain to the lesser of:

- an amount calculated by the usual approach (proceeds of disposition, less adjusted cost base); and

- the excess, if any, of the proceeds of disposition of the old property over the cost of the replacement property. Provided the cost of the new property is equal to or exceeds the proceeds of disposition for the old property, this amount will be nil.

8-148.   In somewhat simplified terms, if the cost of the replacement property is greater than the proceeds of disposition for the replaced property, no capital gain will be recorded if the appropriate election is made. We would remind you that, in those cases where the replacement occurs in a period subsequent to the disposition, this election will have to be applied as an adjustment to the return for the year of disposition.

EXAMPLE   A taxpayer has land with an adjusted cost base of $600,000. It is expropriated by the local municipality. Compensation, which is paid immediately, is $1,000,000. It is replaced in the current taxation year with land which costs $1,200,000.

ANALYSIS   If no election is made under ITA 44(1), there will be a capital gain of $400,000 ($1,000,000 - $600,000) and the new land will have an adjusted cost base of $1,200,000.

Alternatively, if an election is made under ITA 44(1), the capital gain will be the lesser of:

- $400,000; and
- Nil (the excess, if any, of the proceeds of disposition of the old land over the cost of the new land).

Note that when ITA 44(1) is applied, any amount of capital gain that is eliminated must be removed from the cost of the replacement property. This will leave the adjusted cost base of the new land at $800,000 ($1,200,000 - $400,000).

8-149.   If the replacement cost had been less than the expropriation proceeds, it would not have been possible to eliminate all of the capital gain. For example, if the replacement cost had been $700,000, the minimum capital gain would have been $300,000, the excess of the proceeds of disposition of $1,000,000 over the $700,000 replacement cost of the new property. This alternative would leave the adjusted cost base of the replacement property at $600,000 ($700,000, less the deferred capital gain of $100,000).

Application Of ITA 13(4) To Recapture Of CCA

8-150.   The application of ITA 13(4) is more complex. In order to focus on this application we will use an example in which the fair market value of the building is less than its capital cost, thereby avoiding the need to use ITA 44(1) to eliminate a capital gain.

EXAMPLE A company's only building is destroyed in a fire in February, 2016. The original cost of the building was $2,500,000, the fair market value is $2,225,000, and it is an older building with a UCC of only $275,000. The insurance proceeds, all of which are received in 2016 prior to the December 31 year end, equal the fair market value of $2,225,000. The replacement building is acquired in July, 2017 at a cost of $3,000,000.

ANALYSIS Deducting $2,225,000, the lesser of the proceeds of disposition and the capital cost of the building, from the UCC of $275,000 will leave a negative balance of $1,950,000. As there is no replacement of the asset during 2016, this negative balance will remain at the end of this year, resulting in recapture of CCA. This amount will have to be included in income for the 2016 taxation year and will be added back to the UCC, reducing the class balance to nil.

In 2017, the year in which the replacement occurs, the ITA 13(4) election provides for an alternative calculation of the 2016 recapture:

January 1, 2016 UCC Balance		$275,000
Deduction:		
Lesser Of:		
• Proceeds Of Disposition = $2,225,000		
• Capital Cost = $2,500,000	$2,225,000	
Reduced By The Lesser Of:		
• Normal Recapture = $1,950,000		
• Replacement Cost = $3,000,000	(1,950,000)	(275,000)
Recapture Of 2016 CCA (Amended)		**Nil**

8-151.   IT-259R4 indicates that the election, including the relevant calculations, should be made in the form of a letter attached to the tax return in 2017, the year of replacement. In this example, the election would result in a $1,950,000 reduction in the company's 2016 Net Income For Tax Purposes and would likely provide the basis for a tax refund.

8-152.   The $1,950,000 reduction of Net Income For Tax Purposes in the preceding calculation will have to be treated as deemed proceeds of disposition and subtracted from the UCC of the replacement asset. This will leave a balance of $1,050,000 ($3,000,000 - $1,950,000). This balance correctly reflects the economic substance of the events that have occurred:

Original UCC		$ 275,000
Additional Cash:		
Excess Of The Replacement Cost	$3,000,000	
Over The Proceeds Of Disposition	(2,225,000)	775,000
New UCC Balance		**$1,050,000**

8-153.   Note that the reversal of recapture is limited to the cost of the replacement property. In our example, if the cost of the replacement property had only been $1,800,000, this amount would have been the limit on the recapture reversal and the remaining $150,000 [$275,000 - ($2,225,000 - $1,800,000)] would have remained in 2016 income. In this case, the UCC of the replacement building would be nil ($1,800,000 - $1,800,000).

Exercise Eight - 18

Subject: Involuntary Disposition - ITA 13(4) Election For Recapture

Foran Inc., a company with a December 31 year end, has the only building it owns destroyed by a meteorite during 2016. Its original cost was $1,500,000, its fair market value was $1,400,000, and the Class 1 UCC was $650,000. The Company receives $1,400,000 in insurance proceeds during 2016 and replaces the building with a used building at a cost of $2,350,000 in 2017. The Company makes the ITA 13(4) election to defer any recaptured CCA.   What is the UCC of the replacement building?

SOLUTION available in print and online Study Guide.

Combined Application Of ITA 13(4) And 44(1)
Example 1 - Replacement Cost Exceeds Proceeds Of Disposition
8-154.   Our first example of the combined application of ITA 13(4) and ITA 44(1) involves a situation where the replacement cost of the new asset exceeds the proceeds of disposition for the old asset.

EXAMPLE   During its 2016 taxation year, the Martin Company decides to change the location of its operations. Its current property consists of land with an adjusted cost base of $500,000, as well as a building with a capital cost of $1,500,000 and a UCC of $340,000. These assets are sold for a total price of $2,400,000, of which $600,000 is allocated to the land and $1,800,000 is allocated to the building. During January, 2017, a replacement property is acquired at a new location at a cost of $2,800,000, of which $700,000 is allocated to the land and $2,100,000 is allocated to the building.

ANALYSIS - Capital Gain As a result of the disposition, the Martin Company will include the following amounts in its 2016 Net Income For Tax Purposes:

	Old Land	Old Building
Proceeds Of Disposition	$600,000	$1,800,000
Adjusted Cost Base	(500,000)	(1,500,000)
Capital Gain	$100,000	$ 300,000
Inclusion Rate	1/2	1/2
Taxable Capital Gain	$ 50,000	$ 150,000
Recapture Of CCA ($340,000 - $1,500,000)	N/A	$1,160,000

When the replacement occurs in 2017, the cost allocated to the land and building exceeds the proceeds of disposition from these assets. As a consequence, the revised capital gain for 2016 will be nil, a fact that would be reflected in an amended 2016 tax return. However, the capital cost of the replacement assets would be reduced as follows:

	New Land	New Building
Cost	$700,000	$2,100,000
Capital Gain Reversal - ITA 44(1) Election	(100,000)	(300,000)
Deemed Adjusted Cost Base/Capital Cost	$600,000	$1,800,000

8-155. The economic basis for this result can be seen by noting that the combined deemed adjusted cost base of the new land and building is $2,400,000 ($600,000 + $1,800,000). This is equal to the combined adjusted cost base of the old land and building of $2,000,000 ($500,000 + $1,500,000), plus the additional $400,000 in cash ($2,800,000 - $2,400,000) required to finance the acquisition of the new land and building.

8-156. Using the ITA 13(4) formula, the amended 2016 recapture of CCA would be nil, calculated as follows:

UCC Balance		$340,000
Deduction:		
Lesser Of:		
• Proceeds Of Disposition = $1,800,000		
• Capital Cost = $1,500,000	$1,500,000	
Reduced By The Lesser Of:		
• Normal Recapture = $1,160,000		
• Replacement Cost = $2,100,000	(1,160,000)	(340,000)
Recapture Of CCA (Amended)		Nil

8-157. As would be expected when the replacement cost of the new building exceeds the normal recapture of CCA, the amended recapture of CCA will be nil. The reversal of the 2016 recapture of CCA will be reflected in the UCC of the new building as follows:

Deemed Capital Cost Of Building	$1,800,000
Recapture Reversal - ITA 13(4) Election	(1,160,000)
UCC	$ 640,000

8-158. As was the case with the capital cost of the new building, the economic basis for this result can also be explained. The new UCC of $640,000 is equal to the old UCC of $340,000, plus the $300,000 in cash ($2,100,000 - $1,800,000) required to finance the acquisition of the new building.

Example 2 - Proceeds Of Disposition Exceed Replacement Cost

8-159. In the preceding example, we are able to remove 100 percent of the capital gain through the application of the ITA 44 election. This resulted from the fact that the cost of the replacement property exceeded the proceeds of disposition for the old property. If this is not the case, some of the capital gain will have to remain in income. This point can be illustrated by making a small change in our previous example by decreasing the replacement land cost by $150,000.

> **EXAMPLE** During its 2016 taxation year, the Martin Company decides to change the location of its operations. Its current property consists of land with an adjusted cost base of $500,000, as well as a building with a capital cost of $1,500,000 and a UCC of $340,000. These assets are sold for a total price of $2,400,000, of which $600,000 is allocated to the land and $1,800,000 is allocated to the building. During January, 2017, a replacement property is acquired at a new location at a cost of $2,650,000, of which $550,000 is allocated to the land and $2,100,000 is allocated to the building.

8-160. For the 2016 tax return, the capital gains and recapture on the disposition will be as presented in Paragraph 8-154. In 2017, when ITA 44(1) is applied, the minimum capital gain on the land that can be reversed would be the lesser of:

- $100,000 (the excess of the $600,000 proceeds of disposition over the $500,000 adjusted cost base); and

- $50,000 (the excess of the $600,000 proceeds of disposition over the $550,000 replacement cost).

8-161. The lesser amount is $50,000. When this amount of the capital gain is reversed, it leaves $50,000 ($100,000 - $50,000) in capital gains in 2016 income. With respect to the replacement values, the relevant tax values are as follows:

	New Land	New Building
Cost	$550,000	$2,100,000
Capital Gain Reversal - ITA 44(1) Election	(50,000)	(300,000)
Deemed Adjusted Cost Base/Capital Cost	$500,000	$1,800,000
Recapture Reversal - ITA 13(4) Election	N/A	(1,160,000)
UCC	N/A	$ 640,000

Election To Reallocate Proceeds Of Disposition

8-162. In the preceding example, the fact that the replacement cost of the land was less than the proceeds of disposition of the previously owned land, resulted in a situation where a portion of the capital gain on this disposition had to remain in the 2016 tax return. Fortunately, a further election contained in ITA 44 provides, in many cases, a solution to this problem.

8-163. Under ITA 44(6), the taxpayer is allowed to reallocate the total proceeds of disposition on the sale of a former business property, without regard to the respective market values of the land and building. If, in the example presented in Paragraph 8-159, the total proceeds of $2,400,000 are reallocated on the basis of $550,000 (originally $600,000 in Paragraph 8-154) to the land and $1,850,000 (originally $1,800,000) to the building, the 2016 taxable capital gains will be as follows:

	Old Land	Old Building
Proceeds Of Disposition After Election	$550,000	$1,850,000
Adjusted Cost Base	(500,000)	(1,500,000)
Capital Gain	$ 50,000	$ 350,000
Inclusion Rate	1/2	1/2
Taxable Capital Gain	$ 25,000	$ 175,000

8-164.   While the total taxable capital gain remains the same, this reallocation of the total proceeds of disposition results in a situation where the replacement cost of both the land and building are equal to, or exceed, the proceeds of disposition. This, in turn, means that all of the capital gains on both of these capital assets will be removed from the 2016 amended tax return. Under this scenario, the tax values for the replacement assets would be as follows:

	New Land	New Building
Cost	$550,000	$2,100,000
Capital Gain Reversal - ITA 44(1) Election	(50,000)	(350,000)
Deemed Adjusted Cost Base/Capital Cost	$500,000	$1,750,000
Recapture Reversal - ITA 13(4) Election	N/A	(1,160,000)
UCC	N/A	$ 590,000

8-165.   Note that this election is not made without a cost. Had the $50,000 been left as a capital gain, tax would have applied on only one-half of the total. While we have eliminated this $25,000 in income, we have given up future CCA for the full amount of $50,000. In other words, we have given up $50,000 in future deductions in return for eliminating $25,000 of income in 2016. As explained in our Chapters 12 and 13 on corporate taxation, for some corporations, capital gains are initially taxed at higher rates than business income, which could be a factor in this decision. In addition, anticipated future tax rates could be a consideration.

Exercise Eight - 19

Subject: Involuntary Dispositions - ITA 13(4) and 44(1) Elections

Hadfeld Ltd., a company with a December 31 year end, operates out of a single building that cost $725,000 in 2010. At the beginning of 2016, the UCC for its Class 1 was $623,150. On June 30, 2016, the building was completely destroyed in a fire. The building was insured for its fair market value of $950,000 and this amount was received in September, 2016. The building is replaced in 2017 at a cost of $980,000. Hadfeld Ltd. wishes to minimize income taxes. Describe the 2016 and 2017 tax consequences of these events, including the capital cost and UCC for the new building at the end of 2017. Ignore any gain or loss related to the land on which the building is located.

SOLUTION available in print and online Study Guide.

Capital Gains And Tax Planning

8-166.   The capital gains area offers many opportunities for effective tax planning since the realization of capital gains or losses is largely at the discretion of the taxpayer. If the taxpayer desires that gains or losses fall into a particular taxation year, this can often be accomplished by deferring the disposition of the relevant asset until that period. This means that gains can often be deferred, perhaps until retirement, when the taxpayer may be in a lower tax bracket.

8-167.   Other examples of tax planning would include selling securities with accrued losses in order to offset gains realized earlier in the taxation year, deferring the sale of an asset with a significant capital gain until after the year end and delaying the receipt of a portion of the proceeds of disposition to claim capital gains reserves.

8-168.   Tax planning for capital gains is more complex if an individual owns small business corporation shares or a farm or fishing property. This is due to the fact that such properties may be eligible for the lifetime capital gains deduction. Additional complications result from the application of capital losses, particularly with respect to carry overs of such amounts. These issues are discussed in Chapter 11.

We suggest you work Self Study Problems Eight-14 to Eight-18 at this point.

Additional Supplementary Self Study Problems Are Available Online.

Key Terms Used In This Chapter

8-169.   The following is a list of the key terms used in this Chapter. These terms, and their meanings, are compiled in the Glossary located at the back of the Study Guide.

Adjusted Cost Base	Listed Personal Property
Allowable Capital Loss	Personal Use Property
Capital Asset	Principal Residence
Capital Cost	Proceeds Of Disposition
Capital Gain	Real Property
Capital Gains Reserve	Recapture Of CCA
Capital Loss	Replacement Property Rules
Deemed Disposition	Reserve
Deeming Rules	Rollover
Disposition	Small Business Corporation
Election	Superficial Loss - ITA 54
Emigration	Taxable Canadian Property
Former Business Property	Taxable Capital Gain
Identical Property Rules	Terminal Loss
Involuntary Disposition	Undepreciated Capital Cost (UCC)

References

8-170.   For more detailed study of the material in this Chapter, we would refer you to the following:

ITA 38	Taxable Capital Gain And Allowable Capital Loss
ITA 39	Meaning Of Capital Gain And Capital Loss
ITA 40	General Rules
ITA 41	Taxable Net Gain From Disposition Of Listed Personal Property
ITA 42	Dispositions Subject To Warranties
ITA 43	General Rule For Part Dispositions
ITA 44	Exchanges Of Property
ITA 44.1	Definitions (Eligible Small Business Shares)
ITA 45	Property With More Than One Use
ITA 46	Personal Use Property
ITA 47	Identical Properties

References

ITA 49	Granting Of Options
ITA 53	Adjustments To Cost Base
ITA 54	Definitions (Capital Gains)
ITA 69	Inadequate Considerations
ITA 70	Death Of A Taxpayer
ITA 73	Inter Vivos Transfer To Individuals (e.g., Transfers To A Spouse)
IC 88-2	General Anti-Avoidance Rule — Section 245 Of The Income Tax Act
S1-F3-C2	Principal Residence
S1-F5-C1	Related Persons And Dealing At Arm's Length
IT-95R	Foreign Exchange Gains And Losses
IT-96R6	Options Granted By Corporations To Acquire Shares, Bonds Or Debentures And By Trusts To Acquire Trust Units
IT-102R2	Conversion Of Property, Other Than Real Property, From Or To Inventory
IT-159R3	Capital Debts Established To Be Bad Debts
IT-259R4	Exchanges Of Property
IT-262R2	Losses Of Non-Residents And Part-Year Residents
IT-264R	Part Dispositions
IT-268R4	Inter Vivos Transfer Of Farm Property To A Child
IT-381R3	Trusts — Capital Gains And Losses And The Flow Through Of Taxable Capital Gains To Beneficiaries
IT-387R2	Meaning Of Identical Properties (Consolidated)
IT-403R	Options On Real Estate
IT-418	Capital Cost Allowance — Partial Dispositions Of Property
IT-451R	Deemed Disposition And Acquisition On Ceasing To Be Or Becoming Resident In Canada
IT-456R	Capital Property — Some Adjustments To Cost Base
IT-479R	Transactions In Securities
IT-491	Former Business Property

Problems For Self Study (Online)

To provide practice in problem solving, there are Self Study and Supplementary Self Study problems available on the Companion Website.

Within the text we have provided an indication of when it would be appropriate to work each Self Study problem. The detailed solutions for Self Study problems can be found in the print and online Study Guide.

We provide the Supplementary Self Study problems for those who would like additional practice in problem solving. The detailed solutions for the Supplementary Self Study problems are available online, not in the Study Guide.

The .PDF file "Self Study Problems for Volume 1" on the Companion Website contains the following for Chapter 8:

- 18 Self Study problems,
- 9 Supplementary Self Study problems, and
- detailed solutions for the Supplementary Self Study problems.

Assignment Problems

(The solutions for these problems are only available in
the solutions manual that has been provided to your instructor.)

Assignment Problem Eight - 1
(Identical Properties)

Over the last five years, Mary Blaise has bought and sold the shares of two companies, Sadean Ltd. and Dorcan Inc. Both companies are publicly traded and pay eligible dividends on an irregular basis.

Transactions involving Sadean Ltd. shares over this period are as follows:

January, 2013 Purchase	1,250 @	$24
November, 2015 Purchase	860 @	29
June, 2017 Sale	1,750 @	31

Transactions involving Dorcan Inc. shares over this period are as follows:

March, 2013 Purchase	960 @	$ 7.50
September 2014 Purchase	1,230 @	8.75
February, 2015 Purchase	620 @	9.20
July, 2015 Sale	(980) @	10.15
March, 2016 Purchase	375 @	11.23
April, 2017 Sale	(625) @	8.10

Required:

A. Determine the taxable capital gain resulting from the June, 2017 disposition of the Sadean Ltd. shares.

B. With respect to the transactions involving Dorcan Inc., determine the following:

- The adjusted cost base of the shares that are still on hand on December 31, 2017.
- The taxable capital gain or allowable capital loss resulting from the 2015 disposition.
- The taxable capital gain or allowable capital loss resulting from the 2017 disposition.

Assignment Problem Eight - 2
(Identification Of Capital Gains And Reserves)

CL Ltd. is a long distance moving company. In 2015, CL purchased a 40 acre tract of vacant land in an industrial park near Calgary. The cost of this land was $11.8 million.

It was the intention of Casper Lopez, president and driving force of CL Ltd., to relocate all of CL's operations to this site in about 4 to 5 years. He planned to add furniture storage and self storage facilities. However, Casper was aware that he had purchased this land at a very favourable price. It was his belief that, if the plans changed, CL would be able to make a significant gain by reselling the land. He informed the property manager of the industrial park that he might be interested in selling part of the land if the price was right.

Early in 2017, Casper is informed that he has terminal cancer. Shortly afterwards, CL receives an unsolicited offer of $4.3 million for 10 acres of the Calgary site which Casper accepts. In order to facilitate the sale, CL takes back a $2.8 million first mortgage on the property. The mortgage will be repaid in 4 annual instalments of $700,000 each, beginning in 2018.

CL still intends to move its current operations to this site. However, because of Casper's illness, future plans to use the remainder of the site for new storage facilities are unlikely to move forward. CL is considering whether more of the land should be sold as it does not appear it will be needed. There are three purchasers who are interested in buying 1 to 2 acres each.

Required: CL has sought your advice as the appropriate tax treatment of the sale transaction. Provide the required advice.

Assignment Problem Eight - 3
(Warranties, Bad Debts, and Reserves)

For a number of years, Lester Wayne has owned a large tract of undeveloped land near Windsor, Ontario. He had acquired this land at a cost of $1,585,000, all of which was paid in cash.

Despite the dwindling activity in its automobile plants, the relatively mild climate of the Windsor area has encouraged population growth in the surrounding region. Because of this, a local developer has offered Lester $3,650,000 for his land, expecting to turn the area into 100 building lots for large, single family homes. The terms of the offer are as follows:

- An initial payment of $650,000 will be made on January 1, 2017.
- Annual instalments of $1,000,000 will be made on January 1, 2018, January 1, 2019, and January 1, 2020.
- Interest on the outstanding balance will be paid to Lester on December 31 of each of the years 2017 through 2020. It will be calculated at a rate of 5 percent of the balance outstanding on January 1 of each year.

Also, because of the high level of risk involved in the project, Lester is asked to provide a warranty. Specifically, the builder would like to have a payment of $15,000 for each lot that remains unsold on July 1, 2019. Lester agrees to this arrangement.

The required instalment payments due on January 1, 2018 and 2019, as well as the interest due at the end of the years 2017 and 2018 are paid as per agreed upon schedule. However, the developer is not successful in his promotion of the lots. As a result, on July 1, 2019, 40 of the lots remain in his inventory. Lester makes the required warranty payment of $600,000 [(40)($15,000)].

The developer is unable to sell any additional lots after July 1, 2019. Because of these difficulties, he does not make the required interest payment on December 31, 2019, or the required instalment due on January 1, 2020.

When Lester does not receive these payments and grows suspicious of the developer's excuses, he tries very hard to locate the developer. In July, 2020, he finally accepts that this individual has disappeared, leaving many angry creditors. At this point, Lester writes off the interest that was accrued on December 31, 2019, as well as the remaining instalment that was due on January 1, 2020.

During the years 2017 through 2020, Lester does not have any capital gains or losses, other than those related to the sale of this tract of land. He has pension and investment income totalling more than $80,000 each year.

Required: Calculate the tax effects of the transactions that took place during 2017 through 2020 on Lester Wayne's Net Income For Tax Purposes.

Assignment Problem Eight - 4
(Capital Gains Reserves)

Several years ago, Ms. Natasha Simone acquired an existing building to be used in her unincorporated business. The total cost of the property was $1,200,000, with $250,000 of this amount representing the estimated fair market value of the land on which the building was situated.

Natasha had suffered from serious bouts of depression in the past and realized that the stress from running her business was putting her mental health at risk. As a consequence, she decides she must stop operations and sell the assets of the business.

On January 1, 2017, the building that was used in the business was sold for $1,500,000, with $300,000 of this amount representing the estimated fair market value of the land on which the building was situated. The January 1, 2017 UCC balance in Class 1 was $790,742. The building was the only asset in this Class.

The terms of the sale require the buyer to make a down payment at the time of purchase, with the remaining balance payable on January 1, 2019. No payments are required in 2018. Interest on the outstanding balance is paid on December 31 at an annual rate of 6 percent.

Natasha plans to use reserves to defer the payment of taxes on the capital gain which results from this sale.

Required: Indicate the tax effects of these transactions on Natasha's Net Income For Tax Purposes for the years 2017, 2018, and 2019, assuming:

A. that the down payment was equal to 10 percent of the sales price.
B. that the down payment was equal to 30 percent of the sales price.

Assignment Problem Eight - 5
(Capital Gains Reserves)

Several years ago, Erin acquired two tracts of land located near the city of Richmond, British Columbia. These tracts cost $325,000 and $430,000.

His original intention was to develop the tracts into two subdivisions of 40 lots each. However, because of the ongoing responsibilities associated with his position at the University Of British Columbia, he has not found time to undertake this project. Even though he has made no effort to market the tracts, he receives two very attractive offers from a developer to purchase the tracts. The terms of the two offers are as follows:

Tract 1 The offer for the $325,000 tract was $879,000. The terms require a down payment on January 1, 2017 of $395,550 (45 percent of the sales price), with the balance due on December 31, 2020. Interest, calculated at an annual rate of 6 percent of the beginning of the year balance, is due on December 31 of 2018, 2019, and 2020.

Tract 2 The offer for the $430,000 tract was $1,000,000. The terms require a down payment on January 1, 2017 of $100,000. Further payments of $300,000 each will be required on December 31 of 2018, 2019, and 2020. Interest, calculated at an annual rate of 6 percent of the beginning of the year balance, is due on December 31 of 2018, 2019, and 2020.

Erin decides to accept both of these offers.

Required: Determine the amounts that will be included in Erin's Net Income For Tax Purposes as a result of these transactions. Show the effect for each of the years 2017, 2018, 2019, and 2020 separately. You answer should include taxable capital gains and interest receipts.

Assignment Problem Eight - 6
(Short Cases On Capital Gains)
Each of the following independent Cases describes a situation with a proposed tax treatment.

1. Herbert Nash has owned a 200 acre parcel of land for a number of years. He had acquired this land for $250,000 with the intention of eventually building a home on the property. However, he received an offer of $425,000 for 75 acres of the property. Because this 75 acres has waterfront and better road access, he believes that the fair market value of the remaining 125 acres is only $175,000. He accepts the offer and plans to use an adjusted cost base of $177,083 {[$250,000][$425,000 ÷ ($425,000 + $175,000)]} in calculating his gain or loss.

2. Gregory Hayes sells a capital property with an adjusted cost base of $85,000 for $135,000. The $135,000 price includes a warranty on the property which he anticipates will cost him $5,000 to service. He does not anticipate any of the warranty costs will be incurred in the current taxation year. He plans to recognize a capital gain on the transaction of $45,000.

3. During the current year Ms. Kristy Stone sold her sailboat to an arm's length party for $71,000. She had purchased the boat several years ago for $51,000. Also during the year, she sold securities with an adjusted cost base of $22,000 for $12,000. She intends to deduct the loss on the securities against the gain on the sailboat.

4. Nellie Ward has owned a cottage for a number of years, having acquired it for $125,000. It is currently worth more than $500,000. While she has rarely used it, preferring to stay in her penthouse in the city, she believes that it will continue to increase in value. Given this, she decides to convert it to a rental property. While she plans to report her future rental income to the CRA, she does not plan to recognize a gain or loss on the conversion of the property since no disposition has taken place.

5. During the current year, Ignacio Rogers sells a non-depreciable capital asset for $216,000. The adjusted cost base of the asset was $184,000, resulting in a capital gain of $32,000. Under the terms of the sale, he will receive 10 percent ($21,600) of the proceeds in the current year, with the remainder being due early in the following year. As a result, he will recognize $3,200 of the capital gain in the current year.

Required: In each of the preceding Cases, indicate whether or not you believe that the tax treatment being proposed is the correct one. Explain your conclusion.

Assignment Problem Eight - 7
(Principal Residence Designation)

Ms. Annalisa Philson has been married to Spiro Philson for over 10 years. While Annalisa is 32, her husband is 75 and has been in poor health for a number of years. They live in a home in Ottawa which Spiro purchased as a wedding gift for her in 2006 for $628,000. Annalisa is the sole owner of this property.

On a 2008 business trip to Calgary, Annalisa met Arnold Schwarz, a fitness trainer at the hotel where she stayed. The attraction was immediate and mutual and Annalisa has traveled regularly to Calgary to spend time with Arnold since then. In 2009, Annalisa purchased a condo in downtown Calgary for $325,000 and gave Arnold a key. In every year since its purchase, she has spent considerable time with Arnold in this property.

The year 2017 turned out to be an Annus Horribilis for Annalisa. To begin, her husband obtained well documented proof of her infidelity after hiring a private investigator. As a result, he moved out of the Ottawa home and removed her from his will where she had been the sole beneficiary of his considerable estate.

To make matters worse, on her last visit to Calgary, Arnold informed her that, at 32, she was now too mature for his tastes and he had made other living arrangements.

These events have left Annalisa determined to change her life style. She decided to sell both properties and move into a religious community that requires a vow of celibacy from all of its residents.

As Annalisa has spent time in each property during every year of ownership, either one can be designated as her principal residence for any given year of ownership.

Both properties are sold quickly in 2017, with the Ottawa home going for $724,000 and the Calgary condo selling for $415,000. The real estate fees on each sale are 4 percent of the sales price. After receiving the proceeds, Annalisa decides to go on one last trip to Cancun before starting her new life.

Required: Describe how the residences should be designated in order to accomplish Annalisa's goal. In addition, calculate the total amount of the gain that would arise under the designation that you have recommended.

Assignment Problem Eight - 8
(Personal Use Property)

Due to financial difficulties resulting from unfortunate business decisions, Mr. Bo Godina has been forced to sell a number of items.

- An A. Y. Jackson oil painting which he acquired for $140,000 is sold at auction for $180,000, with the auction house claiming a 20 percent commission on the sale price.

- An antique armoire that he acquired for $850 is sold privately for $1,300. No selling costs were involved.

- A vintage Chris Craft boat which he acquired several years ago for $85,000 is sold for $61,000 with no related selling costs.

- As a life long admirer of George Bernard Shaw, he had acquired a first edition of the play Pygmalion for $22,000. Since his purchase, the works of Shaw have become less popular and the sale of this manuscript nets Mr. Godina only $4,200.

- An extensive stamp collection is sold for $16,000. The cost of all of the stamps totalled $12,500. No selling costs were involved.

- Mr. Godina's father left him a vintage automobile in his will several years ago. Mr. Godina's father had purchased it for $23,000 and spent an additional $17,000 restoring the vehicle. The estimated value of the automobile was $60,000 when Mr. Godina received it and he sells it for $110,000, with no related selling costs.

Required: Mr. Godina has asked you to determine the minimum amount that would be included in his Net Income For Tax Purposes as a result of these dispositions. Indicate any amounts that are available for carry over to other years.

Assignment Problem Eight - 9
(Capital Gains On Foreign Securities)

Richie Desjardins is a resident of Canada. On September 4, 2013, he receives an inheritance of $200,000 U.S. dollars (US$, hereafter) from an uncle who is a U.S. resident. The funds are immediately transferred into his brokerage and used to purchase 4,500 shares of Facehow Industries, a tech company that is traded on the New York Stock Exchange. The shares are acquired at US$43 per share, a total investment of US$193,500. The remaining US$6,500 is left in the brokerage account.

The shares pay an annual dividend of US$2.05 per share. Richie receives the dividends of US$9,225 [4,500)(US$2.05)] on the following dates:

June 1, 2014
June 3, 2015
June 1, 2016

All of these funds are left in his brokerage account and his account does not earn interest.

On July 13, 2016, all of the Facehow shares are sold for US$35 per share, a total of US$157,500. The US$157,500 balance is left in the brokerage account until January 31, 2017, at which time they are converted, along with the unused US$6,500 balance and the accumulated dividends, into Canadian dollars (C$, hereafter). He withdraws all the funds in his brokerage account on June 6, 2017 in order to purchase a house.

Assume relevant exchange rates between the Canadian dollar and the U.S. dollar are as follows:

September 4, 2013	C$1.00 = US$0.98
June 1, 2014	C$1.00 = US$1.03
June 2, 2015	C$1.00 = US$1.09
June 1, 2016	C$1.00 = US$1.26
July 13, 2016	C$1.00 = US$1.28
January 31, 2017	C$1.00 = US$1.35
June 6, 2017	C$1.00 = US$1.40

Required: Calculate the minimum amount that will be included in Mr. Desjardins' Net Income For Tax Purposes for each of the years 2013 through 2017.

Assignment Problem Eight - 10
(Changes In Use - Depreciable Property)

Darin Roberts has operated his consulting business out of rented space since 2011. On January 1, 2015, he acquires a property in a suburban location for $1,350,000. The building has 10,000 feet of floor space, and during the year ending December 31, 2015, he uses 2,000 square feet of this space as his principal residence, with the remaining 8,000 square feet being used for his business.

During 2015, his total dedication to work results in significant growth. Because of this, on January 1, 2016, he converts 1,000 of the square feet that was being used as his residence to business usage. This results in 9,000 square feet being used for his business and only 1,000 square feet being used as his residence. This was no hardship as his wife had left him and he spent almost all his time on his business.

Because his business continues to grow, he opens a second location in rented space and hires a business manager. With the availability of space in this new location, he no longer needs as much space in the building that he owns. On January 1, 2017, reflecting this change in his operations, he expands his residential use of the building to 5,000 square feet, leaving the remaining 5,000 square feet for business usage. Since his new girlfriend/business manager has 8 children he has use for the extra space.

Information on the estimated values associated with the building and the land on which it is situated on January 1, 2015, 2016, and 2017 is as follows:

	Land	Building
January 1, 2015	$350,000	$1,000,000
January 1, 2016	375,000	1,150,000
January 1, 2017	390,000	1,300,000

Required: Determine the maximum CCA that can be deducted by Darin in 2015, 2016, and 2017. In addition, ignoring the principal residence gain deduction, indicate any other tax consequences that will result from the changes in use of this property.

Assignment Problem Eight - 11
(Departure From Canada)

Elly Councill is 57 years old and has been a Canadian resident since birth. Having become fed up with Halifax winters, she decides to move to California. Ms. Councill has come to you for advice prior to leaving Canada for good.

She will depart on January 1, 2017 and, on that date, she owns the following assets located in Canada:

	Adjusted Cost Base	Fair Market Value
Oil Painting	$ 33,000	$ 38,000
Coin Collection	11,000	4,000
Shares In Enbridge (A Canadian Public Company)	42,000	68,000
Shares in Veresan (A Canadian Public Company)	63,000	52,000
Vacant Land	87,000	108,000
Personal Residence	220,000	342,000
Power Boat (Recreational Use Only)	72,000	56,000
Shares In Councill Ltd. (A CCPC)	16,000	48,000

Assume she will make no elections related to her departure from Canada.

Required: Determine the amount of the taxable capital gain or allowable capital loss that Ms. Councill will report in her Canadian income tax return for 2017 as a result of her departure from Canada.

Assignment Problem Eight - 12
(Deferral On Small Business Investments)

Alisia Tait actively invests in small venture capital companies. Because of the high risk involved with these companies, she attempts to maintain a diversified group of holdings by periodically selling individual companies and reinvesting the proceeds in new companies. For the purposes of the deferral provisions for investments in small business corporations, all of Alisia's transactions are qualifying dispositions. Other than the shares identified as Royal Bank shares below, all of the shares acquired are shares of small business corporations.

During the 2017 taxation year, she has the following transactions:

Hottone Ltd.   During March, 2017, the shares of this Company are sold for $6,200,000. The adjusted cost base of these shares was $4,800,000. The proceeds are invested as follows:

Funtrax Inc. Common Shares	$1,200,000
Royal Bank Common Shares (A Public Company)	1,800,000
Plexzoomlax Inc. Common Shares	3,200,000

Zenplex Inc.   During July, 2017, the shares of this Company are sold for $3,400,000. The adjusted cost base of these shares was $2,700,000. All of the proceeds are invested in shares of Zertex Ltd. The acquisition involves paying $800,000 for the Company's preferred shares and $2,600,000 for the Company's common shares.

Damtechno Inc.   During October, 2017, the shares of this Company are sold for $4,600,000. The adjusted cost base of these shares was $4,200,000. All of the proceeds, plus an additional $200,000 in cash were used to acquire common shares of Mediadox Ltd. for $4,800,000.

Required: Determine the tax consequences for Ms. Tait of the three sales of shares and the adjusted cost base of each of her new investments, assuming she does not invest in any other eligible small business corporations during the 2017 taxation year.

Assignment Problem Eight - 13
(Voluntary Dispositions - With ITA 44(6) Election)

For many years, Kargo Inc. has operated out of a building in Vancouver. The major assets of this publicly traded Company are as follows:

Land And Building   The building was constructed for the Company at a total cost of $3,100,000. It is the only asset in the Company's Class 1. The January 1, 2017 UCC balance in this Class is $1,286,690. The building is situated on land that the Company acquired at a cost of $430,000.

Equipment   All of the Company's equipment falls into Class 8. It has a capital cost of $670,000. The January 1, 2017 balance in Class 8 is $285,371.

The Company has become aware that, because of the real estate boom in Vancouver, their property has become very valuable. Further, because of the high cost of housing in the area, it has become almost impossible to attract new employees for their operations. Given this, they have decided to re-locate to an alternative site.

They begin the process by selling their Vancouver assets and temporarily suspending operations. The total proceeds for the land and building are $4,800,000, with $1,500,000 of this total reflecting the value of the land. The remaining $3,300,000 is allocated to the building. The equipment is sold for $523,000.

After more investigation than they had anticipated, they finally conclude that Vernon, British Columbia would be an attractive and cost efficient solution. In March, 2018, they acquire an appropriate property in that city for $4,300,000. Based on estimates, $3,500,000 is allocated to the building and $800,000 is allocated to the land. As it is not a new building, it does not qualify for the enhanced CCA rate for Class 1.

The Class 8 equipment is replaced at a cost of $723,000.

The Company's tax year ends on December 31, 2017, and it does not own any buildings or equipment on this date as the building Kargo ultimately purchased was not available yet. The Company would like to minimize any capital gains or recapture resulting from the sale of the Vancouver property.

Required:

A. For the disposition of each property, indicate the tax effects that would be included in the Company's 2017 tax return.

B. Indicate how these tax effects could be altered in an amended 2017 return by using the elections available under ITA 44(1) (to defer capital gains) and ITA 13(4) (to defer recapture), but without the use of the election under ITA 44(6) (to reallocate the proceeds of disposition). Also indicate the adjusted cost base and, where appropriate, the UCC of the replacement properties, subsequent to the application of the ITA 44(1) and ITA 13(4) elections.

C. Indicate the maximum amount of any reduction in income in the amended 2017 Net Income For Tax Purposes that could result from the use of the ITA 44(6) election and calculate the UCC balance that would result from electing to use this amount. Should the Company make the election? Explain your conclusion.

Assignment Problem Eight - 14
(Involuntary Dispositions - No ITA 44(6) Election)

Kontex Ltd. is a Canadian public company with a taxation year that ends on December 31. The Company operates out of a single building which was acquired several years ago at a cost of $1,782,000. Of this total, $400,000 is allocated to the land, with $1,382,000 going to the building. The building is the only asset in Class 1 and, on January 1, 2016, the balance in this Class is $985,926.

On October 1, 2016, the building is completed destroyed in a fire that was started by a disgruntled former executive. While the Company could rebuild on the site of the destroyed building, it expects significant growth in the next few years and would like to have a larger building in which to carry on its operations.

Given this, the Company sells the site for $550,000 on December 5, 2016 and begins to search for a replacement site. As it does not appear that the Company had any involvement in the starting the fire, on December 1, 2016, the Company receives insurance proceeds equal to the $1,600,000 fair market value of the building.

A replacement building is acquired on July 15, 2017 at a cost of $2,500,000, of which $1,700,000 is allocated to the building and $800,000 to the land. It is a new building that will be used 100 percent for non-residential purposes, none of which is manufacturing. It is the intent of Kontex Ltd. to keep this building in a separate Class 1.

Required:

A. Indicate the tax consequences of the involuntary disposition that will be reported in the Company's tax return for the year ending December 31, 2016.

B.   Indicate the changes that will be reported in the amended return for the year ending December 31, 2016, provided the Company makes elections under ITA 13(4) (to defer recapture) and ITA 44(1) (to defer capital gains). In addition, determine the capital cost and UCC for the replacement assets, subsequent to the application of these elections.

C.   Calculate the maximum CCA that Kontex will be able to claim for the building in the taxation year ending December 31, 2017, assuming the Company makes the elections under ITA 13(4) and ITA 44(1).

Assignment Problem Eight - 15

(Comprehensive Tax Payable Covering Chapters 1 to 8)
Family Information

Owen Winehouse is 51 years old and has been married to Arlene Winehouse for over 25 years. Having made his fortune through a wildly successful initial public offering, he devotes most of his time to mentoring young entrepreneurs and participating in volunteer activities.

Arlene is also very active in various charitable causes. For the 2017 taxation year, she has Net Income For Tax Purposes and Taxable Income of $7,650.

Owen and Arlene have two daughters:

Martha is 14 years old and is in good health. She has income from part time summer jobs of $5,620.

Marlene is 19 years old. She is in good health and attends university on a full time basis for 9 months of the year. Owen pays all of her costs including tuition of $11,400, textbook costs of $1,600, and residence fees of $10,400. Marlene has no income of her own. Given this, she has agreed to transfer her tuition credit to her father.

Owen's father, Philip lives with the family. He is 73 years old and in good health. His 2017 Net Income For Tax Purposes totals $17,300.

Other Information

Information relevant to Owen's 2017 tax return follows.

1.   During 2017, Owen received eligible dividends from Canadian public companies in the amount of $32,400.

2.   For several years Owen has owned 100 percent of the shares of an eligible small business corporation. The adjusted cost base of these shares is $520,000. On January 1, 2017, these shares are sold for $600,000. Assume none of the gain is eligible for the lifetime capital gains deduction. Of the total proceeds, $500,000 is immediately invested in another eligible small business corporation. During 2017, the new small business corporation paid non-eligible dividends of $22,000.

3.   The residence occupied by Owen and Arlene was purchased in 2002 for $320,000. As their space needs have grown considerably, particularly since Philip has moved in, they have decided to replace this property. It is sold during February, 2017 for $375,000. Selling costs, including real estate commissions, total $20,000. Their new residence, purchased at the beginning of 2017, cost $458,000.

4.   Owen purchased a cottage for the family's use in 2007 for $215,000, of which $65,000 reflects the cost of the land on which the cottage is situated. The family has made some use of the cottage in every subsequent year. Anticipating spending more time in their new and larger city residence, Owen decides to convert the cottage to a rental property. At this time, it is estimated that the fair market value of the property is $235,000, of which $75,000 can be allocated to the land. As Owen plans to take CCA on this property, he does not elect under ITA 45(2) to have the property continue as his principal residence.

     In addition, Owen spends $42,000 furnishing the cottage. All of the furnishings are Class 8 assets.

On March 1, 2017, it is rented for $3,000 per month for the remainder of the year. Expenses, other than CCA, total $22,000 for March 1 to December 31, 2017.

5. In 2016, Owen purchased 1,000 units of ReCan Investment Trust at $40 per unit. In July, 2017, these units make a distribution of $2 per unit of which $0.75 is designated as a return of capital. All of this distribution is re-invested in ReCan units at a price of $42 per unit. No other distributions are made during the year. In December, 2017, all of the units are sold at a price of $39 per unit.

6. In 2016, Owen sold a piece of undeveloped land for $125,000. This land had been purchased several years before for $100,000. While Owen's original intent was to construct a backwoods retreat on the site, he had not found the time to improve the land and decided the offer of $125,000 was too attractive to resist. Owen had paid a total of $2,000 in property taxes on the land prior to its sale. The terms of the sale required the buyer to provide a down payment of $37,500, with the remaining balance to be paid in 2018. Owen uses reserves to defer as much of his gain as possible.

7. For several years, Owen has been interested in a French common stock Debit Agricole (DA). The stock trades in Euros (€) and Owen's first purchase of 1,000 shares was made on October 1, 2014 for €14.00 per share. Assume he acquired the Euros at a rate of €1 = $1.57. Subsequent transactions were as follows:

Date	Quantity Purchased (Sold)	Price Per Share ( )	Assumed Exchange Rate (Canadian $)
November 4, 2015	300	€14.50	$1.55
January 6, 2016	(400)	15.00	1.54
June 24, 2017	600	15.50	1.51

On December 2, 2017, he sells all of his shares for €13.00 per share. Assume at this time €1 = $1.50. The Euros are immediately converted into Canadian Dollars.

8. As Owen will no longer have use of his cottage, he decides to sell his vintage power boat. He had purchased this boat several years ago in damaged condition for $10,000. He subsequently spent $24,627 restoring it to mint condition. As a result, he was able to sell it for $50,000 during 2017.

9. During 2017 he sold his stamp collection for $12,000. The total cost of the collected stamps was $8,000. He also sold an oil painting for $700. This painting, which he had always hated, had been a gift from Arlene's mother. At the time of the gift, the painting had a fair market value of $4,000.

10. During 2017, Owen spends 225 hours volunteering in a search and rescue program sponsored by the province in which he lives. He receives no compensation for this work.

11. During 2017, Owen makes contributions to registered charities in the amount of $5,000.

12. During 2017, Owen pays for medical services provided to various family members as follows:

Dental Work (Root Canal) For Arlene	$1,500
Dental Work (Cavities) For Martha	875
Physiotherapy (Back Pain) For Arlene	1,300
Surgery (Tummy Tuck) For Owen	1,800
Total	$5,475

Required: Determine Owen's 2017:

A. Minimum Net Income For Tax Purposes.
B. Minimum Taxable Income.
C. Minimum federal Tax Payable.
Ignore GST/HST considerations.

Assignment Problem Eight - 16
(Comprehensive Case Covering Chapters 1 to 8)
Family Information

Mrs. Joan Brockton is 42 years of age and lives with her husband Jack Brockton. They have two children who live with them. Their son Joshua is 15 years old and has 2017 Net Income For Tax Purposes of $5,600, largely from part-time jobs during the summer. Their daughter Anna is 12 and is sufficiently disabled that she qualifies for the disability tax credit. Anna has no 2017 Net Income For Tax Purposes.

Joan's husband Jack is 41 years old and has gone back to university on a full time basis for all of 2017. His tuition fees for this period are $11,500. Jack has 2017 Net Income For Tax Purposes of $8,400, largely from investments that he made while he was still in the work force.

The family's 2017 medical expenses are as follows:

Joan	$ 1,800
Jack	2,500
Joshua	3,400
Anna (No Attendant Care Costs)	11,500
Total	$19,200

Joan makes 2017 donations to registered Canadian charities of $2,300. She does not qualify for the first-time donor's super credit.

Employment Information

Joan is employed by a large public corporation at an annual salary of $122,000. In addition, during 2017, she earned commissions of $46,000. Her employer withholds the following amounts from her income:

RPP Contributions	$2,700
EI	836
CPP	2,564
Professional Association Dues	1,500

Joan's employer makes a matching contribution to her RPP of $2,700.

Her employer requires her to maintain an office in her home and has provided her with a signed Form T2200. The office occupies 15 percent of the floor space in her home. The 2017 costs of operating this property are as follows:

Maintenance And Utilities	$2,200
Property Taxes	4,800
Insurance	950
Mortgage Interest	9,800

Several years ago, Joan's employer granted her options to buy 2,000 shares of the company's stock at a price of $20 per share. This was the market value of the shares at the time the options were granted. In January, 2017, when the shares are trading at $32 per share, Joan exercises all of the options. In December, 2017, the 2,000 shares are sold for $35 per share.

Joan's employer pays her an allowance of $1,500 per month to cover all of her employment related expenses, including her use of an automobile that she owns personally. This automobile was acquired in 2016 at a cost of $29,500. In her 2016 tax return, she claimed CCA based on the automobile being used 75 percent for employment related activity. During 2017, only 60 percent of the automobile usage was employment related. Joan's employment related expenses during the year are as follows:

Automobile Operating Expenses	$4,200
Hotels	5,500
Airline And Other Transportation	7,600
Business Meals And Entertainment	6,400

Other Information

1. During 2017, Joan received eligible dividends of $2,350.

2. At the beginning of 2017, Joan owned 1,000 units of the Torstar Income Trusts. The adjusted cost base of these units at that time was $12 per unit. During 2017, the trust had a distribution of $1.00 per unit, all of which was business income. Joan had all of this distribution invested in additional units at $14 per unit. In December, 2017, all of her Torstar units were sold for $16 per unit.

3. At the beginning of 2017, Joan owned a tract of land with an adjusted cost base of $125,000. Joan had owned the land for a number of years, hoping at some point to construct a rental property on the site. However, in 2017 she receives an unsolicited offer for the property of $375,000. She accepts the offer and immediately receives a payment of $100,000. The remaining $275,000 will be paid in 11 annual instalments of $25,000, beginning in 2017. Joan would like to use a capital gains reserve to defer as much 2017 taxation as possible.

4. For many years, Joan has owned a cottage on a nearby lake. It had cost $75,000, including an estimated value for the land of $20,000. On January 1, 2017, because of her family's declining use of this property, Joan decides to convert the property to a rental property. At this time, the property is appraised for $250,000, including $50,000 for the land. During 2017, net rental income before the deduction of CCA equals $9,000. Joan does not intend to designate the cottage as her principal residence in any of her years of ownership.

5. Joan owns a painting with an adjusted cost base of $2,000. During 2017, she sells this painting for $22,000.

Required: Calculate Mrs. Brockton's minimum 2017 Net Income For Tax Purposes, her 2017 minimum Taxable Income, and her minimum 2017 federal Tax Payable. Ignore provincial income taxes, any instalments she may have paid during the year, any income tax withholdings that would be made by her employer, and GST/HST/PST considerations.

CHAPTER 9

Other Income, Other Deductions, And Other Issues

Introduction

Coverage Of Chapter 9

Subdivisions d and e

9-1.   At this point, we have provided detailed coverage of all of the major components of Net Income For Tax Purposes. There are, however, certain inclusions and deductions that do not fit into any of the categories that we have described. For example, the receipt of a pension benefit cannot be categorized as employment income, business or property income, or a taxable capital gain. Correspondingly, an RRSP deduction cannot be related to any specific type of earned income and, as a consequence, cannot be specifically allocated to any of the previously described income categories. These miscellaneous inclusions and deductions will be given detailed attention in this Chapter.

9-2.   In terms of the *Income Tax Act*, these miscellaneous sources and deductions are covered in two Subdivisions of Division B. Subdivision d, made up of Sections 56 through 59.1, is titled Other Sources Of Income. Subdivision e, made up of Sections 60 through 66.8, is titled Other Deductions.

9-3.   Some of the items in Subdivision d are directly related to a corresponding item in Subdivision e. For example, Subdivision d requires the inclusion of spousal support paid, while Subdivision e provides for the deduction of these amounts by the individual making the payments. In contrast, many of the items in the two subdivisions are not related in any manner (e.g., the inclusion of death benefits under subdivision d).

9-4.   Given this situation, our coverage of this material will be divided into three sections:

- The first section will deal with those Subdivision d inclusions that are not related to Subdivision e deductions, such as scholarships and workers' compensation.

- A second section will deal with those Subdivision e deductions that do not involve Subdivision d inclusions, such as moving costs and child care expenses.

- A third section will give attention to issues that involve Subdivision d inclusions that are related to Subdivision e deductions such as pension income splitting.

Registered Savings Plans

9-5.   As you are likely aware, Canadian taxpayers have access to a number of registered savings plans (e.g., registered retirement savings plans and registered education savings plans). While most of the inclusions and deductions related to these plans are found in subdivisions d and e, the rules related to these plans are complex and involve other components of the *Income Tax Act*.

9-6.   Because of this complexity, our coverage of these plans will be divided between this Chapter 9 and a subsequent Chapter 10 which will provide general coverage of retirement savings. More specifically, in this Chapter we will cover the following plans:

- Registered Education Savings Plans (RESPs)
- Tax Free Savings Accounts (TFSAs)

9-7.   In Chapter 10, our coverage of registered savings plans will be extended to:

- Registered Pension Plans (RPPs);
- Registered Retirement Savings Plans (RRSPs);
- Registered Retirement Income Funds (RRIFs);
- Deferred Profit Sharing Plans (DPSPs); and
- Profit Sharing Plans (PSPs).

9-8.   We are of the belief that this unusually extensive coverage of retirement savings vehicles is justified by the fact that these plans are perhaps the most important generally available form of tax planning that can be used by individuals. In addition, their complexity means that they are not well understood by most individuals, including some of the individuals providing professional advice in this area.

Other Issues - Non-arm's Length Transfers, Death, Income Attribution

9-9.   This Chapter 9 concludes our coverage of the major components of Net Income For Tax Purposes. The calculation of this value requires the application of a number of special rules, some of which we have covered in previous Chapters. However, there are others which we have not covered to this point. These include:

- Non-arm's length transfers of property;
- Deemed dispositions at the death of a taxpayer; and
- Attribution of income to non-arm's length parties.

9-10.   This Chapter will include coverage of these additional rules.

Other Income - Subdivision d Inclusions

Pension Benefits - ITA 56(1)(a)(i)

9-11.   ITA 56(1)(a)(i) requires that payments received from certain types of pension plans be included in the income of individuals. For many individuals, the major item here would be amounts received under the provisions of Registered Pension Plans. Also included would be pension amounts received under the *Old Age Security Act* (OAS), as well as any similar payments received from a province. In addition, benefits received under the Canada Pension Plan (CPP) or a provincial pension plan would also become part of the individual's Net Income For Tax Purposes.

9-12.   CPP recipients can request that their CPP benefits be split and paid separately to a spouse or common-law partner based on the length of time the individuals have been living together relative to the length of the contributory period. As is discussed later in this Chapter, there is also legislation that allows most other types of pension income to be split between spouses or common-law partners. However, this latter type of pension split is implemented entirely in the tax returns and does not involve the actual payments being split.

Retiring Allowances - ITA 56(1)(a)(ii)

9-13.   ITA 56(1)(a)(ii) requires that retiring allowances be included in an individual's Net Income For Tax Purposes. ITA 248(1) defines these payments as follows:

"**retiring allowance**" means an amount (other than a superannuation or pension benefit, an amount received as a consequence of the death of an employee or a benefit described in subparagraph 6(1)(a)(iv)) received

(a) on or after retirement of a taxpayer from an office or employment in recognition of the taxpayer's long service, or

(b) in respect of a loss of an office or employment of a taxpayer, whether or not received as, on account or in lieu of payment of, damages or pursuant to an order or judgment of a competent tribunal,

by the taxpayer or, after the taxpayer's death, by a dependant or a relation of the taxpayer or by the legal representative of the taxpayer.

9-14.   The term "retiring allowance" covers most payments on termination of employment. This includes rewards given for good service, payments related to early retirement (e.g., federal government buyout provisions) at either the request of the employee or the employer, as well as damages related to wrongful dismissal actions.

9-15.   Within specified limits, amounts received as a retiring allowance for service prior to 1996 can be deducted if they are transferred to either a Registered Pension Plan (RPP) or a Registered Retirement Savings Plan (RRSP) within 60 days of the end of the year in which they are received. However, as this only applies to service prior to 1996, this provision declines in importance with each passing year.

Death Benefits - ITA 56(1)(a)(iii)

9-16.   Death benefits are included in the income of the recipient under ITA 56(1)(a)(iii). ITA 248(1) defines these death benefits as follows:

"**death benefit**" means the total of all amounts received by a taxpayer in a taxation year on or after the death of an employee in recognition of the employee's service in an office or employment …

9-17.   When death benefits are received by a surviving spouse or common-law partner, the definition goes on to indicate that only amounts in excess of an exclusion of $10,000 are considered to be a death benefit for purposes of ITA 56(1)(a)(iii). This $10,000 exclusion would be available, even if the benefit was payable over a period of several years. A CPP death benefit is not eligible for the $10,000 exemption as it is not a death benefit paid in recognition of an employee's service.

9-18.   The $10,000 exclusion is also available on payments to individuals other than a spouse or common-law partner, with the amount being reduced to the extent it has been used by the spouse or common-law partner. For example, if Ms. Reid dies and her employer pays a death benefit of $8,000 to her husband and an additional $8,000 to her adult son, the husband could exclude the entire $8,000 from income and the son could use the remaining $2,000 of the exclusion to reduce his income inclusion to $6,000.

9-19.   Although death benefits are normally paid to the family of the deceased, it would appear that the $10,000 exclusion is available without regard to whom the death benefit is paid. This would suggest that an employer could pay any individual, including a related party, a $10,000 tax free death benefit on the death of any employee. Further, it would seem that an employer could repeatedly make such payments on the death of each of his employees.

Income Inclusions From Deferred Income Plans - ITA 56(1)(h), (h.1), (h.2), (i), and (t)

9-20.   Income inclusions from deferred income plans such as Registered Retirement Savings Plans (RRSPs), Registered Retirement Income Funds (RRIFs), and Deferred Profit Sharing Plans (DPSPs) do not fall into any of the major categories of income. Such amounts do not directly relate to employment efforts, business activity, ownership of property, or the disposition of capital assets. However, they clearly constitute income and, as a consequence, the *Income Tax Act* requires that payments from these various deferred income plans be included in the taxpayer's income.

9-21.   The details of these various types of plans are discussed in Chapter 10 where we provide comprehensive coverage of retirement savings arrangements. While you should not expect to understand these plans at this stage, you should note that the various income inclusions that are related to these plans are included in Net Income For Tax Purposes under the provisions of Subdivision d of Division B. Brief descriptions of the various inclusions in this area are as follows:

RRSP Withdrawals   All amounts that are removed from a Registered Retirement Savings Plan must be included in income under ITA 56(1)(h).

Income Inclusions From Home Buyers' And Lifelong Learning Plans   If repayments to the RRSP are not made as per the required schedule for these plans (see Chapter 10), the specified amounts must be included in income. These amounts would be included in income under ITA 56(1)(h.1) and (h.2), respectively.

Payments From DPSPs   Under ITA 56(1)(i), all amounts removed from a Deferred Profit Sharing Plan must be included in income.

RRIF Withdrawals   The required minimum withdrawal, plus any additional withdrawals from Registered Retirement Income Funds, must be included in income under ITA 56(1)(h) and (t). Note that ITA 56(1)(t) would require the inclusion of the minimum withdrawal amount in income, even if the amount was not actually withdrawn.

Scholarships And Prizes - ITA 56(1)(n)

9-22.   ITA 56(1)(n) requires that all amounts received as scholarships, bursaries, grants, and prizes be included in income, to the extent that these amounts exceed the student's scholarship exemption under ITA 56(3). In most situations, these provisions completely exempt from income scholarships and prizes that are received in connection with:

- an education program in which the taxpayer is a qualifying student; and
- an elementary or secondary school education program.

9-23.   Prior to 2017, ITA 56(3) referred to an "education program in which the taxpayer qualified for the education tax credit". However, with the elimination of the education tax credit, the reference was changed to an "education program in which the taxpayer is a qualifying student". ITA 118.6(1) notes that a qualifying student is enrolled as a full time student in a qualifying education program at a designated educational institution. In simplified terms, this refers to a university or college course of at least 3 weeks duration that requires at least 10 hours of effort per week.

9-24.   In our material we will deal only with scholarships that are 100 percent exempt from income. Note that this has become a surprisingly technical area, resulting in the release of IT Folio S1-F2-C3, *Scholarships, Research Grants, And Other Education Assistance*. This complex 25 page document provides detailed coverage of such issues.

Research Grants - ITA 56(1)(o)

9-25.   Research grants are included in income under ITA 56(1)(o). The amount to be included is net of unreimbursed expenses related to carrying on the research work.

Social Assistance And Workers' Compensation Payments - ITA 56(1)(u) And (v)

9-26.   Payments received under various social assistance programs must be included in income under ITA 56(1)(u), while workers' compensation payments are included under ITA 56(1)(v). It is not, however, the intent of the government to tax these amounts. They are sometimes referred to as exempt income, as they have no net effect on Taxable Income. However, they are included in Net Income For Tax Purposes, a figure that is used in a variety of eligibility tests.

9-27.   For example, to get the maximum Canada caregiver tax credit, the dependant's income must be less than a threshold amount ($16,163 for 2017). Since the policy is to reduce this credit in proportion to the dependant's income in excess of that amount, it is important that all types of income be included in the Net Income For Tax Purposes calculation. To accomplish this goal, social assistance and workers' compensation payments are included in the calculation of Net Income For Tax Purposes and then deducted in the calculation of Taxable Income.

Other Deductions - Subdivision e Deductions

CPP Contributions On Self-Employed Earnings - ITA 60(e)

9-28.   As was noted in Chapter 3, individuals who are self-employed are required to contribute larger amounts to the CPP than individuals who are employees. The maximum employee CPP contribution for 2017 is $2,564. This payment is eligible for a tax credit equal to 15 percent of the amount paid, an amount of $385 for employees making the maximum contribution.

9-29.   When an individual is an employee, the employer makes a matching contribution, resulting in a maximum total contribution of $5,128 [(2)($2,564)]. The additional contribution of 2,564 is fully deductible in the determination of the employer's Net Income For Tax Purposes.

9-30.   Self-employed individuals who earn business income do not have an employer. However, the mechanics of the CPP system are such that an individual must have contributions that are the equivalent to those made by the employee/employer combination in order for that individual to receive the same benefits that would accrue to an employee. This goal is accomplished by having individuals with self-employed income make contributions that are the equivalent of both the employee and employer shares, a maximum of $5,128.

9-31.   In order to put the individual with self-employed income on the same tax footing as an employee, the CPP contributions made on self-employed income are treated as follows:

- One-half of the individual's CPP contributions on self-employed income, to a maximum of $2,564, are used to generate a 15 percent credit against Tax Payable.
- The other one-half, to a maximum of $2,564, is deducted under Subdivision e (not in the calculation of business income) in the determination of Net Income For Tax Purposes.

Moving Expenses - ITA 62

General Rules

9-32.   ITA 62(1) indicates that a taxpayer can deduct moving expenses incurred as part of an "eligible relocation". The usual situations that would be considered eligible relocations can be described as follows:

- Taxpayers who move to a new work location (a new work location may or may not involve a new employer), either as:
  - employees,
  - independent contractors, or
  - after ceasing to be a full time student at a post-secondary institution.

- Taxpayers who move in order to commence full time attendance at a post-secondary institution and receive income from the educational institution that increases their Net Income For Tax Purposes.

- An unemployed taxpayer who moves to a new location in Canada to take up employment at that new location.

9-33.   The definition also requires that the taxpayer's residence, both before and after the move, be in Canada. In addition, it specifies that the distance between the old residence and the new work location or institution be not less than 40 kilometres greater than the distance between the new residence and the new work location or institution. This distance is measured using the routes that would normally be traveled by an individual rather than "as the crow flies" (e.g., you can take the bridge, rather than swimming directly across the river).

9-34.   The fact that there is no time limit on such moves has been supported by several court cases (see *Dierckens v. The Queen*, 2011 TCC 169).

> **EXAMPLE**   In 2013, an individual assumes a new job which is 100 kilometres away from his current residence. For several years he commutes this distance on a daily basis. In 2017, he decides to move closer and acquires a residence that is more than 40 kilometres closer to his work location.

> **ANALYSIS**   This would be an eligible relocation despite the fact that he has been working for the same employer at the same work location for more than 4 years.

9-35.   Moving expenses can only be deducted against employment or business income received in a new work location, or from the educational institution (i.e., scholarships, research grants, etc. that increase Net Income For Tax Purposes). If the moving expenses exceed the income earned at the new location during the year of the move, any undeducted amount can be carried forward and deducted against income at the new location in any subsequent year. IT Folio S1-F3-C4, *Moving Expenses*, contains much information on this subject.

9-36.   For employees, to the extent that the moving expenses are directly reimbursed by an employer, they cannot be claimed by the taxpayer. Note, however, if the employer provides a general allowance rather than an item by item reimbursement, the allowance must be included in income, thereby creating a situation in which the employee will be able to deduct the actual amount of expenses incurred.

9-37.   As described in ITA 62(3), moving expenses include:

- Travel costs incurred to move the taxpayer and members of the household from the old residence to the new residence. These include vehicle costs and a reasonable amount expended for meals and lodging for the taxpayer and the taxpayer's family.

- The cost of transporting or storing household effects.

- The cost of meals and lodging for the taxpayer and the taxpayer's family near either the old or new residence for a period not exceeding 15 days. Note that, in measuring the 15 days, days spent while en route to the new location are not included.

- The cost of canceling a lease on the old residence.

- The selling costs of the old residence.

- The legal and other costs associated with the acquisition of the new residence, provided an old residence was sold in conjunction with the move. Note that this does not include any GST/HST/PST paid on the new residence.

- Up to $5,000 of interest, property taxes, insurance, and heating and utilities costs on the old residence, subsequent to the time when the individual has moved out and during which reasonable efforts are being made to sell the property. Deduction of this amount is conditional on the home remaining vacant.

- Costs of revising legal documents to reflect a new address, replacing driver's licenses and non-commercial vehicle permits, and connecting and disconnecting utilities.

9-38.   Any costs associated with decorating or improving the new residence would not be included in the definition of moving expenses, nor would any loss on the sale of the old residence. Also note that, in general, costs associated with trips to find accommodation at the new location are not included in the definition. The exception to this is meals and lodging near the new residence after it has been acquired or a rental lease has been signed.

Vehicle And Meal Expenses - Detailed Vs. Simplified Methods

9-39.   The CRA offers two alternative methods to calculate the vehicle and meal expenses deductible as moving costs. The detailed method requires receipts and uses actual costs while the simplified method provides a flat rate per meal or kilometer and does not require receipts. The detailed method for vehicle expenses is similar to the calculations required for deductible car costs for employees, a pro rata claim of total vehicle expenses based on the kilometers related to the move.

9-40.   The flat rates published by the CRA for the simplified methods have a one year lag. For 2016 (the 2017 rates are not available until 2018), the flat rate for meals is $17 per meal, to a daily maximum of $51. The flat rate for vehicle expenses depends on the province from which the move begins and ranges from $0.435 per kilometre for Alberta to $0.59 per kilometre for the Yukon. The vehicle claim is calculated by multiplying the total kilometres driven during the year related to the move by the rate of the originating province.

Employer Reimbursements

9-41.   As noted in Chapter 3, an employer can reimburse an employee's moving expenses without creating a taxable benefit. It would appear that, for this purpose, the definition of moving expenses is broader than that which applies when an employee is deducting such expenses directly.

> **EXAMPLE**   An employer reimburses costs for an employee to visit a new work location in order to find housing and evaluate local schools.

> **ANALYSIS**   Despite the fact that the employee would not be able to deduct such costs, a reimbursement by the employer does not appear to create a taxable benefit.

9-42.   Another example of this situation involves employer reimbursement for a loss on the sale of a residence at the old work location. An employee would not be able to deduct this type of loss. However, ITA 6(20) indicates that only one-half of any reimbursement in excess of $15,000 will be included in the employee's income as a taxable benefit.

> **EXAMPLE**   An employer provides a $40,000 reimbursement to an employee for his loss on the sale of his house at the old work location.

> **ANALYSIS**   The employee would be assessed a taxable benefit of $12,500 [(1/2)($40,000 - $15,000)]. Note that, if the loss is not related to an eligible relocation (i.e., 40 kilometers closer to a new work location), the full amount of any loss reimbursement would be considered to be a taxable benefit under ITA 6(19).

9-43.   Employers have also attempted to compensate employees for being required to move to a new work location where housing costs are significantly higher. While there has been a considerable amount of litigation in this area, the issues now seem to be clarified:

> **Lump Sum Payments**   In those situations where an employer provides an employee with a lump sum payment to cover the increased cost of equivalent housing at the new work location, the decision in *The Queen v. Phillips* (94 DTC 6177) has established that such an amount will be treated as a taxable benefit to the employee.

> **Interest Rate Relief And Other Subsidies**   ITA 6(23) makes it clear that an amount paid or assistance provided in respect of an individual's office or employment that is related to the acquisition, financing, or use of a residence, is a taxable employment benefit.

Tax Planning

9-44.   In those cases where the employer does not reimburse 100 percent of an employee's moving expenses, the fact that employers can reimburse certain costs that would not be deductible to the employee can be of some tax planning importance.

9-45.   In such partial reimbursement cases, it is to the advantage of the employee to have the employer's reimbursements specifically directed towards those moving costs that the employee would not be able to deduct from Net Income For Tax Purposes. This procedure costs the employer nothing and, at the same time, it permits the employee to maximize the deduction for moving expenses.

> **EXAMPLE**   An employee has total moving expenses of $22,000. This includes an $8,000 loss on his old residence as a result of the relocation. Other than this loss, the remaining moving costs totaling $14,000 are deductible to the employee.   His employer has agreed to pay 60 percent of all moving costs ($13,200 in this case).
>
> **ANALYSIS**   Of the $13,200 that will be paid by the employer, $8,000 should be accounted for as a reimbursement for the loss on the old residence. The remaining $5,200 would be included in employment income. As the $8,000 reimbursement is less than the $15,000 limit that can be reimbursed, there will be no taxable benefit. Under this approach, the employee will include the $5,200 allowance in income and will deduct $14,000 in moving costs, a net deduction of $8,800. If the employer had simply paid an allowance of $13,200, the employee would include all of this amount in income and would deduct the same $14,000 of expenses. This net deduction of $800 is $8,000 less than if the employee had been reimbursed for the housing loss.

Exercise Nine - 1

Subject: Moving Expenses

On December 20, 2017, at the request of her employer, Ms. Martinova Chevlak moves from Edmonton to Regina. She has always lived in a rented apartment and will continue to do so in Regina. The total cost of the actual move, including the costs of moving her personal possessions, was $6,400. In addition, she spent $1,300 on a visit to Regina in a search for appropriate accommodation, and $1,200 as a penalty for breaking her lease in Edmonton. During the year, her salary totalled $64,000, of which $2,000 can be allocated to the period after December 20, 2017. Her employer is prepared to pay $6,000 towards the cost of her move. Indicate how Ms. Chevlak can maximize her moving expense deduction. Determine how much of this total can be deducted in 2017 and any carry forward available.

SOLUTION available in print and online Study Guide.

We suggest you work Self Study Problem Nine-1 at this point.

Child Care Expenses - ITA 63

Basic Definitions

9-46.   The basic idea here is that a taxpayer is permitted to deduct the costs of caring for children if the costs were incurred in order to allow the taxpayer to produce Taxable Income or receive an education.   However, it is the policy of the government to place limits on the amount that can be deducted and, in the process of setting these limits, the rules related to child care costs have become quite complex. As a reflection of this, one of the first Income Tax Folios released was S1-F3-C1, *Child Care Expense Deduction*. In applying the rules, the following terms are relevant:

Eligible Child   An eligible child is defined in ITA 63(3) to include a child of the taxpayer, his spouse or common-law partner, or a child who is dependent on the taxpayer or his spouse or common-law partner and whose income does not exceed the basic personal credit amount ($11,635 for 2017). In addition, the child must be under 16 years of age at some time during the year or dependent on the taxpayer or his spouse or common-law partner by reason of physical or mental infirmity.

There are different limits for disabled children who are eligible to claim the disability tax credit and those who are not (see following material). To be defined as an eligible child in the aged 16 or over category requires only that they be dependent solely as the result of some form of mental or physical disability. S1-F3-C1 does not provide examples of this level of disability, but states that the degree of the infirmity must be such that it requires the child to be dependent for a considerable period of time.

Annual Child Care Expense Amount   There are three annual limits. For a dependent child of any age who is eligible for the disability tax credit (e.g., a blind child), the amount is $11,000. For a child under 7 years of age at the end of the year, the amount is $8,000. For a child aged 7 to 16, or a dependent child over 16 who has a mental or physical infirmity, but is not eligible for the disability tax credit, the amount is $5,000.

Periodic Child Care Expense Amount   This weekly amount is defined as being equal to 2.5 percent (1/40) of the annual child care expense amount applicable to the particular child. Depending on the child, the value per week will be $275 [(2.5%)($11,000)], $200 [(2.5%)($8,000)], or $125 [(2.5%)($5,000)].

Earned Income   For use in determining deductible child care expenses, earned income is defined as gross employment income (for this purpose, taxable benefits, taxable allowances and stock option benefits are included, but no deductions from employment income are taken into consideration), net business income (for this purpose, business losses are ignored), and amounts of scholarships, training allowances, and research grants that have been included in Net Income For Tax Purposes.

Note that the calculation of earned income for child care expense purposes is different than the earned income calculation used to determine RRSP deduction limits (see Chapter 10).

Supporting Person   A supporting person is usually the child's parent, or the spouse or common-law partner of the child's parent. However, a supporting person is also an individual who can claim the amount for an eligible dependant or the Canada care-giver amount for the child. Note that, to qualify as a supporting person, the individual must have resided with the person making the child care expense claim at some time during the relevant taxation year or within 60 days of the following year. This means, for example, that if the mother lives with the children, but the supporting father does not, no child care expense is allowed.

9-47.   Using the definitions, we can now give attention to the rules applicable to determining the deductible amount of child care expenses.

Limits For Lower Income Spouse Or Single Parent

9-48.   There is an implicit assumption in the child care cost legislation that two parent families with a single bread winner should not be able to deduct child care costs. This assumption is implemented through the requirement that, in general, only the spouse (or "supporting person") with the lower income can deduct child care costs. This means that, in most situations, families that have a house parent who is earning no outside income, is not a student, and is capable of taking care of the children, cannot deduct child care costs.

9-49.   The amount that can be deducted by the spouse with the lower Net Income For Tax Purposes in a two parent family, or by the single parent when there is no other supporting person, is the least of three amounts:

1. The amount actually paid for child care services, plus limited amounts (see Paragraph 9-53) paid for lodging at boarding schools and overnight camps.

2. The sum of the **Annual Child Care Expense Amounts** for the taxpayer's eligible children ($11,000, $8,000, or $5,000 per child).

3. 2/3 of the taxpayer's **Earned Income** for child care costs purposes.

9-50.   Note that there is no requirement that these amounts be spent on specific children. For example, a couple with three healthy children under the age of 7 would have an overall amount under limit 2 of $24,000 [(3)($8,000)]. This $24,000 amount would be the applicable limit even, in the unusual situation where all of the $24,000 was spent on care for one child and nothing was spent for the other children.

9-51.   Actual costs include amounts incurred for care for an eligible child in order that the taxpayer may earn employment income, carry on a business, or attend a secondary school (e.g. a high school) or a designated educational institution. In order to be deductible, amounts paid for child care must be supported by proper receipts issued by the payee, including a Social Insurance Number if the payee is an individual. Any amounts paid in the year that are not deductible due to one of the limits, such as earned income, are lost and cannot be carried forward.

9-52.   Other constraints indicated in S1-F3-C1, *Child Care Expense Deduction*, are that payments are not deductible if they are made to:

- the father or mother of the eligible child;
- a supporting person of the eligible child;
- a person in respect of whom the taxpayer or a supporting person of the eligible child has deducted a tax credit under section 118 for the year; or
- a person who is under 18 years of age and related to the taxpayer.

Attendance At Boarding School Or Camp

9-53.   A further limitation on actual costs involves situations where one or more children are attending a boarding school or an overnight camp. The federal government does not wish to provide tax assistance for the cost of facilities that provide services that go beyond child care (e.g., computer lessons). As a consequence, when the actual costs involve overnight camps or boarding school fees, the deductible costs are limited to the Periodic Child Care Expense Amount ($275, $200 or $125 per week, per child). Amounts paid to the camp or boarding school in excess of these amounts would not be deductible.

9-54.   Note that this weekly limit does not apply to fees paid to day camps or sports camps that do not include overnight stays. However, for fees to day camps and day sports schools to be eligible for a child care deduction, the primary goal of the camp must be to care for the children as opposed to providing sports education.

When Deductible By Higher Income Spouse

9-55.   In the preceding material, we noted the general rule that child care costs are to be deducted by the lower income spouse. There are however, a number of exceptions to this general rule. Specifically, the higher income spouse is allowed to make the deduction if:

- the lower income spouse is a student in attendance at a secondary school or a designated educational institution and enrolled in a program of the institution or school that is not less than 3 consecutive weeks duration and provides that each student in the program spend not less than:
  - 10 hours per week on courses or work in the program (i.e., full time attendance); or
  - 12 hours per month on courses or work in the program (i.e., part time attendance);
- the lower income spouse is infirm and incapable of caring for the children for at least 2 weeks because of confinement to a bed, wheelchair, hospital, or asylum (this condition requires a written certificate from a medical doctor supporting the fact that the individual is incapable of caring for children);

- the lower income spouse is likely to be incapable of caring for children for a long and continuous period because of a mental or physical infirmity (this condition requires a written certificate from a medical doctor supporting the fact that the individual is incapable of caring for children);

- the lower income spouse is a person confined to a prison or similar institution throughout a period of not less than 2 weeks in the year; or

- the spouses are separated for more than 90 days beginning in the year.

9-56.   In situations where the higher income spouse is making the deduction, the amount of the deduction would be subject to the same limitations that are applicable when the deduction is being made by the lower income spouse. However, the higher income spouse has a further limitation. This additional limit is calculated by multiplying the sum of the Periodic Child Care Expense Amounts for all eligible children, by the number of weeks that the lower income spouse is infirm, in 91,831, separated from the higher income spouse, or attending an educational institution on a full-time basis. If the attendance is part-time, the sum of the Periodic Amounts is multiplied by the number of months of part-time attendance, not weeks.

Example

9-57.   The following example will help clarify the general rules for child care costs.

EXAMPLE   Jack and Joanna Morris have three children, Bruce, Bobby, and Betty. At the end of 2017, Bruce is aged 18 and, while he is physically disabled, his disability is not severe enough that he qualifies for the disability tax credit. With respect to their other children, Bobby is aged 6 and Betty is aged 5 at the end of the year. Jack has 2017 earned income of $45,000, while Joanna has 2017 earned income of $63,000.

The couple has full time help to care for their children during 49 weeks of the year. The cost of this help is $210 per week ($10,290 for the year). During July, the children are sent to summer camp for three weeks. The camp fees total $3,500 for this period for all three children.

As the result of a substance abuse conviction, Jack spends seven weeks in November and December in prison.

ANALYSIS   The deductible child care costs would be the least of the following amounts:

	Joanna	Jack
Actual child care costs plus maximum deductible camp fees {$10,290 + [(2)($200)(3 weeks) + (1)($125)(3 weeks)]}	$11,865	$11,865
Annual Child Care Expense Amount [(2)($8,000) + (1)($5,000)]	21,000	21,000
2/3 of earned income	42,000	30,000
Periodic Child Care Expense Amounts [(2)($200)(7 weeks) + (1)($125)(7 weeks)]	3,675	N/A

While Joanna is the higher income spouse, she can deduct child care costs for the seven weeks that Jack is in prison. Her maximum deduction is $3,675. Jack's limit is $11,865. This must be reduced by the $3,675 deducted by Joanna to $8,190 ($11,865 - $3,675). Note that, while Bruce, at age 18, is an eligible child because of his disability, the fact that the disability is not severe enough to qualify Bruce for the disability tax credit means that his annual limit is $5,000 rather than $11,000, and that the periodic limit for Joanna and for the camp fees is $125 rather than $275.

Exercise Nine - 2

Subject: Child Care Expenses

Mr. and Mrs. Sampras have three children. The ages of the children are 4, 9, and 14, and they are all in good mental and physical health. During the current year, Mr. Sampras has net employment income of $14,000, after the deduction of employment expenses of $5,500. Mrs. Sampras has net business income during this period of $54,000, after deducting business expenses of $21,000. The child care costs for the current year, all properly documented for tax purposes, are $10,500. Determine the maximum deduction for child care costs and indicate who should claim them.

SOLUTION available in print and online Study Guide.

We suggest you work Self Study Problems Nine-2 and Nine-3 at this point.

Disability Supports Deduction - ITA 64
Eligibility And Coverage

9-58.   In order to assist disabled individuals who work or go to school, ITA 64 provides a disability supports deduction that is available to disabled individuals who are:

• performing duties of an office or employment,
• carrying on a business, either alone or as a partner actively engaged in the business,
• attending a designated educational institution or a secondary school, or
• carrying on research in respect of which the individual received a grant.

9-59.   The deduction is available for an extensive list of costs that can be associated with a disabled person working or going to school. The costs must be paid for by the disabled individual and eligible costs include:

• sign-language interpretation services, a teletypewriter or similar device;
• a Braille printer;
• an optical scanner, an electronic speech synthesizer;
• note-taking services, voice recognition software, tutoring services; and
• talking textbooks.

9-60.   The availability of this deduction is not limited to individuals who qualify for the disability tax credit. As an example, if an individual has a hearing impairment that requires sign language assistance, the costs of such services are deductible, without regard to whether the individual is eligible for the disability tax credit. In most cases, a medical practitioner must provide a prescription, or certify that there is a need for incurring the specific type of cost.

Limits On The Amount Deducted
9-61.   The amount of qualifying costs that can be deducted under ITA 64 is limited to the lesser of:

• An amount determined by the formula:

$$A - B, \text{ where}$$

A   is equal to the qualifying disability support costs and

B   is equal to any reimbursement (such as payments from medical insurance) of amounts included in **A** that were not included in income.

- The total of:

  1. Gross employment income, net business income, and scholarships and research grants to the extent they are included in Net Income For Tax Purposes.

  2. Where the individual is in attendance at a designated educational institution or secondary school, the least of:

     - $15,000;
     - $375 times the number of weeks of school attendance at a designated educational institution or secondary school; and
     - the amount by which the individual's Net Income For Tax Purposes exceeds the amounts of income included in item 1.

Disability Supports Deduction Vs. Medical Expenses Tax Credit

9-62. Since many of the costs that can be deducted under the disability supports deduction could also be claimed for the medical expenses tax credit, it may be difficult for a disabled person to determine the more advantageous way to claim the expenditures. The legislation does not allow amounts that are deducted under the disability supports deduction to be included in the base for the medical expense tax credit.

9-63. In choosing between the alternative uses of these costs, the following factors should be taken into consideration:

- The base for the medical expense tax credit is reduced by 3 percent of the taxpayer's Net Income For Tax Purposes.

- Tax credits are calculated using the lowest tax bracket. If the taxpayer's income places them in a higher tax bracket, the deduction of costs under the disability supports program will provide a larger reduction in taxes.

- If the taxpayer has only limited amounts of Taxable Income, the ability to use the refundable medical expense tax credit may be more beneficial.

- The deduction is only available to the disabled person on costs that have been paid for personally by the disabled person. If a spouse or supporting person has paid the costs, the spouse or supporting person could claim the medical expense credit with respect to these costs, but could not claim the disability supports deduction.

9-64. It is interesting to note that the treatment given to these costs is very different from the treatment given to home accessibility costs which was discussed in Chapter 4. Costs qualifying for the home accessibility credit can also be eligible for inclusion in the base for the medical expense tax credit. With respect to these latter costs, the taxpayer is allowed to double count, including the qualifying amounts in the base of both the home accessibility credit and the medical expense credit. This is in contrast to the situation here where the taxpayer must choose to either deduct disability support costs, or include the costs in the base for the medical expenses credit. It is difficult to understand the conceptual basis for this distinction.

Complications Related To Attendant Care Costs

9-65. If an individual qualifies for the ITA 118.3 disability tax credit, he can claim attendant care costs as a medical expense. As discussed in Chapter 4, if the medical expense claim is for full time attendant care (defined as more than $10,000 per year), the individual loses the ability to claim the disability tax credit. We would note that, if attendant care costs are over $10,000, it may be beneficial to limit the medical expense credit claim to $10,000 in order to stay within the definition of "part time". This would prevent the taxpayer from losing his claim to the disability tax credit.

9-66. Form T929 indicates that only individuals who qualify for the disability tax credit can claim amounts paid for part time attendant care as a disability supports deduction. However, provided the need for such care is certified by a medical practitioner, full time care can be claimed by individuals who do not qualify for the disability tax credit. This results in a very complex situation with respect to these costs. We have tried to simplify the possibilities in the following general summary:

- If an individual qualifies for the disability tax credit, he can claim attendant care costs as either an addition to the base for the medical expense tax credit, or as a disability supports deduction within the limits of ITA 64. If the disabled individual had sufficient income to move them out of the minimum 15 percent federal tax bracket, the latter choice would provide the larger benefit.

- If an individual qualifies for the disability tax credit and has attendant care costs in excess of $10,000, he is faced with a choice. He can add the full amount of the attendant care costs to the medical expenses tax credit base. However, this claim will result in the loss of the disability tax credit. Alternatively, he can claim these costs as a disability supports deduction, provided a medical practitioner will certify the need for such care. This will usually be preferable as he will continue to qualify for the disability tax credit.

- If an individual is disabled, but does not qualify for the disability tax credit, he can deduct full time attendant care costs under ITA 64, provided a medical practitioner certifies the need for full time attendant care. However, this individual cannot deduct the costs of part time attendant care.

Exercise Nine - 3

Subject: Disability Supports Deduction

Jose Morph has visual, speech, and hearing disabilities. However, they are not severe enough to allow him to qualify for the disability tax credit. During 2017, he worked on a full time basis as a programmer for a large public company and his employment income totaled $78,000.

His need for full time attendant care has been certified by a medical practitioner and, during 2017, such care cost Jose $23,000. Other deductible costs required to support his ability to work as a disabled person totaled $18,000, all of which were certified by a medical practitioner. His medical insurance reimbursed him for $5,000 of these expenses. Jose will not include any of these costs in his base for the medical expenses tax credit. Calculate Jose's disability supports deduction for 2017.

SOLUTION available in print and online Study Guide.

Related Inclusions And Deductions

Introduction

9-67.   At the beginning of this Chapter, we noted that there are several Subdivision e deductions that are directly related to an item that is included in Subdivision d. These items will be dealt with in this Section.

Employment Insurance Benefits - ITA 56(1)(a)(iv) And 60(n)

9-68.   ITA 56(1)(a)(iv) requires that Employment Insurance (EI) benefits received be included in income, even if they are subsequently repaid. Repayment of these benefits can be required if an individual has Net Income in excess of a specified level. If EI benefits must be repaid, the repayment can be deducted under ITA 60(n).

Pension Income Splitting - ITA 56(1)(a.2) And 60(c)

General Rules

9-69.   As noted in the Chapter 1 discussion of tax planning, income splitting is one of the most effective techniques that can be used by taxpayers. Here in this Chapter, we will cover pension income splitting. While this can offer significant tax savings, it is only available to individuals who have certain types of pension income. A possible vehicle for limited income splitting among family members is the Tax Free Savings Account (TFSA). It is discussed later in this chapter. Spousal Registered Retirement Savings Plans, which require some long term planning to be effective for income splitting, will be discussed in Chapter 10.

9-70.   The basic provision for the pension income split is found in ITA 60.03. This Section allows a pensioner, defined as any resident Canadian who receives eligible pension income, to file a joint election with a spouse or common-law partner to reallocate up to 50 percent of his pension income to a pension transferee (i.e., the spouse or common-law partner).

9-71.   When the election is made, the pension transferee includes the elected amount in income under ITA 56(1)(a.2) and the same amount is deducted by the pensioner under ITA 60(c). The election requires the filing of a prescribed form T1032. The pensioner can choose to split any amount, from nothing up to a maximum of 50 percent of eligible pension income. The percentage can vary year to year at the discretion of the pensioner.

9-72.   The types of pension income that are eligible for splitting are the same as those that are eligible for the pension income tax credit. You may recall from Chapter 4 that there are different rules for taxpayers who are under 65 years of age and those 65 and over. In general, most types of pension income other than OAS and CPP can be split for those 65 and over.

9-73.   Note, however, that while lump sum withdrawals from Registered Retirement Income Funds are eligible for splitting, lump sum payments from Registered Pension Plans or lump sum withdrawals from Registered Retirement Savings Plans do not qualify for this provision. Also note that while the age of the transferor determines the types of pension income that can be split, the age of the transferee has no influence on this matter.

9-74.   Another point here relates to withholding. Taxes are withheld at the source from most pension amounts that are paid to an individual. ITA 153(2) indicates that, if a portion of this pension income is allocated to a spouse or common-law partner, a proportionate share of the total withholding is deemed to be on behalf of that spouse or common-law partner. This means that this proportionate share of tax withheld will be transferred to the tax return of the spouse or common-law partner to reduce their Tax Payable or increase the amount of their refund.

Complications

9-75.   In some cases, the desirability of pension income splitting is fairly obvious. For example, an individual in the highest tax bracket can transfer a significant amount of income to a spouse who has no income, resulting in a large amount of income being taxed at the lowest rate. In addition, the transfer can create a pension income tax credit for the transferee.

9-76.   There are, however, offsetting factors. These include the loss of the spousal tax credit, the loss of the transferee's age credit, or a decrease in the medical expenses credit. There is also the possibility that the transfer could create or increase a transferee's OAS clawback.

9-77.   Given these complications, it is not possible to have a general rule related to the use of pension income splitting. In cases where one spouse has no pension income, it will generally be desirable to transfer enough pension income to create a pension income tax credit. However, transfer of additional amounts involves a large number of considerations. Fortunately, tax preparation software can assist in determining an optimum solution.

Exercise Nine - 4

Subject: Pension Income Splitting

Joanna Sparks lives with her husband of many years, John Sparks. They are both 67 years of age. During 2017, Joanna received $7,000 in OAS payments. She also receives $85,000 of pension income from a plan that was sponsored by her former employer. She has not, at this point in time, applied for CPP. John's only source of 2017 income is $7,000 in OAS payments. Neither Joanna nor John has any tax credits other than the basic personal credit, age credit, and pension income credit.

Joanna has asked you to indicate the savings in federal tax that would result from making optimum use of pension income splitting for the 2017 taxation year.

SOLUTION available in print and online Study Guide.

We suggest you work Self Study Problems Nine-4 and Nine-5 at this point.

Spousal And Child Support - ITA 56(1)(b) And 60(b)
Definitions
9-78.   ITA 56.1(4) provides definitions for both support and child support:

Support Amount means an amount payable or receivable as an allowance on a periodic basis for the maintenance of the recipient, children of the recipient or both the recipient and children of the recipient, if the recipient has discretion as to the use of the amount, and

(a) the recipient is the spouse or common-law partner or former spouse or common-law partner of the payer, the recipient and payer are living separate and apart because of the breakdown of their marriage or common-law partnership, and the amount is receivable under an order of a competent tribunal or under a written agreement; or

(b) the payer is a legal parent of a child of the recipient and the amount is receivable under an order made by a competent tribunal in accordance with the laws of a province.

Child Support Amount means any support amount that is not identified in the agreement or order under which it is receivable as being solely for the support of a recipient who is a spouse or common-law partner or former spouse or common-law partner of the payer or who is a parent of a child of whom the payer is a legal parent.

9-79.   When read together, these two definitions provide, in effect, a definition of spousal support. For an amount to be treated as spousal support, it must be specifically designated as being solely for the support of a recipient who is a spouse or common-law partner, a recipient who is a former spouse or common-law partner, or a recipient who is the parent of a child of whom the payer is a legal parent.

General Tax Treatment
9-80.   Under the currently applicable rules, only those payments that are clearly designated as spousal support are deductible by the payer under ITA 60(b). Such payments would then be taxable to the recipient under ITA 56(1)(b). As noted in the section which follows, there are other conditions that must be met to qualify the payments for deduction and inclusion.

9-81.   Child support, which would include all support amounts that are not clearly designated as spousal support, cannot be deducted by the payer. Consistent with this, the amounts paid are not taxed in the hands of the recipient.

Conditions For Deduction And Inclusion

9-82.   As described in S1-F3-C3, *Support Payments*, an amount is considered a support payment if:

- it is payable or receivable as an allowance on a periodic basis;
- it is paid for the maintenance of the recipient, the children of the recipient, or both;
- the recipient has discretion as to the use of the amount; and
- where the recipient of the amount is the spouse or common-law partner or former spouse or common-law partner of the payer, the parties are living separate and apart because of a breakdown of their relationship and the amount is receivable under an order of a competent tribunal or under a written agreement; or
- where the recipient is the parent of a child of whom the payer is a legal parent, the amount is receivable under an order of a competent tribunal in accordance with the laws of a province or territory.

9-83.   If an amount is considered to be a support payment, the amount that is deductible to the payor and taxable to the recipient is defined in ITA 60(b) as the total of such support payments, less any amounts that are considered to be child support. Note that, based on the definition in ITA 56.1(4), any amounts that are not clearly designated as spousal support, are considered to be child support.

9-84.   While payments prior to the date of a court decree cannot technically be made pursuant to that decree, ITA 56.1(3) and ITA 60.1(3) deem that payments made in the year of the decree or the preceding year will be considered paid pursuant to the decree, provided that the order or agreement specifies that they are to be so considered.

9-85.   Problems often arise with respect to the requirement that payments be made on a periodic basis. Clearly, a single lump sum payment does not qualify, nor does a payment that releases the payer from future obligations. Payments that are in excess of amounts required to maintain the spouse and/or children in the manner to which they were accustomed are also likely to be disallowed. Other factors that should be considered are the interval at which the payments are made and whether the payments are for an indefinite period, or a fixed term.

9-86.   Under some circumstances, a person who receives support payments and includes the amount received in income may be required to repay some portion of these amounts. In these circumstances, the person making the repayment is allowed to deduct the amount repaid [ITA 60(c.2)]. As you would expect, the recipient is required to include a corresponding amount in income [ITA 56(1)(c.2)].

Additional Considerations

9-87.   There are a number of additional considerations related to the tax treatment of support payments:

- In situations where a required payment includes both child support and spousal support, a problem arises when less than the required amount is remitted. In such cases, the question becomes whether the payments that were made were for child support or, alternatively for spousal support. The required solution in ITA 56(1)(b) and 60(b) is that only payments in excess of the required child support will be deductible/taxable spousal support. For example, consider an individual required to pay $4,000 in child support and $12,000 in spousal support. If a total of $7,000 is paid during the year, only $3,000 of that amount will be deductible/taxable as spousal support.

- In general, payments to third parties that are clearly for the benefit of the spouse are deductible to the payer and taxable to the spouse.

- Deductible support payments reduce the payer's earned income for RRSP purposes. Correspondingly, taxable support payments increase the recipient's earned income for RRSP purposes (see Chapter 10).

- The recipient of child support payments will continue to be eligible for the credit for an eligible dependant (see Chapter 4).

- ITA 118(5) prevents an individual from taking a tax credit for a spouse or eligible dependant and, at the same time, deducting support payments to that spouse or child.

- While it is not part of the legislation, the Government of Canada has published an extensive, province by province list of guidelines for child support. These guidelines are dependent on the number of children involved and the income of the payer.

Exercise Nine - 5

Subject: Support Payments

On June 15, 2017, Sandra and Jerry Groom sign a separation agreement that calls for Sandra to pay Jerry $1,500 per month in child support (Jerry will have custody of their five children) and $2,500 per month in spousal support beginning July 1. During 2017, Sandra pays support for only three months. How will the total support paid of $12,000 be dealt with in Sandra and Jerry's 2017 tax returns?

SOLUTION available in print and online Study Guide.

Annuity Payments Received - ITA 56(1)(d) And 60(a)

Annuities And Their Uses

9-88.   ITA 248(1) defines an annuity as an amount payable on a periodic basis, without regard to whether it is payable at intervals longer or shorter than a year. As the term is usually applied, it refers to the investment contracts that are usually sold by insurance companies. The two basic forms of these contracts involve either payments for a specified period (e.g., annual payments for a period of 10 years), or payments for the life of the annuitant (e.g., annual payments until the recipient of the payment dies).

9-89.   These contracts can also take various types of hybrid forms. For example, a common arrangement would be a life annuity, with payments guaranteed for a minimum of 10 years. In this case, if the annuitant dies prior to the end of 10 years, payments will continue to be made to the deceased's estate until the end of the specified guarantee period.

9-90.   Annuities are widely used in retirement and estate planning because they provide a guaranteed stream of income that is virtually risk free. Also important is the fact that, in the case of life annuities, the annuitant does not have to be concerned with outliving the income stream. As you would expect, these desirable features are offset by low rates of return.

9-91.   The taxation of annuity payments depends on the manner in which the investment contract was acquired:

Acquisition Within A Tax Deferred Plan   Annuities are often purchased by the administrator of such tax deferred plans as Registered Pension Plans (RPPs), Registered Retirement Savings Plans (RRSPs), Registered Retirement Income Funds (RRIFs), and Deferred Profit Sharing Plans (DPSPs). The goal here is to provide the beneficiary of the plan with a fixed and guaranteed stream of income, usually at the time of their retirement. Because contributions to these plans are deductible and earnings on assets held within the plans accumulate on a tax free basis, all payments out of these plans are subject to tax. This means that, the full amount of payments made from annuities that have been purchased within these plans must be included in the recipient's Net Income For Tax Purposes.

Acquisition Outside Tax Deferred Plan   Individuals also purchase annuities outside of tax deferred plans. The potential problem in this case can be illustrated by a simple example:

EXAMPLE Pierre Brissette uses funds from his savings account, (i.e., after tax funds), to purchases a 5 year ordinary annuity with payments of $2,309 at the end of each year. The cost of the annuity is $10,000, providing him with an effective yield of 5 percent.

ANALYSIS The total payments on this annuity would be $11,545. This total is made up of $1,545 of earnings, plus $10,000 which represents a return of Mr. Brissette's capital. It would not be equitable to require Mr. Brissette to include the full amount of the annuity payments in his Net Income For Tax Purposes. Clearly, some type of provision is required to recognize the return of capital components of the annuity payments that he has received.

Capital Element Of An Annuity

9-92. You will recall from Paragraph 9-20 of this Chapter, that payments from registered plans are included under specific provisions of subdivision d [e.g., payments from RRSPs are included under ITA 56(1)(h)].

9-93. In order to distinguish these fully taxable annuity payments from payments made by annuities acquired outside of tax deferred plans, ITA 56(1)(d) requires the inclusion in income of annuity payments that are not "otherwise included in income". As payments from RPPs, RRSPs, RRIFs, and DPSPs, are "otherwise included" under other provisions of the *Income Tax Act*, this means that only annuities purchased with after tax funds would be included here.

9-94. For those annuity payments that are included under ITA 56(1)(d), ITA 60(a) allows a deduction that is designed to reflect the return of capital element that is included in these payments. The capital element that is to be deducted is calculated by multiplying the annuity payment that was included in income for the year by a ratio. As presented in ITR 300, the formula for calculating the capital element of a fixed term annuity payment is as follows:

$$\text{Deduction} = \left[\frac{\text{Capital Outlay To Buy The Annuity}}{\text{Total Payments To Be Received Under The Contract}} \right] [\text{Annuity Payment}]$$

9-95. To illustrate this procedure, refer to the example in Paragraph 9-91. Since this annuity had been purchased with $10,000 in after tax funds, the entire annual payment of $2,309 would be included in income under ITA 56(1)(d). However, this would be offset by a deduction under ITA 60(a) that is calculated as follows:

$$\left[\frac{\$10,000}{\$11,545} \right] [\$2,309] = \$2,000 \text{ Deduction}$$

9-96. Note that this treatment would apply to situations where an individual has made a lump-sum withdrawal from a tax deferred plan and used the funds to acquire an annuity. For example, if an individual withdrew $100,000 from his RRSP, this amount would be subject to tax at the time of withdrawal. This means that payments from this annuity would be included in his income under ITA 56(1)(d) rather than 56(1)(h) and, as a consequence, would be eligible for the ITA 60(a) deduction.

Exercise Nine - 6

Subject: Annuity Payments

On January 1 of the current year, Barry Hollock uses $55,000 of his savings to acquire a fixed term annuity. The term of the annuity is 4 years, the annual payments are $15,873, the payments are received on December 31 of each year, and the rate inherent in the annuity is 6 percent. What is the effect of the $15,873 annual payment on Mr. Hollock's Net Income For Tax Purposes?

SOLUTION available in print and online Study Guide.

Registered Savings Plans

Introduction

9-97.   Registered savings plans allow individuals to make contributions to a trust that is registered with the CRA. The trustees of the plan are required to provide information returns with respect to contributions to, and withdrawals from, these plans.

9-98.   As indicated in Paragraph 9-6, in this Chapter we will provide detailed coverage of two of these plans, Registered Education Savings Plans (RESPs), and Tax Free Savings Accounts (TFSAs). We will also provide a brief description in this Chapter of Registered Disability Savings Plans (RDSPs). Other registered plans will be covered in Chapter 10.

9-99.   Contributions to the plans that are being considered in this Chapter are not deductible in determining the taxpayer's Net Income For Tax Purposes. However, they do have significant tax advantages.

> **Tax Deferral**   Once contributions have been made, they will be invested in various types of income producing assets. There will be no taxation of this income, including compounding amounts, as long as the assets remain in the plan. This provides for significant tax deferral.

> **Tax Reduction (RESPs And RDSPs)**   Contributions to these plans will typically be made by a parent or grandparent who has income that will be taxed at various rates, in most cases at rates higher than the minimum rate. While earnings distributions from RESPs and RDSPs are subject to tax, they will be paid to either a student or a disabled individual.

> In many cases, such individuals will not have sufficient income to use their available tax credits, resulting in a situation where some amounts can be distributed without attracting additional taxation. Even if this is not the case, such individuals are likely to be in a lower tax bracket than the individual who made the contributions, resulting in a tax reduction that may be significant.

9-100.   The basic operation of TFSAs, RESPs, and RDSPs is depicted in Figure 9-1. As shown in that Figure, the contributions to these plans are non-deductible to the taxpayer. This is in contrast to both RPPs and RRSPs where the contributions can be deducted at the time they are made (see Chapter 10).

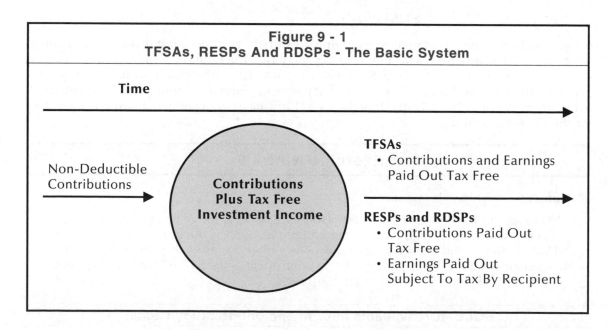

Figure 9 - 1
TFSAs, RESPs And RDSPs - The Basic System

Time

Non-Deductible Contributions

Contributions Plus Tax Free Investment Income

TFSAs
• Contributions and Earnings Paid Out Tax Free

RESPs and RDSPs
• Contributions Paid Out Tax Free
• Earnings Paid Out Subject To Tax By Recipient

Tax Free Savings Accounts (TFSAs)
General Procedures
9-101.   The general procedures for Tax Free Savings Accounts (TFSAs) are as follows:

Eligibility   Any resident individual over 17 years of age can establish a TFSA.

Contribution Room   When TFSAs were introduced in 2009, the maximum annual contribution to the plan was $5,000. This was increased to $5,500 in 2013, with a further increase to $10,000 for 2015. This was for one year only as the 2016 Budget returned the maximum annual contribution to the 2014 limit of $5,500 for 2016. The contribution room accumulates each year the individual is over 17, without regard to whether the individual has established a TFSA or filed a tax return. As of 2017, total TFSA contribution room has accumulated to $52,000 (4@$5,000 + 2@$5,500 + 1@ $10,000 + 2@$5,500) for an individual who was over 17 years of age in 2013.

Unused amounts of this contribution room can be carried forward indefinitely and any withdrawals (consisting of contributions and earnings) are added back to the total contribution room. It is important to note that this addition to contribution room does not occur until the year following the withdrawal. Ignoring this timing lag can result in an excess contribution which will be subject to a penalty. To assist taxpayers, unused TFSA contribution room information can be accessed by using the CRA "My Account" online service. (See Chapter 2.)

Unlike RRSPs, the contributions are not deductible. Contributions in excess of available contribution room will be subject to a tax of 1 percent per month. Interest on money borrowed to make contributions is not deductible. This rule reflects the general principle that interest can only be deducted when the purpose of the borrowing is to produce income from business or property.

Qualified Investments   The *Act* is flexible with respect to the types of investments that can be included in a TFSA. ITR Part XLIX provides a detailed listing of the specific investment categories and includes publicly traded shares, mutual fund units, bonds, mortgages, warrants, and rights. The only significant restrictions relate to investments in the shares of private companies and direct investments in real estate. There is no limit on foreign content. For a more complete discussion of this subject see IT Folio S3-F10-C1, *Qualified Investments - RRSPs, RESPs, RRIFs, RDSPs, and TFSAs*, and IT Folio S3-F10-C2, *Prohibited Investments - RRSPs, RRIFs, and TFSAs*.

Investment Income   As is the case with other registered savings plans, amounts earned on assets held in the plan are not subject to tax while they remain within the plan. However, unlike other registered savings plans, there is no tax on these earnings when they are withdrawn. As their name implies, TFSAs allow investors to receive investment income on a tax free basis. Any losses on the sale of investments in the TFSA have no tax benefit, they simply reduce the TFSA funds available.

Income Attribution Rules   As will be discussed in the final section of this Chapter, when an individual gives assets to a spouse, income on those assets is usually attributed back to that individual. Another attractive feature of TFSAs is that amounts earned in these accounts are not subject to the income attribution rules.

Death Of A Taxpayer   If an individual's spouse or common-law partner is designated as a successor holder, the individual's TFSA can be transferred into the hands of this beneficiary as an ongoing TFSA. It can either be maintained by the individual as a separate TFSA or, alternatively, rolled over into their TFSA without being treated as a contribution. Income on the assets contained in the bequeathed TFSA will continue to accumulate on a tax free basis.

If the decedent's TFSA is transferred to any other beneficiary, that individual can withdraw the funds in the plan at the time of the transferor's death without tax consequences. However, any amounts received in excess of the fair market value of the assets in the plan at the time of the transferor's death will be subject to tax.

Registered Education Savings Plans (RESPs)
Contributions
9-102.   The contribution rules for Registered Education Savings Plans (RESPs) are found in ITA 146.1. As previously noted, like contributions to a TFSA, contributions to an RESP do not provide a deduction for the taxpayer, but earnings in the plan accrue on a tax free basis.

9-103.   As is discussed more completely in Chapter 10, over extended periods of time, there is a very large benefit associated with this tax free accumulation of earnings. Note, however, that in the case of RESPs, this tax free accumulation is limited to 35 years after the plan is established (40 years for plans with a single beneficiary who is eligible for the disability tax credit). At the end of that period, the plan is automatically deregistered.

9-104.   An individual, usually a parent or grandparent becomes a subscriber or a joint subscriber of an RESP by signing a contract with an RESP promoter. Total contributions are limited to $50,000 for each beneficiary with no annual limit on contributions. Although there is complete flexibility with respect to the timing, some consideration should be given to the CESG limits (see Paragraph 9-106).

9-105.   There is a penalty for excess contributions. If, at the end of any month, the contributions for a particular beneficiary exceed the total limit of $50,000, the subscribers to the plan are subject to a 1 percent per month tax on the excess. Note that these limits apply for each beneficiary. If several individuals are contributing to different plans with the same beneficiary (e.g., Joan's father and her grandmother are both contributing to a plan on her behalf), the sum of their contributions to Joan's plans cannot exceed the $50,000 limit. Any tax assessed on excess contributions must be shared on a pro rata basis by the subscriber(s).

Canada Education Savings Grants (CESGs)
9-106.   Under the Canada Education Savings Grant (CESG) program, the federal government will make additional contributions to an RESP to supplement those being made by the subscriber(s).   The CESG has both a basic and "additional" component.

9-107.   The amount of grant eligible contributions is a balance that accumulates at the rate of $2,500 per year, beginning in the year a child is born. The basic CESG is equal to 20 percent of the current year contributions for a beneficiary up to a maximum of $500 [(20%)($2,500)] per beneficiary. If there is unused contribution room from previous years, up to $1,000 in CESG is available in the current year. The lifetime CESG maximum is $7,200.

9-108.   In order to assist low income families, an additional CESG of 10 or 20 percent of the first $500 of contributions in a year for a beneficiary is available. The amount of the additional CESG depends on the net family income for the year. On the first $500 in contributions for 2017, the basic and additional CESG is calculated as follows:

- at 40% (20% + 20%) if 2017 family income is $45,916 or less (maximum of $200),
- at 30% (20% + 10%) if 2017 family income is between $45,916 and $91,831 (maximum of $150), and
- at 20% (20% + 0%) if 2017 family income is greater than $91,831 (maximum of $100).

9-109.   As noted, regardless of family income, for each beneficiary, contributions between $500 and $2,500 in a year earn a grant equal to 20 percent of the contributions.

> **EXAMPLE** Tom is born in February, 2016. Tom's father makes an RESP contribution of $1,300 for Tom in 2016 and $1,300 in 2017. In November of 2017, Tom's grandmother makes a $3,000 contribution to another RESP for Tom.

> **ANALYSIS** Tom's 2017 contribution room for balances eligible for CESGs is $3,700 [(2)($2,500) - $1,300]. As the combined contributions of the father and grandmother total $4,300, $600 of the total contributions will not be eligible for CESGs. Depending on the net family income of Tom's father, the CESG for 2017 ranges from $740 [(20%)($3,700)] to $840 [(40%)($500) + (20%)($3,700 - $500)].

It is important to note that the $600 excess contribution does not carry forward and become eligible for CESGs in the following year when more contribution room accrues to Tom. If it is expected that annual contributions to Tom's RESP will be less than $2,500 in the future, this would suggest that Tom's father should limit his 2017 contribution to $700 and defer the extra $600 to the following year. In that year, it would eligible for a grant. Also note that if there is a large carry forward of grant eligible contribution room, the CESG will be limited to a maximum of $1,000 for a year, ($500 current plus $500 carry forward) regardless of the size of the contribution.

For those subscribers who have substantial funds to invest, there is the option of contributing a large initial sum to take advantage of tax free compounding. Whether this would be more advantageous than contributing less, more often, in order to take full advantage of the CESG requires the consideration of a number of factors. That analysis would go beyond the scope of this text.

9-110.   CESGs will not be paid for RESP beneficiaries for the year in which they turn 18 years of age, or in any subsequent year. In addition, CESG payments are intended to encourage long-term planning for a child's education. Because of this, in a year in which the beneficiary is between the age of 15 and the age of 17, CESG payments will be made only when:

- a minimum of $2,000 of RESP contributions was made in respect of the beneficiary by December 31 of the calendar year in which the beneficiary attains 15 years of age; or

- a minimum of $100 in annual RESP contributions was made in respect of the beneficiary in any four years before the calendar year in which the beneficiary attains 15 years of age.

Exercise Nine - 7

Subject: Canada Education Savings Grants

Jeanine was born in 2016. During 2016, her father establishes a RESP for her and contributes $500 to the plan, while Jeanine's grandfather contributes an additional $1,200. During 2017, her father contributes $1,500 and her grandfather adds a further $2,400. Jeanine's family has never had family income of more than $40,000. Determine the amount of the CESGs that would be added to Jeanine's RESP in 2016 and 2017.

SOLUTION available in print and online Study Guide.

Canada Learning Bonds (CLBs)

9-111.   A further enhancement to the RESP system, Canada Learning Bonds (CLBs), are like the CESGs in that the government makes contributions to a child's RESP. However, unlike the CESGs, the CLB contributions are not based on contributions made to the RESP by others.

9-112.   The CLB provisions apply to children born after 2003 and who have an RESP established in their names. Such children are eligible for a CLB contribution to their RESP in each year that their family is eligible for the child National Child Benefit Supplement (this supplement is an income test benefit that is added to the Canada Child Tax Benefit). Potential eligibility begins in the year the child is born and ends in the year that the child turns 15 years of age.

9-113.   The CLB contributions to individual RESPs are as follows:

- In the first year that the child is eligible for a CLB contribution, an amount of $500 will be provided. In addition, a one-time additional amount of $25 will be added in order to help defray the costs of establishing the RESP.

- In each subsequent year of eligibility, a CLB contribution of $100 will be made. This continues until the year in which the child turns 15 years of age.

9-114.   The child's eligibility will vary with the income of his or her family. In some families, the National Child Benefit supplement will be available every year and, correspondingly, the CLB contributions will be made each year. In situations such as this, the maximum total contribution would be $2,025 {$500 + $25 + [(15)($100)]}. In other cases, eligibility may be present in some years and not present in other years. In such cases, the contributions will total less than $2,025.

9-115.   For families who qualify for the CLB contributions, the establishment of an RESP for each child is clearly a desirable course of action. A potential problem with the CLB program is that families in the income brackets that qualify for this benefit may not be aware of the program or have access to the kind of assistance required to establish an RESP.

Types Of Plans
9-116.   RESP legislation provides for "family plans" in which each of the beneficiaries is related to the subscriber by blood or adoption. Family plans, which are typically established for several siblings under age 18, are subject to the same contribution limits per beneficiary, but provide additional flexibility for the subscriber because the educational assistance payments that will be made are not be limited to each child's "share" of the contributions.

9-117.   This feature is important when an individual has several children and not all of them pursue higher education. Because of the flexibility inherent in family plans, all of the plan distributions could be directed towards the children who are eligible to receive such funds. To ensure that family plans do not provide unintended benefits, no beneficiaries 21 years of age or older can be added to a family plan.

9-118.   In terms of alternatives for investing the funds that have been contributed, there are basically two types of RESPs available. They can be described as follows:

Scholarship Plans are available through "scholarship trust companies" such as the Canadian Scholarship Trust Plan. These plans are distinguished by the fact that all of their funds must be invested in government guaranteed investments. These companies offer group plans (earnings are allocated only to those children who attend college or university), as well as individual plans (subscribers can recover their share of the investment earnings).

Self-Directed Plans allow investors to choose their own investments. The list of qualified investments is similar to that applicable to self-directed RRSPs. For example, publicly traded stocks are eligible, but income producing real estate is not. As is the case with RRSPs, there is no foreign content limit for self-directed RESPs.

Refund Of Contributions
9-119.   Contributions can be paid on a tax free basis to either the subscriber to the plan or to the beneficiary. The only limitations on such payments are those that might be included in the terms and conditions of the plan itself.

Education Assistance Payments
9-120.   Education assistance payments are amounts paid to student beneficiaries from accumulated earnings, CESG amounts, and CLB amounts. These amounts must be included in the income of the recipient.

9-121.   To be eligible for the receipt of such amounts, the individual must be enrolled in a program at the post-secondary level that lasts at least three consecutive weeks. If the student spends not less than 10 hours per week on courses or work it is considered a **qualifying** educational program. If the student spends not less than 12 hours per month on courses or work it is considered a **specified** educational program. In the case of a specified educational program, the student must be at least 16 years old.

9-122. The limits on the amounts to be paid can be described as follows:

- For studies in a qualifying educational program, the limit is $5,000 for the first 13 consecutive weeks. Subsequent to that period, there is no limit on payments, provided the student continues to qualify.

- For studies in a specified educational program, the limit is $2,500 for the first 13 week period, whether or not the student is enrolled in the program throughout this period.

9-123. Note that CESG and CLB amounts can only be paid out as educational assistance payments to beneficiaries. If the beneficiary does not pursue post-secondary education, these benefits must be returned to the government.

Accumulated Income Payments To Subscribers

9-124. Payments made to subscribers out of the accumulated income of the plan are referred to as accumulated income payments. To be eligible to receive such payments, the subscriber must be a resident of Canada. In addition, one of the following conditions must apply:

- The payment is made after the year that includes the 9th anniversary of the plan and, each beneficiary has reached the age of 21 years and is not currently eligible for educational assistance payments.

- The payments are made after the plan has been de-registered (35 or 40 years, depending on the type of plan).

- All of the beneficiaries are deceased.

9-125. The accumulated income payments will be included in the subscriber's Net Income For Tax Purposes and Taxable Income. In calculating the individual's Tax Payable, an additional tax of 20 percent of the accumulated income payments must be added to the total. This additional tax is designed to offset the fact that the individual has enjoyed tax free earnings compounding inside the RESP.

9-126. There is a provision which allows a taxpayer to reduce the amount of accumulated income payments that will be subject to the 20 percent additional tax. Provided the individual has sufficient RRSP contribution room (see Chapter 10 for coverage of this concept), accumulated income payments can be transferred to an RRSP. Such transfers will provide the individual with a deduction for the amounts of accumulated income payments and provide relief from the additional 20 percent tax. The limit on such transfers is $50,000 worth of accumulated income payments.

Repayment Of CESG And CLB Contributions

9-127. As noted in Paragraph 9-123, amounts in the plan that reflect CESG or CLB contributions can only be distributed to a plan beneficiary as an educational assistance payment. They cannot be paid to subscribers.

9-128. In those situations where it is clear that no beneficiary will qualify for educational assistance payments, the plan will likely contain various types of balances. To the extent that these balances include CESG or CLB contributions, these amounts will have to be returned to the government. This means that a withdrawal is likely to include amounts that can be retained by the subscriber as well as amounts that must be repaid to the government.

9-129. Given this situation, a fairly complex set of rules is required to deal with withdrawals from the plan. Such withdrawals must be segregated into: the return of subscriber contributions, the withdrawals of accumulated earnings amounts, and the CESG and CLB contributions that must be repaid to the government. Coverage of these rules goes beyond the scope of this text.

We suggest you work Self Study Problem Nine-6 at this point.

Comparison Of TFSAs And RRSPs

9-130.   For individuals with sufficient resources to maximize contributions to all available types of registered savings plans, making contributions to a TFSA is a no-brainer. However, it appears that, in the real world, such individuals are rare. This means that, for most individuals, a choice must be made among the available alternatives.

9-131.   While the range of available plans can be fairly large for some individuals, the most common choice will be between making contributions to a TFSA and making contributions to a Registered Retirement Savings Plan (RRSP). In comparing these two alternatives, the most significant differences can be described as follows:

- Contributions to an RRSP are tax deductible. Since contributions to a TFSA are not deductible, that means they are funded with after-tax dollars.
- Withdrawals from an RRSP are taxed as income. Withdrawals from a TFSA are not reported as income so they are not subject to tax and do not affect the OAS/EI clawback or government benefits such as the GST credit.

9-132.   Although detailed coverage of RRSPs is found in Chapter 10 and a complete analysis of the impact of these differences goes beyond the scope of this text, a simple example will serve to illustrate their application.

EXAMPLE   In 2017, Sophia Scarponi has $5,000 in pre tax income that she does not need for current consumption. She has asked your advice on whether she should contribute to a TFSA or, alternatively to an RRSP. She indicates that her marginal tax rate is 45 percent, a rate that she expects to be the same for the next 10 years. She anticipates that funds invested in either type of plan will enjoy a compounded annual return of 10 percent. She does not anticipate needing the funds for at least 10 years.

ANALYSIS - TFSA   As the $5,000 is a pre tax amount, she will have after tax funds of $2,750 [($5,000)(1 - .45)] to invest in the TFSA. If this amount is left in the TFSA and earnings are compounded for 10 years at 10 percent, she will have a balance of $7,133. None of this amount will be subject to tax when it is withdrawn.

ANALYSIS - RRSP   As contributions to an RRSP are tax deductible, there will be no need to pay taxes on the $5,000 in pre tax income. This means that the full amount can be contributed. If the $5,000 is left in the RRSP and earnings are compounded for 10 years at 10 percent, the balance will be $12,969. If she withdraws this amount, she will have after tax funds of $7,133 [($12,969)(1 - .45)].

9-133.   In this very simple example, the results under the two approaches are identical. Whether contributions are made to a TFSA or, alternatively, to an RRSP, Ms. Scarponi will wind up with after tax funds of $7,133. However, this result could be altered by a number of considerations. The most obvious factor would be her current tax rate vs. the tax rate after 10 years. If her current tax rate was higher than the rate after 10 years, her year 10 balance using a TFSA would be less than the after tax funds from an RRSP. If her current tax rate was lower, this would favour the use of a TFSA, especially if the OAS clawback was a factor.

Comparison Of TFSAs, RRSPs And RESPs

9-134.   As was noted in our preceding comparison of RRSPs and TFSAs, most families are not able to make maximum contributions to both RRSPs and TFSAs. The situation would be further complicated by the presence of a child or children eligible for the benefits of the RESP program. For an individual with $50,000 in earned income and a child whose RESP contribution would be eligible for a CESG grant, the total funds needed to make these contributions for 2017 would be $17,000 [(18%)($50,000) + $5,500 + $2,500]. It is very unlikely that an individual earning $50,000 per year could divert such a sum from the amounts needed to maintain a family in a comfortable life style.

9-135.   In terms of tax policy, it is worth noting that when one considers these choices as a group, it is clear that their cumulative effect benefits wealthy Canadians. To make maximum use of all these plans, the taxpayer would have to have either a very high level of income and/or a significant accumulation of unneeded resources. It is clear that the average Canadian working individual would rarely, if ever, be able to receive the maximum benefits available from these programs. This fact was recognized when the TFSA limit was dropped from $10,000 in 2015, to $5,500 for 2016 and subsequent years.

9-136. Facing this reality means that most taxpayers will have to make a choice as to which of these registered plans will receive the funds that they have available. We have previously covered some of the factors to be considered in making a choice between TFSAs and RRSPs. With respect to the choice between RRSPs and RESPs, the following points are relevant:

- A major advantage of RESPs relative to RRSPs is the fact that RESP contributions can be eligible for a Canada Education Savings Grant.

- A further advantage of RESPs relative to RRSPs is the fact that the establishment of such plans allows contributions to be made under the Canada Learning Bonds program. Note that this program could justify establishing an RESP for children in low income families, even if no contributions were made to the plan.

- A major advantage of RRSPs relative to RESPs is the fact that RRSP contributions are deductible in the calculation of Net Income For Tax Purposes. Given a particular before tax amount available, this allows for larger contributions to be made to RRSPs.

- Offsetting the deductibility of RRSP contributions, all payments out of RRSPs to plan beneficiaries are normally taxed. While some individuals may be in a lower tax bracket in the period of payment, many individuals will be taxed at the same rates as were applicable when their contributions were deductible. In contrast, RESP distributions are tax free to the extent they represent original contributions to the plan. Further, while RESP earnings are included in the student's income, a university or college student could have sufficient tax credits that no tax is paid on the earnings. As a result, a student can receive a significant amount of income tax free. Even when taxes must be paid, all amounts are likely to be taxed in the minimum tax bracket.

- Both RRSPs and RESPs offer the advantage of having earnings compound on a tax free basis. As is illustrated in detail in Chapter 10, this is a very powerful mechanism for tax deferral. In this area, an advantage for RRSPs is that the tax free compounding period is potentially longer.

- Canada Child Benefit payments are income tested. Because the contributions are deductible, using an RRSP can reduce family income and, in some situations, increase the amount of the Canada Child Benefit payments.

9-137.   In comparing the features of TFSAs vs. RESPs we would add the following points:

- The major advantage of RESPs as compared to TFSAs is the availability of CESG and CLB contributions made by the government.

- The major disadvantage of RESPs as compared to TFSAs is the fact that when earnings are withdrawn they can be subject to tax. Taxation may be avoided if the earnings are distributed to a qualifying student with sufficient credits to eliminate the taxes. However, there is the possibility the beneficiary of the plan may not pursue post-secondary education. In this case, the earnings will be taxed in the hands of the subscribers and subject to the 20 percent penalty.

9-138.   As the preceding makes clear, many taxpayers will be forced to make a choice between these registered plans. Further, an optimum choice involves a great many assumptions about future events, earnings rates, and tax rates. The complexity that is involved is probably well beyond the understanding of most individuals.

Registered Disability Savings Plans (RDSPs)
The Problem
9-139.   Parents of children who are severely disabled are usually faced with a life-long commitment for care and support of these children. Further, the needs of these disabled

individuals for care and support may extend well beyond the lifetime of the parents. Parents facing this possibility would like to ensure that the needed care and support is, in fact, available as long as it is required.

The Solution

9-140.   The government's solution to this problem is legislation which provides for Registered Disability Savings Plans (RDSPs). The mechanics of RDSPs are largely the same as those applicable to RESPs. The general features of these plans are as follows:

- Non-deductible contributions are made to a registered trust with the disabled person as beneficiary.
- The contributions are invested with earnings accumulating on a tax free basis. There is no annual limit. However, contributions are limited to $200,000 over the beneficiary's lifetime.
- The government will supplement contributions to these plans through Canada Disability Savings Grants and Canada Disability Savings Bonds in a manner similar to Canada Education Savings Grants and Canada Learning Bonds.
- Disability assistance payments are made out of the plan assets to the disabled individual. These payments will be divided between a tax free amount which reflects the contributions made to the plans, and a taxable amount which reflects distributions of accumulated earnings.

9-141.   There are many additional rules related to RDSPs, some of them quite complex. Because of this complexity, as well as the fact that these plans are not as widely used as other registered plans, we will not provide detailed coverage of RDSPs. If you have further interest in RDSPs, we would refer you to the CRA's *Registered Disability Savings Plans* (RC4460).

Non-Arm's Length Transfers Of Property

Introduction

The Problem

9-142.   When a capital asset is transferred between arm's length persons, there is an assumption that the transaction takes place at fair market value. Under the usual rules for capital asset dispositions, this fair market value will be used as both the adjusted cost base or capital cost for the newly acquired asset, as well as for the proceeds of disposition to the person disposing of the asset. These proceeds of disposition will then be used to determine tax consequences to the person disposing of the asset (e.g., capital gain or loss).

9-143.   When a non-arm's length transaction is involved, the fair market value assumption cannot be relied on. While many non-arm's length transactions do, in fact, take place at fair market value, there are many situations where it would be to the advantage of a taxpayer to make the transfer at some value that is above or below fair market value (e.g., an individual selling an asset with an accrued capital gain to his low-income spouse for proceeds below fair market value).

9-144.   This situation is further complicated by the fact that the *Income Tax Act* has special rules for determining the UCC when there has been a non-arm's length transfer of depreciable assets. In addition, there are rollover provisions that apply to certain types of non-arm's length transactions.

9-145.   In this material on non-arm's length transactions, we will deal with the following provisions of the *Income Tax Act*:

ITA 69 - Inadequate Considerations   This Section provides rules for dealing with situations where there has been a non-arm's length transfer at a value that is above or below fair market value (including gifts).

ITA 73(1) And (1.01)   These Subsections provide for a tax free rollover of capital properties to a spouse or common-law partner.

ITA 73(3.1) And (4.1) These Subsections provide for a tax free rollover of a farming or fishing property to a child.

ITA 13(7)(e) This Paragraph provides special rules for dealing with non-arm's length transfers of depreciable property.

Non-Arm's Length Defined

9-146. ITA 251(1), in effect, defines the term, "arm's length", by noting that for purposes of the *Act* "related persons shall be deemed not to deal with each other at arm's length". With respect to individuals, ITA 251(2)(a) points out that they are related if they are connected by blood relationship, marriage, common-law partnership or adoption.

9-147. With respect to the question of whether corporations are related, ITA 251(2)(b) and (c) have a fairly long list of possibilities. For example, a corporation is related to the person who controls it, and two corporations are related if they are both controlled by the same person. There are, of course, many complications in this area. However, the examples used in this Chapter involve only situations in which the taxpayers are obviously related. More complex situations will be considered in our coverage of corporate taxation.

Inadequate Considerations - ITA 69

The Problem

9-148. As we have noted, when a transfer of capital property takes place between taxpayers who are dealing with each other at arm's length, there is usually no reason to assume that the transfer took place at a value that was significantly different from the fair market value of the property transferred. In fact, fair market value is often described as the value that would be used by arm's length parties in an exchange transaction.

9-149. The consideration given for the property would normally be used as both the proceeds of the disposition for the vendor and the adjusted cost base for the new owner. However, when a transfer takes place between taxpayers who are not dealing at arm's length, there is the possibility that the consideration can be established at a level that will allow one or both taxpayers to reduce or avoid taxes.

> **EXAMPLE** During 2017, Martin Horst, whose marginal federal tax rate is 29 percent, sells a property with a fair market value of $200,000 to his 25 year old son for its adjusted cost base of $150,000. The son, who has no other source of income in 2017, immediately sells the property for its fair market value of $200,000. The son's only tax credit is the basic personal credit of $1,745.

> **ANALYSIS** If Martin had sold the property for its fair market value of $200,000, he would have paid federal taxes of $7,250 [($200,000 - $150,000)(1/2)(29%)]. In contrast, if the $50,000 capital gain was taxed in the hands of his son, the federal tax would only be $2,005 {[($200,000 - $150,000)(1/2)(15%)] - $1,745}, a savings of $5,245 ($7,250 - $2,005) at the federal level alone.

9-150. The preceding example illustrates the problem associated with non-arm's length transfers in excess of fair market value. In addition, there are two other situations which require special rules. These are:

- A transfer at a positive amount that is below fair market value.
- A transfer for nil consideration (i.e., a gift).

9-151. Section 69 of the *Income Tax Act*, which is somewhat inappropriately titled "Inadequate Considerations", provides rules for dealing with each of these situations.

General Rules

9-152. When a transfer occurs at fair market value, the general rules for determining capital gains and losses are applicable. However, as described in Paragraph 9-150, there are three possible situations that create potential problems. The tax rules for fair market value transfers, and for the three situations described in Paragraph 9-150, are outlined in Figure 9-2.

Figure 9 - 2 Non-Arm's Length Transfers - ITA 69		
Transfer Price	**Proceeds Of Disposition For Transferor**	**Adjusted Cost Base For Transferee**
Fair Market Value	Fair Market Value	Fair Market Value
Above Fair Market Value	Actual Proceeds	Fair Market Value
Below Fair Market Value	Fair Market Value	Actual Proceeds
Nil (Gift)	Fair Market Value	Fair Market Value

Example

9-153.   In order to illustrate the rules presented in Figure 9-2, assume that John Brown has a capital asset with an adjusted cost base of $50,000 and a fair market value of $75,000. If the asset is sold for consideration equal to its fair market value of $75,000, the result will be a capital gain of $25,000 for John Brown and an adjusted cost base for the new owner of $75,000. This would be the result without regard to whether the purchaser was at arm's length with John Brown.

9-154.   If the asset is transferred to a non-arm's length party, and the consideration provided is not equal to its fair market value, ITA 69 becomes applicable. The following three Cases illustrate the various possible alternatives. In each Case, we will assume the transfer is to John Brown's adult brother, Sam Brown.

Case A - Transfer At $100,000 (Above Fair Market Value) In this case, there is no special rule for the transferor. Given this, the proceeds to John Brown will be the actual amount of $100,000 and will result in an immediate capital gain to John Brown of $50,000 ($100,000 - $50,000). The adjusted cost base to Sam Brown will be limited by ITA 69(1)(a) to the $75,000 fair market value. This means that $25,000 of the amount that he has paid is not reflected in his adjusted cost base. If, for example, Sam Brown were to sell the asset for $100,000 (the amount he paid), he would have a capital gain of $25,000 ($100,000 - $75,000) and there will have been double taxation of the $25,000 difference between the transfer price of $100,000 and the fair market value of $75,000.

Case B - Transfer At $60,000 (Below Fair Market Value) If the transfer took place at a price of $60,000, ITA 69(1)(b) would deem John Brown to have received the fair market value of $75,000. As there is no special rule applicable to the purchaser in this case, the adjusted cost base to Sam Brown would be the actual transfer price of $60,000. Here again, double taxation could arise, this time on the difference between the transfer price of $60,000 and the fair market value of $75,000.

Case C - Gift, Bequest, Or Inheritance In this case, ITA 69(1)(b) would deem the proceeds of disposition to be the fair market value of $75,000, and ITA 69(1)(c) would deem Sam Brown's adjusted cost base to be the same value. Note that this is the same result that would be achieved if the asset was sold to Sam Brown at its fair market value of $75,000. However, there is no double taxation involved in this Case.

9-155.   Given the presence of ITA 69, the general rules for transferring property to related parties are very clear. Either transfer the property at a consideration that is equal to its fair market value or, alternatively, gift the property. A non-arm's length transfer, at a value that is either above or below the fair market value of the property, will result in double taxation on some part of any gain recognized when there is a later sale of the property by the transferee.

Applicability Of ITA 69

9-156.   The inadequate consideration rules in ITA 69 are prefaced by the phrase "except as expressly otherwise provided in this Act". This means that if there is a provision that deals with a particular non-arm's length transfer, that provision takes precedence over the general provisions of ITA 69. Examples of such situations that are discussed later in this Chapter are the transfers to a spouse covered in ITA 73(1) and the transfers of farm property to a child covered in ITA 73(3.1). When these provisions are applicable, ITA 69 is not applicable.

Exercise Nine - 8

Subject: Inadequate Consideration - Non-Depreciable Property

Mr. Carl Lipky owns a piece of land with an adjusted cost base of $100,000 and a fair market value of $75,000. He sells the land to his brother for $95,000 who immediately sells it for $75,000. Determine the amount of any capital gain or loss to be recorded by Mr. Lipky and his brother.

SOLUTION available in print and online Study Guide.

Using Leases To Avoid ITA 69

9-157.   At one point, it was possible to avoid the provisions of ITA 69 through the use of leasing arrangements. These arrangements involved the rental of a property to a person with whom the owner/lessor was not dealing at arm's length. The required lease payment was set at a sufficiently low level that the fair market value of the property was significantly reduced. This would allow a sale or gift to be made, with the deemed proceeds of disposition being based on this lower value.

9-158.   As an example of this type of arrangement, consider a situation where an individual has a property with a fair market value of $100,000. If this property was leased on a long-term basis to a spouse or common-law partner for an unrealistically low value, say $2,000 per year, the fair market value of the property might be reduced to about $20,000. If there were no restrictions, it could then be gifted or sold for $20,000 to a child, and there would be no double taxation under the provisions of ITA 69.

9-159.   ITA 69(1.2) is designed to make this an unattractive strategy. Under the provisions of this Subsection, the taxpayer's proceeds of disposition on the gift or sale will be the greater of the actual fair market value at the time of the disposition ($20,000) and the fair market value determined without consideration of the non-arm's length lease ($100,000). This means the transferor will be taxed on the basis of having received the full $100,000 and, under the usual provisions of ITA 69, the transferee will have an adjusted cost base of $20,000. This will result in double taxation of the difference between $100,000 and $20,000 and should serve to discourage this type of avoidance strategy.

Exercise Nine - 9

Subject: Inadequate Consideration - Leased Property

Mr. Ned Bates has land with an adjusted cost base of $33,000 and an unencumbered fair market value of $211,000. He leases this land to his wife for $3,300 per year, for a period of 35 years. Similar leases are based on 10 percent of the value of the property and, as a consequence, the fair market value of the land with the lease in place falls to $33,000. He sells the land to a corporation controlled by his wife for this reduced value. Determine the amount of capital gain or loss to be recorded by Mr. Bates as a result of this sale, as well as the adjusted cost base of the land to the corporation.

SOLUTION available in print and online Study Guide.

We suggest you work Self Study Problem Nine-7 at this point.

Inter Vivos Transfers To A Spouse - ITA 73(1) And 73(1.01)
General Rules For Capital Property

9-160.   An inter vivos transfer is one that occurs while the transferor is still alive, rather than at the time of, or subsequent to, that individual's death. ITA 73(1) contains special rules for certain qualifying transfers as described in ITA 73(1.01). These qualifying transfers are:

- a transfer to the individual's spouse or common-law partner;

- a transfer to the individual's former spouse or former common-law partner in settlement of rights arising out of their marriage or common-law partnership; and

- a transfer to a trust for which the individual's spouse or common-law partner is the income beneficiary (this type of trust has traditionally been referred to as a spousal trust and the conditions related to this concept are discussed in Chapter 19).

9-161.   For the qualifying transfers listed in ITA 73(1.01), ITA 73(1) specifies rules that provide a tax free transfer (such tax free transfers are commonly referred to by tax professionals as rollovers). With respect to the proceeds of disposition for the transferor, the rules for capital property depend on whether it is depreciable or non-depreciable and are as follows:

Proceeds - Non-Depreciable   The proceeds will be deemed to be the adjusted cost base of the property transferred.

Proceeds - Depreciable   The proceeds will be deemed to be the UCC of the class or, if only part of a class is transferred, an appropriate portion of the class.

9-162.   From the point of view of the transferee, ITA 73(1) indicates that he will be deemed to have acquired the capital property at an amount equal to the deemed proceeds to the transferor. Based on this, his values will be as follows:

Tax Cost - Non-Depreciable   The cost to the transferee will be deemed to be the adjusted cost base to the transferor.

Tax Cost - Depreciable   The UCC to the transferee will be the old UCC to the transferor. However, under ITA 73(2), the old capital cost will also be retained by the transferee, with the difference between this and his UCC being considered to be deemed CCA. This rule is very important in that it ensures that if the property is subsequently sold for a value between the old capital cost and the old UCC, the excess over the UCC will be treated as fully taxable recapture, not a capital gain, only one-half of which would be taxed.

9-163.   These rules mean that the transfer will have no tax consequences for the transferor and that the transferee will retain the same tax values that were contained in the transferor's records. This is illustrated by the following example:

EXAMPLE Marg Cardiff gifts land with an adjusted cost base of $100,000 and a fair market value of $250,000 to her husband, Bernie. At the same time, her Class 10 assets are also given to Bernie. The Class 10 assets have a capital cost of $225,000 and a fair market value of $310,000. The UCC for Class 10, prior to the gift, is $195,000.

ANALYSIS Marg would be deemed to have received $100,000 for the disposition of the land and $195,000 for the Class 10 assets. Given these values, the transactions would have no tax consequences for Marg.

For Bernie, the land would have an adjusted cost base of $100,000. The transferred Class 10 assets would have a UCC of $195,000, combined with a capital cost of $225,000. This means that, if Bernie sold all the transferred assets immediately for their combined fair market value of $560,000 ($250,000 + $310,000), there would be a capital gain of $150,000 ($250,000 - $100,000) on the land, a capital gain of $85,000 ($310,000 - $225,000) on the Class 10 assets, as well as recapture of CCA of $30,000 ($195,000 - $225,000) on the Class 10 assets. Note that these are the same tax consequences that would have occurred if Marg had simply sold the assets to an arm's length party.

Electing Out Of The Spousal Rollover

9-164.   The ITA 73(1) rollover automatically applies to spousal rollovers unless the taxpayer takes positive action to remove its applicability. However, the taxpayer can elect out of this approach if he wishes to recognize capital gains or recapture at the time of the transfer. There are a variety of reasons that a taxpayer may wish to make this election. For example, if a taxpayer has unused allowable capital losses, he could choose to trigger taxable capital gains to make use of these losses. Electing out of the ITA 73(1) rollover can also be important when dealing with income attribution. This issue is discussed later in this Chapter.

9-165.   With respect to the process of electing to be taxed on an inter vivos spousal transfer, ITA 73(1) uses the phrase "elects in his return of income". The use of this phrase in the *Income Tax Act* means there is no official tax form required in order to make the election. In contrast, in situations where a form is required, the usual *Income Tax Act* terminology is the phrase "elects in the prescribed manner".

9-166.   For a taxpayer wishing to elect out of ITA 73(1), the only requirement is that they include any income resulting from the spousal transfer in their tax return in the year of disposition.

> **EXAMPLE - Continued**   In the example from Paragraph 9-163, Marg could have elected to record the land transaction at the fair market value of $250,000, resulting in a $150,000 capital gain being recorded at the time of transfer. In this case, the adjusted cost base to Bernie would be $250,000. The election would be made by simply including the $75,000 taxable portion of the $150,000 gain in Marg's tax return.

9-167.   You should note that, if the taxpayer elects out of ITA 73(1), ITA 69 becomes applicable. This means that, in such situations, if the transfer is not a gift, or is made in return for consideration that is not equal to the fair market value of the property, the ITA 69 provisions will result in double taxation as was discussed previously. In addition, if a depreciable asset is transferred, special rules apply when calculating the transferee's capital cost. These rules are covered in the next section of this Chapter.

Exercise Nine - 10

Subject: Inter Vivos Transfer Of Non-Depreciable Asset To A Spouse

Aaron Schwartz owns land with an adjusted cost base of $225,000 and a fair market value of $300,000. He sells this land to his spouse for its fair market value of $300,000. Indicate the tax consequences to Mr. Schwartz and the adjusted cost base of the property to his spouse after the sale assuming Mr. Schwartz does not elect out of ITA 73(1). How would your answer change if Mr. Schwartz elects out of ITA 73(1)?

SOLUTION available in print and online Study Guide.

Non-Arm's Length Transfers Of Depreciable Assets - ITA 13(7)(e)
Problem 1 - Fair Market Value Exceeds Transferor's Capital Cost

9-168.   The problem here relates to the fact that, if the transfer is made at a value in excess of the transferor's capital cost, the result will be a capital gain, only one-half of which will be taxed. If the full amount of the capital gain was added to the transferee's UCC, it would form the basis for fully deductible CCA.

> **EXAMPLE**   Jean Tessier has a depreciable asset with a fair market value of $150,000, a capital cost of $110,000, and a UCC of $85,000. It is the only asset in the Class. He sells this asset to his daughter Francine for its fair market value of $150,000.

Non-Arm's Length Transfers Of Property

ANALYSIS As a result of this disposition, Jean will have recapture of $25,000 ($110,000 - $85,000) and a capital gain of $40,000 ($150,000 - $110,000). Only $20,000 of this capital gain will be subject to tax, resulting in a total increase in his Taxable Income of $45,000 [$25,000 + (1/2)($40,000)].

If Francine was allowed to record the $150,000 as her capital cost for CCA purposes, she would be able to deduct 100 percent of this amount as CCA. This means that, by increasing his Taxable Income by $45,000, the future deductions available on this asset would have increased by $65,000 ($150,000 - $85,000). As related parties, Jean and Francine would clearly have an incentive to make the transfer at this price.

Solution To Problem 1

9-169. Tax legislation acts to prevent such non-arm's length transfers from having this benefit. In those situations where the transfer occurs at a value that exceeds the transferor's capital cost, for the purposes of CCA and recapture calculations **ONLY**, ITA 13(7)(e) deems the transferee's capital cost to be equal to:

$$A + [(1/2)(B - A)], \text{ where:}$$

A = The Transferor's Old Capital Cost
B = The Transferee's New Capital Cost

ITA 13(7)(e) is not applicable when the transfer results from the death of a taxpayer.

ANALYSIS - Continued Applying this rule to the example in Paragraph 9-168, Francine's capital cost and UCC balance would be $130,000 [$110,000 + (1/2)($150,000 - $110,000)]. As a result, the transfer has increased the UCC by $45,000 ($130,000 - $85,000), an amount equal to the increase in Jean's Taxable Income resulting from the transfer.

It is important to note that the $130,000 is only used for recapture and CCA calculations. The capital cost for capital gains purposes would be based on the actual transfer price of $150,000. Assuming Francine later sold the asset for $160,000 without taking any CCA, the taxable capital gain would be $5,000 [(1/2)($160,000 - $150,000)] and there would be no recapture.

UCC Balance At Time Of Sale	$130,000
Deduct Lesser Of:	
• Deemed Capital Cost For CCA Purposes = $130,000	
• Proceeds Of Disposition = $160,000	(130,000)
Recapture	Nil

If these procedures look familiar, they are very similar to those applicable when there is a change in use from personal to business use and the fair market value of the asset exceeds its capital cost. (See coverage of ITA 13(7)(b) in Chapter 8.)

Problem 2 - Fair Market Value Less Than Transferor's Capital Cost

9-170. A similar problem arises when a non-arm's length transfer occurs at a value that is less than the transferor's capital cost.

EXAMPLE Carole Dupre has a depreciable asset with a fair market value of $200,000, a capital cost of $325,000, and a UCC of $150,000. It is the only asset in the Class. She sells this asset to her son Marcel for the fair market value of $200,000.

ANALYSIS As a result of this transaction, the only tax consequence for Carole would be recapture of $50,000 ($150,000 - $200,000).

Under the usual rules, the capital cost to Marcel would be the transfer price of $200,000. The problem with this result is that, if Marcel were to later sell this asset for $250,000, the difference between the $250,000 and this $200,000 would be treated as a capital gain, only one-half of which would be included in his Taxable Income. In contrast, if Carole had sold the asset for $250,000, the difference would have been fully taxable recapture. As in the problem 1 scenario, this situation provides an incentive for Carole and Marcel to make the transfer at this price.

The Solution To Problem 2

9-171. When there is a non-arm's length transfer at a value that is less than the transferor's capital cost, the ITA, including 13(7)(e), deems the transferee's capital cost, for both CCA and capital gains calculations, to be equal to the transferor's old capital cost.

> **ANALYSIS - Continued** Applying this rule to the example in Paragraph 9-170, the deemed capital cost to Marcel would be $325,000, with the $125,000 difference between this amount and the $200,000 paid considered to be deemed CCA. When this rule is applied, a sale by Marcel at $250,000 would result in fully taxable recapture of $50,000 ($200,000 - $250,000). The $250,000 is the lesser of the proceeds of disposition of $250,000 and the deemed capital cost (equal to Carole's capital cost) of $325,000. Unlike the previous case where the transfer is at a value that is greater than the transferor's capital cost, the $325,000 deemed capital cost would be used for determining capital gains as well as for determining recapture.

Application Of ITA 69

9-172. These rules for non-arm's length transfers of depreciable property apply to all such transactions, including those to which ITA 69 is applicable. In such situations, the ITA 13(7)(e) rules will be applied using the amounts that are required by this section. However, the application of ITA 69 to transfers of depreciable assets is very complex. In addition, there are some who believe that the *Income Tax Act* is not entirely clear on how these provisions interact. Given this, we will not include coverage in this text of non-arm's length transfers of depreciable assets at a positive amount that is not fair market value.

Exercise Nine - 11

Subject: Inter Vivos Transfer Of Depreciable Asset To A Spouse

During the current year, Mary Sharp transferred a depreciable property to her spouse. The property had a fair market value of $225,000, a capital cost of $175,000, and a UCC of $110,000. It is the only asset in its class. In return for the property, she received $225,000 in cash. Describe the tax consequences to Ms. Sharp and her spouse, assuming that she does not elect out of ITA 73(1). How would your answer change if she elects out of the rollover provision?

Exercise Nine - 12

Subject: Inter Vivos Transfer Of Depreciable Property To A Parent

Ms. Jennifer Lee owns a depreciable asset that she has used in her unincorporated business. It has a cost of $53,000 and a fair market value of $40,000. It is the only asset in its CCA class, and the UCC balance in the class is $37,200. Ms. Lee sells the asset to her father for the fair market value of $40,000. During the same year, prior to deducting any CCA, the father resells the asset for $44,000. Determine the amount of income to be recorded by Ms. Lee and her father as a result of these transactions.

SOLUTIONS available in print and online Study Guide.

We suggest you work Self Study Problem Nine-8 at this point.

Inter Vivos Transfer Of Farm Or Fishing Property To A Child

9-173.   ITA 73(3.1) and (4.1) provide for direct inter vivos transfers of farm or fishing property, shares of family farm or fishing corporations, or interests in family farm or fishing partnerships, to children on a tax-free basis. As was the case with ITA 73(1), the provisions of ITA 73(3.1) and (4.1) take precedence over the provisions of ITA 69.

9-174.   For the purposes of this Section, "child" refers to children and their spouses, grandchildren, great grandchildren, and any other person who, prior to reaching the age of 19, was dependent on the taxpayer and under his custody or control. To qualify, the child must be a resident of Canada at the time of the transfer. In addition, the property must be in use in a farming or fishing business operated by the taxpayer, the taxpayer's spouse, or any of their children.

9-175.   The transfer is deemed to have taken place at the actual proceeds of disposition, restricted by floor and ceiling amounts.

For **Depreciable Property**, the floor is the property's UCC, while the ceiling is its fair market value. The transferee would retain the original capital cost to the transferor with the difference being treated as deemed CCA.

For **Non-Depreciable Property**, which includes shares in a farm or fishing corporation, the floor is the adjusted cost base, while the ceiling is the fair market value.

9-176.   The following example will illustrate these floor and ceiling rules.

EXAMPLE Tim Johnson's farm consists of land with an adjusted cost base of $200,000 and a fair market value of $350,000, and depreciable assets with a UCC of $400,000, a capital cost of $550,000, and a fair market value of $675,000. It is transferred to Tim's son.

ANALYSIS - Land   If the transfer is for proceeds of disposition below $200,000 (this includes gifts), the deemed proceeds of disposition and adjusted cost base to the child would be $200,000. If the transfer is for an amount in excess of $350,000, the deemed proceeds of disposition and adjusted cost base to the child would be limited to $350,000. For transfers between $200,000 and $350,000, the actual proceeds of disposition would be used.

ANALYSIS - Depreciable Property   For transfers below the UCC of $400,000, (including gifts), the deemed proceeds of disposition and transfer price to the child would be $400,000. Correspondingly, for transfers above $675,000, the deemed proceeds of disposition and capital cost to the child would be $675,000. For transfers between $400,000 and $675,000, the actual proceeds of disposition would be used.

Exercise Nine - 13

Subject: Inter Vivos Farm Property Transfer To A Child

Thomas Nobel owns farm property consisting of land with an adjusted cost base of $250,000 and a fair market value of $325,000, along with a barn with a UCC of $85,000, a capital cost of $115,000, and a fair market value of $101,000. The property is transferred to his 40 year old daughter in return for a payment of $280,000 for the land. No payment is made for the barn. Describe the tax consequences of this transfer, both for Mr. Nobel and for his daughter.

SOLUTION available in print and online Study Guide.

Death Of A Taxpayer

General Rules

9-177.   There are many special rules that may be applicable when an individual dies. In this Chapter, we cover the rules related to capital property. Other material on the death of a taxpayer can be found in the Chapter 11 Appendix titled "Returns For Deceased Taxpayers".

9-178.   ITA 70(5) provides the following general rules for the capital property of a deceased taxpayer:

Capital Property Other Than Depreciable Property   In general, the deceased taxpayer is deemed to have disposed of the property at fair market value immediately before his death. The person receiving the property is deemed to have acquired the property at this time, at a value equal to its fair market value.

Depreciable Property   The basic rules for this type of property are the same. That is, there is a deemed disposition of the property by the deceased taxpayer at fair market value, combined with an acquisition of the property at the same value by the beneficiary. When the fair market value is less than the capital cost of the property for the deceased taxpayer, the beneficiary is required to retain the original capital cost, with the difference being treated as deemed CCA.

9-179.   A simple example will serve to illustrate the rules for depreciable property:

EXAMPLE   Eric Nadon dies, leaving a depreciable property to his son that has a capital cost of $100,000, a fair market value of $60,000, and a UCC of $50,000.

ANALYSIS   Under ITA 70(5), the transfer will take place at the fair market value of $60,000. This means that Mr. Nadon's final tax return will include recaptured CCA of $10,000 ($60,000 - $50,000). While the son's UCC will be the $60,000 transfer price, the capital cost of the asset will remain at Mr. Nadon's original capital cost of $100,000. This means that, if the asset is later sold for a value between $60,000 and $100,000, the resulting gain will be treated as recaptured CCA, rather than as a more favourably taxed capital gain.

9-180.   These deemed disposition rules apply to all capital property, including personal use property and listed personal property.

Rollover To A Spouse, A Common-Law Partner, Or A Spousal Trust

9-181.   ITA 70(6) provides an exception to the general rules contained in ITA 70(5) in situations where the transfer is to a spouse, a common-law partner, or a testamentary spousal or common-law partner trust. This is a rollover provision that allows the transfer of non-depreciable property at its adjusted cost base and depreciable property at its UCC.

9-182.   This means that the transfer does not generate a capital gain or loss, recapture, or terminal loss, and that the surviving spouse or common-law partner will assume the same property values as those carried by the deceased. This has the effect of deferring any capital gains or recapture until the surviving spouse or common-law partner disposes of the property, or dies. As is the case with other transfers at death, if the transfer involves depreciable property, the deceased's old capital cost is retained.

9-183.   It is possible for the legal representative of the deceased to elect in the taxpayer's final return to have one or all asset transfers take place at fair market value. This election could be used to take advantage of charitable donations, medical expenses, unused loss carry forwards, and, in the case of qualified farm property, qualified fishing property, or the shares of a qualified small business corporation, an unused lifetime capital gains deduction. As was the case with electing out of the ITA 73 inter vivos transfer to a spouse rules, electing out of ITA 70(6) is implemented in the deceased's final tax return and does not require the filing of a form.

9-184.   To qualify as a spousal testamentary trust, ITA 70(6) indicates that the surviving spouse or common-law partner must be entitled to receive all of the income of the trust that arises before the death of the surviving spouse or common-law partner. In addition, no person other than the spouse or common-law partner may receive the use of any of the income or capital of the trust, prior to the death of this spouse or common-law partner.

9-185.   Detailed coverage of spousal testamentary trusts can be found in Chapter 19. As discussed in Chapter 19, there are at least two advantages to using a spousal trust:

- Such arrangements can provide for the administration of the assets of the deceased in those situations where the surviving spouse or common-law partner is not experienced in business or financial matters.

- Such arrangements can allow the deceased to determine the ultimate disposition of any property that is left to the spousal trust. For example, if a father wishes the property he bequeathed to the spousal trust to go to his children after his wife's death, this can be specified in the trust arrangement. This would avoid the possibility that his widow might sell it, or redirect the property to a new husband or any children that she might have on remarrying.

Exercise Nine - 14

Subject: Transfers On Death

Ms. Cheryl Lardner, who owns two trucks that were used in her business, dies in July, 2017. Her will transferred truck A to her husband, Michel, and truck B to her daughter, Melinda. Each of the trucks cost $42,000 and had a fair market value at the time of her death of $33,000. The UCC balance for the class that contains the trucks was $51,000. What are the tax consequences resulting from Ms. Lardner's death with respect to these two trucks? Your answer should include the capital cost and the UCC for the trucks in the hands of Michel and Melinda.

SOLUTION available in print and online Study Guide.

Tax Free Transfers Of Farm And Fishing Property At Death

9-186.   As we have seen, the most common situation in which capital property can be transferred at the time of death on a tax free basis is when the transfer is to a spouse or a spousal testamentary trust. However, ITA 70(9) through ITA 70(9.31) provides for other tax free transfers involving specific types of farm and fishing assets. For each of the following types of transfers, the legal representatives of the deceased can elect to transfer the property at any value between its tax value and its fair market value. These elections can be used to utilize any accumulated losses of the deceased, or any unused lifetime capital gains deduction.

- **Farm Or Fishing Property**   When farm or fishing property has been used by a taxpayer or the taxpayer's family, it can be transferred on a tax free basis to a resident child, grandchild, or great grandchild at the time of the taxpayer's death. These provisions can also be used to transfer farm or fishing property from a child to a parent in situations where the child dies before the parent.

- **Shares Of A Family Farm Or Fishing Corporation**   Shares of a family farm or fishing corporation can be transferred on a tax free basis to a resident child, grandchild, or great grandchild at the time of a taxpayer's death. It is possible to have tax free transfers of farm or fishing corporation shares from a child to a parent and, in addition, the rules provide for the rollover of shares in a family farm or fishing holding company.

- **Interests In Family Farm Or Fishing Partnerships**   Rules similar to those described in the two preceding bullets allow for the tax free transfer of interests in family farm or fishing partnerships to a resident child, grandchild, or great grandchild at the time of the taxpayer's death. Here again, it is possible to have a tax free transfer from a child to a parent in the event of the child's death.

We suggest you work Self Study Problem Nine-9 at this point.

Income Attribution

The Problem

9-187.   In the general discussion of tax planning in Chapter 1, it was noted that income splitting can be the most powerful tool available to individuals wishing to reduce their tax burden. The basic goal is to redistribute income from an individual in a high tax bracket to related individuals, usually a spouse or children, in lower tax brackets. As was illustrated in Chapter 1, when such redistribution can be achieved, it can produce very dramatic reductions in the aggregate tax liability of the family unit.

9-188.   It is obvious that, if there were no restrictions associated with transfers of property to related persons, there would be little standing in the way of a complete equalization of tax rates within a family unit and the achievement of maximum income splitting benefits. For many years, it has been the policy of the government to tightly control access to the tax benefits of income splitting and, as a consequence, we have a group of legislative provisions that are commonly referred to as the income attribution rules.

9-189.   These attribution rules could be criticized on the basis of fairness. Many of the most effective income splitting scenarios are complicated and involve the use of complex corporate, partnership, and trust structures. This level of income splitting requires the kind of sophisticated tax assistance that is available only to wealthy Canadians.

9-190.   As mentioned in our coverage of pension income splitting (Paragraph 9-69), there are ways to legitimately split income with family members. However, there are many other potential income splitting opportunities that the attribution rules are designed to prevent. If the goal in transferring a property to a lower income family member is to have the related income taxed at a lower rate, if the attribution rules apply, the income will be taxed in the hands of the transferor and no tax savings will have been achieved.

Basic Rules - ITA 74.1(1) And (2)

Applicable Individuals

9-191.   The income attribution rules are applicable to situations where an individual has transferred property to:

- a spouse or common-law partner [ITA 74.1(1)]; or
- an individual who is under the age of 18 and who does not deal with the individual at arm's length [ITA 74.1(2)].

9-192.   The ITA 74.1(2) rules are applicable, not just to children or grandchildren under the age of 18, but to any non-arm's length individual who is under the age of 18. In addition, this Subsection specifically notes that nieces and nephews are subject to these rules, even though they are not non-arm's length individuals as defined in the *Income Tax Act.*

9-193.   The general idea here is that, unless certain conditions are met, income associated with the transferee holding or disposing of a transferred property may be attributed back to the transferor of the property (i.e., included in the Net Income For Tax Purposes of the transferor). You should also note that losses can be transferred under the attribution rules, a fact that can be used by tax planners to reduce the tax liability of the transferor.

Applicable To Property Income And Capital Gains

9-194.   There are two types of income that may be attributed under these rules. The first type would be property income, such as interest, dividends, rents, and royalties, which accrues while the transferee is holding the transferred assets. This type of income may be attributed back to the transferor without regard to whether the transferee is a spouse, common-law partner, or a related individual under the age of 18.

9-195.   The second type of income that may be subject to the attribution rules is capital gains resulting from a disposition of the transferred property. Whether or not this type of income is subject to the attribution rules will depend on the relationship of the transferee to the transferor:

Transfers To A Spouse   When property is transferred to a spouse or common-law partner, the application of the ITA 73(1) rollover generally means that the property is transferred at the transferor's tax cost, with no taxation at the time of transfer. This means that the transferred property will be recorded at the adjusted cost base value for non-depreciable assets and at the UCC for depreciable assets. Given this, it seems logical that any capital gain or recaptured CCA from a subsequent sale by the spouse would be measured from that tax cost and attributed back to the transferor. This approach is, in fact, required under ITA 74.2.

Transfers To A Related Minor - General Rule   There is no general rollover provision for related minors that corresponds to ITA 73(1) for a spouse or common-law partner. This means that when property is transferred to a related minor, the transfer will normally take place at the fair market value of the property, resulting in the transferor recognizing any capital gains or recaptured CCA that have accrued to the time of transfer. Reflecting this fact, any gain on a subsequent sale by the related minor would be measured using the fair market value at the time of transfer. Further, such gains are not attributed back to the transferor, but are taxed in the hands of the related minor.

Transfers To A Minor Child - Farming Or Fishing Property   As discussed in this Chapter at Paragraph 9-173, ITA 73(3.1) and ITA 73(4.1) provide for a transfer of farm or fishing property to a child at its tax cost. It is not surprising that, when this rollover provision is used, there is attribution of gains arising on a subsequent disposition by the child. More specifically, ITA 75.1 indicates that when a farm or fishing property has been transferred to a child on a rollover basis and the child disposes of that property prior to reaching the age of 18 years, all capital gains and capital losses, both those existing at the time of transfer and those accruing subsequently, are attributed back to the transferor and taxed in the transferor's hands.

Not Applicable After Death Of Transferor

9-196.   Income attribution ceases with the death of the transferor. For example, if a parent made an inter vivos transfer to a minor child, income on the transferred asset would be attributed back to the transferor until the minor reached the age of 18. However, if the transferor died before the minor was 18, attribution of this income would cease on the date of the death.

Not Applicable To Business Income

9-197.   Business income is not subject to the attribution rules. If the assets that are transferred to a spouse, common-law partner, or related minor, are used to produce business income, this type of income will be taxed in the hands of the transferee. The logic of this seems clear. In order to earn business income, an effort is required on the part of the transferee. This means that the resulting business income is not a simple gift, but something that has to be earned. In these circumstances, it would not seem equitable to attribute these amounts to the transferor who provided the property.

9-198.   Note, however, that if a business is transferred to a spouse or common-law partner, any capital gain on a subsequent sale of the business assets will be attributed back to the transferor, despite the fact that business income earned between the transfer and the sale will not be attributed to the transferor.

Not Applicable If Subject To Tax On Split Income

9-199.   A further exception to the income attribution rules is income that is subject to the tax on split income. While this tax is discussed in detail in Chapter 11, we would note here that this is a special tax on certain types of income that are earned by individuals under the age of

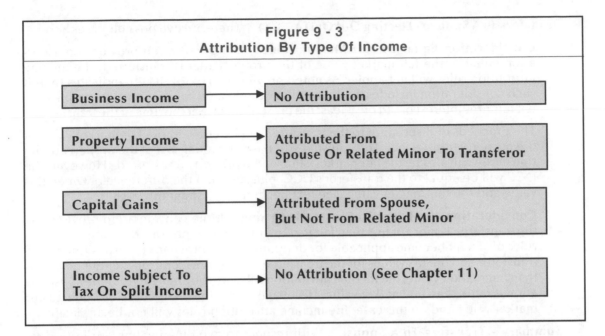

Figure 9 - 3
Attribution By Type Of Income

18 on income that is sourced from related parties. This special tax is assessed on the minor individual at the maximum federal rate of 33 percent, beginning with the first dollar of such income received.

9-200.   With income subject to the tax on split income being taxed at the maximum federal rate of 33 percent, any potential income splitting advantage has been eliminated. As a consequence, there is really no point in applying the income attribution rules to income that is subject to this tax. This view is reflected in ITA 74.5(13) which indicates that the income attribution rules in ITA 74.1(2) are not applicable to income that is subject to the tax on split income.

Summary Of Rules
9-201.   The attribution rules, classified by type of income, are summarized in Figure 9-3.

Avoiding Income Attribution
9-202.   The basic idea behind the income attribution rules is to restrict an individual's ability to simply give a source of income to a related individual for income splitting purposes. The procedure for avoiding these rules on a transfer to a related minor is straightforward:

> **Transfers To A Related Minor**   In this case, ITA 74.5(1)(a) indicates that the income attribution rules are not applicable if the related minor provides, from his own resources, consideration equal to the fair market value of the asset transferred. ITA 74.5(1)(b) indicates that, if such consideration includes debt payable by the related minor, it is acceptable only if it requires interest based on at least the prescribed rate at the time of the transfer.

9-203.   The ITA 73(1) rollover (see inter vivos spousal transfers beginning in Paragraph 9-160) complicates the avoidance of the income attribution rules on transfers to a spouse:

> **Transfers To A Spouse - ITA 73(1) Applicable**   If a property is transferred to a spouse without electing out of the ITA 73(1) rollover, income attribution will always be applicable. Without regard to any amount of consideration provided by the transferee, the proceeds of disposition to the transferor will be the adjusted cost base of the transferred non-depreciable property, or the UCC of the depreciable property. These values will also be used for the adjusted cost base or UCC for the transferee. We would remind you that the transferee will retain the transferor's capital cost for purposes of determining capital gains and recapture.

Transfers To A Spouse - Electing Out Of ITA 73(1)   There are two possible cases here:

Consideration Equal To Fair Market Value   If the transferee provides consideration equal to the fair market value of the property that is transferred, the income attribution rules will not apply. As noted previously, ITA 74.5(1)(b) indicates that, if such consideration includes debt payable by the related spouse, it is acceptable only if it requires interest based on at least the prescribed rate at the time of the transfer.

The proceeds of disposition to the transferor will be equal to the fair market value of the property transferred. The adjusted cost base or capital cost of the property to the transferee will also be the fair market value of the property transferred. However, the UCC will be equal to the transferor's UCC, plus one-half the difference between this value and the fair market value (see text beginning in Paragraph 9-168).

Consideration Not Equal To Fair Market Value   If the consideration provided by the transferee is more or less than fair market, or if there is no consideration given, the rules of ITA 69 become applicable for determining the proceeds of disposition to the transferor and the tax values for the transferee. If the consideration is either nil or less than fair market value, the income attribution rules will be applicable. If the consideration is more than fair market value, ITA 69 will deem the proceeds to be equal to fair market value and, in this case, the income attribution rules will not be applicable.

Summary - Transfers To A Spouse   With respect to avoiding income attribution on transfers to a spouse, the income attribution rules will apply unless:

- The transferor elects out of the ITA 73(1) rollover; and
- The transferee provides consideration equal to or greater than fair market value.

Example

9-204.   The following example will illustrate the provisions that we have just discussed.

EXAMPLE   Mrs. Blaine owns a group of equity securities with an adjusted cost base of $200,000. On December 31, 2016, the fair market value of these securities is $300,000. On this date, she gives one-half of the securities to her unemployed husband Mark, and the other one-half to her 5 year old daughter Belinda.

Both Mark and Belinda hold the securities until December 31, 2017, at which point they are sold for a total of $350,000 ($175,000 each). During 2017, the securities paid $37,500 in eligible dividends ($18,750 to both Mark and Belinda).

ANALYSIS - Transfer To Spouse   Assuming that Mrs. Blaine has not elected out of the ITA 73(1) rules, the transfer to her husband would take place at the adjusted cost base of $100,000 [(1/2)($200,000)] and she would not record a 2016 gain. However, the adjusted cost base of the shares to Mark would be Mrs. Blaine's adjusted cost base of $100,000. This means that when Mark sells the shares, the taxable capital gain will be $37,500 [(1/2)($175,000 - $100,000)], all of which will be attributed to Mrs. Blaine in 2017. In addition, the $18,750 in dividends received by Mark in 2017 would also be attributed to Mrs. Blaine. The taxable amount would be $25,875 [(138%)($18,750)] and Mrs. Blaine would get the related dividend tax credit.

ANALYSIS - Transfer To Minor   As indicated previously, the rules for minors are somewhat different. As there is no general rollover provision for minor children in this case, the gift to Belinda would be treated as a disposition at fair market value, resulting in a 2016 taxable capital gain for Mrs. Blaine of $25,000 [(1/2)($150,000 - $100,000)]. Belinda's adjusted cost base for the shares would then be $150,000. When the shares are sold by Belinda, the additional taxable capital gain of $12,500 [(1/2)($175,000 - $150,000)] would be taxed in Belinda's hands and would not be attributed to Mrs. Blaine. The treatment of the dividends for Belinda is the same as for Mr. Blaine, resulting in an additional $18,750 in dividends being attributed to Mrs. Blaine for 2017. The taxable amount would be $25,875 [(138%)($18,750)] and Mrs. Blaine would get the related dividend tax credit.

9-205.   If either Mark or Belinda reinvests the proceeds from selling the shares, dividend or interest income resulting from the reinvestment will also be attributed back to Mrs. Blaine. Any capital gains on the new investments that are realized by Mark will also be attributed to Mrs. Blaine. This will not be the case with capital gains realized by Belinda. Note, however, that the compound earnings resulting from the reinvestment of the dividends received from the new investment are not subject to the attribution rules.

Exercise Nine - 15

Subject: Income Attribution From A Spouse

On December 31, 2016, Mrs. Norah Moreau gives shares with an adjusted cost base of $23,000 and a fair market value of $37,000 to her husband, Nick Moreau. On February 24, 2017, the shares pay eligible dividends of $2,500 ($3,450 taxable amount) and, on August 31, 2017, Mr. Moreau sells the shares for $42,000. Assume that Mrs. Moreau does not elect out of ITA 73(1). What are the tax consequences for Mr. Moreau and Mrs. Moreau, in each of the years 2016 and 2017? If there are no tax consequences for either individual in a given year, you should clearly state this fact in your answer.

Exercise Nine - 16

Subject: Income Attribution From A Related Minor

On December 31, 2016, Mrs. Norah Moreau gives shares with an adjusted cost base of $23,000 and a fair market value of $37,000 to her 12 year old daughter, Nicki Moreau. On February 24, 2017, the shares pay eligible dividends of $2,500 ($3,450 taxable amount) and, on August 31, 2017, Nicki sells the shares for $42,000. What are the tax consequences for Mrs. Moreau and Nicki in each of the years 2016 and 2017?

Exercise Nine - 17

Subject: Income Attribution - Use Of Loans

On December 31, 2016, Mr. Nadeem Bronski gives corporate bonds to his wife in exchange for a note with a face value of $121,000. The corporate bonds have an adjusted cost base of $115,000 and a fair market value of $121,000. The note from his wife does not pay interest and has no specific maturity date. Mr. Bronski does not report a gain on these bonds in 2016. During 2017, the bonds pay interest to Mrs. Bronski in the amount of $6,100. On October 1, 2017, immediately after an interest payment, Mrs. Bronski sells the bonds for $129,000. She uses $121,000 of the proceeds to pay off the loan owing to her husband. What are the tax consequences for Mr. and Mrs. Bronski in each of the years 2016 and 2017?

SOLUTIONS available in print and online Study Guide.

Income Attribution - Other Related Parties

9-206.   The applicability of the income attribution rules that were previously discussed is limited to transfers and loans to spouses and related individuals under the age of 18. There is another income attribution provision that applies to a broader group of individuals. This is found in ITA 56(4.1) and indicates that, if an interest free or low rate loan is made to a related party for the purpose of producing property income, the income can be attributed back to the individual making the loan. A further condition for this attribution is that one of the main reasons for making the loan is to reduce or avoid tax.

9-207.   The most important application of this provision is to loans made by parents to their adult children. For children 18 or over, the general income attribution rules do not apply. Although there are no tax consequences associated with cash gifts to adult children, parents interested in providing some financial assistance to their children can be reluctant to completely lose control over the resources involved.

9-208.   As an example, a parent might extend an interest free loan to an adult child to assist with the purchase of a property. If the child decides to live in the property, there is no attribution related to the interest free loan used to purchase the principal residence. However, if the child uses the property to produce rental income, this income can potentially be attributed back to the parent making the loan.

9-209.   The tax planning conclusion in this situation is obvious. If a parent wishes to provide financial assistance to an adult child to earn property income, the appropriate route is to use an outright gift. While an interest free loan can accomplish the goal of providing financial assistance to the child, ITA 56(4.1) can eliminate the potential tax savings associated with this form of income splitting.

> **We suggest you work Self Study Problems Nine-10 and Nine-11 at this point.**

Anti-Avoidance Provisions

9-210.   Given the attractiveness of income splitting, it is not surprising that tax planners have shown considerable ingenuity in devising procedures to avoid these attribution rules. It is equally unsurprising that the federal government has continued to come up with new rules to deal with these procedures.

9-211.   Current legislation contains a number of provisions directed at preventing the use of indirect transfers, corporations, or trusts to circumvent the attribution rules. Complete coverage of these anti-avoidance rules is beyond the scope of this material. However, some of the more important anti-avoidance rules can be described as follows:

- ITA 74.1(3) prevents the substitution of a new low rate or interest free loan for an existing commercial rate loan.

- ITA 74.5(6) prevents a loan from being made to a person who is not subject to the attribution rules, who then makes a similar loan to a person who would be subject to the attribution rules if the loan had been directly made to that individual. The use of the intermediary would be disregarded and indirect attribution would apply.

- ITA 74.5(7) prevents the use of loan guarantees to avoid the attribution rules. That is, a higher income spouse cannot get around the attribution rules by providing a guarantee on a low rate or interest free loan to a spouse that is made by a third party.

- ITA 74.3 and 74.4 contain a variety of rules designed to prevent the avoidance of the attribution rules through the use of a trust (ITA 74.3) or a corporation (ITA 74.4).

Tax Planning And Income Attribution

9-212.   In recent years it has become increasingly difficult to avoid the income attribution rules. Further, many of the plans that are available for this purpose involve corporations and trusts and are too complex to be dealt with in detail in an introductory level text such as this. However, there are a number of relatively simple points that can be helpful:

Split Pension Income   As discussed in this Chapter, it is possible to transfer up to 50 percent of qualified pension income to a lower income spouse. This is an important provision which can provide for a significant reduction in family unit taxes.

TFSAs   As discussed in this Chapter, Tax Free Savings Accounts can be used for income splitting as these plans are not subject to the income attribution rules.

RESPs   As discussed in this Chapter, Registered Education Savings Plans can be used for a limited amount of income splitting.

Spousal RRSPs   As is discussed in Chapter 10, the spousal Registered Retirement Savings Plan is a readily available device for a limited amount of income splitting.

Assets With Capital Gains Potential   As there is no attribution of capital gains on transfers to related minors, assets with capital gains potential should be given to children, rather than to a spouse.

Loans   The prescribed rate is currently 1 percent (2nd quarter of 2017). With the rate at this level, it is possible to find safe investments that have a higher yield. Given this, it may be useful to loan funds at this prescribed rate to a low income family member who reinvests the funds at a rate higher than 1 percent.

Segregating Gifts To Spouses And Minors   If a spouse or minor child receives a gift or inheritance from a source to which attribution would not apply, the funds should be segregated for investment purposes and, if possible, should not be used for such non-deductible purposes as vacations, reducing the mortgage on the family home, or purchases of personal effects.

Detailed Records   In order to have low income family members acquire investment income, it is necessary for them to have funds to invest. Having the higher income spouse pay for non-deductible expenditures such as household expenses, clothing, vacations, and the lower income spouse's income tax liability can help provide for this. Although tuition fees can be eligible for a tax credit (see Chapter 4), they do not have to be paid by the student to be eligible for the credit. It may be desirable to maintain separate bank accounts and relatively detailed records to ensure that it is clear that the lower income family members' funds are being used for investment purposes.

New Businesses   When a new business is started, low income family members should be allowed to acquire an equity position, particularly if the capital requirements are small. Note, however, if the business experiences losses in its first years of operation, this may not be the best alternative.

Salaries To Family Members   When business income is earned in the family unit, or through a related corporation, the lower income spouse and any children should be paid reasonable salaries for any activity that can be justified as business related. Examples would include bookkeeping, filing, and other administrative work.

We suggest you work Self Study Problems Nine-12 and Nine-13 at this point.

Additional Supplementary Self Study Problems Are Available Online.

Key Terms Used In This Chapter

9-213.   The following is a list of the key terms used in this Chapter. These terms, and their meanings, are compiled in the Glossary located at the back of the Study Guide.

Alimony	Eligible Child
Annual Child Care Expense Amount	Inadequate Consideration
Annuity	Income Attribution
Anti-Avoidance Provision	Income Splitting
Arm's Length	Inter Vivos Transfer
Canada Disability Savings Bonds	Moving Expenses
Canada Disability Savings Grants	Non-Arm's Length

Canada Education Savings Grants	Periodic Child Care Expense Amount
Canada Learning Bonds	Registered Disability Savings Plan (RDSP)
Child Care Expenses	Registered Education Savings Plan (RESP)
Child Support	Retiring Allowance
Common-Law Partner	Spousal Support
Death Benefit	Spouse
Deferred Income Plans	Support Amount
Disability Supports Deduction	Tax Free Savings Account (TFSA)
Earned Income (Child Care Expenses)	

References

9-214.   For more detailed study of the material in this Chapter, we refer you to the following:

ITA 56	Amounts To Be Included In Income For Year
ITA 56.1	Support
ITA 60	Other Deductions
ITA 60.1	Support
ITA 62	Moving Expenses
ITA 63	Child Care Expenses
ITA 64	Disability Supports Deduction
ITA 74.1(1)	Transfers And Loans To Spouse Or Common-Law Partner
ITA 74.1(2)	Transfers And Loans To Minors
ITA 74.2	Gain Or Loss Deemed That Of Lender Or Transferor
ITA 74.5	Transfers For Fair Market Consideration
ITA 146.1	Registered Education Savings Plans
ITA 146.2	Tax-Free Savings Accounts
ITA 146.4	Registered Disability Savings Plan
ITR 300	Capital Element Of Annuity Payments
IC 93-3R2	Registered Education Savings Plans
S1-F1-C3	Disability Supports Deduction
S1-F2-C3	Scholarships, Research Grants, And Other Education Assistance
S1-F3-C1	Child Care Expense Deduction
S1-F3-C3	Support Payments
S1-F3-C4	Moving Expenses
S1-F5-C1	Related Persons And Dealing At Arm's Length
S2-F1-C2	Retiring Allowances
S3-F10-C1	Qualified Investments - RRSPs, RESPs, RRIFs, RDSPs, and TFSAs.
S3-F10-C2	Prohibited Investments - RRSPs, RRIFs and TFSAs.
IT-209R	Inter Vivos Gifts Of Capital Property To Individuals Directly or Through Trusts
IT-325R2	Property Transfers After Separation, Divorce And Annulment
IT-499R	Superannuation Or Pension Benefits
IT-508R	Death Benefits
IT-510	Transfers And Loans Of Property Made After May 22, 1985 To A Related Minor
IT-511R	Interspousal And Certain Other Transfers And Loans Of Property
RC4092	Registered Education Savings Plans
RC4460	Registered Disability Savings Plan
RC4466	Tax Free Savings Account

Problems For Self Study (Online)

To provide practice in problem solving, there are Self Study and Supplementary Self Study problems available on the Companion Website.

Within the text we have provided an indication of when it would be appropriate to work each Self Study problem. The detailed solutions for Self Study problems can be found in the print and online Study Guide.

We provide the Supplementary Self Study problems for those who would like additional practice in problem solving. The detailed solutions for the Supplementary Self Study problems are available online, not in the Study Guide.

The .PDF file "Self Study Problems for Volume 1" on the Companion Website contains the following for Chapter 9:

- 13 Self Study problems,
- 8 Supplementary Self Study problems, and
- detailed solutions for the Supplementary Self Study problems.

Assignment Problems

(The solutions for these problems are only available in
the solutions manual that has been provided to your instructor.)

Assignment Problem Nine - 1
(Death Benefits)
On December 15, 2017, Jasmine Li dies when the motorcycle she was driving hit a raccoon. She was 52 years old at the time of her death. She is survived only by her 23 year old son, Mark Li.

Jasmine had been a full time employee of Arboor Landscapers for many years. In recognition of her long time service, the business decides to pay her a death benefit of $12,000. It will be in annual instalments of $4,000 per year, beginning on December 31, 2017. The payments will be made to her son, Mark.

Required: What effect will this death benefit have on the Net Income For Tax Purposes of Mark Li and Ms. Li in 2017 and in subsequent years?

Assignment Problem Nine - 2
(Moving Expenses)
Ms. Latricia Mode has worked diligently for a small company in Edmonton for several years, but has become increasingly dissatisfied with her progress in the organization. After the president's totally incompetent daughter was promoted, she resigned as of May 1, 2017.

She had already been searching for a new position and, after a much needed vacation in Europe, she found a position in Winnipeg that offered her outstanding opportunities for promotion. After some negotiation about benefits, she agreed to accept the position at a starting salary of $4,000 per month. She assumed her new duties on November 1, 2017.

After accepting the job, Latricia flew to Winnipeg in order to find living quarters. After 3 days she purchased a suitable house. In order to acquire furnishings, she remained in Winnipeg an additional four days after the acquisition. Her expenses for this 7 day trip were as follows:

Assignment Problems

Air Fare (Edmonton - Winnipeg, Return)	$ 586
Car Rental (7 Days At $45)	315
Hotel (7 Nights At $122)	854
Food (7 Days - Total)	455

On her return to Edmonton, she received the following statements from her attorney:

Real Estate Commission - Old Home	$ 16,800
Legal Fees - Old Home	1,800
Unpaid Property Taxes On Old Home To Date Of Sale	1,350
Legal Fees - New Home	1,950

On October 1, after supervising the final packing of her property and its removal from the old house, Latricia spent 2 days in an Edmonton hotel while she finalized arrangements for her departure. Expenses during these 2 days were as follows:

Hotel (2 Nights At $115)	$230
Food (2 Days - Total)	26

On October 3, she leaves Edmonton by automobile, arriving in Winnipeg on October 7. The trip is 1,304 kilometers. As her new residence is not yet available, she lives in a hotel in Winnipeg until October 28. Her expenses for the period October 3 through 28 are as follows:

Gasoline Purchased During The Trip	$ 297
Hotel (4 Nights En Route+21 Nights In Winnipeg At $135)	3,375
Food (25 Days - Total)	1,820

On moving into the new residence, Latricia is required to pay the moving company a total of $2,850. This fee includes $725 for the 23 days of storage required because the new home was not available when the furnishings arrived.

Latricia's only income for 2017 was employment income and the net amounts to be included in her Net Income For Tax Purposes are as follows:

Old Job (4 Months)	$14,000
New Job (2 Months)	8,000
Net Employment Income	**$22,000**

Latricia's new employer did not provide any reimbursement for moving expenses. Latricia will use the simplified method of determining vehicle and food costs in calculating her moving expenses. Assume that the relevant flat rate for vehicle expenses is $0.435 for Alberta and $0.469 for Manitoba, and the flat rate for meals is $51 per day.

Required: Calculate the maximum allowable moving expenses that Latricia can deduct from her Net Income For Tax Purposes for 2017 and any amount that can be carried forward to a subsequent year.

Assignment Problem Nine - 3
(Child Care Expenses)

Andrew Brock operates an unincorporated business which, in most years, has been very successful, producing a net business income of more than $200,000 per year. However, in 2017, due to some very bad inventory decisions, his gross revenues are only $125,000 which result in net business income for tax purposes of $24,000. Andrew has no other source of income during 2017.

During a slack period of business activity, Andrew enrolled in an organizational behaviour course at a local university. The course lasted 7 weeks and required a minimum of 12 hours of work each week.

His wife, Andrea Brock is an accountant for a large publicly traded company. For 2017, her Taxable Income includes the following amounts:

Gross Salary	$ 92,300
Registered Pension Plan Contributions	(4,000)
Fees For Preparing Tax Returns For Friends And Family	12,700
Stock Option Benefit	4,100
Taxable Capital Gains	8,500
Interest Income	7,200
Taxable Income	**$120,800**

In January of 2017, as the result of a serious snowboarding accident, Andrea was hospitalized for a period of one week. Subsequent to her release, she was in a wheel chair for an additional 6 weeks. A doctor has certified that, during this 7 week period, Andrea was not capable of caring for her children.

During 2017, the couple incurred actual child costs of $350 per week for 50 weeks. During the remaining two weeks of the year, the couple arranged their schedules so that they could provide their own child care.

Required: Determine the maximum amount that can be deducted by Mr. and Mrs. Brock for the year ending December 31, 2017 for child care expenses under the following assumptions:

A. They have two children, neither of whom qualify for the disability tax credit. The children are 2 and 12 years old.

B. They have three children. Their ages are 2, 4, and 12 years old. The 2 year old is sufficiently disabled that he qualifies for the disability tax credit.

Assignment Problem Nine - 4
(Pension Income Splitting With OAS)

Alex Barrett is 68 years old and his wife of many years, Laura Barrett, is 70 years old. They are both retired and, other than the aches and pains that go with advancing years, they are both in good health.

They have no deductions to be used in the determination of Taxable Income and their respective incomes for the 2017 taxation year are as follows:

	Alex	Laura
OAS Payments	$ 7,000	$ 7,000
Canada Pension Plan Receipts	11,000	3,000
RPP Receipts	52,000	Nil
Interest	2,000	500
Net Income For Tax Purposes And Taxable Income	**$72,000**	**$10,500**

The only tax credits that are available to Alex and Laura are the following:

- basic personal
- spousal
- age
- pension income

Required: Determine the savings in federal Tax Payable that would arise if Alex and Laura made maximum use of the pension income splitting provisions. Describe (without calculations) the factors that created the difference in the combined Tax Payable.

Assignment Problem Nine - 5
(Other Income And Deductions Including RESP)

Viva Houde's divorce settlement resulted in her having custody of her two children. Her daughter Lacy is 8 years old and her son Mark is 10 years old. They are both in good health. The agreement calls for her to receive child support payments of $2,000 per month, as well as spousal support of $1,500 per month. During 2017, she received all of these payments.

In order to get a fresh start in life, she enrolled in a co-op program at Western University in London, Ontario. She was very successful during the winter term (January through April, 2017). The program requires her to work in her field during the summer, with her first placement being Timmins, Ontario during the period May to August, 2017. Her employment income for this period was $8,000.

In late August she returned to London and resumed full time studies during the fall term (September through December, 2017). She was also able to obtain a part time job in her field in London. During these four months she had employment income of $1,600.

The eligible moving costs associated with moving herself and her children to Timmins for the summer work term totaled $1,200. The costs for the move back to London were $1,350.

In addition to her support payments and employment income, Viva received the following amounts:

Scholarship Granted By University For The Fall Semester	4,300
Eligible Dividends Received	2,600
Inheritance From Rich Uncle	22,000
TFSA Withdrawal	4,000

Throughout the year, Viva required assistance with her children. During the period January through April, the costs in London totaled $1,950. In Timmins, she incurred costs of $1,725. After returning to London for the fall term, her costs for the September through December period were $2,175.

During 2017, Viva establishes RESPs for both of her children. She contributes $1,500 to each of these plans.

Required: Determine the minimum Net Income For Tax Purposes that Viva will report for the 2017 taxation year. Provide reasons for omitting items that you have not included in your calculations. Also, indicate any amounts that can be carried forward to future years.

Assignment Problem Nine - 6
(Non-Arm's Length Transfer Of Shares)

Erik Gladstone owns 10,000 shares of Publix Inc., a publicly traded Canadian corporation. These shares were acquired at a cost, including brokerage fees, of $125,000. Based on current trading values, the shares are now worth $175,000.

The following four Cases make different assumptions as to the identity of the purchaser, the circumstances of the sale, and the proceeds of disposition. In each Case, assume that the purchaser immediately resells the shares for their fair market value of $175,000.

Case 1   Because Erik needs cash to acquire a condominium for his new girl friend, he sells the shares to an arm's length party for $175,000.

Case 2   As part of a settlement with his previous spouse, Erik gifts the shares to his 16 year old daughter. She sells the shares and uses the proceeds to finance her continued education abroad.

Case 3   Erik sells the shares to his impoverished sister for $100,000 to create a loss as he has realized significant capital gains during the current year. Since his sister has no other source of income, she will be taxed on the gain from the resale at the minimum federal rate.

Case 4   Erik's mother has realized a large amount of capital gains during the current year. To help his mother (and because he could really use the cash), Erik sells the shares to her for $250,000. She plans to use the loss on the immediate resale to offset her capital gains.

Required: For each of the Cases, advise Erik of the tax consequences that will result from the disposition and indicate the tax consequences to the purchaser of the shares when they are resold. In addition, in Cases 3 and 4, indicate whether the stated tax planning objective was achieved.

Assignment Problem Nine - 7
(Non-Arm's Length Transfer Of Depreciable Asset)

During 2017, Joey Zieman sells three depreciable assets. In each case, the asset that is sold is the last one in its class.

Asset A   This asset has a capital cost of $123,400 and, at January 1, 2017, the UCC balance in its class was $87,323. The asset is sold to Joey's father for its fair market value of $53,200.

Asset B   This asset has a capital cost of $87,600 and, at January 1, 2017, the UCC balance in its class was $62,246. The asset is sold to Joey's mother for its fair market value of $92,500.

Asset C   This asset has a capital cost of $163,400 and, at January 1, 2017, the UCC balance in its class is $93,472. The asset is sold to Joey's sister for its fair market value of $110,000.

Required: For each of the three dispositions, indicate the tax consequences for Joey that result from the sale. In addition, indicate the tax values that will be used by the transferee subsequent to the transfer.

Assignment Problem Nine - 8
(Deemed Dispositions On Death And Emigration)

Kacy Conner is 67 years old and has been married to Jason Conner for over 30 years. They have one son, Karson who is a very successful organic farmer.

On January 1, 2017, Kacy owns the following properties:

Farm Land   Kacy owns farm land with a cost of $340,000 and a current fair market value of $525,000. The land is farmed by Kacy's son Karson.

Conner Ltd.   Conner Ltd. is a Canadian controlled private company. Kacy started this Company several years ago with an investment of $210,000. She owns 100 percent of the voting shares. It is estimated that these shares are now worth $450,000. It is not a qualified small business corporation for purposes of the lifetime capital gains deduction.

Sololex Inc.   Kacy owns 4,000 shares of Sololex Inc., a Canadian public company. These shares were purchased for $8.00 per share. They are currently trading at $8.50 per share.

Rental Property   Kacy owns a rental property that was acquired for $850,000. At the time of the acquisition, the estimated value of the land was $150,000. The property has been appraised at a value of $975,000, with the land component contributing $175,000 to this value. The UCC balance for the building is $632,218

Assignment Problems

Required: Assuming that no elections are made and that normal deemed disposition values apply, explain the tax consequences to Kacy or her estate in each of the following Cases:

A. Kacy dies on January 4, 2017, leaving all of her property to her son Karson.
B. Kacy dies on January 4, 2017, leaving all of her property to her husband Jason.
C. Kacy departs from Canada and ceases to be a resident on January 4, 2017.

Assignment Problem Nine - 9
(Transfers To A Spouse - Income Attribution)

Jason Holt has owned a number of rental properties for many years. He has been married to Geena Holt for 5 years. Their pre-nuptial agreement requires Jason to gift a rental property to Geena on each 5th anniversary of their marriage.

On January 1, 2017, as required by their pre-nuptial agreement, Jason gifts one of the rental properties to Geena. Information on this property is as follows:

	Land	Building
Original Cost	$123,000	$387,000
Fair Market Value - Date Of Transfer	167,000	426,000
UCC - Date Of Transfer	N/A	299,772

During 2017, the property had a net rental income, before the deduction of CCA, of $23,451. Geena plans to deduct maximum CCA.

On January 1, 2018, after concluding that other investments would provide a better return, Geena sells the rental property for $650,000. At this time, an appraisal indicates that the fair market value of the land has increased to $175,000, leaving $475,000 ($650,000 - $175,000) to be allocated to the building.

Required: Determine the tax effects associated with the transfer and subsequent sale of the property for both Mr. and Mrs. Holt assuming:

A. The facts are as stated in the problem and that Mr. Holt does not elect out of ITA 73(1).

B. The pre-nuptial agreement requires that Geena purchase the property for its fair market value, using her own funds. On this sale, Mr. Holt elects out of ITA 73(1).

Assignment Problem Nine - 10
(Income Attribution)

On January 1, 2017, Ms. Fawn Halpern owned 9,500 shares of Zunit Inc., a Canadian public company. These shares were acquired several years ago at a cost of $23.50 per share, a total investment of $223,250.

During 2017, the following transactions occur:

- On February 1, she gives 3,500 of these shares to her common-law partner Melvin Young. On this date, the shares are trading at $25.00 per share. Fawn does not elect out of ITA 73(1).

- On March 1, she gives the remaining 6,000 shares to her 15 year old daughter Clare. At this time the price of the shares has fallen to $22.50.

- On July 1 and September 1, the Zunit Inc. shares pay an eligible dividend of $0.80 per share.

- On December 1, both Melvin and Clare sell all of the shares they have received for $26.25 per share.

Required:

A. Determine the total Net Income For Tax Purposes to be recorded for the 2017 taxation year by Fawn, her common-law partner Melvin, and her daughter Clare, as a result of the preceding transactions.

B. How would your answer change if Fawn died on July 15, 2017?

Assignment Problem Nine - 11
(Gifts And Income Attribution)

Valerie Nixon is a partner in a national CPA firm. Her income normally exceeds $350,000. She is married to Bunny Blake, a former Ms. World contestant.

Valerie and Bunny have two adopted children. Their son, Richard is 14 years old while their daughter, Patricia is 19 years old. To this point in time, Valerie has not gifted or sold property to any of the members of her immediate family.

With her high level of income, Valerie has accumulated a significant amount of investment assets. Her current portfolio contains the following items:

- Shares in a Canadian controlled private company, **Nixon Distributors**. Valerie is the only shareholder of this Company, an enterprise she started several years ago with an investment of $$823,000. It is estimated that the shares are currently worth $1,800,000. Nixon Distributors is not a qualified small business corporation for purposes of the lifetime capital gains deduction.

- Shares of **Royal Bank**. The 15,000 shares that she holds have an adjusted cost base of $1,050,000. Their current fair market value is $1,230,000.

- As she grew up in rural Ontario, Valerie has always had a love of farming. This is reflected in a holding of **Farm Land** that she acquired several years ago for $650,000. It is estimated that the current fair market value of this land is $960,000. Bunny operates the farm on a full time basis to grow organic vegetables.

- A 10 unit residential **Rental Property** that she purchased for $1,300,000. At the time of the purchase, the value of the land was estimated to be $400,000. At January 1 of the current year, the UCC of the property was $749,124. A recent appraisal indicates that the fair market value of the land has increased to $600,000 and the fair market value of the building has increased to $1,300,000.

Valerie has been diagnosed with terminal cancer, with her doctor indicating that she has less than two years to live. Given this, she would like to begin gifting her properties to Bunny, Richard, and Patricia. In the case of gifts to Bunny, she will not elect out of ITA 73(1).

Assume the recipient of the gift sells the property prior to Valerie's death.

Required: For each of the four listed properties, provide the following information. Your answer should include the different results related to the three possible gift recipients.

1. The tax consequences to Valerie at the time of the gift.

2. The tax cost of the properties to the recipient of the gift.

3. The tax treatment of any income on the property subsequent to the gift and before the property is sold.

4. The tax consequences that would result from a subsequent sale of the gifted property, (prior to Valerie's death), at a price that is $100,000 more than the fair market value at the time of the gift. In the case of the rental property, assume that the extra $100,000 is allocated to the building, with no change in the value of the land. Also in the case of the rental property, assume that the recipient of the gift does not deduct CCA prior to the sale.

Assignment Problems

Assignment Problem Nine - 12
(Comprehensive Case Covering Chapters 1 to 9)
Family Information

Spencer James is 41 years old. He has been married to Suzanne James for over 20 years. The couple have three children. All members of the family are in good health. Information on the children is as follows:

Charles And Charlene are 8 year old twins. During 2017, each of the twins received eligible dividends of $1,000 on public company shares that were gifted to them by their father in July, 2016. At the time of the gift, each block of shares had a fair market value of $9,500. Spencer had acquired the two blocks of shares at a cost of $8,000 each. In December, 2017, each twin sold the shares for $10,000.

Charlton is 19 years old and attends university on a full time basis for 4 months of the year. Spencer and Suzanne pay his tuition fees of $6,300, along with textbook costs of $650. He has agreed to transfer the maximum amount of his tuition credit to his father. Charlton lives with Spencer and Suzanne. His only income for the year is from the sale of shares purchased from Spencer as described in the following text.

In June, 2017, Spencer sells shares with an adjusted cost base of $28,000 and a fair market value of $36,500 to his son, Charlton. In order to provide Charlton with money to buy a car and to create a capital loss for himself, he sells the shares to Charlton for $5,000. Charlton sells the shares in September for $42,000.

Because of their work demands, Spencer and Suzanne have child care costs for the two twins of $250 per week for 48 weeks. During the remaining 4 weeks, the twins are sent to summer camp at a cost of $250 per child per week.

Suzanne's Income Information

Suzanne operates a mail order business out of rented space. As it is furnished business space, the business does not own any capital assets. For 2017, her net business income, calculated on the basis of tax rules was $70,544.

During 2017, Suzanne spent 6 consecutive weeks attending a specialized business accounting program at a designated educational institution. She received a tuition tax receipt that stated she had paid $2,000 in tuition fees.

In January, 2016, Spencer gifted Suzanne a residential rental property. This property had cost Spencer $500,000 several years ago, with $100,000 of this amount allocated to the land and $400,000 allocated to the building. At the time of the gift, an appraisal indicates that the fair market value of the building was $530,000, allocated $110,000 to the land and $420,000 to the building. The building had a January 1, 2016 UCC of $376,320. Spencer did not recognize this transaction in his 2016 tax return.

For the year ending December 31, 2016, Suzanne had net rental income, after the deduction of maximum CCA, of $16,400.

In November, 2017, after experiencing significant difficulties with tenants, Suzanne lists the property for sale. It sells within a month for $555,000, with $120,000 of this total allocated to the land and $435,000 allocated to the building. The net rental income, prior to the deduction of CCA, was $15,300 for 2017.

Spencer's Employment Information

Spencer is employed by a Canadian public company. His annual salary is $105,500, none of which is commissions. His employer withheld the following amounts from his remuneration:

EI Premiums	$ 836
CPP Contributions	2,564
Professional Association Dues	1,200
Registered Pension Plan Contributions	4,200

Spencer's employer made a matching RPP contribution of $4,200.

Because of his excellent performance during 2017, Spencer was awarded a bonus of $20,000. Of this total, $10,000 will be paid in 2017, with the balance being paid in June, 2018.

Spencer is provided with an automobile by his employer. The vehicle is leased by the employer at a rate of $523 per month, including a payment of $51 per month for insurance. The automobile is available to Spencer for 11 months during 2017. During the remaining month, the employer required that it be returned to their garage. Total milage for 2017 is 58,000 kilometers, only 5,000 of which are for personal use.

On their birthday, Spencer's employer provides every employee with a $1,000 gift certificate that can be used for merchandise on Amazon (one of the largest online retailers). In addition, at Christmas, each employee receives a basket of gourmet food and wine. The value of this basket is $350.

During 2017, Spencer spent $5,600 on meals and entertainment of his employer's customers. The employer's policy is to reimburse 80 percent of these costs.

For the last ten years, Spencer has worked in a rural office of his employer. The rural office is located 110 kilometers from the Company's head office in a major Canadian city. As his family has become less enchanted with the country life style, Spencer has transferred to the Company's city office. The move involves selling his rural home and acquiring a city home. The various cash outflows associated with the move are as follows:

Real Estate Commissions - Old Home	$11,620
Legal Fees - Old Home	1,250
Loss - Old Home	18,000
Unpaid Property Taxes - Old Home	625
Cleaning And Minor Repairs - Old Home	450
Legal Fees - New Home	1,460
Cost Of Moving Household Goods	3,460

While Spencer's employer does not provide a moving allowance, the company agrees to compensate him for his $18,000 loss on his old home as management expects him to spend the time he spent commuting at the office.

Other Information

1. The family's medical expenses for 2017 were as follows:

Spencer	$ 4,600
Suzanne*	8,600
Charles	4,700
Charlene	3,600
Total Medical Expenses	$21,500

*This medical expense was for a brow lift to remove wrinkles and improve the appearance of Suzanne's forehead.

2. In January, 2017, Spencer's father dies. He was an unsuccessful pig farmer who agonized over the death of each pig. The major asset in his father's estate is a family farm operation which is left to Spencer (other assets go to Spencer's mother and siblings). Information on the farm's assets is as follows:

Land   The farm land had an adjusted cost base of $250,000. At the time of the father's death, the fair market value was $375,000.

Building   The building had a capital cost of $325,000, a fair market value at the time of the father's death of $275,000, and a UCC of $253,000.

Equipment   The equipment had a capital cost $130,000, a fair market value at the time of death of $110,000, and a UCC of $95,000.

The executors of the father's estate elect to transfer the land at its fair market value in order to use up accumulated capital losses on other assets. The building and equipment are transferred at the UCC values.

3. As Spencer, and especially his family, have no interest in running a pig farm, he sells the inherited property to his brother in March, as soon as he has title. His brother agrees to purchase the assets for the fair market values determined by the executors, specifically $375,000 for the land, $275,000 for the building and $110,000 for the equipment.

4. In memory of his father, Spencer donates $8,400 on his father's birthday in 2017 to Hearts On Noses - A Mini Pig Sanctuary. This registered charity helps preserve the lives of injured, abused, abandoned and neglected pot bellied pigs. This was the first time that either Spencer or Suzanne have ever made a contribution to a registered charity.

5. During 2017, Spencer makes a $4,000 contribution to his Tax Free Savings Account and $5,000 to Suzanne's. He also makes a $2,000 contribution ($1,000 per child) to the family Registered Education Savings Plan established for Charles and Charlene.

Required:

A. Determine Suzanne's federal Tax Payable and her CPP liability for 2017. In calculating Suzanne's federal Tax Payable, assume that Spencer's Taxable Income exceeds $200,000.

B. Determine Spencer's federal Tax Payable for 2017.

In determining these amounts, ignore GST, PST and HST considerations.

Assignment Problem Nine - 13
(Comprehensive Case Covering Chapters 1 to 9)

Ms. Peta Jansan is 37 years old and divorced from her former spouse. She has two children from the marriage, Lotte, aged 5 and Bram, aged 9. Neither of these children have any 2017 income.

The divorce decree, which was issued in 2015, requires her former spouse to pay $3,000 per month in child support and an additional $1,000 per month in spousal support. While all of the payments for previous years have been made, during 2017, her former spouse has experienced financial difficulties and has paid only $40,000 of the required amounts.

Ms. Jansan also provides care for her 85 year old grandfather who lives with her and her children. While her grandfather is not mentally or physically infirm, his 2017 income was only $7,950, leaving him as a dependant of Ms. Jansan.

Ms. Jansan is employed by Dutch Foods Ltd., a large public company. For 2017, she has a base salary of $75,000 per year. During 2016, she was awarded a bonus of $19,500, all of which was paid in January, 2017.

For her employment related travel, the company provides her with an automobile which the company leases for $560 per month. Ms. Jansan is required to pay all of her own operating and maintenance costs on the automobile. During 2017, these costs totaled $6,300. The automobile was available for use for 11 months during 2017 and was driven a total of 43,360 kilometers. Of these kilometers, all but 8,240 were for employment related use.

Her employer withheld the following amounts from her 2017 earnings:

RPP Contributions	$3,400
EI Premiums	836
CPP Contributions	2,564
Life Insurance Premiums	250

Her employer pays her Alberta provincial health care premium of $44 per month.

During 2017, Ms. Jansan is transferred by Dutch Foods Ltd. from their Edmonton office to their Calgary office. The Company has agreed to fully compensate her for any loss on the sale of her Edmonton house, but will not compensate her for the legal fees associated with the sale. The Company will provide her with a $15,000 payment when she purchases a home in order to compensate her for the higher cost of Calgary housing.

Dutch Foods Ltd. is also providing her with a $200,000 interest free housing loan to help finance her new house purchase. This loan is granted on April 1, 2017 and must be repaid at the end of five years. In addition to these other amounts, the Company is providing a $10,000 allowance to cover any additional costs of the move.

On January 3, 2017, Ms. Jansan flies to Calgary at a cost of $325 to locate a new residence for her and her family. During the three days that she is there, her food and lodging costs total $575. Both the air fare and the food and lodging costs are reimbursed by Dutch Foods Ltd. After considering the properties that she has seen, she makes an offer on a property on January 10. The offer is accepted that same day.

Later that month she sells her Edmonton home which she purchased for $265,000 in 2015. The house is sold for $257,800. While Ms. Jansan managed to sell the house without using a real estate agent, legal fees associated with the sale total $950.

Ms. Jansan and her family leave Edmonton on March 15 and arrive in Calgary that same day. She uses her Company's car to transport herself and her family. This milage is included in the 43,360 kilometer total and is viewed as being employment related. As the family brought a picnic lunch for the trip, she ignores food costs for the day.

Unfortunately, her new Calgary home is not available until April 3 and, as a consequence, she, her children and her grandfather stay in a Calgary suite hotel from March 15 through April 3 (19 days).

The rate for a two room suite is $325 per day, but Ms. Jansan has a discount voucher that gives her a rate of $200 per day for a week (7 nights).

Assume that the 2017 rate for meals is $51 per day per person.

The cost for moving her household effects and leaving them in storage until her Calgary home was ready totaled $3,540. Her legal fees associated with acquiring the Calgary home are $600.

Ms. Jansan has belonged to her employer's stock purchase plan since 2015. In that year she acquired 360 shares at $5.00 per share. In 2016, she acquired an additional 500 shares at $5.25 per share.

On February 1, 2017, she acquired 400 more shares at $6.00 per share. On July 1, 2017, all of her shares paid an eligible dividend of $0.30 per share. In order to help finance some of the costs of the move, she sold 900 of these shares in December, 2017 at $6.10 per share.

On January 1, 2017, Ms. Jansan purchases an annuity for $28,733. The annuity was purchased with after-tax funds and will provide a payment of $5,000 at the end of each year for eight years. Given its price, the effective yield on the annuity is 8 percent.

During 2017, Ms. Jansan contributes $5,500 to her Tax Free Savings Account (TFSA) and $5,500 to a TFSA that she opens in her grandfather's name.

Before moving to Calgary, child care costs in Edmonton were $200 per week for 11 weeks. In Calgary, the weekly cost increased to $250 per week and was paid for a total of 36 weeks. In the summer, both children spent four weeks at an exclusive summer camp. The fees at this camp were $500 per child per week.

The 2017 medical expenses for Ms. Jansan and her dependants, which were all paid for by Ms. Jansan, are as follows:

Ms. Jansan	$ 465
Lotte	493
Bram	245
Grandfather	12,473
Total Medical Expenses	$13,676

Assume a prescribed rate of 2 percent during all four quarters of 2017.

Required: Calculate the following for Ms. Jansan:

- her minimum 2017 Net Income For Tax Purposes,
- her minimum 2017 Taxable Income,
- her minimum 2017 federal Tax Payable.

Ignore GST and HST considerations, as well as any amounts of income tax that would have been withheld by Ms. Jansan's employer.

CHAPTER 10

Retirement Savings And Other Special Income Arrangements

Planning For Retirement

Introduction

10-1.   Increasing life expectancies and lower birth rates are creating a situation in which the portion of the Canadian population that is of retirement age has been increasing, and will continue to do so. This, in turn, leads to the need to allocate a growing proportion of our society's resources to caring for this older segment of the population. There are enormous social and economic considerations resulting from this trend and, given the large and growing political clout of Canadian senior citizens, it is not a situation that the government can ignore.

Providing Consistency

10-2.   Minimal financial requirements for the retirement years are provided by Old Age Security (OAS) payments and the Canada Pension Plan (CPP) system. However, for 2017, the maximum payment under the Canada Pension Plan is $13,300 per year for a person with no disability. When this is combined with the current OAS payments of about $7,000 per year, the total does not provide for the lifestyle most individuals would like to enjoy during their retirement years. In response to this situation, the Canadian income tax system contains a number of provisions that encourage the development of various private retirement savings arrangements to supplement benefits provided under the government provided plans. These include:

- Registered Retirement Savings Plans (RRSPs)
- Registered Pension Plans (RPPs), including Individual Pension Plans
- Target Benefit Plans
- Pooled Registered Pension Plans
- Registered Retirement Income Funds (RRIFs)
- Deferred Profit Sharing Plans (DPSPs)

10-3.   The current retirement savings system was initiated in 1990. At the heart of this system is the concept that retirement savings should have an annual limit that is consistently applied to all types of plans. In general, this limit is defined in terms of an annual amount of contributions to a money purchase (a.k.a., defined contribution) Registered Pension Plan. The amount of this limit, designated the money purchase limit, is subject to annual indexing.

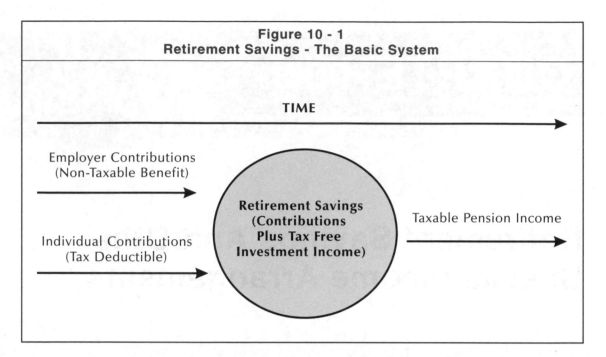

Figure 10 - 1
Retirement Savings - The Basic System

10-4. The major problem faced by the government in designing the current system was to ensure that, despite the variety of retirement savings vehicles available, the annual contribution limit was applied in a consistent manner, without regard to the variety of retirement savings vehicles used by an individual, or the manner in which the ultimate retirement benefit was determined.

10-5. The detailed provisions related to the different types of tax assisted retirement savings plans show considerable variation. For example, Registered Pension Plans and Deferred Profit Sharing Plans require employer sponsorship. In contrast, any Canadian resident can establish a Registered Retirement Savings Plan or a Registered Retirement Income Fund.

10-6. Despite such variations, the basic idea underlying all of these plans is the same. They allow individuals to invest a considerable amount of funds into a trusteed arrangement. The amounts invested are either deductible to the taxpayer (RRSP contributions and employee RPP contributions) or can be paid by an employer without creating a taxable benefit (employer RPP and DPSP contributions). Inside the trusteed arrangement, the invested funds can earn income on a tax free basis for long periods of time. While all amounts will ultimately be subject to taxation, there is a substantial amount of tax deferral. This arrangement can be seen graphically in Figure 10-1.

10-7. You will recall that we also discussed registered savings plans in Chapter 9. The discussion in that Chapter covered Tax Free Savings Accounts (TFSAs), Registered Education Savings Plans (RESPs) and Registered Disability Savings Plans (RDSP). There is a major difference between those plans and the ones that are under consideration here. The contributions made to TFSAs, RESPs and RDSPs are not deductible. In contrast, the retirement savings plans covered in this chapter provide tax advantaged contribution arrangements. Contributions made by beneficiaries are tax deductible and contributions made by employers are not treated as taxable benefits. We would remind you that employer contributions to RPPs and DPSPs can be deducted when made by the employer.

Tax Deferred Savings
Sources Of Deferral
10-8. As shown in Figure 10-1, there are two basic sources for the investment funds going into retirement savings plans. First, for employed individuals, employers may make contributions to RPPs and DPSPs. As these contributions do not create a taxable benefit until they are withdrawn as retirement income, the employee has received a benefit on which the payment

of tax has been deferred, despite the fact that the employer has an immediate deduction.

10-9.   The second source of investment funds is the contributions made by employed individuals to RPPs, and by all individuals to RRSPs. As the individual can deduct these contributions against all types of income, they are the equivalent of receiving income on which the tax has been deferred.

10-10.   This means that, whether an employer has made contributions on behalf of the individual, or the individual has personally made the contributions, the taxes on the amounts involved have been deferred from the year of contribution to the year of withdrawal from the plan. This period may exceed 45 years for contributions made at the beginning of an individual's working life.

Tax Free Compounding

10-11.   Also of great importance is the fact that the income earned by investments contained in these plans is not taxed until it is withdrawn. This allows earnings to accumulate at before tax rates, rather than after tax rates. Given that such plans may be in place over long periods of time, this provides for a significantly larger accumulation of assets.   As illustrated in the following example, the importance of tax free accumulation should not be underestimated.

> **EXAMPLE** Mr. Kerr is a 35 year old taxpayer who pays taxes at a marginal rate of 45 percent. For the next 30 years, he has $5,000 per year of pre-tax income that he wishes to put aside for his anticipated retirement at age 65.
>
> **ANALYSIS**   If Mr. Kerr contributes this amount to an RRSP, it can be deducted and no taxes will be paid on the $5,000 per year of pre-tax income. If this $5,000 per year is invested in an RRSP at a 10 percent per annum rate of return, it will accumulate to $822,470 at the end of 30 years. If the full amount is withdrawn when he reaches age 65, and he is still paying taxes at a marginal rate of 45 percent, he will be left with after tax funds of $452,359.
>
> If Mr. Kerr had not invested in an RRSP, taxes at 45 percent would have been paid on the $5,000, leaving only $2,750 per year to invest. Further, if he invests these funds at 10 percent outside of an RRSP, his after tax return will only be 5.5 percent [(10%)(1-.45)]. At this after tax rate, the investment of $2,750 per year for 30 years would result in an accumulation of only $199,198 by the time Mr. Kerr is 65 years old, less than half of the after tax accumulation resulting from using the RRSP approach.

10-12.   In effect, the deferral of taxes on the deductible contributions, as well as the deferral of tax on the income from fund investments, has allowed for a larger amount of resources being available for retirement. As this fairly realistic example illustrates, the amounts involved can be very substantial.

Early Contributions

10-13.   The availability of tax free compounding in an RRSP makes it advantageous to contribute as early as possible. RRSP contributions for 2017 can be made as early as January 1, 2017, or as late as 60 days after the end of 2017. It can be demonstrated that, over a contribution period of 35 years, making contributions at the earliest date as opposed to the latest date can result in a 10 percent increase in the balance in the plan.

Advantages At Retirement

10-14.   The use of these tax deferred retirement savings plans may have additional advantages. If either federal or provincial tax rates have been lowered, the effective tax rate at the time of withdrawal may be lower than the rate when the contributions are made. Note, however, the opposite effect may arise if federal or provincial rates are increased.

10-15.   In addition, for some individuals, retirement may result in a sufficient reduction in income that they find themselves in a lower tax bracket. Someone who spends their working life subject to a 50 percent tax rate could find that, subsequent to retirement, they are subject to taxes at 25 percent. As this lower rate would apply to amounts withdrawn from a retirement savings plan, the deferral of taxation on contributions and investment earnings will result in an absolute reduction in taxes paid (tax avoidance).

10-16.   Even if the individual is not paying taxes at a lower rate after retirement, there are additional advantages associated with the funds taken out of these plans. The first $2,000 of eligible pension income entitles the recipient to a credit against federal Tax Payable each year equal to 15 percent of amounts received. This is worth $300 at the federal level alone, and can be increased to $600 per couple through the pension income splitting provisions. (See Chapter 9.)

Defined Benefit Vs. Money Purchase Plans

10-17.   A major problem in the design of Canada's retirement savings system is the fact that, unlike RRSPs, DPSPs, and RRIFs, RPPs may be designed to provide a specified benefit after retirement. Such plans are normally referred to as defined benefit plans, while other types of RPPs are referred to as money purchase (a.k.a., defined contribution) plans. A basic understanding of the difference between these two types of plans is essential to the comprehension of the material in this Chapter. In view of this, the following brief descriptions are provided:

Defined Benefit Plans   In defined benefit plans, the plan sponsor undertakes to provide a specified benefit, usually expressed as a percentage of earnings, for each year of qualifying service. For example, such a plan might require an employer to provide a retirement benefit equal to 2 percent of an employee's average lifetime earnings for each year of service. Thus, if an employee worked for 20 years and earned an average salary of $50,000 per year, the retirement benefit would be $20,000 per year [(2%)(20)($50,000)].

In promising this benefit, the employer has effectively agreed to make whatever amount of contributions is required to provide these benefits. The required amount of contributions will vary depending on a number of factors, the most important of which is earnings on fund assets. Employee turnover and employee life expectancy at retirement are also influential. In this type of plan, the employer is assuming all of the risk and uncertainty associated with these factors.

Money Purchase Plans (a.k.a. Defined Contribution Plans)   These plans are distinguished by the fact that the employer agrees to make specified contributions for each plan participant. A typical plan might find an employer agreeing to contribute 3 percent of each employee's annual wages to a fund that would be established to provide retirement benefits.   The employer would have no obligations beyond making the specified contributions and the employee would have no guarantee as to the amount of the retirement benefit that is to be received.

The actual benefit that will be received will be based on the amounts contributed and the rates of return earned on the investment of these contributions. In money purchase plans, it is the employee who is assuming the risk and uncertainty associated with investment of the contributed funds.

10-18.   Before leaving these descriptions we would note that, while the term is not usually applied to them, RRSPs, DPSPs, and RRIFs are essentially money purchase plans. That is, the benefits to be received from such plans are based on the amounts transferred into the plan and the earnings resulting from the investment of these amounts. Such plans do not guarantee that the individual will receive a specified benefit after retirement. Currently, the only widely used retirement savings arrangement that uses the defined benefit approach is the employer sponsored RPP. However, RPPs can take either form and, for some time now, employers have been moving away from assuming the risks associated with defined benefit plans.

10-19.   It is perhaps because of this trend that the government introduced Pooled Registered Pension Plans (PRPPs). These plans allow employers with a small number of employees to provide a defined contribution plan (a.k.a. money purchase plan) on a pooled basis with other employers. More recently they have introduced Target Benefit Plans for some employers. Both of these types of plans will be given some attention later in this Chapter.

Registered Retirement Savings Plans (RRSPs)

Basic Operations

Establishment

10-20.   The general rules for Registered Retirement Savings Plans (RRSPs) are contained in ITA 146. Under these rules, an RRSP is a trust with the individual as the beneficiary and a financial institution acting as the administrator. Financial institutions offering such plans include Canadian chartered banks, Canadian mutual funds, Canadian trust companies, Canadian credit unions, Canadian brokerage firms, and Canadian insurance companies.

10-21.   Registration of the plan results in the investor being able to deduct a limited amount of contributions to the plan for income tax purposes. Further, the individual is not subject to tax on the income earned by the assets in the plan until it is withdrawn.

Withdrawals

10-22.   Amounts that an individual withdraws from an RRSP must be included in income unless received under the Home Buyers' Plan or the Lifelong Learning Plan (these programs are discussed in Paragraphs 10-103 and 10-114, respectively). Depending on the amount withdrawn, the trustee will be required to withhold a percentage of the amount withdrawn as a partial payment towards the tax that will be assessed on the withdrawal.

10-23.   Withdrawals are treated as an ordinary income inclusion under ITA 56(1)(h), even if they were earned as dividends or capital gains within the plan. This latter point is important in that dividends and capital gains are normally taxed at more favourable rates than other types of income. This favourable treatment is lost when the amounts are earned inside an RRSP.

Investment Options For An RRSP

10-24.   There are two basic types of RRSPs. The managed RRSP is managed by the financial institution that holds the fund assets. The self-administered (a.k.a. self-directed) RRSP is managed by the taxpayer. For individuals who prefer to make their own investment decisions with respect to the fund assets, the self-administered type of plan is the obvious choice.

10-25.   An additional advantage of the self-administered type of plan is that the taxpayer can transfer securities that he already owns into the plan. However, with the availability of discount brokers charging minimal commissions, the importance of this advantage for many taxpayers has declined over time. As the RRSP is a separate taxable entity, such transfers are dispositions and any gains arising on the transfer will be subject to tax. Note, however, that ITA 40(2)(g)(iv) prevents the recognition of losses on such transfers.

> **EXAMPLE**   An individual transfers securities to his RRSP. The shares of Company A have an adjusted cost base of $5,000 and a fair market value of $7,000. The shares of Company B have an adjusted cost base of $5,000 and a fair market value of $4,000.

> **ANALYSIS**   While the individual would have to record a capital gain on the Company A shares of $2,000, the $1,000 loss on the shares of Company B cannot be deducted. Given this, if the taxpayer wishes to have Company B in his RRSP, it would be preferable to sell his holding and, at a later point in time, purchase the shares within the RRSP. Care should be taken to avoid the superficial loss rules (see Chapter 8).

10-26.   If the taxpayer's preference is to have a financial institution manage the plan, he will be confronted with a wide variety of choices. Managed funds include those that invest entirely in equity securities, funds that hold only long-term bonds, funds with mixed portfolios, and funds that specialize in one type of asset such as mortgages.

10-27.   Choosing between the alternatives involves an assessment of many factors, including the investment goals of the taxpayer, and the fees charged by the various plans. With hundreds of choices available, the decision can be a very difficult one. However, considering the amount of financial resources that may eventually be invested in RRSP assets, it is not a decision that should be made without a thorough investigation of the alternatives.

10-28.   Since an individual can own any number of separate RRSPs, it is possible to have both a self-administered and a managed plan. Further diversification could be achieved by having two or more types of managed plans. However, the extra effort and costs required to keep track of the multiple plans should be considered.

10-29.   The *Act* is flexible with respect to the types of investments that can be included in either a self-administered or a managed RRSP. ITR Part XLIX provides a detailed listing of the specific investment categories and includes publicly traded shares, mutual fund units, bonds, mortgages, warrants, and rights. The only significant restrictions relate to investments in the shares of private companies that are under the influence of the taxpayer, and direct investments in real estate.   There is no limit on foreign content (e.g., shares of U.S. public companies).   For a more complete discussion of qualified investments, see IT Folio S3-F10-C1, *Qualified Investments - RRSPs, RESPs, RRIFs, RDSPs, and TFSAs.*

10-30.   While it is not likely that this is a common problem, there are rules applicable to holdings of publicly traded securities where the RRSP registrant holds more than a 10 percent interest (number of shares or fair market value). These holdings are referred to as "prohibited investments" and, significant penalties apply if they are contained in either an RRSP, a RRIF or a TFSA. These investments are discussed in detail in IT Folio S3-F10-C2, *Prohibited Investments - RRSPs, RRIFs, and TFSAs.*

10-31.   It is interesting to note that an RRSP can provide a mortgage on Canadian real property to the registrant of the plan, provided that the mortgage is insured under the National Housing Act, or by some other company providing mortgage insurance. The extra costs associated with this insurance have served to limit the use of this option.

The Capital Gains And Dividend Problems

10-32.   As you are aware, when capital gains or eligible dividends are received directly by an individual, they are taxed at very favourable rates. We will not consider non-eligible dividends here as, in many circumstances, the shares of private companies cannot be held in RRSPs. As we noted in Chapter 7, an individual subject to Ontario's maximum rate of 53.5 percent, would be taxed on capital gains at 26.8 percent and eligible dividends at 39.3 percent.

10-33.   In contrast, when these types of income are earned inside an RRSP, they will be taxed as ordinary income when the amounts are distributed to the registrant. In effect, for an Ontario resident in the maximum tax bracket, any capital gains or eligible dividends earned inside an RRSP will be taxed at 53.5 percent.

10-34.   At first glance, this appears to be a very undesirable consequence of investing in an RRSP. However, this is mitigated by the fact that, for an individual with a specified amount of before tax funds to invest, a larger amount of funds can be invested since RRSP contributions are deductible.

> **EXAMPLE**   An individual has $10,000 in pre-tax income that he does not require for his current needs. His marginal tax rate is 52 percent on ordinary income and 37 percent on eligible dividends. He is considering investing in the shares of a Canadian public company in three alternative ways:
>
> - Investing the full $10,000 through an RRSP. Note that he can invest the full amount because the contribution is deductible.
> - Investing the after tax amount of $4,800 [($10,000)(1 - .52)] through a TFSA.
> - Investing the after tax amount of $4,800 directly, i.e., without using either type of plan, through a trading account.
>
> Assume that over the following 2 years the shares of the Canadian public company will increase in value by 50 percent. No dividends will be paid by the company during this period.
>
> At the end of the 2 year period, all available funds, including maximum withdrawals from the RRSP and the TFSA, will be used to acquire a residence.

ANALYSIS The result for the three alternatives are as follows:

RRSP Result

Deductible Contribution	$10,000
Increase In Value [(50%)($10,000)]	5,000
Available Withdrawal	$15,000
Tax On Withdrawal [(52%)($15,000)]	(7,800)
After Tax Funds Available	$ 7,200

TFSA Result

Initial Investment [($10,000)(1 - .52)]	$4,800
Increase In Value [(50%)($4,800)]	2,400
Available Withdrawal	$7,200
Tax On Withdrawal	Nil
After Tax Funds Available	$7,200

Direct Investment Result

Initial Investment [($10,000)(1 - .52)]	$4,800
Increase In Value [(50%)($4,800)]	2,400
Available Funds	$7,200
Tax On Capital Gain [(1/2)(52%)($2,400)]	(624)
After Tax Funds Available	$6,576

10-35. This simple example indicates that the benefits of being able to deduct contributions to an RRSP can more than offset the unfavourable tax treatment that is given to capital gains that are withdrawn from such plans. Using the RRSP results in an additional $624 ($7,200 - $6,576) in funds being available.

10-36. Note also that the deductibility of RRSP contributions and the resulting ability to invest a larger amount of funds offsets the fact that no taxes are assessed on the TFSA investment. Both the RRSP and the TFSA result in the individual having $7,200 in funds to use in acquiring a new residence.

Exercise Ten - 1

Subject: Comparison Of Dividends Earned In RRSP, TFSA And Directly

Brian Forthright has $20,000 in pre tax income that he does not need currently. He is trying to decide whether it would be better to contribute the $20,000 to his RRSP and deduct the full amount, or invest the after tax amount of these funds either in a TFSA or outside either plan. He will invest the available funds in preferred shares that pay an annual eligible dividend of 5 percent. At the end of 5 years, he will use all of the available funds for an extended vacation.

Brian's combined marginal tax rate on ordinary income is 40 percent and his combined tax rate on eligible dividends is 22 percent. Ignoring the effect of any reinvestment of the dividend income, determine which of the three alternatives will provide more funds for Brian's trip.

SOLUTION available in print and online Study Guide.

Figure 10 - 2
RRSP Deduction Limit Formula - ITA 146(1)

"RRSP deduction limit" of a taxpayer for a taxation year means the amount determined by the formula

$$A + B + R - C, \text{ where}$$

A is the taxpayer's **unused RRSP deduction room** at the end of the preceding taxation year,

B is the amount, if any, by which

(a) the lesser of the **RRSP dollar limit** for the year and 18% of the taxpayer's **earned income** for the preceding taxation year,

exceeds the total of all amounts each of which is

(b) the taxpayer's **pension adjustment** for the preceding taxation year in respect of an employer, or

(c) a **prescribed amount** in respect of the taxpayer for the year,

C is the taxpayer's net **past service pension adjustment** for the year, and

R is the taxpayer's total **pension adjustment reversal** for the year.

Example of relevant years   Contributions made during the first 60 days of 2018 and undeducted contributions made in years prior to 2017 can be deducted against the RRSP Deduction Limit for 2017. Adding to the confusion is the fact that the RRSP Deduction Limit for 2017 is based on Earned Income for the previous year (2016), as well as a Pension Adjustment that is calculated using 2016 figures.

Non-Deductible Financing Costs

10-37.   As a final point, it is important to note that interest paid on funds borrowed to finance RRSP contributions is not deductible. This suggests that it may not be desirable for an individual to borrow in order to make RRSP contributions. A complete analysis of this issue requires an estimate of how long the loan will be outstanding and a comparison of the individual's borrowing rate with his expected return on funds invested in the plan.

RRSP Deduction Limit

The Basic Formula

10-38.   At the heart of this retirement savings system is the RRSP Deduction Limit. It is this amount that determines the maximum contribution to an RRSP that can be deducted in a year. While this amount is sometimes referred to as the contribution limit, this is not an accurate description. The definition of RRSP Deduction Limit is found in ITA 146(1) and is reproduced in Figure 10-2. There are several technical terms included in this definition and they are highlighted in Figure 10-2 with bold, italic type. Explanations for each term will be provided in the material which follows.

10-39.   The RRSP Deduction Limit is neither a limit on contributions that can be made during the current year, nor a requirement that the contributions deducted in the current year be made in that year. A limited amount of non-deductible contributions can be made that are in excess of the RRSP Deduction Limit. Further, contributions made in earlier years that were not deducted in those years, or contributions made in the first 60 days of the following year, can be deducted under the RRSP Deduction Limit for the current year.

10-40.   The reason for using an Earned Income figure from a previous year is to allow an individual to determine his maximum contribution for the current year during the early part of that year. If the limit had been based on the current year's Earned Income, an individual would have to make contributions during the year based only on an estimate of his Earned Income, a situation that would often result in contributions that are over or under the limit.

10-41.   To assist taxpayers in dealing with this deduction limit calculation, the CRA issues an RRSP Deduction Limit Statement to individuals who have filed income tax returns. It is included with the Notice of Assessment and, assuming the return is filed on time, calculates the individual's maximum RRSP deduction for the year after the assessed year. The RRSP Statement is also available online through the CRA's My Account portal.

> **EXAMPLE**   The RRSP Statement for the 2017 return will normally be available online or through the mail during April or May, 2017. This Statement indicates the maximum RRSP deduction for 2017. Note that this maximum deduction can be made using contributions made prior to 2017 or in the first 60 days of 2018. There is no requirement that the deduction for 2017 be based on contributions made during 2017.

Unused RRSP Deduction Room

10-42.   As it is used in the Figure 10-2 formula, a taxpayer's Unused RRSP Deduction Room at the end of the preceding year is simply the cumulative total of all of the amounts determined under the formula for years prior to the current year, less any amounts that have been deducted in those years.

10-43.   This approach provides for a carry forward of deduction room that is not time limited. As a result, a taxpayer who lacks the funds to make a deductible contribution in a particular year does not lose the deduction room applicable to that year. The deduction room is carried forward and provides the basis for a deductible contribution in any future year.

RRSP Dollar Limit

10-44.   The RRSP Dollar Limit is defined in terms of the Money Purchase Limit that is specified in quantitative terms in ITA 147.1(1). The Money Purchase Limit is the annual ceiling applicable to contributions made to RPPs. Because of the one year lag in the data used for the RRSP Deduction Limit, the RRSP Dollar Limit is generally defined as the Money Purchase Limit for the preceding year.

10-45.   Money Purchase Limits and the RRSP Dollar Limits for years 2014 through 2018 are as follows:

Year	Money Purchase Limit	RRSP Dollar Limit
2014	24,930	24,270
2015	25,370	24,930
2016	26,010	25,370
2017	**26,230**	**26,010**
2018	Indexed	26,230

Earned Income

10-46.   Earned Income for RRSP purposes is defined in ITA 146(1). Note that Earned Income for child care expense purposes (see Chapter 9) is different than Earned Income for RRSP purposes. The basic idea underlying this definition of Earned Income for RRSP purposes is that the income to be included in this designation is earned by the individual, rather than received as the result of owning property. This means that interest, dividends, and capital gains are excluded from the definition.

10-47.   Surprisingly, however, net rental income is included, despite the fact that, for individuals, rental income is usually a form of property income. Another unusual feature of the definition is that it does not include either net or gross employment income in unaltered form. Rather, the net employment income component of Earned Income is a hybrid concept that excludes RPP contributions and is not used anywhere else in the determination of Net Income

For Tax Purposes. Note that the deductible portion of CPP contributions payable because of self employed income are deducted under subdivision e [ITA 60(e)]. Since this means that they do not affect the calculation of net business income, they do not affect the calculation of earned income for RRSP purposes.

10-48. As found in ITA 146(1), the basic components of Earned Income are as follows:

Additions

- Net employment income, computed without the deduction for RPP contributions
- Income from carrying on a business
- Net rental income from real property
- Income earned as an active partner
- Royalties, provided the recipient is the author, composer, or inventor of the work
- Taxable support payments received by a spouse.
- Research grants, net of certain related expenses
- Canada and Quebec Pension Plan disability benefits received
- Supplementary unemployment benefit plan payments (This does not include the regular Employment Insurance benefit payments)

Deductions

- Deductible support payments (This does not include non-deductible child support payments)
- Losses from carrying on a business
- Losses allocated to an active partner
- Losses from the rental of real property

Exercise Ten - 2

Subject: Earned Income

Mr. Jarwhol Nacari has net employment income of $56,000 (he is not a member of an RPP), interest income of $22,000, net rental income of $2,500, and receives taxable support payments from his former spouse of $12,000 during the current year. What is Mr. Nacari's Earned Income for RRSP purposes for the current year?

Exercise Ten - 3

Subject: Earned Income

Ms. Shelly Devine has net employment income of $82,000 (after the deduction of $3,000 in RPP contributions), a business loss of $12,500, taxable dividends of $4,200, and pays deductible support to her former spouse of $18,000 during the current year. What is Ms. Devine's Earned Income for RRSP purposes for the current year?

SOLUTIONS available in print and online Study Guide.

Pension Adjustments (PAs) - Overview

10-49. If an individual participates in an RPP or a DPSP, his RRSP Deduction Limit must be reduced to reflect retirement savings that are taking place in these plans. If this did not happen, individuals belonging to RPPs and DPSPs could have access to larger amounts of tax deferred retirement savings than would be the case for other individuals.

10-50. Pension Adjustments (PAs) are designed to reflect the benefits earned by an individual through defined benefit RPPs or contributions made to money purchase RPPs and DPSPs by an individual or his employer during a particular year. As RPPs and DPSPs are always sponsored by an employer, the CRA requires the employer to calculate an annual PA for each employee who is a member of that employer's RPP or DPSP. This amount is reported on the employee's T4.

10-51. Employers do not issue T4s until January or February of the year following the calendar year in which contributions are made or benefits granted. Because of this, the PA that is deducted in the calculation of the taxpayer's RRSP Deduction Limit for the current year, is based on the employer's contributions or benefits granted during the preceding year. More specifically, the 2017 RRSP Deduction Limit is reduced by PAs calculated with reference to 2016 RPP benefits earned and RPP and DPSP contributions made. These PAs are reported to the CRA and the taxpayer in the 2016 T4s that are issued in January or February of 2017. These PAs are also incorporated into the 2017 RRSP Deduction Limit Statement that the CRA issues for the 2017 taxation year.

Exercise Ten - 4

Subject: Retirement Savings

How does the Canadian retirement savings system prevent individuals who are a member of their employer's RPP or DPSP from being treated more favourably than individuals who can only use an RRSP for retirement savings?

SOLUTION available in print and online Study Guide.

Pension Adjustments - Money Purchase RPPs And DPSPs

10-52. The calculation of PAs for money purchase plans is relatively straightforward. As RRSPs operate in the same general format as money purchase plans (i.e., they do not promise a specific benefit), contributions to money purchase plans are directly comparable, on a dollar for dollar basis, with contributions to an RRSP.

10-53. As a consequence, the PA for a money purchase RPP is simply the sum of all employee and employer contributions for the year. Following the same reasoning, an employee's PA for a DPSP is simply the employer's contributions for the year that are allocated to the individual (employees cannot contribute to a DPSP). Since the PA that is deducted already includes the employee's contributions to the RPP, the net employment figure used to calculate earned income must add back RPP contributions so they are not deducted twice. A simple example will illustrate these calculations:

EXAMPLE Ms. Jones' employer sponsors a money purchase RPP and a DPSP. Ms. Jones is a member of both. During 2016, she has net employment income of $68,000 after the deduction of her $2,000 contribution to the RPP. This results in Earned Income of $70,000 ($68,000 + $2,000). Her employer contributes $2,000 to the RPP and $1,500 to the DPSP on her behalf. She has no Unused RRSP Deduction Room at the end of 2016.

ANALYSIS Ms. Jones' 2016 PA is $5,500 ($2,000 + $2,000 + $1,500), an amount that will be reported on the 2016 T4 that she will receive in early 2017. After filing her 2016 tax return, Ms. Jones will have access to her RRSP Deduction Limit Statement for 2017 from the CRA that will calculate her 2017 maximum RRSP contribution.

As she has no Unused RRSP Deduction Room at the end of 2016, her RRSP Deduction Limit will be calculated by taking the lesser of the $26,010 RRSP Dollar Limit for 2017 and $12,600, 18 percent of Ms. Jones' 2016 Earned Income of $70,000. The 2016 PA of $5,500 will be subtracted from the lesser figure of $12,600, to arrive at her maximum deductible RRSP contribution for 2017 of $7,100.

Pension Adjustments - Defined Benefit RPPs

10-54.   As defined benefit plans guarantee the benefit to be provided, rather than specify the amount of contributions required, contributions made to these plans cannot be compared directly to contributions made to RRSPs, DPSPs, or money purchase RPPs. However, if retirement savings limits are to be applied equitably to all individuals, without regard to the type of arrangements available to them, it is necessary to find a basis for equating the benefits earned under these plans with the contributions made to the other types of plans.

10-55.   It is unfortunate that there is no simple way to convert a benefit earned into an equivalent amount of contributions. While there are a number of problems in dealing with this conversion, the most significant is the age of the employee. Because of the difference in years during which earnings will accumulate, it costs an employer much less in terms of current contributions to provide a $1 per year retirement benefit to an employee who is 25 years old and 40 years away from receiving that benefit, than it does to provide the same retirement benefit to an employee who is 60 years old and only 5 years away from receiving the benefit.

10-56.   To have a completely equitable system for dealing with this problem, different values would have to be assigned to benefits that are earned by employees of different ages. Benefits earned by older employees would have to be assigned a higher value than those earned by younger employees. Unfortunately, it appears that the government believes that the benefits of such an equitable system do not warrant the costs of associating different levels of benefits with individuals of differing ages.

10-57.   Rather than a system that takes into account the different ages of participants in defined benefit RPPs, the current solution is to equate $1 of benefits earned with $9 of contributions. If, during the current year, an individual earns $1 of future benefits under the provisions of a defined benefit RPP, in the calculation of his PA for the year, this will be viewed as the equivalent of $9 in contributions to a money purchase RPP or DPSP. Unlike the case of money purchase plans, the amounts contributed to the plan by the employer and employee during the year do not affect the PA.

10-58.   The use of the multiple 9 is an arbitrary solution that fails to give any consideration to the age of the employee (there is an unconfirmed rumour that this number was selected because it was the shoe size of the Minister of Finance at the time the legislation was passed). It is systematically unfair to younger individuals as it overstates the cost of providing their pension benefits, thereby generating an excessive PA which, in turn, creates a corresponding reduction in their ability to contribute to their RRSP.

> **EXAMPLE**   Bryan is 25 years of age. In 2017, he earns a pension benefit in his employer's defined benefit RPP of $1,000 to be received beginning in 2057 when Bryan reaches 65 years of age. His PA for 2017 is $9,000 which decreases his RRSP deduction room by $9,000.

> **ANALYSIS**   In return for a $1,000 per year pension after 40 years, Bryan has lost $9,000 in RRSP contribution room. Assuming that he would have used this room to make a $9,000 contribution in 2017, this contribution would have accumulated, assuming a 10 percent rate of return, to $407,331 in 2057. This balance would clearly produce an income stream well in excess of the pension benefit of $1,000 per year.

> While this comparison is not a complete analysis of the situation (it does not consider the costs of the two alternatives), it does illustrate the fact that, when a pension benefit given to a young individual is multiplied by 9, there is a very high cost in terms of lost RRSP contribution room.

10-59.   While it was probably essential to the implementation of this system that some type of averaging process be used, it is unfortunate that the selected alternative has such a systematic bias against younger individuals. It is unlikely that the government could have arrived at any administratively convenient solution that would not appear inequitable to some individuals. However, it would have been more equitable to have used some type of age dependent sliding scale, as opposed to the inflexible application of the factor of 9.

Exercise Ten - 5

Subject: Pension Adjustments

Mr. Arnett's employer sponsors both a money purchase RPP and a DPSP. During the current year, his employer contributes $2,300 to the RPP and $1,800 to the DPSP on behalf of Mr. Arnett. Mr. Arnett contributes $2,300 to the RPP. Calculate the amount of the Pension Adjustment that will be included on Mr. Arnett's T4 for the current year.

SOLUTION available in print and online Study Guide.

Prescribed Amount - ITA 146(1)

10-60.   The Prescribed Amount (see Figure 10-2) is a deduction that may arise as the result of an individual transferring accumulated benefits from one RPP to a different RPP. We will not give any attention to the calculation of this amount in this text.

Past Service Pension Adjustments (PSPAs)

10-61.   Past Service Pension Adjustments (PSPAs) are designed to deal with benefits under defined benefit RPPs related to credit for past service. They are far less common than PAs. Some of the events giving rise to PSPAs are as follows:

- A new RPP is implemented by an employer and benefits are extended retroactively for years of service prior to the plan initiation.

- The benefit formula is changed, increasing the percentage that is applied to pensionable earnings to determine benefits earned. Again, a PSPA is created only if the increased benefits are extended retroactively to years of service prior to the plan amendment.

- An individual, either voluntarily or because of terms contained in the plan, works for a number of years without being a member of the plan. On joining the plan, the employee is credited for years of service prior to entry into the plan.

10-62.   If an individual were to receive such past service benefits without experiencing any reduction in his RRSP Deduction Limit, he would have effectively beaten the system. That is, he would be receiving additional pension benefits over and above the limits that are normally applicable to individual taxpayers. The role of PSPAs is to prevent this from happening.

10-63.   PSPAs are calculated on the basis of all of the PAs that would have applied in the years prior to the year of change if the plan or improvement had been in effect, or if the individual had been a member in those years. From these "as if" PAs, the actual PAs reported would be deducted. The resulting difference is then reported as a PSPA for the current year.

10-64.   As with PAs, the employer is responsible for calculating and reporting PSPAs, normally within 60 days of the past service event. The amount is reported on a PSPA information form (not on a T4) that is sent to both the employee and the CRA. Since the current year's PA will reflect the new benefits, only years prior to the year of change are used to calculate the PSPA. As a result, unlike the one year lag in deducting PAs, PSPAs are deducted from the RRSP deduction room formula in the year in which they occur.

10-65.   The following simplified example illustrates very basic PSPA calculations:

EXAMPLE   Wally Oats has been a member of his employer's defined benefit RPP since 2011. Until 2017, the benefit formula provided a retirement benefit equal to 1.5 percent of pensionable earnings for each year of service. During 2017, the benefit formula was increased to 1.75 percent of pensionable earnings for each year of service, a change that is to be applied to all prior years of service. Mr. Oats has had $48,000 in pensionable earnings in each prior year.

ANALYSIS The calculation of the PSPA for 2017 would be based on the six years of service prior to the current year (2011 to 2016) as follows:

New Formula PAs [(1.75%)($48,000)(9)(6 Years)]	$45,360
Previously Reported PAs [(1.50%)($48,000)(9)(6 Years)]	(38,880)
2017 PSPA	$ 6,480

10-66.   Note that PSPAs only occur in the context of defined benefit plans. If additional contributions for past service are made to a money purchase plan, these amounts will be included in the regular Pension Adjustment for the year in which the contributions are made. This eliminates the need for any sort of catch up adjustment.

Pension Adjustment Reversals (PARs)

10-67.   A vested pension benefit is one in which the employee has an irrevocable property right. That is, he is entitled to receive the value of the benefit, without regard to whether he remains an employee of the employer providing the benefit.

10-68.   In order to give their employees an incentive to remain with them, many employers grant pension benefits that do not become vested unless the employee remains for a specified period of time. A common arrangement would be for an employer to grant benefits that do not vest until the employee has completed 5 years of service. If an employee leaves before the end of this 5 year period, he loses the benefits that he has earned to that point in time.

10-69.   This creates a problem in that employers are required to report PAs for all benefits or contributions earned by an employee during the year, regardless of when the pension benefits become vested. This means that an employer may report PAs for benefits that will not, in fact, be received by the employee. This, in turn, means that the RRSP deduction room that was eliminated by these PAs would also be lost.

10-70.   To deal with this problem, Pension Adjustment Reversals (PARs) were added to the pension legislation. Note that this is only an issue with the employer's share of contributions made or benefits earned. Provincial legislation requires that employees have a vested right to all of their own contributions.

10-71.   A PAR is calculated by the employer whenever an employee terminates membership in an RPP or DPSP and receives less from the plan than the total of the PAs and PSPAs reported for the employee. The PAR is reported to the CRA and to the employee, and will be added to the individual's RRSP deduction room in the year of termination.   The following simple example illustrates the use of a PAR:

EXAMPLE Stan Kapitany is a member of an RPP in which benefits are not vested until the fourth year of service. He leaves after 3 years when he is offered an opportunity to develop high performance race cars. His employer was required to report PAs for the first 3 years of his employment and this, in turn, reduced Mr. Kapitany's ability to make deductible contributions to an RRSP.

ANALYSIS Since he ceases to work for his employer prior to the benefits becoming vested, the benefits for which PAs were previously reported will not be transferred to him. This means that there will be no retirement benefits corresponding to the previously reported PAs and, as a consequence, Mr. Kapitany has lost a portion of his entitlement to tax deferred retirement savings. This problem is solved with the addition of a PAR to Mr. Kapitany's RRSP deduction room.

We suggest you work Self Study Problem Ten-1 at this point.

Examples Of RRSP Deduction Calculations

10-72.   The following three examples illustrate the calculation of the RRSP Deduction Limit, Unused RRSP Deduction Room, and the carry forward of undeducted RRSP contributions.

Example A

Miss Brown has 2016 net employment income of $30,000, 2016 net rental income of $10,000, and 2016 interest income of $5,000. She is not a member of an RPP or a DPSP. She contributes $5,000 to her RRSP in October, 2017 and $800 in January, 2018. At the end of 2016, her Unused RRSP Deduction Room was nil and she had undeducted contributions of $1,000 in her RRSP account.

Unused Deduction Room Carried Forward From 2016	Nil
Lesser Of:	
• 2017 RRSP Dollar Limit = $26,010	
• 18% Of 2016 Earned Income Of $40,000 = $7,200	$7,200
2017 RRSP Deduction Limit	$7,200
RRSP Deduction ($5,000 + $800 + $1,000)	(6,800)
Unused Deduction Room - End Of 2017	**$ 400**

The interest income is not included in Earned Income as defined in ITA 146(1).

Example B

After deducting an RPP contribution of $2,000, Mrs. Blue has 2016 net employment income of $34,000. Her employer reports a PA of $4,500 on her 2016 T4. Her 2017 RRSP contributions total $5,000 and she deducts $3,200 in her 2017 tax return. At the end of 2016, her Unused RRSP Deduction Room was $2,500 and there were no undeducted contributions in her RRSP account.

Unused Deduction Room Carried Forward From 2016	$2,500
Lesser Of:	
• 2017 RRSP Dollar Limit = $26,010	
• 18% Of 2016 Earned Income Of $36,000 = $6,480	6,480
Less 2016 PA	(4,500)
2017 RRSP Deduction Limit	$4,480
RRSP Deduction ($5,000 Contributed)	(3,200)
Unused Deduction Room - End Of 2017	**$1,280**

Mrs. Blue has 2016 Earned Income of $36,000 (net employment income of $34,000, plus her $2,000 RPP contribution that was deducted). She has an undeducted RRSP contribution of $1,800 ($5,000 - $3,200). She can deduct $1,280 in any subsequent year, but needs $520 of additional RRSP deduction room to deduct the remainder.

Example C

Mr. Green receives taxable 2016 spousal support of $150,000 and has no other source of income during 2016. He is not a member of an RPP or DPSP. In January, 2018, he contributes $11,500 to his RRSP. This full amount is deducted in his 2017 tax return. His Unused RRSP Deduction Room carried forward from 2016 was $1,200 and there were no undeducted contributions in his RRSP account.

Unused Deduction Room Carried Forward From 2016	$ 1,200
Lesser Of:	
• 2017 RRSP Dollar Limit = $26,010	
• 18% Of 2016 Earned Income Of $150,000 = $27,000	26,010
2017 RRSP Deduction Limit	$27,210
RRSP Deduction ($11,500 Contributed)	(11,500)
Unused Deduction Room - End Of 2017	**$15,710**

Exercise Ten - 6

Subject: Unused RRSP Deduction Room

Mr. Victor Haslich has 2016 Earned Income for RRSP purposes of $38,000. He is not a member of an RPP or a DPSP. His Unused RRSP Deduction Room carried forward from 2016 was $4,800. During 2017, he contributes $6,000 to his RRSP and makes an RRSP deduction of $4,500. What is the amount of Mr. Haslich's Unused RRSP Deduction Room and undeducted RRSP contributions at the end of 2017? If instead of deducting only $4,500, Mr. Haslich wanted to deduct his maximum RRSP deduction, how much more would he have to contribute to do so?

Exercise Ten - 7

Subject: Maximum RRSP Deduction

During 2016, Mr. Black has taxable capital gains of $23,650, net rental income of $6,530, pays spousal support of $18,000, and has net employment income of $75,600. Based on his RPP contributions of $2,400 and the matching contributions made by his employer, his employer reports a 2016 PA of $4,800. Mr. Black has Unused RRSP Deduction Room carried forward from 2016 of $10,750. Also at this time, his RRSP contains undeducted contributions of $6,560. During 2017, he makes contributions to his RRSP of $13,200.

Determine Mr. Black's maximum RRSP deduction for 2017. Assuming he deducts his maximum, determine the amount of any Unused RRSP Deduction Room that he will have available at the end of 2017, and indicate whether he has any undeducted contributions remaining at the end of 2017.

SOLUTIONS available in print and online Study Guide.

Undeducted RRSP Contributions
General Rules

10-73.   As we have previously noted, there is no requirement that contributions made to an RRSP be deducted immediately. If an individual has available funds to invest, it may be desirable to transfer these funds into an RRSP in order to enjoy the tax deferral on investment earnings that these arrangements provide. However, in some situations, it may be desirable to defer the deduction of all or part of these contributions.

10-74.   An example of this type of situation would be a taxpayer who is currently in a low tax bracket and expects to be in a higher bracket in the future. Contributions made now can be deducted in any subsequent year. There is no time limit on the deductibility of unused contributions.

Excess RRSP Contributions

10-75.   As long as an individual has a corresponding amount of available deduction room, the CRA is not concerned about undeducted contributions. However, because of the desirability of having earnings accumulate on a tax free basis inside an RRSP, it is not surprising that rules have been developed to limit the amount of contributions that are in excess of an individual's deduction room.

10-76.   The basic limiting provision is found in ITA 204.1(2.1) which imposes a tax of 1 percent per month on the "cumulative excess amount in respect of registered retirement savings plans". The "cumulative excess" is defined in ITA 204.2(1.1), as undeducted contributions in excess of the sum of the RRSP Deduction Limit, plus a $2,000 cushion. This, in effect, means that the penalty applies to undeducted contributions that are more than $2,000 greater than the individual's RRSP Deduction Limit.

10-77. This $2,000 cushion provides for a margin of error when a taxpayer makes contributions early in the taxation year on the basis of estimates of the amount that will be deductible. Note, however, the $2,000 cushion is only available to individuals who are 18 years of age or older throughout the year. This is to prevent parents from making undeducted contributions to an RRSP in the name of their minor children.

10-78. The following simple example illustrates the application of this rule.

EXAMPLE At the beginning of 2016, Mr. Woods has an RRSP Deduction Limit of nil and no undeducted contributions in his plan. During 2016, his RRSP Deduction Limit increases by $9,000. On April 1, 2016, Mr. Woods makes a contribution of $10,000 to his RRSP. No RRSP deduction is taken for 2016.

During 2017, his RRSP Deduction Limit increases by $10,000. On July 1, 2017, $15,000 is contributed to the plan. No RRSP deduction is taken for 2017.

ANALYSIS There would be no penalty for 2016 as his $10,000 in undeducted contributions is only $1,000 more than his $9,000 unused deduction room for 2016. There would, however, be a penalty in 2017. It would be calculated as follows:

	January To June	July To December
Undeducted RRSP Contributions	$10,000	$25,000
RRSP Deduction Limit ($9,000 + $10,000)	(19,000)	(19,000)
Cushion	(2,000)	(2,000)
Monthly Cumulative Excess Amount	$ Nil	$ 4,000
Penalty Rate	1%	1%
Monthly Penalty	$ Nil	$ 40
Number Of Months	N/A	6
Total Penalty	$ Nil	$ 240

Exercise Ten - 8

Subject: Excess RRSP Contributions

Ms. Lucie Brownell is not a member of an RPP or a DPSP. At the beginning of 2016, Ms. Brownell has no Unused RRSP Deduction Room. During 2015 and 2016 she has Earned Income of $160,000 each year. On July 1, 2016, she makes a $27,350 RRSP contribution, but does not take any deduction for the year. In 2017, she has Earned Income of $50,000, makes a $30,000 contribution on May 1, but still does not take a deduction for the year. Determine any penalty that will be assessed to Ms. Brownell for excess contributions during either 2016 or 2017.

SOLUTION available in print and online Study Guide.

Tax Planning - Excess RRSP Contributions

10-79. It would be very difficult to find an investment for which the elimination of tax effects would offset a non-deductible penalty of 1 percent per month (12 percent annually). Clearly, excess contributions that subject the taxpayer to this penalty should be avoided.

10-80 If excess contributions are withdrawn from the RRSP prior to the end of the year following the year in which an assessment is received for the year in which the contribution is made, an offsetting deduction is available. If, however, any excess is not withdrawn within this specified time frame, it will be included in income and taxed on withdrawal, even though it was never deducted from income.

10-81.   This still leaves the question of whether it is worthwhile to make use of the $2,000 penalty free cushion. If an individual has no contribution room left in his TFSA and still has an additional $2,000 in available funds, the ability to have earnings compound on a tax free basis within the RRSP would usually make this a desirable strategy.

10-82.   Alternatively, if an individual has not contributed the maximum allowable to his TFSA and only has limited funds available for investment, the TFSA would be the preferable alternative. This reflects the fact that, while both the TFSA and the non-deductible contributions to an RRSP enjoy tax-free compounding of earnings, withdrawals from a TFSA are not subject to tax. In contrast, any withdrawal from an RRSP, even amounts that have not been deducted, will be subject to tax.

> **We suggest you work Self Study Problems Ten-2, 3, 4, and 5 at this point.**

RRSP And RRIF Administration Fees

10-83.   Administration fees for these plans, as well as investment counseling fees related to investments in these plans, cannot be deducted by an individual. As a consequence, such fees should be paid with funds that are in the plan. While there was some controversy associated with this issue, it has been concluded that such payments are not a withdrawal from the plan, nor do they create a taxable benefit for the taxpayer.

RRSP Withdrawals And Voluntary Conversions

Lump Sum Withdrawals

10-84.   A lump sum withdrawal from an RRSP is possible at any point in time. The tax consequences of partial or complete withdrawals are very straightforward. In general, the amount withdrawn must be added to income in the year of withdrawal. Further, as a withdrawal does not result in an increase in the ability to make future contributions, such transactions result in a permanent reduction in the balances that will enjoy tax free earnings accumulation.

10-85.   Even when the individual is at or approaching retirement, a lump-sum withdrawal of all funds would not usually be a reasonable alternative. This course of action could subject a large portion of the withdrawal to maximum tax rates at that time and, in the absence of other retirement income, would result in lost tax credits in subsequent years.

10-86.   We would also call your attention to the fact that lump sum withdrawals are subject to withholding. The trustee of the plan is required to withhold a portion of the funds withdrawn and remit them to the government. The taxpayer will, of course, be able to use these withholdings to offset the taxes that will be assessed on the amounts withdrawn. Withholding is based on the following schedule:

Amount	Rate
Less Than $5,001	10%
$5,001 To $15,000	20%
More Than $15,000	30%

10-87.   An additional point with respect to lump sum RRSP withdrawals is that such amounts are not eligible for the pension income tax credit or the pension income splitting provisions that are available to couples (see Chapter 9).

Conversion To Income Stream

10-88.   Besides lump sum withdrawals, the following options are available for converting an RRSP into an income stream:

Life Annuity   Funds from within an RRSP can be used to purchase a single life annuity or, alternatively, a joint life annuity with a spouse or common-law partner. Taxation occurs only as the annuity payments are received.

Note that a life annuity can guarantee that it is paid for a minimum number of periods. For example, a life annuity with a ten year guaranteed term would make payments for a minimum of ten years, even if the annuitant died prior to the end of the period.

A possible point of confusion here is the use of the term annuitant. In most dictionaries, this term refers to someone who is actually receiving an annuity. In contrast, the *Income Tax Act* uses the term to refer to someone who is entitled to receive an annuity, even if payments under the annuity arrangement have not commenced.

Fixed Term Annuity   In a similar fashion, a fixed term annuity can be purchased. As with the life annuity, taxation would occur as the annuity payments are received.

10-89.   Note that these conversions can be made at any age, and without regard to whether the taxpayer has retired. Further, there are no tax consequences resulting from the conversion. However, the income stream from the annuity will be fully taxable as it is received (see the discussion in Chapter 9 with respect to the taxation of annuity payments).

10-90.   Unlike lump sum withdrawals, annuity payments resulting from RRSP conversions are eligible for both the pension income tax credit and the pension income splitting provisions.

Conversion To RRIF

10-91.   A final alternative for winding up an RRSP is as follows:

Registered Retirement Income Fund (RRIF)   The funds can be transferred on a tax free basis to one or more Registered Retirement Income Funds (RRIFs). This arrangement will be described beginning in Paragraph 10-168.

Involuntary Termination Due To Age Limitation

Objective

10-92.   The options for termination of an RRSP that were discussed in the preceding section are available at any age and without regard to whether the individual actually retires. However, government policy in this area takes the view that the tax sheltering features of RRSPs should not continue to be available to taxpayers in periods that are substantially beyond normal retirement age. Because of this view, RRSPs must be terminated in the year an individual turns 71.

Post Termination

10-93.   While individuals cannot have their own RRSP after reaching the age of 71, it is still possible for such individuals to make deductible RRSP contributions. If their spouse or common-law partner has not reached the age of 71, and if the individual continues to have income that qualifies as Earned Income for RRSP purposes (pension income does not), contributions can still be made to an RRSP in the name of the spouse or common-law partner.

Spousal RRSP

Benefits

10-94.   Under ITA 146(5.1), a taxpayer can deduct payments that are made to a plan that is registered in the name of a spouse or common-law partner. Any RRSP that is registered with the taxpayer's spouse or common-law partner as the registrant, and to which the taxpayer has made a contribution, is considered to be a spousal RRSP. This means that, if an individual makes any contribution to his spouse or common-law partner's existing RRSP, that plan becomes a spousal RRSP, even if the great majority of the contributions were made by the individual's spouse or common-law partner. Note that this term is still the most commonly used, despite the fact that the legislation covers both spouses and common-law partners.

10-95.   Unlike the pension income splitting provision which is only available to couples who have eligible pension income, a spousal RRSP is an income splitting plan that is available to all couples. In situations where one spouse or common-law partner is likely to have either no retirement income or a significantly lower amount, having the spouse or common-law partner with the higher expected retirement income make contributions to a plan in which the spouse or common-law partner is the registrant will generally result in the withdrawals from the plan being taxed at lower rates.

10-96.   In addition, if one spouse or common-law partner has no other source of qualifying pension income, a spousal RRSP allows that individual to make use of the $300 [(15%)($2,000)] annual pension income credit against Tax Payable. Note, however, that in most circumstances, the provision for splitting pension income could accomplish this same goal.

10-97.   When an individual makes contributions to an RRSP in the name of his spouse or common-law partner, the contributions will be deductible in the contributor's tax return. However, the contributor must have available deduction room and, as you would expect, contributions to a spousal plan erode this room in exactly the same manner as would contributions to an RRSP in the contributor's name.

10-98.   We have noted previously that an individual can continue making contributions to a spousal RRSP, even if his own plan has been collapsed because he is over 71 years of age. In addition, a deceased taxpayer's representative can make contributions to a spousal RRSP for up to 60 days after the end of the year in which the taxpayer dies.

Attribution Rules

10-99.   The objective of all of the RRSP legislation is to encourage retirement savings. In the case of spousal RRSPs, the legislation also provides for an element of income splitting. However, as the federal government does not want this element of income splitting to over-ride the basic objective of retirement savings, there is an income attribution provision that discourages the use of spousal RRSPs in a manner that, in effect, provides for an immediate transfer of income to a lower income spouse.

10-100.   ITA 146(8.3) contains an income attribution provision that requires certain with-drawals from a spousal RRSP to be attributed to the spouse or common-law partner who made the contribution. Withdrawals from non-spousal RRSPs are normally taxed in the hands of the registrant. However, if a registrant makes a withdrawal from a spousal RRSP, and the registrant's spouse or common-law partner has made a contribution to the plan, either in the current year or in the two preceding calendar years, the lesser of the withdrawal or the total of the spousal contributions in the 3 years will be attributed to the contributing spouse or common-law partner. The registrant of the plan will not be taxed on this amount.

10-101.   Other considerations related to the application of this rule are as follows:

- This attribution rule applies to withdrawals up to the amount of the relevant contributions, but does not apply to withdrawals in excess of this amount.

- This attribution rule applies without regard to whether the contributing spouse or common-law partner has deducted the contributions.

- This attribution rule is applicable even when there are funds that were contributed by the registrant of the plan prior to the spouse or common-law partner making additional contributions.

- This attribution rule does not apply when the taxpayer and spouse or common-law partner are living apart due to a marital breakdown at the time of the withdrawal.

- It is the calendar year in which the spousal contributions are made that is relevant, as a February 1, 2018 contribution is counted in 2018, even if it is deducted in 2017.

10-102.   When the taxpayer's spouse or common-law partner is eligible to make his or her own contributions to an RRSP, it can be useful to have these contributions made to a separate, non-spousal RRSP. If there is a need to withdraw funds, this precaution allows the withdrawal to be made from a plan that has not received spousal contributions. As a result, there would be no attribution and the withdrawal would be taxed in the hands of the individual making the withdrawal. However, if no withdrawals are anticipated in the foreseeable future, there is no tax related need to have a separate, non-spousal plan.

Exercise Ten - 9

Subject: Spousal RRSP

During 2015, Mr. Garveau makes a $5,000 contribution to a new RRSP in which he is the registrant. His wife, Mrs. Charron Garveau also makes a $5,000 contribution to his RRSP in 2015. In 2016, Mrs. Garveau does not make any further contribution to her husband's RRSP. However, Mr. Garveau makes a $6,500 contribution. During 2017, Mr. Garveau withdraws $9,000 from his RRSP. How will this withdrawal be taxed?

SOLUTION available in print and online Study Guide.

Home Buyers' Plan (HBP)

Qualifying HBP Withdrawals

10-103. The Home Buyers' Plan (HBP) permits a non-taxable withdrawal of "eligible amounts" from one or more of an individual's RRSPs. The current limit on non-taxable withdrawals is $25,000. In order to receive this withdrawal without tax consequences, the individual must meet several conditions:

- On January 1 of the year of withdrawal, all amounts related to previous HBP withdrawals must have been repaid.

- All amounts, up to the limit of $25,000 per individual, must have been received in a single year or by the end of January of the following year.

- The individual must have bought or built a "qualifying home" before October 1 of the year following the year of withdrawal(s). Extensions of the deadline are available where there is a written agreement to purchase a home, or payments have been made towards the construction of a home, by the October 1 deadline. A "qualifying home" is defined as a housing unit located in Canada, including a share of the capital stock of a cooperative housing corporation that provides an equity interest in the housing unit.

- Within one year of the acquisition of this "qualifying home", the taxpayer must begin, or intend to begin, using it as a principal place of residence. Note, however, there is no minimum holding period for the home, provided that at some point it becomes a principal residence.

- Neither the individual nor his spouse or common-law partner can have owned a home that he or she has occupied during the four calendar years preceding the withdrawal. However, there is an exception to this constraint for disabled individuals. More specifically, if the home purchase is being made by, or for the benefit of, an individual who qualifies for the disability tax credit (see Chapter 4), and the home is more accessible for the individual, or is better suited for the care of the individual, the HBP can be used even if the individual owned a home that was occupied during the specified four year period.

- The individual must complete Form T1036, Home Buyers' Plan Request To Withdraw Funds From An RRSP.

10-104. There is nothing in these rules to prevent withdrawals by both an individual and his or her spouse or common-law partner, provided all of the withdrawn funds are used to acquire a single property. This would allow couples to make withdrawals totaling $50,000 towards the purchase of a home.

Restrictions On The Deduction Of New RRSP Contributions

10-105.   The intent of this legislation is to allow individuals, who have not recently owned a home, to use accumulated RRSP contributions to acquire a residence. The government does not want to allow individuals to abuse the HBP by making contributions that are immediately withdrawn. To prevent this from happening, a special rule denies a tax deduction for contributions to an RRSP or a spousal RRSP that are withdrawn within 90 days under the Home Buyers' Plan.

10-106.   For this purpose, contributions to an RRSP within the 90 day period will not be considered to be part of the funds withdrawn, except to the extent that the RRSP balance after the withdrawal is less than the amount of the new contributions. This means that an individual can make the maximum $25,000 withdrawal and still make deductible contributions in the preceding 90 days, provided they had at least $25,000 in the RRSP prior to making the additional contributions.

> **EXAMPLE**   At the beginning of 2017, Mr. Garth has an accumulated RRSP balance of $20,000. In order to make the maximum $25,000 HBP withdrawal, he makes a $5,000 contribution to the RRSP on June 1, 2017. If he then withdraws the $25,000 within 90 days of making the $5,000 contribution, the resulting nil balance will be less than the amount of the contribution and no deduction will be allowed for the $5,000 contribution. If Mr. Garth withdrew only $17,000, the resulting $8,000 balance will be greater than the $5,000 contribution and the contribution will be deductible.

10-107.   As a final point you should note that this rule is applied on a plan by plan basis. If a withdrawal under the HBP serves to reduce the balance of a particular plan below the level of contributions made in the preceding 90 days, the contributions will not be deductible to the extent of this deficiency. This would be the case even if the taxpayer has balances in excess of $25,000 in other RRSPs.

Repayment Of HBP

10-108.   Eligible amounts are not taxed when they are withdrawn from the RRSP and, if there was not a requirement for these funds to be returned to the plan at some point in time, they would constitute a significant tax free leakage from the retirement savings system. As a consequence, repayment of amounts withdrawn must begin as per a specified schedule in the second calendar year following the year of withdrawal.

10-109.   Any RRSP contribution made during the year, or in the first 60 days of the following year, can be designated an HBP repayment. These designated repayments are not deductible in the determination of Net Income For Tax Purposes. Repayments under the specified schedule must begin in the second year following the withdrawal.

10-110.   Any amounts that are not returned to the plan as per the required schedule will be included in the taxpayer's income in the year in which they were scheduled to be repaid and deducted from the outstanding HBP balance. There is no upper limit on the amounts that can be repaid in any year subsequent to withdrawal, but repayment must be made within 16 years. This is accomplished by requiring a minimum repayment based on the following balance:

Eligible Amounts Withdrawn	$xx,xxx
Repayments In Previous Years	(xxx)
Amounts Included In Income In Previous Years	(xxx)
Balance	$ x,xxx

10-111.   A fraction is then applied to this balance, beginning at 1/15 for the second year following the withdrawal. In each subsequent year, the denominator of the fraction is then reduced by one, resulting in 1/14 for the third year after withdrawal, 1/13 for the fourth year after withdrawal, and so on, until the fraction reaches 1/1 in the sixteenth year following the withdrawal. These are minimum payments and, if they are made as per this schedule, there will be a 15 year, straight line repayment of the eligible amounts.

10-112.   If the payments are less than these minimum amounts, any deficiency must be included in that year's Net Income For Tax Purposes. As any income inclusions will be deducted from the balance to which the fraction is applied in the same manner as if they were repayments, this will not alter the schedule for the remaining payments.

10-113.   However, if payments are accelerated in any year, the schedule is changed. While the multiplier fractions remain the same, the excess payments will reduce the balance to which the fractions are applied. A simple example will help clarify these points:

> **EXAMPLE**   Ms. Ritchie withdraws an eligible amount of $15,000 from her RRSP in July, 2015, and uses the funds for a down payment on a qualifying home. In 2017, a repayment of $2,400 is made and, in 2018, a repayment of $600 is made.

> **ANALYSIS**   The minimum payment for 2017 is $1,000 [(1/15)($15,000)] and, since this is less than the actual payment, no income inclusion is required. The required payment for 2018 is $900 [(1/14)($15,000 - $2,400)]. As the actual payment is $600, an income inclusion of $300 will be required. This is the case, despite the fact that the $3,000 in cumulative payments for the two years exceeds the $2,000 minimum that would have been required for the two years. This illustrates the fact that making payments in excess of the required level in one year does not provide an equivalent reduction in the payment for the following year. Note that the required payment for 2019 is also $900 [(1/13)($15,000 - $2,400 - $600 - $300)].

Exercise Ten - 10

Subject: Home Buyers' Plan

During 2015, Ms. Farah DeBoo withdraws $18,000 from her RRSP under the provisions of the Home Buyers' Plan. Due to some unexpected income received during 2016, she repays $5,000 in that year. What is the amount of her minimum repayment during 2017?

SOLUTION available in print and online Study Guide.

Lifelong Learning Plan (LLP)
General Format
10-114.   ITA 146.02 contains provisions that allow an individual to make tax free withdrawals from their RRSPs in order to finance the education of themselves or their spouse or common-law partner. Withdrawals under this Lifelong Learning Plan (LLP) must be repaid over a period of ten years. The repayment amounts are not deductible and, if they are not made as per the required schedule, deficiencies will be included in the individual's income.

Withdrawals
10-115.   To qualify for the tax free withdrawals, the individual or his spouse or common-law partner must be enrolled as a full-time student in a qualifying educational program at a designated educational institution. In general, a qualifying educational program is a post-secondary program that requires students to spend ten hours or more per week on courses that last three consecutive months or more. A designated educational institution is a university, college, or other designated educational institution. See S1-F2-C1, *Education and Textbook Tax Credits*, for more information on designated educational institutions.

10-116.   The maximum withdrawal is $10,000 in any one calendar year, to a maximum of $20,000 over a period of up to four calendar years. While the designated person for these withdrawals can be either the individual or his spouse or common-law partner, an individual cannot have a positive LLP balance (withdrawals, less repayments) for more than one person at any point in time. However, both an individual and his spouse or common-law partner can participate at the same time, provided they use funds from their own RRSPs.

10-117.   As with HBPs (see Paragraph 10-105), if an RRSP contribution is withdrawn within 90 days as a non-taxable amount under the LLP provisions, it is not deductible in the calculation of the individual's Net Income For Tax Purposes.

Repayment Of LLP

10-118.   Minimum repayments must be made on a straight line basis over a period of ten years. In a manner similar to that used for HBPs, this is accomplished by using a formula in which 1/10 is repaid the first year of repayment, 1/9 the second year, 1/8 the third year, etc. Also in a manner similar to HBPs, deficient repayments will be included in the taxpayer's income and deducted from the outstanding LLP balance. Repayments in excess of the required minimum reduce the balance to which the fractions will be applied.

10-119.   Any RRSP contribution made during the year, or in the first 60 days of the following year, can be designated an LLP repayment. These designated repayments are not deductible in the determination of Net Income For Tax Purposes. Repayments must begin no later than the fifth year after the year of the first LLP withdrawal (actually the sixth year if payments are made within 60 days of the end of the fifth year).

EXAMPLE   Sarah makes LLP withdrawals from 2015 to 2018. She continues in a qualifying education program from 2015 to 2020. Since 2020 is the fifth year after the year of her first LLP withdrawal, Sarah's repayment period is from 2020 to 2029. The due date for her first repayment is no later than March 1, 2021, which is 60 days after the end of 2020, her first repayment year.

10-120.   Repayments must begin earlier if the beneficiary of the program does not continue in a qualifying educational program. Specifically, repayment must begin in the second year in which the individual is not enrolled in a qualifying educational program

EXAMPLE   Joseph makes an LLP withdrawal in 2016 for a qualifying educational program he is enrolled in during 2016. Joseph completes the educational program in 2017. He is not enrolled in a qualifying education program in either 2018 or 2019 and, as a consequence, Joseph's first repayment year is 2019.

Other Considerations

10-121.   There is no limit on the number of times an individual can participate in the LLP. However, an individual may not participate in a new plan before the end of the year in which all repayments from any previous participation have been made.

10-122.   For a withdrawal to be eligible for tax free status, the designated person must complete the qualified educational program before April of the year following the withdrawal or, alternatively, be enrolled in a qualified educational program at the end of March of the year following the withdrawal. If this is not the case, the withdrawal will still be eligible for tax free treatment, provided less than 75 percent of the tuition paid for the program is refunded.

Exercise Ten - 11

Subject: Lifelong Learning Plan

Jean Paul Riopelle makes a Lifelong Learning Plan (LPP) withdrawal of $5,000 in July, 2015. This is subsequent to his acceptance in a community college art program that runs from September to November, 2015. He completes the course. On February 28 of each year from 2018 through 2027, he makes payments of $500 per year to his RRSP. These amounts are designated as LLP repayments in his tax returns for the years 2017 through 2026. Indicate the tax consequences to Jean Paul of these transactions.

SOLUTION available in print and online Study Guide.

Departure From Canada

RRSP Balances

10-123.   ITA 128.1(4)(b) requires a deemed disposition of most capital property when an individual departs from Canada (see coverage of this subject in Chapter 8). However, most pension benefits are exempt from these rules and, as a consequence, a departure from Canada will not automatically result in the collapse of an RRSP.

10-124.   Once the taxpayer has ceased to be a resident of Canada, he may find it desirable to collapse the plan. The collapse and subsequent payment to a non-resident will result in taxation under ITA Part XIII. The Part XIII tax is a 25 percent tax on payments to a non-resident and, for those countries with which Canada has a tax treaty, the rate can be as low as 10 percent. Unlike the withholding tax that is assessed on withdrawals by Canadian residents, this is a final tax, and the withdrawn balances will not be subject to further taxation in Canada.

10-125.   Whether or not the proceeds resulting from the collapse of the plan will be taxed in the new country of residence will depend on a number of factors, including which country is involved and the manner in which the RRSP income was reported prior to the individual leaving Canada. While there are significant tax planning opportunities in this area, detailed coverage of this subject goes beyond the scope of this text.

10-126.   If the plan is not collapsed and payments are made to a non-resident, such payments are also subject to Part XIII tax at a 10 percent, or greater, rate. As was the case with the proceeds resulting from collapsing the plan, how this will be taxed in the individual's new country of residence is determined by a number of factors.

Home Buyers' Plan Balances

10-127.   If an individual ceases to be a resident of Canada, any unpaid balance under the HBP must be repaid before the date the tax return for the year of departure should be filed, or 60 days after becoming a non-resident, whichever date is earlier. If this deadline is not met, the unpaid balance must be included in income.

Lifelong Learning Plan Balances

10-128.   Similar to the provisions under the HBP, if an individual ceases to be a resident of Canada, any unpaid balance under the LLP must be repaid before the date the tax return for the year of departure should be filed, or 60 days after becoming a non-resident, whichever date is earlier. If this deadline is not met, the unpaid balance must be included in income.

Death Of The RRSP Registrant

General Rules

10-129.   When an individual dies, there can be many tax implications. In this Chapter 10, we will cover the complications associated with RRSPs owned by an individual at the time of death.

10-130.   The general rules for RRSPs depend on whether the plan is an unmatured plan (i.e., the registrant has not converted the plan to an annuity) or a matured plan (i.e., the plan has been converted to an annuity which is producing a regular stream of income). As described in RC4177, "Death Of An RRSP Annuitant", the general rules are as follows:

Unmatured RRSPs When the registrant of an unmatured RRSP dies, he or she is considered to have received, immediately before death, an amount equal to the fair market value of all the property held in the RRSP at the time of death. This amount, and all other amounts the registrant received in the year from the RRSP, have to be reported on the registrant's return for the year of death.

Matured RRSPs When the annuitant of a matured RRSP dies, the annuitant is considered to have received, immediately before death, an amount equal to the fair market value of all remaining annuity payments under the RRSP at the time of death. This amount, and all other amounts the annuitant received in the year from the RRSP, have to be reported on the annuitant's return for the year of death. Note that, if a straight life annuity was involved, there would be no further payments after death.

10-131.   If these general rules are applied, with the lump-sum or annuity amounts included in the decedent's final tax return, the assets will pass to the specified beneficiaries at fair market value, with no immediate tax consequences for the beneficiaries. However, when the RRSP assets or annuity are transferred to certain qualified beneficiaries, there are important exceptions to this general rule. (See material which follows.)

10-132.   An additional point here is that there are two different ways in which RRSP assets can be transferred at death. The preferable approach is for the registrant to specify the beneficiary, or beneficiaries, in the RRSP contract. This will result in the assets being passed immediately at death. Perhaps more importantly, probate fees will be avoided.

10-133.   If this approach is not used, the RRSP assets will pass into the deceased's estate. If this happens, their distribution will be subject to probate fees. In Ontario, these fees are 0.5 percent of the first $50,000, plus 1.5 percent of any amount in excess of $50,000.

Exception - Transfers To A Spouse Or Common-Law Partner
10-134.   The various possibilities that could arise when the disposition of an RRSP after death is to a spouse or common-law partner can be described as follows:

Unmatured RRSP - Spouse Is Beneficiary If the spouse is the sole beneficiary and there is a transfer to an RRSP with the spouse as the registrant, there will be no tax consequences for either the decedent or the spouse. The assets in the decedent's RRSP simply become assets in the spouse's RRSP. This is usually the most tax advantageous arrangement for dealing with an unmatured RRSP.

Matured RRSP - Spouse Is Beneficiary If the RRSP is in the form of an annuity with the spouse as the sole beneficiary, the RRSP will continue with the spouse receiving the payments. There will be no tax consequences for the decedent and the spouse will be taxed as the annuity payments are received. For matured RRSPs, this is clearly the most tax advantageous arrangement.

Estate Is Beneficiary Whether the RRSP has or has not matured, the general rules will be applicable here. If the spouse is the beneficiary of the estate, the same rollover results can be achieved here through the use of elections. However, probate fees will be applicable and the procedures will be more complex.

Exception - Transfers To A Financially Dependent Child Or Grandchild
10-135.   Without becoming involved in the details, there are provisions that allow both matured and unmatured RRSPs to be transferred to a financially dependent child or grandchild on a basis that shifts the tax burden from the decedent to the transferee.

10-136.   While the relevant amounts could be taxed in the hands of the dependant, there are other options. If the child has a physical or mental infirmity, the dependant can avoid current taxation by transferring the amounts to an RRSP, RRIF, Registered Disability Savings Plan (RDSP as described in Chapter 9) or an annuity. If there is no physical or mental infirmity, the only option that avoids current taxation is to purchase an annuity. In this case, the life of the annuity cannot exceed 18 years, minus the age of the child or grandchild when the annuity is purchased. As a result, if the child is over 17 years of age, this option cannot be used.

Home Buyers' Plan Balances
10-137.   If a participant in the HBP dies prior to repaying all amounts to the RRSP, any unpaid balance will be included in income in the final tax return. However, a surviving spouse may elect with the legal representatives of the deceased to avoid the income inclusion. If this election is made, the surviving spouse assumes the position of the deceased by being treated as having received an eligible amount equal to the unpaid balance outstanding at the time of the deceased's death. This amount is added to any balance of eligible amounts received by the surviving spouse that have not been previously repaid to the RRSPs.

Lifelong Learning Plan Balances

10-138.   If an individual dies and has a positive LLP balance, this balance must be included in the individual's income for the year of death. As is the case with HBPs, there is an election that allows a spouse to make the repayments under the deceased's LLP terms.

We suggest you work Self Study Problem Ten-6 at this point.

Registered Pension Plans (RPPs)

Establishing An RPP

Types Of Plans

10-139.   The most important type of Canadian pension arrangement is the Registered Pension Plan (RPP) provided by some employers for their employees. Such plans are established by a contract between the employer and the employees and provide either for a pension benefit that is determined under a prescribed formula (a defined benefit or benefit based plan), or for a specified annual contribution by the employer that will provide a benefit that will be based on the funds available at the time of retirement (a money purchase or contribution based plan).

10-140.   An additional variable is the question of whether, in addition to the contributions made by the employer, the employees make contributions to the plan. If they do, it is referred to as a contributory plan.   Both employer and employee contributions to the RPPs are normally deposited with a trustee who is responsible for safeguarding and managing the funds deposited.

Registration Of The Plan

10-141.   It would be possible for an employer to have a pension plan that is not registered. However, such an arrangement would make very little sense. In order to deduct contributions for tax purposes, an employer sponsored pension plan must be registered with the CRA.

10-142.   In most situations, the basic requirements for registration are not difficult to meet. The plan must provide a definite arrangement, established as a continuing policy by an employer, under which benefits are provided to employees after their retirement. The terms and conditions must be set out in writing and the amounts of benefits to be provided must be reasonable in the circumstances.

Employer Contributions To The RPP

General Rules

10-143.   As is noted in Chapter 6 on business income, ITA 20(1)(q) allows an employer to deduct contributions to an RPP in the determination of Net Income For Tax Purposes. It indicates that such amounts can be deducted to the extent that they are provided for by ITA 147.2(1) or 147.5(10).

10-144.   Turning to these subsections, we find that contributions to money purchase plans are deductible as long as they are made in accordance with the plan as registered. For defined benefit plans there is a similar requirement. Contributions made during the year, or within 120 days after the year end, are deductible as long as they have not been deducted previously.

10-145.   Note that the reference is to contributions made, establishing the fact that the availability of deductions for pension costs is on a cash basis. As deductions under GAAP must be determined on an accrual basis, there are likely to be differences between the accounting expense for the period and the tax deduction for the period.

Restrictions

10-146.   The preceding general rules appear to provide for any level of deductions, as long as the amount is consistent with the plan as registered.   As we have noted, however, the restrictions on contributions are implemented through the registration process. More specifically, ITA 147.1(8) indicates that RPPs become revocable if the PA of a member of the plan exceeds the lesser of:

- the money purchase limit for the year, and
- 18 percent of the member's compensation from the employer for the year.

10-147.   Given the fact that the RRSP Deduction Limit is also based on these same factors (with a one year lag), this restriction means that, in general, an RPP cannot provide for more retirement savings than would be available to an individual whose only retirement savings vehicle is an RRSP. To illustrate this, consider a member of a money purchase RPP who always has employment income in excess of $200,000. As 18 percent of this individual's income will always be larger than the money purchase limit, his maximum retirement savings will be determined by that limit. This means that for 2017, his limit will be $26,230.

10-148.   If that same individual was not a member of an RPP, his maximum retirement savings would be based on the RRSP dollar limit, a figure that lags the money purchase limit by one year. Given this, his 2017 maximum retirement savings would be $26,010, $220 less than would be the case if he were a member of an RPP.

10-149.   An RPP that provides benefits to an employee that creates a PA in excess of the money purchase limit for the year, or 18 percent of the employee's compensation, will have its registration revoked. Given that registration is required for RPP contributions to be deductible, this requirement should ensure that benefits are limited to the specified levels.

10-150.   Before leaving this discussion of employer contributions, you should note that this restriction on PAs would effectively restrict both employer and employee contributions to an RPP. Both types of contributions go into the PA calculation and, as a consequence, placing the limit on this measure of pension benefits ensures that the combined employee/employer contributions will be restricted to the desired maximum level.

Employee Contributions To The RPP

10-151.   As is noted in Chapter 3, the basic provision here is ITA 8(1)(m) which indicates that, in the determination of employment income, individuals can deduct contributions to an employer's RPP as specified in ITA 147.2(4). Taking the same approach that was used for employer contributions, this Subsection indicates that amounts contributed for current service are deductible if they are made in accordance with the terms of the plan. This places employee contributions under the same overall limit as employer contributions. That is, they must be made under the terms of a plan that does not produce a PA that exceeds the lesser of the money purchase limit for the year and 18 percent of the employee's compensation for the year.

Options At Retirement

10-152.   Retirement options for RPPs are not established in tax legislation. Each employer sponsored plan has a set of rules that are applicable to the participants of that plan. Most plans only allow the individual to receive the periodic benefit to which he or she is entitled. Less frequently, some plans may allow for a lump sum withdrawal, a transfer to a different type of plan, or a transfer to another employer's plan. Transfers to other plans are discussed beginning in Paragraph 10-197.

Phased Retirement

The Problem

10-153.   At one time, an employee could not accrue benefits under a defined benefit RPP if he was currently receiving benefits from that plan. This prohibition also applied if the employee was receiving benefits from another defined benefit RPP sponsored by the same employer or an employer related to that employer. This meant that:

- If an individual had wanted to phase in retirement by working on a part time basis after he had started to receive his basic pension benefits, he could not receive any further pension benefits for this part time work.

- If an individual continued on a full time basis after beginning to receive his basic pension benefit, he could not be rewarded with a partial pension benefit for this additional work.

The Solution

10-154. The problem has been dealt with in ITR 8503(16) through (25). An employer can pay employees up to 60 percent of their accrued defined benefit pension entitlement, while they continue to accrue additional pension benefits on a current service basis with respect to their post-pension commencement employment. This program is limited to employees who are at least 55 years of age and who are otherwise eligible to receive a pension without being subject to an early retirement reduction.

Inadequate Retirement Savings

The Problem

10-155. It is very clear that a large majority of Canadian individuals are not making adequate financial arrangements for their retirement years. While this is not a problem for those fortunate individuals who are members of a generous RPP sponsored by a government organization, a large public company, or a large union, there are many other individuals who will be facing a bleak future once their working years have ended.

10-156. To some extent, RRSPs provide a solution to this problem. In 2014, Canadians had $951 billion in unused and new contribution room. In that year, only 23 percent of eligible Canadians made contributions to these plans. The average contribution of those who did make contributions was only $3,000, with the total amount for all contributions only $39 billion. This leaves over $900 billion in unused contribution room.

10-157. An obvious solution to these problems is to have a larger percentage of Canadians enrolled in plans that require regular contributions. RPPs sponsored by a single employer are not likely to provide a general solution to this problem as the maintenance of a registered pension plan is very expensive. This makes it difficult for small or even medium sized employers to provide an RPP. Further, RRSPs do not provide a totally satisfactory solution in that the size of these individual plans is not sufficient to justify the cost of either professional management or adequate diversification of assets.

Pooled Registered Pension Plans (PRPPs)

10-158. One proposed solution to the problem of inadequate retirement savings is what the government refers to as Pooled Registered Pension Plans (PRPPs). These are, in effect, registered pension plans offered and managed by financial institutions such as trust and insurance companies. The basic features of these plans can be described as follows:

- These are money purchase plans sponsored by a financial institution capable of taking on a fiduciary role (trust and insurance companies). The sponsoring financial institutions are the administrators of the plan. They are responsible for receiving contributions, thereby creating a large pool of capital that can be used to construct asset portfolios designed to appeal to various potential registrants. They are also responsible for complying with tax rules, particularly with respect to administrative and reporting requirements related to contributions and withdrawals.

- An employer can select a particular plan for its employees. While the financial institution retains primary responsibility for the management of the plan, the employer would be responsible for enrolling its employees in the plan, determining the level of contributions, and collecting contributions to the plan. There is no requirement that the employer would have to make contributions to the plan and employees can opt out of participating.

- In addition to employed members, individual members who are either employees of employers who choose not to participate in a PRPP or are self-employed individuals can also participate in PRPPs.

- Without going into detail, the PRPPs operate under the general rules applicable to all types of retirement savings (e.g., contributions cannot exceed the annual money purchase limits and there will be penalties for excess contributions).

- The plans will generally be portable, with members being able to move the benefits they've accrued to another plan or retirement savings vehicle.

- The PRPP legislation allows interested jurisdictions to require mandatory participation for employers.

10-159.   It is hoped that the introduction of PRPPs will result in a large increase in the number of individuals that participate in a registered pension plan that requires regular contributions. While regulations for the operation of PRPPs have been issued at the federal level, additional legislation is required in each province. It is likely that most provinces will provide for these plans.

Target Benefit Plans

10-160.   A different solution to the problem of inadequate retirement savings has been proposed by the federal government. Target benefit plans, a.k.a. shared risk plans are something of a compromise between defined contribution plans and defined benefit plans:

- Like defined contribution plans, target benefit plans have either fixed contribution rates or, in some cases, contribution rates that vary within a narrow range.
- Like defined benefit plans, target benefit plans have a targeted pension benefit.
- The compromise is that, unlike a regular defined benefit plan, target benefit plans allow for benefits to be reduced if the fund assets are not sufficient to provide the targeted benefit.

10-161.   At this point, several provinces have introduced legislation to provide for plans with these characteristics. While target benefit plans may become widespread in the future, they are not currently of sufficient importance to cover in this general text.

Expanded Canada Pension Plan

10-162.   It is a fact that, given current levels of retirement savings, many individuals will find themselves in a very difficult financial situation in their retirement years. It is clear that the existing retirement savings programs are not capable of coping with this large scale problem. The portion of workers who are members of an employer sponsored RPP is declining and the generous provisions of the RRSP legislation are not being used in anything approaching an adequate fashion. In addition, for various reasons, expected life spans are getting longer.

10-163.   Like the existing programs, pooled registered pension plans and target benefit plans require the participation of employers or voluntary actions by the plan participants. It is unlikely that these programs will fully solve what is becoming an increasingly urgent problem.

10-164.   Unlike other retirement savings vehicles, the CPP is not an optional program. If you have employment income, you and your employer must participate. If you have business income as an individual, you are also required to participate.

10-165.   The problem, however, is the adequacy of the benefits that are provided under this program. The maximum benefit is currently in the $13,000 per year range, below anyone's definition of the poverty line, even when combined with OAS of less than $7,000 annually.

10-166.   In the U.S., the Social Security system is a similar system to the CPP (required participation by employers and individuals earning business income). In contrast to the low benefits provided under the CPP program, the maximum benefit in the U.S. for an individual retiring at age 65 is around US$32,000 per year. If Canadians wish to enjoy a more financially secure retirement, CPP benefits must move closer to the amounts paid in the U.S.

10-167. It appears that this will happen. In June, 2016, the federal and provincial governments reached an agreement in principle to enhance the benefits available under the Canada Pension Plan. In general terms, the agreement calls for the annual benefit to be increased to around $20,000 by the year 2025. To finance this change, the upper income limit for requiring CPP contributions will be increased and, in addition, the contribution rate will be increased. There will also be an increase to the Working Income Tax Benefit to assist low-income workers. At this point, no legislation has been passed to implement this agreement.

Registered Retirement Income Funds (RRIFs)

Establishment

Only Transfers From Other Plans

10-168. A RRIF is a trusteed arrangement, administered in much the same manner as an RRSP. A basic difference, however, is the fact that deductible contributions cannot be made to a RRIF. ITA 146.3(2)(f) makes it clear that the only types of property that can be accepted by the RRIF trustee are transfers from other types of retirement savings arrangements. The most common type of transfer would be the tax free rollover that can be made from an RRSP. As was indicated previously, this commonly occurs when an individual reaches age 71 and can no longer maintain an RRSP.

10-169. There is no limit on the number of RRIFs that can be owned by a taxpayer and, in addition, the taxpayer has complete flexibility as to the number of RRSPs that can be transferred to a RRIF on a tax free basis. Further, the taxpayer is free to divide any RRSP and only transfer a portion of the funds to a RRIF. This in no way limits the options available for any remaining balance from the RRSP.

10-170. A RRIF can be established by an individual of any age and without regard to whether the individual is retiring. However, the individual must have an eligible savings plan, such as an RRSP, from which funds can be transferred.

Other Considerations

10-171. Any amount transferred from an RRSP to a RRIF is not subject to taxation until it is withdrawn by the taxpayer from the RRIF. As was the case with RRSPs, withdrawals are taxed as ordinary income, without regard to how they were earned inside the RRIF (e.g., capital gains realized within the RRIF are taxed in full on withdrawal from the plan).

10-172. Once inside the RRIF, the assets can be managed by the trustee of the plan according to the directions of the taxpayer. The list of qualified investments for RRIFs is similar to that for RRSPs and allows for considerable latitude in investment policies. As is the case with RRSPs, fees paid by an individual for the administration of a RRIF are not deductible.

RRIF Withdrawals

Pension Income Tax Credit And Pension Income Splitting

10-173. In our discussion of RRSP withdrawals, we noted that lump sum withdrawals from RRSPs are not eligible for the pension income tax credit or the pension income splitting provision. Fortunately, this is not the case with lump sum withdrawals from a RRIF. If the taxpayer is aged 65 or over, all taxable withdrawals from a RRIF qualify for the pension income tax credit and can be split with a spouse or common-law partner.

Withdrawals Greater Than The Minimum Withdrawal

10-174. While legislation establishes the minimum withdrawal from a RRIF (see the following paragraph), there is no maximum withdrawal. The entire balance in the RRIF can be withdrawn at any time. However, as was noted, any amounts removed from the RRIF must be included in Net Income For Tax Purposes in the year of withdrawal. In contrast to RRSPs where tax is withheld on any regular withdrawals, tax is only withheld on RRIF withdrawals in excess of the minimum withdrawal.

Calculating The Amount Of The Minimum Withdrawal

10-175.   We noted previously that, unlike the situation with RRSPs, an individual cannot make deductible contributions to a RRIF. Another difference between an RRSP and a RRIF is that a minimum annual withdrawal must be made from a RRIF beginning in the year following the year it is established.

10-176.   For an individual who is under 71 at the beginning of the year, the minimum withdrawal is determined by dividing the fair market value of the RRIF assets at the beginning of the year, by 90 minus the age of the individual at the beginning of the year.

10-177.   Once an individual is 71, the amount that must be withdrawn is determined by a prescribed percentage applied to the RRIF assets at the beginning of the year. This percentage is found in ITR 7308(4). It increases each year starting at 5.28 percent for an individual who is 71 years old at the beginning of the year, until it reaches 20 percent for individuals who are aged 95 at the beginning of the year. It remains at 20 percent for each subsequent year until the individual dies. This, of course, means that the RRIF balance will never reach zero if minimum withdrawals are made.

> **EXAMPLE**   A 70 year old individual had $1,000,000 in RRIF assets at the beginning of 2016 and $1,000,000 at the beginning of 2017. The RRIF was established in 2014.
>
> **ANALYSIS**   This individual would have to withdraw a minimum of $50,000 [$1,000,000 ÷ (90 - 70)] during 2016 and $52,800 [($1,000,000)(5.28%)] during 2017.

Use Of Spouse's Age For Minimum Withdrawal

10-178.   It is possible to irrevocably elect to use a spouse's age to calculate the minimum RRIF withdrawal. If the spouse is younger, the minimum amount is lower and offers an opportunity to defer the tax effect of the withdrawals.

Exercise Ten - 12

Subject: Minimum RRIF Withdrawal

On January 1, 2017, Mr. Larry Harold transfers all of his RRSP funds into a RRIF. Mr. Harold is 65 years old on that date. The fair market value of these assets on January 1, 2017 is $625,000. The corresponding figure on January 1, 2018 is $660,000. What is the minimum withdrawal that Mr. Harold must make from the RRIF during 2017 and during 2018?

SOLUTION available in print and online Study Guide.

Death Of The RRIF Registrant

General Rules

10-179.   As was the case with an RRSP, the general rule is that, when a taxpayer dies, the fair market value of the assets in his RRIF will be included as income in his final tax return. Also following this pattern, there are exceptions when the RRIF is transferred to either a spouse or common-law partner, or a financially dependent child or grandchild of the taxpayer.

Rollovers

10-180.   If an individual has a spouse or common-law partner, the most tax advantageous approach to estate planning is usually to name that person as the successor registrant of the RRIF. In this situation, the RRIF will simply continue with the surviving spouse receiving the payments. There will be no tax consequences for the decedent and future withdrawals from the RRIF will be taxed in the hands of the spouse.

10-181.   If a RRIF is left to the decedent's estate, the alternatives for transfers to a spouse or common-law partner, or to a financially dependent child or grandchild, are the same as those for an RRSP (see Paragraphs 10-134 to 10-136).

10-182.   As was the case with RRSPs, a tax free rollover to a spouse or common-law partner is available by making appropriate elections. Also as with RRSPs, if a financially dependent child or grandchild is physically or mentally infirm, current taxation can be avoided if the assets are transferred to an RRSP, a RRIF, a RDSP, or an annuity. In the absence of a physical or mental infirmity, the only option is the purchase of a limited term annuity.

Evaluation Of RRIFs

10-183.   For individuals required by age to terminate their RRSP, lump sum withdrawals are usually not a good choice. This reflects the fact that such withdrawals can often result in a large portion of the income being taxed at high rates. In addition, the pension income splitting provisions cannot be utilized. A possible exception to this view would be situations in which the taxpayer plans to give up Canadian residency.

10-184.   This leaves individuals with a choice between using a RRIF and purchasing an annuity. The fact that life annuities are only available through life insurance companies means that the rates of return implicit in these financial instruments are often not competitive with other investments.

10-185.   Further, annuities lack flexibility. Once an individual has entered into an annuity contract, there is usually no possibility of acquiring larger payments if they are required by some unforeseen event. In contrast, RRIFs offer some degree of flexibility with respect to amounts available to the taxpayer.

10-186.   As a final point, the wide range of qualifying investments that can be acquired in RRIFs provide individuals with the opportunity to achieve better rates of return than those available through the purchase of annuities. It would appear that, for most individuals, the use of a RRIF is the most desirable option when the individual's age forces the collapse of an RRSP.

Deferred Profit Sharing Plans

General Rules

10-187.   ITA 147 provides for an arrangement where an employer can deduct contributions made to a trustee of a Deferred Profit Sharing Plan (DPSP, hereafter) for the benefit of the employees. Employees cannot make contributions to an employer sponsored DPSP. However, certain direct transfers of balances from other plans belonging to the employee can be made (see Paragraph 10-197).

10-188.   Amounts placed in the plan will be invested, with investment earnings accruing on a tax fee basis. As with the other retirement savings vehicles, the beneficiary of the plan is taxed only when assets are distributed from the plan.

10-189.   As was the case with RPPs, the employer's contributions to these plans are limited by a maximum PA that must be complied with to avoid having the DPSP revoked. This is found in ITA 147(5.1) and is more restrictive than the corresponding limit for RPPs. Like the situation with RPPs, contributions to DPSPs cannot result in a PA that exceeds 18 percent of a beneficiary's employment income for the year. However, contributions to these plans are limited to only one-half of the money purchase limit for the year.

Tax Planning

10-190.   From the point of view of the employer, DPSPs are similar to RPPs. However, they have the advantage of providing greater flexibility in the scheduling of payments. Such plans are tied to the profits of the business and, if the business has a bad year, it will normally result in a reduction of payments into the DPSP. Further, no specific benefits are promised to the employees. This relieves the employer from any responsibility for bad investment decisions by the fund trustee or estimation errors in the actuarial valuation process, factors that can cause significant uncertainty for the sponsors of defined benefit RPPs.

10-191.   From the point of view of the employee, a DPSP operates in a manner similar to an RPP. The major difference is that employees are not permitted to contribute to DPSPs. A further difference is that DPSPs cannot be designed to provide a defined benefit. They are always defined contribution plans.

10-192.   DPSPs must invest in certain qualified investments and there are penalties for purchases of non-qualified investments. A final important consideration is that DPSPs cannot be registered if the employer or a member of the employer's family is a beneficiary under the plan. This would include major shareholders if the employer is a corporation, individual owners if the employer is a proprietorship or partnership, and beneficiaries when the employer is a trust.

Profit Sharing Plans

General Rules

10-193.   ITA 144 provides for Profit Sharing Plans. These plans are similar to DPSPs in that the employer can deduct contributions made on behalf of employees. Unlike the DPSPs, there are no specified limits on the employer's contributions as long as they are reasonable and are paid out of profits.

10-194.   However, these plans have not achieved the popularity of DPSPs for a very simple reason. The employer's contributions to Profit Sharing Plans are taxable income to the employee in the year in which they are made. In addition, any income that accrues on the assets in the fund is allocated to the employee as it accrues. Although payments to the employees out of the fund are received on a tax free basis, this form of compensation offers no deferral of tax and requires the payment of taxes on amounts that have not been realized by the employee. Given these facts, it is not surprising that such Profit Sharing Plans have not been a popular compensation mechanism.

Part XI.4 Tax On Excess PSP Contributions

10-195.   The preceding suggests that there are not really any tax advantages associated with the use of Profit Sharing Plans. However, the CRA has found that such plans are being used:

- to direct business profits to family members in order to reduce taxes; and
- to avoid employee withholding requirements, as well as CPP and EI payments.

10-196.   To curtail these practices, there is a Part XI.4 tax on excess contributions for specified employees. A "specified employee" is defined in ITA 248(1) as a person who is a specified shareholder of the employer, or who does not deal at arm's length with the employer. The tax is assessed on amounts paid by the employer into the profit sharing plan for the benefit of a specified employee that exceed 20 percent of that individual's employment income for the year. It will be assessed at the maximum federal/provincial rate applicable to individuals in their province of residence.

Transfers Between Plans

Accumulated Benefits

10-197.   As individuals may belong to several different retirement savings plans over their working lives, it is important that tax free transfers between different types of retirement savings plans can be made. For example, an individual who goes from a position where the employer provides RPP benefits, to a different position where no such benefits are provided, may wish to have his accumulated RPP benefits transferred to his RRSP. In the absence of a special provision to deal with this transfer, the benefits transferred from the RPP would have to be included in the individual's Net Income For Tax Purposes in the year of withdrawal. This, of course, would make such a transfer very unattractive.

10-198.   Fortunately, the *Act* allows for great flexibility in this area. Provided the transfer is made directly between the plans, the following transfers can be made on a tax free basis:

Registered Pension Plans   ITA 147.3 provides for the direct transfer of a lump sum amount from an RPP to a different RPP, to an RRSP, and to a RRIF. The Section also permits a transfer from a taxpayer's RPP to an RPP, RRSP, or RRIF of his or her spouse, former spouse, common-law partner or former common-law partner under a court order or written separation agreement in the event of a marriage or common-law partnership breakdown.

Registered Retirement Savings Plans   ITA 146(16) provides for the transfer of lump sum amounts from an RRSP to a RRIF, an RPP, or to another RRSP. The Subsection also permits a transfer from a taxpayer's RRSP to an RRSP or RRIF of his or her spouse, former spouse, common-law partner or former common-law partner under a court order or written separation agreement in the event of a marriage or common-law partnership breakdown.

Deferred Profit Sharing Plans   ITA 147(19) provides for the direct transfer of a lump sum amount from a DPSP to an RPP, an RRSP, or to a different DPSP. There are additional tax free transfers to the taxpayer's RRIF and to an RPP, RRSP, DPSP or RRIF of his or her spouse, former spouse, common-law partner or former common-law partner under a court order or written separation agreement in the event of a marriage or common-law partnership breakdown.

Retiring Allowances

10-199.   The full amount of any retiring allowance, which includes amounts received for loss of office or employment and unused sick leave, must be included in the taxpayer's income in the year received. However, a deduction is available under ITA 60(j.1) for certain amounts transferred to either an RPP or an RRSP. This, in effect, creates a tax free transfer of all, or part, of a retiring allowance into an RRSP, without using up any of the available RRSP deduction room. The limit on this tax free transfer is as follows:

- $2,000 for each year, or part year, the taxpayer was employed by the employer prior to 1996. This includes non-continuous service with the same employer.

- An additional $1,500 for each year, or part year, the taxpayer was employed by the employer prior to 1989 for which the employer's contributions to an RPP or DPSP had not vested by the time the retiring allowance was paid.

10-200.   This transfer does not have to be directly from the employer to the RRSP. The deduction is available if the taxpayer receives the funds and deposits the eligible amount into his RRSP within 60 days of the end of the year it is received. The eligible amount must be contributed to the employee's RRSP (not a spousal RRSP) to be deducted. However, if a direct transfer is used, the taxpayer will avoid having income tax withheld on the retiring allowance. It should also be noted that, for the individual to deduct the amount transferred to his RRSP, the trustee must issue the usual RRSP contribution receipt.

EXAMPLE   Joan Marx retires at the end of 2017, receiving from her employer a retiring allowance of $150,000. She began working for this employer in 1982. The employer has never sponsored an RPP or a DPSP.

ANALYSIS   The entire $150,000 must be included in Ms. Marx's 2017 Net Income For Tax Purposes. Provided she makes a $38,500 [($2,000)(the 14 years 1982 through 1995) + ($1,500)(the 7 years 1982 through 1988)] contribution to her RRSP, she will be able to deduct the $38,500 RRSP contribution, without eroding her RRSP deduction room.

Exercise Ten - 13

Subject: Retiring Allowance

On December, 31, 2017, Mr. Giovanni Bartoli retires after 42 years of service with his present employer. In recognition of his outstanding service during these years, his employer pays him a retiring allowance of $100,000. His employer has never sponsored an RPP or a DPSP. What is the maximum deductible contribution that Mr. Bartoli can make to his RRSP as a result of receiving this retiring allowance?

SOLUTION available in print and online Study Guide.

We suggest you work Self Study Problems Ten-7 and Ten-8 at this point.

Retirement Compensation Arrangements

The Problem

10-201.   As we have seen throughout this Chapter, the rules related to maximum contributions by employers to RPPs and DPSPs are very specific. While these maximum limits are sufficient to provide a reasonable level of retirement income to the majority of employees, they fall short of this goal for highly paid senior executives. Such individuals are often accustomed to a lifestyle that cannot be sustained by the maximum amounts that can be produced by RPPs and DPSPs. A similar analysis can be made for owner/managers of successful private corporations.

10-202.   Given this situation, both public and private corporations use plans other than RPPs and DPSPs to provide benefits that are not limited by the rules applicable to the more conventional plans. In general, such arrangements can be classified as Retirement Compensation Arrangements (RCAs).

Arrangements Defined

10-203.   RCAs are defined in the *Income Tax Act* as follows:

> **ITA 248(1)   Retirement compensation arrangement** means a plan or arrangement under which contributions are made by an employer or former employer of a taxpayer, or by a person with whom the employer or former employer does not deal at arm's length, to another person or partnership in connection with benefits that are to be received or may be received or enjoyed by any person on, after, or in contemplation of any substantial change in the services rendered by the taxpayer, the retirement of the taxpayer or the loss of an office or employment of the taxpayer.

10-204.   The definition goes on to indicate that the term retirement compensation arrangement does not include RPPs, PRPPs, DPSPs, RRSPs, profit sharing plans, supplementary unemployment benefit plans, or plans established for the purpose of deferring the salary or wages of a professional athlete.

10-205.   Provided the arrangement involves a contractual obligation to ultimately make payments to the covered employees, a corporation's contributions to a RCA are fully deductible when made. However, as we shall see in the following material, both contributions and subsequent earnings on the invested contributions are subject to a special refundable tax.

Part XI.3 Refundable Tax

10-206.   Contributions made to a RCA are subject to a 50 percent refundable tax under ITA Part XI.3. In addition, earnings on the assets contained in the plan are subject to this same 50 percent refundable tax. The tax amounts are refunded at a 50 percent rate when distributions are made to the beneficiaries of the plan.

EXAMPLE During 2016, Borscan Ltd. contributes $50,000 to a plan established for several of its senior executives. The funds are used to purchase investments that earn interest of $4,500, and no payments are made to the executives during the year. On January 1, 2017, $20,000 is distributed to the beneficiaries of the plan.

ANALYSIS Borscan Ltd. would be able to deduct the $50,000 payment into the plan in determining its 2016 Net Income For Tax Purposes. However, the Company would be required to pay Part XI.3 tax of $27,250 [(50%)($50,000 + $4,500)]. In 2017, when the $20,000 distribution is made to the beneficiaries, the Company would receive a refund of $10,000 [(50%)($20,000)].

10-207.   In legislating this tax provision, it was clearly the intent of the government to discourage the use of RCAs. The 50 percent tax that is required at the corporate level is higher, in some provinces significantly so, than the rate that would be paid by an individual if the equivalent funds were simply distributed as salary.

10-208.   As a result, this means that more taxes will be paid initially, in situations where a RCA is used to compensate employees. Although the Part XI.3 tax is totally refundable, the corporation will not receive any refund of the tax until distributions from the RCA are made.

10-209.   Despite this analysis, the use of RCAs appears to be on the rise, particularly with respect to providing retirement benefits to the owner/managers of private corporations. The explanation for this phenomenon probably lies in the not always rational preference that such owner/managers have for having taxation occur at the corporate, rather than the personal level.

10-210.   In addition, it appears that the CRA has discovered the use of "tax motivated arrangements" that are perceived to be an abuse of the retirement compensation arrangement rules. These arrangements are very technical and covering them goes beyond the scope of this text. However, we would note that there are a number of special rules which assess penalties in some situations where retirement compensation arrangements are established between non-arm's length parties.

Salary Deferral Arrangements

The Problem

10-211.   The fact that business income is on an accrual basis while employment income is on a cash basis has made it advantageous for employers to accrue bonuses prior to the actual payment of the amount to the employee. As was discussed in Chapter 3, if payment to the employee is made within 180 days of the employer's year end, the employer can deduct the amount when accrued, while the employee will not be taxed until the bonus is paid.

10-212.   If, however, the actual payment occurs more than 180 days after the employer's year end, ITA 78(4) defers the deductibility of the bonus until the point in time when it is actually paid. However, even if the employer cannot deduct the amounts until they are paid, it may still be attractive to make an arrangement that will defer compensation and postpone the payment of taxes by the employee. The concept of a salary deferral arrangement serves to place a time limit on the ability of employers and employees to make such arrangements.

The Solution

10-213.   The *Act* defines a salary deferral arrangement as follows:

ITA 248(1)   Salary deferral arrangement   A plan or arrangement, whether funded or not, under which any person has a right in a taxation year to receive an amount after the year where it is reasonable to consider that one of the main purposes for the creation or existence of the right is to postpone tax payable under this Act by the taxpayer in respect of an amount that is, or is on account or in lieu of, salary or wages of the taxpayer for services rendered by the taxpayer in the year or a preceding taxation year (including such a right that is subject to one or more conditions unless there is a substantial risk that any one of those conditions will not be satisfied).

10-214. Converting this to everyday terms, a salary deferral arrangement involves an amount of salary that has been earned by an individual during the taxation year. However, the employee has made an arrangement with his employer to defer the actual receipt of the amount with the intent of postponing the payment of taxes.

10-215. The definition of a salary deferral arrangement also contains a number of exclusions from its scope. These include RPPs, DPSPs, profit sharing plans, supplementary unemployment benefit plans, plans for providing education or training (sabbaticals), or plans established for the purpose of deferring the salary of a professional athlete.

10-216. A further important exception is that the definition of a salary deferral arrangement excludes bonus arrangements where the amount is paid within three years of the end of the calendar year in which the employee provided his services. This means that the ITA 78(4) rules deferring deductibility by the employer apply to amounts that are paid more than 180 days after the employer's year end, but within three years of the end of the calendar year in which the services were rendered. If the payment is beyond three years, it is subject to the salary deferral arrangement rules.

10-217. Under the salary deferral arrangement rules, employers deduct amounts that fall within this definition in the fiscal year the bonus is declared and employees cannot defer taxation on these amounts. They are required to include such amounts in their Net Income For Tax Purposes on an accrual basis, rather than on the cash basis that is the normal basis for employment income. In many cases, this will serve to remove any tax incentive from this type of arrangement and will discourage their continued use.

10-218. Despite these restrictions, certain deferral arrangements can be effective in that they do not fall within the ITA 248(1) definition. These include:

- self funded leave of absence arrangements (sabbaticals);
- bonus arrangements with payment deferred not more than three years, provided the employer accepts the loss of deductibility that occurs after 180 days;
- deferred compensation for professional athletes; and
- retiring allowances. (These escape the salary deferral arrangement rules and, within limits, can be transferred on a tax free basis to an RRSP as discussed in Paragraph 10-199.)

Individual Pension Plans (IPPs)

10-219. It is possible to establish a defined benefit plan for a single individual. These plans are defined in ITR 8300(1) as follows:

> ... a registered pension plan that contains a defined benefit provision if, at any time in the year or a preceding year, the plan has fewer than four members and at least one of them is related to a participating employer in the plan.

10-220. Such plans are usually marketed in conjunction with insurance products and their establishment requires the use of an actuarial valuation for the specific individual covered by the plan.

10-221. These plans have grown in popularity in recent years, particularly for successful owner/managers of private companies. However, the actuarial concepts involved in these plans go beyond the scope of this text. As a consequence, we will not provide detailed coverage of these specialized arrangements.

We suggest you work Self Study Problems Ten-9 and Ten-10 at this point.

Additional Supplementary Self Study Problems Are Available Online.

Key Terms Used In This Chapter

10-222.   The following is a list of the key terms used in this Chapter. These terms, and their meanings, are compiled in the Glossary located at the back of the Study Guide.

Annuitant

Annuity

Beneficiary

Canada Pension Plan (CPP)

Deferred Income Plans

Deferred Profit Sharing Plan

Defined Benefit Plan

Defined Contribution Plan

Earned Income (RRSP Limit)

Employment Income

Fixed Term Annuity

Home Buyer's Plan (HBP)

Income Attribution

Income Splitting

Individual Pension Plan

Life Annuity

Lifelong Learning Plan (LLP)

Money Purchase Limit

Money Purchase Plan

Past Service Cost

Past Service Pension Adjustment (PSPA)

Pension Adjustment (PA)

Pension Adjustment Reversal (PAR)

Pension Income Tax Credit

Phased Retirement

Pooled Registered Pension Plan

Profit Sharing Plan

Refundable Part XI.3 Tax

Registered Pension Plan (RPP)

Registered Retirement Income Fund (RRIF)

Registered Retirement Savings Plan (RRSP)

Retirement Compensation Arrangement

Retiring Allowance

Rollover

RRSP Deduction Limit

RRSP Deduction Room

RRSP Dollar Limit

Salary Deferral Arrangement

Spousal RRSP

Spouse

Target Benefit Plans

Tax Deferral

Unused RRSP Deduction Room

Vested Benefit

Vested Contribution

References

10-223.   For more detailed study of the material in this Chapter, we would refer you to the following:

ITA 144	Employees Profit Sharing Plans
ITA 146	Registered Retirement Savings Plans
ITA 146.01	Home Buyers' Plan
ITA 146.02	Lifelong Learning Plan
ITA 146.3	Registered Retirement Income Funds
ITA 147	Deferred Profit Sharing Plans
ITA 147.1	Definitions, Registration And Other Rules (Registered Pension Plans)
ITA 147.2	Pension Contributions Deductible – Employer Contributions
ITA 147.3	Transfer – Money Purchase To Money Purchase, RRSP Or RRIF
ITA 147.4	RPP Annuity Contract

ITR 8503	
(16) to (25)	Defined Benefit Provisions - Phased Retirement

IC 13-1R1	Pooled Registered Pension Plans (PRPPs)
IC 72-13R8	Employees' Pension Plans
IC 72-22R9	Registered Retirement Savings Plans
IC 78-18R6	Registered Retirement Income Funds

S2-F1-C2	Retiring Allowances
S3-F10-C1	Qualified Investments - RRSPS, RESPs, RRIFs, RDSPs, and TFSAs.
S3-F10-C2	Prohibited Investments - RRSPs, RRIFs, and TFSAs.

References

IT-124R6	Contributions To Registered Retirement Savings Plans
IT-167R6	Registered Pension Plans — Employees' Contributions
IT-280R	Employees Profit Sharing Plans - Payments Computed By Reference To Profits
IT-307R4	Spousal Or Common-Law Partner Registered Retirement Savings Plans
IT-379R	Employees Profit Sharing Plans — Allocations To Beneficiaries
IT-500R	Registered Retirement Savings Plans — Death of An Annuitant
IT-528	Transfer Of Funds Between Registered Plans
RC4112	Lifelong Learning Plan (Guide)
RC4135	Home Buyers' Plan (Guide)
RC4177	Death Of An RRSP Annuitant (Pamphlet)
T4040	RRSPs And Other Registered Plans For Retirement (Guide)
T4041	Retirement Compensation Arrangements (Guide)

Problems For Self Study (Online)

To provide practice in problem solving, there are Self Study and Supplementary Self Study problems available on the Companion Website.

Within the text we have provided an indication of when it would be appropriate to work each Self Study problem. The detailed solutions for Self Study problems can be found in the print and online Study Guide.

We provide the Supplementary Self Study problems for those who would like additional practice in problem solving. The detailed solutions for the Supplementary Self Study problems are available online, not in the Study Guide.

The .PDF file "Self Study Problems for Volume 1" on the Companion Website contains the following for Chapter 10:

- 10 Self Study problems,
- 5 Supplementary Self Study problems, and
- detailed solutions for the Supplementary Self Study problems.

Assignment Problems

(The solutions for these problems are only available in
the solutions manual that has been provided to your instructor.)

Assignment Problem Ten - 1
(Calculation Of PAs, PSPAs, And PARs)

The Canadian retirement savings system makes an effort to treat all taxpayers in an equitable manner, without regard to the retirement savings vehicle they are using. In order to implement this objective, it is necessary to have Pension Adjustments (PAs), Past Service Pension Adjustments (PSPAs), and Pension Adjustment Reversals (PARs). The following **independent** Cases serve to illustrate the calculations that are required for these adjustments.

Lorina Heyman

Ms. Heyman began working for Unafase Ltd. in 2014. The Company sponsors a defined contribution pension plan which requires 5 years of service prior to pension benefits becoming vested. For the 3 years 2014 through 2016, a total of $16,000 in Pension Adjustments were reported for Ms. Heyman by the Company.

In January 2017, it was discovered that Ms. Heyman had been operating an escort service out of her Company office. She was immediately terminated, losing all of her non-vested pension benefits.

Required: Calculate Ms. Heyman's Pension Adjustment Reversal (PAR) for 2017.

Reyes Club

Mr. Club has worked for Konlane Inc. since January 1, 2015. On January 1, 2017, the Company implements a defined benefit pension plan. The pension agreement requires the Company to extend benefits for all years of service prior to its inception.

The plan provides a benefit of 1.2 percent of pensionable earnings for year of service. Mr. Club's pensionable earnings for his years of service are as follows:

2015	$72,000
2016	76,000
2017	82,000

Required: Calculate Mr. Club's Past Service Pension Adjustment (PSPA) for 2017, as well as his Pension Adjustment (PA) for 2017.

Carrie Salisbury

Ms. Salisbury's employer sponsors both a defined contribution registered pension plan and a deferred profit sharing plan. During 2017, the employer contributed $4,600 to the registered pension plan and $2,100 to the deferred profit sharing plan. Ms. Salisbury was required to make a matching contribution of $4,600 to the registered pension plan.

Required: Calculate Ms. Salisbury's 2017 Pension Adjustment (PA).

Pablo Godley

Mr. Godley's employer sponsors a defined benefit registered pension plan. During 2017, Mr. Godley's employer contributes $4,500 to the registered pension plan on his behalf. In addition, Pablo is required to make a matching contribution of $4,500. The plan provides a benefit of 1.35 percent of pensionable earnings for each year of service. For 2017, Mr. Godley has pensionable earnings of $103,000.

Required: Calculate Mr. Godley's 2017 Pension Adjustment (PA).

Willis Hack

Mr. Hack has worked for his current employer since 2015. He earns vested benefits under a defined benefit registered pension plan that is sponsored by his employer. Mr. Hack and his employer contribute the same amount to the plan each year. Mr. Hack's total RPP contributions to the plan (employer and employee) and pensionable earnings for these years were as follows:

Year	Total RPP Contributions	Earnings
2015	$4,200	$71,000
2016	$4,400	73,000
2017	$4,800	69,000

Prior to 2017, the plan provided a benefit of 1.1 percent of pensionable earnings for each year of service. As of 2017 the benefit percentage was increased to 1.2 percent. This change will be applied retroactively to all prior years of service.

Required: Calculate Mr. Hack's 2017 Past Service Pension Adjustment (PSPA), as well as his 2017 Pension Adjustment (PA).

Assignment Problem Ten - 2
(Excess RRSP Contributions)

On January 1, 2015, Kerri Kmatz had unused RRSP deduction room of $18,500. In addition, because she was unemployed in the two previous years, she had undeducted contributions of $14,700. She had no Earned Income for RRSP purposes in either 2013 or 2014. While she manages to live on accumulated savings during the year, she has no 2015 Earned Income for RRSP purposes.

During 2016 she has several periods of part time employment and has Earned Income for RRSP purposes totalling $17,300. In addition, as the result of an incredible lucky streak at the blackjack tables in the Montreal Casino, she has accumulated winnings of over $100,000. In her excitement, she immediately makes a $20,000 contribution to her RRSP, on October 1, 2016. Without deducting any RRSP contributions for 2016, she has no Tax Payable for the year.

During 2017, she finally finds full time employment, resulting in a 2017 Earned Income for RRSP purposes of $45,000. She makes no further contributions during this year and claims her maximum RRSP deduction for 2017.

Required:

A. Determine Kerri's maximum RRSP deduction for 2017.

B. Determine the ITA 204.1 penalty (excess RRSP contributions) that would be assessed to Kerri for the year ending December 31, 2017.

C. Determine the amount of contributions that Kerri would have to withdraw from her RRSP on January 2, 2018 in order to avoid being assessed a penalty under ITA 204.1. What advice would you give to Kerri regarding her retirement savings?

Assignment Problem Ten - 3
(Net Income With RRSP Contributions)

During 2016, Mr. Jeff Singer has the following amounts of income and deductions that will be used in calculating his Net Income For Tax Purposes:

Net Employment Income Jeff's net employment income was $59,000. This included commissions of $12,000 and taxable benefits of $6,000. It was after deductions which totaled $8,000. This $8,000 amount included contributions to the employer's RPP of $1,500. The employer made a matching contribution of $1,500 and, in addition, contributed $1,000 to a deferred profit sharing plan on Jeff's behalf.

Property Income Jeff's property income was made up of interest of $2,300, eligible dividends received of $1,400, and royalties of $5,000. The royalties were on a software application that he developed in a previous year. He also had a net rental loss of $27,200.

Capital Gains And Losses During 2016, Jeff had taxable capital gains of $62,000 and allowable capital losses of $6,000. In the determination of his 2016 Taxable Income, he deducted a net capital loss carry forward of $56,000 [(1/2)($112,000)].

Other Income And Deductions During 2016, Jeff received $12,000 in spousal support payments from his first wife. As he has custody of his 14 year old son from this marriage, he also receives $11,000 in child support payments. In addition, Jeff paid $24,000 in spousal support payments to his second wife. As he has decided to remain single for the rest of his life, he has deductible child care costs during 2016 of $5,000.

Jeff has $18,000 in unused deduction room and $20,000 in undeducted contributions at the end of 2016, but Jeff did not make an RRSP deduction in 2016. This is as the result of advice from his brother, who read on an investing blog that this would protect him if his RRSP investments lost value.

Required:

A. Calculate Jeff's 2016 Net Income For Tax Purposes.

B. Based on the information provided, calculate:

   - the maximum RRSP contribution that Jeff can make for 2017 without incurring a penalty;

   - Jeff's maximum RRSP deduction for 2017 and any remaining undeducted contributions, assuming he makes the maximum contribution that you have calculated.

C. Assume that, in addition to the information provided in the problem, Jeff has 2016 net business income of $175,000. Using this new information, provide the information required in Part B.

Assignment Problem Ten - 4
(RRSPs, TFSAs And Tax Planning)

For more than 10 years, Hazel Swilling had been living with and supported by her husband, Giorgio. As he had become increasingly abusive when he was drinking (which was often), she moved out in May, 2016 and commenced divorce proceedings. She had married shortly after graduating from college at the age of 22 and had no earned income prior to 2016.

After an extensive search for employment, in November, 2016, she found a position with an annual salary of $36,000 per year. Her gross employment income for the November and December months of 2016 was $6,000.

Hazel's new employer sponsors a defined benefit pension plan. For 2016, $400 was withheld from Hazel's wages as a contribution to this plan. In addition, the employer made a matching contribution of $400.

Once Giorgio realized that Hazel had left him for good, he joined Alcoholics Anonymous. He eventually accepted they had irreconcilable differences and decided to work out equitable terms for an amiable split. In July, they decided that Giorgio would retain their principal residence and that on August 31, he would give Hazel a rental property that he had purchased after they had married. He had paid $423,000 for this property, with $100,000 of this total being the estimated fair market value of the land. Information on this property is as follows:

August 31, 2016 Fair Market Values	
Land	$120,000
Building	375,000
January 1, 2016 UCC Of Building	280,054
Net Rental Loss (Before CCA)	
For September 1 to December 31, 2016	2,600

The September 1, 2016 divorce settlement required him to make a lump-sum payment of $98,000, plus $2,500 per month in spousal support. The $98,000 was deposited in a savings account and, during the September 1 through December 31, 2016 period, interest of $653 was accrued in this account. The required $2,500 per month payments were made for September through December, 2016.

Other sources of funds for Hazel during 2016 are as follows:

- An inheritance from her mother's estate of $62,000.
- Eligible dividends from Canadian public companies of $1,800.

For both 2016 and 2017, Hazel does not anticipate that her income will exceed the limit for the lowest federal tax bracket of 15 percent. However, she anticipates that for the 2018 taxation year, her income will place her in the 26 percent tax bracket.

Required:

A. Calculate Hazel's net employment income for 2016.

B. Determine Hazel's maximum deductible RRSP contribution for 2017.

C. As Hazel's personal financial consultant, what advice would you give her regarding her TFSA and RRSP contribution and deduction for 2017?

Assignment Problem Ten - 5
(RRSP Contributions)

Prior to 2014, Ms. Sherly Sam had no Earned Income for RRSP purposes. In 2014 and 2015, she had sufficient Earned Income to allow for maximum allowable RRSP deductions in 2015 and 2016. However, she did not make any contributions in either of those years.

Sherly has been employed by a Canadian public corporation since 2015. The following information pertains to her income over the past two years:

	2017	2016
Salary Before Benefits	$150,000	$150,000
Automobile Benefit	7,000	6,500
Employee Stock Option Benefit	4,000	3,000
Benefit On Interest Free Loan	2,000	1,500
Registered Pension Plan Contributions	(4,500)	(5,000)
Deductible Employment Expenses	(3,200)	(3,400)
Interest Income	2,200	2,100
Taxable Capital Gains	14,500	6,300
Net Business Income (Note 1)	21,300	14,600
Royalty Income (Note 2)	6,400	6,600
Net Rental Loss	(5,000)	(10,000)
Spousal Support Payments Received	24,000	24,000
Eligible Dividends	1,400	1,500
Totals	$220,100	$197,700

Note 1 The business income is from a mail order business that Sherly runs out of her home.

Note 2 The royalty income is from a manual that she wrote on how to write instruction manuals.

Sherly participates in her employer's money purchase Registered Pension Plan. Her employer contributes twice the amount contributed by each employee to the plan. Her Pension Adjustment for 2016 is $15,000.

Required Ignore all GST considerations.

A. Calculate Sherly's Earned Income for the purpose of determining her maximum 2017 RRSP contribution by listing the items and amounts that would be included in her Earned Income. List separately the items that are not included in the Earned Income calculation.

B. Calculate Sherly's maximum deductible RRSP contribution for 2017.

Assignment Problem Ten - 6
(Net Income And RRSP Contributions)

Stefanie Heiner provides you with the following tax related information for the year ending December 31, 2017:

1. Her savings account earned interest of $875.
2. She realized capital gains on personal assets of $32,180.
3. She had losses on the sale of shares of $7,250.
4. She received eligible dividends of $4,620.
5. She paid spousal support totaling $12,000.
6. She received royalties on a text for the elementary school market totaling $8,600.

Also during the year ending December 31, 2017, she operated an unincorporated business. Under GAAP rules, the business had a Net Income of $156,470. Other business related information for the year is as follows:

- Amortization in the amount of $23,400 was deducted in the determination of accounting net income. Maximum CCA, which Stefanie intends to deduct, was determined to be $31,460.
- As a result of meetings with various clients and suppliers, Stefanie incurred meal and entertainment costs of $8,560. This amount was deducted in determining accounting income.
- During the year, the business sold depreciable assets for $26,500. The net book value of these assets was $15,900, their capital cost was $31,000, and the January 1, 2017 UCC balance was $12,349. There were no additions to the class during the year.

At the beginning of 2017, Stefanie had Unused RRSP Deduction Room of $7,300. She also had undeducted contributions of $3,200.

Required:

A. For the 2017 taxation year, calculate Stefanie's minimum Net Income For Tax Purposes before any deduction is made for RRSP purposes. Ignore CPP contributions in your calculations.

B. Calculate the maximum RRSP deduction that can be made by Stefanie for 2017. In making this calculation, assume that Stefanie's 2016 Earned Income is equal to her 2017 Earned Income. Determine the amount of additional contributions that she would have to make in order to make the maximum RRSP deduction.

Assignment Problem Ten - 7
(Retiring Allowance And Tax Planning)

Saul Brundige has worked for the same Company, Vilaflex Ltd., since 1984. In 2017, in an effort to develop a younger, more diversified workforce, Vilaflex instituted an early retirement program. The program offers a cash payment of $40,000 to individuals over the age of 60, provided they are willing to resign immediately.

As Saul qualifies for this program, he is considering acceptance of this offer.

Required: Describe the tax consequences to Saul if he accepts this offer. Explain any alternatives that he might have in this regard and advise Saul as to an appropriate course of action.

Assignment Problem Ten - 8
(Comprehensive Case Covering Chapters 1 to 10)

Family Information

Roland Sorter has been married to Rachel since their graduation from university. They have two healthy children:

Richard   Their son, Richard is 14 years old. He has 2017 income from part time jobs of $2,300.

Roxanne   Their daughter, Roxanne is 11 years old. Her 2017 income, also from part time jobs, is $3,600.

The family's medical expenses, all paid for by Rachel are as follows:

Prescription Glasses For Roland	$ 625
Rhinoplasty For Rachel (See Rachel's Business Income)	9,350
Physiotherapy Fees For Richard And Roxanne	1,475
Dental Braces For Richard	8,560
Psychologist Consulting Fees For Roxanne	2,450
Total	$22,460

During 2017, Roland worked 225 hours as a voluntary firefighter. He did not receive any compensation for his work.

Rachel's Business Income

Rachel is a lawyer who has an unincorporated professional practice specializing in lucrative contracts for TV and movie actresses. Her practice has a December 31 year end.

From childhood, Rachel has been embarrassed by the size and shape of her nose. Since her clients put a lot of emphasis on looking beautiful, Rachel felt that her nose stood in the way of getting more important clients and had rhinoplasty surgery in 2016. It was not required for medical reasons. Unfortunately, complications from Rachel's surgery in 2016 resulted in a significant decrease in her revenues for that year. She was also very disappointed with the results of the rhinoplasty surgery.

In 2017, she was introduced to a doctor who said he could greatly improve the look of her nose. She was convinced and the operation was a success.

During 2017, the revenues from her legal practice totalled $411,000, double what she anticipated. Rachel credited her perfected nose for much of the increase in business.

She operates her practice out of a building that she purchased for this purpose in 2013. The building was acquired for $675,000 of which $175,000 reflected the estimated fair market value of the land. When purchased, the building was new and it has been allocated to a separate Class 1 for CCA purposes. Rachel's practice uses all of the building. On January 1, 2017, the building has a UCC value of $433,521.

During the year 2017, Rachel renovated her offices, replacing the old furniture and fixtures with new furniture and fixtures at a cost of $67,000. The older furniture and fixtures were sold for $13,000. These older assets had a capital cost of $29,500 and a January 1, 2017 UCC of $13,594.

During 2017, Rachel acquired other assets as follows:

- A client list from a retiring lawyer for $23,000.
- A new laptop computer for $1,400.
- Applications software for $3,600.

As she offers mobile legal services as part of her practice, Rachel uses an automobile in her business. She retired her previous vehicle at the end of 2016 and, on January 1, 2017, she aquired a new BMW for $53,000. During 2017, it was driven 21,000 kilometers, 3,000 of which involved personal use. Operating costs for the vehicle during 2017 totaled $4,200.

Other 2017 costs of operating her business, determined on an accrual basis, are as follows:

Building Operating Costs	$29,400
Salaries And Wages	53,200
Office Costs	21,800
Meals With Clients	8,600

Roland's Employment Income

Roland works for a large Canadian public company. His 2017 salary is $66,500, none of which involves commissions. His employer withholds the following amounts during the year:

Registered Pension Plan Contributions*	$2,300
EI Premiums	836
CPP Contributions	2,564
Union Dues	460

*Roland's employer makes a matching contribution of $2,300.

Assignment Problems

Roland's work requires some amount of travel. He uses his own vehicle for this travel. This vehicle was acquired on January 1, 2017 at a cost of $29,500. During 2017, he drove the vehicle 28,000 kilometers, of which 22,600 were employment related. His total operating costs for the year were $5,600.

In addition to automobile costs, Roland has other travel costs as follows:

Hotels	$2,800
Food On Out Of Town Trips	930

In addition to his salary, Roland's employer provides him with the following allowances for travel:

Hotels And Out Of Town Meals	$3,800
Use Of Personal Automobile ($700 Per Month)	8,400

Investment Information

All of the family's investments are in Rachel's name. During 2017, these investments produced the following amounts of income:

Capital Gains	$12,750
Eligible Dividends	11,500
Interest Income	6,300
Total	$30,550

Roland has no 2017 investment income.

RRSP Information

Roland and Rachel have both invested on a regular basis in RRSPs. Information related to these plans is as follows:

Rachel's Plan   At the beginning of 2017 there was $6,500 of unused deduction room in Rachel's plan. Due to her decreased income in 2016, she did not deduct all of her RRSP contributions. As of January 1, 2017 there was $8,800 in undeducted contributions. During 2017, Rachel contributes an additional $14,500 to her plan.

Rachel's 2016 Earned Income for RRSP purposes was $116,000. She did not have a pension adjustment.

She would like to take the maximum deduction that is available on the basis of this information.

Three years earlier, during 2014, Rachel removed $18,000 from her RRSP under the provisions of the Home Buyers' Plan. After selling the family's existing residence in early 2015, Rachel used these funds, along with the proceeds from the old home, to acquire a new residence. Due to a continued oversight on the part of her myopic accountant, she did not designate any of her RRSP contributions as repayments of the Home Buyers' Plan funds in either 2016 or 2017.

Roland's Plan   At the beginning of 2017, Roland had unused deduction room in his plan of $5,500. He had no undeducted contributions. During 2017, Roland contributes $4,500 to his plan. He plans to take the maximum deduction available for 2017.

At the beginning of 2017, after lengthy negotiations with his union, Roland's employer agrees to increase the benefit formula in the Company's defined benefit plan. The annual benefit will be increased from 1.75 of pensionable earnings to 2.00 percent of pensionable earnings. This change will be applied retroactively to the years 2015 and 2016. Roland has been a member of the plan for over 10 years. His pensionable earnings during the retroactive years were as follows:

Year	Pensionable Earnings
2015	$37,000
2016	42,000

Roland's 2016 Earned Income for RRSP purposes was $48,000. His employer reported a pension adjustment for that year of $4,100.

Roland and Rachel will allocate tax credits between them to minimize the family's tax liability. Where either spouse can claim the credit and it makes no difference in the combined tax payable, Rachel will claim the credit.

Required: Ignore GST/HST/PST considerations in your solution.

A. Determine Rachel's Net Income For Tax Purposes and Taxable Income for 2017.

B. Determine Rachel's federal Tax Payable and her CPP liability for 2017.

C. Determine Roland's Net Income For Tax Purposes and Taxable Income for 2017.

D. Determine Roland's federal Tax Payable for 2017.

Assignment Problem Ten - 9

(Comprehensive Case Covering Chapters 1 to 10 - Three Individuals)

Zhi and Meng Liu are both 45 years old. They are married and support Zhi's 19 year old son from his former marriage, Sheng. In January, 2017, the family moved from Edmonton, Alberta to London, Ontario, so that Zhi could accept a new position. Meng continued her party planning business in London. What follows is information about the income of each of the three family members.

1. **Information About Zhi's Income**

   a. In 2017, Zhi earned $170,000 from employment, all of it after the move from Edmonton to London. CPP of $2,674 and EI of $836 were deducted from Zhi's employment income during 2017.

   b. The following expenses were incurred as a result of the move from Edmonton to London:

Air Fare - House Hunting Trip To London	$ 550
Hotel And Meals (3 Days) - London Trip	500
Airfare For Moving Family (1 Day Of Travel)	2,000
Costs - Waiting For New Home (20 Days)	
Hotel (All Receipts Available)	3,000
Meals (No Receipts Available)	unknown
Cost Of Repairing Old Home For Sale	1,000
Legal Fees And Commission - Old Home	3,700
Actual Loss On Sale Of Old Home	27,000
Transportation Of Household Goods	4,900
Legal Fees - New Home	2,900
Decorations For New Home	9,500

   c. Zhi received a moving allowance of $8,000 from his new employer.

   d. Zhi and his former spouse divorced in 2007. As per their divorce settlement, Zhi's former spouse has paid him an annual amount of $6,000 in spousal support payments since then.

   e. Zhi and Meng share a joint personal chequing and savings account. The interest earned on the account for 2017 was $350. Both Zhi and Meng contribute equally to this account.

f. Zhi had invested in Matel Industries Inc. (a public company) over the years, and on January 30, 2017 he sold 250 shares for $20 each. His history of trading in these shares was as follows:

> May 24, 2009 - Purchased 130 shares @ $26 per share
> June 30, 2010 - Purchased 170 shares @ $31 per share
> October 31, 2012 - Purchased 300 shares @ $29 per share
> June 9, 2013 - Sold 400 shares @ $15 per share
> July 5, 2013 - Purchased 400 shares @ $12 per share
> June 3, 2016 - Purchased 385 shares @ $18 per share

g. Zhi borrowed $10,000 to make an RRSP contribution in 2016. Interest on this loan paid in 2017 was $500. The RRSP contribution was properly deducted in 2016. Zhi had a Notice of Assessment from 2016 that indicated his 2017 deduction limit was $4,000, and also indicated that there were no undeducted contributions. In 2012, Zhi withdrew RRSP funds under the Home Buyers' Plan. His Notice of Assessment indicated that a repayment of $1,500 was required under the Home Buyers' Plan for 2017. Zhi did not make the necessary contribution in 2017 or the first 60 days of 2018. A repayment of the same amount will be required on the Home Buyers' Plan in 2018 or the first 60 days of 2019.

h. Zhi inherited a rental property from his mother, Mrs. Liu, who passed away in 2017. The relevant details are provided in Appendix A.

2. Information About Meng's Income

a. Meng's income is business income from her business, Meng's Party Services. Financial information related to this business is provided in Appendix B.

b. Meng made an RRSP contribution on October 31, 2017 in the amount of $12,000. According to her 2016 Notice of Assessment, her deduction limit for 2017 was $8,000. She had no undeducted contributions after filing her 2016 tax return.

c. See Zhi's information for interest on the joint chequing account.

3. Information About Sheng

a. Sheng is a full time university student. He paid $6,000 in tuition in 2017. Of this total, $3,000 was for the 4 months he attended in 2017, and the balance was for 2018. He was enrolled in University full time for 4 months in 2017. Sheng is willing to transfer any unused part of his tuition tax credit to his mother.

b. Zhi's wealthy ailing father, a Canadian resident and Sheng's grandfather, has given Sheng $100,000 to make him more marriageable in the hopes he will marry soon and have a son to carry on the lineage. The grandfather has promised more funds at the wedding if he is still alive. Sheng was uncertain as to how to deal with this situation, so on February 15, 2017, he invested the $100,000 in an interest bearing term deposit at 4 percent. Interest is paid every 6 months.

c. Sheng was the successful applicant for a scholarship and was awarded $1,000 to assist him with his tuition costs.

d. Sheng's payments from his RESP in 2017 consisted of the following:

Accumulated Earnings	$1,000
Canada Education Savings Grant Payment	2,500
Payment Of Contributions By Zhi And Meng	7,500

e. Sheng had employment income of $10,000 which he earned working as a server for his mother's business. He has worked in the business since he was 10 years old. As Sheng is related to his employer, these earnings are not insurable and no EI was deducted from his pay. CPP premiums of $322 were correctly calculated and deducted by his employer.

Required: In determining the following amounts, ignore GST, PST and HST considerations.

A. For the 2017 taxation year, calculate Zhi Liu's minimum:

1. Net Income For Tax Purposes,
2. Taxable Income,
3. Federal Balance Owing Or Refund (Tax Plus Any CPP Contributions).

B. For the 2017 taxation year, calculate Sheng Liu's minimum:

1. Net Income For Tax Purposes,
2. Taxable Income,
3. Federal Tax Payable.

C. For the 2017 taxation year, calculate Meng Liu's minimum:

1. Net Income For Tax Purposes,
2. Taxable Income,
3. Federal Balance Owing Or Refund (Tax Plus Any CPP Contributions).

D. Determine the amounts of any carry forwards available to Zhi or Meng. In addition, indicate the ending UCC balances for Meng's business assets.

E. Determine the maximum deductible RRSP contribution for Zhi and Meng for 2018. What advice would you give them regarding their RRSP contributions and other tax planning considerations?

Appendix A - Inherited Rental Property

On October 10, 2017, Zhi's mother, Ms. Liu, passed away. At her death, Ms. Liu owned a small apartment building with a cost of $350,000. Of the total cost, $100,000 was allocated to the land with the $250,000 balance going to the building. For CCA purposes, the building was included in Class 1. At the beginning of 2017, the UCC of the building was $170,000.

At the time of her death, the fair market value of the land was $212,000 and the fair market value of the building was $325,000. The property was transferred to Zhi on October 11, 2017. Rental income received by Zhi for his period of ownership from October 11 until December 31, 2017 was $26,000. Rental expenses before CCA totalled $22,000.

Appendix B - Meng's Business Income

The business provides complete party planning services for all occasions. A summarized Income Statement is as follows:

Meng's Party Services
Statement Of Income
For the year ended December 31, 2017

Sales		$561,000
Expenses:		
General And Administrative	($485,120)	
Amortization Of Fixed Assets	(28,170)	(513,290)
Operating Profit		$ 47,710
Gain On Disposal Of Fixed Assets (See Details Below)		99,290
Net Income		$147,000

General and administrative expenses includes a payment of $50,000 in drawings to Meng.

The UCC balances of the business assets as at January 1, 2017 were:

Class 1	$30,000
Class 6 (Fence)	2,100
Class 8	2,000
Class 10	11,000

In January, 2017, as a result of the move to London, Meng sold the owned business premises and some other business assets. The Class 6 asset listed is the fence that was erected around the former business premises. On the sale of these premises, no proceeds were allocated to the fence. This was the only asset in Class 6.

The details of the asset sales at the time of the move are as follows:

	Proceeds	Original Cost	Net book value
Land	$ 20,000	$ 5,000	$ 5,000
Class 1 building	125,000	45,000	40,000
Class 8 chairs and tables	6,000	8,000	5,120
Delivery van	4,500	18,000	6,175
Office equipment	5,000	15,000	4,915
Class 6 fence	Nil	3,000	Nil

To facilitate the sale, Meng agreed to take 10 percent of the total purchase price as a down payment, with the balance due in 2018.

Meng found leased premises in London that meet her needs, however, she was not happy with the external appearance of the leased premises. She had landscaping work completed around the new leased office space at a cost of $12,000. For 2017, no amortization of this work was deducted in the determination of accounting Net Income.

During the year, the business purchased the following new depreciable assets:

Office Furniture	$15,000
Delivery Van	30,000
Computer Equipment And Systems Software	10,000
Photocopier (No Separate Class Election Was Filed)	2,600

INDEX

This index includes the entries for both Volume I and II. Volume II begins on page 511.

This index includes the entries for both Volume I and II. Volume II begins on page 511.

This index includes the entries for both Volume I and II. Volume II begins on page 511.

This index includes the entries for both Volume I and II. Volume II begins on page 511.

Division B Income

This index includes the entries for both Volume I and II. Volume II begins on page 511.

This index includes the entries for both Volume I and II. Volume II begins on page 511.

This index includes the entries for both Volume I and II. Volume II begins on page 511.

This index includes the entries for both Volume I and II. Volume II begins on page 511.

This index includes the entries for both Volume I and II. Volume II begins on page 511.

This index includes the entries for both Volume I and II. Volume II begins on page 511.

This index includes the entries for both Volume I and II. Volume II begins on page 511.

This index includes the entries for both Volume I and II. Volume II begins on page 511.

This index includes the entries for both Volume I and II. Volume II begins on page 511.

This index includes the entries for both Volume I and II. Volume II begins on page 511.

Undepreciated Capital Cost - Defined

This index includes the entries for both Volume I and II. Volume II begins on page 511.